American College of Physicians

# MKSAP® 15

## Medical Knowledge Self-Assessment Program®

*General Internal Medicine*

# General Internal Medicine

## Contributors

**Kurt Kroenke, MD, MACP, Book Editor[2]**
Professor of Medicine
Indiana University School of Medicine
Research Scientist, Regenstrief Institute
Indianapolis, Indiana

**Jack Ende, MD, MACP, Associate Editor[1]**
Professor of Medicine
University of Pennsylvania
Chief, Department of Medicine
Penn Presbyterian Medical Center
Philadelphia, Pennsylvania

**Brent W. Beasley, MD, FACP[1]**
Associate Professor of Medicine
University of Missouri—Kansas City
Program Director, Internal Medicine Residency
Kansas City, Missouri

**Steven L. Cohn, MD, FACP[2]**
Director, Medical Consultation Service
Kings County Hospital Center
Clinical Professor of Medicine
SUNY Downstate
Brooklyn, New York

**Paul A. Hemmer, MD, MPH, FACP[1]\***
Bethesda, Maryland

**John T. Philbrick, MD, FACP[1]**
Professor of Medicine
Division of General Medicine, Geriatrics, and Palliative
    Medicine
University of Virginia School of Medicine
Charlottesville, Virginia

**Michael J. Roy, MD, MPH, FACP[1]\***
Colonel, Medical Corps, US Army
Professor of Medicine
Uniformed Services University of the Health Sciences
Bethesda, Maryland

**Stephen M. Salerno, MD, MPH, FACP[1]\***
Associate Professor of Medicine, USUHS
Director of Medical Education
Madigan Army Medical Center
Tacoma, Washington

**Gary H. Tabas, MD, FACP[1]**
Professor of Medicine
Division of General Internal Medicine
University of Pittsburgh School of Medicine
Pittsburgh, Pennsylvania

---

\* The views expressed here are those of the authors only and are not to be construed as those
  of the Department of Army, Department of Air Force, or Department of Defense.

## Editor-in-Chief

**Patrick C. Alguire, MD, FACP[1]**
Director, Education and Career Development
American College of Physicians
Philadelphia, Pennsylvania

## General Internal Medicine Reviewers

Raymond F. Bianchi, MD, FACP[1]
John K. Chamberlain, MD, MACP[1]
John H. Holbrook, MD, FACP[1]
Robert T. Means, Jr., MD, FACP[2]
Patrick G. O'Malley, MD, MPH, FACP[1]
Amir Qaseem, MD, PhD, MHA, FACP[1]
Darius A. Rastegar, MD, FACP[1]
Robert E. Wright, MD, FACP[1]

## General Internal Medicine ACP Editorial Staff

**Becky Krumm**, Senior Staff Editor
**Sean McKinney**, Director, Self-Assessment Programs
**Margaret Wells**, Managing Editor
**Charles Rossi**, Senior Associate of Clinical Content
    Development
**Shannon O'Sullivan**, Editorial Coordinator

## ACP Principal Staff

**Steven E. Weinberger, MD, FACP[2]**
*Deputy Executive Vice President*
*Senior Vice President, Medical Education and Publishing*

**D. Theresa Kanya, MBA[1]**
*Vice President, Medical Education and Publishing*

Sean McKinney[1]
*Director, Self-Assessment Programs*

Margaret Wells[1]
*Managing Editor*

Charles Rossi[1]
*Senior Associate of Clinical Content Development*

Becky Krumm[1]
*Senior Staff Editor*

Ellen McDonald, PhD[1]
*Senior Staff Editor*

Amanda Neiley[1]
*Staff Editor*

Katie Idell[1]
*Production Administrator/Editor*

Valerie Dangovetsky[1]
*Program Administrator*

John Murray[1]
*Editorial Coordinator*

Shannon O'Sullivan[1]
*Editorial Coordinator*

**Developed by the American College of Physicians**

---

1. Has no relationships with any entity producing, marketing, re-selling, or distributing health care goods or services consumed by, or used on, patients.

2. Has disclosed relationships with entities producing, marketing, re-selling, or distributing health care goods or services consumed by, or used on, patients. See below.

## Conflicts of Interest

The following contributors and ACP staff members have disclosed relationships with commercial companies:

**Steven L. Cohn, MD, FACP**
*Stock Options/Holdings*
Pfizer, GlaxoSmithKline, Merck, AstraZeneca
*Speakers Bureau*
Sanofi-Aventis, Pfizer

**Kurt Kroenke, MD, MACP**
*Research Grants/Contracts*
Eli Lilly
*Consultantship*
Eli Lilly, Pfizer, Forest

**Robert T. Means, Jr., MD, FACP**
*Honoraria*
Beckman Coulter

**Steven E. Weinberger, MD, FACP**
*Stock Options/Holdings*
Abbott, GlaxoSmithKline

## Acknowledgments

The American College of Physicians (ACP) gratefully acknowledges the special contributions to the development and production of the 15th edition of the Medical Knowledge Self-Assessment Program® (MKSAP 15) of Scott Thomas Hurd (Senior Systems Analyst/Developer), Ricki Jo Kauffman (Manager, Systems Development), Michael Ripca (Technical Administrator/Graphics Designer), and Lisa Torrieri (Graphic Designer). The Digital version (CD-ROM and Online components) was developed within the ACP's Interactive Product Development Department by Steven Spadt (Director), Christopher Forrest (Senior Software Developer), Ryan Hinkel (Senior Software Developer), John McKnight (Software Developer), Sean O'Donnell (Senior Software Developer), and Brian Sweigard (Senior Software Developer). Computer scoring and reporting are being performed by ACT, Inc., Iowa City, Iowa. The College also wishes to acknowledge that many other persons, too numerous to mention, have contributed to the production of this program. Without their dedicated efforts, this program would not have been possible.

## Continuing Medical Education

The American College of Physicians is accredited by the Accreditation Council for Continuing Medical Education (ACCME) to provide continuing medical education for physicians.

The American College of Physicians designates this educational activity for a maximum of 166 *AMA PRA Category 1 Credits*™. Physicians should only claim credit commensurate with the extent of their participation in the activity.

*AMA PRA Category 1 Credit*™ is available from July 31, 2009, to July 31, 2012.

## Learning Objectives

The learning objectives of MKSAP 15 are to:
- Close gaps between actual care in your practice and preferred standards of care, based on best evidence
- Diagnose disease states that are less common and sometimes overlooked and confusing
- Improve management of comorbidities that can complicate patient care
- Determine when to refer patients for surgery or care by subspecialists
- Pass the ABIM certification examination
- Pass the ABIM maintenance of certification examination

## Target Audience

- General internists and primary care physicians
- Subspecialists who need to remain up-to-date in internal medicine
- Residents preparing for the certifying examination in internal medicine
- Physicians preparing for maintenance of certification in internal medicine (recertification)

## How to Submit for CME Credits

To earn CME credits, complete a MKSAP 15 answer sheet. Use the enclosed, self-addressed envelope to mail your completed answer sheet(s) to the MKSAP Processing Center for scoring. Remember to provide your MKSAP 15 order and ACP ID numbers in the appropriate spaces on the answer sheet. The order and ACP ID numbers are printed on your mailing label. If you have not received these numbers with your MKSAP 15 purchase, you will need to acquire them to earn CME credits. E-mail ACP's customer service center at custserv@acponline.org. In the subject line, write "MKSAP 15 order/ACP ID numbers." In the body of the e-mail, make sure you include your e-mail address as well as your full name, address, city, state, ZIP code, country, and telephone number. Also identify where you have made your MKSAP 15 purchase. You will receive your MKSAP 15 order and ACP ID numbers by e-mail within 72 business hours.

## Permission/Consent for Use of Figures Shown in MKSAP 15 General Internal Medicine Multiple-Choice Questions

Figure shown in Self-Assessment Test Item 51 appears courtesy of Linda Lippa, MD, University of California, Irvine.

## Disclosure Policy

It is the policy of the American College of Physicians (ACP) to ensure balance, independence, objectivity, and scientific rigor in all its educational activities. To this end, and consistent with the policies of the ACP and the Accreditation Council for Continuing Medical Education (ACCME), contributors to all ACP continuing medical education activities are required to disclose all relevant financial relationships with any entity producing, marketing, re-selling, or distributing health care goods or services consumed by, or used on, patients. Contributors are required to use generic names in the discussion of therapeutic options and are required to identify any unapproved, off-label, or investigative use of commercial products or devices. Where a trade name is used, all available trade names for the same product type are also included. If trade-name products manufactured by compa-

nies with whom contributors have relationships are discussed, contributors are asked to provide evidence-based citations in support of the discussion. The information is reviewed by the committee responsible for producing this text. If necessary, adjustments to topics or contributors' roles in content development are made to balance the discussion. Further, all readers of this text are asked to evaluate the content for evidence of commercial bias so that future decisions about content and contributors can be made in light of this information.

## Resolution of Conflicts

To resolve all conflicts of interest and influences of vested interests, the ACP precluded members of the content-creation committee from deciding on any content issues that involved generic or trade-name products associated with proprietary entities with which these committee members had relationships. In addition, content was based on best evidence and updated clinical care guidelines, when such evidence and guidelines were available. Contributors' disclosure information can be found with the list of contributors' names and those of ACP principal staff listed in the beginning of this book.

## Educational Disclaimer

The editors and publisher of MKSAP 15 recognize that the development of new material offers many opportunities for error. Despite our best efforts, some errors may persist in print. Drug dosage schedules are, we believe, accurate and in accordance with current standards. Readers are advised, however, to ensure that the recommended dosages in MKSAP 15 concur with the information provided in the product information material. This is especially important in cases of new, infrequently used, or highly toxic drugs. Application of the information in MKSAP 15 remains the professional responsibility of the practitioner.

The primary purpose of MKSAP 15 is educational. Information presented, as well as publications, technologies, products, and/or services discussed, is intended to inform subscribers about the knowledge, techniques, and experiences of the contributors. A diversity of professional opinion exists, and the views of the contributors are their own and not those of the ACP. Inclusion of any material in the program does not constitute endorsement or recommendation by the ACP. The ACP does not warrant the safety, reliability, accuracy, completeness, or usefulness of and disclaims any and all liability for damages and claims that may result from the use of information, publications, technologies, products, and/or services discussed in this program.

## Publisher's Information

## Unauthorized Use of This Book Is Against the Law

MKSAP 15 ISBN: 978-1-934465-25-7
General Internal Medicine ISBN: 978-1-934465-36-3

Printed in the United States of America.

For order information in the U.S. or Canada call 800-523-1546, extension 2600. All other countries call 215-351-2600. Fax inquiries to 215-351-2799 or e-mail to custserv@acponline.org.

## Errata and Norm Tables

Errata for MKSAP 15 will be posted at http://mksap.acponline.org/errata as new information becomes known to the editors.

MKSAP 15 Performance Interpretation Guidelines with Norm Tables, available December 31, 2010, will reflect the knowledge of physicians who have completed the self-assessment tests before the program was published. These physicians took the tests without being able to refer to the syllabus, answers, and critiques. For your convenience, the tables are available in a printable PDF file at http://mksap.acponline.org/normtables.

# Table of Contents

# General Internal Medicine

## Routine Care of the Healthy Patient

### Screening

Screening—an evaluation to detect a disease at an asymptomatic stage—is appropriate when the population to be screened is accessible and willing to undergo testing, the disease causes significant burden of illness to the patient or to society, and the test has adequate sensitivity and specificity to detect disease without excessive false-positive results. In addition, treatment during the asymptomatic phase should be more effective than treatment after symptoms have appeared.

The gold standard for efficacy of screening is decreased mortality as demonstrated by randomized clinical trials. In evaluating studies of screening tests, clinicians must be aware of two common fallacies that occur in studies of effectiveness. *Lead-time bias* occurs when survival appears to be longer because of earlier detection. *Length bias* occurs when survival appears to be longer because persons who are able to participate in clinical trials often have less aggressive disease.

Screening can result in harm to the patient. False-positive tests can lead to anxiety, extra testing, and increased costs. Conversely, a false-negative test can give patients and physicians a false sense of reassurance. The U.S. Preventive Services Task Force (USPSTF) uses rigorous methodology to assess the effectiveness of screening tests (www.ahrq.gov/clinic/uspstfix.htm).

See **Table 1** for a summary of USPSTF age-specific and sex-specific preventive medicine (screening and counseling) recommendations.

### Screening During the History and Physical Examination

Screening and brief office-based interventions for several behavioral risk factors, including tobacco use and alcohol misuse, have been shown to be effective (see Lifestyle Risk Factors). The USPSTF recommends screening for depression in clinical practices with systems in place to ensure accurate diagnosis, effective treatment, and follow-up. In screening for depression, no single instrument has been shown to be superior; however, the two-question screen for abnormal mood and anhedonia ("Over the past 2 weeks have you felt down, depressed or hopeless?" and "Over the past 2 weeks, have you felt little interest or pleasure in doing things?") seems to be as effective as longer instruments. Begin a full diagnostic assessment for mood disorders in patients with either depressed mood or anhedonia by assessing symptoms directly using

case-finding tools such as the Patient Health Questionnaire (see Mental and Behavioral Health).

Although there is insufficient evidence to recommend screening all adults for dementia, physicians should assess cognitive function whenever there are self-reports or family reports of change in cognitive function.

Although the USPSTF did not find sufficient evidence to recommend for or against screening for family and intimate partner violence, clinicians should be alert to signs and symptoms suggestive of abuse of partners and elders.

| **TABLE 1** Recommended Interventions for Preventive Care |
|---|
| **Screening** |
| Height and weight (periodically) |
| Blood pressure |
| Alcohol and tobacco use |
| Depression (if appropriate follow-up is available) |
| Diabetes mellitus (patients with hypertension) |
| Dyslipidemia (total and HDL cholesterol): men ≥35 y; men or women ≥20 y who have cardiovascular risk factors; measure every 5 y if normal |
| Colorectal cancer screening (men and women 50-75 y) |
| Mammogram every 1 to 2 y for all women ≥40 y. Evaluation for *BRCA* testing in high-risk women only. |
| Papanicolaou test (at least every 3 y until age 65 y) |
| Chlamydial infection (sexually active women ≤25 y and older at-risk women) |
| Routine voluntary HIV screening (ages 13-64 y) |
| Bone mineral density test (women ≥65 y and at-risk women 60-64 y) |
| AAA screening (one time in men 65-75 y who have ever smoked) |
| **Counseling—Substance Abuse** |
| Tobacco cessation counseling |
| Alcohol misuse: brief office behavioral counseling; alcohol abuse: referral for specialty treatment |
| **Counseling—Diet and Exercise** |
| Behavioral dietary counseling in patients with hyperlipidemia, risks for CHD and other diet-related chronic disease |
| Regular physical activity (at least 30 minutes per day most days of the week) |
| Intensive counseling/behavioral interventions for obese patients |

AAA = abdominal aortic aneurysm; *BRCA* = breast cancer susceptibility gene; CHD = coronary heart disease.

Based on recommendations from the U.S. Preventive Services Task Force.

Blood pressure screening is indicated to identify hypertension and is recommended by the USPSTF. The USPSTF recommends screening every 2 years if the index systolic and diastolic pressures are below 120 mm Hg and 80 mm Hg, respectively, and yearly if the systolic pressure is 120 to 139 mm Hg or diastolic pressure is 80 to 89 mm Hg. The major benefits of identifying hypertension include reduced morbidity and mortality from stroke and heart failure and reduced all-cause mortality.

Screening for obesity by measuring weight and height to determine body mass index (BMI) is recommended by the USPSTF. The Task Force also recommends that obese adults receive intensive counseling and behavioral interventions to promote sustained weight loss. Waist circumference greater than 102 cm (40 in) for men and 88 cm (35 in) for women is associated with increased risk for cardiovascular disease. Waist-hip ratio appears to be a better predictor of cardiovascular disease and overall mortality than BMI in research settings; however, measurement errors may limit its use in the office setting.

The value of the periodic health examination has recently been the subject of debate. A recent systematic review concluded that the periodic health examination improved the delivery of some preventive health services and reduced patient worry. Benefits regarding short- and long-term clinical outcomes have not yet been clearly demonstrated. Complete blood counts, chemistry profiles, and urinalyses are not recommended as part of the periodic health examination.

## Specific Screening Tests

The USPSTF recommends screening for lipid disorders in men aged 35 years and older and in men or women aged 20 years and older who are at increased risk for cardiovascular disease. The standard screening test is a lipid panel obtained after a 12-hour fast. Screening using nonfasting total cholesterol and HDL cholesterol is as predictive of cardiovascular disease risk as obtaining a complete fasting lipid panel and can be performed during a regular office visit. If the results show a total cholesterol level greater than 200 mg/dL (5.18 mmol/L) or HDL cholesterol level below 40 mg/dL (1.04 mmol/L), then a fasting lipid panel is indicated. The Adult Treatment Panel of the National Cholesterol Education Program (ATP III) guidelines recommend that patients with 0 to 1 risk factor and a normal fasting lipid profile or normal nonfasting total cholesterol and HDL cholesterol levels do not have to be screened again for 5 years; the USPSTF acknowledges that the optimal screening interval is uncertain but that every 5 years is reasonable for low-risk persons. There is no clear age cutoff at which to stop screening, but for older patients, clinicians should take into account the presence of comorbid conditions and life expectancy.

The USPSTF recommends screening for type 2 diabetes mellitus in adults with sustained blood pressure (either treated or untreated) greater than 135/80 mm Hg. The rationale for this recommendation is that in adults with diabetes and hypertension, lowering blood pressure below standard target values reduces cardiovascular risk. Similarly, screening for type 2 diabetes in adults with dyslipidemia should be considered because diabetes is one of the conditions that lowers LDL cholesterol target levels.

Screening for osteoporosis is recommended for women 65 years and older and for women aged 60 to 64 years who are at increased risk. The USPSTF notes that weight below 70 kg (154 lb) is the single best predictor of low bone mineral density, although older age and no current use of estrogen therapy are also important predictors used in determining who should be screened. The American College of Physicians recommends that physicians perform individualized assessments of risk factors for osteoporosis in older men. The preferred screening test is dual-energy x-ray absorptiometry at the femoral neck. A screening interval of 2 years is appropriate for women 65 years or older, but can reasonably be extended to 5 years for women younger than 65 years.

One-time screening for abdominal aortic aneurysm using ultrasonography is recommended by the USPSTF in men aged 65 to 75 years who have ever smoked. A recent study including nonsmokers showed that the mortality benefit of screening persisted for 7 years.

The USPSTF concludes that there is insufficient evidence to recommend for or against routine screening for thyroid disease. The USPSTF recommends against routine screening for hemochromatosis. Pregnant women should be screened for iron-deficiency anemia.

The USPSTF recommends against screening for carotid artery stenosis with duplex ultrasonography or by listening for carotid bruits with a stethoscope. Screening for coronary artery disease in asymptomatic patients using electrocardiography, exercise treadmill testing, or electron-beam CT is not recommended for patients at low risk for cardiovascular disease and has unknown utility for patients at increased risk.

There is insufficient evidence to recommend for or against screening adults for glaucoma, according to the USPSTF. Intraocular pressure is only part of the definition of the disease, and many patients with primary open-angle glaucoma do not have increased intraocular pressure.

### Screening for Infectious Diseases

All pregnant women should be screened for asymptomatic bacteriuria using urine culture at 12 to 16 weeks' gestation to reduce symptomatic urinary tract infection, low birth weight, and preterm delivery. Screening in nonpregnant women and men is not recommended.

The American College of Physicians recommends routine voluntary HIV screening for adolescents and adults. The U.S. Centers for Disease Control and Prevention (CDC) recommend routine voluntary HIV screening for all persons aged 13 to 64 years as well as routine prenatal HIV screening. In addition, pregnant women at increased risk or in areas of high prevalence should have an additional HIV test during their third trimester.

The USPSTF recommends that all pregnant women should be screened for hepatitis B virus at their first prenatal visit. The general population should not be screened for hepatitis B or hepatitis C virus. All pregnant and nonpregnant women should be screened for gonorrhea if they are at increased risk (history of gonorrhea or other sexually transmitted diseases, new or multiple sexual partners, inconsistent condom use, sex work, and drug use). Evidence is less clear for men at increased risk. The USPSTF recommends screening for chlamydial infection in all sexually active women aged 24 years and younger (including pregnant women) and for older pregnant and nonpregnant women only if they are at increased risk. Persons at risk and all pregnant women should be screened for syphilis. Screening for herpes simplex virus is not recommended for any individuals.

### Cancer Screening Tests

#### Colorectal Cancer Screening

Colorectal cancer screening is recommended for men and women beginning at age 50 years. The USPSTF does not recommend routine screening in patients 75 to 85 years of age, although considerations in individual patients may support screening. The USPSTF does not recommend screening in patients older than age 85 years. Screening of high-risk patients (for example, those with multiple relatives with colon cancer) may begin at younger than 50 years. Several screening methods are acceptable, and the choice depends on patient preference, an evaluation of risks and benefits, and costs. Current USPSTF guidelines recommend either colonoscopy every 10 years, fecal occult blood testing annually, or flexible sigmoidoscopy every 5 years combined with fecal occult blood testing every 3 years.

A randomized trial showed mortality benefit for patients assigned to screening with biannual home fecal occult blood testing followed by colonoscopy for positive results, but most authorities recommend annual screening. Digital rectal examination or performing a single office guaiac test does not constitute adequate screening because sensitivity is only 4.9% for advanced neoplasia and only 9% for colorectal cancer. The various screening tests are discussed more fully in MKSAP 15 Gastroenterology and Hepatology.

#### Breast Cancer Screening

The USPSTF and the American Cancer Society (ACS) recommend screening for breast cancer using mammography with or without clinical breast examination for women 40 years and older. Some experts recommend annual screening, although there is little evidence that annual screening is better than biannual screening. The evidence for screening in women from 40 to 49 years of age is not as strong as for older women, and the optimal screening interval in this age group is unclear. The Canadian Task Force on Preventive Health Care concluded that there was insufficient evidence to make a recommendation regarding screening mammography in women aged 40 to 49 years.

Mammography is the only imaging technique that is currently approved for screening. Ultrasonography may be considered for the evaluation of a pregnant or breastfeeding patient or a patient younger than 30 years with breast-related symptoms. The USPSTF notes that there is insufficient evidence to determine whether clinical breast examination or breast self-examination affects breast cancer mortality. The ACS recommends clinical breast examinations beginning at age 20 years and recommends mammography with clinical breast examination beginning at age 40 years; the ACS does not make a firm recommendation regarding breast self-examination. Testing for the breast cancer susceptibility gene (*BRCA*) is recommended only for women whose family history is suggestive of increased risk for mutations in the *BRCA1* or *BRCA2* gene (see Family History and Genetic Testing).

#### Cervical and Anal Cancer Screening

The USPSTF recommends cervical cancer screening for women who are sexually active and have a cervix. Screening should begin within 3 years of onset of sexual activity but no later than age 21 years. After age 65 years, the effectiveness of screening is low in women who have had recent negative Pap smears; however, the ACS recommends screening until age 70 years. Women at normal risk can be screened every 3 years, although the ACS recommends waiting until age 30 years before lengthening the screening interval from an annual basis. Liquid-based cytology is not superior to standard testing and is more costly. The USPSTF has indicated that the evidence is insufficient to recommend either for or against routine screening for human papillomavirus (HPV).

Anal cytologic screening (anal Pap smear) in high-risk groups (HIV- and HPV-infected men and women) has been recommended by some groups to detect anal intraepithelial neoplasia, a purported precursor of anal cancer. Neither the USPSTF, the ACS, nor the CDC recommends screening with anal Pap smear testing at this time.

#### Prostate Cancer Screening

Screening for prostate cancer is commonly performed but remains controversial because clear evidence for effectiveness is lacking. In men younger than 75 years, the USPSTF does not recommend for or against screening because of insufficient evidence for morbidity or mortality benefit. The USPSTF recommends against screening men 75 years or older. The ACS recommends offering digital rectal examination and prostate-specific antigen (PSA) testing to men beginning at age 50 years. Men should be counseled as to risks and possible benefits prior to receiving PSA testing. False-positive test results may be due to other diseases (benign prostate hyperplasia), and inconsequential positive results can be seen with indolent prostate cancer that will not become clinically evident. Known harms include unnecessary biopsies, anxiety, and complications of treatment.

*Additional Cancer Screening Tests*

The ACS recommends examination of the thyroid, testicles, ovaries, lymph nodes, oral region, and skin during periodic health examinations. However, the USPSTF recommends against screening for testicular cancer, ovarian cancer, pancreatic cancer, and bladder cancer because of lack of evidence showing benefit. Benefits from routine screening for skin cancer are unproved, but clinicians should remain alert for changing moles or suspicious lesions.

Although low-dose CT is more sensitive than chest radiograph for the detection of lung cancer, there is insufficient evidence to recommend for or against these tests or sputum cytology to screen for lung cancer. Clinicians should remain alert to the possibility of oral cancer in patients who smoke or use alcohol, but there is insufficient evidence to recommend for or against routine screening.

### KEY POINTS

- The U.S. Preventive Services Task Force recommends routine periodic screening for hypertension, obesity, dyslipidemia (men ≥35 years), osteoporosis (women ≥65 years), abdominal aortic aneurysm (one-time-screening), depression, and HIV infection.

- The U.S. Preventive Services Task Force recommends routine periodic screening for colorectal cancer (persons 50-74 years of age), breast cancer (women ≥40 years), and cervical cancer.

- The U.S. Preventive Services Task Force recommends that all pregnant women be screened for asymptomatic bacteriuria, iron-deficiency anemia, hepatitis B virus, and syphilis.

- The U.S. Preventive Services Task Force recommends against screening for hemochromatosis; carotid artery stenosis; coronary artery disease; herpes simplex virus; or testicular, ovarian, pancreatic, or bladder cancer.

## Family History and Genetic Testing

The Human Genome Project has increased public awareness of the heritable basis of disease and encouraged the development of genetic tests. Recent discoveries of gene alterations associated with increased risk for cancer, diabetes, cardiac diseases, and other common conditions have fostered the hope that these advances will be translated into medical benefits, including prevention strategies and new treatments. An example of the potential for success with regard to inherited disease is screening newborns for phenylketonuria so that provision of a phenylalanine-poor diet can be instituted to prevent mental retardation and other complications. In contrast, the reality of our limits in genetic medicine is illustrated by how our detailed understanding of the genetic basis of sickle cell anemia has not led to improvements in treatment.

### Taking a Family History

The process of taking a family history typically employed by medical genetics professionals is both labor- and time-intensive. It typically involves a three-generation pedigree and may require hours to complete. Given the multiple demands on the internist during the clinical encounter, this degree of detail is not feasible. A family history by the internist should be approached from two directions: first, an inquiry regarding any diseases that "run in the family"; and second, specific inquiry into family history of the more common and important inherited diseases, including breast, ovarian, prostate, and colon cancer; as well as early cardiovascular disease. A detailed family history should follow for those conditions identified through this preliminary questioning. Patient-reported family histories for first-degree relatives have been shown to be accurate and valuable for breast and colon cancer, but a negative family history for ovarian and endometrial cancer is less accurate. **Table 2** lists family history patterns suggestive of genetic disorders.

### Caveats to Genetic Testing

Although it is standard of care to perform genetic testing for certain mutations in unselected preconception, prenatal, and

| TABLE 2 Family History Patterns Suggestive of Inherited Disorders |
|---|
| **Autosomal Dominant** |
| Multiple generations of affected relatives, both males and females |
| **Autosomal Recessive** |
| Siblings more likely to be affected than parents |
| **X-linked Recessive** |
| Males only affected; all related through their mothers and no male-to-male transmission |
| **X-linked Dominant** |
| Half of male and female children of affected mothers will be affected. For affected fathers, no male-to-male transmission, but all daughters will be affected; some X-linked dominant conditions are fatal to males, so only affected females survive. |
| **Other Factors** |
| Multiple affected individuals in multiple generations |
| Occurrence of the disease at an earlier age than expected |
| Close degree of relatedness of affected relatives |
| Presence of associated conditions (e.g., breast and ovarian cancers) |
| Unusual presentations (e.g., bilateral breast cancer, breast cancer in males) |

newborn populations, at least three important issues make it unwise to perform genetic testing in unselected populations seen by internists: the clinical validity of such a test may be lacking, there may be a high likelihood of false-positive tests, and the harms of performing a genetic test may outweigh any benefits.

Genetic testing is offered to a member of a family to determine the risk of a particular disorder occurring in an asymptomatic person. In many cases, genetic testing of at-risk family members provides a highly accurate estimate of disease risk for the individual in question. However, having a mutation does not mean that a person will necessarily experience the clinical consequences associated with it. *Penetrance* is the likelihood of developing a disease given the inheritance of an autosomal dominant mutation. Usually, a genetic mutation is first discovered in families with many affected members. In these families, presence of a gene mutation is very likely to have associated expression of the disease (high penetrance). However, when population-based studies of the mutation are carried out, it is often discovered that penetrance is "incomplete." That is, compared with individuals in the high-risk families, persons in other populations with the mutation have a lower risk of the disease. Thus, the genetic test may have a high "analytic validity" (that is, the test accurately detects the mutation) but may have a lower "clinical validity" (that is, there is a lower likelihood of the patient developing the disease—a function of gene penetrance). For example, as many as 85% of women with the *BRCA1* or *BRCA2* mutation identified by a family history of breast cancer develop breast cancer by age 70 years. However, women identified with the mutation in population-based studies have a lower risk, ranging from 40% to 55%. Some disorders also display variable expression of the genotype, meaning that a given mutation may cause different severity/manifestations of disease in different patients. This can result in variations in age of disease onset, disease severity, disease characteristics, and disease progression. For example, some patients with Marfan syndrome may show only mild physical manifestations, whereas others develop life-threatening aortic aneurysms.

In interpreting diagnostic tests, the clinician must estimate the positive and negative predictive values. Even if a test has very high sensitivity and specificity, the positive predictive value will be quite low in patients with a low pretest probability. To minimize the false positives, patients selected for genetic testing should have a higher risk than the general population of having a mutation (higher pretest probability). For genetic testing in internal medicine populations, this determination is best made with an appropriate family history.

Genetic testing may carry benefits, especially when a unique intervention is available for persons with a particular genotype. For example, testing for the *BRCA* mutations or for familial adenomatous polyposis may lead to aggressive preventive interventions for the few persons at high risk for cancer. In contrast, testing for diseases for which there are no measures either for prevention or for delaying onset—for example, age-related macular degeneration—may result in little benefit except the relief that results from a negative test. Potential harms include emotional distress from the knowledge of having a "genetic illness"; genetic labeling with accompanying worry regarding employment or insurance discrimination; and survivor guilt in family members found not to have the mutation.

## Referral for Genetic Counseling

Because of the potential harms from genetic test information and the need for patients and their families to receive appropriate information for decision-making, patients with possible inherited diseases should be referred for genetic testing only in the context of genetic counseling. Genetic counseling should include discussion of possible risks and benefits of early detection and prevention modalities. Genetic counseling with the option for testing should be offered when: (1) the patient has a personal or family history suggestive of a genetic susceptibility condition; (2) the genetic test can be adequately interpreted; and (3) the test results will aid in diagnosis or influence the medical or surgical management of the patient or family at hereditary risk.

There are a number of useful on-line resources to assist practitioners and patients; several include links to other sites:

- GeneTests (www.genetests.org): A publicly funded directory of genetic counseling clinics and laboratories, plus information and educational materials
- Human Genome Epidemiology Network (www.cdc.gov/genomics/hugenet/default.htm): The Centers for Disease Control and Prevention's Web site addressing public health aspects of genomics
- National Cancer Institute (www.cancer.gov/cancer-topics/prevention-genetics-causes/genetics): Information regarding the genetic aspects of cancer
- U.S. Surgeon General's Family History Initiative (www.hhs.gov/familyhistory): Web-based or downloadable family history software

---

**KEY POINTS**

- Outside of prenatal, preconception, and newborn care, genetic testing should not be performed in unselected populations because of lower clinical validity; potential for false positives; and potential for harm, including "genetic labeling."
- For patients for whom genetic testing may be appropriate, referral for genetic counseling should be provided before and after testing.

---

# Immunization

The CDC Advisory Committee on Immunization Practices (ACIP) publishes yearly updates on recommended vaccines and schedules for immunization that can be found on their Web site (www.cdc.gov/vaccines/pubs/ACIP-list.htm). The commonly used vaccines, exclusive of travel immunization, are discussed here. All of these vaccines are safe to give in combination and are appropriate to give to patients with concurrent minor—but not moderate or severe—acute illness. Any vaccine can cause anaphylactic shock, but this is rare, occurring in fewer than one case per million vaccine doses.

## Hepatitis A Vaccine

The major use of hepatitis A vaccine is in patients with medical, occupational, and lifestyle risk factors for infection. The major populations of patients requiring hepatitis A vaccine include men who have sex with men, illicit drug users, individuals with chronic liver disease, and travelers to developing countries with a high prevalence of disease. Food handlers are also candidates for the vaccine, if local health authorities or private employers deem vaccination appropriate. The safety of the vaccine during pregnancy is uncertain. The vaccine is an inactivated virus. The dose varies with age; two doses are needed, with a minimum interval between doses of 6 months. If the second dose is delayed, it should be administered without repeating the first. No revaccination is needed after the two-dose series.

## Hepatitis B Vaccine

In addition to populations for which hepatitis A vaccination is recommended, the hepatitis B vaccine is indicated for all children through age 18 years, patients with HIV or other recent sexually transmitted diseases, persons who are sexually active but not monogamous, workers with occupational exposure to blood, clients and staff of institutions for the developmentally disabled, correctional facility inmates, illicit drug users, and patients with advanced chronic kidney disease who are approaching hemodialysis. Pregnant women who need protection from hepatitis B infection may be vaccinated. The vaccine contains recombinant noninfectious viral surface elements. Three doses are needed to confer optimal immunity. The second and third doses may be given 1 and 6 months, 1 and 4 months, or 2 and 4 months after the initial dose. If doses are delayed, the series should be continued from where it was left off. Hepatitis A and hepatitis B vaccination may be delivered in a combination vaccine for patients 18 years and older. The hepatitis A component is an inactivated virus and the hepatitis B component is a recombinant hepatitis B surface antigen protein. An initial vaccine dose is administered, and repeat doses are given at 1 and 6 months after the initial dose.

## Human Papillomavirus Vaccine

A vaccine against common strains of HPV causing cervical cancer was licensed in 2006. This vaccine is composed of noninfectious particles similar to HPV virions of strains 6, 11, 16, and 18. The vaccine is recommended for females ages 9 through 26 years regardless of sexual activity. It is not for use in pregnant women. Two subsequent doses at 2 and 6 months follow an initial dose. The minimum interval between the first two doses is 4 weeks and between the second two doses is 12 weeks. No revaccination is required after the three-dose regimen. In a randomized placebo-controlled, double blind trial, the vaccine was 100% successful in preventing vaginal, vulvar, perineal, and perianal intraepithelial lesions and warts, as well as cervical intraepithelial neoplasia and adenocarcinoma in situ in association with vaccine-type HPV.

## Influenza Vaccine

The influenza vaccine is indicated in all adults wishing to reduce their likelihood of influenza infection, but is especially recommended in patients ages 50 years and older, in whom the disease causes significant morbidity and mortality. The importance of vaccination is also emphasized in those with certain medical, occupational, and lifestyle risk factors. These populations include persons residing in high–population density areas such as chronic care facilities and dormitories as well as persons such as health care workers who work or live with those in whom influenza infection poses a major mortality risk. Vaccination is also indicated in pregnant women whose last two trimesters coincide with influenza season and persons with diabetes, chronic cardiopulmonary or kidney disease, hemoglobinopathies, and suppressed immune systems. Finally, it is recommended in patients with conditions increasing the risk of aspiration.

There are two vaccine types, a trivalent inactivated virus appropriate for all age groups given intramuscularly and an intranasal live attenuated influenza vaccine appropriate for patients aged 2 to 49 years. The live attenuated vaccine should be avoided in pregnant women as well as patients with chronic metabolic diseases, diabetes, renal dysfunction, hemoglobinopathies, immunosuppression, and chronic diseases that can compromise respiratory function or the handling of respiratory secretions. The vaccine can be administered to family members of immunosuppressed patients not requiring a protected environment (such as a hematopoietic stem cell recipient). The influenza vaccine should not be given to persons allergic to eggs or to those with a history of Guillain-Barré syndrome. Revaccination in target populations is indicated every year in the fall, at the beginning of the influenza season.

## Measles-Mumps-Rubella Vaccine

Internists rarely need to deliver the measles-mumps-rubella vaccine, a live attenuated virus vaccine given in a two-dose series. Children typically get one dose of the vaccine at 1 year of age and a second at 4 to 6 years of age. Revaccination is not required after the two-dose series. Persons born after 1956 require the measles, mumps, rubella vaccine unless there is documentation of prior administration, physician-confirmed disease, or laboratory evidence of immunity to all three diseases. High-risk groups include health care workers, students at post–high school institutions, and international travelers. The vaccine should not be administered during pregnancy or in women considering pregnancy within the next 28 days and should not be administered to patients allergic to vaccine components, such as gelatin or neomycin.

## Meningococcal Vaccine

The meningococcal vaccine is important to administer in young adults, especially those living in dormitories or barracks. The vaccine is also recommended in persons exposed in meningitis outbreaks and in patients with asplenia or terminal complement deficiencies. Indications also exist for travelers to endemic regions, and in laboratory workers routinely exposed to isolates of *Neisseria meningitides.*

There are two types of meningococcal vaccine, both made from noninfectious polysaccharide components of the meningococcus. The older type, the MPSV4 polysaccharide vaccine, is now used only for children 2 to 10 years old and adults older than 55 years. Revaccination is indicated if a patient had one injection of MPSV4 five or more years ago and is still in a high-risk category. Studies of vaccination with MPSV4 during pregnancy have not documented adverse effects among pregnant women or newborns. However, no specific studies have been performed on the vaccine's safety in pregnancy. A newer conjugate vaccine, the MCV4 vaccine, generates a more robust immunologic response, eliminating the need for revaccination, and is preferred for patients 11 to 55 years of age. Serious side effects, such as Guillain-Barré syndrome, have been reported in proximity to vaccine administration, but so few adverse events have occurred that causality remains in question.

## Pneumococcal Pneumonia Vaccine

Adults 65 years and older should be immunized against pneumococcal pneumonia. The vaccine contains 23 antigen types of *Streptococcus pneumoniae* and protects against 60% of bacteremic disease. The vaccine is also recommended in some populations of younger patients, including Alaskan natives and certain American Indian populations; residents of long-term care facilities; patients who are undergoing radiation therapy or are on immunosuppressive medication; and patients with chronic pulmonary disorders, diabetes, cardiovascular disease, chronic liver or kidney disease, cochlear implants, asplenia, immune disorders, or malignancies. There is no information on vaccine safety during pregnancy. For patients older than 65 years, one-time revaccination is warranted if they were vaccinated more than 5 years ago and were younger than 65 years at the time of primary vaccination. One-time revaccination is also recommended in 5 years for patients with chronic kidney disease, asplenia, immune disorders or malignancies, or who are on immunosuppressive medication.

## Polio Vaccine

The polio vaccine is not routinely recommended for adult patients, even those who have not completed a primary series, unless they intend to travel to areas of the developing world where exposure to wild-type virus is likely.

## Tetanus-Diphtheria–Acellular Pertussis Vaccine

The tetanus-diphtheria (Td) vaccine is recommended for all adults who have not completed a primary series. The vaccine is composed of modified bacterial toxins that elicit an immune response but are rendered nontoxic. To administer a primary series, the vaccine is given in three doses, with the second dose 1 to 2 months and the third dose 6 to 12 months after the initial dose. Interruption of the recommended schedule does not require starting the series over. Boosters are administered at 10-year intervals. The tetanus-diphtheria–acellular pertussis (Tdap) vaccine, discussed below, can substitute for any one of the doses of Td in the three-dose primary series.

The ACIP recommends routine use of a single dose of Tdap in adults aged 19 to 64 years to replace the next Td booster. Tdap can be administered earlier than the usual 10-year Td booster cycle to protect against pertussis. Administration as soon as 2 years from the most recent Td vaccine has proved safe. The ACIP also recommends that health care providers and adults who anticipate having close contact with an infant younger than 12 months receive a Tdap vaccine as soon as 2 years have passed since their most recent Td vaccine to obtain maximal protection against pertussis. After the one Tdap booster is administered, traditional 10-year interval cycles of Td boosters resume. The utility of further Tdap boosters beyond the first is unknown.

In patients presenting with acute wounds, special considerations are required. In patients with wounds of any type, Td revaccination is indicated if the patient has had fewer than three doses of vaccine or status is unknown. A patient who presents with a clean, minor wound and has had three or more documented Td doses should be revaccinated if the last vaccination was 10 or more years ago. In all other wounds, a booster is administered if the last vaccination was 5 or more years ago.

## Varicella Vaccine

The varicella vaccine is a live attenuated virus vaccine recommended by the ACIP for administration to patients 13 years and older who do not have evidence of varicella immunity. Evidence of immunity consists of birth prior to 1980, documentation of age-appropriate vaccination with a varicella vaccine, laboratory evidence of immunity, evidence of prior varicella disease as documented by a health care provider or laboratory testing, or diagnosis of herpes zoster by a health care provider. For health care personnel, pregnant women, and immunocompromised persons, birth before 1980 should not be considered evidence of immunity. Two vaccine doses are needed, with the second dose given 4 to 8 weeks after the initial dose. If the second dose is delayed, it is administered without repeating the series. This vaccine should not be given to patients with diseases of the immune system or who are on immunosuppressive medications. It is also not indicated in pregnancy or in patients allergic to vaccine components such as gelatin or neomycin. Women of childbearing age are advised to not become pregnant for 3 months after receiving the vaccine.

## Zoster Vaccine

The zoster vaccine is a live attenuated virus vaccine recommended for persons ages 60 years and older for prevention of shingles. As it is possible for a person to have a second herpes zoster infection, the vaccine is indicated regardless of whether there is a history of shingles. It should not be used for treatment of herpes zoster or postherpetic neuralgia or for prevention of primary varicella infection (chickenpox). It should also not be used in pregnant women, patients with active untreated tuberculosis, patients with diseases or malignancies of the immune system, or patients on immunosuppressive medications. It is not necessary to test for exposure to varicella prior to vaccine administration. Unlike the vaccine against primary varicella, a booster vaccination is not required.

The vaccine is the most effective (64% risk reduction) in patients aged 60 to 69 years. Its effectiveness declines with increasing age and only provides an 18% risk reduction for patients 80 years and older. All Medicare Part D plans cover the zoster vaccine. In those who developed herpes zoster, the duration of symptomatic infection was shortened by 3 days in the vaccinated group compared with the placebo group. The incidence of postherpetic neuralgia was reduced as well.

### KEY POINTS

- A human papillomavirus vaccine series is indicated in females ages 9 through 26 years, regardless of sexual activity, for prevention of cervical cancer.
- A single dose of tetanus-diphtheria–acellular pertussis (Tdap) vaccine should be given to adults ages 19 through 64 years to replace the next tetanus-diphtheria toxoid (Td) booster.
- A zoster (shingles) vaccine is given to all patients 60 years and older regardless of history of prior shingles or varicella infection.

# Lifestyle Risk Factors

## Behavioral Counseling

There is increasing evidence for the effectiveness of brief primary care–based interventions for changing individual health risk behaviors, particularly for smoking cessation and risky alcohol use. The USPSTF advocates the "five A's" model of brief counseling for changing behaviors (**Table 3**). Additional resources useful to support brief office counseling include:

### TABLE 3 "Five A's" Framework for Brief Counseling

| | |
|---|---|
| Assess | Ask about behavioral health risks, such as smoking, substance use, diet, and exercise. Assess beliefs, behaviors, knowledge, motivation, and past experience. |
| Advise | Give clear, specific, well-timed, and personalized behavior change advice. Advise in a noncoercive, nonjudgmental manner that respects readiness for change and patient autonomy. |
| Agree | Collaboratively select appropriate goals and methods based on the patient's interest and willingness to change. For those with multiple risks, agree on what to tackle first. |
| Assist | Aid the patient in achieving agreed-upon goals with use of social/environmental supports and adjunctive medical treatments when appropriate (including pharmacotherapy). |
| Arrange | Schedule follow-up (in person or by phone) to provide ongoing support and to adjust the plan as needed, including referral for more specialized interventions. |

- Involvement of office staff: Office staff may participate in a team-based approach by providing teaching and counseling and by providing follow-up assessment.
- Screening/reminder systems: Patient questionnaires and chart reminders can be used to screen for health risks and prompt staff for when interventions are due. Patient registries and electronic medical records can facilitate these systems.
- Patient education materials: Written patient information materials are useful to reinforce brief counseling and support behavioral change. They should be at the proper literacy level and in the needed language (for example, the ACP Foundation's patient information "Health Tips" pads: http://foundation.acponline.org/hl/htips.htm).
- Referral network: For patients who require a more intensive intervention, a referral network might include nutritionists; weight loss programs; exercise trainers; patient educators; and counselors in smoking cessation, obesity, and substance abuse issues.
- Nonprofessional role models: Referral to patients or others willing to serve as informal counselors or to self-change support groups such as Alcoholics Anonymous or Overeaters Anonymous may be helpful.
- Documentation: Documenting the counseling intervention along with the action plan is important to track progress.

## Physical Inactivity

The American College of Sports Medicine and the American Heart Association recently updated their recommendations for physical activity. Evidence affirms a dose-response relationship between physical activity and health benefits, particularly the lowering of risk of cardiovascular disease, premature death, hypertension, adult-onset diabetes, obesity, and osteoporosis. **Table 4** highlights key recommendations.

**TABLE 4** Recommendations for Physical Activity in Healthy Adults

| Topic | Recommendation |
|---|---|
| Aerobic (endurance) exercise | Moderate-intensity physical activity for at least 30 minutes 5 days per week, or vigorous-intensity activity for at least 20 minutes 3 days per week. |
| Muscle-strengthening exercise | Perform activities that maintain or increase muscular strength and endurance at least 2 days per week. This should be 8 to 10 exercises on 2 or more nonconsecutive days using the major muscles. A resistance or weight should be used that results in substantial fatigue after 8 to 12 repetitions of each exercise. |
| Benefits of greater amounts of activity | Because there is a dose-response curve relationship between physical activity and health, persons who wish to further improve their personal fitness, reduce their risk for chronic diseases, or prevent unhealthy weight gain may exceed these minimum recommended amounts of physical activity. |
| Injury risk | Physically active adults do not appear to have a higher injury rate than inactive adults. The risk of cardiac arrest or myocardial infarction is very low in generally healthy adults during moderate-intensity activities. |
| Screening/clearance | Asymptomatic adults who plan to be physically active at the recommended levels do not need to consult with a physician prior to beginning exercise unless they have a specific medical question. |
|  | Routine stress tests prior to exercise are not warranted owing to their poor predictive value for acute cardiac events, the uncertainties in interpreting abnormal tests in persons with a low pretest risk of coronary disease, and high cost. |
|  | Symptomatic persons or those with cardiovascular disease, diabetes, other active chronic disease, or any other medical concern should consult a physician before any substantive increase in physical activity. |

Recommendations from Haskell WL, Lee IM, Pate RR, et al; American College of Sports Medicine; American Heart Association. Physical activity and public health: updated recommendations for adults from the American College of Sports Medicine and the American Heart Association. Circulation. 2007;116(9):1081-1093. [PMID: 17671237]

For all adults ages 65 years and older and those ages 50 to 64 years with clinically significant chronic conditions or functional limitations, the emphasis of physical activity recommendations is on reducing sedentary behavior and increasing moderate activity rather than attaining high levels of activity, and taking a gradual or stepwise approach.

**KEY POINT**

- Asymptomatic adults who plan to be physically active at the recommended levels do not need to consult with a physician prior to beginning exercise unless they have a specific medical question.

## Substance Use Disorders

### Tobacco

It is recommended that smoking status be determined on all patients. The U.S. Public Health Service suggests asking all patients two questions: "Do you smoke?" and "Do you want to quit?"

The U.S. Public Health Service recommends the "five A's" approach for brief smoking cessation intervention (see Table 3) and further counseling for those unwilling to quit using the "five R's" approach (**Table 5**). The U.S. Public Health Service recommends that health care providers encourage tobacco users to use both counseling and medication to help them to quit. In addition, providers should promote the use of telephone quit lines, which have been shown to be effective (for example, the National Smoking

Cessation Hotline: 1-800-QUIT NOW). Quitters should be warned of withdrawal symptoms (which will improve in several weeks), plan a coping strategy for cravings (such as chewing gum), avoid high-risk smoking situations, and anticipate some weight gain.

Cochrane systematic reviews have evaluated evidence on several aspects of smoking cessation. Individual counseling by a smoking cessation specialist increases the quit rate by about 50%. Intensive counseling has not proved more effective than brief counseling. Standard self-help materials on smoking cessation may increase quit rates, but the effect is likely to be small. All nicotine replacement therapies (gum, patch, nasal

**TABLE 5** "Five R's" of Counseling for Smokers Who Are Unwilling to Quit

| | |
|---|---|
| Relevance | Encourage the smoker to discuss why quitting is personally relevant. Motivation is greatest if smoking has relevance to disease risk, family, or social situation. |
| Risks | Ask the patient to identify negative consequences of smoking. |
| Rewards | Ask the patient to identify potential benefits of stopping tobacco use. |
| Roadblocks | Ask the patient to identify barriers or impediments to quitting. Note elements of treatment that could address the barriers. |
| Repetition | Repeat the motivational intervention at subsequent office visits. |

spray, inhaler, and lozenges) increase the quit rate by 50% to 70%, regardless of setting. Nicotine replacement is likely safer than smoking in pregnant women but is generally recommended only after failure of behavioral programs. Contraindications to nicotine replacement are myocardial infarction within 2 weeks, severe arrhythmias, and worsening or severe angina.

When used as sole pharmacotherapy, antidepressants (bupropion and nortriptyline) doubled the odds of cessation compared with placebo. Bupropion and nortriptyline appeared to be equally effective and of similar efficacy to nicotine replacement therapy. Bupropion is a category B drug for pregnancy. There was insufficient evidence that adding nicotine replacement therapy provided additional benefit. Contraindications to bupropion include history of a seizure disorder, situations that lower seizure threshold such as alcohol or benzodiazepine withdrawal, and recent monoamine oxidase (MAO) inhibitor use. Contraindications to nortriptyline are recovery from an acute myocardial infarction, recent MAO inhibitor use, and risk of urinary retention. Selective serotonin reuptake inhibitors showed no evidence of significant benefit.

The nicotine receptor partial agonist, varenicline, given for 12 weeks increased the odds of long-term smoking cessation approximately three-fold compared with placebo. When compared directly with bupropion, varenicline was more effective. The main side effect of varenicline was nausea, which usually subsided over time. Two trials tested varenicline

for an additional 12 weeks without adverse effects. Varenicline is a pregnancy category C drug and is considered only when the potential benefits outweigh the potential risks to the fetus. Possible links between varenicline and depression, agitation, and suicidal behavior/ideation are under review by the FDA; until this is clarified, caution should be exercised with varenicline use if a patient has a history of psychiatric illness.

### Alcohol

Alcohol misuse definitions include "risky/hazardous" and "harmful" drinking. Risky drinkers consume alcohol above levels considered moderate. Harmful drinkers experience current harm associated with alcohol use but do not meet criteria for dependence (**Table 6**). The USPSTF recommends routine screening to identify persons whose alcohol use puts them at risk. Although the optimal interval for screening is not known, persons more likely to be at risk are those with prior alcohol problems, young adults, and smokers; more frequent screening may be beneficial in these populations. There are several screening instruments. A single question, "How many times in the past have you had five or more drinks (for men) or four or more drinks (for women) in a day?" can be used to screen for at-risk drinkers. The CAGE questionnaire is a commonly used instrument to identify alcohol problems:

**C** Have you ever felt you should **cut down** on your drinking?

**A** Have people **annoyed** you by criticizing your drinking?

**TABLE 6** Categories and Definitions for Patterns of Alcohol Use

| Category | Organization | Definition |
| --- | --- | --- |
| Moderate drinking | NIAAA | Men, ≤2 drinks per day<br>Women, ≤1 drink per day<br>Over 65 years, ≤1 drink per day |
| At-risk drinking | NIAAA | Men, >14 drinks per week or >4 drinks per occasion<br>Women, >7 drinks per week or >3 drinks per occasion |
| Hazardous drinking | WHO | At risk for adverse consequences from alcohol |
| Harmful drinking | WHO | Alcohol is causing physical or psychological harm |
| Alcohol abuse (DSM-IV) | APA | One or more of the following events in a 12-month period:<br>• Recurrent use resulting in failure to fulfill major role obligations<br>• Recurrent use in hazardous situations<br>• Recurrent alcohol-related legal problems<br>• Continued use despite social or interpersonal problems caused or exacerbated by alcohol use |
| Alcohol dependence (DSM-IV) | APA | Three or more of the following events in a 12-month period:<br>• Tolerance (increased amounts to achieve effect *or* diminished effect from same amount)<br>• Withdrawal<br>• Great deal of time spent obtaining alcohol, using it, or recovering from its effects<br>• Important activities given up or reduced because of alcohol<br>• Drinking more or longer than intended<br>• Persistent desire or unsuccessful efforts to cut down or control alcohol use<br>• Use continued despite knowledge of having a psychological problem caused or exacerbated by alcohol |

APA = American Psychiatric Association; DSM-IV = Diagnostic and Statistical Manual of Mental Disorders IV; NIAAA = National Institute on Alcohol Abuse and Alcoholism; WHO = World Health Organization.

**G** Have you ever felt bad or **guilty** about your drinking?

**E Eye opener**: Have you ever had a drink first thing in the morning to steady your nerves or to get rid of a hangover?

With a cutoff of two positive answers, the CAGE questionnaire is 77% to 94% sensitive and 79% to 97% specific for detecting alcohol abuse or dependence in primary care settings and indicates that further assessment is warranted; the test may be less accurate in women and blacks. Other screening instruments are available at www.niaaa.nih.gov/Publications/AlcoholResearch/.

Laboratory findings such as an elevated mean corpuscular volume (sensitivity 63%; specificity 48%) and an elevated aspartate aminotransferase/alanine aminotransferase ratio (sensitivity 12%; specificity 91%) can be suggestive but are not diagnostic of alcohol abuse and dependence.

For management of alcohol abuse and dependence, the USPSTF recommends referral for specialty treatment. For alcohol misuse, brief behavioral counseling (such as the five A's and the five R's) may be useful.

Adjunctive drug therapy may be considered for patients who previously failed to benefit from psychosocial approaches alone and those who have recently stopped drinking but are experiencing cravings or relapses. Three oral medications are currently approved for treating alcohol dependence, but they are most effective when combined with some behavioral support. Disulfiram causes a reaction of flushing, sweating, nausea, and tachycardia when the patient ingests alcohol. It is most effective when medication compliance can be monitored. Contraindications are use of alcohol-containing preparations, metronidazole, severe cardiac disease, and unwillingness to completely abstain from alcohol. Naltrexone reduces alcohol cravings and causes a lesser reward in response to drinking. It is contraindicated if a patient is dependent on or taking opioids or has liver disease. Acamprosate's alcohol-related action is unclear, but it may reduce abstinence-related symptoms, such as anxiety, restlessness, and dysphoria. It is contraindicated in severe renal disease. There is no proven benefit for combining these medications. A reasonable minimum duration of adjunctive drug therapy is 3 months, with treatment continuing a year or longer if the patient responds. A clinician's guide for using these medications is available at www.niaaa.nih.gov/guide.

### Drugs

The USPSTF does not recommend for or against screening for substance abuse in the general population. However, if the internist wishes to inquire about substance abuse, it is often best to start with socially accepted substances such as nicotine and caffeine, move on to alcohol, and finally ask about illicit drugs. The CAGE-AID questionnaire—the CAGE instrument with the phrase "or drug use" added to each item—has been found to be useful in settings of high likelihood of alcohol or drug abuse, such as emergency departments or sexually transmitted disease clinics. Family members, friends, and other contacts may provide useful information.

Clues for chemical dependency include unexpected behavioral changes, acute intoxication, frequent job changes, unexplained financial problems, family history of substance abuse, frequent problems with law enforcement agencies, having a partner with substance abuse, and medical sequelae of drug abuse (for example, endocarditis, nasal perforation, hepatitis, needle tracks). Patients addicted to prescription drugs may request increased doses and refills more often than anticipated, repeatedly "lose" prescriptions, and get prescriptions from multiple physicians (often revealed by calls to or from pharmacies). Urine testing is widely used to confirm recent drug use.

Drug abusers often deny their addiction and express ambivalence about discontinuing their drug use. In the office, the internist may use brief counseling techniques similar to those used for smoking and alcohol abuse to motivate patients to take action to change their behavior. Often this means the patient following through with a referral to a substance abuse treatment program.

**KEY POINTS**

- Smoking status should be determined for all patients.
- Patients who want to quit smoking should be offered pharmacologic therapy in addition to counseling, including telephone quit lines.
- Routine screening is recommended to identify persons whose alcohol use puts them at risk.
- For management of alcohol abuse and dependence, referral for specialty treatment is recommended; for management of alcohol misuse, brief behavioral counseling may be useful.
- Clues for chemical dependency include unexpected behavioral changes, acute intoxication, frequent job changes, unexplained financial problems, family history of substance abuse, frequent problems with law enforcement agencies, having a partner with substance abuse, and medical sequelae of drug abuse.

## Sexual Behavior

A sexual history should be obtained with respect and a nonjudgmental attitude. Because rates of many sexually transmitted diseases (STDs) are highest among adolescents and men who have sex with men, a sexual history is particularly important for those groups. **Table 7** provides one recommended approach to obtaining a sexual history. Risk factors for acquiring an STD include history of an STD, multiple sex partners, contact with sex workers, new sex partner, meeting partners on the Internet, illegal drug use, imprisonment or admission to a juvenile detention center, younger age, unmarried status,

| TABLE 7 "Five P's" of a Sexual History |
| --- |
| **1. Partners** |
| "Do you have sex with men, women, or both?" |
| "In the past 2 months, how many partners have you had sex with?" |
| "In the past 12 months, how many partners have you had sex with?" |
| **2. Prevention of Pregnancy** |
| "Are you or your partner trying to get pregnant?" If no, "What are you doing to prevent pregnancy?" |
| **3. Protection from STDs** |
| "What do you do to protect yourself from STDs and HIV?" |
| **4. Practices** |
| "To understand your risks for STDs, I need to understand the kind of sex you have had recently." |
| "Have you had vaginal sex, meaning 'penis in vagina sex'"? |
| If yes, "Do you use condoms: never, sometimes, or always?" |
| "Have you had anal sex, meaning 'penis in rectum/anus sex'"? |
| If yes, "Do you use condoms: never, sometimes, or always?" |
| "Have you had oral sex, meaning 'mouth on penis/vagina'"? |
| For condom answers: |
|   If "never": "Why don't you use condoms?" |
|   If "sometimes": "In what situations, or with whom, do you not use condoms?" |
| **5. Past History of STDs** |
| "Have you ever had an STD?" |
| "Have any of your partners had an STD?" |
| **Additional Questions to Identify HIV and Hepatitis Risk:** |
| "Have you or any of your partners ever injected drugs?" |
| "Have any of your partners exchanged money or drugs for sex?" |
| "Is there anything else about your sexual practices that I need to know about?" |

STD = sexually transmitted disease.

Information from Centers for Disease Control and Prevention, Workowski KA, Berman SM. Sexually transmitted diseases treatment guidelines, 2006. MMWR Recomm Rep. 2006;55(RR-11):1-94. [PMID: 16888612]

| TABLE 8 Recommendations for Screening and Prevention of Sexually Transmitted Diseases |
| --- |
| Effective prevention strategies include reducing the number of sex partners, being in a mutually monogamous relationship with a person free of sexually transmitted diseases (STDs), screening for STDs before initiating sexual contact with a new partner, and abstinence. |
| Condom use by men reduces transmission of HIV, *Chlamydia*, gonorrhea, *Trichomonas*, herpes virus, and human papillomavirus. The female condom, if used correctly, may provide similar benefits. |
| HIV testing and prevention counseling should be offered when evaluating for STDs. |
| Asymptomatic women with risk factors for STDs should be screened for gonorrhea and chlamydial infection during their annual pelvic examinations. Immunization for hepatitis A and B viruses and human papillomavirus should be offered as appropriate. |
| Herpes simplex virus-2 sexual transmission can be reduced by the use of suppressive antiviral agents by the infected person, by using condoms, or by both. Partners of infected persons should be advised that sexual transmission can occur during asymptomatic periods. |
| Men who have sex with men should have annual testing for HIV infections, gonorrhea, chlamydial infection, and syphilis. |
| Pregnant women should be screened for syphilis, chlamydial infection, HIV infection, and hepatitis B. |

Recommendations from the Centers for Disease Control and Prevention.

and living in an urban area. **Table 8** outlines CDC recommendations for STD screening and prevention.

- Condom use reduces transmission of HIV, *Chlamydia*, gonorrhea, *Trichomonas*, herpesvirus, and human papillomavirus.

## Domestic Violence

Domestic violence is defined as intentional controlling or violent behavior by a person who is or was in an intimate relationship with the victim. The behavior may take the form of physical abuse, sexual assault, emotional abuse, economic control, or social isolation of the victim. Domestic violence frequently remains undiagnosed because patients conceal that they are in abusive relationships, and the signs and symptoms of abuse may be subtle or absent. As many as 31% of women report abuse at some time in their lifetime. Elder abuse occurs in 4% to 6% of the elderly and can result in loss of independence, home, life savings, health, and dignity.

There is controversy regarding routine screening for domestic violence. While such screening is acceptable to patients and increases the identification of domestic violence, the USPSTF has concluded that there is insufficient evidence that the subsequent interventions lead to improved outcomes. Other groups, however, advocate routine screening, particularly at initial visits.

When screening for domestic violence, it is important to provide a safe environment, including assurances regarding confidentiality, a private examination room, and availability of posters, pamphlets, and referral cards. Screening questions should be integrated into history taking. Consider introducing the subject in a general way; for example: "Because violence is so common in many people's lives, I've started to ask about it routinely." Finally, the choice of screening question or questions used is important. A screen consisting of the following single question has been shown to increase detection: "At any time, has a partner (or family member or caretaker) hit, kicked, or otherwise hurt or threatened you?" However, the single question "Do you feel safe at home?" has been found to be insensitive for detection of domestic violence and should not be used alone. The four-item SAFE screening questionnaire also can be used:

**S Stress/safety:** "Do you feel safe in your relationship?"

**A Afraid/abused:** "Have you ever been in a relationship where you were threatened, hurt, or afraid?"

**F Friends/family:** "Are your friends or family aware that you have been hurt? Could you tell them and would they be able to give you support?"

**E Emergency plan:** "Do you have a safe place to go and the resources you need in an emergency?"

Clues to an abusive relationship that could trigger an inquiry are shown in **Table 9**. When an abusive situation is identified, a patient may not be ready to leave his or her abuser because of fear of retaliation, financial dependence on the abuser, having no place to go, a belief that the abuse will stop, or a belief that the abuse is the patient's fault. Important interventions for patients who are in abusive situations include:

- Validate the patient's perceptions that he or she is being abused, confirm the patient's worth, and assure the patient that you will support him or her.

- Assess for safety: Inquire about escalating verbal or physical abuse and recent weapons purchases. Discuss safety planning in detail, including whether the patient wants to leave home, return home, or have the abuser removed from the household.

- Ask if the patient wants to file a police report or obtain a restraining order.

- Provide information about community resources, including local domestic violence hot lines, the National Domestic Violence Hotline (800-799-SAFE; www.ndvh.org), shelters, legal advocacy groups, and social services. In some instances, calling from the office and going directly to a shelter may be appropriate.

- Refer to mental health services if appropriate.

- Carefully document the encounter in case the patient decides to seek legal redress. Documentation may include photographs or detailed sketches of injuries.

- For domestic violence involving a child or an incompetent adult, reporting to the local department of social services is mandatory. A minority of states require reporting injuries from domestic violence against competent adults.

**KEY POINTS**

- It is important to ask about domestic violence when patients present with symptoms or behaviors that may be associated with abuse.

- When an abusive situation is identified, address immediate safety needs.

**TABLE 9 Potential Clues to an Abusive Relationship**

Inconsistent explanation of injuries or a delay in seeking treatment

Somatic complaints (abdominal and pelvic pain, headaches, fatigue)

Depression, anxiety, or sleep disturbances

Exacerbations or poor control of chronic medical conditions

Sexually transmitted diseases and unplanned pregnancies

Frequent, unexplained appointment changes

Overly solicitous partner or one who refuses to leave the examination room

Suicide attempts

Substance abuse

## Bibliography

Armstrong K, Moye E, Williams S, Berlin JA, Reynolds EE. Screening mammography in women 40 to 49 years of age: a systematic review for the American College of Physicians. Ann Intern Med. 2007;146(7):516-526. [PMID: 17404354]

Barry MJ. Screening for Prostate Cancer–The controversy that refuses to die. N Engl J Med. 2009;360(13):1351-1354. [PMID: 19297564]

Boulware LE, Marinopoulos S, Phillips KA, et al. Systematic review: the value of the periodic health evaluation. Ann Intern Med. 2007;146(4):289-300. [PMID 17310053]

Burke W, Psaty BM. Personalized medicine in the era of genomics. JAMA. 2007;298(14):1682-1684. [PMID: 17925520]

Centers for Disease Control and Prevention, Workowski KA, Berman SM. Sexually transmitted diseases treatment guidelines, 2006. MMWR Recomm Rep. 2006;55(RR-11):1-94. [PMID: 16888612]

Fiore MC, Jaén CR, Baker TB, et al. Treating Tobacco Use and Dependence: 2008 Update. Clinical Practice Guideline. Rockville, MD: U.S. Department of Health and Human Services. Public Health Service. May 2008.

Fraser CG, Matthew CM, Mowat NA, Wilson JA, Carey FA, Steele RJ. Immunochemical testing of individuals positive for guaiac faecal occult blood test in a screening programme for colorectal cancer: an observational study. Lancet Oncol. 2006;7(2):127-131. [PMID: 16455476]

Garland SM, Hernandez-Avila M, Wheeler CM, et al; Females United to Unilaterally Reduce Endo/Ectocervical Disease (FUTURE) I Investigators. Quadrivalent Vaccine against Human Papillomavirus to Prevent Anogenital Diseases. N Engl J Med. 2007;356(19):1928-1943. [PMID: 17494926]

Goldstein MG, Whitlock EP, DePue J; Planning Committee of the Addressing Multiple Behavioral Risk Factors in Primary Care Project. Multiple behavioral risk factor interventions in primary care: summary of research evidence. Am J Prev Med. 2004;27(2 Suppl):61-79. [PMID: 15275675]

Haskell WL, Lee IM, Pate RR, et al. Physical activity and public health: updated recommendations for adults from the American College of Sports Medicine and the American Heart Association. Circulation. 2007;116(9):1081-1093. [PMID: 17671237]

Levin B, Lieberman DA, McFarland B, et al; Screening and surveillance for the early detection of colorectal cancer and adenomatous polyps, 2008: a joint guideline from the American Cancer Society, the US Multi-Society Task Force on Colorectal Cancer, and the American College of Radiology. CA Cancer J Clin. 2008;58(3):130-160. [PMID: 18322143]

Murff HJ, Spigel DR, Syngal S. Does this patient have a family history of cancer? An evidence-based analysis of the accuracy of family cancer history. JAMA. 2004;292(12):1480-1489. [PMID: 15383520]

Oxman MN, Levin MJ, Johnson GR, et al. A vaccine to prevent herpes zoster and postherpetic neuralgia in older adults. N Engl J Med. 2005;352(22):2271-2284. [PMID: 15930418]

Qaseem A, Snow V, Shekelle P, Hopkins R Jr., Owens DK; Clinical Efficacy Assessment Subcommittee, American College of Physicians. Screening for HIV in health care settings: a guidance statement from the American College of Physicians and HIV Medicine Association. Ann Intern Med. 2009;150(2):125-31. [PMID: 19047022]

Rich EC, Burke W, Heaton CJ, et al. Reconsidering the family history in primary care. J Gen Intern Med. 2004;19(3):273-280. [PMID: 15009784]

U.S. Preventive Services Task Force. Screening and behavioral counseling interventions in primary care to reduce alcohol misuse: recommendation statement. Ann Intern Med. 2004;140(7):554-556. [PMID: 15068984]

U.S. Preventive Services Task Force. Screening for family and intimate partner violence: recommendation statement. Ann Intern Med. 2004;140(5):382-386. [PMID: 14996680]

# Patient Safety

## Data on Adverse Events

The Institute of Medicine (IOM) reported in 2000 that nearly 100,000 patients die as a result of medical errors each year. A Brigham and Women's Hospital self-audit from 2005 found 233 serious errors and 54 preventable adverse events during 1490 patient-days. The most common serious errors were medication-related (61%); 53% of performance-level failures were slips and lapses (rather than rule-based or knowledge-based errors). Two-thirds of adverse events do not cause direct harm to the patient, and many are "near-misses." The IOM estimates that preventable errors cost approximately $20 billion in hospitals alone.

## Principles of Patient Safety

A *root-cause analysis* is a group exercise used to determine the contributors to an adverse event. Often, a fishbone pattern is used to illustrate causation, beginning with a problem or error at the fish's head. Working back down the spine, the team is asked repetitively, "And what contributed to this?" This continues until an investigatory team has reached as many prime factors as possible. Factors that should be addressed in such a root-cause analysis are outlined in **Table 10**.

Graber and colleagues studied factors that contributed to diagnostic error in 100 cases and found an average of 5.9 system-related or cognitive factors contributing to the diagnostic error in each case. This finding confirms the "Swiss cheese" model of error in a medical environment—that there must be a breakdown of several layers in a system to actually cause an injury (**Figure 1**). Therefore, a health system must build redundancy into its safety processes with the factors listed in Table 10 addressed in order to build in multiple layers of protection between a patient and any potential harm. For example, an airline pilots' checklist model has been used

| **TABLE 10** Questions to Consider in a Root-Cause Analysis of an Adverse Event |
| --- |
| Were issues related to patient assessment a factor in this situation? |
| Were issues related to staff training or staff competency a factor in this event? |
| Was equipment involved in this event in any way? |
| Was the work environment a factor in this event? |
| Was the lack of information (or misinterpretation of information) a factor in this event? |
| Was communication a factor in this event? |
| Were appropriate rules/policies/procedures—or the lack thereof—a factor in this event? |
| Was the failure of a barrier—designed to protect the patient, staff, equipment, or environment—a factor in this event? |
| Were personnel or personal issues a factor in this event? |

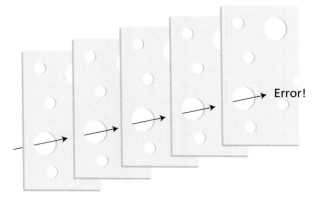

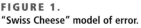

**FIGURE 1.**
"Swiss Cheese" model of error.

Adapted with permission from Reason J. Human error: models and management. BMJ. 2000;320(7237):768-770. [PMID: 10720363] Copyright 2000, BMJ Publishing Group Ltd.

in intensive care units to ensure that important initiatives, such as sedation holidays, ventilator weaning, and infection prophylaxis, are addressed daily on morning rounds. Likewise, a "time-out" policy to ensure proper matching of patient with procedure has quickly become a national norm. As an example, a surgical nurse may be the point person empowered to call "time out" before an operation commences. Then, the patient and the team, including the anesthesiologist, the surgeons, and any technicians, confirm the correct patient name, the kind of planned surgery, and the correct surgical site.

Technology initiatives, such as electronic medical record (EMR) systems, can be used to design "force functions" to decrease human error. For example, an EMR's physician order entry screen can ensure medication safety with automatic checks and offer reminders for important quality indicators (*"Please consider an ACE inhibitor in this patient with heart failure"*). Safe health care systems set up a culture of safety, in which the health care team openly discusses errors, teams are encouraged to analyze problems, and collaboration occurs across disciplines to find solutions in a systems-based approach.

## Quality Improvement Models

Most major health care organizations now have quality departments that are being converted from reporting groups (for reporting quality data measures) into proactive departments that facilitate performance improvement (PI) teams that are chartered to address particular problems. Rather than labeling *people* in the health care team as the source of errors, these teams focus on the *processes* involved in care delivery. A common methodology used by such teams is the PDSA, or Plan-Do-Study-Act, cycle (**Figure 2**). For example, to improve the timing of administering antibiotics to patients with pneumonia, a PI team might *plan* a test of a simplified system (consisting of fewer steps) for giving antibiotics after an order is given, *do* the test by trying the new protocol on a limited number of patients, *study* the results and summarize what was learned, and *act* by refining the protocol based on what was learned and planning the next test.

Another quality management model used in health care is total quality management (TQM), typified by the Baldrige National Quality Program, which publishes evidence-based criteria by which an organization can judge its management (www.quality.nist.gov). The goal of TQM is to build quality processes into every level of the health care organization.

## Diagnostic Errors

A burgeoning science has evolved to teach physicians how to avoid errors in diagnosis. Analyses of clinicians' heuristics seek to understand common shortcuts in reasoning and how these shortcuts can lead to diagnostic errors. *Availability heuristic* errors arise when a clinician has encountered a similar presentation and jumps to the conclusion that the current diagnosis must be the same as in the previous case. *Anchoring heuristic* errors occur when a clinician holds to an initial impression, such as might occur when a referring physician has provided a diagnosis that is then accepted at face value. *Blind obedience* to an authority (such as of a resident to an attending physician) as well as *premature closure* of the thought process can prevent the important expansion of a differential diagnosis.

Strategies to reduce diagnostic errors include: (1) orienting physicians to common diagnostic pitfalls using simulations; (2) compiling a complete differential diagnosis to avoid premature closure (the most common cognitive factor leading to error); and (3) using "prospective hindsight" by assuming that a working diagnosis is incorrect and asking, "What alternatives should be considered?"

## National Patient Safety Goals

Beyond individual organizations and clinicians, external organizations have required major quality initiatives for accreditation, payment, insurance contracts, and national recognition. The Joint Commission's 2009 National Patient Safety Goals (**Table 11**) encourage wholesale organizational commitment to standards to improve health care safety on a national level (www.jointcommission.org/PatientSafety/NationalPatientSafetyGoals). Organizations without safety initiatives in these areas may be judged to be out of compliance and receive sanctions. A survey of the goals reveals a focus on making safe the day-to-day activities of the hospital environment, including communication, medication administration, and risk reduction (infection, surgery, falls).

The Joint Commission's goal to implement a standardized approach to hand-off communications is particularly crucial for physicians. With the advent of resident work-hour

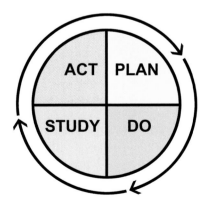

**FIGURE 2.**
**Plan-Do-Study-Act (PDSA) cycle.**
The Plan-Do-Study-Act cycle is a widely used method for rapidly testing a change.

| **TABLE 11** The Joint Commission's 2009 National Patient Safety Goals for Hospitals |
| --- |
| Improve the accuracy of patient identification |
| Improve the effectiveness of communication among caregivers |
| Improve the safety of using medications |
| Reduce the risk of health care–associated infections |
| Accurately and completely reconcile medications across the continuum of care |
| Reduce the risk of patient harm resulting from falls |
| Encourage patients' active involvement in their own care as a patient safety strategy |
| Identify safety risks inherent in the organization's patient population |
| Improve recognition and response to changes in a patient's condition |
| Universal Protocol: Conducting a pre-procedure verification process, marking the procedure site, performing a time-out |

Adapted from The Joint Commission. 2009 National Patient Safety Goals. www.joint-commission.org/PatientSafety/NationalPatientSafetyGoals. Accessed July 13, 2009.

restrictions and the increased use of hospitalist teams, there has been a corresponding increase in the number of patient hand-offs between physicians. This increases the potential for error, given the likely omission of important information (such as allergies, important past history, pending tests). The best practice for hand-off includes person-to-person communication, providing an opportunity to ask and respond to questions, and providing information that is accurate and concise (including name, location, history, diagnoses, medication and problem lists, status, recent procedures, a "to do" list that has "if/then" statements, severity of illness, and contingency plans).

**KEY POINTS**

- Diagnostic error is typically multifactorial, with an average of 5.9 system-related or cognitive factors contributing to a single diagnostic error.

- Strategies for building redundancy into a health care system's safety processes include checklist systems, time-out policies, and force functions, such as automatic checks and reminders.

- The Plan-Do-Study-Act (PDSA) cycle is an effective means for performance improvement teams to implement changes to address specific patient safety problems.

- A key strategy for reducing diagnostic error is to compile a complete differential diagnosis to avoid "premature closure."

- The best practice for patient hand-off includes person-to-person communication and information that is accurate and concise.

### Bibliography

Graber ML, Franklin N, Gordon R. Diagnostic Error in Internal Medicine. Arch Intern Med. 2005;165(13):1493-1499. [PMID: 16009864]

Redelmeier DA. Improving patient care. The cognitive psychology of missed diagnoses. Ann Intern Med. 2005;142(2):115-120. [PMID: 15657159]

Rothschild JM, Landrigan CP, Cronin JW, et al. The Critical Care Safety Study: The incidence and nature of adverse events and serious medical errors in intensive care. Crit Care Med. 2005;33(8):1694-1700. [PMID: 16096443]

Vidyarthi A, Arora V, Schnipper J, Wall S, Wachter R. Managing discontinuity in academic medical centers: strategies for a safe and effective resident sign-out. J Hosp Med. 2006;1(4):257-266. [PMID: 17219508]

# Professionalism and Ethics

## Professionalism

The Charter on Medical Professionalism was a product of several years of collaborative work by leading organizations of internal medicine. The charter contains three fundamental principles and ten professional commitments (**Table 12**). The first principle, that of the *primacy of patient welfare*, dates from ancient times. There is concern, however, that in today's health care environment, the physician's commitment to the patient is being challenged by the conditions of medical practice and external forces. The second principle, that of *patient autonomy*, has a more recent history. Only in the latter part of the twentieth century did the public begin to view the physician as an advisor, often one of many, to an autonomous patient. Finally, the principle of *social justice* calls upon the profession to promote a fair distribution of health care resources.

The American College of Physicians (ACP) has highlighted four areas for professional commitment on the part of physicians and their professional organizations as part of an initiative to revitalize internal medicine: (1) advocacy for patients and for the patient-physician relationship; (2) enhanced communications with patients and colleagues in order to foster health care partnerships and improve coordination of the health care team; (3) a renewed commitment to "mastery," both in expanding and applying the internal medicine knowledge base and in developing and implementing improvements in the processes and coordination of care; and (4) development and implementation of performance measures linked to quality improvement and accountability in a manner that respects the patient-physician relationship. To achieve these goals, it was acknowledged that society—comprising health plans, purchasers, government, clinicians, and patients—must promote the appropriate context for health care delivery by providing consistent support for sustained patient-physician relationships within which physicians can fulfill their ethical obligations to patients. Finally, the ACP affirms that all parties to health care delivery should foster an ethical health care environment, including universal access and a reimbursement mechanism that encourages physicians to take the time required to provide and coordinate appropriate care for adult patients throughout the aging process.

**KEY POINT**

- The three fundamental principles of medical professionalism are the primacy of patient welfare, patient autonomy, and social justice.

## Decision-Making and Informed Consent

### Assessing Decision-Making Capacity

The legal concept of competency covers a wide range of decision-making abilities, including both medical (competency to make treatment decisions, competency to consent to research) as well as nonmedical (competency to manage one's financial affairs, competency to stand trial). Whereas competency is a legal concept, its application in a clinical setting requires the assessment of a patient's ability to exercise his or her autonomy. To avoid confusion, many clinicians

| TABLE 12 Principles and Commitments of Professionalism | |
| --- | --- |
| **Principle or Commitment** | **Comment** |
| **Fundamental Principle** | |
| Primacy of patient welfare | Altruism is a central trust factor in the physician-patient relationship. Market forces, societal pressures, and administrative exigencies must not compromise this principle. |
| Patient autonomy | Patients' decisions about their care must be paramount, as long as those decisions are in keeping with ethical practice and do not lead to demands for inappropriate care. |
| Social justice | Physicians should work actively to eliminate discrimination in health care, whether based on race, gender, socioeconomic status, ethnicity, religion, or any other social category. |
| **Professional Commitment** | |
| Competence | Physicians must be committed to lifelong learning and to maintaining the medical knowledge and clinical and team skills necessary for the provision of quality care. |
| Honesty with patients | Obtain informed consent for treatment or research. Report and analyze medical errors in order to maintain trust, improve care, and provide appropriate compensation to injured parties. |
| Patient confidentiality | Privacy of information is essential to patient trust and even more pressing with electronic medical records. |
| Appropriate patient relations | Given the inherent vulnerability and dependency of patients, physicians should never exploit patients for any sexual advantage, personal financial gain, or other private purpose. |
| Improve quality of care | Work collaboratively with other professionals to reduce medical errors, increase patient safety, minimize overuse of health care resources, and optimize the outcomes of care. |
| Improve access to care | Work to eliminate barriers to access based on education, laws, finances, geography, and social discrimination. Equity requires the promotion of public health and preventive medicine, as well as public advocacy, without concern for the self-interest of the physician or the profession. |
| Just distribution of resources | Work with other physicians, hospitals, and payers to develop guidelines for cost-effective care. Providing unnecessary services not only exposes one's patients to avoidable harm and expense but also diminishes the resources available for others. |
| Scientific knowledge | Uphold scientific standards, promote research, create new knowledge, and ensure its appropriate use. |
| Manage conflicts of interest | Medical professionals and their organizations have many opportunities to compromise their professional responsibilities by pursuing private gain or personal advantage. Such compromises are especially threatening with for-profit industries, including medical equipment manufacturers, insurance companies, and pharmaceutical firms. Physicians have an obligation to recognize, disclose to the general public, and deal with conflicts of interest that arise. |
| Professional responsibilities | Undergo self-assessment and external scrutiny of all aspects of one's performance. Participate in the processes of self-regulation, including remediation and discipline of members who have failed to meet professional standards. |

Adapted with permission from ABIM Foundation. American Board of Internal Medicine; ACP-ASIM Foundation. American College of Physicians-American Society of Internal Medicine; European Federation of Internal Medicine. Medical professionalism in the new millennium: a physician charter. Ann Intern Med. 2002;136(3):243-246. [PMID: 11827500] Copyright 2002, American College of Physicians.

and researchers use competency as the legal ability and capacity as the medical or psychological ability to make certain decisions.

There is no single or absolute standard for determining a patient's medical decision-making capacity. Instead, there are various criteria levels ranging from low to high stringency (**Table 13**). More stringent criteria typically come into play as the consequences of what the clinician deems an uninformed or incompetent decision become more serious, especially in terms of risk-benefit ratio. For example, one might demand more stringent evidence of decision-making capacity in a young person who is septic and confused who refuses antibiotic therapy compared with an elderly person with advanced dementia and metastatic cancer with a gram-negative bacteremia who refuses treatment.

## Advance Directives and Surrogate Decision-Making

Advance directives include instructions about what kind of care should be provided (living wills) and who should make the decisions if the patient cannot do so (proxy designations). Though helpful as a means of expressing general views regarding end-of-life care, living wills often use vague terms such as "heroic measures," "terminally ill," or "facing imminent death." Some living wills provide concrete instructions for care in a variety of clinical situations, such as the use of feeding tubes or ventilators in the event of permanent unconsciousness. Even detailed directives, however, cannot describe all of the situations and special circumstances in which patients may find themselves. Thus, it is also desirable, either instead of or in addition to a living will, to specify a surrogate decision-maker

**TABLE 13** Criteria Clinicians May Consider in Assessing Medical Decision-Making Capacity

| Criterion | Stringency | Test | Who Might Fail? |
|---|---|---|---|
| Evidencing a choice | Low | Answer *yes* or *no* | Comatose |
| Capacity: Ability to understand in general sense | Medium | Mental status testing | Dementia (advanced) |
| Comprehension: Actual understanding of specific information provided | Medium | *Can you repeat what I have just told you?* | Anxiety<br>Low education<br>Language barriers<br>Cultural barriers |
| Rational reasons for choice | High | *Why are you choosing this?* | Psychosis; delirium |
| Reasonable outcome expected | High | Does the decision make sense in terms of:<br>    Disease prognosis<br>    Patient's values | Depression |

rather than focusing solely on all of the possible decisions that may be necessary. Naming a family member or friend to serve as a health care proxy through a durable power of attorney for health care identifies someone physicians can talk to if and when clinical circumstances occur wherein the patient is not able to speak for him- or herself. A surrogate decision-maker should be that person most familiar with the patient's previous beliefs and aims, and having no conflicts of interest. Sometimes, but not always, a surrogate decision-maker is formally identified by means of a durable power of attorney. If the patient's preference has not been designated in advance, the surrogate is typically a family member; for adults, this may be the spouse, an adult child, parents, and siblings, in order of priority. However, other factors may determine who is the surrogate in the absence of the patient's expressed preferences, including the presence of a domestic partner, estrangement of a spouse or other family members, disagreement among family members, and differences among state laws.

## Informed Consent

Three elements of informed consent are required when discussing a medical treatment or course of action: (1) disclosure of all relevant information, including the benefits, risks, and alternatives with respect to the treatment or research study; (2) adequate understanding of the information by the patient or subject; and (3) voluntary decision-making by the patient or subject. These can be thought of as the "three C's" of informed consent—communication, comprehension, and no coercion.

What information should be disclosed? At the beginning of the twentieth century, disclosure was guided by the *professional practice standard* (whatever the physician felt should be disclosed). Case law and contemporary bioethics have gradually transitioned informed consent to the *prudent person standard*, whereby the physician must disclose what a reasonable person would want to know before making a decision, particularly potential risks. A reasonable guideline is to describe the complications or side effects that either have a high likelihood of occurring even if they are minor (nausea or transient fever) or have a low likelihood of occurring but are so serious

that a prudent person would want to know when making decisions (for example, 5% chance of dying). After disclosing what a reasonable person would want to know, it is important to ask the patient or subject whether he or she needs any other information to make a decision. This allows the person to ask questions that may be unique to their own values and concerns and thus sets an even higher standard, a subjective or individual patient standard.

**KEY POINTS**

- Advance directives include instructions about what kind of care should be provided (living wills) and who should make the decisions if the patient cannot do so (proxy designations).

- The three elements required for informed consent include disclosure of relevant information, comprehension by the patient, and lack of coercion.

- Decision-making competency assessment can range from less to more stringent, depending on the consequences of the decision, and may include the patient's ability to express a choice, general decision-making capacity, comprehension of specific information, rational reasons, and reasonable outcomes.

## Withholding or Withdrawing Treatment

Withholding or withdrawing therapy that is deemed futile or according to patient preference is justifiable from both an ethical and a legal perspective. The best strategy to avoid subjecting a patient to a life support measure that was unwanted is to discuss end-of-life care with the patient as early as possible. Patient preferences for do-not-resuscitate orders as well as issues of artificial feeding, hydration, and other life prolonging measures, should be clearly documented in the medical record. While patients have a right to refuse unwanted life-sustaining treatments, it is less clear whether these treatments must be provided (if requested by a patient or family member) once it is clear the prognosis is dismal. *Qualitative futility* means that the treatment will not improve the patient's already poor quality of life. *Quantitative futility* uses a numeric probability to decide when treatment should not be offered, as the patient is unlikely to survive even with the intervention. *Physiologic futility* means that it is impossible for the intervention to significantly improve the patient's condition. In discussing decisions to withhold or withdraw treatments, the physician should carefully address any family concerns regarding the decision, such as the belief that discontinuing a feeding tube will result in the patient suffering from hunger or thirst, despite evidence to the contrary.

Cardiopulmonary resuscitation is not appropriate for patients with terminal, irreversible disease or imminent death. However, do-not-resuscitate orders do not preclude provision of other life-prolonging measures or palliative care. Occasionally, treatments are withheld based on the fear that once started, they cannot be withdrawn. A limited trial of a therapy can be used to assess a patient's response, after which the treatment plan can be reviewed and revised. The decision to institute or withdraw life-prolonging measures needs to be discussed with the patient (if competent) and family. If the patient is unable to make these decisions, an advance directive allows health care providers to follow the patient's wishes or have a surrogate make decisions. When there is no advance directive, the physicians and surrogate should make decisions based on *substituted judgment*—what do they think the patient would have wanted—or, if this is not possible, based on what they believe is in the patient's best interests. Laws and processes for these decisions vary from state to state.

In making quality-of-life determinations, priority tends to be given to patient or surrogate assessment of whether the treatment is worthwhile; however, when there is a significant conflict, the physician should not be forced to administer a treatment that violates his or her values or is medically futile. In these instances, a discussion with the family and an ethics committee is warranted, and if no consensus can be reached, consideration should be given to transferring the patient to another physician or health care facility. Rarely, a legal decision may be necessary.

> **KEY POINT**
>
> • Life support measures need not be started or continued if they are thought to be medically futile; however, legal opinion may vary and if doubt exists, the wishes of the patient or surrogate are usually favored.

## Physician-Assisted Suicide and Euthanasia

Physician-assisted suicide involves knowingly prescribing a potentially lethal amount of medication to a patient for self-administration. Whether or not it is ever ethical for a physi-

cian to do this has been debated for years. The Hippocratic Oath does not support physician-assisted suicide, and both the ACP and American Medical Association have issued statements opposing the practice. However, some physicians feel that it is not immoral to honor patient autonomy and assist in the rational suicide of a terminally ill patient. In the United States, physician-assisted suicide is currently illegal in all states except Oregon and Washington, where legal safeguards have been established to protect the autonomy of the patient. Active euthanasia, whereby a physician, with the patient's consent, directly and intentionally administers a substance to cause death, is illegal in all states.

A request for physician-assisted suicide should be construed as a signal that the patient has unmet needs and should trigger further assessment to determine the fears, social circumstances, and level of pain and suffering that may have brought about this decision. The physician's obligations are to provide appropriate palliative care, including relief of pain; control of symptoms related to the illness; evaluation and treatment of depression; and counseling and support. Inadequate pain management remains a problem, often owing to physician inexperience or fear of prescribing high-dose narcotics.

> **KEY POINTS**
>
> • A request for physician-assisted suicide is often a signal that a patient has unmet needs, including fear, hopelessness, difficult social circumstances, and severe pain and suffering.
>
> • Despite mixed public opinion, physician-assisted suicide is illegal in most of the United States, and active euthanasia is illegal in all states.

## Confidentiality

Confidentiality is fundamental to medical care, and the physician should respect patient privacy and encourage candid discussion of any problems the patient may have. The physician should not release any private, identifiable patient information ("privileged communication") without the patient's consent. If a patient is incapacitated, the physician can disclose protected health information to a caregiver (for example, a spouse or relative) if, in the physician's professional judgment, the disclosure is in the best interests of the patient. Discussions about patients in a public place (office waiting room, hospital elevator, hallway, cafeteria) violate confidentiality and must be avoided. The Health Insurance Portability and Accountability Act (HIPAA) established federal standards for privacy protection of medical records, and physicians, clinical practices, and institutions must have policies and procedures related to disclosure of medical information to ensure confidentiality of these records. However, the advent of electronic medical records, prescriptions, and computerized databases has raised concerns regarding the security of confidential information. This information should still be protected under the physician-patient relationship, and legislation provides guidelines and penalties with respect to standards for handling and disclosure of patient information contained in these electronic media. Strategies to maintain protection of electronic medical records include not sharing passwords or allowing unauthorized persons access to the system and logging off before leaving a computer station.

A delicate situation may arise when a patient requests that certain information not be recorded in the medical record (substance abuse, sexual preference, test results). Although the physician has an ethical obligation to maintain a complete and accurate record, release of this sensitive information may be detrimental to the patient, and the physician cannot guarantee confidentiality. Confidentiality, however, is not absolute and may need to be overridden in certain cases. Some of these possible exceptions to confidentiality include exceptions to protect the patient (for example, disclosure of domestic violence) and exceptions to protect third parties (reporting infectious diseases or impaired drivers to public health officials, partner notification by public health officials, injuries caused by weapons or crimes, warnings by physicians to persons at risk, and violence by psychiatric patients). In such cases, the physician should attempt to discuss these issues with the patient whenever possible prior to breaching confidentiality, and the disclosure should be done in a manner to minimize harm to the patient and to comply with the law.

A physician may receive information from sources other than the patient and be asked to withhold that information or its source from the patient. Although the physician is not legally obligated to keep such information from the patient, he or she should first encourage discussion between the informant and the patient and then decide, based on the best interests of the patient, whether or not to reveal the information.

**KEY POINTS**

- Discussions of patient information should not take place in public places.
- The physician should not release any private, identifiable patient information without the patient's consent.

## Conflicts of Interest

A conflict of interest exists when a physician's professional duty to the patient conflicts (or gives the appearance that it conflicts) with another interest, such as personal financial gain, insurance or contractual obligation, or other arrangements or commitments. The physician's main responsibility is to the patient—to make recommendations based on medical merit and to practice effective and efficient health care using available resources wisely.

Financial conflicts of interest arise when physician reimbursement potentially drives decision making and actions that are not necessarily in the patient's best interest. Examples include

financial incentives for overuse in a fee-for-service setting or underuse in a managed care setting. Physicians must be cognizant of the system conditions under which they practice and should always act to benefit the patient. Participating in certain business arrangements involving referrals within a group or to an outside group or facility in which the physician or a family member has a financial interest is potentially illegal under the so-called *Stark laws*, which govern physician self-referral.

Gifts, trips, and subsidies offered by pharmaceutical and medical device industries may create conflicts of interest wherein the physician's interest coincides more with the business than with the patient. These influences may subtly change the physician's attitude and behavior in a manner favoring the company involved, resulting in higher medical costs to the patient. Even more subtle may be the influence of industry on continuing medical education (CME) and clinical practice guidelines. As a result, new policies and standards have been developed that demand explicit disclosure of financial conflicts of interest by guideline committee members and CME providers.

The two primary methods for dealing with conflicts of interest are *disclosure* and *avoidance*. Disclosure alone does little to protect patients, however, and avoidance is preferable. Physicians should try to avoid all significant conflicts of interest; if a potential conflict is unavoidable or less serious, it should be acknowledged and disclosed to the patient.

**KEY POINTS**

- Conflicts of interest include potential for overuse in a fee-for-service setting, for underuse in a managed care setting, acceptance of gifts from pharmaceutical companies or medical device manufacturers, and certain business arrangements regarding referrals.
- Conflicts of interest should be avoided, if possible; if avoidance is not possible, they should be disclosed.

## Medical Error Reporting

The Institute of Medicine defines a medical error as the failure of a planned action to be completed as intended (error of execution) or the use of a wrong plan to achieve an aim (error of planning). Knowledge of previous medical errors is important to efforts to reduce the incidence of future errors; however, the frequent failure to report medical errors hampers these efforts. Although failure to report a medical error is considered unethical, fear of damage to reputation and potential legal ramifications often hinder physicians and hospitals from disclosing these errors.

The Patient Safety and Quality Improvement Act established a federal system for voluntary reporting of medical errors (www.pso.ahrq.gov/index.html) and provides protection for health care providers who submit information intended to improve patient safety. (See Patient Safety section for strategies to reduce medical errors.)

## Sexual Contact between Physician and Patient

The American Medical Association and the ACP both state that it is unethical for a physician to become sexually involved with a current patient even if the patient initiates or consents to the relationship. The rationale for these recommendations is that there is inequality between the parties (one-way intimacy with the patient in a vulnerable and dependent position), and the physician may betray the patient's trust (using confidential information) or not act in the patient's best interest. There are legal and regulatory sanctions against these relationships, ranging from criminal charges to sanctions by state licensing boards. Sexual contact or a romantic relationship between a physician and a former patient may also be unethical irrespective of the length of time elapsed since ending the professional relationship. It has also been suggested that physicians refrain from such relationships with a family member or surrogate of a patient if there may be an appearance that the professional relationship has been exploited. Increased patient autonomy has attenuated the imbalance of power, however, theoretically reducing patient vulnerability. In any case, a physician should consult with a colleague or other professional prior to becoming sexually involved with a former patient.

Despite these prohibitions, it has been reported that 5% to 10% of psychiatrists have had sexual contact with a patient; it is unknown what percentage of practitioners in other specialties have had similar relationships. Physicians aware of instances of sexual misconduct have an obligation to report them.

A request by a patient or physician for a chaperone to be present during the physical examination should be accommodated, but the physician should respect the patient's right to confidentiality and not discuss patient issues while the chaperone is in the room.

### KEY POINT

- Sexual relationships between a physician and a patient are considered unethical because of the inequality of power, potentially placing the patient in a vulnerable and dependent role.

## The Impaired Physician and Colleague Responsibility

The impaired physician is one who is no longer able to safely carry out his or her professional duties because of physical, psychological, or substance abuse problems. Approximately 15% of physicians will be impaired at some point in their career. Risks for abuse include male sex and underlying mood or personality disorders. The highest rates of substance abuse are among emergency department physicians (most commonly using marijuana and cocaine), psychiatrists (most commonly using benzodiazepines), and solo practitioners.

An increasing number of impaired physicians are older physicians, impaired by age-related conditions, who delay retirement.

The first signs of impairment may occur at home and include marital strife. Signs at work may include frequent absences, missed appointments, secretive or inappropriate behavior, mood swings, conflict with colleagues, and heavy drinking at hospital functions. Impaired physicians may exhibit poor personal hygiene, bloodshot eyes, stumbling, or changes in speech patterns. Substance abuse should be considered in residents who experience academic or interpersonal difficulties. Changes in professional performance indicate advanced impairment.

Many physicians are reluctant to report suspected physician impairment because of the desire to protect colleagues, fear of mislabeling them as impaired, and fear of reprisals. The American Medical Association states that physicians have an ethical obligation to report impaired colleagues, but only 20% of states in the United States require the reporting of suspected substance abuse. Physicians should report concerns about colleagues to the hospital impaired physician program or other appropriate authority.

Treatment for substance abuse is more effective among physicians than in the general population. Approximately 75% to 85% of physicians return to work after treatment. Treatment should always be confidential and may include referral to an employee assistance program or an addiction specialist. All states now have treatment programs sponsored by state medical societies, and these programs are independent of state licensing boards. The best success is seen in treatment programs that include 2 to 4 weeks of intensive inpatient treatment.

### KEY POINTS

- Signs of impairment in a physician colleague may include frequent absences from work, missed appointments, secretive or inappropriate behavior, mood swings, conflict with colleagues, and poor personal hygiene.
- Every physician is responsible for protecting patients from an impaired physician and should report any concerns to the hospital impaired physician program or other appropriate authority.

### Bibliography

American College of Physicians. Medical Professionalism in the Changing Health Care Environment: Revitalizing Internal Medicine by Focusing on the Patient–Physician Relationship. Philadelphia: American College of Physicians;2005: Position Paper.

Baldisseri MR. Impaired healthcare professional. Crit Care Med. 2007;35(2 Suppl):S106-S116. [PMID: 17242598]

Gillick MR. Advance care planning. N Engl J Med. 2004;350(1):7-8. [PMID: 14702421]

Jones JW, McCullough LB, Richman BW. Ethical nuances of combining romance with medical practice. J Vasc Surg. 2005;41(1):174-175. [PMID: 15696065]

Murphy JG, Stee L, McEvoy MT, Oshiro J. Journal reporting of medical errors: the wisdom of Solomon, the bravery of Achilles, and the foolishness of Pan. Chest. 2007;131(3):890-896. [PMID: 17356109]

Snyder L, Leffler C; Ethics and Human Rights Committee; American College of Physicians. Ethics Manual: fifth edition. Ann Intern Med. 2005;142(7):560-582. [PMID: 15809467]

Terry PB. Informed consent in clinical medicine. Chest. 2007;131(2): 563-568. [PMID: 17296662]

Tonelli MR. Conflict of interest in clinical practice. Chest. 2007; 132(2):664-670. [PMID: 17699138]

# Palliative Care

## Palliative Care Assessment and Communication

Many terminally ill patients are reluctant to initiate end-of-life discussions with their families, and the physician can play an important role as facilitator. The dialogue may be emotionally charged, and a series of visits may be needed to cover all appropriate areas. It is important to stress to patients that a discussion of end-of-life care is not a discussion of withdrawal of treatment or patient abandonment. A comprehensive palliative care discussion should include information about the diagnosis causing the terminal condition, with expected clinical symptoms and strategies to relieve them. Patients should be asked what symptoms they fear most, and they should be presented with a plan for symptom assessment and treatment titration. The discussion should also include patient preferences for surrogate decision making, an assessment of the patient's emotional and spiritual health, and an understanding of family support systems and community resources that are available. The patient should be asked to give his or her opinion on advance directives for cardiopulmonary resuscitation, other invasive procedures, and artificial nutrition and hydration.

Patients with medical hardware such as pacemakers and intracardiac defibrillators or who undergo chronic life-sustaining treatments such as dialysis require special consideration, as such technologies may unduly prolong life unless decisions are made regarding explicitly discontinuing them. Patients may also wish to discontinue other treatment not directly related to their comfort, especially medications when swallowing becomes difficult. Physicians must be clear about the possible consequences of treatment withdrawal with patients and their surrogate decision makers and not infer consent to discontinue these treatments under the broader context of an advance directive. Discussions on withdrawal of active treatments should take place when patients' functional status and quality of life start to decline but before they lose their ability to vocalize their preferences. Some physicians may feel uncomfortable honoring a patient's request to discontinue treatment for a disorder not related to the underlying cause of death. The input of a clinical ethics committee may be helpful in such situations.

Determining prognosis in terminally ill patients, especially those with nonmalignant disorders, can be challenging for physicians and frustrating for patients. The Palliative Performance Scale is a useful validated tool to provide general estimates of prognosis (**Table 14**).

## Symptom Management

In palliative care, physicians focus on short-term outcomes designed to improve patient comfort and quality of life. The most common patient symptoms encountered are pain, dyspnea, anorexia and weight loss, depression, and delirium.

### Pain

The World Health Organization pain relief ladder represents a useful framework for pharmacologic treatment of pain (**Figure 3**). Non-narcotic treatments, such as aspirin, acetaminophen, or NSAIDs, are used for mild pain (a score of 1-3 on the 0-10 pain intensity scale). Moderate pain (pain score

**Severe Pain (7-10/10)**

| **Strong Opioids** +/- **Nonopioids** +/- **Adjuvants** | **Strong Opioids** ▪ Morphine (immediate or sustained release) ▪ Oxycodone (immediate or sustained release) ▪ Hydromorphone ▪ Fentanyl transdermal |
|---|---|

**Moderate Pain (4-6/10)**

| **Weak Opioids** +/- **Nonopioids** +/- **Adjuvants** | **Weak Opioids** ▪ Codeine ▪ Hydrocodone bitartrate |
|---|---|

**Mild Pain (1-3/10)**

| **Nonopioids** +/- **Adjuvants** | **Nonopioids** ▪ NSAIDs ▪ Salicylates ▪ Acetaminophen |
|---|---|

**Adjuvant Therapy**

| ▪ Anticonvulsants | ▪ Dermal analgesics |
|---|---|
| ▪ Antidepressants | ▪ Muscle relaxants |
| ▪ Corticosteroids | ▪ Stimulants |

**FIGURE 3.**
**World Health Organization three-step analgesic ladder.**

**TABLE 14** Palliative Performance Scale

| Score[a,b] | Ambulation | Activity Level/ Evidence of Disease | Self-Care | Intake | Level of Consciousness |
|---|---|---|---|---|---|
| 100 | Full | Normal activity and work (no evidence of disease) | Full | Normal | Full |
| 90 | Full | Normal activity and work (some evidence of disease) | Full | Normal | Full |
| 80 | Full | Normal activity and work with effort (some disease) | Full | Normal or reduced | Full |
| 70 | Reduced | Unable to do normal job or work (significant disease) | Full | Normal or reduced | Full |
| 60 | Reduced | Unable to do hobbies or housework (significant disease) | Occasional assistance | Normal or reduced | Full or confusion |
| 50 | Reduced | Unable to do any work (extensive disease) | Considerable assistance | Normal or reduced | Full or confusion |
| 40 | Mainly sit or lie | Unable to do most activities (extensive disease) | Mainly assistance | Normal or reduced | Full or drowsy +/– confusion |
| 30 | Bed-bound | Unable to do any activity (extensive disease) | Total care | Normal or reduced | Full or drowsy +/– confusion |
| 20 | Bed-bound | Unable to do any activity (extensive disease) | Total care | Minimal to sips | Full or drowsy +/– confusion |
| 10 | Bed-bound | Unable to do any activity (extensive disease) | Total care | Mouth care only | Drowsy or coma +/– confusion |
| 0 | Death | — | — | — | — |

[a]In a mixed cohort of cancer and noncancer patients, 100% of patients with a score of ≤60 died within 1 year, more than 96% of patients with a score of ≤30 died within 2 months, and more than 95% of those with a score of ≤20 died within 2 weeks.

[b]Begin at the left column and read downwards until the appropriate ambulation level is reached, then read across to the next column and downwards again until the activity/evidence of disease is located. These steps are repeated until all five columns are covered before assigning the actual palliative performance scale score for that patient.

Adapted with permission from Lau F, Downing GM, Lesperance M, Shaw J, Kuziemsky C. Use of Palliative Performance Scale in End-of-Life Prognostication. J Palliat Med. 2006;9(5):1066-1075. [PMID: 17040144] Copyright 2006, Mary Ann Leibert, Inc. publishers.

of 4-6) is treated with a combination of opioids and non-narcotic pain relievers. If these agents are combined in a single pill (such as oxycodone and acetaminophen) to reduce polypharmacy, care must be taken to avoid inadvertent overdosing of the non-narcotic component when need for the opioid ingredient increases. The daily cumulative acetaminophen dose (<4 g) limits the dosing of the opioid in combination medications. Severe pain (pain score 7-10) is mainly treated by opioids. Adjunct therapies can be used at all levels of the ladder. Starting doses of opioid pain medications, given in morphine equivalents, are detailed in **Table 15**. Oral administration is the preferred route for opioid analgesics because of its convenience, low cost, and ability to produce stable opioid blood levels. Intramuscular injections are not recommended because of the associated pain, unreliable absorption, and relatively long interval to peak drug concentrations. If a parenteral route is needed, intravenous or subcutaneous administration is preferred. Intravenous administration is associated with the most rapid onset of analgesia but also the shortest duration of action. A transdermal opioid patch is available for the treatment of chronic pain. Codeine,

tramadol, and morphine can accumulate in patients with renal failure and should be used with caution in this setting.

When a patient begins having pain constantly and uses opioid analgesics the entire day, a shift of treatment strategy is required. Typically, a longer-acting opioid is started to ensure basal pain relief for the entire day. The three most common long-acting narcotic agents are extended-release morphine, oxycodone, and transdermal fentanyl. Fentanyl is also available as a solid sweetened lozenge and mucosal patch. A shorter-acting opioid with or without a non-opioid analgesic is used for breakthrough pain relief. To avoid overmedication, a typical starting dose of long-acting basal pain medication is 30% to 50% (based on morphine equivalents) of the patient's average 24-hour narcotic dosage. The long-acting narcotic can be titrated upward every 3 to 4 days to avoid frequent administration of the breakthrough medication. A typical starting dose for breakthrough therapy is 10% of the patient's total daily narcotic need.

As these medications may take 1 to 3 days to take full effect, the patient must be followed carefully for over- or undersedation. Ideally, to allow ease in dose titration, the

**TABLE 15** Common Noninjected Narcotics Used in Palliative Care for Chronic Pain

| Agent | Drug:Morphine Potency Ratio[a] | Form | Starting Dose | Onset | Duration | Comments |
|---|---|---|---|---|---|---|
| Morphine | — | Immediate release | 10 mg q 3-4 h | 30 min | 4 h | Tablet, solution, and rectal suppository |
| | | Controlled/ sustained release[b] | 15-30 mg q 12 h | 2-4 h | 12 h | Tablets, ranging from 15-200 mg |
| Oxycodone | 2:1 | Immediate release | 2.5-5 mg q 6 h | 10-15 min | 3-6 h | Tablet and solution form |
| | | Extended release[b] | 10 mg q 12 h | 1 h | 12 h | Tablets 60 mg or higher for use only in opioid-tolerant patients. |
| Fentanyl | 4:1[c] | Immediate release | 200-µg lozenge: may repeat once in 15 min, then q 6 h<br><br>100-µg buccal tablet: may repeat once in 30 min, then q 4 h | 5-15 min | 4-8 h | Not recommended for opioid-naïve patients.<br><br>Transmucosal lozenge or buccal tablet should be used only in patients who are already receiving narcotics and are opioid tolerant.<br><br>Limit to 4 or fewer daily—additional doses mark need for adjustment of basal pain medication. |
| | | Extended release | 25-µg patch q 72 h | 12-24 h | 72 h | Not recommended for opioid-naive patients.<br><br>Patients should be on at least 60 mg oral morphine equivalents/d before starting.<br><br>Dose should not be adjusted upward based on supplemental opiate need for 3 days after initial placement or 6 days after subsequent dose changes.<br><br>17 hours are required for 50% decrease in fentanyl levels after removal. |
| Codeine | 1:3-8 (variable) | Immediate release | 30-60 mg q 4-6 h | 30-60 min | 4-6 h | Tablet and liquid, usually taken with adjunct analgesics due to weak strength.<br><br>Variable efficacy due to differences in metabolism to morphine with CYP2D6 enzyme. |
| Hydro-morphone | 4:1 | Immediate release | 2-4 mg q 3-6 h | 15-30 min | 4-5 h | Oral, liquid, rectal suppository |
| Hydrocodone | 1:1 | Immediate release | 5-15 mg q 3-8 h | 30-60 min | 4-8 h | Available as combination product with adjunct analgesics |

q = every.

[a]A ratio of 2:1 indicates that the medication is twice as powerful as an equivalent mg strength of morphine. No fixed conversion ratio is likely to be satisfactory in all patients, especially patients receiving large opioid doses.

[b]Divide cumulative daily dose of short-acting narcotic into two divided doses of the longer-acting narcotic.

[c]The fentanyl comparison is a µg-to-mg conversion.

same agents should be used for breakthrough and basal pain relief. Bone metastases represent a special situation in which other adjunct measures, such as radiation therapy and bisphosphonates, may provide additional pain relief.

Several narcotics should be avoided when treating chronic pain. Meperidine is rarely appropriate for oral use owing to variable oral bioavailability and the accumulation of active metabolites with prolonged use at high doses or in renal failure. Such accumulation lowers the seizure threshold and causes central nervous system symptoms, such as tremors, twitching, and nervousness. Partial opioid receptor agonists and agonist/antagonist agents, such as buprenorphine, dezocine, nalbuphine, pentazocine, and butorphanol, may also cause delirium and provide less incremental analgesia when used alone. Methadone is difficult to titrate as its onset of action is far shorter than its half life. For this reason, it should only be administered by providers experienced in its use.

Opioids have a number of side effects, including nausea, constipation, pruritus, and sedation. Mild sedation usually dissipates as the patient builds tolerance to the medication, and more significant sedation is usually reversible with dose reduction. Constipation is one of the most common side effects of opioids. Stool softeners and laxatives should be prescribed for patients who use opioids daily. A combination of docusate as a stool softener and senna or bisacodyl as a mild laxative is a popular initial prophylactic therapy. Osmotic laxatives, such as magnesium citrate, lactulose, and polyethylene glycol, are used if the prophylactic regimen does not produce daily bowel movements. Opioid-related itching and urticaria are due to the release of histamine. For these patients, an antihistamine is useful. Oxymorphone and fentanyl are two opioids that do not release histamine, and switching to these opioids can be considered. Opioid-induced nausea can be treated with metoclopramide, meclizine, or another phenothiazine medication. Corticosteroids and benzodiazepines may be useful in refractory cases. Some patients will experience less nausea if the opioid blood level remains constant throughout the day rather than experiencing periodic peaks. Changing the dosing interval of an immediate-release preparation from every 4 hours to a smaller dose every 3 hours may even out the blood level and reduce nausea and vomiting. Changing to a sustained-release opioid or the transdermal route also produces more constant opioid blood levels and may be helpful.

Pain arising from internal organs (visceral pain) is usually dull, colicky, and poorly localized. Visceral pain is typically caused by distention, torsion, or inflammation, and it most frequently occurs in the settings of pancreatic, liver, renal, and gastrointestinal malignancies. The discomfort may be associated with autonomic symptoms, such as nausea or diaphoresis. At times, the pain can be referred. For example, liver, small bowel, and gallbladder pain may present as right shoulder discomfort. Visceral pain can also be caused by severe constipation due to opioid analgesics used to treat other forms of pain. Palliative surgery can be useful to relieve visceral pain caused by bowel obstruction. Blockade of the celiac plexus, sympathetic plexus, or splanchnic nerve may also be useful in patients refractory to pain control using opioid analgesics.

Neuropathic pain is usually caused by direct pathologic changes to the central or peripheral nervous system. In terminally ill patients, this is most often related to a malignancy causing nerve root compression or encroachment on a plexus of nerve fibers. In patients without cancer, structural problems, such as diabetic peripheral neuropathy or nerve root impingement, are common sources of patient discomfort. Neuropathic pain may be constant or episodic and is usually characterized as burning, tingling, lancinating, or shooting in nature. Symptoms caused by central nervous system involvement more frequently cause headache or focal neurologic changes than neuropathic pain syndromes. Several therapies are effective for neuropathic pain. Tricyclic antidepressants, venlafaxine, and duloxetine may be especially useful in patients with both neuropathic pain and depression. Tramadol, gabapentin, and pregabalin are also effective for neuropathic pain. However, the efficacy of all these drugs is better established for nonmalignant pain disorders (such as diabetic peripheral neuropathy and postherpetic neuralgia) and less extensively tested for cancer-related neuropathic pain. Corticosteroids can reduce edema and lyse certain tumors, thereby enhancing the analgesic effect of non-opioid and opioid drugs. They are effective in the management of malignant infiltration of the brachial and lumbar plexus and spinal cord compression, as well as headache pain due to brain tumors.

### KEY POINTS

- Mild pain can usually be adequately treated with aspirin, acetaminophen, and NSAIDs.

- In the treatment of moderate pain, low-dose opioid drugs are added to aspirin, acetaminophen, or NSAIDS.

- A strategy incorporating long-acting narcotics with a plan for breakthrough pain control should be started in patients requiring multiple doses of daily narcotics.

- Patients requiring daily narcotics should receive scheduled doses of a stool softener and laxative to prevent narcotic-related constipation.

- Tricyclic antidepressants, venlafaxine, duloxetine, gabapentin, and pregabalin may be useful as adjunct therapy for neuropathic pain.

## Dyspnea

Dyspnea is one of the most common symptoms encountered in palliative care. It is most often the result of direct cardiothoracic pathology, such as pleural effusions, heart failure, chronic obstructive pulmonary disease, pulmonary embolism, pneumonia, or lung metastases. Dyspnea can also be caused by systemic conditions, such as anemia, muscle weakness, or conditions causing abdominal distention. The patient's self-report of discomfort should be the driving factor for treatment. The patient's self-report often has little correlation with respiratory rate, arterial blood gases, oxygen saturation, or use of accessory musculature.

Patients with underlying lung disease on bronchodilator therapy should have this therapy continued to maintain comfort. Opioids are effective in reducing dyspnea in patients with underlying cardiopulmonary disease and malignancy. In patients already receiving opioids, using the breakthrough pain dose for dyspnea as well and increasing this dose by 25% if not fully effective may be helpful. A 5-mg dose of oral morphine given four times daily has been shown to help relieve dyspnea in patients with end-stage heart failure. Low-dose (20 mg) extended-release morphine given daily has been used to relieve dyspnea in patients with advanced chronic obstructive pulmonary disease.

In contrast to opioids, benzodiazepines have not demonstrated consistent benefit in treating dyspnea, but may have a special use in patients with dyspnea caused by anxiety. Oxygen may be useful in relieving dyspnea in terminally ill patients with hypoxemia, but a meta-analysis suggests that it has limited use in symptom relief in patients without hypoxemia. If severe anemia is uncovered as a cause of dyspnea, a blood transfusion may help relieve symptoms.

**KEY POINTS**

- Oxygen is not helpful in treating cancer-related dyspnea in the absence of hypoxemia.
- Morphine is effective in treating cancer-related dyspnea as well as dyspnea related to end-stage cardiopulmonary disorders.

## Nutrition

Reduced appetite and weight loss is a common symptom in patients dying of malignancy or chronic disease. As eating and enjoying food is an essential component of social interaction, a lack of interest in food and poor nutrition are viewed with distress by many families. Distress may be caused by caregiver concern that food preparation is not appropriate for the patient, patient guilt about snubbing caregiver efforts to demonstrate help, and family distress over the knowledge that anorexia, poor nutrition, and weight loss are ominous indicators of poor prognosis. Pressure may be placed on the patient to eat larger portions even if it is uncomfortable. Caregivers may accuse patients of "giving up" to their disease by not forcing themselves to eat. Patient and caregiver education on how the disease process may cause anorexia and cachexia is often helpful in relieving guilt and promoting acceptance of a dying patient's altered eating habits. A realistic discussion regarding nutrition and hydration advance directives is also useful. Caregivers should make every effort to allow the patient to participate in the social aspects of meals, realizing that the patient may just enjoy a bite or two of a favorite food.

If prognosis is uncertain and death is not imminent, appetite stimulants may be considered. In cancer-related anorexia, the most commonly studied medications are progestins, such as megestrol (in doses of 400-800 mg/d) or medroxyprogesterone (typically 500 mg twice daily). In a systematic review, these medications improved anorexia and promoted weight gain but had an uncertain impact on quality of life. Side effects include an increased incidence of thromboembolic disease, hyperglycemia, adrenal suppression, and vaginal bleeding. Prokinetic agents such as metoclopramide significantly reduce nausea but have no impact on weight gain and anorexia. Short-term corticosteroids improved nausea and anorexia in advanced cancer patients in several trials, but little data have been published on corticosteroid use in palliative care populations. Insufficient data exist to recommend dronabinol, fish oil supplements, ghrelin, melatonin, nandrolone, and NSAIDs. The use of enteral and parenteral feeding in terminally ill patients is controversial. The benefits of these modalities are most pronounced in patients with good functional status and with gastrointestinal disease affecting nutritional intake. There is scant evidence for improved quality of life in patients with anorexia and weight loss due to terminal disease in a palliative care setting. In addition, there are important risks associated with therapy, such as line infection or dislodgement, hyperglycemia, electrolyte imbalances, and fluid overload. Discussing patient nutrition preferences before extreme weight loss and anorexia occur is important to avoid emotional distress for the patient and family.

## Depression

The diagnosis of depression in terminally ill patients can often be problematic. First, it is difficult to separate symptoms such as anorexia and weight loss traditionally associated with depression from the patient's underlying disease. Both patients and providers may have the misconception that depression is a normal or untreatable symptom of terminal disease. Patients may be concerned about the stigma of taking an antidepressant. Finally, physicians may be concerned about drug interactions with pain medications.

Techniques to screen for depression may require modification in the palliative care setting. Many models have been proposed with varying rates of sensitivity and specificity for different populations of patients requiring end-of-life care. One key feature of many adapted models is the elimination of somatic symptoms from the depression screen. A meta-analysis of depression screening tools in the palliative care setting also found that two questions (low mood and low interest) were effective across five studies incorporating 900 patients. The pooled data from the meta-analysis found a sensitivity of 91% and a specificity of 86% for the two-question approach. Given the low risk of short-term complications of therapy and potential benefit of improving the patient's remaining quality of life, physicians should have a low threshold for initiating therapy in this setting.

Tricyclic antidepressants, selective serotonin reuptake inhibitors, and psychotherapy are all effective in improving symptoms of depression in the terminally ill. There is less literature on the use of psychostimulants such as dextroamphetamine. In patients with a prognosis of less than 1 month, some experts recommend psychostimulants owing to their short onset of action compared with antidepressants.

---

**KEY POINT**

- Depression is common in terminally ill patients, and physicians should have a low threshold for initiating therapy.

---

### Altered Mental Status

Delirium is common in the palliative care setting, and most patients in the last days of life experience some form of altered mental status. It is caused by a variety of conditions, many of which are reversible. Titration of opioid pain medication can result in altered mental status. Physicians and caregivers should be vigilant for altered mental status each time an opioid pain medication dose is increased. This is especially common with titration of longer-acting extended-release medications. In some conditions, such as progressive renal failure, the mechanism of elimination is altered, and the dose of narcotic requires downward titration. Psychoactive medications, such as benzodiazepines used for anxiety or antidepressants, also may be responsible. Finally, progression of the underlying disease, which may cause hypoxia, brain metastases, or metabolic problems (for example, hypercalcemia, volume depletion) should be considered.

Prior to initiating an extensive evaluation for altered mental status, physicians should carefully consider the patient's prognosis and functional status, prior written advance directives, and the opinion of the surrogate decision maker. For delirium associated with agitation, antipsychotic medications may be useful for sedation and symptom relief. Haloperidol, in doses starting at 0.5 mg with escalating repeat doses every hour titrated against symptoms, is usually effective. When antipsychotic medications fail, further sedation may be required with benzodiazepines or propofol. Sedation may cause respiratory depression and hypotension, and careful discussion with the patient's surrogate decision maker is indicated prior to initiation. In most cases, family members are willing to take judicious risks to support patient comfort.

---

**KEY POINT**

- Delirium is common in terminally ill patients and can be treated with small doses of haloperidol while reversible causes are investigated.

---

## Caregiver Stressors and Bereavement

Prolonged and intense caregiver duties have an adverse impact on their health and mortality. Even when adjusted for comorbidities, spousal caregivers reporting strain are 63% more likely to die within 4 years than non-caregiving spouses. Physicians must be vigilant to health concerns vocalized by caregivers and encourage them to seek respite from their duties and maintain their own health needs. Physicians should also provide family members and caregivers with information about the normal grieving process. Physicians should schedule a follow-up appointment after the funeral and several months later for family members under their care to screen for complicated grief and depression.

After a loved one dies, caregivers and family members may experience symptoms of anger or bitterness over the death; a sense of disbelief in accepting the death; recurrent feelings of intense longing for the deceased; preoccupation with thoughts of the loved one, including intrusive thoughts related to the death; and a feeling that life is empty and the future has no meaning without the deceased. When these symptoms persist for 6 or more months after the death, they are defined as *complicated grief*. Complicated grief causes barriers in forming other relationships, engaging in other rewarding activities, and moving beyond a state of mourning. About 20% to 30% of caregivers experience complicated grief or depression within a year of the death. Family members and caregivers at risk for complicated grief include those with pre-existing mental health disorders, high levels of caregiver burden, and competing responsibilities, such as work or caring for others. Depression persisting for 2 or more weeks longer than 2 months after the death should be considered for treatment. Treatment improves some symptoms of depression but does not reduce the intensity of grief. Complicated grief and depression resulting from bereavement are treated with specialized grief programs or psychotherapy alone or in combination with medications.

### Bibliography

Breitbart W, Strout D. Delirium in the terminally ill. Clin Geriatr Med. 2000;16(2):357-372. [PMID: 10783433]

Johnson MJ, McDonagh TA, Harkness A, McKay SE, Dargie HJ. Morphine for the relief of breathlessness in patients with chronic heart failure: a pilot study. Eur J Heart Fail. 2002;4(6):753-756. [PMID: 12453546]

Mitchell AJ. Are one or two simple questions sufficient to detect depression in cancer and palliative care? A Bayesian meta-analysis. Br J Cancer. 2008;98(12):1934-1943. [PMID: 18506146]

Qaseem A, Snow V, Shekelle P, et al; Clinical Efficacy Assessment Subcommittee of the American College of Physicians. Evidence-Based Interventions to Improve the Palliative Care of Pain, Dyspnea, and Depression at the End of Life: A Clinical Practice Guideline from the American College of Physicians. Ann Intern Med. 2008;148(2):141-146. [PMID: 18195338]

Schultz R, Beach SR. Caregiving as a risk factor for mortality: the caregiver health effects study. JAMA. 1999;282(23):2215-2219. [PMID: 10605972]

Uronis HE, Currow DC, McCrory DC, Samsa GP, Abernethy AP. Oxygen for relief of dyspnoea in mildly- or non-hypoxaemic patients with cancer: a systematic review and meta-analysis. Brit J Cancer. 2008;98(2):294-299. [PMID: 18182991]

Yavuzsen T, Davis MP, Walsh D, LeGrand S, Lagman R. Systematic review of the treatment of cancer-associated anorexia and weight loss. J Clin Oncol. 2005;23(33):8500-8511. [PMID: 16293879]

# Common Symptoms

## Overview

Symptoms account for more than half of all outpatient encounters or, in the United States alone, nearly 400 million office visits annually. Approximately half of these visits are for pain (headache, back pain, joint pain, chest pain, abdominal pain); a quarter are for upper respiratory tract symptoms (cough, sore throat, ear, nasal); and the remainder are for nonpain, non–upper respiratory tract symptoms, such as fatigue, dizziness, or palpitations. Approximately 75% of outpatients presenting with physical symptoms experience improvement within 2 weeks, whereas 20% to 25% have chronic or recurrent symptoms. Studies in the general population, as well as in primary care and specialty clinics, have shown that at least one third to one half of symptoms are medically unexplained (that is, no physical cause is found after clinical evaluation).

The most common comorbid psychiatric conditions in patients presenting with physical complaints are depressive, anxiety, and somatoform disorders. Predictors of psychiatric comorbidity include recent stress, total physical symptom count, three or more unexplained symptoms, pain in at least two different regions of the body, high symptom severity, poor self-rated health, high health care use, and the clinician's perception of a difficult encounter.

Although symptoms are ubiquitous (80% of persons in the general population report at least one symptom in the past month), only a minority of symptomatic persons seek health care. Although seeking health care can be prompted by symptom severity or persistence, many patients visit their physicians because of symptom-related concerns and expectations. One of the most common concerns is worry about serious illness, either disease-specific ("Could this headache be a brain tumor?") or generic ("I don't know what this might be, but is it something to worry about?") Prognosis is another frequent concern ("How long is this likely to last? Will it interfere with my work or recreational activities?"). Common expectations for provider actions include medication prescriptions, diagnostic tests, or subspecialty referrals. Patients may be reluctant to share their concerns because of embarrassment, fear of wasting the physician's time, or the mistaken assumption that if it is important, the physician will ask. Addressing the patient's concerns and expectations can improve patient and physician satisfaction, adherence with the physician's recom-

mendations, and possibly symptom outcome. Two useful questions to ask at the end of the initial visit are: "Is there anything else you were worried about?" and "Is there anything else you wanted or thought might be helpful?"

### KEY POINTS

- One third to one half of physical symptoms are medically unexplained.
- Predictors of comorbid depression and anxiety include the number of physical symptoms, presence of three or more unexplained symptoms, and two or more pain symptoms.
- Approximately 75% of symptomatic patients report improvement within 1 month.

## Chronic Pain

### Characterizing and Assessing Pain

Pain has received significantly more attention in recent years; the Joint Commission has mandated that every patient be queried about the presence and intensity of pain. Pain adversely impacts prognosis in conditions such as depression, reinforcing the need to identify and treat pain. Because individual tolerance for pain varies widely and there are no physical correlates for objectively quantifying pain, it is important to use the patient's subjective report of pain to guide management. Asking patients about their pain helps physicians to better characterize the pain.

Chronic pain is one of the most common and challenging problems confronting primary care physicians. Hippocrates noted that whereas it is the patient's responsibility to accurately characterize the pain, it is the physician's responsibility to listen carefully. Chronic pain often seems to take on a life of its own, becoming all-encompassing and adversely influencing many aspects of daily life. There may or may not be a clear precipitating cause associated with the onset of pain.

A working definition for chronic pain is pain, with or without a clear precipitant, which has persisted for at least 3 months. Pain may be categorized in various ways, and there is a considerable body of literature addressing certain subtypes of pain, such as postoperative pain and cancer-related pain. One broad approach comprises three categories: somatic pain (attributable to injury to the skin or musculoskeletal system, such as osteoarthritis or spinal stenosis), central sensitization pain (such as fibromyalgia), and neuropathic pain (such as diabetic peripheral neuropathy). There may be some overlap between these categories; however, they are helpful in selecting therapies that are likely to be effective.

Somatic (also called nociceptive) pain, which frequently has an inflammatory component, often responds well to NSAIDs, such as ibuprofen or naproxen. Patients who do not respond to one NSAID may benefit by switching to another

NSAID. For those in whom trials of two or more NSAIDs are not helpful or who either have a contraindication to or do not tolerate NSAIDs (such as the elderly or those with renal impairment), an analgesic such as acetaminophen, or topical remedies such as an aspirin-based cream or capsaicin cream, may be considered. For patients concerned about the adverse gastrointestinal effects of NSAIDs, a nonacetylated salicylate, such as choline magnesium trisalicylate, may be a suitable alternative with less platelet inhibition.

Central sensitization pain tends to be diffuse and difficult to localize, is often based upon symptoms with little or no objective findings, and is more likely to be labeled as functional. In this type of pain, the central nervous system's processing of sensation is altered, leading to amplification of signals. Manifestations include a sensation of pain with stimuli that are usually not painful (allodynia) and more severe pain with stimuli that are typically associated with less severe pain (hyperalgesia). In addition, the relationship between the degree of pain and functional status is often less clear than for other types of pain; therefore, relief of pain with NSAIDs or opioids does not necessarily lead to improvement in functional status. Medications that modulate neurotransmitter levels, such as tricyclic antidepressants and serotonin-norepinephrine reuptake inhibitors (SNRIs), seem to have greater efficacy for central sensitization pain. A meta-analysis documented that patients with fibromyalgia who were treated with antidepressants had significant improvements in pain, depression, fatigue, sleep, and health-related quality of life; the most robust data are available for the SNRI duloxetine and the tricyclic antidepressant amitriptyline, although it appears likely that their efficacy can be generalized to their respective medication classes. Cognitive-behavioral therapy may have a particularly durable benefit.

If the specific etiology of pain is unclear, evaluation should begin with a careful medical history and physical examination. Because depression and anxiety disorders are common in persons with chronic pain, screening questions to identify these conditions should be a part of the history. The history and physical examination should guide the ordering of additional laboratory, imaging, and other diagnostic studies. An erythrocyte sedimentation rate may be helpful in older patients to rule out an active inflammatory process or help in the identification of polymyalgia rheumatica. Localized radiography can be useful in confirming osteoarthritis, as well as in ruling out less common causes of skeletal pain, although the physical examination is usually sufficient for diagnosing osteoarthritis.

Systemic symptoms such as weight loss and anorexia should lead to additional diagnostic tests, such as chest radiography to assess for lung cancer or abdominal ultrasound or CT to screen for pancreatic cancer, either of which may have pain as a primary feature. Otherwise, in the absence of specific abnormalities, there is little evidence to support going beyond age-appropriate screening for breast, prostate, and colon cancer.

## Managing Pain

Treatment of patients with chronic pain is difficult and often inadequate. Initially, non-opioid pain medications, such as acetaminophen or NSAIDs, should be used either alone or in combination with adjuvant measures such as antidepressants, antiepileptics, and dermal analgesics as appropriate. Non-opioid pain medications often have significant adverse effects, whereas opioids carry concerns about addiction and abuse as well as suppression of breathing or consciousness. Such concerns are well-founded, and available evidence more strongly supports the benefit of opioids in short-term pain relief than in the chronic use that is common in practice; thus, alternatives should be fully explored first, reserving opioids for the treatment of chronic pain that is not relieved by a combination of nonpharmacologic and non-opioid pharmacologic measures. The World Health Organization analgesic ladder (see Palliative Care) was developed to guide the management of cancer pain; however, it also serves as a valid construct for the management of non-cancer chronic pain. Epidural and intrathecal injections and regional blocks can improve pain relief with less central nervous system depression, particularly for somatic pain syndromes such as spinal stenosis and sciatica.

Because elderly patients are at greater risk for adverse effects with many pain medications (such as falls with sedating medications and gastric bleeding with NSAIDs), the American Geriatric Society (AGS) recently published a guideline to assist clinicians that features a similar stepped approach. The AGS recommends acetaminophen as the initial therapy for most older patients with persistent pain, especially if it is musculoskeletal. NSAIDs, owing to the greater risk for gastrointestinal and renal complications in the elderly, are only a secondary alternative for those with contraindications (such as cirrhosis) or lack of efficacy with acetaminophen. In addition, gastrointestinal protection with a medication such as a proton pump inhibitor is strongly advised. The AGS also recommends a trial of topical lidocaine, particularly for localized neuropathic pain.

Prior to starting an opioid for chronic pain, patients should undergo an appropriate history and physical examination—including an assessment of the potential for abuse, misuse, and addiction—as well as an explanation of the relative benefits and risks of opioids. The goals of treatment and an appropriate follow-up schedule should be agreed upon. For example, the patient's preferences should be elicited regarding balancing the completeness of pain relief against drowsiness or suppression of consciousness. Opioids should then be initiated in a graduated, stepwise manner to minimize the side effects and risks of addiction while still providing effective pain relief, utilizing effective adjunctive therapy as well (see Palliative Care). Opioids with higher abuse or addiction potential tend to have a rapid onset of action, either because of their route of administration or because they are more lipophilic, and possess a relatively short duration of action.

Patients on chronic opioid therapy require periodic reassessment of their pain, the efficacy of the regimen, side effects, and comorbidities that might impact the efficacy of, or otherwise interact with, pain medications. For patients deemed at higher risk for misuse or abuse of pain medications, urine drug screens should be incorporated in the monitoring. Those with repeated misuse or abuse should have their medications tapered. Common side effects of chronic opiates, such as nausea and constipation, should be monitored for and managed with appropriate lifestyle modifications or medications.

Tramadol is a unique drug that may be helpful with all three categories of pain, although U.S. Food and Drug Administration (FDA) approval is for moderate to moderately severe pain, and it has not received specific approval for treatment of osteoarthritis or neuropathic pain. Tramadol is available in both immediate-release and extended-release oral formulations. It can be used in conjunction with, or in place of, anti-inflammatory agents for relief of somatic pain or to avoid or limit the dose of more sedating and addictive opioids. Tramadol is a synthetic analogue of codeine that has a dual mechanism of action, acting as both a μ-opioid receptor agonist and a weak inhibitor of serotonin and norepinephrine reuptake. Although tramadol's lesser affinity for opioid receptors gives it less potential for respiratory suppression or abuse or addiction, physicians should keep in mind that it still can be associated with these complications.

Gabapentin, pregabalin, and duloxetine are approved by the FDA for treatment of neuropathic pain, including diabetic neuropathy and postherpetic neuralgia. Pregabalin, duloxetine, and milnacipran are approved for treatment of fibromyalgia. Due to their lower cost, tricyclic antidepressants or gabapentin may be tried first for neuropathic or central sensitization pain. If these agents are ineffective or not tolerated, the newer agents may be warranted.

Nonpharmacologic methods of pain control, either alone or in combination, can be important adjuncts to pain management. Whereas ice can be helpful in acute pain, topical heat is more useful with chronic pain. A graduated exercise regimen can benefit patients with either somatic or central sensitization pain. Music, as well as immersion in a virtual environment (for example, a virtual representation of the sights, sounds, and smells of the beach or a meadow on a sunny day), appears to have some utility in reducing anxiety and providing adjunctive pain relief that enables a reduction in pain medication dosage, although studies of larger size and longer duration are needed to better delineate their niche in pain treatment. Acupuncture may provide adjunctive pain relief for some patients, although in blinded studies, meaningful differences between acupuncture and sham acupuncture treatment arms have been small or nonexistent. A meta-analysis of studies on electrical nerve stimulation found evidence of efficacy in the treatment of chronic pain. Multidisciplinary pain treatment programs that bring together diverse specialties, such as anesthesiology and psychiatry, have been highly successful in combining pharmacologic and nonpharmacologic measures.

**KEY POINTS**

- Initial therapies for somatic pain include acetaminophen, NSAIDs, and topical remedies.
- In elderly patients, because of the risk of adverse effects, NSAIDs should be reserved for those with contraindications to or lack of efficacy with acetaminophen.
- Central sensitization pain (for example, fibromyalgia) is more likely to respond to tricyclic antidepressants, serotonin-norepinephrine reuptake inhibitors, and pregabalin.
- Gabapentin, pregabalin, and duloxetine are effective for neuropathic pain.

## Acute and Chronic Cough

### Acute Cough

An acute cough is a cough that has been present for less than 3 weeks. Viral upper respiratory tract infection is the most common cause of acute cough. Other causes include pneumonia (viral or bacterial); acute tracheobronchitis; rhinitis due to allergens or environmental irritants; influenza; exacerbations of chronic pulmonary disease or left ventricular failure; malignancy; aspiration or foreign body; medication reactions (angiotensin-converting enzyme [ACE] inhibitors); and, less commonly, pulmonary embolism.

Because pneumonia is the third most common cause of acute cough illness, and the most serious, the primary diagnostic objective when evaluating acute cough is to exclude the presence of pneumonia. The absence of abnormal vital signs (heart rate ≥100/min, respiration rate ≥24/min, or oral temperature ≥38 °C [100.4 °F]) and chest examination findings (crackles, egophony, and fremitus) sufficiently reduces the likelihood of pneumonia to the point where further diagnostic testing is unnecessary.

The common cold is characterized by rhinorrhea, sneezing, nasal congestion, and postnasal drainage with or without fever, headache, tearing, and throat discomfort. The chest examination in these patients is normal. The cough from the common cold should improve within 1 week, although 25% of patients may still have a cough at 2 weeks; worsening or persistence of the cough suggests another underlying reason.

Acute bronchitis is also a self-limiting condition that should be considered when coughing, with or without sputum production, persists for more than 5 days after the onset of an upper respiratory tract infection. It is associated with a normal chest examination. The cause of acute bronchitis is usually viral; common pathogens include rhinovirus, adenovirus, and influenza A and B viruses. Atypical bacteria that can cause the syndrome include *Bordetella pertussis, Chlamydia pneumoniae,* and *Mycoplasma pneumoniae.* Because Gram stain and culture of sputum do not reliably detect *B. pertussis, C. pneumoniae,* or *M. pneumoniae,* these tests and other diagnostic tests are not recommended.

Improvement in cough due to the common cold may occur with a first-generation antihistamine/decongestant combination (for example, brompheniramine and pseudoephedrine) but is associated with dizziness and dry mouth. Zinc lozenges and over-the-counter cough medications have not been shown to be helpful in alleviating cough. Nasal anticholinergic medications may help alleviate some symptoms, but their effect on cough is unclear. Peripherally and centrally acting cough suppressants have limited efficacy for upper respiratory tract infections and are not recommended. For patients with acute bronchitis and wheezing, an inhaled β-agonist may be helpful.

As the likely etiology of the common cold and most cases of acute bronchitis is viral, antibiotics are not indicated and should not be given routinely. The one exception to this is acute infection with *B. pertussis.* Pertussis should be suspected in adolescents or young adults without fever in the setting of an epidemic, when there has been contact with a person with pertussis or persistent cough (more than 2 weeks), or if there is whooping or post-tussive vomiting. The diagnostic gold standard is recovery of bacteria in culture or by polymerase chain reaction. Antimicrobial therapy (a macrolide or trimethoprim/sulfamethoxazole) for suspected pertussis in adults is recommended primarily to decrease shedding of the pathogen and spread of disease because antibiotic treatment does not appear to improve resolution of symptoms if it is initiated beyond 7 to 10 days after the onset of illness.

Influenza is characterized by the sudden onset of fever and malaise, followed by cough, headache, myalgia, and nasal and pulmonary symptoms. Clinical criteria for influenza include temperature 37.8 °C or higher (≥100.0 °F) and at least one of the following: cough, sore throat, or rhinorrhea. A diagnosis of influenza can be established by analysis of viral cultures or secretions or results of several rapid diagnostic tests (immunofluorescence, polymerase chain reaction, and enzyme immunoassays). The neuroaminidase inhibitors zanamivir and oseltamivir are active against both influenza A and B. Anti-influenza drugs decrease illness by about 1 day and allow return to normal activities one-half day sooner. For these antiviral agents to be effective, influenza must be diagnosed and treatment initiated within 48 hours of symptom onset. Because of emergence of resistance, the U.S. Centers for Disease Control and Prevention no longer recommend amantadine or rimantadine for prophylaxis or treatment of influenza.

Asthma is a consideration in patients presenting with an acute cough illness. However, in the setting of acute cough, the diagnosis of asthma is difficult to establish unless there is a reliable history of asthma and episodes of wheezing and shortness of breath in addition to the cough. This is because transient bronchial hyperresponsiveness (and abnormal results on spirometry) is common to all causes of uncomplicated acute bronchitis. Postinfectious airflow obstruction on pulmonary function tests or methacholine challenge testing may be present up to 8 weeks after an acute bronchitis episode, making the distinction from asthma difficult.

Acute exacerbations of chronic bronchitis and bronchiectasis present with an abrupt increase in cough, sputum production, sputum purulence, and shortness of breath over baseline (see below).

## Chronic Cough

Subacute cough lasts 3 to 8 weeks, chronic cough last 8 weeks or longer, and the two categories of cough are evaluated similarly. Upper airway cough syndrome (UACS), asthma, and gastroesophageal reflux are responsible for approximately 90% of cases of chronic cough but are responsible for 99% of cases of chronic cough if the patient is a nonsmoker, has a normal chest radiograph, and is not taking an ACE inhibitor. Neither the patient's description of the cough, its timing (for example, when supine), nor the presence or absence of sputum production has predictive value in the evaluation of chronic cough. Chronic cough is often multifactorial.

UACS (formerly called postnasal drip) refers to a recurrent cough triggered when mucus draining from the sinuses through the oropharynx triggers cough receptors. The diagnosis is confirmed when drug therapy eliminates the discharge and cough. Most patients with UACS have symptoms or evidence of one or more of the following: postnasal drainage, frequent throat clearing, nasal discharge, cobblestone appearance of the oropharyngeal mucosa, or mucus dripping down the oropharynx. First-generation antihistamines, in combination with a decongestant, are the most consistently effective form of therapy for patients with UACS not due to sinusitis. Additionally, the avoidance of allergens and daily use of intranasal corticosteroids or cromolyn sodium are recommended for patients with allergic rhinitis. Patients who do not respond to empiric therapy should undergo sinus imaging to diagnose "silent" chronic sinusitis.

Cough-variant asthma (cough is the predominant symptom) occurs in up to 57% of patients with asthma. Cough-variant asthma is suggested by the presence of airway hyperresponsiveness and confirmed when cough resolves with asthma medications. If the diagnosis is uncertain, inhalational challenge testing with methacholine should be considered. A normal test result essentially rules out asthma, but a positive test result is less helpful because it is not specific for asthma; other conditions, such as chronic obstructive pulmonary disease or postinfectious airway hyperresponsiveness, can be associated with a positive test. The treatment of cough-variant asthma is the same as asthma in general, but the maximum symptomatic benefit may not occur for 6 to 8 weeks in cough-variant asthma.

Although gastroesophageal reflux disease (GERD) can cause cough by aspiration, the most common mechanism is a vagally mediated distal esophageal-tracheobronchial reflex. There is nothing about the character or timing of chronic cough due to GERD that distinguishes it from other causes of cough. Up to 75% of patients with GERD-induced cough may have no other GERD symptoms. The most sensitive (96%) and specific (98%) test for GERD is 24-hour esophageal pH monitoring; however, a therapeutic trial with a proton pump inhibitor is recommended before invasive testing. The data supporting the effectiveness of proton pump inhibitors are not robust, however, and symptom relief may not occur until 3 months after treatment is begun.

In patients with chronic cough who have normal chest radiograph findings, normal spirometry, and a negative methacholine challenge test, the diagnosis of nonasthmatic eosinophilic bronchitis (NAEB) should be considered. NAEB is confirmed as a cause of chronic cough by the presence of airway eosinophilia (obtained by sputum induction or bronchial wash during bronchoscopy) and improvement with treatment. Patients with NAEB should be evaluated for possible occupational exposure to a sensitizer. First-line treatment for NAEB is inhaled corticosteroids and avoidance of responsible allergens.

Chronic cough with sputum is the hallmark symptom of chronic bronchitis. Treatment is targeted at reducing sputum production and airway inflammation by removing environmental irritants, particularly cigarettes. Ipratropium bromide can decrease sputum production, and systemic corticosteroids and antibiotics may be helpful in decreasing cough during severe exacerbations. Bronchiectasis, a type of chronic bronchitis, causes a chronic or recurrent cough characterized by voluminous (>30 mL/d) sputum production with purulent exacerbations. Chest radiograph and high-resolution CT may be diagnostic, showing thickened bronchial walls in a "tramline" pattern. Bronchiectasis should be treated with antibiotics selected on the basis of sputum cultures and with chest physiotherapy.

Although most smokers have a chronic cough, they are not the group of patients who commonly seek medical attention for cough. After smoking cessation, cough has been shown to resolve or markedly decrease in 94% to 100% of patients. In 54% of these patients, cough resolution occurred within 4 weeks.

Cough due to ACE inhibitors is a class effect, not dose related, and may occur a few hours to weeks or months after a patient takes the first dose of an ACE inhibitor. The diagnosis of ACE inhibitor–induced cough can only be established when cough disappears with elimination of the drug. The median time to resolution is 26 days. Substituting an angiotensin-receptor blocker for the ACE inhibitor can also eliminate an ACE inhibitor–induced cough. Other drugs may induce cough as well (**Table 16**).

Clinical evaluation of chronic cough includes a careful history and physical examination focusing on the common causes of chronic cough (**Figure 4**). All patients should undergo chest radiography. Smoking cessation and discontinuation of ACE inhibitors should be recommended for 4 weeks before additional workup. Causes of cough may be determined by observing which therapy eliminates the symptoms associated with cough. Because cough may be caused by more than one condition, a second or third intervention should be added in the event of partial initial response. If chronic cough does not abate with empiric therapeutic trials, objective assessment should be undertaken and can include spirometry, methacholine challenge testing (if spirometry is normal), 24-hour esophageal pH monitoring, and chest CT.

## Cough in the Immunocompromised Patient

Management of acute, subacute, and chronic cough in immunocompromised patients should be similar to management in the general population, but with the patient's specific immune deficiency and geographic location addressed as important factors in the history. Immunocompromised patients are more susceptible to a wide variety of pathogens that may be specific to where they live or have traveled. HIV-positive patients with cough and a CD4 cell count below $200/\mu L$ (or above $200/\mu L$ and with warning signs such as fever, weight loss, night sweats, or thrush) should be evaluated for opportunistic infections, tuberculosis, and pneumocystis pneumonia.

## Hemoptysis

Hemoptysis is defined as coughing up blood from the lower respiratory tract. It can sometimes be difficult to differentiate from hematemesis (vomiting blood) or pseudohemoptysis

| TABLE 16 Potential Causes of Drug-Induced Cough |
| --- |
| Angiotensin-converting enzyme inhibitors |
| Inhaled medications |
| Mycophenolate mofetil |
| Nitrofurantoin |
| Propofol |
| Aspirin |
| NSAIDs |
| β-Blockers |
| Antibiotics (amphotericin B, erythromycin, sulfonamides, aminoglycosides) |
| Chemotherapeutic agents |

Information from Prakash UB. Uncommon causes of cough: ACCP evidence-based clinical practice guidelines. Chest. 2006;129(1 Suppl):206S-219S. [PMID: 16428713]

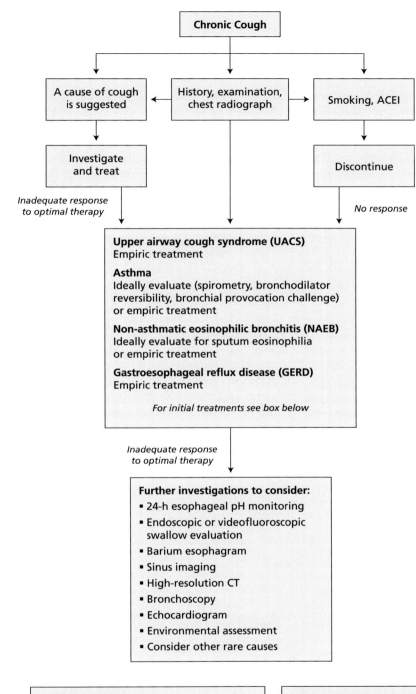

**FIGURE 4.**
**Evaluation of chronic cough.**

ACEI = angiotensin-converting enzyme inhibitor; LTRA = leukotriene receptor antagonist.

Reproduced with permission from: Irwin RS, Baumann MH, Bolser DC, et al; American College of Chest Physicians (ACCP). Diagnosis and management of cough executive summary: ACCP evidence-based clinical practice guidelines. Chest. 2006;129(1 Suppl):4S. [PMID: 16428686] Copyright 2006 American College of Chest Physicians.

(spitting of blood from sources other than the lungs or bronchial system). The sputum from hemoptysis is often frothy, bright red or pink, liquid, or clotted.

Treatment of hemoptysis is directed at the underlying cause. The most commonly encountered causes of hemoptysis in ambulatory patients are infection (bronchitis or pneumonia) and malignancy. Elevated pulmonary pressure from left-sided heart failure or pulmonary embolism may cause hemoptysis, although hemoptysis alone is not sufficiently sensitive or specific to diagnose pulmonary embolism. In up to 30% of patients, the cause is not identified (cryptogenic hemoptysis). A diagnosis of cryptogenic hemoptysis should not be made until the patient has undergone thorough evaluation.

All patients with hemoptysis should have a chest radiograph. Risk factors that increase the risk of malignancy include male sex, age older than 40 years, a smoking history of more than 40 pack-years, and symptoms lasting for more than 1 week. These patients should be referred for chest CT and fiberoptic bronchoscopy even if the chest radiograph is normal.

Massive hemoptysis (>200 mL/d of blood) represents a medical emergency. Such high rates of bleeding may indicate bleeding from the bronchial arterial system rather than the pulmonary venous system. These patients should be managed in an intensive care unit with hemodynamic and airway stabilization and prompt consultation with a pulmonologist and cardiothoracic surgeon for diagnostic and therapeutic intervention.

### KEY POINTS

- Upper airway cough syndrome, asthma, and gastroesophageal reflux are responsible for approximately 99% of cases of chronic cough if the patient is a nonsmoker, has a normal chest radiograph, and is not taking an angiotensin-converting enzyme inhibitor.

- Cough caused by an angiotensin-converting enzyme (ACE) inhibitor may develop at any time during treatment; stopping the ACE inhibitor may be both diagnostic and therapeutic.

- The treatment of choice for cough due to either the common cold or upper airway cough syndrome is a first-generation antihistamine combined with a decongestant.

- Cough presumed due to gastroesophageal reflux disease is treated empirically with a proton pump inhibitor prior to invasive testing.

## Chronic Fatigue and Chronic Fatigue Syndrome

Chronic fatigue is fatigue that has been present for at least 6 months and is associated with functional impairment. Chronic fatigue is common, identified in nearly 20% of respondents to a large community survey. For approximately two thirds of these cases, however, the fatigue was attributable to a known medical or psychiatric condition, leaving about 6% to 7% of respondents with idiopathic chronic fatigue. The chronic fatigue *syndrome* was defined for research purposes by the U.S. Centers for Disease Control and Prevention, but the definition does have some prognostic utility, as those who meet full criteria have worse outcomes than those who do not. Chronic fatigue syndrome is defined by 6 months or more of medically unexplained, debilitating fatigue, with four or more of the following features: subjective memory impairment, sore throat, tender lymph nodes, muscle pain, joint pain, headache, unrefreshing sleep, and postexertional malaise that lasts at least 24 hours. Chronic fatigue syndrome has a highly variable prevalence in community surveys, from 0.2% to 2.6%.

### Evaluation of Chronic Fatigue

There is no test that is diagnostic for chronic fatigue syndrome. An appropriate medical history and physical examination in a patient presenting with chronic fatigue should include an assessment for common causes of fatigue. This should include a sleep history, and those with a history of loud snoring, apneic spells, or frequent limb movements during sleep should be considered for a sleep study to evaluate for sleep apnea or restless legs syndrome. All patients with fatigue should be assessed for depression and anxiety disorders. Because patients with hypothyroidism may present with fatigue in the absence of other clear findings, it is reasonable to order a thyroid-stimulating hormone level. If significant weight loss, lymphadenopathy, or fever is detected on physical examination, assessment for malignancy and chronic infections such as tuberculosis should ensue. A complete blood count should be obtained to rule out anemia as well as to look for evidence of lymphoma or leukemia. A metabolic profile is reasonable to rule out diabetes mellitus, kidney disease, and liver disease. An erythrocyte sedimentation rate can help assess for polymyalgia rheumatica or an active inflammatory process in older patients. No additional studies are routinely indicated, but such studies may be warranted in selected patients based on the history and physical examination findings. Although Epstein-Barr virus and a host of other infectious agents have been considered in the pathogenesis of chronic fatigue syndrome, none have been borne out by careful study, and testing for such agents is not routinely indicated.

### Treatment of Chronic Fatigue

There is no evidence that management of chronic fatigue syndrome should differ from that for chronic fatigue that does not meet full criteria for the syndrome. Treatment of chronic fatigue syndrome has proved difficult, but a few interventions have shown some benefit, although study results have been mixed. A graded exercise program can help reduce fatigue and improve functional status. It is important to start slowly and very gradually increase the duration and intensity of the exercise regimen. Physicians or ancillary staff may need to be quite specific in their instructions and follow up closely to ensure that patients avoid progressing too quickly, resulting in relapse. One sensible approach favors exercise in the form of walking, jogging, biking, or swimming at a comfortable intensity level every other day, with an initial duration of 10 minutes or less for the first 2 weeks. Patients record their rating of perceived exertion with each session (for example, using the Borg Rating of Perceived Exertion Scale, which runs from "very, very light" at 6-7 points, to "very, very hard" at 19-20 points). This should be followed by a medical appointment to review the 2-week experience and to establish a plan for the ensuing 2 weeks, with an increase in duration of 2 to 5 minutes if the exertion ratings were at an acceptable level (for example, "somewhat hard," or 14 or lower, on the Borg scale), while holding the intensity level constant. Ensuing 2-week cycles should be maintained until the duration of exercise reaches 30 minutes, with progression in the intensity of the exercise to be initiated only at that point (for example, by increasing to a "hard" exertion level for the first 1-2 minutes of the exercise session).

There is also evidence to support the use of cognitive-behavioral therapy for chronic fatigue syndrome. Cognitive-behavioral therapy in this setting is targeted in part at breaking the cycle of effort avoidance, decline in physical conditioning, and increase in fatigue, and can work well in combination with graduated exercise in this regard. Cognitive-behavioral therapy reduces fatigue and improves functional status. Interestingly, one study found that cognitive-behavioral therapy reduced self-reported cognitive impairment despite failure to improve neuropsychological test performance. This suggests that the patient's perception of impairment may be more significant than the actual level of function.

Finally, for the large percentage of patients with chronic fatigue syndrome with significant symptoms of depression, there is some evidence that treatment with an antidepressant such as the selective serotonin reuptake inhibitor fluoxetine may improve the depressive symptoms, although not necessarily the nondepressive symptoms. Pharmacotherapy should not, therefore, be initiated as the sole intervention. A variety of other medications have been tried, including corticosteroids, mineralocorticoids, growth hormone, melatonin, and acyclovir, but with no clear evidence of benefit.

### KEY POINTS

- Hypothyroidism, sleep disorders, depression, anxiety disorders, cancer, and chronic infection should be considered in the initial evaluation of chronic fatigue, but if the history and physical examination are unremarkable, an extensive workup is not necessary.

- A graded exercise program with clear instructions and close follow up can improve chronic fatigue syndrome.

- Cognitive-behavioral therapy is an effective treatment for chronic fatigue syndrome.

## Dizziness

The clinical syndrome of dizziness may be divided into vertigo, presyncope, disequilibrium, and nonspecific dizziness. Vertigo is the illusion of motion, often spinning, and is commonly associated with vestibular and central nervous system causes. Presyncope is the sensation of nearly losing consciousness. Disequilibrium is a general feeling of being unsteady when moving. Nonspecific dizziness is dizziness that does not fit neatly into the other categories.

### Evaluation of Dizziness

Patients with dizziness often have difficulty precisely articulating the quality of their symptoms. One study showed that patients had poor internal validity when asked to classify their symptoms as light-headedness, vertigo, or unsteadiness and were asked the same questions 6 minutes later. In contrast, patients were able to consistently identify the length and periodicity, as well as the triggers, for their dizzy spells. These features may be just as useful in the differential diagnosis and more reliable than the quality of the dizziness. New medications are a common cause of dizziness, and a complete medication history is especially important.

As the history is often nonspecific, a thorough physical examination and selected testing are important to help make a diagnosis (**Table 17**). Orthostatic vital signs and a complete cardiac examination are important in patients with a history of presyncope or an unclear history. An electrocardiogram has a low yield in the evaluation of dizziness but may be indicated in the elderly, patients with cardiovascular disease, or patients with syncope. A neurologic and otologic examination is useful for detecting vestibular and central nervous system causes of dizziness. Nystagmus elicited by a Dix-Hallpike maneuver may be helpful in differentiating peripheral vestibular from central nervous system causes of vertigo. While seated on the examination table, the patient is asked to lie down quickly, first with one ear turned toward the table, and then with the other ear turned toward the table. The finding of 10 to 20 seconds of nystagmus (and possibly vertigo) is abnormal. With peripheral causes of vertigo, the nystagmus is horizontal or rotatory, lasts seconds in duration, may be delayed in onset, and fatigues with repetition. Symptoms of vertigo are typically more pronounced with peripheral causes. Central causes of vertigo typically elicit nystagmus that is vertical or changes direction with different head positions, is longer in duration, has no latent period, and is nonfatiguing. Although head-hanging maneuvers may be suggestive of a diagnosis, they can be difficult to perform and have insufficient sensitivity and specificity to conclusively pinpoint the source of vertigo.

### Vestibular and Peripheral Nerve Causes of Dizziness

Vestibular causes of dizziness are often—but not always—associated with vertigo. Vestibular dizziness is typically of

**TABLE 17** Differential Diagnosis of Dizziness Syndromes

| Type of Dizziness | Suggestive History and Examination Features | Diagnostic Testing Results |
|---|---|---|
| Benign paroxysmal positional vertigo | Recurrent, brief episodes of vertigo precipitated by head motion with otherwise normal neurologic examination | Peripheral nystagmus and reproduction of symptoms on Dix-Hallpike maneuver |
| Vestibular neuritis | Sudden onset of severe and persistent vertigo with nausea and vomiting but no other neurologic symptoms. Antecedent infection may be present. Lasts days to weeks. | Peripheral nystagmus on examination |
| Migraine headache | Headache, duration of vertigo minutes to hours, may have associated triggers | Central or peripheral nystagmus |
| Meniere disease | Vertigo, tinnitus, fullness in ear, and hearing loss. Recurrent episodes lasting hours. | Peripheral nystagmus, unilateral low-frequency hearing loss on audiometry |
| Disequilibrium | Nonspecific sense of unsteadiness, typically while moving. Typically a geriatric patient with multifactorial causes, such as impaired eyesight, peripheral neuropathy, deconditioning, and polypharmacy. | Risk factors revealed by history and physical examination |
| Stroke or transient ischemic attack | Older patient with cardiovascular risk factors. Typically single episode (stroke) or one or more transient episodes lasting at least minutes. Associated neurologic symptoms, such as motor paresis, dysarthria, and other cranial nerve abnormalities, are common. | Central nystagmus, abnormal neurologic examination, abnormal MRI or angiography |
| Acoustic neuroma | Mild to moderate unsteadiness when walking; unilateral tinnitus; hearing loss | Central nystagmus, abnormal MRI |
| Hyperventilation | Triggered by stressful situations; builds up slowly and persists for 20 minutes or longer | Reproduction of symptoms during 2-minute hyperventilation test |
| Psychiatric | History of psychiatric illness, especially anxiety disorders | Diagnosis of exclusion after other causes ruled out |
| Presyncope | Sensation of almost passing out | Depends on cause |

short duration and is recurrent or episodic. Unlike orthostatic hypotension, vestibular dizziness may occur in the supine position. It is most commonly exacerbated by head movement. A recent upper respiratory tract infection, hearing loss, tinnitus, or head trauma may suggest vestibular causes of dizziness.

Benign paroxysmal positional vertigo (BPPV) is the most common cause of vestibular dizziness. BPPV is thought to be caused by otolith debris within the semicircular canal. Patients typically describe vertigo lasting minutes in duration, with multiple episodes occurring over weeks to months. Tinnitus, ear pain, and hearing loss are absent, and nausea that is sufficiently severe or prolonged to cause vomiting is rare. Further diagnostic testing of BPPV is not needed in the absence of other central nervous system symptoms. The natural history of BPPV is to spontaneously remit over a period of several weeks. Recurrences are common, with up to a 30% relapse rate over 3 years.

Otolith repositioning, commonly known as the *Epley maneuver*, has been shown helpful in resolving symptoms of BPPV (**Figure 5**). In this maneuver, the head is sequentially moved in four different positions after waiting for 30 seconds on each turn. The maneuver has no significant adverse effects, and variants of the maneuver can be taught to patients if the symptoms of BPPV return. If these maneuvers fail, medications may be considered in patients with frequently recurring episodes. Anticholinergic medications (scopolamine), antihistamines (meclizine or diphenhydramine), benzodiazepines, or phenothiazine may be useful until symptoms subside.

Vestibular neuronitis is another common cause of peripheral vertigo and dizziness. The suspected cause is postviral inflammation of the vestibular portion of the eighth cranial nerve, but a history of antecedent infection is found in fewer than 50% of patients. Symptoms of vertigo, nausea, vomiting, and gait instability are often disabling. Patients do not usually have other neurologic findings, and hearing is usually preserved. When hearing is impaired, the disorder is termed *acute viral labyrinthitis.*

Vestibular neuronitis differs from BPPV in that the symptoms are usually persistent and tend to be more severe. Patients with vestibular neuronitis do not have recurrent bouts of disease and over several days have a progressive return of equilibrium and cessation of vertigo. A 21-day taper of methylprednisolone may result in faster symptom resolution. Herpes zoster oticus (Ramsay Hunt syndrome) is a specific type of vestibular neuronitis associated with vertigo, hearing loss, ipsilateral facial paralysis, ear pain, and vesicles in the auditory canal and auricle (see Ear, Nose, Mouth, and Throat Disorders). It is treated with standard therapy for herpes zoster (corticosteroids, appropriate antiviral agents).

Meniere disease is a cause of episodic vertigo accompanied by sensorineural hearing loss, fullness, and tinnitus in the affected ear. The vertigo tends to last from 20 minutes up to

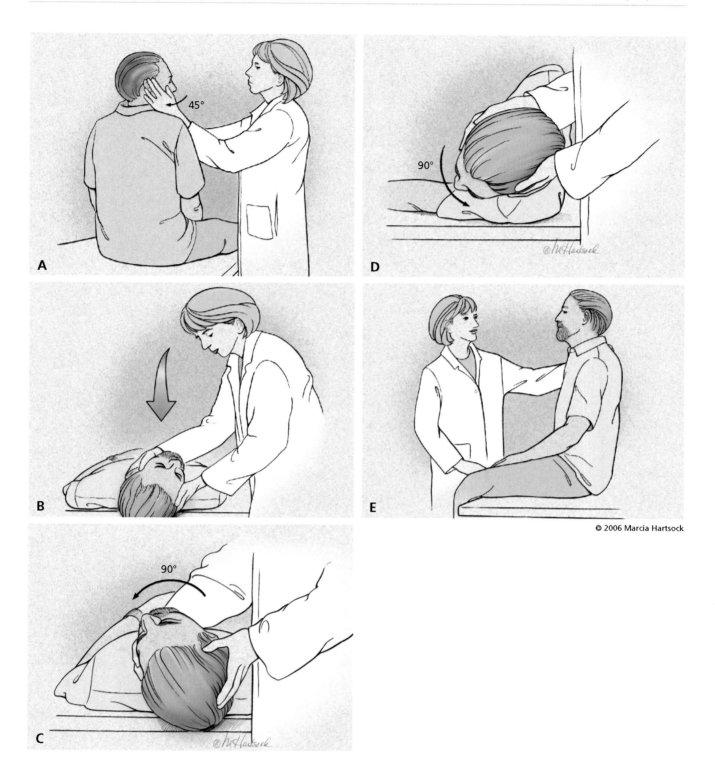

© 2006 Marcia Hartsock

**FIGURE 5.**

**Epley maneuver for relieving benign paroxysmal positional vertigo.**

The patient sits on the examination table, with eyes open and head turned 45 degrees to the right (*A*). The physician supports the patient's head as the patient lies back quickly from a sitting to supine position, ending with the head hanging 20 degrees off the end of the examination table (*B*). The physician turns the patient's head 90 degrees to the left side. The patient remains in this position for 30 seconds (*C*). The physician turns the patient's head an additional 90 degrees to the left while the patient rotates his or her body 90 degrees in the same direction. The patient remains in this position for 30 seconds (*D*). The patient sits up on the left side of the examination table (*E*). The procedure may be repeated on either side until the patient experiences relief of symptoms.

several hours at a time, in contrast to shorter episodes with BPPV. Fixed hearing loss involving tones of all pitches develops over time. Autoimmune vasculitis, trauma, aminoglycoside toxicity, and acoustic neuroma are less common causes of vertigo. Audiometry may be useful in determining the etiology of dizziness symptoms associated with cochlear symptoms.

### Central Nervous System Causes of Dizziness

Tumors are found in fewer than 1% of dizzy patients. The most common tumor associated with dizziness is acoustic neuroma, for which cochlear symptoms (tinnitus and hearing loss) often predominate. Unilateral cochlear symptoms raise the suspicion of acoustic neuroma, whereas bilateral symptoms more likely represent presbycusis rather than a tumor.

Posterior circulation cerebrovascular disease can also cause vertigo but is usually associated with other neurologic symptoms and findings, such as ipsilateral limb ataxia, temperature and pain sensation loss on the contralateral body and ipsilateral face, ipsilateral Horner syndrome, dysarthria, and dysphagia. A high index of suspicion should be observed in older patients with vascular risk factors, such as smoking, hypertension, diabetes, and hyperlipidemia. Duration of symptoms for longer than a few seconds is useful in differentiating either a vertebrobasilar transient ischemic attack or stroke from BPPV. Unlike Meniere disease, simultaneous vestibular and cochlear symptoms are uncommon in patients with cerebrovascular disease. However, it can be difficult to differentiate posterior cerebrovascular ischemic syndromes from vestibular neuronitis.

Migraine headaches may be associated with dizziness described as vertigo. Clues may include antecedent aura and a recurrent nature of symptoms that last from minutes to hours. As headaches and vertigo may occur with more serious disorders such as cerebellar hemorrhage, the initial diagnosis of migrainous vertigo is one of exclusion.

MRI is indicated when clinical symptoms, audiometric testing, and the neurologic examination suggest an infarct, a tumor, or a demyelinating disorder such as multiple sclerosis. The addition of MRI angiography may be useful in ruling out posterior circulation vascular disease in a patient with intermittent neurologic symptoms.

### Disequilibrium

Disequilibrium is a sensation of unsteadiness while walking. It often has multiple causes, with deconditioning, peripheral neuropathy, poor hearing, poor eyesight, and polypharmacy the most common contributing factors. Medications that contribute to disequilibrium include anticholinergic agents, narcotics, benzodiazepines, and antihypertensive agents. In a study of 1087 community-living persons older than 72 years, 24% had dizziness. More than half of those with dizziness had multiple symptom descriptions, and nearly 75% of those with dizziness reported more than one triggering activity. Risk factors for dizziness were impaired hearing, anxiety, depressive symptoms, polypharmacy, postural hypotension, prior myocardial infarction, and impaired balance. Treatment of disequilibrium involves reducing polypharmacy, installing safety features in patient's homes, providing assistive devices such as walkers and canes, correcting eyesight and hearing if possible, and instituting physical therapy to improve muscle strength.

### Nonspecific Dizziness

Often, after an exhaustive evaluation, no specific neurologic or cardiovascular cause of dizziness is revealed. Other systemic problems that may cause a feeling of dizziness include hypoglycemia, medications, thyroid disease, and anemia. Dizziness associated with hyperventilation is typically triggered by stressful situations. Reproduction of the dizziness in an office setting is useful but does not rule out other underlying causes, and hyperventilation is a common secondary component of multifactorial dizziness.

Diagnosis of psychiatric illness may be related to nonspecific dizziness. In a study of 345 patients with dizziness present most days for more than 3 months, 60% met criteria for diagnosis of an anxiety disorder; in 30% of these patients with anxiety, no other potential causes of dizziness were found. Other common causes of chronic dizziness in the study included traumatic brain injury and migraine headache.

**KEY POINTS**

- Benign paroxysmal positional vertigo is associated with increased dizziness with lying down or rolling over while supine.
- The Dix-Hallpike maneuver may be helpful in differentiating peripheral vestibular from central nervous system causes of vertigo.
- The Epley maneuver is effective at relieving short-term symptoms of benign paroxysmal positional vertigo and has minimal adverse effects.
- Corticosteroids may reduce the length and severity of symptoms in patients with acute vestibular neuronitis.
- Anxiety disorders are common in patients with chronic unexplained dizziness.

## Insomnia

Insomnia is difficulty falling asleep or maintaining sleep, waking up too early, or sleep that is chronically nonrestorative despite the opportunity and circumstances for sleep; and is associated with daytime impairment or distress. Acute insomnia lasts less than 1 week, short-term insomnia lasts 1 to 3 weeks, and chronic insomnia occurs at least three times weekly for more than 1 month. One in three Americans have insomnia at some point in their lives, and one in ten have chronic insomnia. Insomnia can occur at any age but is more common as people age, with prevalence rates of 12% to 30% in patients older than 65 years. Older adults take longer to initiate sleep, the amount of time in lighter levels of sleep increases, overall sleep time decreases, and the amount of rapid eye movement (REM) sleep also decreases. Regardless of age, adults need approximately 7 to 8 hours of sleep nightly.

Insomnia has significant personal and societal costs. Insomnia can lead to daytime somnolence, irritability, increased health care utilization, decreased quality of life, higher accident rates (2.5-4.5 times more likely than controls), and impaired job performance (including higher rates of absenteeism). Insomnia may be a harbinger to or a consequence of depression, anxiety, and mood disorders. Insomnia may lead to substance abuse such as alcohol and other medications (prescription and nonprescription). The total direct costs related to insomnia in the United States in 1995 were $13.9 billion.

At least 80% of insomnia cases are secondary to an underlying condition such as pain, mental health disorders, dementia, cardiopulmonary disease, situational worry, a primary sleep disorder, or medications (**Table 18**). Primary insomnia

is that which is not due to an underlying condition and lasts for a period of more than 1 month. It can be triggered by long-lasting emotional distress, travel (jet lag), or work-related changes (shift work). Some of the habits that develop to deal with the insomnia, such as napping, going to bed early, or worrying about sleep, can perpetuate the problem.

The medical history should focus on underlying medical conditions (heart failure, chronic obstructive pulmonary disease), psychiatric conditions (depression, anxiety, posttraumatic stress disorder), and environmental conditions (light, circadian rhythm disturbances, noise, sleep partner problems) that may cause or contribute to the insomnia. A sleep history is essential for characterizing the patient's concerns and identifying any possible underlying sleep disorder (**Table 19**). Self-administered questionnaires such as the Pittsburgh Sleep Quality Index may be helpful to establish the cause of insomnia and to plan effective treatment. A patient-recorded sleep diary for 1 to 2 weeks documenting bedtime, wake time, hours of sleep, and number of awakenings may help obtain a more accurate record of sleep habits than general questioning.

| **TABLE 18** Common Causes of Insomnia | |
|---|---|
| **Cause** | **Characteristics** |
| Psychophysiologic insomnia | Disturbed sleep resulting from conditioned arousal usually to the bedroom. Look for a history of sleep improvement when away from the bedroom. Patients may have an inordinate concern over sleep. |
| Restless legs syndrome | An uncomfortable or restless feeling in legs most prominent at night and at rest associated with an urge to move and alleviated by movement. Approximately 80% of patients with RLS have PLMD on polysomnography. |
| Periodic limb movement disorder | Repetitive stereotypic leg movement during sleep. Polysomnography is necessary for diagnosis. |
| Sleep state misperception | Objectively normal sleep in the face of the patient's report of insufficient sleep. |
| Central sleep apnea syndrome | Repetitive pauses in breathing during sleep without upper airway occlusion. Look for associated history of CHF or CNS disease. Polysomnography is necessary for diagnosis. |
| Obstructive sleep apnea syndrome | Upper airway obstruction during inspiration in sleep. Look for a history of snoring, witnessed pauses in respiration, and daytime sleepiness. Polysomnography is necessary for diagnosis. |
| Inadequate sleep hygiene | Disturbed sleep associated with caffeine, tobacco, alcohol use, or irregular sleep habits (e.g., college students). Comprehensive sleep history will facilitate the diagnosis. |
| Environmental sleep disorder | Disturbed sleep associated with environmental elements. Comprehensive sleep history will facilitate the diagnosis. |
| Hypnotic-dependent sleep disorder | Disturbed sleep associated with tolerance to or withdrawal from hypnotic drugs. Positive history of sustained hypnotic drug use with development of tolerance leading to increased dose. |
| Alcohol-dependent sleep disorder | Alcohol used to initiate sleep; sleep that follows is fragmented. Ask for patient's history of alcohol use to facilitate sleep for at least the last 30 days. |
| Shift-work sleep disorder | Symptoms of insomnia as a consequence of shift-work. Shift work includes those patients working a permanent night shift. |
| Time zone change syndrome (jet lag) | Time zone changes secondary to travel, leading to poor sleep, daytime sleepiness, or both. |
| Anxiety and depressive disorders | May trigger sleep initiation or sleep maintenance problem. Most patients with anxiety and insomnia will present with anxiety first or concomitant with insomnia. In contrast, depression tends to follow insomnia. |
| Dementia | Insomnia associated with dementia and manifested by wandering, aggressive behavior, verbalization, and delirium in the early evening hours. |

CHF = congestive heart failure; CNS = central nervous system; PLMD = periodic limb movement disorder; RLS = restless legs syndrome.

**TABLE 19 Elements of a Comprehensive Sleep History**

Problems of sleep initiation, sleep maintenance, early morning waking, or nonrestorative sleep

Duration of symptoms

Stability or progression of symptoms (stable, worsening, or improving)

Precipitating causes of insomnia

Bedtime, waking time, length of sleep time

Bedtime routine, including activities 1-2 hours before sleep and activities while in bed (such as watching television) that may delay sleep

Caffeine use (within 8 hours of bedtime)

Alcohol use (in general or as sleep aid)

Any current or previous behavioral therapies used to treat insomnia

Previous over-the-counter or prescription sleep remedies

Shift work or irregular sleep schedule

Potential acute stressors, such as:
   Medical or psychiatric illness
   Medication use, both prescribed and illicit
   Acute stress at home or work
   Circadian rhythm stressors (jet lag)

**TABLE 20 Sleep Hygiene and Stimulus Control Behaviors**

Maintain stable bedtimes and rising times, even if there is trouble initiating or maintaining sleep on a given night

Spend no more than 8 hours in bed

Experience regular daytime light exposure

Maintain a quiet, dark bedroom
   Associate the bedroom with rest and sleep: avoid activities such as watching television or reading in bed

Maintain adequate nutrition

Avoid sleep-fragmenting substances, such as caffeine, nicotine, and alcohol
   Caffeine within 8 hours of bedtime can fragment sleep

Avoid using alcohol to initiate sleep
   Alcohol may promote drowsiness but impairs deeper levels of sleep

Avoid clock-watching
   If unable to initiate sleep within 20 minutes of attempting sleep, advise patients to leave the bedroom, undertake nonstimulating activities (such as reading) elsewhere, and return to bed when sleepy

Maintain regular exercise

Avoid heavy exercise within 2 hours of bedtime

Avoid bright light before bedtime

Maintain a 30-minute relaxation period before bedtime

The physical examination should be tailored to confirming problems identified in the history. Any diagnostic testing should be guided by judgment about associated medical conditions (for example, iron deficiency and renal disease with restless legs syndrome). Referral for polysomnography is indicated when a primary sleep disorder is suspected (obstructive sleep apnea, restless legs syndrome, periodic limb movement disorder). A sleep study may also include multiple sleep latency testing, in which a patient takes four or five 20-minute naps, and sleep latency (the time from deciding to sleep to actually falling asleep) is measured. Sleep latency of less than 8 minutes is associated with hypersomnia, which occurs with sleep disorders such as narcolepsy, insufficient sleep syndrome, medication adverse effects, sleep apnea syndromes, and periodic limb movements in sleep. Treatment of insomnia involves addressing and correcting precipitating factors. Any intervention—pharmacologic or nonpharmacologic—begins by focusing on ensuring adequate sleep hygiene, as poor sleep hygiene can contribute to sleep fragmentation, circadian rhythm disturbance, discomfort, and overstimulation. Sleep hygiene should be tailored to an individual patient's needs (**Table 20**).

The technique of sleep restriction should be considered in patients with insomnia with no underlying medical or psychological disorder in whom sleep hygiene measures have been unsuccessful. Sleep restriction involves limiting the time spent in bed and gradually moving bedtime later in an effort to consolidate sleep. A patient undergoing sleep restriction should maintain a sleep log for 1 to 2 weeks documenting

bedtime, sleep time, nocturnal waking, and rising time. The patient should then limit the time spent in bed to the average time reported sleeping in the sleep log, but no less than 5 hours. A strict rising time each day should be maintained. If sleep efficiency (total time asleep/total time in bed) is greater than 90%, bedtime can be moved earlier in 15-minute increments, being careful to maintain 90% sleep efficiency. Successful sleep restriction technique results in improved total sleep time. Patients should be warned that sleep restriction has the potential to significantly increase daytime sleepiness and to be cautious driving or engaging in other daytime activities that require attention.

In cognitive-behavioral therapy for insomnia, patients are provided with correct information about sleep (such as the need for 7-8 hours/night and normal changes in sleep associated with aging), and negative concerns and beliefs that have arisen about sleep are addressed. In certain populations, behavioral techniques such as cognitive-behavioral therapy have been shown to decrease awake time more effectively than drugs in randomized trials. Biofeedback and progressive muscle relaxation techniques may also be helpful.

Pharmacologic therapy for insomnia involves both nonprescription and prescription medications. Nonprescription antihistamines (diphenhydramine or doxylamine) are widely available, but evidence of their efficacy is limited and they are associated with significant adverse effects (daytime somnolence, impairment of complex tasks such as driving, anticholinergic side effects). Melatonin may be effective for circadian rhythm disturbances (for example, jet lag) but its role, as well as that of alternative therapies such as St. John's wort, valerian, and kava, is unproven, and these agents are generally discouraged for chronic insomnia.

Prescription medications are commonly used for treating insomnia but caution must be exercised. Consensus opinion and the FDA recommend limiting the use of sedative hypnotics to 1 month. The FDA has issued warnings regarding severe allergic reactions and anaphylaxis as well as complex sleep-related behaviors (such as sleep-driving or sleep-eating; often associated with amnesia of the events) for many commonly used agents. It is important to avoid hypnotics in patients with underlying disorders in which their use can be counterproductive. For example, a patient with obstructive sleep apnea syndrome would not be aided and would potentially be harmed by sleeping pills. In addition, patients should be cautioned to avoid using alcohol while taking any sedative-hypnotic sleep medication. Finally, several studies suggest that nondrug therapies may be more effective if not used in conjunction with drugs. In general, nonbenzodiazepine hypnotics, such as zolpidem, zaleplon, and eszopiclone, have more favorable effects on sleep and fewer side effects than benzodiazepines. Benzodiazepines have the potential for dependency and may lose effectiveness after 30 days; tapering the dose at discontinuation may mitigate withdrawal or rebound insomnia. The minimally effective dose for the shortest duration should be used. Antidepressants should be used to treat underlying depression and should not be used solely to treat insomnia. Dopaminergic agents can be helpful in treating symptoms of restless legs syndrome (when other reversible causes such as iron deficiency, thyroid disease, and caffeine use have been eliminated); if these agents are unhelpful or contraindicated, clonazepam or gabapentin may help restless legs syndrome.

**KEY POINTS**

- Insomnia may be a symptom or consequence of mental health problems.
- Antidepressants should not be used solely to treat insomnia.
- Instruction on sleep hygiene is a key element in the treatment of insomnia.
- Over-the-counter sleep medications have potential for adverse effects and limited efficacy.
- In the treatment of insomnia, the use of sedative hypnotics should be limited to 1 month.

# Syncope

Syncope is a sudden and transient loss of consciousness and posture, typically caused by a lack of blood flow to the brain. Presyncope is a sensation of nearly losing consciousness and has the same general causes as syncope. Common findings on the history and physical examination associated with various types of syncope are described in **Table 21**.

## Neurologic Causes of Syncope

Seizures are a common cause of loss of consciousness and should be considered when there are no witnesses to the event or a suggestive history is elicited. There are several clues on history that may help differentiate syncope from seizures. Loss of consciousness associated with tongue biting, incontinence, preceding emotional stress, loss of memory or confusion after the event, head turning during the event, and a prodrome of déjà vu or jamais vu (a false sensation of unfamiliarity with a situation) are all suggestive of seizure. A

| **TABLE 21** Differential Diagnosis of Syncope | |
|---|---|
| **Possible Diagnosis** | **Associated Findings** |
| Seizures | Tongue biting, incontinence, preceding emotional stress, loss of memory or confusion after the event, a prodrome of déjà vu or jamais vu |
| Vasovagal syncope | Prodrome of nausea, diaphoresis, and pallor before syncope. Triggers such as fear, pain, prolonged standing, phlebotomy, coughing, urinating, defecating, and drinking cold liquids. |
| Carotid sinus syncope | Head turning or other pressure on carotid sinus |
| Orthostatic hypotension | Syncope on standing from sitting or supine position, history of drugs associated with orthostatic hypotension, diseases associated with autonomic failure (such as Parkinson disease) |
| Stroke | Associated focal neurologic symptoms, headache |
| Structural heart disease | Abnormal murmur on cardiac examination, exertional syncope, abnormal ECG, history of heart disease |
| Arrhythmia | History of coronary artery disease or heart failure, exertional syncope, palpitations, absence of a prodrome, family history of sudden death, drugs prolonging QT interval, abnormal baseline ECG |
| Systemic causes | History of labile diabetes, anemia, volume depletion, adrenal insufficiency |
| Psychiatric syncope | Frequent episodes, odd associated symptoms, no heart disease |

ECG = electrocardiogram.

history of prior lightheaded spells, diaphoresis preceding spells, and spells after prolonged sitting or standing are more suggestive of causes of syncope that are not seizure related.

Cerebrovascular disease is an uncommon cause of syncope. Syncope can be associated with stroke, subarachnoid hemorrhage, vertebrobasilar insufficiency, and subclavian steal syndrome but rarely occurs without other findings on neurologic examination. In some disorders, such as large subdural hematomas, it is difficult to determine whether the finding is a result of a fall caused by syncope or a contributing factor to the syncope itself.

### Neurocardiogenic Syncope

Neurocardiogenic or vasovagal syncope is one of the most common causes of syncope. In neurocardiogenic syncope, triggers lead to increased parasympathetic tone, causing a drop in heart rate and blood pressure (cardioinhibitory response); decreased sympathetic tone, causing vasodilation and hypotension (vasodepressor response); or a combination of the two. The increased vagal tone seen in neurocardiogenic syncope typically causes a prodrome of nausea, diaphoresis, and pallor. Common triggers include fear, pain, prolonged standing, phlebotomy, coughing, urinating, defecating, and drinking cold liquids. Neurocardiogenic syncope is frequently diagnosed when other causes of syncope are excluded or with a suggestive history in a low-risk patient. It may also be diagnosed by characteristic bradycardia and hypotension during an upright tilt-table test.

Carotid sinus hypersensitivity causes neurocardiogenic syncope when mechanical pressure on the carotid sinus stimulates the glossopharyngeal nerve, altering sympathetic and parasympathetic tone. Recent studies suggest that carotid sinus hypersensitivity is common in the elderly, occurring in up to 35% of asymptomatic patients. It is a diagnosis of exclusion when other causes of syncope have been eliminated.

Treatment of neurocardiogenic syncope is based on trigger avoidance and assumption of a supine position with legs elevated when symptoms arise. Other nonpharmacologic treatments include compression stockings, tilt training, and volume expansion. In patients with frequent episodes, pharmacologic therapy with β-blockers may be considered. A dual-chamber pacemaker can be considered in selected patients with inappropriate bradycardia when medical therapy is ineffective, episodes are particularly severe and frequent, and a predominant cardioinhibitory response is found on tilt-table testing.

### Orthostatic Hypotension

Orthostatic hypotension is a frequent cause of syncope and presyncope. It is defined as a systolic blood pressure decrease of at least 20 mm Hg or a diastolic blood pressure decrease of at least 10 mm Hg within 3 minutes of standing. Orthostatic hypotension may be classified into medication-induced, neurogenic, and nonneurogenic categories.

Common medications associated with orthostatic hypotension include α-adrenergic blockers, nitrates, diuretics and other antihypertensive agents, phosphodiesterase inhibitors, and antidepressants. Initiation of a new medicine is often temporally related to symptoms. Examples of diseases causing neurogenic orthostatic hypotension are diabetic or alcoholic polyneuropathy, multiple sclerosis, and multiple systems atrophy. Nonneurogenic orthostatic hypotension may be caused by disorders such as adrenal insufficiency, venous pooling, or volume depletion from an acute medical illness.

Patients with orthostatic hypotension should be educated to avoid rising to standing positions quickly, to wear elastic support hose, and to avoid volume depletion and large meals. In patients in whom these measures fail and no offending medications are being given, a trial of fludrocortisone or a sympathomimetic agent may be useful.

### Cardiac Disease

Three major groups of disorders cause syncope of cardiac origin. These disorders are cardiac outflow obstruction, arrhythmias, and cardiac ischemia. Causes of obstructed cardiac output leading to syncope include severe aortic stenosis, hypertrophic obstructive cardiomyopathy, and pulmonary embolism. Coronary artery disease is an uncommon cause of syncope and typically occurs with symptoms of cardiac ischemia, abnormal cardiac enzyme levels, or an abnormal electrocardiogram.

Ventricular tachycardia, atrial arrhythmias, and bradyarrhythmias can cause syncope. Atrial tachyarrhythmias are more likely to cause palpitations and lightheadedness than syncope. Ventricular tachycardia (VT) is perhaps the most feared cause of syncope because of its tendency to recur and cause sudden cardiac death. VT is most commonly seen in patients with advanced systolic heart failure and underlying ischemic heart disease (see MKSAP 15 Cardiovascular Medicine). Less common causes include long QT syndrome, catecholaminergic polymorphic VT, and Brugada syndrome. Patients at risk for recurrent VT should receive electrophysiologic testing and consideration of an implantable cardioverter-defibrillator. Syncope may also be associated with long (>3 seconds) sinus pauses and advanced heart block. These conditions are readily treated by pacemaker insertion.

### Risk Stratification and Hospitalization

The decision to hospitalize a patient with syncope should be based on concern for a short-term risk for arrhythmia or sudden death that will be detected during the observation period. Several recent studies have tried and failed to define prediction rules with sufficient sensitivity to detect life-threatening causes. While no rule has been validated for widespread use, the literature has identified several factors associated with a significantly increased risk of adverse events (**Table 22**). Patients with these characteristics should be considered for admission or observation. Age and other comorbidities are also important factors in

**TABLE 22** Risk Factors for Short-Term Adverse Outcomes from Syncope (American College of Emergency Physicians)

Abnormal ECG

　Acute ischemia

　New changes on ECG

　Any rhythm other than sinus

　Significant conduction abnormalities

Hematocrit <30%

History of heart failure, coronary artery disease, or structural heart disease

Older age

ECG = electrocardiogram.

Information from Huff JS, Decker WW, Quinn JV, et al. Clinical policy: critical issues in the evaluation and management of adult patients presenting to the emergency department with syncope. Ann Emerg Med. 2007;49(4):431-444. [PMID: 17371707]

deciding whether to admit a patient. The American College of Emergency Physicians considers age a risk factor for adverse longer-term outcomes in patients with syncope but felt there were insufficient data to recommend a specific age cutoff for which they would recommend admission.

## Diagnostic Evaluation of Syncope

A general approach to the evaluation of syncope is outlined in **Figure 6**. All patients should undergo a thorough history, physical examination, 12-lead electrocardiogram, and orthostatic vital sign evaluation. Serum electrolytes and a hematocrit are often useful to screen for common systemic disorders. In patients deemed low risk with a suggestive history for neurocardiogenic syncope, no further evaluation may be needed. In patients with normal orthostatic vital signs but with a history strongly suggestive of neurocardiogenic syncope, tilt-table testing may be indicated. Carotid sinus massage can be attempted with monitoring in patients without bruits or cerebrovascular disease when other causes of syncope have been excluded. The massage attempts to reproduce index symptoms with a characteristic heart rate and blood pressure response.

If the cause of syncope is unexplained from the initial evaluation, continuous telemetry may be useful to screen for paroxysmal arrhythmias. If symptoms are frequent, 24-hour ambulatory monitoring may be useful to exclude arrhythmia as a cause of symptoms. If symptoms are infrequent, an event monitor or loop recorder should be used. If structural heart disease is suspected, an echocardiogram is indicated. In patients with coronary artery disease or heart failure, electrophysiologic testing is often performed because these patients have a high incidence of malignant ventricular arrhythmias. If syncope occurs during exercise, a graded exercise test may reveal useful information.

Neuroimaging, such as CT scanning, is of limited use in evaluating syncope. It has the highest yield in patients who are older than 65 years and have neurologic symptoms such as headache, neurologic examination abnormalities, head trauma, or are on anticoagulants. Bilateral carotid stenosis is a rare cause of syncope, and routine carotid duplex ultrasonography is not recommended. An electroencephalogram may be useful in patients with historical features more consistent with seizures than syncope.

**KEY POINTS**

- History, physical examination, and a screening electrocardiogram are usually sufficient to diagnose most causes of syncope.
- Seizure may be suggested by tongue biting, incontinence, loss of memory or confusion after the event, head turning during the event, and a prodrome of déjà vu.
- The increased vagal tone seen in neurocardiogenic syncope typically causes a prodrome of nausea, diaphoresis, and pallor.
- Carotid sinus hypersensitivity causes neurocardiogenic syncope when mechanical pressure on the carotid sinus alters sympathetic and parasympathetic tone.
- Patients with syncope associated with dyspnea, an abnormal electrocardiogram, a systolic blood pressure below 90 mm Hg, a hematocrit below 30%, or a history of congestive heart failure or structural heart disease have an increased short-term risk of an adverse event, and hospitalization should be considered.

## Chest Pain

In outpatients, the most common cause of chest pain is musculoskeletal; in emergency settings, approximately 50% of patients have an acute coronary syndrome. The differential diagnosis of chest pain can be approached as cardiac, pulmonary, gastrointestinal, musculoskeletal, and psychiatric causes (**Table 23**).

Ischemic chest pain classically presents as substernal pressure, tightness, or heaviness with radiation to the jaw, shoulders, back, or arms. The most powerful clinical features that increase the probability of myocardial infarction include chest pain that simultaneously radiates to both arms (positive likelihood ratio = 7.1), an $S_3$ (positive likelihood ratio = 3.2), and hypotension (positive likelihood ratio = 3.1). In contrast, a normal electrocardiogram result (negative likelihood ratio = 0.1-0.3), chest pain that is positional (negative likelihood ratio = 0.3) or reproduced by palpation (negative likelihood ratio = 0.2-0.4), or pain that is sharp or stabbing (negative likelihood ratio = 0.3), makes an ischemic etiology less likely. Patients suspected of having acute coronary syndrome are hospitalized and evaluated with serial electrocardiograms and measurement of cardiac biomarkers, chest radiography, and, often, echocardiography. Low-risk patients without evidence

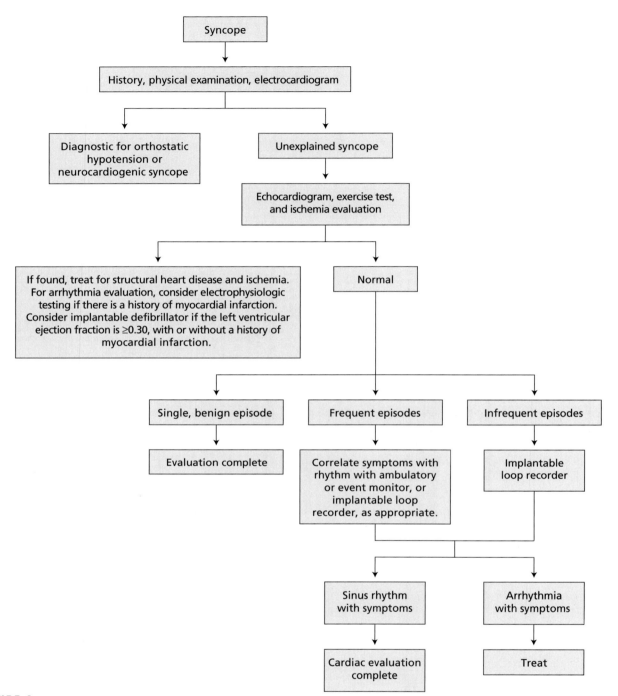

**FIGURE 6.**
Evaluation of syncope.

of myocardial infarction are evaluated with an exercise or pharmacologic stress test.

Acute pericarditis (viral or bacterial) is characterized by sudden onset of substernal chest pain with radiation along the trapezius ridge; the pain is often worse with inspiration and lying flat and is frequently alleviated with sitting and leaning forward. Pericarditis may be preceded or accompanied by symptoms of an upper respiratory tract infection and fever. A pericardial friction rub is present in 85% to 100% of patients at some time during its course. A confirmatory electrocardiogram will show diffuse ST-segment elevation and PR-segment depression, findings that are specific but not sensitive.

**TABLE 23** Differential Diagnosis of Chest Pain

| Disease | Notes |
|---|---|
| Acute coronary syndrome | Chest pain, nausea, or dyspnea. Associated with specific ECG and echocardiographic changes. Cardiac enzymes help establish diagnosis of myocardial infarction. |
| Aortic dissection | Substernal chest pain with radiation to the back, midscapular region. Often described as "tearing" or "ripping" type pain. Chest radiograph may show a widened mediastinal silhouette, a pleural effusion, or both. |
| Aortic stenosis | Chest pain with exertion, heart failure, syncope. Typical systolic murmur at the base of the heart radiating to the neck. |
| Esophagitis | Burning-type chest discomfort, usually precipitated by meals, not related to exertion. Often worse lying down, improved with sitting. |
| Musculoskeletal pain | Typically more reproducible chest pain. Includes muscle strain, costochondritis, and fracture. Should be a diagnosis of exclusion. |
| Panic attack | May be indistinguishable from angina. Often diagnosed after a negative evaluation for ischemic heart disease. Often associated with palpitations, sweating, and anxiety. |
| Pericarditis | Substernal chest discomfort that can be sharp, dull, or pressure-like, often relieved with sitting forward. Usually pleuritic. ECG changes may include ST-segment elevation (usually diffuse) or more specifically (but less commonly) PR-segment depression. |
| Pneumothorax | Sudden onset of pleuritic chest pain and dyspnea. Chest radiograph or CT confirms the diagnosis. |
| Pulmonary embolism | Commonly presents with dyspnea. Pleuritic chest pain is present in approximately 30% of patients. Look for risk factors (immobilization, recent surgery, stroke, cancer, previous VTE). |

CT = computed tomography; ECG = electrocardiography; VTE = venous thromboembolism.

Patients with dissection of the thoracic aorta typically present with abrupt onset of back pain or severe, sharp, or "tearing" chest pain that may radiate to the abdomen. A pulse differential (diminished pulse compared with the contralateral side) is one of the most useful findings (positive likelihood ratio = 5.7). Focal neurologic deficits are present in a minority of patients, but in the proper clinical context, such findings are highly suggestive. A wide mediastinum on a chest radiograph is a common initial finding, and the absence of this finding helps rule out dissection (negative likelihood ratio = 0.3). However, the "classic" manifestations of aortic dissection, including widened mediastinum, a pulse deficit, and radiation of the pain, are often absent; this diagnosis should, therefore, be considered in any patient who presents with sudden severe thoracic pain. CT of the chest, MRI, transesophageal echocardiography, and aortic root angiography all have a high sensitivity and specificity for detection of a dissection flap.

Aortic stenosis is a cause of exertional chest pain. Physical examination reveals a systolic crescendo-decrescendo murmur best heard at the second right intercostal space with radiation to the carotids. A transthoracic echocardiogram is the diagnostic test of choice for suspected aortic stenosis.

Pulmonary causes of chest pain include embolism, pneumonia, and pneumothorax. Pulmonary embolism may present with acute pleuritic chest pain, dyspnea, and, less often, cough and hemoptysis. The presence of risk factors for pulmonary embolism, such as recent surgery, immobilization, history of previous venous thromboembolism, and malignancy, may suggest the diagnosis. Physical examination findings are nonspecific. Pleuritic chest pain associated with pneumonia is often accompanied by fever, chills, cough, purulent sputum, and dyspnea. The physical examination may show wheezing or crackles and signs of consolidation such as dullness to percussion, egophony, and bronchophony. Pneumothorax should be considered in any patient with sudden onset of pleuritic chest pain and dyspnea. The physical examination may show decreased breath sounds on the affected side; if a tension pneumothorax is present, hypotension and tracheal deviation to the opposite side of the pneumothorax can be seen.

Pulmonary causes of chest pain are initially evaluated with a chest radiograph. In patients with dyspnea, pulse oximetry or an arterial blood gas analysis is indicated. In the setting of moderate to high suspicion for pulmonary embolism, a helical CT scan of the chest or a ventilation/perfusion lung scan with or without duplex Doppler examination of the lower extremities is an appropriate initial approach. A negative D-dimer test helps exclude the diagnosis of pulmonary embolism and is most helpful when the clinical suspicion is low.

Pain associated with gastroesophageal reflux can mimic ischemic chest pain. Important distinctions include gastroesophageal pain lasting minutes to hours and resolving either spontaneously or with antacids. However, response to antacids cannot be relied on to rule out a cardiac cause. Discomfort associated with reflux is often positional (worse when lying down), increases after meals, or awakens patients from sleep. In unclear cases, it is appropriate to exclude cardiac causes of chest pain before evaluating gastrointestinal etiologies. For patients with a high probability of gastroesophageal reflux disease, empiric treatment with a proton pump inhibitor for 4 to 6 weeks is an appropriate initial diagnostic and therapeutic approach.

Musculoskeletal causes of chest pain are more common in women than men; common causes include costochondritis, arthritis, and fibromyalgia. Musculoskeletal chest pain has an insidious onset and may last for hours to weeks. It is most recognizable when sharp and localized to a specific area of the chest; however, it can also be poorly localized. The pain may be worsened by turning, deep breathing, or arm movement. Chest pain may or may not be reproducible by chest palpation (pain reproduced by palpation does not exclude ischemic heart disease), and the cardiovascular examination is often normal. For musculoskeletal chest pain, the history and physical examination are keys to the diagnosis; selected imaging and laboratory tests may be indicated depending upon the clinical circumstances.

Chest pain can also be a manifestation of severe anxiety and panic attack. Patients may complain of sweating; trembling or shaking; sensations of choking, shortness of breath, or smothering; nausea or abdominal distress; and feeling dizzy, unsteady, or lightheaded. On physical examination, tachycardia and tachypnea may be present, but the remainder of the cardiovascular and pulmonary examinations is unremarkable. Psychosomatic chest pain is a clinical diagnosis; other causes of chest pain are usually excluded by careful history and physical examination.

**KEY POINTS**

- The most powerful clinical features that increase the probability of myocardial infarction include chest pain that simultaneously radiates to both arms, an $S_3$, and hypotension.

- Aortic dissection should be considered in any patient who presents with sudden severe thoracic pain, particularly when the pain is maximal at onset.

- D-dimer testing is most helpful in ruling out pulmonary embolism when it is normal in a low-risk patient.

- Panic attack may be clinically indistinguishable from angina and is a diagnosis of exclusion.

### Bibliography

Chou R, Fanciullo GJ, Fine PG, et al; American Pain Society-American Academy of Pain Medicine Opioids Guidelines Panel. Clinical guidelines for the use of chronic opioid therapy in chronic noncancer pain. J Pain. 2009;10(2):113-130. [PMID: 19187889]

Häuser W, Bernardy K, Uçeyler N, Sommer C. Treatment of fibromyalgia syndrome with antidepressants: a meta-analysis. JAMA. 2009;301(2):198-209. [PMID: 19141768]

Huff JS, Decker WW, Quinn JV, et al; American College of Emergency Physicians. Critical issues in the evaluation and management of adult patients presenting to the emergency department with syncope. Ann Emerg Med. 2007;49(4):431-444. [PMID: 17371707]

Irwin RS. Guidelines for treating adults with acute cough. Am Fam Physician. 2007;75(4):476, 479, 482. [PMID: 17323709]

Irwin RS, Baumann MH, Bolser DC, et al; American College of Chest Physicians (ACCP). Diagnosis and management of cough executive summary: ACCP evidence-based clinical practice guidelines. Chest. 2006;129(1 Suppl):1S-23S. [PMID: 16428686]

Johnson M, Martinson M. Efficacy of electrical nerve stimulation for chronic musculoskeletal pain: a meta-analysis of randomized controlled trials. Pain. 2007;130(1-2):157-165. [PMID: 17383095]

Jackson JL, O'Malley PG, Kroenke K. Antidepressants and cognitive-behavioral therapy for symptom syndromes. CNS Spectr. 2006;11(3):212-222. [PMID: 16575378]

Kelly BS. Evaluation of the elderly patient with acute chest pain. Clin Geriatr Med. 2007;23(2):327-349. [PMID: 17462520]

Kerr SR, Pearce MS, Brayne C, Davis RJ, Kenny RA. Carotid sinus hypersensitivity in asymptomatic older persons: implications for diagnosis of syncope and falls. Arch Intern Med. 2006;166(5):515-520. [PMID: 16534037]

Kroenke K, Rosmalen JGM. Symptoms, syndromes and the value of psychiatric diagnostics in patients with functional somatic disorders. Med Clin N Am. 2006;90(4):603-626. [PMID: 16843765]

Martell BA, O'Connor PG, Kerns RD, et al. Systematic review: opioid treatment for chronic back pain: prevalence, efficacy, and association with addiction. Ann Intern Med. 2007;146(2):116-127. [PMID: 17227935]

Newman-Toker DE, Cannon LM, Stofferahn ME, Rothman RE, Hsieh YH, Zee DS. Imprecision in patient reports of dizziness symptom quality: a cross-sectional study conducted in an acute care setting. Mayo Clin Proc. 2007;82(11):1329-1340. [PMID: 17976352]

Pharmacologic management of persistent pain in older persons. J Am Geriatr Soc. In press. Available at www.americangeriatrics.org/education/pharm_management.shtml.

Reeves WC, Jones JF, Maloney E, et al. Prevalence of chronic fatigue syndrome in metropolitan, urban, and rural Georgia. Popul Health Metr. 2007;5:5. [PMID: 17559660]

Ringstrom E, Freedman J. Approach to undifferentiated chest pain in the emergency department: a review of recent medical literature and published practice guidelines. Mt Sinai J Med. 2006;73(2):499-505. [PMID: 16568192]

Roth T. Insomnia: definition, prevalence, etiology, and consequences. J Clin Sleep Med. 2007;3(5 Suppl):S7-10. [PMID: 17824495]

Staab JP, Ruckenstein MJ. Expanding the differential diagnosis of chronic dizziness. Arch Otolaryngol Head Neck Surg. 2007;133(2):170-176. [PMID: 17309987]

Tinetti ME, Williams CS, Gill TM. Dizziness among older adults: a possible geriatric syndrome. Ann Intern Med. 2000;132(5):337-344. [PMID: 10691583]

Wenzel PR, Fowler AA 3rd. Clinical Practice. Acute bronchitis. N Engl J Med. 2006;355(2):2125-2130. [PMID: 17108344]

Wilson JF. In the clinic. Insomnia. Ann Intern Med. 2008;148(1): ITC13-1-ITC13-16. [PMID: 18166757]

# Musculoskeletal Pain

## Acute Low Back Pain

Acute low back pain is the fifth most common reason for ambulatory physician visits in the United States. It is defined as pain between the costal margin and the gluteal folds for less than 6 weeks. Seventy percent of patients will have an occurrence over their lifetime, usually during middle age. It is usually self-limited, with full recovery in 6 weeks in 90% of individuals. Of patients presenting with acute low back pain, approximately 4% have compression fractures, 1% to 3% have prolapsed intervertebral disks, and 3% have spinal stenosis; neoplasia, ankylosing spondylitis, and spinal infections are even rarer. An age of onset of greater than 50 years denotes a higher risk for concerning diagnoses.

## Diagnosis and Evaluation

The goal of performing a diagnostic triage is to look for "red flags" that might denote a more serious injury (**Table 24**). The American College of Physicians and the American Pain Society recommend that the initial history and physical examination of a patient with low back pain be directed toward categorizing the patient as having nonspecific low back pain, back pain that may be associated with radiculopathy or spinal stenosis, or back pain that may be caused by some other specific spinal pathology. Psychosocial factors that predict risk for chronic disabling back pain should also be assessed; these include depression, somatoform disorders, job dissatisfaction, and higher levels of disability. Thoracic rather than lumbar pain may indicate more severe pathology, as may pain that is constant, progressive, nonmechanical in nature (no relief with bed rest), or lasting for more than 4 weeks. Patients initially presenting with back pain who are treated conservatively should be instructed to call the office immediately if they develop neurologic symptoms (distal muscle weakness, foot drop) or urinary retention, which is 90% sensitive for the presence of cauda equina syndrome.

During the physical examination, the clinician should percuss the spinous processes (painful in compression fracture or pathologic fracture) and palpate in between the spinous processes looking for tenderness (seen in disk space abscesses). Next, palpating the paravertebral musculature helps to locate the level of the injury. Palpating over the sacroiliac joints may elicit tenderness in sacroiliitis. Asking the patient to point to the most tender location on the back with one finger helps establish the level. Checking range of motion is not beneficial in an examination for acute back pain, as range is usually decreased from any condition causing acute back pain.

A careful, focused neurologic examination is essential. The deep tendon reflexes at the patellar and Achilles tendons should be assessed bilaterally. The strength in the quadriceps muscles may be assessed by asking the patient to stand up from a sitting position without using the arms. Calf strength is best demonstrated by the ability to stand on tiptoes, and distal strength can be demonstrated by dorsiflexion of the toes

**TABLE 24** "Red Flags" in the Evaluation of Low Back Pain

| Possible Cause | Key Features on History/Physical Examination | Imaging[a] | Additional Studies[a] |
|---|---|---|---|
| Cancer | History of cancer with new onset of low back pain | MRI | ESR |
| | Unexplained weight loss; failure to improve after 1 month; age >50 y | Lumbosacral plain radiography | ESR |
| | Multiple risk factors present | Plain radiography or MRI | ESR |
| Vertebral infection | Fever; injection drug use; recent infection | MRI | ESR and/or CRP |
| Cauda equina syndrome | Urinary retention; motor deficits at multiple levels; fecal incontinence; saddle anesthesia | Emergent MRI | None |
| Vertebral compression fracture | History of osteoporosis; use of corticosteroids; older age | Lumbosacral plain radiography | None |
| Ankylosing spondylitis | Morning stiffness; improvement with exercise; alternating buttock pain; awakening due to back pain during the second part of the night; younger age | Anterior-posterior pelvis plain radiography | ESR and/or CRP, HLA-B27 |
| Severe/progressive neurologic deficits | Progressive motor weakness | MRI | Consider EMG/NCV |
| Herniated disk | Back pain with leg pain in an L4, L5, or S1 nerve root distribution; positive straight-leg-raise test or crossed straight-leg-raise test | None | None |
| | Symptoms present >1 month | MRI | Consider EMG/NCV |
| Spinal stenosis | Radiating leg pain; older age (pseudoclaudication a weak predictor) | None | None |
| | Symptoms present >1 month | MRI | Consider EMG/NCV |

CRP = C-reactive protein; EMG = electromyography; ESR = erythrocyte sedimentation rate; NCV = nerve conduction velocity.

[a]Level of evidence for diagnostic evaluation is variable.

Adapted with permission from Chou R, Qaseem A, Snow V, et al; Clinical Efficacy Assessment Subcommittee of the American College of Physicians; American College of Physicians; American Pain Society Low Back Pain Guidelines Panel. Diagnosis and treatment of low back pain: a joint clinical practice guideline from the American College of Physicians and the American Pain Society [erratum in Ann Intern Med. 2008;148(3):247-248]. Ann Intern Med. 2007;147(7):481. [PMID: 17909209] Copyright 2007, American College of Physicians.

against resistance. The patient's gait should be observed for the presence of foot drop. Sensation in the perineum, buttocks, legs, and feet should be assessed, and assessing rectal tone and signs of urinary retention may be considered, depending on the level of symptoms and signs.

Symptoms and signs in the sciatic nerve distribution are fairly sensitive for lumbar disk herniation, of which 90% of cases occur in the L4-L5 distribution. The straight-leg-raise maneuver has a sensitivity of 91% in diagnosing disk herniation. If a nerve is tethered by a compressive problem, such as a herniated disk, stretching the leg by raising it off the table 30 to 70 degrees while the patient is in a supine position will pull on the nerve, sending a shooting "electric shock" sensation from the hip down to the ankle. (A stretching pain in the tendons or tendon sheaths in the low back or posterior leg should not be confused with the nerve pain of a positive test.)

In general, plain film findings correlate poorly with symptoms and should not be ordered in patients with nonspecific low back pain. Disk degeneration is found in 33% of asymptomatic patients younger than 30 years, in 60% of patients between 40 and 60 years, and in almost all patients older than 60 years. Spondylolisthesis (anterior slippage of the vertebral body due to bilateral separation of vertebral pars interarticularis) is found in 1% to 5% of normal persons, and spondylolysis (unilateral or bilateral separation in the vertebral pars interarticularis) is equally prevalent in normal and symptomatic persons. Other findings in asymptomatic patients include congenital anomalies, disk calcification, Schmorl nodes (disk material within a vertebral body), and mild to moderate scoliosis. The utility of lumbar plain films lies mainly in the workup of a potential compression fracture in patients at risk (for example, owing to corticosteroid use, trauma, or osteoporosis).

Disk herniation and spinal stenosis cannot be detected with plain films. On advanced imaging studies, even in asymptomatic patients, a herniated disk may be found in 20% to 30% of patients. Spinal stenosis, a common cause of back and leg pain in elderly patients, has been found in more than 20% of asymptomatic persons older than 60 years.

In general, diagnostic imaging and testing should be ordered when severe or progressive neurologic deficits are present or when a serious underlying condition is suspected on the basis of red flags. When radiculopathy is not resolving or spinal stenosis is a major consideration, and if the patient is a candidate for surgery or epidural corticosteroid injection (for radiculopathy), MRI or CT should be considered.

## Treatment

A patient-centered approach is important in the management of acute episodes of low back pain. Patients should be provided with evidence-based information regarding their expected course as well as effective self-care options. Patients should be advised to stay active and continue normal activities if possible; bed rest is not an effective treatment plan and may actually lengthen disability.

First-line medications for low back pain are acetaminophen and NSAIDs. Opiates increase the risk of side effects (odds ratio = 2.5) compared with acetaminophen alone, and muscle relaxants have twice the number of central nervous system side effects. In addition, muscle relaxants have a risk of dependency after just 1 week of treatment. Most patients with a herniated disk without major neurologic concern experience resolution of their pain spontaneously over the course of a few weeks. For those who do not, diskectomy or epidural corticosteroid injections may be an option.

Exercise during the acute phase has the potential to increase the time to recovery; however, exercise, spinal manipulation, and yoga have some evidence of efficacy in the management of subacute or chronic low back pain in selected patients. Spinal manipulation may be helpful in some patients with acute low back pain. Patients are most likely to benefit from spinal manipulation if they meet four of the following five criteria: symptom duration less than 16 days, no symptoms distal to knee, a score of less than 19 on the Fear-Avoidance Beliefs Questionnaire (FABQ), at least one hypomobile lumbar segment (as compared with the mobility in the segment above and below), and at least one hip with more than 35 degrees of internal rotation.

For chronic back pain, tricyclic antidepressants are an option and may be of added benefit in treating depressive syndromes that often accompany chronic pain. Patients with psychosocial factors that place them at greater risk for chronic pain and disability may respond better to a multidisciplinary approach to rehabilitation.

**KEY POINTS**

- Low back pain is usually self-limited, with a 90% full recovery rate at 6 weeks.
- Cauda equina syndrome most often presents with urinary retention.
- A positive straight-leg-raise test has a sensitivity of 91% in diagnosing disk herniation.
- In nonspecific low back pain, imaging results correlate poorly with symptoms.
- Diagnostic imaging with CT or MRI is typically reserved for patients with low back pain associated with severe or progressive neurologic deficits or "red flags" suggesting a serious condition.
- First-line medications for low back pain are acetaminophen and NSAIDs.

## Neck Pain

### Diagnosis and Evaluation

Population studies have shown a lifetime prevalence of neck pain of 66%. The evidence is less robust for the optimal workup and treatment of neck pain than for back pain but centers on similar diagnostic triage, dividing neck pain into three categories: soft tissue strain, neurologic pain, and systemic disease.

Important elements in the history of a patient with neck pain include trauma, gradual versus sudden onset, radiation into the arms or frank muscle weakness (associated with disk herniation), fever and weight loss, and characteristics of the pain. There is evidence that neck pain is associated with work-related risk factors: neck flexion, arm force, arm posture, duration of sitting, twisting or bending of the trunk, hand-arm vibration, and workplace design. Gradual onset of pain is associated with repetitive motion.

The physical examination should focus on palpation to elicit tender points (facets, disk spaces, musculature), evaluation of strength and reflexes in the upper extremities, lower extremity strength and gait, and a search for upper motor neuron signs (**Table 25**). Laboratory data (including complete blood count, erythrocyte sedimentation rate, alkaline phosphatase level) are mainly important when considering systemic disease.

Radiography is necessary to rule out fracture if there is a history of trauma; it is not helpful in evaluating acute nontraumatic injury. Three-view plain radiography may be useful if pain has not resolved after 4 to 8 weeks. In patients with distal neurologic changes, cervical MRI or CT myelography should be obtained. Diseases involving the deeper neck structures (carotid arteritis, carotid artery dissection, thyroiditis, lymphadenitis) at times can cause neck pain and must be considered when no musculoskeletal cause can be found.

## Treatment

For patients with neck pain caused by musculoskeletal strain, the mainstays of therapy are NSAIDs and physical therapy. The rationale for physical therapy is the belief that exercise helps to maintain posture and strengthen the neck muscles, thereby decreasing pain and preventing progression of symptoms. Although clinical studies may show some degree of effectiveness of various nondrug therapies for neck pain, the effectiveness of these therapies is dependent entirely on the skill of the therapist. Most industries have workplace analysis to reduce the risk of repetitive motion injuries to the neck.

Mobilization, manipulation, and exercise may play a role in recovery. There is little evidence that transcutaneous electrical nerve stimulation (TENS) units or massage is helpful. Isometric resistance exercises of the neck and shoulder

| **TABLE 25** Evaluation of Neck Pain | | |
| --- | --- | --- |
| **Category** | **History** | **Physical Examination** |
| Mechanical neck pain (muscle, ligament, facet, intervertebral disk) | Pain (usually episodic, deep, dull, and aching) and stiffness | Decrease in active and passive range of motion |
| | Symptom may be precipitated or aggravated by excessive or unaccustomed activity or sustaining an awkward posture without a specific injury | Superficial tenderness indicates soft tissue pain; deep tenderness indicates muscle or bone pain |
| | Ligament, muscle, and facet pain are localized and asymmetric | Pain on extension or ipsilateral lateral flexion usually indicates facet pain; pain on flexion or contralateral lateral flexion usually indicates soft tissue pain |
| | Pain from upper cervical segments is referred toward the head; pain from lower segments is referred to the upper limb girdle | |
| Neurologic neck pain (cervical nerve root and/or spinal cord) | Significant root pain; sharp, intense, often described as a burning sensation; may radiate to the trapezial and periscapular regions or down the arm | Neurologic examination may show motor weakness, usually involving several cervical levels and often asymmetric, affecting one or both arms |
| | Numbness in a dermatomal distribution and motor weakness in a myotomal distribution | Look for plantar extensor response, gait disorder, and spasticity in patients with spinal cord involvement |
| | Symptoms often more severe with certain movement | Bilateral or multilevel involvement indicates more severe pathology |
| Neck pain associated with systemic disease | Fever, malaise, or pain in areas in addition to the neck | Complete physical examination may show underlying systemic disease, such as inflammatory joint disease, organ infection, or neoplastic process |
| | Pain is usually severe, relentless, and progressive | |
| | Symptoms or signs may be progressive despite treatment | |

Adapted with permission from Huang S, Tsang IK. Neck Pain. http://pier.acponline.org/physicians/diseases/d103/tables/d103-tables.html. In PIER (online database). Philadelphia: American College of Physicians, 2009. Accessed July 7, 2009.

musculature for chronic or frequent neck disorders appear to be somewhat helpful in preventing recurrence of pain.

In patients with radicular symptoms, epidural corticosteroid injections have improved patient recovery at 2 weeks and may be worth trying before consulting a surgeon. Surgery is not indicated in patients without neurologic symptoms and signs.

### KEY POINTS

- NSAIDs and physical therapy are the mainstays of treatment for musculoskeletal neck pain.
- Surgery is not indicated in patients with neck pain without neurologic manifestations.

## Shoulder Pain

### Diagnosis and Evaluation

Causes of shoulder pain and associated findings on history and physical examination are listed in **Table 26**. Pain in the shoulder after a traumatic injury or fall may be caused by a partial or full rupture of a rotator cuff tendon. Pain that has gradually developed and is associated with repetitive motion may be more indicative of tendinitis. Bursa pain is often described as a burning sensation. Poorly localized pain may be referred pain caused by disease in other structures, such as cervical radiculopathy, cardiac ischemia, diaphragmatic irritation, or pulmonary diseases. These external causes of shoulder pain are not related to shoulder movement and do not impair range of motion.

On inspection of the shoulder, asymmetry indicates a possible dislocation. The major anatomic landmarks should be palpated, including the subacromial space below the tip of the acromion process, the acromioclavicular joint, the biceps tendon groove, the cervical spine, and the scapula. Range of motion testing should be performed in several directions. The patient should be asked to fully extend the arms above the head; if the patient is unable to do so, the examiner should attempt with gentle pressure to assist (passive range of motion). The Apley scratch tests consist of several maneuvers to assess range of motion (**Figure 7**). Checking passive range

| TABLE 26 Common Causes of Shoulder Pain | |
| --- | --- |
| **Condition** | **Characteristics** |
| Rotator cuff tendinitis | Lateral shoulder pain aggravated by reaching, raising arm overhead, lying on side. Subacromial pain on palpation and with passive/resisted abduction. |
| Rotator cuff tear | Shoulder weakness, loss of function, tendinitis symptoms, nocturnal pain. Similar to tendinitis examination plus weakness with abduction and external rotation, positive drop-arm test. |
| Bicipital tendinitis/rupture | Anterior shoulder pain with lifting, overhead reaching, flexion; reduced pain after rupture. Bicipital groove tenderness, pain with resisted elbow flexion, "Popeye" lump in antecubital fossa following rupture. |
| Adhesive capsulitis | Progressive decrease in range of motion, more from stiffness than pain. Loss of external rotation, abduction: unable to scratch lower back or fully lift arm straight overhead. |
| Acromioclavicular syndromes | Anterior shoulder pain/deformity, usually from trauma or overuse. Localized joint tenderness and deformity (osteophytes, separation), pain with adduction. |
| Glenohumeral arthritis | An uncommon cause of shoulder pain. Gradual onset of anterior pain, stiffness. Anterior joint-line tenderness, decreased range of motion, crepitation. |

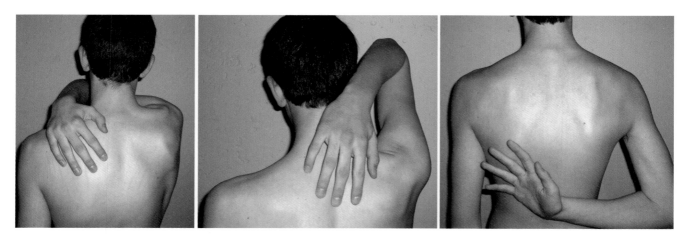

**FIGURE 7.**
**Apley scratch test.**
This test assesses range of motion of the rotator cuff. The patient attempts to reach across the chest with the ipsilateral hand to scratch the contralateral shoulder (*left*), reach over the ipsilateral trapezius muscle to scratch the spinous processes of the thoracic spine (*center*), and reach behind the back by internal rotation of the shoulder to scratch the contralateral scapula (*right*).

of motion if the patient is unable to achieve the expected range helps define areas of pain or weakness.

Particular tests of the rotator cuff tendons may be performed by standing across from the patient and assuming a posture of "shaking hands" with the patient and holding the patient's elbow with the other hand (**Figure 8**). From this position, the examiner can direct the patient to apply pressure in various directions to check the strength and competence of the rotator cuff tendons. Frank weakness, sometimes without pain, occurs if there is a complete tear of the tendon. To test for impingement, the Hawkins test (**Figure 9**) is 92% sensi-

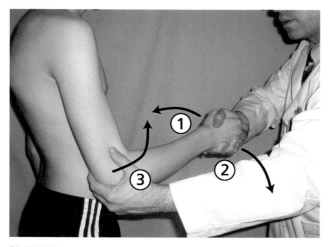

**FIGURE 8.**
**Rotator cuff tendon assessment maneuvers.**
To assess rotator cuff function, the examiner stands across from the patient and assumes a posture of shaking hands with the patient, holding the patient's elbow with the other hand. Pain with resistance in these directions may indicate tendinitis: (1) resisted internal rotation (subscapularis); (2) resisted external rotation (infraspinatus); (3) resisted abduction (supraspinatus).

tive. In order to determine the stability of a shoulder, the apprehension test is performed (**Figure 10**). If the patient has pain or apprehension of possible dislocation of the shoulder, the test is positive and indicative of a loose shoulder, as seen in weak musculature or in rotator cuff tears.

## Rotator Cuff Tendinitis

The most common cause of shoulder pain in primary care practices is rotator cuff tendinitis (29%). When the history and physical examination are consistent with rotator cuff tendinitis and there is no history of trauma, radiography will not likely add to the management. If the pain is relieved by a subacromial lidocaine injection in the affected shoulder and the strength is normal, the diagnosis is nearly confirmed. During the acute phase (2 weeks), patients may be treated with corticosteroid injection, NSAIDs, and rest; physical therapy can be added in the subacute phase. Subacromial corticosteroid injections are effective for rotator cuff tendinitis for up to 9 months. These injections have been found more effective in higher doses and are probably more effective than NSAIDs. Physical therapy alone, however, is insufficient. Patients should be instructed that during the resting (acute) phase, range of motion exercises must be done daily to help prevent adhesive capsulitis, or frozen shoulder.

## Impingement Syndrome

Impingement syndrome is a special category of supraspinatus tendinitis caused by irritation of the subacromial bursa or rotator cuff tendon from mechanical impingement between the humeral head and the coracoacromial arch, which includes the acromion, coracoacromial ligament, and the coracoid process (**Figure 11**). Chronic overhead activity may contribute to narrowing of this space, which can lead to

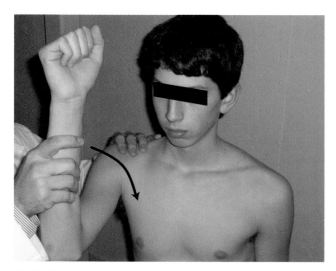

**FIGURE 9.**
**Hawkins test for shoulder impingement.**
The patient holds the arm extended anteriorly at 90 degrees with the forearm bent to 90 degrees (at 12 o'clock), as if holding a shield. The scapula should be stabilized by the examiner. The arm is then internally rotated to cross in front of the body. A positive test elicits pain in the shoulder.

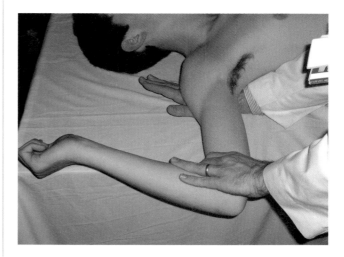

**FIGURE 10.**
**Apprehension test.**
The patient is placed supine on a table. With the arm abducted at 90 degrees and the forearm flexed, the examiner stands at the bedside facing the patient and places one hand under the affected shoulder. With the other hand, gentle pressure is placed on the forearm. Pain or apprehension constitutes a positive test.

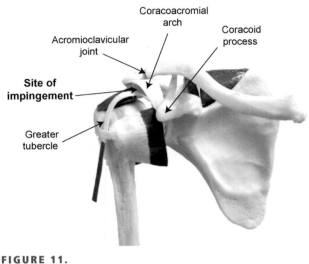

**FIGURE 11.**
**Shoulder impingement syndrome.**

Reproduced with permission from Rencic J. Approach to knee and shoulder pain. In: Internal Medicine Essentials for Clerkship Students 2. Philadelphia, PA: American College of Physicians; 2009:310. Copyright 2009, American College of Physicians.

recurrent microtrauma and chronic local inflammation of rotator cuff tendons. Pain on the Hawkins test that resolves with injection of lidocaine into the subacromial space helps establish the diagnosis. Initial treatment is similar to rotator cuff tendinitis; however, persistence of symptoms after 3 months, which occurs in 10% to 25% of patients, may warrant an orthopedic referral.

## Adhesive Capsulitis

Range that is limited on both active and passive motion may be a sign of adhesive capsulitis. Chronic adhesive capsulitis may be painless. Adhesive capsulitis typically occurs in patients with long-standing shoulder problems; occasionally, however, the patient does not recall an initial insult. Adhesive capsulitis usually occurs in middle or older age. When NSAIDs, joint corticosteroid injection, and physical therapy are ineffective after 3 months, a patient's shoulder may need to be manipulated under general anesthesia, or alternatively undergo arthroscopy, to break the adhesions.

## Acromioclavicular Ligament Injuries

A fall onto the superior portion of the shoulder or onto an outstretched hand (FOOSH injury) is a common cause of acromioclavicular ligament strain or tear. These injuries are graded into six categories based on the severity of involvement of both the acromioclavicular (A-C) ligament and the coracoclavicular (C-C) ligament. Grade I is a partial tear of the A-C ligament, and is recognized by the physical examination maneuver of bringing the outstretched arm across the chest, which elicits sharp pain in the A-C joint. Grade II is a full tear of the A-C ligament and a partial tear of the C-C ligament, possibly accompanied by A-C joint widening (normal is <4 cm) on an anteroposterior radiograph comparing both

shoulders. Grade III and above are full tears of both the A-C and the C-C ligaments, and displacement of the clavicle upwards is usually obvious on examination. Grades IV through VI involve severe clavicular displacement or dislocation into fascial planes or through muscle and require surgical referral.

The key initial management of injuries in grades I through III is rest and immobilization. Surgical correction of a grade III injury is becoming less common, as studies have shown equivalent outcomes between surgical and conservative approaches, with more complications from a surgical approach. When the patient's pain is resolved, a physical therapy program may be designed to slowly increase strength and mobility in the shoulder. If pain persists or the rehabilitation is not optimal, the patient should be referred to an orthopedist to consider a surgical correction.

**KEY POINTS**

- In patients with rotator cuff tendinitis, range-of-motion exercises must be done daily during the resting phase to prevent adhesive capsulitis.
- Most acromioclavicular injuries (grade I-III) do not require a surgical approach.
- Severe clavicular displacements (grades IV-VI) should be referred for surgery immediately.

# Elbow Pain

## Diagnosis and Evaluation

Elbow pain is usually related to periarticular structures. Because it is not a weight-bearing joint, the elbow is not normally affected by osteoarthritis. Examination of a painful elbow begins with noting any erythema or swelling. It is useful to use the contralateral elbow to compare the passive range of motion. The humeroulnar joint should extend to 0 degrees and flex to approximately 135 degrees. The radiohumeral joint should rotate 180 degrees; however, bony abnormalities (such as from previous fracture) may restrict this. Bursitis and epicondylitis do not restrict range of motion, but inflammatory intra-articular conditions, such as rheumatoid arthritis or a crystal-induced arthropathy, do.

Tenderness at either the medial or lateral epicondyle should lead to palpation of the tendons that extend distally. The joint line of the radiohumeral joint may be tender if inflamed. In elbow injuries stemming from throwing motions (for example, in baseball pitchers), the medial and lateral collateral ligaments of the elbow may be tender on palpation or even lax when the examiner applies lateral stress.

## Epicondylitis

Epicondylitis is caused by microtearing of the tendons resulting from repetitive motions. Lateral epicondylitis, or tennis elbow, is the most common cause of elbow pain. Symptoms are tenderness of the lateral epicondyle and pain on resisted wrist extension and hand gripping. Medial epicondylitis, or golfer's elbow, is less common. There is tenderness in the medial epicondyle and pain with wrist flexion.

Treatment options for epicondylitis include NSAIDs, corticosteroid injection, and physiotherapy. Corticosteroid injection achieves a faster resolution of symptoms than NSAIDs. Although corticosteroid injection provides rapid improvement in pain, physiotherapy provides better long-term results. A systematic review found evidence of short-term relief of lateral epicondyle pain with acupuncture. In about 20% of patients with epicondylitis, surgery may be required to achieve resolution. In patients with lateral epicondylitis, employment in a manual job is associated with a poor prognosis.

### Olecranon Bursitis

Olecranon bursitis, or carpet-layers elbow, occurs when the olecranon bursa develops an effusion, either from trauma, an inflammatory process, or infection. On examination, an inflamed bursa does not cause restriction or pain with range of motion of the elbow, providing evidence that the joint is not involved. However, the bursa can be extremely tender to palpation. An effusion should be aspirated for Gram stain, culture, and crystal analysis to rule out infection or gout. When the acute process has resolved, the bursa may thicken and remain swollen chronically and may not be painful.

### Cubital Tunnel Syndrome

Cubital tunnel syndrome, or ulnar nerve entrapment, is a common cause for pain and sensory and motor loss in the ulnar region and for paresthesias in the ulnar aspect of the arm and hand. Systemic diseases such as end-stage renal disease may be involved; extrinsic causes such as ganglion cysts or external pressure are common as well. The clinician should explore with the patient any activities in which the ulnar nerve may be compressed (such as resting the elbow on the car door while driving). Electromyography (EMG) is useful for differentiating the level of the ulnar nerve lesion (cubital tunnel, wrist, thoracic outlet, cervical disk), assessing the severity, and determining the need for surgery. Treatment is avoidance of any pressure to the area, NSAIDs, and surgical decompression when severe.

**KEY POINT**

- Restricted range of motion of the elbow may indicate an inflammatory arthropathy.

## Wrist and Hand Pain

### Fractures

The scaphoid bone is the pivotal bone for the wrist and is the carpal bone most vulnerable to fractures, particularly when the hand is used to break a fall. The lunate is the next most likely to fracture. If there is any history of a fall, plain film radiography is required. Clinicians often miss injury to the hook of the hamate, which is prone to fracture during the downstroke of a golf swing upon striking the ground.

### Carpal Tunnel Syndrome

The prevalence of carpal tunnel syndrome is 1% to 3% in the general population and up to 15% in workers in certain industries (manufacturing, use of tools that vibrate). It is still uncertain whether computer use contributes to carpal tunnel syndrome. Previous wrist fracture predisposes to carpal tunnel syndrome, as do pregnancy and certain systemic disorders, including rheumatoid and osteoarthritis, renal failure, diabetes mellitus, hypothyroidism, and obesity. Symptoms include aching wrist pain with sparing of the palm, numbness and tingling in the median nerve sensory distribution of the fingers, and weakness of the thenar muscles.

On sensory examination, the median nerve territory should be assessed for hypalgesia. Abduction weakness in the thumb is tested by placing the patient's hand open on a table, with the dorsal surface down. The patient is instructed to raise his or her thumb perpendicular to the palm as the examiner applies downward pressure on the distal phalanx. Notably, the Phalen (LR+ = 1.3) and Tinel (LR+ = 1.4) signs have limited ability to discriminate carpal tunnel syndrome from other causes of hand dysesthesia. An EMG study is useful when the diagnosis is uncertain, when a patient is not responding to therapy, or when surgery is under consideration. EMG is 85% sensitive and 95% specific in diagnosing carpal tunnel syndrome.

Initial treatment of carpal tunnel syndrome should be conservative. Although most guidelines emphasize noninvasive therapies before invasive treatment for mild to moderate carpal tunnel syndrome, there is not sufficient evidence to show whether drug or nondrug modalities are more effective, which should be tried first, or whether a combination of therapeutic approaches would be more useful. Although NSAIDs are recommended and widely used as the initial drug therapy, there is no strong evidence that they are useful. Splinting, yoga, ultrasonic treatment, and carpal tunnel mobilization exercises are also beneficial. Oral corticosteroid therapy has shown short-term, but not long-term, benefits. Similarly, corticosteroid injections may provide short-term (first month) relief but do not improve the long-term outcome compared with NSAIDs and splinting. Patients with symptoms for more than 1 year are less likely to receive benefit from corticosteroid injection. Carpal tunnel release surgery is indicated for severe carpal tunnel syndrome (by clinical or EMG evidence) and has an excellent outcome in more than 90% of patients.

### Other Causes of Wrist Pain

Ulnar nerve compression at the wrist is also called Guyon tunnel syndrome, because the entrapment occurs where the ulnar nerve transverses the Guyon tunnel between the pisiform and hamate bones on the anterolateral side of the wrist, and cyclist's palsy, because the compression of the ulnar nerve often occurs as the hand rests on the handlebars. However, the ulnar nerve can be compressed by muscles, tumors (lipomas), scar tissue, synovial cysts, or any other internal structure that passes close to the tunnel. The presentation is similar to that of carpal tunnel syndrome, but with symptoms and signs on the ulnar distribution of the hand. The workup and treatment are also similar to those of carpal tunnel syndrome.

De Quervain tenosynovitis is an exercise-related injury associated with knitting, and sports involving extensive wrist action. Tenderness may be elicited in the anatomic snuffbox (the extensor pollicis brevis and abductor pollicis longus tendons). Pain elicited by flexing the thumb into the palm, closing the fingers over the thumb, and then bending the wrist in the ulnar direction (Finkelstein test) is confirmatory. Conservative treatment measures (splinting the thumb, ice, NSAIDs) or injection of corticosteroid into the snuffbox is usually effective.

Ganglion cysts are synovia-filled cysts arising from joints or tendon sheaths that typically appear on the dorsal hand or ventral wrist. They can cause pain and compress other structures. They transilluminate because of the clear fluid. These may be aspirated, and corticosteroid injection into the collapsed cyst may prevent recurrence. Surgical correction is often required.

---

**KEY POINTS**

- De Quervain tenosynovitis is diagnosed by the finding of pain on extreme extension of the extensor tendon of the thumb.

- Carpal tunnel syndrome is a common cause of wrist and hand pain, typically caused by repetitive overuse of the wrist.

---

# Hip Pain

Hip pain may be indicative of hip joint pathology but may also be referred from the pelvis, intra-abdomen, or retroperitoneum. True hip pain usually presents as groin pain. Weight bearing increases pain originating from the hip joint. Bursal pain is typically situated laterally or posteriorly and is worse when lying on the affected bursa. Thigh pain, buttock pain, and pain radiating below the knee are more often attributable to disorders of the lumbar spine. Pain that has a paresthesia quality (burning, numbness, or an electric shock sensation) may indicate a nerve entrapment syndrome. A history of hip surgery, corticosteroid injections, collagen vascular disease, or malignancy may suggest important causes of hip pain. In patients with a history of prostate, breast, lung, thyroid, or kidney cancer, a diagnosis of metastatic disease should always be considered. Occupational and recreational activities are also important considerations in patients with hip pain, particularly with a history of trauma.

## Diagnosis and Evaluation

Patients should be asked to point with one finger to the place where the pain is the greatest. Poor localization may be a sign of referred pain. The FABER test assesses the ability to Flex, ABduct, and Externally Rotate the hip (**Figure 12**). If there is pain in the sacroiliac joint with the FABER test but no pain with passive range of motion of the hip, sacroiliac joint pathology is likely.

Plain film radiography is used to rule out a fracture and may provide evidence of osteoarthritis in the hip joints, with osteophytes and joint space narrowing with weight bearing. An MRI is able to determine signs of osteonecrosis or an occult fracture. A bone scan may be useful if an MRI is contraindicated.

## Specific Causes of Hip Pain

Meralgia paresthetica is a nerve entrapment syndrome of the lateral cutaneous nerve of the anterior thigh typified by pain and burning. The nerve runs under the inguinal ligament and may be compressed by obesity or tight clothing or belts. Diabetes mellitus may predispose to this condition. The diagnosis is clinical, with decreased sensation in the skin of the distal lateral thigh. The treatment is conservative: treatment of the diabetes (if present), weight loss, and looser clothing.

Piriformis syndrome is a sciatic nerve compression neuropathy that causes chronic posterior pain. The piriformis muscle overlies the sciatic notch where the nerve exits the sacrum. It occurs in persons who are subject to prolonged sitting, such as truck drivers. An EMG can determine the level of the neuropathy (nerve root compression

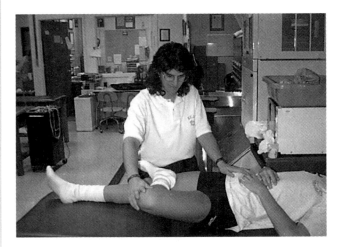

**FIGURE 12.**
**FABER test.**
The FABER test assesses flexion, abduction, and external rotation of the hip. With the leg in a figure-four position, the normal leg should attain a parallel plane with the table. Gentle downward pressure on the knee in this position simultaneously places stress on the ipsilateral sacroiliac joint.

versus more distal sciatic nerve compression) and whether the piriformis muscle is contributory. Stretching exercises and NSAIDs are the initial treatment, but a surgical release may be needed.

Osteonecrosis is most often found when already advanced. Risk factors (corticosteroid use, sickle cell anemia) may provide a clue for early identification. Diagnosis is made with MRI (early) or plain radiography (late). Other than pain control, the optimal treatment for osteonecrosis is unclear; specialty referral is almost always indicated.

The trochanteric bursa lies directly over the greater trochanter, making it amenable to examination as well as injection. Trochanteric bursitis can be confirmed in patients in whom hip adduction intensifies the pain or in those in whom the examination reveals pain and tenderness over the bursa. Relief of pain with lidocaine injection into the bursa can be diagnostic. Heat and stretching exercises are commonly prescribed as initial therapy for acute trochanteric bursitis. Corticosteroid injection may provide prolonged relief when conservative measures fail. On rare occasions, the bursa must be removed surgically to provide relief.

Rectus femoris strains, hamstring strains, and adductor tendinopathies are more likely to occur in athletes. In minor strains, the extremity may be relatively painless with passive range of motion but painful with resisted muscle contraction. In complete tears, there may be evidence of frank hemorrhage (purpura) around the tear and a painful, tender muscle throughout the length of the thigh. Treatment depends on the severity. A minor strain may need only rest (sometimes prolonged), NSAIDs, and rehabilitation. Tears require surgical management.

Labral tears, which may be associated with running activities, are regarded as an early stage of hip osteoarthritis and can be identified on MRI. Surgical correction may be required if conservative therapy (rest, NSAIDs) is not effective. The management of osteoarthritis is addressed in MKSAP 15 Rheumatology.

**KEY POINTS**

- True hip pain usually presents as groin pain and is increased by weight bearing.
- Bursal pain is typically situated laterally or posteriorly and is worsened by lying on the affected bursa.

## Knee Pain

Osteoarthritis is, by far, the most common cause of chronic knee pain in older persons. Acute knee pain may be due to trauma, overuse syndromes, inflammation (crystalline arthritis, rheumatoid arthritis), or infection (**Table 27**). The knee is the most commonly infected joint, and septic arthritis must be considered in all patients with unilateral knee pain. Underlying chronic diseases, such as osteoarthritis or a systemic rheumatologic disorder, can also be associated with an acute presentation of knee pain. Referred hip pain or L5-S1 root radiculopathy can cause knee pain; in these patients, the results of the knee examination will be normal. This section will focus on common mechanical causes of knee pain that are associated with trauma, soft tissue inflammation, and overuse syndromes.

In chronic pain syndromes, such as osteoarthritis and rheumatoid arthritis, radiographs are unlikely to alter management. If an effusion is present (2.4% of patients with acute knee pain), arthrocentesis may be warranted to rule out crystalline or infectious causes.

### Trauma

Trauma may result in a fracture or ligament tear, which produces a noticeable "popping" sensation in 50% of patients. Typically, a large effusion collects rapidly. Anterior cruciate ligament tears occur with sudden twisting and hyperextension

---

| **TABLE 27** Initial Approach for Work-up of Acute Knee Pain | |
|---|---|
| **Question** | **Action** |
| Ottawa Decision Rules: Has there been a recent injury and at least one of the following predictors of fracture?<br><br>• Age >55 y<br>• Tenderness at the head of the fibula or isolated to the patella<br>• Inability to bear weight for at least four steps of walking<br>• Inability to flex knee to at least 90 degrees | Plain films |
| Is there an effusion? | Arthrocentesis (especially to rule out infectious or crystalline arthritis) |
| Does the physical examination suggest meniscal or ligamentous injury or history of locking or give-way sensation? | Orthopedic referral (for examination and decision on need for MRI or arthroscopy) |

Adapted with permission from Jackson JL, O'Malley PG, Kroenke K. Evaluation of acute knee pain in primary care. Ann Intern Med. 2003;139(7):575-88. [PMID: 14530229] Copyright 2003, American College of Physicians.

injuries, collateral ligament tears occur with medial or lateral force without twisting, and posterior cruciate ligament tears occur with trauma to a flexed knee. Only 10% of knee radiographs ordered for acute knee pain demonstrate a fracture; therefore, candidates for knee radiography must be carefully selected. The Ottawa Decision Rules are nearly 100% sensitive for fracture following a fall, and radiography should not be ordered unless these criteria are met.

When the history suggests meniscal or ligamentous injury (the knee locking or giving way), several physical examination maneuvers have a high degree of specificity for identifying these injuries (**Figure 13**). An audible or palpable snap on the McMurray test has a 97% specificity for meniscal damage. The Lachman test is 87% sensitive and 93% specific for anterior cruciate ligamentous injury. If a meniscal or ligamentous injury is suspected based on the physical examination, the patient should be referred to an orthopedic surgeon. The decision to order an MRI should generally be made by a specialist, rather than by the internist prior to referral.

## Patellofemoral Syndrome

The most common cause of knee pain in patients younger than 45 years, especially in women, is the patellofemoral syndrome. The pain is peripatellar and exacerbated by overuse (such as running), descending stairs, or prolonged sitting. Diagnosis is confirmed by firmly compressing the patella against the femur and moving it up and down along the groove of the femur, reproducing pain or crepitation. The condition is self-limited; NSAIDs and minimizing high-impact activity improve symptoms.

## Bursitis

Bursitis, which may result from either trauma or overuse, is characterized by local tenderness and burning pain. The pes anserine bursa is palpated on the medial side of the knee, approximately 6 cm below the joint line and at about the same level as the tibial tuberosity. Pes anserine bursitis cause medial pain that worsens with activity and at night. The prepatellar bursa sits directly over the patella; prepatellar bursitis is associated with anterior knee pain and swelling anterior to the patella and is often caused by trauma or repetitive kneeling. The suprapatellar bursa sits directly under the distal portion of the gastrocnemius muscle; suprapatellar bursitis can be confused with the pain associated with chondromalacia of the patella, given that the location of the pain is in the same general area. However, suprapatellar bursitis is very tender when the examiner presses above the patella on a passively extended leg. Treatment of knee bursitis may include rest, ice, NSAIDs, and corticosteroid injections.

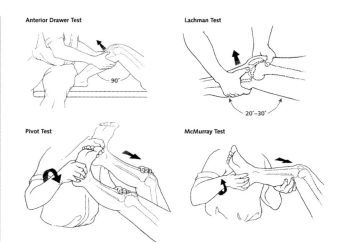

**FIGURE 13.**

**Common knee maneuvers for assessing possible ligamentous and meniscal damage.**

(*Top left*) Anterior drawer test (anterior cruciate ligament): Place patient supine, flex the hip to 45 degrees and the knee to 90 degrees. Sit on the dorsum of the foot, wrap your hands around the hamstrings (ensuring that these muscles are relaxed), then pull and push the proximal part of the leg, testing the movement of the tibia on the femur. Do these maneuvers in three positions of tibial rotation: neutral, 30 degrees externally, and 30 degrees internally rotated. A normal test result is no more than 6 to 8 mm of laxity. (*Top right*) Lachman test (anterior cruciate ligament): Place patient supine on examining table, leg at the examiner's side, slightly externally rotated and flexed (20-30 degrees). Stabilize the femur with one hand and apply pressure to the back of the knee with the other hand with the thumb of the hand exerting pressure placed on the joint line. A positive test result is movement of the knee with a soft or mushy end point. (*Bottom left*) Pivot test (anterior cruciate ligament): Fully extend the knee, rotate the foot internally. Apply a valgus stress while progressively flexing the knee, watching and feeling for translation of the tibia on the femur. (*Bottom right*) McMurray test (meniscus): Flex the hip and knee maximally. Apply a valgus (abduction) force to the knee while externally rotating the foot and passively extending the knee. An audible or palpable snap during extension suggests a tear of the medial meniscus. For the lateral meniscus, apply a varus (adduction) stress during internal rotation of the foot and passive extension of the knee.

## Iliotibial Band Syndrome

Iliotibial band syndrome is a common cause of knife-like lateral knee pain that occurs with vigorous flexion-extension activities of the knee, such as running. It is treated conservatively with rest and stretching exercises.

## Baker Cyst

In the popliteal fossa, Baker cysts can form from synovia because of arthritis or torn cartilage. A Baker cyst can be painful if it ruptures. Ultrasonography is useful for diagnosing a ruptured Baker cyst, as it may be confused with a deep venous thrombosis.

- The most common cause of knee pain in patients younger than 45 years, especially in women, is the patellofemoral syndrome.

- Prepatellar bursitis is associated with anterior knee pain and swelling anterior to the patella and is often caused by trauma or repetitive kneeling.

- Pes anserine bursitis causes pain located medially, about 6 cm below the joint line, which is worse with activity and at night.

- Iliotibial band syndrome is a common cause of knife-like lateral knee pain that occurs with running.

- Plain films are only needed in evaluating acute knee pain after a fall if at least one of the following is present: age older than 55 years, tenderness at the head of the fibula or patella, inability to flex knee to 90 degrees, or inability to bear weight for four steps.

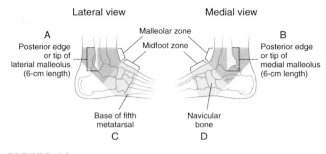

**FIGURE 14.**
**Ottawa ankle and foot rules.**
An ankle radiographic series is indicated if a patient has pain in the malleolar zone and any of these findings: bone tenderness at *A*, bone tenderness at *B*, or inability to bear weight immediately and in the emergency department (or physician's office). A foot radiographic series is indicated if a patient has pain in the midfoot zone and any of these findings: bone tenderness at *C*, bone tenderness at *D*, or inability to bear weight immediately and in the emergency department (or physician's office).

Reproduced with permission from Davis MF, Davis PF, Ross DS. ACP Expert Guide to Sports Medicine. Philadelphia, PA: American College of Physicians, 2005:404. Copyright 2009, American College of Physicians.

## Ankle and Foot Pain

### Ankle Sprain

Eighty-five percent of ankle injuries are from inversion sprains. Grade I sprains have no evidence of ligamentous tear and carry an excellent prognosis. Grade II sprains involve partial tears and are accompanied by moderate pain and disability and some difficulty bearing weight. Grade III sprains involve complete rupture of ligaments with an inability to bear weight. Although the inability to bear weight is common with severe sprains, it also raises the suspicion of a fracture. Pain in other locations along with the ankle also raises the possibility of fracture. The age of the patient is important in assessment of ankle injuries because an epiphyseal injury may occur in younger bones.

Examination of an injured ankle begins with noting any petechiae or ecchymoses around the joint (suggesting bleeding in the region of a torn ligament) and any swelling or obvious deformity. Pain elicited by the "squeeze test" (squeezing the tibia and fibula together at the distal calf) indicates rupture of the syndesmotic ligaments joining the two bones at their distal ends. A normal gait rules out fracture or severe sprain. The Ottawa ankle and foot rules (**Figure 14**) are a highly sensitive means of selecting appropriate patients for radiography. If a patient has none of the indications for radiography, the negative likelihood ratio of fracture is 0.08.

Conservative treatment is recommended for ankle sprains. The Institute for Clinical Systems Improvement has developed an evidence-based guideline using the acronym PRICE: Protect against further injury with support; Rest and avoid activities that can exacerbate the injury; and control swelling by applying Ice, applying Compression, and Elevating the injured limb. Evidence regarding the efficacy of a surgical versus a conservative approach to ligament tears is inconclusive.

### Hind Foot Pain

Plantar fasciitis is the most common cause of heel pain and is a major source of concern for runners. Symptoms are worse in the mornings. Diagnosis is based on demonstrating palpable tenderness at the anterior base of the calcaneus. Pain that is more posterior on the calcaneus may indicate a calcaneal stress fracture. The windlass test looks for pain in the plantar fascia by simulating the motion of a step. With the patient's foot in a weight-bearing position, the toes are dorsiflexed by the examiner, maximally stretching the plantar fascia. When the windlass test produces the foot pain, the diagnosis is almost certainly plantar fasciitis. Radiography adds little to the evaluation for plantar fasciitis (15% of foot radiographs for heel pain find a heel spur that is unrelated to the pain) unless alternative sources for the pain are being sought.

Conservative treatment of plantar fasciitis includes arch supports, ice after exercise, morning massage, fascia stretching (rolling the foot over a tennis ball while sitting), and orthotic devices, although most patients improve eventually regardless of the therapy. Corticosteroid injection has been used with some efficacy; however, rupture of the plantar fascia may occur after injection in a small number (7%) of patients.

Fat pad syndrome is a condition seen in older runners in which the natural fat pad overlying the calcaneus becomes thinned. Pain increases with prolonged exercise, distinguishing it from plantar fasciitis. Shoe inserts may cushion the impact of the foot.

Achilles tendinitis presents with tenderness in runners. NSAIDs and rest are the first-line treatment. Achilles tendinitis usually resolves with conservative treatment within 2 weeks. Corticosteroid injections should be avoided so as not to precipitate Achilles tendon rupture.

Fluoroquinolone antibiotics may also precipitate Achilles tendon ruptures, probably by potentiating the production of matrix metalloproteinases in tendons. While it is unusual for this tendon to rupture without heavy exertional stress, patients on corticosteroids and those who have been on fluoroquinolones can rupture an Achilles tendon with no more than low-level walking. Patients who undergo percutaneous surgical repair have less chance of re-rupture than patients with nonoperative treatment. However, in patients at higher surgical risks, a nonoperative approach with a cast or a functional brace is reasonable.

## Midfoot Pain

The tarsal tunnel syndrome is a nerve entrapment condition that causes foot pain and paresthesias. Stretching the posterior tibial nerve by dorsiflexion of the toes and simultaneous eversion of the foot may replicate the pain. Treatment measures are similar to those for carpal tunnel syndrome.

Tarsal and metatarsal bone fractures are rare, but do occur in high-impact sports. They require a high index of suspicion to diagnose and should be considered when presumed diagnoses are not responding to standard therapies.

## Forefoot Pain

Metatarsalgia is a painful condition, more frequent in athletes, in which the distal head of the metatarsal is tender and painful. It may be caused by poorly fitting footwear and usually responds to improved shoeware.

Morton neuroma is an entrapment syndrome of the interdigital nerve, characterized by tenderness between the third and fourth metatarsals. Unilateral presentation is most common in patients with this condition, and women, usually in their fifth decade, are affected more often than men. Lateral compression of the forefoot can reproduce symptoms. Wider shoes and corticosteroid injection may help, but severe cases may only respond to surgery.

### KEY POINTS

- In an ankle sprain, ecchymoses around the joint suggest bleeding in the region of a torn ligament.

- The Ottawa ankle and foot rules are highly sensitive for ruling out fracture.

- Plantar fasciitis is the most common cause of heel pain, and reproduction of the pain with toe dorsiflexion confirms the diagnosis.

## Bibliography

Aldridge T. Diagnosing heel pain in adults [erratum in Am Fam Physician. 2006;73(5):776]. Am Fam Physician, 2004;70(2):332-338. [PMID: 15291091]

Bachmann LM, Kolb E, Koller MT, Steurer J, ter Riet G. Accuracy of Ottawa ankle rules to exclude fractures of the ankle and mid-foot: systematic review. BMJ. 2003;326(7386):417. [PMID: 12595378]

Childs JD, Fritz JM, Flynn TW, et al. A clinical prediction rule to identify patients with low back pain most likely to benefit from spinal manipulation: a validation study. Ann Intern Med. 2004;141(12): 920-928. [PMID: 15611489]

Chou R, Qaseem A, Snow V, et al; Clinical Efficacy Assessment Subcommittee of the American College of Physicians; American College of Physicians; American Pain Society Low Back Pain Guidelines Panel. Diagnosis and treatment of low back pain: a joint clinical practice guideline from the American College of Physicians and the American Pain Society [erratum in Ann Intern Med. 2008;148(3):247-248]. Ann Intern Med. 2007;147(7):478-491. [PMID: 17909209]

Gerritsen AA, de Vet HC, Scholten RJ, Bertelsmann FW, de Krom MC, Bouter LM. Splinting vs. surgery in the treatment of carpal tunnel syndrome: a randomized controlled trial. JAMA, 2002;288(10): 1245-1251. [PMID: 12215131]

Gross AR, Goldsmith C, Hoving JL, et al; Cervical Overview Group. Conservative management of mechanical neck disorders: a systematic review. J Rheumatol. 2007;34(5):1083-1102. [PMID: 17295434]

Hunt D, Clohisy J, Prather H. Acetabular labral tears of the hip in women. Phys Med Rehabil Clin N Am. 2007;18(3):497-520, ix-x. [PMID: 17678764]

Peat G, Thomas E, Duncan R, Wood L, Hay E, Croft P. Clinical classification criteria for knee osteoarthritis: performance in the general population and primary care. Ann Rheum Dis. 2006;65(10):1363-1367. [PMID: 16627539]

Sherman KJ, Cherkin DC, Erro J, Miglioretti DL, Deyo RA. Comparing yoga, exercise, and a self-care book for chronic low back pain: a randomized, controlled trial. Ann Intern Med 2005;143(120:849-856. [PMID: 16365466]

Trinh KV, Phillips SD, Ho E, Damasma K. Acupuncture for the alleviation of lateral epicondyle pain: a systematic review. Rheumatology (Oxford). 2004;43(9):1085-1090. [PMID: 15213328]

# Hyperlipidemia

## Screening for Lipid Disorders

The standard screening test for lipid disorders is a lipid panel obtained after a 12-hour fast. Abnormal results are interpreted according to the number of risk factors present in the patient (see Routine Care of the Healthy Patient). Two samples should be obtained at least 1 week apart before making treatment decisions.

## Evaluation of Lipid Levels

### LDL Cholesterol

Dyslipidemia (hyperlipidemia and/or low HDL cholesterol) is diagnosed when there are one or more lipid abnormalities found on a whole blood lipid panel after a 12-hour fast. Although a total cholesterol level above 200 mg/dL (5.18

mmol/L) is considered abnormal, therapy is targeted at the individual components of total cholesterol.

LDL cholesterol is the major atherogenic lipoprotein and is the primary target for therapy. Elevations are primarily related to dietary and genetic factors. Secondary causes include hypothyroidism, obstructive liver disease, nephrotic syndrome, estrogen use, antipsychotic medications, and protease inhibitors (used to treat HIV disease). Individual LDL cholesterol goals are determined by the presence or absence of five major risk factors (**Table 28**). LDL cholesterol goals and therapy are provided in **Table 29**. The Adult Treatment Panel of the National Cholesterol Education Program (ATP III) recommends that patients with two or more risk factors

whose LDL cholesterol is above 130 mg/dL (3.37 mmol/L) should be further stratified using the Framingham risk equation, which predicts the 10-year absolute risk of a major cardiovascular event, to determine treatment goals and options. (See http://hp2010.nhlbihin.net/atpiii/calculator.asp?usertype=prof for an on-line Framingham risk calculator.) For patients at greatest risk (those with at least two major risk factors, such as coronary artery disease [CAD] and smoking, or CAD and diabetes mellitus), achieving an LDL cholesterol of less than 70 mg/dL (1.81 mmol/L) is considered an optional goal. Total cholesterol/HDL cholesterol ratio is a predictor of CAD risk but should not replace LDL cholesterol as the primary target of therapy.

## Triglycerides

Hypertriglyceridemia is usually related to obesity and physical inactivity but also can be due to genetic factors, high carbohydrate intake, type 2 diabetes, renal disease, alcohol abuse, and certain drugs (corticosteroids, β-blockers, estrogens, protease inhibitors). Hypertriglyceridemia is a predictor of development of CAD but not after adjustment for LDL or HDL cholesterol subfractions.

Determining goal triglyceride level is an indirect process based on non–HDL cholesterol level (total cholesterol minus HDL cholesterol). This value, which comprises very-low-density lipoprotein (VLDL) and LDL cholesterol levels, is a good estimate of the level of atherogenic lipid particles and is a better estimate of CAD risk than LDL cholesterol alone. The non–HDL cholesterol goal equals the patient's LDL cholesterol goal plus 30 mg/dL (0.78 mmol/L) (accounting for a top-normal VLDL cholesterol of 30 mg/dL

---

**TABLE 28** Major Risk Factors (Exclusive of LDL Cholesterol) Used To Individualize LDL Cholesterol Goals

**C**igarette smoking

**H**ypertension (blood pressure ≥140/90 mm Hg or taking antihypertensive medication)

**O**lder age (men ≥45 y; women ≥55 y)

**L**ow HDL cholesterol (<40 mg/dL [1.04 mmol/L])[a]

**E**lder (family) history of premature coronary artery disease (male first-degree relative age <55 y; female first-degree relative age <65 y)

[a]HDL cholesterol ≥60 mg/dL (1.55 mmol/L) is a "negative" risk factor. This removes one risk factor from the total count.

Data from the National Heart Lung and Blood Institute. National Cholesterol Education Program. Third Report of the Expert Panel on Detection, Evaluation, and Treatment of High Blood Cholesterol in Adults (Adult Treatment Panel III): Executive Summary. www.nhlbi.nih.gov/guidelines/cholesterol/atp_iii.htm. Published May 2001. Accessed July 14, 2009.

---

**TABLE 29** Adult Treatment Panel III Recommendations for LDL Cholesterol Level Management

| Risk Category | LDL Cholesterol Goal | Initiate TLC | Consider Drug Therapy[a] |
|---|---|---|---|
| High risk: CAD or CAD equivalents[b] (10-year risk >20%) | <100 mg/dL (2.59 mmol/L) (optional goal: <70 mg/dL [1.81 mmol/L])[c] | ≥100 mg/dL (2.59 mmol/L) | ≥130 mg/dL (3.37 mmol/L) 100 to 129 mg/dL (2.59 to 3.34 mmol/L): drug optional[d] |
| Moderately high risk: ≥2 risk factors (10-year risk 10% to 20%) | <130 mg/dL (3.37 mmol/L) | ≥130 mg/dL (3.37 mmol/L) | ≥130 mg/dL (3.37 mmol/L) |
| Moderate risk: ≥2 risk factors (10-year risk <10%) | <130 mg/dL (3.37 mmol/L) | ≥130 mg/dL (3.37 mmol/L) | ≥160 mg/dL (4.14 mmol/L) |
| Lower risk: 0 to 1 risk factor | <160 mg/dL (4.14 mmol/L) | ≥160 mg/dL (4.14 mmol/L) | ≥190 mg/dL (4.92 mmol/L) 160 to 189 mg/dL (4.14 to 4.90 mmol/L): drug optional |

CAD = coronary artery disease; TLC = therapeutic lifestyle changes.

[a]When LDL cholesterol–lowering drug therapy is employed, intensity of therapy should be sufficient to achieve at least a 30% to 40% reduction in LDL cholesterol levels.

[b]CAD risk equivalents include peripheral arterial disease, abdominal aortic aneurysm, carotid artery disease, transient ischemic attacks or stroke of carotid origin or 50% obstruction of a carotid artery, diabetes, and 10-year risk for CAD ≥20%.

[c]ATP III Update 2004: Implications of recent clinical trials for the ATP III Guidelines. Available at www.nhlbi.nih.gov/guidelines/cholesterol/atp3upd04.htm.

[d]If a high-risk person has high triglycerides or low HDL cholesterol, combining a fibrate or nicotinic acid with an LDL cholesterol–lowering drug can be considered.

Data from the National Heart Lung and Blood Institute. National Cholesterol Education Program. Third Report of the Expert Panel on Detection, Evaluation, and Treatment of High Blood Cholesterol in Adults (Adult Treatment Panel III): Executive Summary. www.nhlbi.nih.gov/guidelines/cholesterol/atp_iii.htm. Published May 2001. Accessed July 14, 2009.

[0.78 mmol/L]). The ATP III recommends treatment of moderate triglyceride elevation (200-499 mg/dL [2.26-5.64 mmol/L]) only if non–HDL cholesterol is elevated. An alternative approach in patients with a family history of premature CAD is to obtain specialized lipoprotein testing to detect genetic disorders associated with hypertriglyceridemia and increased risk of CAD.

## HDL Cholesterol

HDL cholesterol level is inversely related to cardiovascular risk. The increased risk associated with low HDL cholesterol (<40 mg/dL [1.04 mmol/L]) appears to persist somewhat even at very low levels of LDL cholesterol. Factors contributing to low HDL cholesterol are physical inactivity, obesity, cigarette smoking, type 2 diabetes, renal failure, high triglyceride level, high carbohydrate intake, thiazide diuretics, β-blockers without intrinsic sympathetic activity (propanolol and most others), progestational agents, and anabolic steroids. (The effect of thiazide diuretics and β-blockers on lipids may have limited significance, and overall benefits of using these drugs likely exceed harms.) Genetic factors account for about half of the variability in HDL cholesterol levels.

Because of insufficient evidence of risk reduction from controlled trials, ATP III has not set a specific goal for raising HDL cholesterol. ATP III guidelines emphasize LDL cholesterol as the primary therapeutic target and non–HDL cholesterol as a secondary therapeutic target. The approach to low HDL cholesterol is discussed in the management section.

## Nonstandard Lipid Risk Factors

Measurement of nonstandard risk factors, such as lipoprotein(a) and lipid particle size, is discussed in MKSAP 15 Cardiovascular Medicine. The vertical auto profile (VAP) test is available at some commercial laboratories and includes common lipid panel values as well as non–HDL cholesterol, lipoprotein(a), intermediate-density lipoprotein (IDL), LDL particle size pattern, and remnant lipoproteins. Neither the VAP test nor other newer lipid tests can currently be recommended for routine practice.

## Metabolic Syndrome

Even if standard lipid measurements are normal, patients should be evaluated for the metabolic syndrome (**Table 30**) because of the additional risk it confers for adverse cardiovascular outcomes at any level of LDL cholesterol.

ATP III recommends that metabolic syndrome be considered a secondary target for risk reduction therapy after LDL cholesterol is evaluated and managed as a primary target. Any person at high risk or moderately high risk who has lifestyle-related risk factors such as the metabolic syndrome is a candidate for therapeutic lifestyle changes to modify these risk factors regardless of LDL cholesterol level. However, it is not clear whether the metabolic syndrome in itself confers an

**TABLE 30** Criteria for Metabolic Syndrome

**Any Three of the Following:**

| Risk Factor | Defining Level |
|---|---|
| Abdominal obesity (waist circumference) | >40 in (>102 cm) in men; >35 in (>88 cm) in women |
| Triglycerides[a] | ≥150 mg/dL (1.70 mmol/L) |
| HDL cholesterol | <40 mg/dL in men (1.04 mmol/L); <50 mg/dL (1.30 mmol/L) in women |
| Blood pressure | ≥130/≥85 mm Hg |
| Fasting glucose | ≥110 mg/dL (6.11 mmol/L) |

[a]Triglycerides ≥150 mg/dL (1.70 mmol/L) as a single factor correlates highly with presence of metabolic syndrome.

Data from the National Heart Lung and Blood Institute. National Cholesterol Education Program. Third Report of the Expert Panel on Detection, Evaluation, and Treatment of High Blood Cholesterol in Adults (Adult Treatment Panel III): Executive Summary. www.nhlbi.nih.gov/guidelines/cholesterol/atp_iii.htm. Published May 2001. Accessed July 14, 2009.

independent risk beyond that associated with the specific individual risk factors that comprise this syndrome.

# Management of Dyslipidemias

## Therapeutic Lifestyle Changes

Dietary modification is always indicated in patients with dyslipidemia and can be the only therapeutic regimen when lipid values are near goal. When medication is indicated, dietary modification should be continued, because drugs used for dyslipidemia are less effective with an unrestricted diet. Total fat should be restricted to 25% to 35% of total calories, and saturated fat should be restricted to less than 7% of total calories, or about 15 g of saturated fat daily. Replacement of saturated fat with monounsaturated and polyunsaturated fats or complex carbohydrates results in less of a decrease in HDL cholesterol compared with replacement by simple sugars. In patients with hypertriglyceridemia, carbohydrate restriction is indicated.

Plant stanol and sterol esters are naturally occurring substances that are chemically similar to cholesterol and compete with cholesterol for uptake in the gastrointestinal tract. ATP III recommends increasing intake of stanols and sterols as a therapeutic option for lowering LDL cholesterol. Sterol esters can be found in small quantities in fruits, vegetables, nuts, seeds, cereals, and legumes, but in order to achieve the recommended 2 g per day, supplemental dietary sources (plant sterol table spreads) are recommended. ATP III also recommends increased intake of viscous (soluble) fiber (10-25 g/d), found in psyllium seeds, barley, oatmeal, and oat bran. Some studies show a reduction in cardiovascular risk with foods containing flavonoids (including cocoa and chocolate), but total caloric intake should not be increased. Neither supplemental vitamins (E, C, B$_6$, B$_{12}$, β-carotene) nor alternative therapies (such as garlic) have proved effective. Weight loss can decrease the triglyceride level by 22% and increase HDL cholesterol by 9%. Even moderate weight loss is helpful. Exercise (4 hours per week, moderate intensity) improves cardiovascular fitness and results in increased HDL cholesterol and decreased triglyceride levels.

---

**KEY POINT**

- Dietary intervention is always indicated for patients with dyslipidemia, with total fat limited to 25% to 35% of total calories and saturated fat to less than 7% of total calories.

---

## Statin Therapy

### Principles of Therapy

Statins are the most effective drugs for lowering LDL cholesterol and can lower LDL cholesterol by 18% to 55% (**Table 31**). All statins are effective, and differences in potency can be equalized by using recommended doses. In addition to lowering LDL cholesterol, statins improve endothelial function and have anti-inflammatory and plaque-stabilizing (pleiotropic) effects.

In patients without known CAD (primary prevention), treatment of elevated LDL cholesterol with statins has been shown to decrease major coronary events, with a trend toward decreased mortality. A long-term follow-up study of one of the major primary prevention trials (West of Scotland Coronary Prevention Study) showed that the benefit of reduced cardiac events persisted for 10 years after the trial.

The greatest impact of LDL cholesterol–lowering therapy is in patients with CAD or CAD-equivalent disease (secondary prevention), including diabetes. In one trial, high-dose statin therapy was more effective than moderate-dose therapy in reducing major cardiovascular events in patients with stable CAD, but this result was not seen in another trial among patients with previous myocardial infarction. LDL cholesterol–lowering therapy is associated with coronary lesion regression in patients with high LDL cholesterol (170-190 mg/dL [4.40-4.92 mmol/L]) who achieve 30% to 40% lower LDL cholesterol values with medication.

| **TABLE 31** Drugs for Treating Lipid Disorders | | |
|---|---|---|
| **Agent** | **Effectiveness** | **Notes** |
| Bile acid binders | Lower LDL cholesterol 12%-16% | Good long-term safety record. Drugs of choice for LDL-cholesterol lowering in children and in women with childbearing potential. Often used as second-line drug with statins because they act synergistically to induce LDL receptors. Do not use in patients with triglycerides >300 mg/dL (3.39 mmol/L) or those with gastrointestinal motility disorders. Bloating can occur. Can interfere with absorption of drugs given at the same time (less so with colesevelam). |
| Statins | Lower LDL cholesterol 18%-55% <br><br> Raise HDL cholesterol 5%-10% <br><br> Lower triglycerides 15%-25% | Drugs of choice for elevated LDL cholesterol based on safety and efficacy. Adverse effects include elevated liver enzymes, myalgia, and myositis. Used in combination with bile acid binders or ezetimibe to synergistically lower LDL cholesterol. Used in combination with niacin and fibrates in patients with combined hyperlipidemia. Use cautiously in patients on fibrates owing to increased risk of myositis and do not use in women of childbearing age unless pregnancy is highly unlikely. Pravastatin is least likely to cause myalgia. |
| Fibrates | Do not lower LDL cholesterol reliably <br><br> Raise HDL cholesterol 15% <br><br> Lower triglycerides 50% | Most effective triglyceride-reducing drugs. Use with caution in patients with renal insufficiency or gallbladder disease. Fenofibrate is less risky than gemfibrozil when combined with a statin. |
| Nicotinic acid | Lowers LDL cholesterol 5%-25% <br><br> Lowers triglycerides 20%-50% <br><br> Raises HDL cholesterol 15%-35% | Most effective HDL cholesterol–raising drug. Adverse effects include flushing, liver toxicity, nausea, glucose intolerance, gout, and elevated uric acid levels. |
| Ezetimibe | Lowers LDL cholesterol 18% <br><br> Lowers triglycerides 8% | When used in combination with statins, yields an additional LDL cholesterol reduction of 12% (total reduction 26% to 60%), an increase in HDL cholesterol of 3%, and a triglyceride reduction of 8%, although in a study using surrogate endpoints no benefits were shown. Do not use in combination with resins or fibrates. Contraindicated in patients with active liver disease or elevated liver enzymes. |

The ATP III update on recent clinical trials recommends that patients with diabetes and CAD be treated with statins regardless of LDL cholesterol level. In a meta-analysis, the number-needed-to-treat (NNT) to achieve benefit in this group was approximately 14 for a trial average of approximately 5 years. Treatment in persons with diabetes but without CAD results in about half that benefit and is recommended for those with concomitant risk factors (age >55 years, hypertension, smoking, left ventricular hypertrophy, history of stroke, peripheral vascular disease). The ATP III recommends achieving a target LDL cholesterol level of less than 100 mg/dL (2.59 mmol/L) for patients with diabetes who do not have CAD, whereas the American College of Physicians and others, noting disagreement in the literature regarding the effectiveness of selecting specific LDL cholesterol targets, recommend the use of moderate doses of statins (atorvastatin, 20 mg/d; or 40 mg/d of lovastatin, pravastatin, or simvastatin) for these patients regardless of LDL cholesterol level. Statins are also indicated for patients who have experienced an acute coronary syndrome (ACS) and should be prescribed to these patients before they leave the hospital.

Referral to a lipid specialist should be considered for patients whose LDL cholesterol goals cannot be met using conventional therapy and for those with severe hyperlipidemia or suspected genetic syndromes.

### Adverse Effects

Side effects of statins include elevated liver enzymes, myalgia, and rhabdomyolysis. Baseline serum creatine kinase (CK), alanine aminotransferase (ALT), and aspartate aminotransferase (AST) measurements should be obtained in patients initiating statin therapy. During statin therapy, liver enzyme abnormalities occur no more frequently than with placebo (~1%) for most statins. Monitoring of patients taking statins with periodic laboratory screening is recommended by many groups, but the American College of Physicians recommends such monitoring only in patients with symptoms or baseline abnormalities or who are taking other drugs concomitantly that increase the risk of side effects. If AST/ALT is three times the upper limit of normal, the statin should be discontinued and other causes of liver injury should be sought. Liver failure due to statins is rare, and another statin can be substituted after liver enzyme levels have returned to normal.

Myalgia is common and may not be caused by statin therapy. In clinical trials, myalgia occurs no more often with statins than with placebo, and a substitute statin may be tried in patients with myalgia. If myalgia is persistent and a statin must be used, coenzyme Q10 (ubiquinone), 100 mg/d, may be effective in resolving the symptoms. CK levels should be obtained in patients with myalgia to detect myopathy because progression to rhabdomyolysis, myoglobinuria, and acute renal failure is possible if myopathy is present. Rhabdomyolysis must be treated promptly to avoid renal failure. Myopathy is more likely to occur with higher doses of statins and when statins are used in combination with other drugs, including fibrates, nicotinic acid (niacin), macrolide antibiotics, some antifungal agents, and cyclosporine. Although grapefruit is a cytochrome P-450 inhibitor, large amounts (a quart of juice or more) would need to be consumed to pose a serious risk for rhabdomyolysis.

### KEY POINTS

- LDL cholesterol–lowering therapy is twice as effective for secondary prevention of cardiovascular disease compared with primary prevention.
- Statins are usually well tolerated but may cause myositis or rhabdomyolysis in elderly patients, those with comorbid illnesses, or those taking certain other medications, including fibrates and nicotinic acid.

## Combination Drug Therapy

When LDL cholesterol goals are not met by using a statin alone, other medications can be used safely in combination with statins. The bile acid binders (see Table 31) lower LDL cholesterol another 12% to 16% when used with statins. Colesevelam is more easily administered, better tolerated, and interacts less with other drugs than other bile acid binders.

Ezetimibe decreases the delivery of intestinal cholesterol to the liver and lowers LDL cholesterol by 18%. A combination product consisting of ezetimibe, 10 mg/d, with simvastatin lowers LDL cholesterol by 45% to 60%, depending on the dosage of simvastatin. However, the ENHANCE trial, which used carotid intimal thickness as a surrogate measure of atherosclerosis progression, did not show a benefit of adding ezetimibe to simvastatin, despite significant reductions in LDL cholesterol and C-reactive protein levels. The American College of Cardiology statement regarding the ENHANCE trial concluded that major decisions cannot be made on the basis of the trial and that ezetimibe remains a reasonable option for patients who cannot tolerate statins or do not reach goal with statins alone (www.acc.org/enhance.htm). Statins, ezetimibe, and bile acid binders can be used together.

Other drugs can also be used to lower LDL cholesterol, particularly when multiple lipid components are targeted. Nicotinic acid lowers LDL cholesterol level by 5% to 25% and triglyceride level by 20% to 50%; it raises HDL cholesterol by 15% to 35%. A combined nicotinic acid and lovastatin preparation lowers LDL cholesterol and triglyceride levels by 30% to 42% and raises HDL cholesterol by 20% to 30%. Although these drugs yield a moderate reduction in cardiovascular disease when used to modify atherogenic dyslipidemia, recommendations for their use are based mainly on improved lipoprotein profiles and several indirect lines of evidence.

- If initial therapy to lower LDL cholesterol fails to achieve lipid goals, combination therapy using moderate doses of statins and another drug is an alternative option to using maximum doses of statins.

## Management of Hypertriglyceridemia

When a patient has a high triglyceride level as well as a non–HDL cholesterol value that is more than 30 mg/dL (0.78 mmol/L) above the LDL cholesterol goal, medication is indicated to treat the high triglyceride level as well as the dyslipidemia associated with it. If the LDL cholesterol is above goal, statins can be used to treat the dyslipidemia even if LDL cholesterol does not otherwise meet primary criteria for treatment. If LDL cholesterol is already at goal, treatment is directed at the triglyceride elevation. If triglyceride level is greater than 500 mg/dL (5.65 mmol/L), the ATP III guidelines recommend reducing the triglyceride level regardless of non–HDL cholesterol level because of the potential for acute pancreatitis.

Fibrates are most effective for reducing triglycerides and can lower triglyceride level by 50%. Routine monitoring for patients taking fibrates should include AST/ALT levels. When fibrates are used in combination with statins, rhabdomyolysis is more common than with either drug alone. Since fenofibrate does not raise statin levels, it is preferred over gemfibrozil for combination with statins. Nicotinic acid also lowers triglyceride levels. Omega-3 fatty acids can be used as an adjunct in lowering triglyceride levels, but studies have disagreed regarding mortality benefit. ATP III withholds a strong recommendation for using omega-3 fatty acids.

- Treatment for hypertriglyceridemia is indicated for patients with non–HDL cholesterol that is 30 mg/dL (0.78 mmol/L) above the patient's LDL cholesterol goal or with a triglyceride level above 500 mg/dL (5.65 mmol/L).

## Management of Low HDL Cholesterol

In evaluating and managing low HDL cholesterol, it is important to remember that the primary target of therapy is LDL cholesterol. Low HDL cholesterol (<40 mg/dL [1.04 mmol/L]) is one of the five major risk factors used to set the LDL cholesterol target. Once LDL cholesterol has been evaluated and managed, non–HDL cholesterol is evaluated as a secondary target in patients with elevated triglycerides (>200 mg/dL [2.26 mmol/L]). Because of insufficient evidence of risk reduction from controlled trials, ATP III has not set a specific goal for raising HDL cholesterol. In patients in whom the HDL cholesterol remains low despite use of statins and/or fibrates to treat high LDL or non–HDL cholesterol,

low HDL cholesterol should first be treated with lifestyle interventions, including exercise, tobacco cessation, and weight management. Exercise can increase HDL cholesterol level by 1 to 4 mg/dL (0.03-0.1 mmol/L), depending on intensity of activity. ATP III states that fibrates, especially in combination with statins (fenofibrate is preferred when used with a statin because of less risk of myopathy) may have an adjunctive role in the treatment of patients with high triglycerides and low HDL cholesterol, particularly in patients with diabetes or metabolic syndrome. Nicotinic acid alone or in combination with statins effectively lowers LDL cholesterol and raises HDL cholesterol, and its use for CAD risk reduction in similar patients is supported by several clinical trials.

There is more evidence for the use of the medication regimens listed above when low HDL cholesterol is present in patients who have CAD. In the VA-HIT trial, gemfibrozil reduced future CAD events by 24% in patients with low HDL cholesterol and a history of CAD. Some authors state that using nicotinic acid in similar patients is a reasonable alternative. Nicotinic acid raises HDL cholesterol levels 2 to 3 times more than gemfibrozil but is associated with a flushing sensation that limits its use in some patients.

- Pharmacologic treatment for low HDL cholesterol is only indicated for patients with established coronary artery disease.

## Management of the Metabolic Syndrome

In patients meeting the criteria for the metabolic syndrome (see Table 30), lifestyle modifications, including weight loss in overweight patients, exercise in sedentary patients, and salt reduction in those with elevated blood pressure, should be initiated. If these measures do not result in normalization of the metabolic syndrome components, drug therapy is indicated. Evidence-based therapies recommended by the ATP III for patients with the metabolic syndrome include intensified lowering of LDL cholesterol and non–HDL cholesterol, antihypertensive therapy, and, in patients with CAD, aspirin to treat the prothrombotic state associated with the metabolic syndrome. Treating hyperglycemia in patients with the metabolic syndrome has not been shown to reduce risk for CAD.

A step-wise approach to diagnosing and treating lipid disorders is shown in **Table 32**.

## Management at the Extremes of Age

Approximately two-thirds of first coronary events occur in men 65 years or older and women 75 years or older, making the elderly an important group in which to consider therapy to reduce cardiovascular risk. ATP III supports the use of statins for primary prevention in the elderly (following the treatment goals and principles outlined in Table 29), stating that statin therapy beginning at age 65 years and continuing for 15 years results in a number needed to treat (NNT) of 10

**TABLE 32** Stepwise Evaluation and Management of Hyperlipidemia

| Step | Action | Key Features |
|---|---|---|
| 1 | Determine lipoprotein levels | Fasting lipid profile |
| 2 | Identify presence of CAD or CAD equivalent | CAD: myocardial infarction, unstable angina, coronary artery procedures, or evidence of myocardial ischemia |
| | | CAD equivalent: diabetes mellitus, symptomatic carotid artery disease, peripheral arterial disease, and abdominal aortic aneurysm |
| 3 | Determine presence of major risk factors other than LDL cholesterol level | Cigarette smoking, hypertension (blood pressure ≥140/90 mm Hg or taking antihypertensive medication), older age (men ≥45 y; women ≥55 y), HDL cholesterol <40 mg/dL (1.04 mmol/L), family history of premature CAD |
| 4 | If ≥2 risk factors (other than LDL cholesterol) are present without CAD or CAD equivalent, calculate 10-year risk of CAD | Online risk calculator available at: http://hp2010.nhlbihin.net/atpiii/calculator.asp?usertype=prof |
| 5 | Determine risk category | See Table 29 |
| 6 | Initiate TLC if LDL cholesterol is above goal | Dietary changes, weight management, increased physical activity |
| 7 | Add drug therapy if indicated | See Table 29 |
| 8 | Identify and treat metabolic syndrome | See Table 30 |
| | | TLC (weight loss, exercise); if risk factors persist despite 3 months of TLC, treat hypertension, treat lipid abnormalities, and, in patients with CAD, prescribe aspirin to reduce prothrombic state |
| 9 | Treat elevated triglycerides | Encourage increased physical activity and weight loss; use fibrates or a nicotinic acid if drug treatment indicated |

CAD = coronary artery disease; TLC = therapeutic lifestyle changes.

Adapted from National Cholesterol Education Program: ATP III Guidelines At-A-Glance Quick Desk Reference. www.nhlbi.nih.gov/guidelines/cholesterol/atglance.pdf. Published May 2001. Accessed July 14, 2009.

to prevent one CAD death in patients with a 40% 10-year risk and a NNT of 42 in patients with a 10% 10-year risk. The largest trial evaluating treatment of the elderly, however, showed no benefit for primary prevention. Clinical trials have shown that secondary prevention in the elderly is effective. When considering therapy in the elderly, several factors, including functional and chronologic age, comorbid illness, social and financial circumstances, and increased risk of drug side effects, should be considered. Because lipid levels and Framingham scores are less predictive of risk in the elderly, other tests, including ankle-brachial index and resting or stress electrocardiograms, may be used to further stratify risk in elderly patients.

CAD is rare in men younger than 35 years and women younger than 45 years, occurring mainly in those with diabetes, heavy smoking, and familial hypercholesterolemia. Screening for dyslipidemia in these age groups should be selective, based on the presence of cardiovascular risk factors. Screening is recommended for adolescents and children with CAD risk factors, a family history of CAD, or one parent with a total cholesterol level greater than or equal to 240 mg/dL (6.22 mmol/L). Physical findings of familial hypercholesterolemia include xanthelasma and xanthoma (see MKSAP 15 Dermatology). Lipid abnormalities include a total cholesterol level of 350 to 500 mg/dL (9.06-12.95 mmol/L) and elevated LDL cholesterol with a normal triglyceride level.

**KEY POINT**

- Treating the elderly for hyperlipidemia requires an individualized approach; both primary and secondary prevention of cardiovascular disease should be considered in those with reasonable life expectancy and few comorbid illnesses.

## Stroke Prevention

Major clinical trials and meta-analyses show that lowering LDL cholesterol decreases the incidence of stroke in patients with CAD by 27% to 31%. The mechanism of action is likely related to plaque stabilization and slowing of plaque progression. The SPARCL trial showed a 2.1% absolute reduction of stroke risk among patients with previous stroke or transient ischemic attack (secondary prevention) treated with 80 mg/d of atorvastatin. A worrisome side effect in the study was an increase in hemorrhagic stroke (NNT to prevent one stroke, 51; number needed to harm (NNH) to cause one hemorrhagic stroke, 110). Physicians should consider risk factors for hemorrhagic stroke, including older age, previous hemorrhagic stroke, chronic hypertension, male sex, and use of anticoagulation, before prescribing high-dose atorvastatin for stroke prevention. The effectiveness of statins for primary prevention of stroke has not been proved.

## Hyperlipidemia in Special Populations

In women with CAD or CAD-equivalent disease, statins result in a 29% risk reduction, as compared with a 31% risk reduction in men. The presence of diabetes mitigates lower overall risk in women. For primary prevention, because relatively few trials have included women, the estimates of benefit have been extrapolated from studies of men.

Blacks have the highest cardiovascular mortality rate of any ethnic group in the United States; this is most likely secondary to the high prevalence of major risk factors in this population. Screening and treatment recommendations for blacks are the same as for the general population.

## Bibliography

Amarenco P, Bogousslavsky J, Callahan A 3rd, et al; Stroke Prevention by Aggressive Reduction in Cholesterol Levels (SPARCL) Investigators. High-dose atorvastatin after stroke or transient ischemic attack. N Engl J Med. 2006;355(6):549-559. [PMID: 16899775]

Brunzell JD. Hypertriglyceridemia. N Engl J Med. 2007;357(10):1009-1017. [PMID: 17804845]

Ford I, Murray H, Packard CJ, Shepherd J, Macfarlane PW, Cobbe SM; West of Scotland Coronary Prevention Study Group. Long-term follow-up of the West of Scotland Coronary Prevention Study. N Engl J Med. 2007;357(15):1477-1486. [PMID: 17928595]

Hayward RA, Hofer TP, Vijan S. Narrative review: lack of evidence for recommending low-density lipoprotein treatment targets: a solvable problem. Ann Intern Med. 2006;145(7):520-530. [PMID: 17015870]

Kastelein JJ, Akdim F, Stroes ES, et al; ENHANCE Investigators. Simvastatin with or without ezetimibe in familial hypercholesterolemia [erratum in N Engl J Med. 2008;358(18):1977]. N Engl J Med. 2008;358(14):1431-1443. [PMID: 18376000]

LaRosa JC, Grundy SM, Waters DD, et al; Treating to New Targets (TNT) Investigators. Intensive lipid lowering with atorvastatin in patients with stable coronary disease. N Engl J Med. 2005; 352(14):1425-1435. [PMID: 15755765]

Pedersen TR, Faergeman O, Kastelein JJ, et al; Incremental Decrease in End Points Through Aggressive Lipid Lowering (IDEAL) Study Group. High-dose atorvastatin vs usual-dose simvastatin for secondary prevention after myocardial infarction: the IDEAL study: a randomized controlled trial [erratum in JAMA. 2005;294(24):3092]. JAMA. 2005;294(19):2437-2445. [PMID: 16287954]

Vijan S, Hayward RA; American College of Physicians. Pharmacologic lipid-lowering therapy in type 2 diabetes mellitus: background paper for the American College of Physicians. Ann Intern Med. 2004;140(8):650-658. [PMID: 15096337]

# Obesity

## Definition and Epidemiology of Obesity

Obesity in adults is a serious public health problem, with a lifetime risk exceeding 25% in the United States. The National Institutes of Health and the World Health Organization have established criteria for the diagnosis of obesity using the body mass index (BMI). The BMI is the patient's weight in kilograms divided by height in meters squared. *Overweight* is defined as a BMI of 25 to 29.9 and *obesity* as a BMI of 30 or higher. Obesity is further divided into three classes: class I (BMI 30-34.9), class II (BMI 35-39.9) and class III (BMI >40). Severe, or morbid, obesity is defined as class III obesity

or class II obesity in the presence of significant comorbidities caused by obesity (**Table 33**). The U.S. Preventive Services Task Force recommends that adult patients be screened for obesity by calculating BMI. Their recommendation is based on the rationale that BMI calculations are a noninvasive, reliable, and low-cost screening tool for diagnosis and on the premise that high-intensity counseling and behavioral interventions may lead to improved outcomes. A calculator to compute BMI is available at http://diabetes.acponline.org/custom_resources/tools/bmi_calculator.html?dbp.

Obesity is associated with an increased risk of chronic disease and overall mortality. The magnitude of risk generally rises with the degree of obesity. In a large cohort study of middle-aged patients, mortality was assessed after adjustment for chronic disease and smoking. The mortality risk among overweight patients was 20% to 40% higher and the risk among obese patients was 200% to 300% higher than those with a normal BMI. When obesity is diagnosed, the patient should be screened and treated for the obesity-related health problems listed in **Table 33**.

The distribution of adipose tissue is important when assessing health risks from obesity. Higher levels of abdominal obesity are associated with increased risk of coronary

**TABLE 33 Diseases with Higher Prevalence in Patients with Obesity**

Atrial fibrillation

Cholelithiasis

Chronic kidney disease

Coronary artery disease

Dyslipidemia

Heart failure

Hypertension

Gastroesophageal reflux disease

Malignancy
  Colorectal
  Esophageal
  Gallbladder
  Liver
  Lymphoma (non-Hodgkin)
  Multiple myeloma
  Pancreatic
  Renal

Nephrolithiasis

Nonalcoholic steatohepatitis

Obstructive sleep apnea

Osteoarthritis

Stroke

Type 2 diabetes mellitus

artery disease, type 2 diabetes mellitus, dyslipidemia, and hypertension. In adults with a BMI of 25 to 34.9, a waist circumference greater than 102 cm (40 in) for men and 88 cm (35 in) for women is associated with greater risk than that determined by BMI alone. In patients with a BMI of 35 or greater, the measurement is less helpful, as nearly all these patients have abdominal obesity. There are some racial variations in measuring abdominal obesity. In Asian populations, a male waist circumference of greater than 90 cm (35 in) and a female waist circumference of greater than 80 cm (32 in) are considered abnormal. Waist circumference is measured with a flexible tape placed horizontally around the abdomen at the level of the iliac crest.

**KEY POINTS**

- All adults should be screened for obesity by calculating BMI.

- Mortality risk among persons with obesity is 2 to 3 times higher than for those with normal weight.

- In adults with a BMI of 25 to 34.9, a waist circumference greater than 102 cm (40 in) in men and 88 cm (35 in) in women is associated with higher mortality risk than that determined by BMI alone.

- Morbid obesity is defined as class III (BMI >40) obesity or class II (BMI 35-39.9) obesity in the presence of significant comorbidities caused by obesity.

# Evaluation for Underlying Causes of Obesity

Patients diagnosed with obesity should be screened for evidence of secondary diseases, medications, and behavioral conditions that can cause or worsen the condition. The time course over which the obesity developed, the patient's eating habits, and a medication and psychiatric history are all important components of the initial evaluation. Life events commonly associated with weight gain include pregnancy, marital status changes, occupational changes, and smoking cessation. A careful history and physical examination should determine the extent of testing for secondary causes of obesity and obesity-related diseases. Most obese patients do not have a readily identifiable secondary cause; many patients do have behaviors that contribute to weight gain and are potential barriers to weight loss.

Medications can cause weight gain. In patients with diabetes, thiazolidinediones, oral hypoglycemic medications, and insulin can all cause modest weight gain. Certain psychiatric medications, including tricyclic antidepressants, selective serotonin reuptake inhibitors, lithium, and many antipsychotic agents (thioridazine, clozapine, olanzapine) are also associated with weight gain. Finally, several anticonvulsants such as valproic acid and carbamazepine can cause weight gain.

In the occasional patient in whom a secondary cause of obesity is found, endocrine disorders are often the underlying cause. The reduced metabolic activity resulting from hypothyroidism may result in weight gain. Excess glucocorticoids from iatrogenic or primary disease states leading to Cushing syndrome can also cause progressive obesity. Growth hormone deficiency, insulinomas, and hypothalamic damage (by surgery, trauma, tumor, or inflammatory disease) can also result in obesity. About half of women with the polycystic ovary syndrome are obese, but the precise relationship between this disorder and obesity is not known.

# Treatment of Obesity

## Behavioral Interventions

Behavioral therapies, including dietary and exercise interventions, are traditional and effective approaches to obesity therapy. They are often used to augment pharmacologic and surgical approaches in morbidly obese patients or as monotherapy in patients with less severe disease (**Figure 15**). While many patients desire to lose as much as one third of their weight, this is a difficult, and usually unrealistic, goal to achieve, even with surgery. A more modest long-term weight loss goal of 5% to 15% will reduce the risk of many of the medical complications of obesity.

Behavioral interventions typically involve self-monitoring of food intake, learning about and controlling stressors that activate eating, establishing a supportive social network, slowing food intake during meals, nutrition education about portion size and meal content, goal setting and behavioral contracting, and education about appropriate physical activity. Group and individual therapy sessions are both effective but result in only modest weight loss—on average, 3 kg or less. Active monthly interventions with face-to-face or Internet engagement with patients can be effective in preventing weight from being regained.

Physical activity is often recommended for treatment of obesity and overweight. Low-intensity workouts equivalent to walking 30 minutes per day are effective in maintaining stable weights; high-intensity/high-amount workouts provide proportionately greater benefits. Exercise has additional benefits of improved cardiovascular health and decreased abdominal and hip circumference measurements. Physical activity is generally felt to be a useful adjunct in preventing further weight gain, but it is probably not adequate as monotherapy for obesity without behavioral therapy, diet, medication, or surgery.

**KEY POINTS**

- A sustained weight loss of 5% to 15% will reduce the risk of many medical complications of obesity.

- Physical activity programs without diet achieve only modest weight loss but are useful in maintaining lost weight and reducing abdominal fat, metabolic abnormalities, and cardiovascular risk.

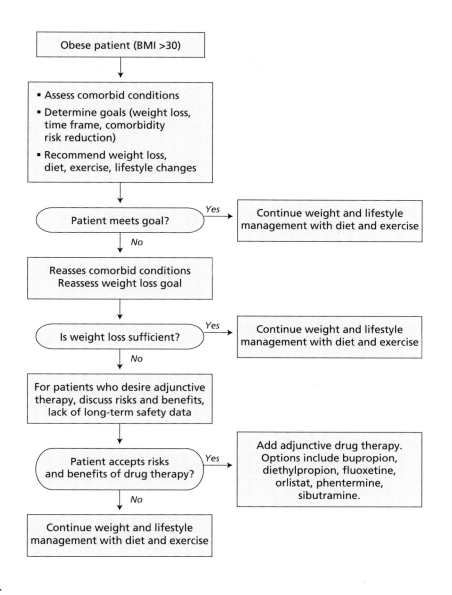

**FIGURE 15.**
**Management of obesity.**

## Dietary Therapy

Restricting caloric intake is a key component of any weight loss program. Very-low-calorie diets of under 800 kcal/d are difficult to administer and can be associated with a higher incidence of adverse effects. They are not recommended for routine use. The amount of ideal caloric restriction in patients depends on the patient's age, sex, degree of obesity, and physical activity. Diets are often best planned with input from a dietician.

Calorie-restricted diets generally fall into three major categories: balanced low-calorie diets, low-fat diets, and low-carbohydrate diets. Data are conflicting regarding which dietary strategies have the most favorable outcome on sustained weight loss and metabolic parameters. Nearly all diets target

a cumulative daily reduction of calories compared with the patient's normal baseline. Low-carbohydrate diets, including variants of the Atkins diet, target an initial goal of 20 g/d or less of carbohydrate for several months, followed by a goal of 50 g/d or less for subsequent continued weight loss and maintenance. Low-fat diets, such as the Ornish diet, generally restrict fat intake to 10% or less of total dietary calories. Balanced low-calorie diets, such as the Zone diet, have a balance of carbohydrate, protein, and fat, typically in a 40%/30%/30% distribution.

Comparisons between diets have yielded conflicting results. A meta-analysis comparing low-fat to low-carbohydrate diets demonstrated a short-term increase in weight loss with low-carbohydrate diets with no difference between the two types of diet after 12 months in terms of either weight loss or blood pressure. Low-carbohydrate diets improve triglyceride and HDL cholesterol levels more than low-fat diets, whereas low-fat diets improve LDL and total cholesterol levels more than low-carbohydrate diets. In a randomized trial comparing several diets in obese postmenopausal women for 12 months, a low-carbohydrate diet resulted in a mean weight loss of 4.7 kg, compared with 1.6 kg with a balanced low-calorie diet and 2.2 kg with a low-fat diet. HDL cholesterol, triglycerides, and both systolic and diastolic blood pressure were more favorable in the low-carbohydrate diet group. Longer-term studies assessing dietary compliance and maintenance strategies are required to definitively recommend one diet over another. The existing data demonstrate that both low-carbohydrate and low-fat diets work in the short term, giving physicians wide latitude to work with patients and dietitians to find a diet that is most likely to result in adherence and maintenance of weight loss.

---

**KEY POINT**

- Calorie restriction is effective for weight loss; however, dieting rarely causes more than 5 kg of sustained weight loss.

---

## Pharmacologic Therapy

Pharmacologic therapy can be offered to obese patients who have failed to achieve their weight loss goals through diet and exercise alone. Before initiating therapy, however, it is important to discuss with patients the drugs' side effects, the lack of long-term safety data, and the temporary nature of the weight loss achieved with medications. Many medications have been tried for treatment of obesity (**Table 34**), but long-term data are only available for orlistat, sibutramine, and rimonabant. (Rimonabant is not available in the United States and is not discussed here.) The U.S. Food and Drug Administration has approved sibutramine for a 2-year course of therapy and orlistat for a 4-year course. In many studies, cessation of the obesity medication is associated with recurrent weight gain. Obesity medications should be used in combination with diet and exercise. Guidelines from the National Institute for Health

and Clinical Excellence (NICE) recommend discontinuation of drug treatment if a 5% threshold in weight loss has not been reached by the end of 3 months of therapy.

Orlistat, which is available over the counter, inhibits pancreatic lipases and alters fat digestion. This results in dose-dependent incomplete digestion of fat with elimination of the excess fat in the stool. Less than 1% of orlistat is absorbed systemically, so it has few drug-drug interactions. Major side effects, occurring in up to 30% of patients, include abdominal cramping, flatus, oily stool, and fecal incontinence. A meta-analysis of 16 orlistat trials demonstrated an average weight reduction of 2.9 kg. The study also demonstrated that orlistat reduced the incidence of diabetes and improved glycemic control in patients with diabetes. Orlistat also reduces blood pressure as well as total cholesterol and LDL cholesterol levels and is associated with a small increase in HDL cholesterol level.

Sibutramine is a sympathomimetic agent that suppresses appetite and food intake. It inhibits norepinephrine, serotonin, and dopamine reuptake into nerve terminals.

A meta-analysis of ten sibutramine trials demonstrated an average of 4.2 kg of weight loss compared with placebo. Sibutramine mildly increased concentrations of HDL cholesterol and lowered triglyceride levels. Sibutramine increased systolic blood pressure by an average of 1.7 mm Hg, diastolic blood pressure by 2.4 mm Hg, and pulse by 4.5/min. Other adverse effects occurred in up to 20% of patients and included insomnia, nausea, dry mouth, and constipation. Sibutramine should not be used in patients with uncontrolled or poorly controlled hypertension or a history of cardiovascular disease.

---

**KEY POINTS**

- Pharmacologic therapy with sibutramine or orlistat should be considered in obese patients in whom behavioral interventions have been ineffective and may result in an additional 3 to 4 kg of weight loss.
- Sibutramine should not be used in patients with poorly controlled or uncontrolled hypertension or cardiovascular disease.

---

| **TABLE 34** FDA-Approved Drugs for the Treatment of Obesity | | |
|---|---|---|
| **Drug** | **Mechanism of Action** | **Approved Indication** |
| Orlistat | Pancreatic lipase inhibitor | Long-term use and maintenance |
| Sibutramine[a] | Sympathomimetic | Long-term use and maintenance |
| Benzphetamine[b] | Sympathomimetic | Short-term use |
| Diethylpropion[a] | Sympathomimetic | Short-term use |
| Phendimetrazine[b] | Sympathomimetic | Short-term use |
| Phentermine (HCl or resin)[a] | Sympathomimetic | Short-term use |

FDA = U.S. Food and Drug Administration.

[a]U.S. Drug Enforcement Administration schedule IV drug.

[b]U.S. Drug Enforcement Administration schedule III drug.

## Surgical Treatment

The goal of bariatric surgery is to improve mortality, reduce morbidity from obesity-related illnesses, and improve patient quality of life. A 1991 NIH consensus panel recommended that surgical therapy for obesity be considered in well-informed, motivated patients with a BMI above 40 who have an acceptable surgical risk and who have failed to benefit from previous nonsurgical weight loss therapies. The panel also suggested that adults with a BMI above 35 with serious comorbidities, such as diabetes, sleep apnea, obesity-related cardiomyopathy, or severe joint disease, may be considered for surgery. Bariatric surgery in elderly patients and children remains controversial. Most surgeons will also not perform bariatric surgery on patients with untreated major psychiatric disorders, including binge eating disorders and current drug or alcohol abuse, or on patients who are unable to comply with postoperative nutritional, dietary, and follow-up requirements.

Some bariatric procedures reduce gastric size and leave small-bowel absorptive function intact. Caloric intake is reduced by causing early satiety. These restrictive procedures are generally simpler and less invasive but produce less long-term weight loss. Vertical banded gastroplasty and laparoscopic adjustable gastric banding are examples of restrictive procedures. The vertical banded gastroplasty has fallen out of favor owing to a high rate of re-operation and has been largely replaced with vertical sleeve gastrectomy, a procedure that does not have a lengthy long-term outcome record.

Procedures utilizing malabsorption shorten the length of functional small bowel and induce more dramatic weight loss, but at the cost of an increased risk of nutritional deficiencies. These procedures may be combined with restrictive approaches. The Roux-en-Y gastric bypass is a dual-mechanism bariatric surgery combining a small gastric reservoir, which restricts oral intake, with a small-bowel bypass, which induces mild malabsorption. The two most common types of bariatric procedures performed are laparoscopic adjustable gastric banding and Roux-en-Y gastric bypass (**Table 35**).

A meta-analysis demonstrated that bariatric surgery improved or resolved diabetes, hyperlipidemia, hypertension, and obstructive sleep apnea in 70% or more of patients. Patients who underwent gastric banding lost approximately 48% of excess weight, and those who underwent gastric bypass lost approximately 60% to 70% of excess weight. Another study of obese patients (men with BMI >34 and women with BMI >38) compared bariatric surgery outcomes to conventional (nonsurgical) treatment outcomes over an 11-year period. The nonsurgical group remained within 2% of study entry weight. At the study conclusion, weight losses from baseline were 25% for gastric bypass and 14% for gastric banding. When adjusted for age, sex, and comorbidities, the surgical group had a significant 29% reduction in mortality compared with the control group.

Whereas the mortality rate of bariatric surgery is generally less than 1%, adverse effects and complications are common, with unexpected rehospitalization rates ranging from 6% to 20%. Complications of gastric banding procedures include intractable nausea and vomiting, staple line disruption, band erosion, marginal ulcers, stomal obstruction, and severe gastroesophageal reflux disease. Complications of gastric bypass include anastomotic leaks, ventral hernias, bleeding, vitamin deficiencies, wound infection, stomal stenosis, cholelithiasis, and wound infections. Dumping syndrome may occur (see MKSAP 15 Gastroenterology and Hepatology). Nutritional deficiencies of vitamin $B_{12}$, iron, calcium, folic acid, and 25-hydroxyvitamin D are common in patients after gastric bypass. Less frequently, deficiencies of magnesium, copper, zinc, vitamin A, other B-complex

| TABLE 35 Comparison of Commonly Used Bariatric Surgery Techniques | | |
|---|---|---|
| Characteristic | Laparoscopic Adjustable Gastric Banding | Roux-en-Y Gastric Bypass |
| Mechanism | Restrictive | Restrictive and malabsorptive |
| Technique | Adjustable silicone ring is placed around the top part of the stomach, creating a 15-30 mL pouch. | 7-10 mL gastric pouch is separated from the rest of the stomach and connected to the small intestine, bypassing the rest of the stomach and duodenum. |
| Dietary program | Patients must consume <800 kcal/d for 18-36 months, 1000-1200 kcal/d thereafter. Certain foods can get "stuck" (rice, bread, dense meats, nuts), causing pain and vomiting. | Patients must consume <800 kcal/d in the first 12-18 months; 1000-1200 kcal/d thereafter in three small, high-protein meals per day. Patients must avoid sugar and fats to prevent "dumping syndrome." |
| Initial hospital length of stay | <1 d | 3-4 d |
| Weight loss | 27% excess weight loss | 60%-70% excess weight loss |
| 30-day mortality | 0.1% | 0.5% |
| Incidence of postoperative complications | 10% | 15% |

vitamins, and vitamin C may occur. Pulmonary embolism is a common but preventable complication in bariatric surgery.

### Bibliography

Adams KF, Schatzkin A, Harris TB, et al. Overweight, obesity, and mortality in a large prospective cohort of persons 50 to 71 years old. N Engl J Med. 2006;355(8):763-778. [PMID: 16926275]

Buchwald H, Avidor Y, Braunwald E, et al. Bariatric surgery: a systematic review and meta-analysis [erratum in JAMA. 2005; 293(14):1728]. JAMA. 2004;292(14):1724-3177. [PMID: 15479938]

Gardner CD, Kiazand A, Alhassan S. Comparison of the Atkins, Zone, Ornish, and LEARN diets for change in weight and related risk factors among overweight premenopausal women: the A TO Z Weight Loss Study: a randomized trial [erratum in JAMA. 2007;298(2):178]. JAMA. 2007;297(9):969-977. [PMID: 17341711]

Nordmann AJ, Nordmann A, Briel M, et al. Effects of low-carbohydrate vs low-fat diets on weight loss and cardiovascular risk factors: a meta-analysis of randomized controlled trials [erratum in Arch Intern Med. 2006;166(8):932]. Arch Intern Med. 2006;166(3):285-293. [PMID: 16476868]

Rucker D, Padwal R, Li SK, Curioni C, Lau DC. Long term pharmacotherapy for obesity and overweight: updated meta-analysis [erratum in BMJ. 2007;335(7629):doi: 10.1136/bmj.39406.519132.AD]. BMJ. 2007;335(7631);1194-1199. [PMID: 18006966]

Sjöström L, Narbro K, Sjöström CD, et al; Swedish Obese Subjects Study. Effects of bariatric surgery on mortality in Swedish obese subjects. N Engl J Med. 2007;357(8):741-752. [PMID: 17715408]

# Men's Health

## Sexual Dysfunction

Sexual dysfunction is more prevalent than previously recognized and can adversely affect quality of life. It is important to ascertain the specific sexual problem—erectile dysfunction, decreased libido, or premature ejaculation—as the workup and treatment will differ.

## Erectile Dysfunction

Erectile dysfunction (ED) is defined as the consistent or recurrent inability to attain or maintain a penile erection adequate for sexual performance. The etiology of ED, previously assumed to be mainly psychogenic, is now thought to be more organic or multifactorial. The presence of nocturnal or early morning erections and rapid onset of erectile dysfunction suggest a psychogenic rather than organic cause. Of the organic etiologies, vascular disease and diabetes mellitus predominate.

### Risk Factors

The prevalence of ED increases significantly with age, increasing approximately 10% per decade from the fifth decade on.

Besides a decline in physiologic function, older age is usually associated with other conditions that increase the risk of ED, most commonly hypertension, hyperlipidemia, diabetes mellitus, and the metabolic syndrome. Diabetes may increase risk of ED as much as four-fold; ED in this population is associated with duration of disease, glycemic control, and associated complications (neurogenic and vascular). Other endocrine problems associated with ED include hypogonadism and thyroid disease. Other risk factors include smoking, obesity, cardiovascular disease, certain medications (antidepressants and antihypertensive agents), and alcohol and drug abuse. ED and cardiovascular disease share many risk factors, and whereas cardiovascular disease can cause ED, a diagnosis of ED often precedes and may be a marker for silent heart disease. Lower urinary tract symptoms (filling symptoms—frequency, urgency, dysuria, nocturia; or voiding symptoms—hesitancy, dribbling, overflow incontinence), radical prostatectomy, and spinal cord injury are also associated with ED.

### Diagnosis and Evaluation

Many men are reluctant to volunteer information about sexual dysfunction, and it is incumbent on the physician to open the discussion and ask appropriate questions in such a manner that the patient feels comfortable to answer. The sexual history should include a detailed description of the symptoms, including onset, severity, and duration. Standardized questionnaires such as the Sexual Health Inventory for Men (SHIM) and International Index of Erectile Function (IIEF) may be helpful. (The SHIM can be downloaded at www.erectilefunction.org/tool_kit/Shim.pdf; an interactive version of the five-item version of the IIEF is available at www.medal-reg.com/qhc/medal/ch16/16_09/16-09-07-ver9.php3.)

Although it is not usually informative in the patient with ED, a physical examination should be performed, with a focus on the cardiovascular system (including blood pressure and peripheral pulses), genitalia (penile plaques, Peyronie disease, small testes) and secondary sexual characteristics, rectal examination (diminished sphincter tone, absent bulbocavernous reflex, prostate gland enlargement), and evidence of neuropathy.

Laboratory testing (blood glucose, lipid profile, thyroid-stimulating hormone, blood urea nitrogen/creatinine) and electrocardiogram should be performed to identify any systemic diseases commonly associated with ED. Measurement of morning total or free serum testosterone level is controversial, as is prostate-specific antigen (PSA) testing. Vascular evaluation, including nocturnal penile tumescence, is not recommended routinely for patients with ED.

### Treatment

Therapies for ED should be based on the preferences of the patient and partner. Options include lifestyle modifications, oral erectogenic agents, vacuum constriction devices (for patients with contraindications to oral therapy), injection therapies (intraurethral or intrapenile), testosterone replacement (in patients with hypogonadism), psychological counseling, and penile prostheses (**Figure 16**). Lifestyle modifications often suggested for patients with ED include smoking cessation, diet and exercise, and weight loss; although small studies have shown some improvement in ED scores with these modifications, their value may be more related to the elevated cardiovascular risk that accompanies ED.

Phosphodiesterase-5 (PDE-5) inhibitors are generally considered first-line therapy for ED and include sildenafil, vardenafil, and tadalafil. These agents increase penile cyclic guanosine monophosphate (cGMP), facilitating smooth muscle relaxation and allowing inflow of blood. All of these drugs have been shown to improve erectile function, as

measured by successful sexual intercourse attempts and improved scores on various survey instruments. There are no direct comparisons to support superiority of any one agent, as the populations studied differ in various characteristics.

The PDE-5 inhibitors vary in their duration of action, interaction with food and other medications, and adverse effects (**Table 36**). Limited case reports of nonarteritic anterior ischemic optic neuropathy in men taking PDE-5 inhibitors have raised the possibility of an association with this condition. Treatment failure may result from lack of patient education or improper use (timing, taking with food, inadequate sexual stimulation), inadequate dose, performance anxiety or unrealistic expectations, an inadequate trial (see Figure

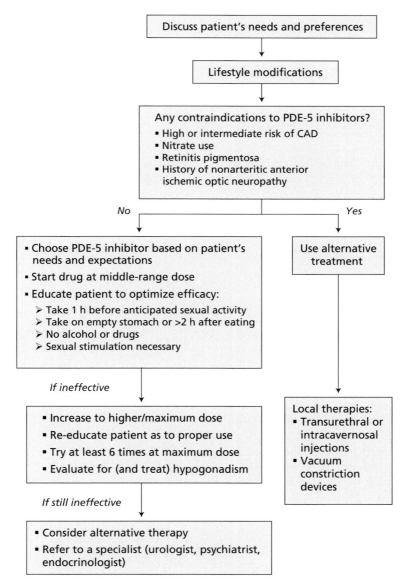

**FIGURE 16.**
**Treatment of erectile dysfunction.**

CAD = coronary artery disease; PDE = phosphodiesterase.

| **TABLE 36** Characteristics of Phosphodiesterase-5 Inhibitors for Erectile Dysfunction | | | |
|---|---|---|---|
| **Characteristic** | **Sildenafil** | **Tadalafil** | **Vardenafil** |
| Dose range | 25-100 mg | 5-20 mg[a] | 5-20 mg |
| Tmax (median) | 1 h (30 min-2 h) | 2 h (30 min-6 h) | 1 h (30 min-2 h) |
| Duration of action | At least 4 h | Up to 36 h | At least 4 h |
| Change in Cmax with high-fat meal | ↓ 29% Tmax delay: 1 h | No change | ↓ 18-50% Tmax delay: 1-2 h |
| Metabolism | Hepatic | Hepatic | Hepatic |
| Side effects | | | |
|   Headache | +++ | +++ | +++ |
|   Flushing | ++ | + | ++ |
|   Dyspepsia | +/++ | ++ | + |
|   Rhinitis | + | + | ++ |
|   Visual disturbances | + (blue tinge) | +/− | +/− |
|   Back pain/myalgia | ? | + | ? |

Cmax = maximum concentration; Tmax = time of maximal drug concentration.

[a]Dose range listed is for taking as needed, prior to anticipated sexual activity. The dosage for once-daily use (without regard to timing of sexual activity) is 2.5-5 mg.

16), hypogonadism, or an incorrect diagnosis (premature ejaculation or hypoactive sexual desire disorder).

Prior to prescribing a PDE-5 inhibitor, the patient's cardiovascular risk category and subsequent evaluation should be based on the Princeton Guidelines (**Table 37**). Sexual activity is usually associated with an exercise level of 4 or fewer metabolic equivalents, and although the relative risk of myocardial infarction with exercise is increased, the absolute risk is extremely low. PDE-5 inhibitors should be avoided in patients using organic nitrates (owing to a risk of severe hypotension) or in whom sexual activity is inadvisable owing to significant cardiac disease.

Intracavernous injection and transurethral administration of alprostadil (prostaglandin E$_1$) increase the rate of successful intercourse and may be used in patients who cannot take or fail to respond to PDE-5 inhibitors. Adverse effects include pain and burning. Testosterone therapy (intramuscular or transdermal) is helpful in patients with hypogonadism. Psychosexual therapy may be helpful if a psychogenic cause is suspected. However, selective serotonin reuptake inhibitors (SSRIs) can cause erectile dysfunction and delay ejaculation, although the latter effect may be helpful in treating premature ejaculation. In men who do not respond to any of the above therapies (or who have contraindications to them), vacuum erection devices and penile implants may be considered.

## Premature Ejaculation

Premature ejaculation is one of the most prevalent male sexual dysfunctions, but it is often misdiagnosed or overlooked. Although there is no universally used definition or validated assessments to make this diagnosis, the American Urological Association (AUA) recommends the diagnosis be based solely upon sexual history of a shortened intravaginal latency time, reduced control over ejaculation, low satisfaction with sexual intercourse, and distress regarding the condition. Treatment of premature ejaculation involves behavioral techniques to

decrease sensory input and off-label use of selective serotonin reuptake inhibitors, tricyclic antidepressants, PDE-5 inhibitors, and topical anesthetics.

## Decreased Libido

Decreased libido (hypoactive sexual desire disorder, or HSDD) may be caused by hormonal deficiency, psychogenic causes, or medication effects. Low testosterone levels are associated with declines in androgen-related sexual behavior in men. Hyperprolactinemia may cause hypogonadism, and the neuroleptic activity of prolactin may lead to depression and anxiety. Relationship difficulties often coexist with HSDD, and it may be difficult to establish the cause-effect relationship. HSDD is often seen in patients with psychiatric disorders (schizophrenia, depression), and the effects of medications for these disorders on sexual function may vary. Drugs with neuroleptic activity may worsen HSDD, whereas antidepressant medications may actually result in improved sexual function more frequently than causing deterioration. Aging, chronic medical conditions (coronary artery disease, heart failure, renal failure, HIV disease) may also be associated with HSDD. The evaluation and treatment of hypogonadism is discussed in more detail in MKSAP 15 Endocrinology and Metabolism.

### KEY POINTS

- Erectile dysfunction and cardiovascular disease share similar risk factors, and erectile dysfunction may precede or be a marker for cardiovascular disease.
- Phosphodiesterase-5 inhibitors are contraindicated in patients who use nitrates.
- Intracavernosal injection or transurethral administration of alprostadil are effective alternatives for patients with erectile dysfunction who cannot take or do not respond to phosphodiesterase-5 inhibitors.

**TABLE 37** Second Princeton Consensus Conference Guidelines for Treatment of Erectile Dysfunction in Patients with Cardiovascular Disease or Cardiac Risk Factors

| Risk Level | Treatment Recommendation |
|---|---|
| **Low risk** | |
| Asymptomatic and <3 major cardiac risk factors[a] <br> Controlled hypertension <br> Mild stable angina <br> Post successful coronary revascularization <br> MI (>6-8 weeks before) <br> Mild valvular disease <br> Left ventricular dysfunction (NYHA functional class I) | Can initiate or resume sexual activity or treat for ED with PDE-5 inhibitor (if not using nitrates) |
| **Intermediate/indeterminate risk** | |
| Asymptomatic and ≥3 major cardiac risk factors[a] <br> Moderate stable angina <br> Recent MI (2-6 weeks) <br> Left ventricular dysfunction (ejection fraction <40%) or heart failure (NYHA class II) <br> Noncardiac atherosclerotic disease (clinically evident PAD, history of stroke/TIA) | Further cardiac evaluation (stress test or cardiology consultation) and restratification prior to resumption of sexual activity or treatment for ED |
| **High risk** | |
| Unstable or refractory angina <br> Uncontrolled hypertension <br> Moderate to severe heart failure (NYHA class III-IV) <br> Recent MI (<2 weeks) <br> High-risk arrhythmia <br> Obstructive hypertrophic cardiomyopathy <br> Moderate to severe valvular disease (particularly aortic stenosis) | Defer sexual activity or ED treatment until cardiac condition is stabilized and reassessed |

ED = erectile dysfunction; MI = myocardial infarction; NYHA = New York Heart Association; PAD = peripheral arterial disease; PDE = phosphodiesterase; TIA = transient ischemic attack.

[a]Major cardiac risk factors are: age, hypertension, diabetes mellitus, smoking, dyslipidemia, sedentary lifestyle, family history of premature coronary artery disease. (Male sex is excluded.)

Data from Kostis JB, Jackson G, Rosen R, et al. Sexual dysfunction and cardiac risk (the Second Princeton Consensus Conference). Am J Cardiol. 2005;96(2):313-321. [PMID: 16018863]

# Benign Prostatic Hyperplasia

## Diagnosis and Evaluation

Benign prostatic hyperplasia (BPH) is a common cause of lower urinary tract symptoms in older men. A symptom-free 46-year-old man has a 45% risk of developing BPH over a period of 30 years. Symptoms include increased urinary frequency and urgency, nocturia, poor urinary stream, a sense of incomplete emptying of the bladder, postvoid dribbling, and, less commonly, incontinence. Because these symptoms are sensitive but not specific for BPH, the differential diagnosis should include medications (diuretics, drugs with autonomic effects), neurologic conditions (spinal cord injury, stroke, dementia, multiple sclerosis), and bladder obstruction due to conditions other than BPH. A rectal examination to assess prostate size and nodularity as well as anal sphincter tone and an abdominal examination to evaluate for a palpable bladder are warranted. However, lower urinary tract symptoms are often poorly correlated with prostate gland size. A urinalysis is indicated and, if pyuria or hematuria is present, a urine culture should be performed.

The AUA guidelines recommend a baseline assessment with the AUA Symptom Index (www.prostate-cancer.org/tools/forms/aua_symptom_form.html). A score of 0 to 7 represents mild symptoms, 8 to 19, moderate symptoms; and 20 to 35, severe symptoms. Because prostate cancer seldom causes lower urinary tract symptoms, AUA guidelines do not advocate PSA testing in all patients but rather, only in those who have more than a 10-year life expectancy and those for whom PSA levels may influence BPH treatment. In fact, BPH itself often causes a mildly elevated PSA level.

## Treatment

For patients with mild BPH symptoms, watchful waiting with conservative measures may be appropriate, including the following:

- Reduce fluid intake and limit intake of caffeinated drinks and alcohol
- Review aggravating medications (diuretics, drugs with autonomic effects)
- Evaluate for cognitive impairment, especially correctible causes
- Optimize mobility

For patients in whom these measures are insufficient, two classes of medications are effective for BPH symptoms, α-antagonists and 5α-reductase inhibitors (**Table 38**). α-Antagonists relax the prostatic smooth muscle in the bladder outflow tract, act rapidly (usually within 48 hours), and are considered first-line treatment, producing a clinical response in 70% of men. All drugs in this class have similar efficacy and tend to improve symptoms by 30% to 40%. Abnormal ejaculation is a side effect and appears similar for all α-antagonists. Elderly patients are less likely to discontinue treatment because of ejaculatory dysfunction than because of cardiovascular side effects, such as postural hypotension, dizziness, and headaches.

5α-Reductase inhibitors decrease the production of dihydrotestosterone, thereby arresting prostatic hyperplasia. Because shrinkage is slow, symptoms often do not improve until after 6 months of therapy. Side effects include erectile and ejaculatory dysfunction, reduced libido, gynecomastia, and breast tenderness. 5α-Reductase inhibitors may be suitable in patients who have failed to respond to or do not tolerate α-antagonists, those with severe symptoms, and those with an obviously enlarged prostate or a PSA level above 1.4 ng/mL (1.4 µg/L). The latter two factors—prostate size and PSA level—are strong predictors of BPH disease progression. 5α-Reductase inhibitors decrease serum PSA levels by about half, and reference levels need to be adjusted if a patient is suspected of having or is being followed for prostate cancer.

The Medical Therapy of Prostatic Symptoms (MTOPS) multicenter trial looked at the long-term progress (mean 4.5 years) of patients randomized to either placebo, finasteride (a 5α-reductase inhibitor), doxazosin (an α-antagonist), or both. Monotherapy with either drug had a similar ability to prevent progression of disease (34%-39% compared with placebo) but combination therapy was more effective (66% compared with placebo). Events such as urinary retention or a need for surgery were reduced significantly by finasteride and combination therapy but not by doxazosin alone. However, combination therapy produced more side effects. Surgery is effective but can often be avoided or delayed if the patient responds to pharmacotherapy. Indications for referral for surgery include the following:

- Urinary retention (>1 episode)
- Urinary tract infection
- Bladder stones
- Renal failure with hydronephrosis
- Urinary symptoms with history of urologic surgery or trauma (including traumatic catheterizations)
- Severe BPH symptoms that have not responded to medical therapy

Open prostatectomy may be the procedure of choice for a severely enlarged or obstructive prostate. Long-term results from randomized trials comparing transurethral resection of the prostate and transurethral microwave thermotherapy show similar outcomes, suggesting the latter may be the preferred minimally invasive option.

**KEY POINTS**

- The two effective pharmacologic treatments for benign prostatic hyperplasia are α-antagonists and 5α-reductase inhibitors.
- Symptom improvement in benign prostatic hyperplasia occurs more quickly with α-antagonists (within 48 hours) than with 5α-reductase inhibitors (up to 6 months).

## Acute Testicular and Scrotal Pain

### Initial Evaluation

The history of patients presenting with acute scrotal pain should focus on onset (abrupt or gradual); quality; prior episodes; any other locations of pain (younger men may report hip or abdominal pain as the manifestation of scrotal or testicular pathology); sexual activity; any associated symptoms of dysuria, urgency, frequency, fever, or nausea/vomiting; and

**TABLE 38** Pharmacologic Treatment of Benign Prostatic Hyperplasia

| Agent | Recommended Dosage |
|---|---|
| **α-Antagonists** | |
| Tamsulosin | 0.4 mg/d (less if postural hypotension and dizziness) |
| Alfuzosin | 10 mg/d (less if postural hypotension and dizziness) |
| Doxazosin | 2-4 mg/d |
| Terazosin | 5-10 mg/d (start at 1 mg and titrate up slowly) |
| **5α-Reductase inhibitors** | |
| Finasteride | 5 mg/d |
| Dutasteride | 0.5 mg/d |

any history of trauma or surgery. On physical examination, the scrotum should be inspected and palpated and the contents transilluminated, beginning with the unaffected side. The presence of erythema or edema, any fullness or mass, and the position of the testes should be noted. Before palpation of the testicles, the cremasteric reflex should be tested, beginning with the unaffected side. The reflex is elicited by stroking the upper inner aspect of the thigh, and the testicle on the same side should rise. Other findings on palpation may include a knot in the spermatic cord in testicular torsion, crepitus of the scrotum, fluid collection (hydrocele), or fluctuance (abscess).

### Testicular Torsion

Testicular torsion occurs when the testis twists on the spermatic cord, often causing ischemia. Testicular torsion has a bimodal distribution, occurring most often in early childhood and again in preadolescence; it is rare in men older than 30 years. Patients with torsion may be in severe pain (more so than with epididymitis) and may have nausea and vomiting. Absence of the cremasteric reflex on the affected side is nearly 99% sensitive for torsion.

In torsion, the testis is usually high within the scrotum and may lie transversely, with the epididymis lying anteriorly, medially, or laterally, depending on the number of twists. Doppler flow ultrasonography is the preferred imaging method to assess blood flow to the affected testicle; however, definitive surgical intervention should never be delayed to obtain an ultrasound when torsion is the likely diagnosis.

Treatment of testicular torsion is surgical exploration and reduction. Salvage of the testicle depends upon the duration of symptoms. In patients with fewer than 6 hours of pain, salvage rates exceed 90%; if pain has been present for 24 to 48 hours, the salvage rate is reported to be from 10% to 75%; beyond 48 hours, the salvage rate is essentially 0%. Manual detorsion of the testicle can be attempted if surgery cannot be performed immediately.

### Epididymitis and Orchitis

Infectious causes of acute scrotal pain, such as epididymitis and orchitis, begin to peak in adolescence, corresponding to increased sexual activity. Inflammation and infection of the epididymis cause pain localizing to the posterior and superior aspect of the testicle. The onset of pain may be more subacute than that of torsion and may be accompanied by dysuria, increased urinary urgency and frequency, pyuria, fever, and leukocytosis. The scrotum may be edematous and erythematous. On color Doppler flow ultrasound, blood flow to the testicle and epididymis is normal or increased, in marked contrast to torsion. In men younger than 35 years, gonorrhea or chlamydial disease should be considered, based on history (see MKSAP 15 Infectious Disease). In men older than 35 years and men who practice anal intercourse, *Escherichia coli* and Enterobacteriaceae are more likely culprits, and treatment is an oral fluoroquinolone.

Orchitis, an inflammation of the testicle, is usually caused by viral infection (mumps) or extension of a bacterial infection from epididymitis or urinary tract infection; in mumps, parotiditis begins about 5 days prior to orchitis. The testicle is diffusely tender. Treatment is based on the likely causative organism.

### Other Causes of Acute Scrotal Pain

Indirect hernias may incarcerate or strangulate within the scrotum, causing severe pain with an associated mass. Ruptured aortic aneurysms may bleed into the scrotum, but this is unlikely to be the sole manifestation of a ruptured aortic aneurysm. Peritonitis may cause scrotal pain due to leaking of contents and/or pus into the scrotum through a patent processus vaginalis. Renal colic classically radiates to the ipsilateral testicle. Necrotizing fasciitis, or Fournier gangrene, is a life-threatening polymicrobial infection of the perineum, scrotum, and penis (see MKSAP 15 Infectious Disease).

---

**KEY POINTS**

- In the patient with acute scrotal pain, absence of the cremasteric reflex on the affected side is nearly 99% sensitive for testicular torsion.
- Definitive surgical intervention should never be delayed to obtain an ultrasound when testicular torsion is the likely diagnosis.

---

## Chronic Prostatitis and Pelvic Pain

### Clinical Presentation

Prostatitis has an estimated prevalence of 5% to 8% in the United States. More than 90% of symptomatic patients have chronic prostatitis/chronic pelvic pain syndrome (CP/CPPS) for which the cause remains uncertain. Conditions similar, if not identical, to what is now labeled CP/CPPS include coccygodynia, proctalgia fugax, levator ani spasm syndrome, and piriformis syndrome. Patients with CP/CPPS typically have two types of symptoms: genitourinary/pelvic pain and voiding symptoms. Pain may be located in the perineum, testicles, the tip of the penis, and the suprapubic area and may occur during or after ejaculation. Voiding symptoms include dysuria, a sense of incomplete bladder emptying, and increased frequency. Depression and anxiety are common comorbid conditions, present in at least half to two thirds of patients. There is no diagnostic physical or laboratory finding, and urine cultures are typically negative. Although leukocytes may be found in expressed prostatic secretions, post–prostate massage urine, or semen of some patients, the presence or absence of leukocytes is currently felt to have limited clinical utility in diagnosis or in predicting treatment response.

Patients with acute bacterial prostatitis present with acute symptoms of a urinary tract infection (urinary frequency and dysuria) and, occasionally, systemic symptoms, such as malaise, fever, and myalgia. Bacteriuria and pyuria typically represent infection by gram-negative bacteria such as *Escherichia coli* or by enterococci. Chronic bacterial prostatitis is characterized by recurrent infections with the same type of organisms.

## Treatment

A meta-analysis of randomized controlled trials evaluating pharmacologic treatments for CP/CPPS showed that α-blockers have the strongest evidence of efficacy, although their impact on outcomes is modest and not consistent across all trials. Antibiotics (typically a 6-week course) are the most commonly prescribed treatment, yet were not proved effective in the only two high-quality randomized controlled trials to date. Anti-inflammatory drugs are a third frequently recommended treatment, yet have only been tested in a single randomized controlled trial, and this involved a COX-2 inhibitor rather than the more commonly used NSAIDs.

Other pharmacologic treatments tested in single small trials with benefits on some but not other outcomes include finasteride, pentosan polysulfate, mepartricin (an estrogen-lowering agent), and quercetin (a bioflavonoid found in red wine, onions, and other food and considered an herbal therapy). More studies are needed before any of these can be recommended. Other popular "prostatic health" supplements, including saw palmetto, stinging nettle, *Pygeum africanum*, and zinc, do not appear effective for CP/CPPS.

### KEY POINTS

- α-Blockers are modestly effective for chronic prostatitis/chronic pelvic pain syndrome symptoms.
- Antibiotics are commonly prescribed for chronic prostatitis/chronic pelvic pain syndrome, but evidence for their efficacy is lacking.

# Hernias

Approximately 75% of hernias occur in the groin, with indirect hernias being more common than direct, right-sided more common than left, and the incidence in men greater than in women. Incisional, ventral, umbilical, and other hernias are less common. Presumed causes of inguinal hernias include acquired or congenital connective tissue disorders, maneuvers that increase intra-abdominal pressure (cough, straining from constipation or prostatism, heavy lifting), marked obesity, ascites, pregnancy, pelvic tumors, previous lower abdominal surgery, and older age.

## Diagnosis and Evaluation

Clinical presentations of hernia vary. A hernia may be asymptomatic, and a bulge may or may not be present. The patient may describe a heavy feeling or a dragging sensation that is intermittent and may radiate to the testicle, a sharp pain improved by reclining or changing position, or, if the hernia is incarcerated, severe pain. Direct hernias tend to cause fewer symptoms than indirect hernias and are less likely to become incarcerated or strangulated.

Diagnosis is made by inspection (presence of a visible bulge) or digital examination of the inguinal canal in the prone and standing positions. Various findings have been described to differentiate direct from indirect hernias, but the distinction is often difficult with reported low accuracy; in either type, most symptomatic groin hernias are surgically repaired.

## Treatment

The standard recommendation that inguinal hernias should always be surgically repaired to prevent incarceration and strangulation has been questioned in recent years. Several studies have indicated that watchful waiting rather than surgical repair is an acceptable option in men with minimal symptoms. Although a number of patients in such studies crossed over to surgery as symptoms worsened, the risk of incarceration was very low. Surgical repair usually results in improved symptoms but may be associated with long-term complications, such as postoperative neuralgia. Prior to surgical repair, underlying conditions, such as prostatic hyperplasia, should be addressed.

The standard surgical procedures are tension-free repairs with mesh (with or without a plug) and may be open or laparoscopic and either transabdominal preperitoneal (TAPP) or total extraperitoneal (TEP). Potential advantages of laparoscopic repair include less incisional pain, less persistent pain and numbness, and earlier return to work, and this approach may be preferable for bilateral or recurrent hernias. These benefits are offset, however, by the need for general anesthesia, longer operative times, and a higher risk for rare but serious complications. Cost-effectiveness analyses have reported variable findings. Risk of recurrence is low (although probably underreported) and comparable with either approach.

### KEY POINTS

- Watchful waiting is an acceptable option for men with minimally symptomatic hernias because acute hernia incarcerations are rare.
- Laparoscopic hernia repair takes longer and has a higher rate of rare but more serious complications than open mesh repair; however, recovery is quicker with less persisting pain and numbness.

## Bibliography

Dimitrakov JD, Kaplan SA, Kroenke K, Jackson JL, Freeman MR. Management of chronic prostatitis/chronic pelvic pain syndrome: an evidence-based approach. Urology. 2006;67(5):881-888. [PMID: 16698346]

Fitzgibbons RJ Jr, Giobbie-Hurder A, Gibbs JO, et al. Watchful waiting vs repair of inguinal hernia in minimally symptomatic men: a randomized clinical trial [erratum in JAMA. 2006;295(23):2726]. JAMA. 2006;295(3):285-292. [PMID: 16418463]

Kostis JB, Jackson G, Rosen R, et al. Sexual dysfunction and cardiac risk (the Second Princeton Consensus Conference). Am J Cardiol. 2005;96(12B):85M-93M. [PMID: 16387575]

McConnell JD, Roehrborn CB, Bautista OM, et al; Medical Therapy of Prostatic Symptoms (MTOPS) Research Group. The long-term effect of doxazosin, finasteride, and combination therapy on the clinical prognosis of benign prostatic hyperplasia. N Engl J Med. 2003;349(25):2387-2398. [PMID: 14681504]

McVary KT. Clinical practice. Erectile dysfunction. N Engl J Med. 2007;357(24):2472-2481. [PMID: 18077811]

Patel AK, Chapple CR. Benign prostatic hyperplasia: treatment in primary care. BMJ. 2006;333(7567):535-559. [PMID: 16960209]

Ringdahl E, Teague L. Testicular torsion. Am Fam Physician. 2006;74(10):1739-1743. [PMID: 17137004]

Rosenstein D, McAninch JW. Urologic emergencies. Med Clin North Am. 2004;88(2):495-518. [PMID: 15049590]

# Women's Health

## Sexual Dysfunction

### Approach to the Patient

Sexual dysfunction in women is common, affecting nearly half of all women at some time. Sexual dysfunction occurs at any age, may follow events such as childbirth or surgery, and is more common as women age. Nevertheless, women are often hesitant to raise their concerns and physicians rarely inquire about sexual health. Importantly, personal or relationship distress resulting from the concern is part of defining sexual dysfunction.

A brief sexual history can be integrated into an examination as a routine part of the review of systems (**Figure 17**). Validated screening instruments, such as the Female Sexual Function Index (www.fsfi-questionnaire.com/), may also be useful. In response to a concern or anticipated event (such as surgery), a more in-depth sexual history may involve seeing a patient and her partner together as well as individually (**Table 39**). This comprehensive approach is based on expert opinion and should be tailored based on the specific concern, with referral to a specialist (such as a psychiatrist, sex therapist, or marital counselor) if warranted.

Medical disorders (**Table 40**) and medications (**Table 41**) can affect the sexual response, either directly or through alterations in body image, disfigurement, fatigue, and dependency. Pelvic examination is necessary to confirm or exclude causes such as vaginal atrophy, infection, sexually transmitted diseases, uterine abnormalities, or malignancy. Laboratory testing alone is unlikely to be helpful in uncovering a cause of sexual dysfunction, but testing should be considered as indicated by the history and physical examination.

The sexual response involves *desire* (thoughts and fantasies about sexual activity), *arousal* (characterized by pelvic vasocongestion, vaginal lubrication, and swelling of the external genitalia), *orgasm*, and *resolution*. For women, there normally may not be a consistent progression from desire to arousal to orgasm. Sexual function evolves with age and with issues of intimacy, relationships, and social and cultural variations and expectations. Adults remain sexually active into the eighth and ninth decades of life, and it is important not to assume sexual inactivity, presume sexual preferences, or assume that sexual activity is limited to intercourse.

### Female Sexual Desire Disorders

#### Hypoactive Sexual Desire Disorder

Hypoactive sexual desire disorder affects up to 30% of women. It can be associated with aging or surgical menopause (probably due to a combination of lack of estrogen and falling androgen levels), medication side effects, or endocrinopathies. Desire may be considered to have three components: *drive*—spontaneous sexual interest or wanting to be sexual (which declines with age in both men and women); *cognition*—an individual's beliefs and values about sex; and *motivation*—the interpersonal connection, which can

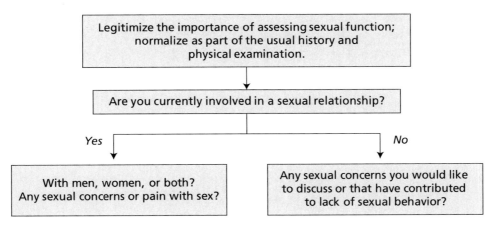

**FIGURE 17.**
Two-to-three minute basic screening sexual history for women.

| TABLE 39 Information Needed to Assess and Diagnose Sexual Dysfunction in Women | |
|---|---|
| **Information Requested** | **Details from the Couple** |
| Sexual problem and reason for seeking help at this time | Ask patients to describe problems in their own words, request clarification with direct questions, provide options rather than ask leading questions, provide support and encouragement, acknowledge their embarrassment, and reassure patients that sexual problems are common. |
| Duration, consistency, and priority of problems | Clarify whether problems are present in all situations. If there is more than one problem, which is most troubling? |
| Context of sexual problems | Assess the emotional intimacy of the couple, activity or behavior just before sexual activity, degree of privacy they have during sexual activity, degree of sexual communication, time of day and fatigue level when sexual activity occurs, use of birth control (adequacy, type), risk of sexually transmitted diseases, usefulness of sexual stimulation, and sexual knowledge. |
| Each partner's sexual response other than that related to the problem | Elicit this information with respect to the present and the period before the onset of the problem. |
| Reaction of each partner to the problem | Determine how each has reacted emotionally, sexually, and behaviorally. |
| Previous help sought by either partner | Assess compliance with the previous recommendations and their effectiveness. |
| **Details from Each Partner When Seen Alone** | |
| Partner's own assessment of the problem | Symptom severity (such as a total lack of desire) may be easier to disclose in the partner's absence. |
| Sexual response with self-stimulation | Also inquire about sexual thoughts and fantasies. |
| Past sexual experiences | Discuss positive and negative aspects. |
| Developmental history | Determine relationships to others in the home during childhood and adolescence. Were there losses or traumas? Was he or she emotionally close to anyone? Was he or she given physical affection, love, and respect? |
| Past or current sexual, emotional, or physical abuse | Explain that questions about abuse are routine and do not necessarily imply causation of sexual problems. It is helpful to ask whether the partner has ever felt hurt or threatened in the current relationship and, if so, whether he or she wishes to give more information. |
| Physical health, especially conditions leading to debility and fatigue, impaired mobility, or difficulties with self-image (e.g., from the presence of stomas, disfiguring surgery, or incontinence) | Ask specifically about medications with known sexual side effects, including selective serotonin reuptake inhibitors, β-blockers, antiandrogens, gonadotropin-releasing hormone agonists, and oral contraceptives. |
| Evaluation of mood | Correlation of sexual function and mood (including anxiety and depression) warrants routine screening for a mood disorder, by means of either a questionnaire (such as the Beck Depression Inventory) or a semistructured series of questions. |

be affected by relationship issues, worries, and stress. Treatment can involve treatment of an identifiable underlying cause, psychotherapy, and/or sex therapy (individual or couples). There are no treatments approved by the U.S. Food and Drug Administration (FDA). Testosterone preparations used in addition to estrogen hormone replacement therapy (HRT) have improved sexual function (desire) in surgically-induced postmenopausal women, but such use of testosterone is considered off-label and may not be generalizable to women after natural menopause. In addition, its use must be balanced against the risks of testosterone therapy (such as insulin resistance, lower HDL cholesterol levels) and the known adverse effects associated with postmenopausal HRT. Currently, the use of testosterone for low desire without concomitant HRT has no safety or efficacy data to support its use.

### Female Sexual Aversion Disorder

Female sexual aversion disorder is a sexual desire disorder in which there is a persistent or recurrent aversion to and avoidance of genital contact with a partner. The aversions may be caused by general or specific thoughts or activities and may have manifestations of revulsion, nausea, shortness of breath, or even panic response. Treatment is behavioral therapy to uncover the underlying events that triggered the aversion and help the woman and her partner address the ongoing avoidance and aversion.

### Female Sexual Arousal Disorder

Female sexual arousal disorder is the persistent or recurrent inability to maintain the vaginal lubrication/swelling response to completion of sexual activity. However, this definition fails to account for the lack of lubrication that is considered to be

**TABLE 40** Medical Conditions that Can Contribute to Sexual Dysfunction

| Conditions | Notes |
|---|---|
| Endocrine system | Diabetes mellitus: impaired arousal, orgasm |
| | Androgen insufficiency (levels decrease with age): hypoactive desire |
| | Estrogen deficiency (menopausal or surgical): desire and arousal impacted; vaginal atrophy |
| | Thyroid disease: impaired sexual desire |
| | Hyperprolactinemia: impaired arousal and orgasm |
| Neurologic and cerebrovascular diseases | Multiple sclerosis and spinal cord injuries: can impair desire, arousal, and orgasm; direct damage to neurologic structures involved in processing sexual stimuli |
| | Parkinson disease: low desire common |
| | Head injury: direct injury to structures to process stimuli and/or hypothalamic/pituitary injury |
| Cardiovascular disease, including myocardial infarction | Impaired desire, arousal. Low motivation to trigger or act on desire for fear of recurrent symptoms; coexisting depression in 50% of patients; symptoms are unlikely if no symptoms on exercise testing to 6 METs. |
| Psychiatric illness | Depression: impaired desire. Low desire in 50% to 60% of untreated patients. |
| Renal failure | Desire, arousal affected; low desire during sexual encounter may be triggered by knowing outcome will be painful owing to estrogen deficiency and associated dyspareunia. |
| Lower urinary tract disease, including incontinence | Desire, arousal, orgasm affected. Leakage of urine during intercourse or orgasm reduces desire. |

MET = metabolic equivalent.

Information from Kingsberg SA. Taking a sexual history. Obstet Gynecol Clin North Am. 2006;33(4):535-547. [PMID: 17116499] and Basson R, Schultz WW. Sexual sequelae of general medical disorders. Lancet. 2007 Feb 3;369(9559):409-424. [PMID: 17276781]

**TABLE 41** Medications that Can Affect Sexual Response

| Category | Specific Agents |
|---|---|
| Psychotropic medications | Antidepressants (SSRIs, SNRIs, tricyclic antidepressants, monoamine oxidase inhibitors), antipsychotics, benzodiazepines, mood stabilizers |
| Antihypertensive agents | $\beta$-Blockers, $\alpha$-blockers, diuretics |
| Cardiovascular agents | Lipid-lowering drugs, digoxin |
| Histamine $H_2$-receptor blockers | |
| Hormonal therapies | Oral contraceptives, estrogens, progestins, antiandrogens, gonadotropin-releasing hormone agonists |
| Narcotics | |
| Amphetamines | |
| Anticonvulsants | |
| Corticosteroids | |
| Protease inhibitors | |

SNRI = serotonin-norepinephrine reuptake inhibitor; SSRI = selective serotonin reuptake inhibitor.

Adapted with permission from Kingsberg SA. Taking a sexual history. Obstet Gynecol Clin North Am. 2006;33(4):535-547. [PMID: 17116499] Copyright 2006, with permission from Elsevier.

a normal part of aging; it also does not explicitly incorporate the importance of the subjective experience of arousal that may or may not occur. Arousal disorders can be common after pelvic surgery. Treatment involves using over-the-counter lubricants, behavioral techniques, and partner counseling to draw awareness to the arousal response. The only FDA-approved therapy is a clitoral vacuum device that enhances clitoral and genital blood flow and arousal. Phosphodiesterase inhibitors have not been shown to be effective.

### Female Orgasmic Disorder

There is significant variability in the normal orgasmic response in women, and some activities, such as manual stimulation, more reliably produce orgasm than do other activities, such as sexual intercourse. Female orgasmic disorder is the persistent or recurrent delay in or absence of orgasm following a normal excitement phase, with resulting personal or interpersonal distress. Female orgasmic disorder has a prevalence of 20% to 40% and is more common in younger women,

women with diabetes mellitus, and those who engage less frequently in sexual activity. Many factors can play a role, including performance anxiety, social and cultural factors, and religious beliefs.

Treatment involves cognitive-behavioral approaches in which negative attitudes and anxiety are addressed along with behavioral treatments such as directed masturbation, sensate focus, and systematic desensitization done in private. The clitoral vacuum device may also be used for female orgasmic disorder. Selective serotonin reuptake inhibitors (SSRIs) commonly cause difficulty in achieving orgasm and may even cause anorgasmia. Treatment for SSRI-associated orgasm disorders includes reducing the medication dose, changing the medication (if possible), and/or cognitive-behavioral therapy. There is no conclusive evidence supporting the use of phosphodiesterase inhibitors, $\alpha_2$-adrenergic receptor antagonists (yohimbine), or dopaminergic agents.

### Female Sexual Pain Disorders

Any woman with pain associated with sexual activity must have a pelvic examination to evaluate for pelvic pathology.

#### Dyspareunia

Dyspareunia is coital pain that is persistent and recurrent; occurs before, during, or after sexual intercourse; and is not explicitly caused by lack of lubrication or vaginismus (although this can be difficult to differentiate). It affects 15% to 20% of women and may be more common in younger women. Patients may describe pain on entry or deep pain. Pain on entry may be due to vulvodynia (poorly localized pain, which may be unprovoked), lack of lubrication, vaginismus, or other processes involving the external genitalia, such as herpes simplex virus infection, Bartholin gland inflammation, vestibulitis, and lichen sclerosus. Deeper pain may reflect a pelvic pathology (such as chronic pelvic inflammatory disease, malignancy, endometriosis, inflammatory bowel disease, or lower urinary tract disease).

#### Vaginismus

Vaginismus is a persistent or recurrent involuntary spasm of the outer third of the pelvic floor musculature, which can make insertion of a penis, finger, speculum, tampon, or other object difficult or impossible. Patients may describe pain, burning, or a sensation of "hitting a wall" with attempted intercourse. The response often occurs in anticipation of pain but is involuntary. This response may be to specific stimuli only (such as intercourse or pelvic examination) or may be generalized to any object. Treatment involves cognitive-behavioral approaches including individual and partner therapy and systematic desensitization. In systematic desensitization therapy, patients learn deep muscle relaxation techniques; they then learn to insert dilators of increasing size into the vagina over a period of several weeks. Initially, the woman does this privately; the partner is involved in counseling

throughout, and attempts at intercourse are delayed until the final stages of treatment. Although systematic desensitization is widely recommended as treatment, there are no controlled trials of its effectiveness. Finally, vaginismus should prompt an exploration of possible sexual trauma.

**KEY POINTS**

- Women with pain associated with sexual activity must undergo a pelvic examination.
- The diagnosis of sexual dysfunction requires that the concern causes personal or interpersonal distress.
- Selective serotonin reuptake inhibitors often cause orgasm disorders.

## Breast Mass

### Epidemiology and Clinical Presentation

Palpable breast lesions include discrete masses (cystic or solid), thickenings, and generalized nodularity. Although most of these findings are benign, especially in premenopausal women, failure to diagnose breast cancer is one of the most common causes of litigation. The differential diagnosis of a breast mass varies by age and includes cysts, fibroadenomas, fibrocystic changes, fat necrosis, and carcinoma (**Table 42**).

Diffuse lumpiness is usually caused by fibrocystic changes, which may be painful and vary with the menstrual cycle. Breast cysts occur most often in women younger than 40 years and also fluctuate with the menstrual cycle. In women younger than 30 years, a firm rubbery lump is most likely a fibroadenoma. A firm discrete lump in a woman between ages 30 to 50 years most commonly represents a fibroadenoma, cyst, fibrocystic changes, or ductal or lobular hyperplasia. A firm discrete mass in women older than 50 years may be a cyst or carcinoma (in situ or invasive).

Important risk factors for breast cancer include older age, early menarche, late first childbirth, late menopause, and presence of proliferative breast disease. Additional risk factors are discussed in MKSAP 15 Hematology and Oncology.

### Diagnosis and Evaluation

The absence of risk factors should not alter management of the patient with a breast mass, and usual clinical practice requires the "triple test"—palpation, mammography (with or without ultrasound), and surgical evaluation for biopsy. When vague nodularity or thickening is present (as opposed to a discrete mass) in premenopausal women, physical examination should be repeated at mid-cycle 1 month later and if still present, managed as noted above; postmenopausal women should undergo immediate evaluation. Imaging is indicated not only to evaluate the palpable mass but also to screen for other masses on the same or contralateral breast. Because 10% to 15% of palpable breast cancers are not detected by mammography, a negative mammogram does not eliminate the

**TABLE 42** Evaluation of Clinical Breast Abnormalities

| Breast Abnormality | Diagnostic Test |
|---|---|
| Palpable lump or mass and age <30 y | US. (Consider observation to assess resolution within 1 or 2 menstrual cycles. If persistent, do US.) If asymptomatic and cystic on US, observe. If symptomatic or not clearly cystic on US, aspirate. If aspirate fluid is bloody or a mass persists following aspiration, biopsy or excise for diagnosis. If mass is solid on US, do mammogram and obtain tissue diagnosis (fine needle aspiration, core biopsy, or surgical excision). If not visualized on US, obtain mammogram and obtain tissue diagnosis. |
| Palpable lump or mass and age ≥30 y | Mammogram: if BI-RADS[a] category 1-3 obtain US and follow protocol above. If BI-RADS category 4-5 obtain tissue diagnosis. |
| Nipple discharge, no mass, any age | Bilateral, milky: pregnancy test (if negative, endocrine evaluation). Persistent, spontaneous, unilateral, one duct, or serous/bloody: cytology optional, obtain mammogram and surgical referral for duct exploration. |
| Thickening or asymmetry and age <30 y | Consider unilateral mammogram; if normal, reassess in 3-6 months; if abnormal, obtain tissue diagnosis. |
| Thickening or asymmetry and age ≥30 y | Obtain bilateral mammogram; if normal, reassess in 3-6 months; if abnormal, obtain tissue diagnosis. |
| Skin changes (erythema, peau d'orange, scaling, nipple excoriation, eczema) and age <30 y | Consider mastitis: treat with antibiotics if appropriate and reevaluate in 2 weeks. Otherwise, evaluate as below. |
| Skin changes (erythema, peau d'orange, scaling, nipple excoriation, eczema) and age ≥30 y | Obtain bilateral mammogram; if normal, obtain skin biopsy; if abnormal or indeterminate, obtain needle biopsy or excision (also consider skin punch biopsy). |

US = ultrasonography.

[a]Breast Imaging Reporting and Data System: BI-RADS 1: negative; BI-RADS 2: benign finding; BI-RADS 3: probably benign finding—short-interval follow-up suggested; BI-RADS 4: suspicious abnormality—consider biopsy; BI-RADS 5: highly suggests malignancy—take appropriate action.

need for a biopsy. Ultrasound serves to distinguish cystic from solid masses. A cystic mass should be aspirated and the fluid sent for cytologic evaluation if bloody or recurrent. A solid mass requires biopsy by fine-needle aspiration, core needle, or excision. A benign biopsy in a woman with a negative mammogram still requires close follow-up, as documented by a study in which breast cancer developed in 707 of 9087 women with previous benign breast biopsies followed for a median of 15 years. Risk factors were noted to be histologic classification (atypia or proliferative changes) and family history of breast cancer.

**KEY POINTS**

- Although most breast masses are benign, workup to exclude cancer is mandatory.

- Basic workup of a breast mass includes bilateral mammography and fine-needle aspiration or ultrasonography.

- A negative mammogram does not exclude breast cancer, particularly in a patient with a palpable mass.

# Breast Pain

## Clinical Presentation

Breast pain can be classified as cyclic mastalgia, noncyclic mastalgia, or extramammary pain (chest wall syndromes). Cyclic mastalgia is the most common and is related to the menstrual cycle. Pain is dull, heavy, or aching; diffuse and bilateral; and involves the upper outer breast region with radiation to the upper arm and axilla. Although histologic, hormonal, fluid-electrolyte, nutritional, and psychological associations have been described, the cause of cyclic mastalgia is unknown. Cyclic mastalgia may be weakly associated with breast cancer (odds ratios from 1.35 to 3.32 depending on severity of symptoms), but there is conflicting evidence with noncyclic mastalgia (2% to 7% presenting with pain in one study and odds ratio of 0.63 in another).

Noncyclic mastalgia is constant or intermittent and is not associated with the menstrual cycle. It tends to occur at a later age, and it is usually unilateral and localized within a quadrant. The cause of most cases of noncyclic mastalgia is unknown but may be related more to an anatomic than a hormonal cause. However, estrogens, progestagens, antidepressants, antihypertensive agents, and other medications have been associated with noncyclic breast pain.

## Evaluation

The history should include the quality and location of the pain, severity and limitation of activities, relationship to physical activity, other breast symptoms, and medications. A careful clinical breast examination and evaluation of the chest wall and surrounding structures should be performed. Breast pain often prompts women to seek medical care because of concerns for cancer, but malignancy is uncommon in women with a normal clinical examination. Ultrasonography should be considered for focal, persistent breast pain and mammography for women older than 30 years or with risk factors for breast cancer (although the yield is usually low).

## Treatment

Severe pain may warrant treatment. Nonpharmacologic interventions include reassurance; using a supportive, well-fitting bra; and dietary change (low fat, methylxanthine restriction, vitamin E, evening primrose oil), although the supporting evidence for these measures is mixed. Pharmacologic interventions include NSAIDs and the hormonally active agents danazol, tamoxifen, and bromocriptine. Danazol is the only FDA-approved medication for mastalgia, but it is teratogenic and is contraindicated in women with a history of venous thromboembolism. An adjustment in dose or preparation of hormonal therapy may be considered. Cyclic mastalgia typically responds better to treatment than noncyclic mastalgia with a significant percentage of patients' symptoms resolving spontaneously; however, the rate of recurrent symptoms is high.

### KEY POINTS

- Most women with breast pain respond to reassurance and nonpharmacologic measures.
- Pharmacologic therapy options for women with severe breast pain include NSAIDs, danazol, tamoxifen, and bromocriptine.

## Contraception

### Oral Contraceptive Pills

Oral contraceptive pills (OCPs) are the most popular method of contraception in the United States, and recent modifications have improved their safety and tolerability without reducing efficacy. Newer alternative preparations generally have lower doses of estrogen, reducing the risk of complications such as thromboembolic disease (an especially significant risk in women who smoke cigarettes). In addition, whereas the earlier generation of OCPs typically provide 7 out of 28 hormone-free days in each cycle, inducing menses, newer pill regimens often reduce the hormone-free days in each cycle or extend the time between hormone-free cycles to as long as 3 months. This decreases the extent or frequency of menstrual bleeding while also reducing hormone-related mood swings and bloating. Some OCPs may even induce amenorrhea, but numerous studies document that extended-cycle and continuous OCP regimens are safe and effective. Because the estrogen dose in OCPs is usually significantly lower than what has been used in postmenopausal estrogen replacement, the cardiovascular risks are not as great, although there is still a greater risk of myocardial infarction for women older than 35 years who smoke or have hypertension. Iron-deficiency anemia is much less common in women who take OCPs owing to less menstrual blood loss. The failure rate

(usually defined as experiencing unintended pregnancy within the first year of use) with OCPs is 0.3% with perfect use, but in practice is as high as 8%, most often due to missing pills.

### Long-Acting Progesterone Compounds

A contraceptive method that has been particularly useful in reducing pregnancy in teens is long-acting progesterone compounds with intramuscular depot medroxyprogesterone acetate; implantable and subcutaneous forms are also available. This approach is particularly useful for those who are more likely to forget to take a pill each day, such as teenagers. Whereas there is evidence that the use of long-acting progesterone compounds reduces bone mineral density, this effect is fully reversible. Other recently approved alternatives include an ethinyl estradiol-norelgestromin patch that is changed weekly and etonogestrel in an ethylene vinyl acetate rod that can be placed in the subcutaneous tissue of the upper arm to provide 3 years of contraceptive action. Like OCPs, long-acting progesterone compounds have a failure rate of 0.3% with ideal use, but in practice pregnancy occurs in up to 3% of women in the first year, with missed or delayed appointments largely responsible.

### Barrier Methods

Barrier methods avoid hormone-induced side effects but have several disadvantages, such as the need for placement, which may be awkward; less comfort; messiness; and, most troublesome, a higher failure rate. Barrier methods include male and female condoms (15%-20% failure rate in actual practice), diaphragms (15%), cervical caps (15%-30%), and vaginal rings (7%-10%). Silicone vaginal devices have proved superior to older latex models by providing greater durability while avoiding problems with allergies and odor. Spermicides are insufficient by themselves, but do provide added efficacy when used in conjunction with barrier methods. Male and female condoms are a particularly good choice, whether used alone or in conjunction with other methods, for the prevention of sexually transmitted diseases (STDs) in those who are not monogamous. Microbicides have the potential to decrease STD transmission, but the only one currently approved in the United States, nonoxynol-9, is ineffective in this regard, and may even increase the risk of HIV transmission through disruption of the vaginal epithelium.

### Intrauterine Devices

Intrauterine devices (IUDs) are the most widely used method of contraception worldwide, with efficacy greater than 99%. IUDs that incorporate a levonorgestrel intrauterine system are particularly effective, with only 1/1000 users becoming pregnant in 1 year, comparable to rates with male or female sterilization. However, their use is relatively infrequent in the United States (1% compared with 15%-30% or more in other nations), likely due largely to repercussions of the Dalkon Shield controversy, which, by virtue of its design, significantly increased the risk of pelvic inflammatory disease. One of the greatest advantages of IUDs is that after being put in place, they do not require action by the user, as do condoms or oral contraceptives, for example, and they can remain effective for 7 to 10 years or more. The likelihood of pregnancy or adverse effects, including expulsion or removal because of bleeding or pain, decreases with age, making the IUD particularly well-suited to older women who already have children and desire to prevent further pregnancies. A long-term World Health Organization study of copper IUDs (one of the more commonly used types) found that whereas the risk of expulsion is 6% in the first year, and removal because of pain, bleeding, or another medical indication is approximately 12% in the first year, such complications are much less common after the first year, with efficacy remaining high for up to 10 to 12 years.

## Sterilization

Among the most effective contraceptive methods, with failure rates approximately 1 in 1000 in 1 year, are sterilization techniques—vasectomy in men and tubal ligation in women. Vasectomy is the simplest, safest, and most effective sterilization method, with failure exceedingly rare when postprocedure oligospermia is documented. Concerns about an increased risk of heart disease, prostate cancer, or testicular cancer do not appear to be credible. Reversibility of surgical vasectomy for those who change their minds can be difficult. A reversible, nonsurgical vasectomy, involving injection of a plug into the vas deferens, has achieved popularity in China but has not been approved in the United States. Tubal ligation has a slightly higher failure rate than vasectomy, and in women who do become pregnant, the rate of ectopic pregnancy is high.

## Emergency Contraception

Emergency contraception is defined as the use of a drug or device to prevent pregnancy after either unprotected sexual intercourse or contraceptive failure (such as rupture of a condom). Three forms of emergency contraception are available: oral levonorgestrel (Plan B), oral mifepristone (RU-486), and a copper IUD. Levonorgestrel and mifepristone have comparable tolerability and efficacy, with failure rates slightly over 1%, and they do not require professional insertion like the IUD. Because mifepristone is currently approved in the United States only for termination of pregnancy and is not available in pharmacies, levonorgestrel, taken in two 0.75-mg doses 12 to 24 hours apart within 5 days of having had intercourse, is the preferred regimen. However, the efficacy is greater when taken closer to the time of intercourse and diminishes over the ensuing 5 days. A series of studies found no adverse events with the use of levonorgestrel; the rate of condom use was no lower and sexually transmitted diseases were no more common than in control groups. Postcoital insertion of a copper IUD within 5 days of intercourse is the most effective emergency contraceptive, with a failure rate of

only 0.1% to 0.2% when properly inserted, and there are no systemic metabolic effects, although there is a risk of fundal perforation with insertion, at a rate of approximately 1 in 3000. Once inserted, the IUD can be kept in place for up to 10 years to prevent subsequent pregnancy.

### KEY POINTS

- Newer oral contraceptives have lower doses of estrogen, decreasing the risk of thromboembolic or cardiovascular events compared with older formulations.
- Long-acting depot or implantable progesterone compounds provide effective contraception in teens or others more likely to forget to take daily pills.
- Levonorgestrel is the preferred method of emergency contraception, although a copper intrauterine device has some significant advantages.

# Menopause

Menopause is the permanent cessation of ovarian function, resulting in amenorrhea. However, since most women experience an average of 4 years of perimenopause, a period of time in which hormonal changes begin to occur and the menstrual cycle becomes irregular, menopause can usually only be diagnosed retrospectively. In the United States, the average age of menopause is 51 years, meaning that women spend one-third of their lives in a postmenopausal state. Genetics have by far the greatest influence on the age of menopause, with black and Hispanic women having an earlier onset than white women. Tobacco use and higher socioeconomic status are associated with an earlier onset of menopause, whereas greater parity predicts a later age of onset.

Hormonal changes that herald menopause begin with a decrease in ovarian inhibin production and an increase in follicle-stimulating hormone release from the pituitary gland, followed by a drop in ovarian estradiol production 6 to 12 months before menopause. The diagnosis of menopause can be established clinically, and a follicle-stimulating hormone level does not need to be obtained routinely. It may, however, be helpful in selected patients; for example, an elevated follicle-stimulating hormone level might confirm the cause of a patient's symptoms when there is some doubt, such as in a woman who enters menopause earlier than usual.

## Management of Symptoms

Vasomotor symptoms such as hot flushes and night sweats represent the single most frequent menopause-related complaint. Even so, whereas three-quarters of menopausal women in the United States experience hot flushes, only a fraction of these women actually seek medical attention for this symptom. Hot flushes gradually diminish over time, but 26% to 50% of women continue to experience them for up to 10 years, and 10% report a duration of 11 years or more. Hot flushes are more common at night, often interfering with sleep. They typically last anywhere from 30 seconds to a few minutes and may be accompanied by palpitations or other symptoms of anxiety. Estrogen is the most effective treatment for the relief of hot flushes, with a 50% to 90% response rate, and evidence shows that even low doses provide effective symptom relief. Relief of hot flushes is now considered the primary reason for initiating HRT, and HRT is worth considering in nonsmokers without other significant cardiovascular risks, a history of thromboembolic disease, a personal history of breast cancer, or a first-degree relative with breast cancer. Although the USPSTF recommended against the routine use of combined estrogen and progesterone (or unopposed estrogen in women who have had a hysterectomy) for the prevention of chronic conditions, they deferred to others the evaluation of the utility of hormone replacement for the management of menopausal symptoms. The North American Menopause Society (NAMS) reviewed the available evidence and concluded that the absolute risk of HRT is low and that although the use of such therapy should be individualized, estrogen replacement (with progesterone for women with an intact uterus) is the most effective treatment for vasomotor symptoms. For women in whom HRT is contraindicated, there are modest data suggesting some benefit from antidepressants (SSRIs, the serotonin-norepinephrine reuptake inhibitor venlafaxine), clonidine, and gabapentin. There is currently insufficient evidence for the effectiveness of either physical exercise or herbal remedies such as soy proteins, black cohosh, red clover, dong quai, evening primrose, or ginseng.

Irregular menstrual bleeding typically occurs for 2 to 8 years before cessation of menses. Usually, bleeding becomes lighter and less frequent. Further evaluation is indicated for bleeding that lasts more than 7 to 10 days, is highly irregular compared with prior patterns, is more frequent than every 21 days, or recurs after at least 6 months of amenorrhea.

Vaginal atrophy and dryness are common during menopause and may result in vaginal burning and pruritus, dyspareunia, and dysuria. The NAMS review concluded that estrogen therapy is the most effective treatment of vulvar and vaginal atrophy and that estrogen vaginal cream is the preferred method of administration for women with primarily vaginal symptoms.

## Systemic Risks and Benefits of Hormone Replacement Therapy

The Women's Health Initiative (WHI) identified an increase in the risk of cardiovascular events (fatal and nonfatal myocardial infarction) during the first year of HRT; while this risk declined over time, the magnitude of the initial increase led to persistence of the effect over a mean of 5.2 years of follow-up. However, the WHI design initiated HRT in women ages 50 to 79 years, many of whom already had significant coronary artery disease risks. In fact, subgroup analysis indicates that perimenopausal or recently menopausal women may actually derive cardiovascular benefit from HRT. Women ages 50 to 59 years in the estrogen-only arm of the WHI trial had a statistically significant decrease in a global coronary score (relative risk, 0.66; CI, 0.45-0.96), and a decrease in coronary events that was nearly significant (relative risk, 0.63; CI, 0.36-1.08). The Heart and Estrogen/Progestin Replacement Study (HERS), as well as an additional follow-up study (HERS II), found no increased risk of cardiovascular events in an average of 6.8 years of follow-up. In addition, a meta-analysis of 23 randomized, controlled trials of HRT found that women within 10 years of menopause had a significant reduction in coronary events (relative risk, 0.68; CI, 0.45-0.96). The USPSTF concluded on the basis of the HERS and WHI trials that HRT should not be prescribed for prevention of cardiovascular disease in postmenopausal women.

The initiation of HRT in women well past menopause is unwise. However, low-dose HRT may in fact have a beneficial cardiovascular profile when prescribed in perimenopausal women, although further study is indicated. The WHI found increased rates of stroke in women on HRT, but again, the strokes occurred in older women. An increase was not identified for women in their 50s, although the absolute rates were low, limiting power to discern a difference. Overall, 50- to 59-year-old women receiving HRT in the WHI trial had only 70% of the mortality seen in nonusers, providing compelling evidence for benefit in the early menopausal years.

Another controversial issue is the impact of HRT on breast cancer. The WHI indicated that estrogen-progestin combination therapy appears to be associated with an increase in the risk of breast cancer. For the estrogen-only arm in the WHI, however, the overall risk of breast cancer was lower; more specifically, ductal and localized cancer decreased, while lobular or tubular cancers (which are typically small, slow growing, low grade, and well differentiated) were more common. Because unopposed estrogen increases the risk of endometrial cancer, it should only be used in women who have had hysterectomy; otherwise, it should be combined with a progestin.

Estrogen has a significant positive impact on bone mineral density, and the onset of menopause accelerates bone loss, often bringing on osteoporosis and consequent increased risk of vertebral, hip, and distal forearm fractures. The role of HRT in osteoporosis is covered in MKSAP 15 Endocrinology and Metabolism.

In summary, HRT provides symptomatic relief of hot flushes as well as vaginal atrophy and dryness, but the decision to treat must be individualized and weighed against potential risks, including thromboembolism and breast cancer. Overall, the risk-benefit ratio is greater for women closer to the start of menopause than for older women.

## KEY POINTS

- During the perimenopause period, heavier or more frequent bleeding, or menstruation after at least 6 months of amenorrhea, warrants further evaluation.

- Estrogen replacement provides the most effective relief of hot flushes, with some evidence of benefit with selective serotonin reuptake inhibitors, venlafaxine, clonidine, and gabapentin.

- Estrogen replacement provides the most effective relief of vaginal atrophy and dryness, with vaginal administration preferred when these are the most prominent menopausal symptoms.

- Initiation of hormone replacement therapy should be avoided in women who smoke, have known coronary artery disease, a history of breast cancer, or who are well past menopause.

- Hormone replacement therapy is not recommended for the prevention of chronic disease after menopause.

# Abnormal Uterine Bleeding and Dysmenorrhea

## Clinical Presentation and Evaluation

Abnormal uterine bleeding can take many forms, including infrequent menses, excessive flow, prolonged duration of menses, intermenstrual bleeding, and postmenopausal bleeding. Normal menstrual cycles are typically consistent in ovulating women, with duration of flow of 4 days (range, 2-6 days) and cycle length of 28 days (range, 21-35 days). Abnormal uterine bleeding is one of the more common gynecologic problems seen by primary care physicians with an annual prevalence of 5% in women between 30 and 49 years of age. The differential diagnosis of abnormal uterine bleeding is broad and includes structural disorders, endocrine disorders, neoplasia, and bleeding disorders (**Table 43**). Amenorrhea and polycystic ovary syndrome are addressed in MKSAP 15 Endocrinology and Metabolism.

| **TABLE 43** Causes of Abnormal Uterine Bleeding by Age | |
|---|---|
| **Cause** | **Diagnostic Clues** |
| **Menarche to teenage years** | |
| Pregnancy | Irregular or absent periods |
| Anovulation | Cycle length falls outside normal range or varies by 10 days or more |
| Stress | Physical or mental |
| Bleeding disorders | Associated with other sources of bleeding (gums, nose) |
| Infection (cervical or vaginal) | Postcoital bleeding and/or vaginal discharge |
| **Teens to 40s** | |
| Pregnancy | Irregular or absent periods |
| Malignancy (uterine, cervical, vaginal, or vulvar) | Postcoital bleeding and/or vaginal discharge |
| Infection (cervical or vaginal) | Postcoital bleeding and/or vaginal discharge |
| Cervical polyps, endometrial polyps | Dysmenorrhea |
| Adenomyosis, fibroids | Dysmenorrhea |
| Anovulation | Irregular periods |
| Bleeding disorders | Associated with other sources of bleeding (gums, nose) |
| Endocrine abnormalities | Signs of hypothyroidism, diabetes, hyperprolactinemia, polycystic ovary syndrome |
| Ovarian or adrenal tumor | New-onset virilization or hirsutism |
| **Perimenopausal** | |
| Anovulation | Irregular periods |
| Endometrial hyperplasia and polyps; fibroids | Dysmenorrhea |
| Malignancy (uterine, cervical, vaginal, or vulvar) | Postcoital bleeding and/or vaginal discharge |
| **Postmenopausal** | |
| Malignancy (uterine, cervical, vaginal, or vulvar) | Postcoital bleeding and/or vaginal discharge |
| Atrophy of vaginal mucosa | Vaginal dryness, dyspareunia |
| Estrogen replacement therapy | Estrogen withdrawal bleeding |

When evaluating a patient with abnormal uterine bleeding, the clinician should attempt to quantify the patient's menstrual flow by asking about the number of tampons or pads used. Typically, 10 to 15 pads or tampons are used during the course of a normal cycle. Twenty-five or more pads used on average indicate heavy menstruation.

In all patients with abnormal bleeding, physical examination should include a pelvic examination and Pap smear. A bimanual pelvic examination may detect abnormal cervical or uterine anatomy, such as cervical polyps, neoplasia, or fibroids. Fibroids are the most common anatomic cause of menorrhagia and are often palpable on examination. If the patient is premenopausal, a pregnancy test should be obtained to rule out intrauterine pregnancy (amenorrhea) or an ectopic pregnancy or threatened abortion (abnormal bleeding). Laboratory testing may also include an assessment of thyroid function. In patients with anovulatory bleeding as determined by irregularity of periods (that is, the cycle length falls out of the normal range or cycle length varies by more than 10 days), measurement of prolactin levels is indicated, especially in the presence of galactorrhea. A platelet count, activated partial thromboplastin time, and bleeding time may be indicated in a patient with a history of excessive menstrual bleeding since menarche, a family history of bleeding disorders, easy bruising, or menorrhagia that is refractory to treatment. A bleeding diathesis is found in 17% of women referred for menorrhagia with no sign of anatomic abnormalities.

If a bimanual pelvic examination suggests abnormal uterine anatomy or the patient's body habitus makes a bimanual examination difficult, a pelvic ultrasound is indicated. Endometrial biopsy should be strongly considered in all patients with a hyper–estrogen-stimulation state (postmenopausal unopposed estrogen stimulation, polycystic ovary syndrome), although no guidelines currently address this. A referral for hysteroscopy and dilation and curettage also may be necessary.

## Management

Single anovulatory cycles may happen once or twice a year in women who are either close to menarche or close to menopause. Assuming pregnancy, hypothyroidism, and structural abnormalities have been ruled out, patients with excessive menstrual bleeding can be treated with high-dose estrogens (off-label use) to stop bleeding quickly. The patient is instructed to take all of the pills from a pack of estrogen-containing oral contraceptive pills for the particular weekday at one time ("Take all four Sunday pills at one time, all four Monday pills the next day, all four Tuesday pills the following day, etc."), finishing the whole pack in 1 week. The patient is instructed that she should expect menstruation to slow and cease after the first few days. After finishing the pack, she should expect to have a large period that should end. This process should "reset" her menstrual cycles. She should call the physician if the expected outcome does not occur. Once excessive bleeding is controlled, options to control the amount of bleeding occurring with each cycle include cyclical progesterone, oral contraceptives, and levonorgestrel IUD (off-label use). According to a Cochrane Collaboration review, women prefer a progesterone-releasing IUD rather than cyclical progesterone therapy or oral contraceptive pills, each of which is efficacious in decreasing abnormal uterine bleeding. NSAID therapy before and during menses has been shown to be superior to placebo in decreasing heavy menses.

As a general rule, a primary care physician should consult a gynecologist when:

- There is no response to initial therapy
- The cause of anovulation is unclear
- Hospitalization is required
- Gynecologic procedures are required for diagnosis or therapy

## Dysmenorrhea

Patients with a history of menstrual pain that begins within 1 to 2 years of menarche and sometimes worsens over time usually have primary dysmenorrhea, in which no pathologic cause for the menstrual pain exists. This symptom is in contrast to secondary dysmenorrhea, defined as menstrual pain for which an organic cause exists. An underlying cause for dysmenorrhea is likely in the setting of noncyclic pain, abnormal discharge, dyspareunia, or heavy or irregular bleeding. Primary dysmenorrhea is common, with prevalence rates estimated as high as 90%. Prostaglandins play a role in the pathophysiology of primary dysmenorrhea, and NSAIDs are an effective first-line therapy. For women who are not trying to conceive, OCPs are also effective therapy. A Cochrane systematic review has concluded that high-frequency transcutaneous electrical nerve stimulation (TENS) and vitamin $B_1$ (100 mg/d) are also effective therapies for primary dysmenorrhea. Nitroglycerin may also decrease pain associated with dysmenorrhea. Typically, primary dysmenorrhea decreases after the first pregnancy.

Secondary dysmenorrhea has many causes, including fibroids, adenomyosis, endometriosis, infections, adhesions, pelvic inflammatory disease, and uterine displacement. Treatment for secondary dysmenorrhea is directed toward the cause.

### KEY POINTS

- Fibroids are the most common anatomic cause of menorrhagia and are often palpable on examination.
- A progesterone-releasing intrauterine device, cyclical progesterone therapy, and oral contraceptive pills are efficacious in decreasing excessive cyclical bleeding.
- For treatment of primary dysmenorrhea, NSAIDs and oral contraceptive pills are first-line therapies.

# Vaginitis

The three common causes of vaginitis are bacterial vaginosis, vulvovaginal candidiasis, and trichomoniasis, and these conditions often coexist. Laboratory studies for the evaluation of vaginitis are summarized in **Table 44**.

Bacterial vaginosis is the most common cause of vaginitis, present in 29% of women, 50% of whom are asymptomatic. It is more prevalent in lower socioeconomic groups. It is not a disease caused by a particular organism, but has been termed an "imbalance" of normal flora, particularly between *Lactobacillus* and *Gardnerella* organisms. This imbalance creates a decrease in lactic acid and a less acidic vaginal milieu. Symptoms include a typical "fishy" odor, pruritus, and discharge. On vaginal examination, there is no evidence of inflammation, but a homogeneous, white, noninflammatory discharge that smoothly coats the vaginal walls is commonly observed. The pH is elevated (>4.5), the "whiff test" is positive (a fishy odor is present when potassium hydroxide is added to vaginal secretions), and "clue cells" are found on wet mount (**Figure 18**). Treatment is oral metronidazole, 500 mg twice daily for 1 week. There is currently no evidence to suggest that partners should be concomitantly treated. For a patient with recurrent bacterial vaginosis, prophylaxis includes metronidazole gel twice weekly and encouraging condom use.

Yeast infection is the second most common cause of vaginitis, and most women have an occurrence at some time during their life. *Candida albicans* is part of the normal vaginal flora. Overgrowth is known to occur as a result of antibiotic usage and is more common in women with diabetes; however, it may also occur without a recognized provocation. Examination reveals a "cottage cheese" discharge and a normal vaginal pH (<4.5). A potassium hydroxide wet mount preparation may reveal the hyphae and spores of yeast, but this test is only 60% sensitive, and patients may be treated based on the appearance of the

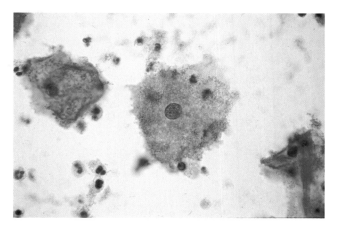

**FIGURE 18.**
Clue cells.

exudates and symptoms alone. Patients with recurrent episodes may self-treat with over-the-counter medications without consulting their physician. A single 150-mg oral dose of fluconazole provides high patient satisfaction but may be more costly than many over-the-counter treatments, such as miconazole or clotrimazole creams or vaginal suppositories.

Trichomoniasis is a sexually transmitted disease, unlike the other two causes of vaginitis, and is responsible for fewer than 25% of cases of vaginitis. *Trichomonas vaginalis* is a flagellated protozoan. It is a fastidious organism and may be spread through shared moist objects (including bathing suits). Examination may reveal a green bubbly discharge and the prototypical "strawberry cervix." The pH is very elevated (up to 6.0), and mobile trichomonads are usually visible on microscopy (100% specific). Treatment is oral metronidazole, 2 g in one dose for all infected nonpregnant women and symptomatic pregnant women. Most experts also recommend treating the partner to prevent recurrent infection, although actual trials of patient-delivered partner treatment are ongoing.

| **TABLE 44** Laboratory and Other Studies for Vaginitis and Cervicitis | |
|---|---|
| **Test** | **Notes** |
| Vaginal pH | Normal pH is <4.5; blood, semen, cervical secretions may interfere with test; pH usually normal in candidiasis and >4.5 in bacterial vaginosis and trichomoniasis. |
| "Whiff" test on vaginal secretions | Add 10% potassium hydroxide to vaginal secretions; test is positive if a fishy smell is present (volatilization of amines produced by anaerobes); positive in bacterial vaginosis and sometimes in trichomoniasis. |
| Microscopic examination of vaginal fluid | Mix secretions in small amount of saline and observe using "high dry" 40× lens. Note the presence of budding yeast and pseudohyphae, motile trichomonads, and clue cells (squamous epithelial cells covered with bacteria whose edges are obscured). Observe number and type of bacteria: moderate numbers of large rods represent lactobacilli (normal flora); large numbers of coccobacilli or motile curved rods highly suggest bacterial vaginosis.<br><br>Use of potassium hydroxide preparation may be helpful for yeast infection; demonstration of yeast infection is subject to sampling error; examination of repeated slide preparations can be helpful. |
| Amsel criteria for bacterial vaginosis | Must have 3 of the following 4 signs: vaginal pH >4.5, positive "whiff" test, presence of clue cells, and homogeneous vaginal discharge. |

Adapted from Schwebke JR. http://pier.acponline.org/physicians/diseases/d196/tables/d196-tables.html. In PIER (online database). Philadelphia: American College of Physicians, 2008. Accessed March 9, 2008.

## Chronic Pelvic Pain

Chronic pelvic pain (CPP) is pelvic pain that has been present for more than 6 months, lacks an apparent physical cause, and is accompanied by changes in behaviors involving sexual life, work, recreation, and/or mood. One study identified a point prevalence of 12% and a lifetime prevalence of 33%. Women with CPP are also more likely to have chronic somatic syndromes, such as fibromyalgia, low-back pain, and chronic headaches, as well as psychological conditions, such as depression and alcohol or substance abuse. A history of sexual abuse or domestic violence is quite common as well.

Initial evaluation of CPP should include a history and physical examination, with psychological screening for depression, anxiety, and somatization. Attention should be paid to determining whether there is a pattern to the onset of pain, such as relation to meals, bowel movements, or menstrual cycle. The abdominal, pelvic, and rectovaginal examinations are particularly important, assessing for tenderness, masses, bleeding, or discharge. Urinalysis, complete blood count, and serum chemistries, as well as vaginal cultures and a transvaginal ultrasound, are all useful to rule out potential causes, with other studies needed only when indicated by the history and physical examination. The most commonly identified contributory conditions are endometriosis, interstitial cystitis, irritable bowel syndrome, and adhesions. In many patients, there are likely multiple factors, and most have no identifiable organic cause. CPP due to endometriosis (as well as adenomyosis) is often, although not always, cyclic, and is more likely to improve with hormonal therapy or hysterectomy. However, up to 30% of women presenting with CPP have already had a hysterectomy. CPP due to interstitial cystitis may improve with pentosan polysulfate sodium, although the evidence is modest.

Treatment of CPP has largely proved ineffective in women with no identifiable underlying disorder, with no evidence of benefit for NSAIDs, antibiotics, antidepressants, or muscle relaxants. Extrapolation from other chronic pain syndromes suggests that cognitive-behavioral therapy may be the best approach; there is some evidence to suggest that it is beneficial for CPP, but additional studies are needed to confirm this.

## Bibliography

Allsworth JE, Peipert JF. Prevalence of bacterial vaginosis: 2001-2004 National Health and Nutrition Examination Survey data. Obstet Gynecol. 2007;109(1):114-120. [PMID: 17197596]

Basson R. Clinical practice. Sexual desire and arousal disorders in women. N Engl J Med. 2006;354(14):1497-1506. [PMID: 16598046]

Cheong Y, William Stones R. Chronic pelvic pain: Aetiology and therapy. Best Pract Res Clin Obstet Gynaecol. 2006;20(5):695-711. [PMID: 16765092]

Eckert LO. Clinical practice. Acute vulvovaginitis [erratum in N Engl J Med. 2006;355(26):2797]. N Engl J Med, 2006;355(12):1244-1252. [PMID: 16990387]

Grimes DA, Lopez LM, Manion C, Schulz KF. Cochrane reviews of IUD trials: lessons learned. Contraception 2007;75:S55-9.

Haugstad GK, Haugstad TS, Kirste UM, Leganger S, Klemmetsen I, Malt UF. Mensendieck somatocognitive therapy as treatment approach to chronic pelvic pain: results of a randomized controlled intervention study. Am J Obstet Gynecol. 2006;194(5):1303-1310. [PMID: 16647914]

James AH, Kouides PA, Abdul-Kadir R, et al. Von Willebrand disease and other bleeding disorders in women: Consensus on diagnosis and management from an international expert panel. Am J Obstet Gynecol. 2009;201(1):12.e1-8. [PMID: 19481722]

Kingsberg SA, Janata JW. Female sexual disorders: assessment, diagnosis, and treatment. Urol Clin North Am. 2007;34(4):497-506, v-vi. [PMID: 17983890]

Klaiber EL, Vogel W, Rako S. A critique of the Women's Health Initiative hormone therapy study. Fertil Steril. 2005;84(6):1589-1601. [PMID: 16359951]

Lobo RA. Postmenopausal hormones and coronary artery disease: potential benefits and risks. Climacteric. 2007;10 Suppl 2:21-26. [PMID: 17882668]

Morgan PJ, Kung R, Tarshis J. Nitroglycerin as a uterine relaxant: a systematic review. J Obstet Gynaecol Can. 2002;24(5):403-409. [PMID: 12196860]

Nestler JE. Metformin for the treatment of the polycystic ovary syndrome. N Engl J Med 2008;358(1):47-54. [PMID: 18172174]

Santen RJ, Mansel R. Benign breast disorders. N Engl J Med. 2005;353(3):275-285. [PMID: 16034013]

Smith RL, Pruthi S, Fitzpatrick LA. Evaluation and management of breast pain. Mayo Clin Proc. 2004;79(3):353-372. [PMID: 15008609]

Utian WH, Archer DF, Bachman GA, et al. Estrogen and progestogen use in postmenopausal women: July 2008 position statement of The North American Menopause Society. 2008;15(4 Pt 1):584-602. [PMID: 18580541]

Zurawin RK, Ayensu-Coker L. Innovations in contraception: a review. Clin Obstet Gynecol 2007;50:425-439. [PMID: 17513928]

# Eye Disorders

## Red Eye

### Clinical Presentation

The most common eye disorder in the ambulatory setting is the red eye. Most causes of red eye are readily apparent, benign, and self-limiting, but a few are manifestations of serious underlying disease. A systematic approach is needed to separate benign from serious causes.

Historical features of importance in evaluating the patient with a red eye include the onset (abrupt or gradual), duration, presence and quality of ocular pain (foreign body sensation versus orbital or periorbital pain), recent trauma, recurrent symptoms (seasonally or otherwise), concomitant illness, underlying medical problems, and associated visual disturbance (**Table 45**). Physical examination findings that may help narrow the diagnosis include photophobia, localization and appearance of the erythema, unilateral versus bilateral eye involvement, skin eruptions (such as herpes zoster), and eye discharge (mucopurulent versus watery). The presence of visual disturbance, photophobia, pupillary changes, decreased visual acuity, pain, or trauma should raise concern for a problem that requires urgent consultation with an ophthalmologist. Nausea, vomiting, and other constitutional symptoms are not associated with benign disease and warrant immediate referral.

### Specific Conditions

#### Conjunctivitis

Conjunctivitis is the most common cause of red eye (**Figure 19**). Allergic conjunctivitis may be recurrent and seasonal and

**TABLE 45 Historical Clues in the Diagnosis of the Red Eye**

| Clue | Suggested Diagnosis | Comment |
|---|---|---|
| Onset following use of striking tools or sharp, superficial pain | Foreign body | Inspect fornices, perform fluorescein test, and consider referral. |
| Deep, aching pain; nausea; vomiting | Acute angle-closure glaucoma | Check depth of anterior chamber. Emergency referral. |
| Pain with reading or photophobia | Iridocyclitis or keratitis | Inflammation confined to corneal limbus; corneal irregularity or edema. Emergency referral. |
| Halos around lights or decreased visual acuity | Keratitis, iridocyclitis, glaucoma | Inflammation confined to corneal limbus; corneal irregularity or edema; or narrow anterior chamber. Emergency referral. |
| Itching with mucoid or watery discharge | Allergic conjunctivitis | Diffuse conjunctival redness and other atopic symptoms. |
| Upper respiratory tract infection followed by one, then a second red eye | Viral conjunctivitis | Adenovirus most common virus. |
| Diffuse unilateral redness with morning crusting of eyelashes | Bacterial conjunctivitis | Pneumococci most common bacteria. |
| Profusely purulent discharge in a sexually active adult | Gonorrhea | Systemic antibiotics and referral. |
| Chronic red eye in a sexually active adult | Chlamydial infection | Preauricular lymphadenopathy. Systemic antibiotics and referral. |
| Constitutional symptoms | Keratitis, iritis, scleritis | Consider collagen vascular diseases. |

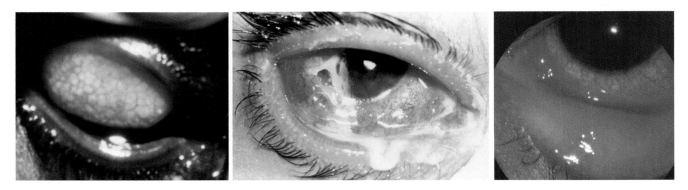

**FIGURE 19.**
**Conjunctivitis.**
Allergic conjunctivitis (*left*): prominent cobblestoning of the palpebral conjunctiva is present. Bacterial conjunctivitis (*center*): the conjunctiva is diffusely erythematous with mucopurulent discharge. Viral conjunctivitis (*right*): the palpebral and bulbar conjunctivae are diffusely injected with pseudomembrane formation involving the palpebral conjunctiva.

Images courtesy of Linda Lippa, MD, University of California, Irvine.

presents with itching, conjunctival edema, and cobblestoning under the upper lid. It usually responds to topical antihistamines, short-course topical NSAIDs (3 days maximum), and cool compresses. Topical corticosteroids may be used by an ophthalmologist for difficult cases.

Bacterial conjunctivitis may be caused by staphylococcal, pneumococcal, gonorrheal, or *Haemophilus* species. Typical symptoms include a mucopurulent discharge from one or both eyes (often worse in the morning) and preserved visual acuity. Warm water soaks and gentle scrubbing with cotton balls or a clean washcloth may help relieve crusting. Most causes of bacterial conjunctivitis are self-limited, and with the exception of gonorrhea and chlamydial infection, the evidence for treatment with topical or systemic antibiotics is inconclusive.

Viral conjunctivitis is highly contagious, and scrupulous handwashing and hygiene are necessary to prevent transmission to an unaffected eye or close contacts. Adenovirus is the typical agent, and patients may have bilateral eye involvement, prominent tearing, significant foreign body sensation, and enlargement of preauricular and/or submandibular nodes, which may be associated with pharyngitis and a fever (pharyngoconjunctival fever). When pharyngoconjunctival fever or keratoconjunctivitis is suspected, an ophthalmology referral should be considered, as adenovirus may involve the cornea.

Herpes zoster infection may present with a unilateral red eye and represents an ophthalmologic emergency. Patients often have an associated headache or brow ache, which precedes the vesicular skin eruption in the distribution of the ophthalmic branch of the trigeminal nerve. Involvement of the tip of the nose (Hutchinson sign) is particularly serious, as the nasociliary nerve innervates this and the cornea. Untreated, herpes zoster ophthalmicus can lead to permanent blindness, and patients should be started on antiviral therapy (acyclovir, valacyclovir, or famciclovir) and immediately referred to an ophthalmologist.

In young, sexually active adults, hyperpurulent conjunctivitis, characterized by copious purulent discharge, suggests gonococcal infection and requires culture and immediate ophthalmologic consultation. Gonococcal conjunctivitis is a potentially blinding disease and is treated with systemic and topical antibiotics. Chlamydial conjunctivitis should be suspected in patients with bilateral involvement, which may be chronic, that is associated with urethritis or salpingitis, and in those whose symptoms persist despite traditional treatment. Oral tetracycline is an effective therapy.

## Subconjunctival Hematoma

Subconjunctival hematomas (**Figure 20**) may result from straining or coughing; such lesions are painless and spontaneously resolve over 2 weeks. The history is critical because subconjunctival hematomas also may be caused by trauma or foreign bodies and be a sign of possible globe penetration, requiring immediate consultation with an ophthalmologist.

## Episcleritis and Scleritis

Scleritis is characterized by severe, constant, boring ocular pain that typically worsens with eye movement; photophobia; and a raised hyperemic lesion, which may be localized or diffuse, that obscures the underlying vasculature. It is commonly associated with collagen vascular and rheumatoid diseases. Scleritis may progress to orbital rupture, and patients with scleritis should be urgently referred to an ophthalmologist for management while investigating for underlying or associated conditions. Episcleritis is characterized by a red, flat, more superficial lesion (**Figure 21**) that allows visualization of the underlying vasculature and sometimes white sclera, and that usually is not painful. Episcleritis is typically a self-limited condition not associated with systemic disease.

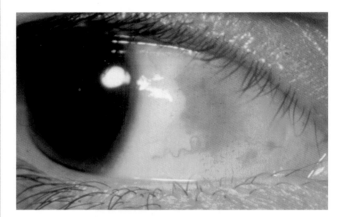

**FIGURE 20.**
**Subconjunctival hematoma.**
A well-localized (nonpainful) superficial collection of extravasated blood is visible; the sclera and conjunctiva are not involved.

Image courtesy of Linda Lippa, MD, University of California, Irvine.

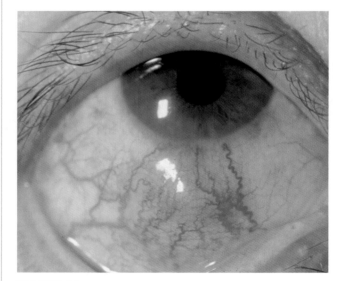

**FIGURE 21.**
**Episcleritis.**
Superficial dilated blood vessels are seen (nonpainful), with white sclera visible between the blood vessels.

Image courtesy of Linda Lippa, MD, University of California, Irvine.

## Corneal Conditions

Patients with corneal involvement usually have a prominent foreign body sensation, excessive blinking and tearing, and may have visible pus in the anterior chamber (hypopyon). Corneal staining with fluorescein is helpful in diagnosing epithelial defects. Areas of bright-green staining denote absent or diseased epithelium. The use of a cobalt blue light enhances the fluorescein staining.

Common corneal problems include keratitis (viral, bacterial, or noninfectious), ulceration, and abrasion. Corneal ulcers may appear as a white infiltrate (**Figure 22**), while abrasions may not be evident without ophthalmologic examination. Herpes simplex infection involving the cornea is characterized on fluorescein staining by dendritic branching, and these patients should be referred to an ophthalmologist. Corneal abrasions are usually the result of trauma and cause intense discomfort, tearing, and even blepharospasm and are typically associated with linear or geographic fluorescein staining. Eye patching is not necessary and symptoms usually resolve in 1 to 2 days.

Contact lens wearers who present with red eye must remove the lenses immediately. While lenses may cause an abrasion, if an ulcer is present or infection is suspected, patients should be referred to an ophthalmologist immediately to aid with culture and intensive treatment for possible pseudomonal infection.

### Iritis

Inflammation of the anterior uveal tract (iris and ciliary body) is often referred to as *iritis* or *iridocyclitis* (**Figure 23**). Iritis may be caused by extension of an infection from another part of the eye or may be associated with underlying diseases, such as the seronegative spondyloarthropathies, sarcoidosis, herpes zoster, tuberculosis, or syphilis. Patients present with intense pain, photophobia, ciliary injection (redness at the junction

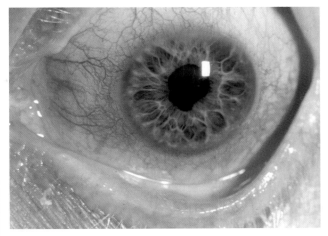

**FIGURE 23.**
**Iritis.**
Injection extends to the limbus (corneal-scleral junction); pupil is irregularly shaped.

Image courtesy of Linda Lippa, MD, University of California, Irvine.

between the cornea and sclera), and miosis. Patients should be referred to an ophthalmologist for management.

### Blepharitis

Blepharitis is a chronic inflammation of the eyelid margin. Staphylococcal blepharitis leads to scales and crusts around the eyelashes; seborrheic blepharitis is characterized by dandruff-like skin changes and greasy scales around the eyelashes. Initial treatment of staphylococcal blepharitis includes topical antibiotics. The treatment for seborrheic blepharitis, and other forms of blepharitis once the underlying condition is controlled, is twice-daily gentle scrubbing of the lid margins with cotton tip applicators and a dilute solution of a nontearing shampoo.

### KEY POINTS

- In patients with a red eye, the presence of visual disturbance, photophobia, pupillary changes, decreased visual acuity, pain, or trauma should raise concern for a problem that requires urgent consultation with an ophthalmologist.

- Hyperpurulent conjunctivitis in young, sexually active adults suggests gonococcal infection and requires culture and immediate ophthalmologic consultation.

- Scleritis is an ophthalmologic emergency characterized by severe, constant, boring ocular pain that typically worsens with eye movement; photophobia; and a raised hyperemic lesion that may be focal or diffuse.

## Macular Degeneration

### Pathophysiology

Age-related macular degeneration (AMD) is a leading cause of blindness and visual impairment. AMD is a chronic,

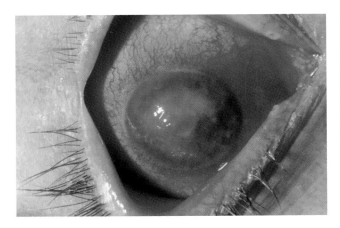

**FIGURE 22.**
**Corneal ulcer.**
Corneal infiltrate (areas of whitened opacification) is visible, secondary to purulent cells in the corneal stroma.

Image courtesy of Linda Lippa, MD, University of California, Irvine.

progressive disease affecting the macula, leading to central visual field loss and impairment of such crucial tasks as reading, driving, and recognition of faces. Peripheral vision is usually preserved. The underlying pathologic processes in macular degeneration are not fully understood, but likely represent both genetic and environmental factors.

There are two types of AMD: atrophic or dry (80% of cases) and exudative or wet (20% of cases) (**Figure 24**). In dry AMD, there is geographic thinning and atrophy of the macula. Dry AMD usually affects both eyes, and the visual loss may be gradual. In wet AMD, the predominant process is choroidal neovascularization; new blood vessels form near the macula, which may bleed, leak fluid, and lead to scar formation. In wet AMD, visual loss is usually more rapid and profound, accounting for nearly 90% of the cases of severe visual impairment associated with AMD.

In addition to increasing age, smoking is one of the few identified risk factors for AMD. The odds ratios for AMD-related retinal changes vary in smokers compared with non-smokers from 2.2 for women to 3.2 for men. Quitting smoking reduces the risk of developing AMD. Hypertension may play a role, but the benefits of blood pressure control are uncertain. Advanced AMD is more common among whites and possibly Chinese Americans.

Dilated fundus examination by an ophthalmologist is the gold standard for diagnosing AMD. Obtaining risk factor information as part of the general history and physical examination may identify at-risk patients who should be scheduled for routine eye examinations.

## Clinical Presentation and Evaluation

In the early stages, AMD is often asymptomatic. Common symptoms, when present, include distortion of vision or a notable loss of central vision. Those with advanced AMD and profound visual loss may experience visual hallucinations (Charles Bonnet syndrome). The hallucinations, which are often self-limited, may also occur following photodynamic therapy.

In both dry and wet AMD, drusen are common findings. Drusen are amorphous deposits behind the retina that lead to visual loss through direct (space occupying) and indirect (inflammatory response) means. A few small, hard drusen are common as people age, but numerous large, soft drusen are a harbinger of severe AMD. The drusen of AMD should not be confused with the common, normal finding of optic head drusen.

## Treatment

There is no clear evidence to support any specific medication or supplement to prevent either the development of AMD or its progression in those with early AMD. Antioxidant and mineral supplementation may be mildly protective in preventing visual loss and disease progression in selected patients. In the Age-Related Eye Disease Study, there was a 6% absolute risk reduction in progression of visual loss over 6.3 years in patients taking antioxidants plus zinc. β-Carotene should be avoided in smokers, owing to an increased risk of lung cancer, and vitamin E should be avoided in patients with vascular disease and diabetes mellitus, owing to an increased risk of heart failure.

More aggressive therapies are used for AMD with neovascularization. Photodynamic therapy is effective at slowing visual loss, but approximately 1 in 50 patients will respond with an abrupt decline in visual acuity. Laser photocoagulation destroys the neovascularization in AMD. It is effective in the long term (approximately 2 years) at preventing visual loss

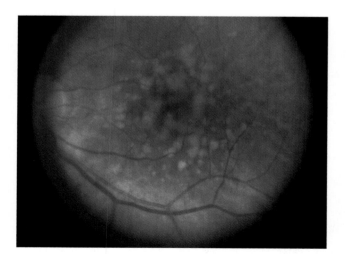 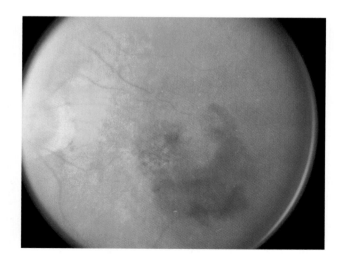

**FIGURE 24.**
**Age-related macular degeneration.**
Dry form (*left*), showing distinct yellow-white lesions (drusen) surrounding the macular region and areas of pigment mottling. Wet form (*right*), showing clumps of hyperpigmentation, hypopigmentation, and evidence of subretinal hemorrhage.

Images courtesy of Edward A. Jaeger, MD, Jefferson Medical College, Wills Eye Institute, Philadelphia, PA.

(number needed to treat = 6), but at the cost of significant early visual loss in some patients. External beam irradiation has not shown clear evidence of benefit. More recent efforts are focusing on medications with anti-angiogenic properties, such as pegaptanib sodium, which binds to vascular endothelial growth factor and is administered intravitreally every 6 weeks for at least 1 year.

**KEY POINTS**

- Age-related macular degeneration causes distorted vision and central visual field loss.
- Neovascularization is the hallmark of wet age-related macular degeneration and can lead to rapid visual loss.
- Smoking is a clear, modifiable risk factor for age-related macular degeneration.

## Glaucoma

### Clinical Presentation and Evaluation

Primary open-angle glaucoma (POAG) is an insidious, progressive optic neuropathy associated with elevated intraocular pressure (IOP). POAG is the most prevalent form of glaucoma, affecting nearly 2.5 million people in the United States, with nearly 130,000 becoming blind as a result. It typically affects both eyes, although there may be asymmetric involvement. Ocular hypertension is the finding of elevated IOP ($\geq$21 mm Hg) without the associated optic neuropathy or visual field defects. Normotensive glaucoma is probably in the spectrum of POAG, with optic neuropathy and visual field defects but normal IOP. Angle-closure glaucoma is caused by obstruction of the outflow of aqueous humor from the anterior chamber (such as due to obstruction by the iris) with resultant increased IOP and optic neuropathy and visual field defects.

POAG is typically asymptomatic, initially causing visual field loss in the peripheral vision before affecting the central vision, and may go unrecognized by patients for several years. Funduscopic findings include vertical extension of the central cup, disc hemorrhages, and an increased optic cup:disc ratio (>0.5). All of these findings are nonspecific, however, as they may be seen in those without glaucoma.

There is no evidence from randomized, controlled trials to recommend for or against routine screening for glaucoma. Because glaucoma initially affects the peripheral vision, standard visual acuity testing in the primary care setting is unlikely to be helpful. Formal testing by eye care professionals is necessary and may be best targeted to those at higher risk: (1) African-American or African-Caribbean patients older than 40 years (prevalence of glaucoma 1.2%-11.3% versus 0.9%-2.1% in white patients older than 40 years); (2) all other patients older than 64 years; (3) patients with a family history of glaucoma (begin screening at age 40 years); (4) those with a personal history of high IOP; and (5) those with myopia.

### Treatment

Although the treatment of glaucoma is in the realm of the eye care specialist, internists should be aware of the common medical and surgical treatments and their potential impact on coexistent medical conditions (**Table 46**). Medical therapy is the mainstay of treatment and currently consists predominantly of topical therapy. Treatment of ocular hypertension

**TABLE 46** Drug Treatment for Primary Open-Angle Glaucoma

| Agent | Mechanism of Action | Systemic Side Effects |
|---|---|---|
| β-Blockers (timolol) | Decreases inflow | Bradycardia, heart block, bronchospasm, decreased libido, central nervous system depression, mood swings |
| Nonselective adrenergic agonists (epinephrine) | Improves outflow and decreases inflow | Hypertension, headaches, extra systoles |
| Selective $\alpha_2$-adrenergic agonists (brimonidine) | Decreases inflow and increases outflow | Hypotension, vasovagal attack, dry mouth, fatigue, insomnia, depression, syncope, dizziness, anxiety |
| Parasympathomimetic agents (pilocarpine, echothiophate iodide) | Increases outflow | Increased salivation, increased gastric secretion, abdominal cramps, frequency, and shock |
| Oral carbonic anhydrase inhibitors (acetazolamide) | Decreases inflow | Acidosis, depression, malaise, hirsutism, paresthesias, numbness, blood dyscrasias, diarrhea, weight loss, renal stones, loss of libido, bone marrow depression, hypokalemia, bad taste, increased serum urate |
| Topical carbonic anhydrase inhibitors (dorzolamide) | Decreases inflow | Lower incidence of systemic effects compared with oral carbonic anhydrase inhibitors |
| Prostaglandin analogues (latanoprost) | Increases outflow | Flu-like symptoms, joint and muscle pain |
| Hyperosmotic agents (mannitol) | Reduces vitreous and aqueous volume | Headache, heart failure, expansion of blood volume, nausea, vomiting, diarrhea, electrolyte disturbance, renal failure |

Adapted from Smith OU, Seligsohn AL, Khan SJ, Spaeth GL. Primary open angle glaucoma. http://pier.acponline.org/physicians/diseases/d602/tables/d602-tables.html. In PIER (online database). Philadelphia: American College of Physicians, 2009. Accessed July 7, 2009.

with topical agents to reduce IOP decreases the risk (OR = 0.62) of developing glaucomatous visual field defects.

Surgical treatment for POAG consists of trabeculectomy or the Scheie procedure (iridectomy with a thermal sclerostomy). Trials comparing medication with surgical intervention have not been conducted with the most currently used medications.

> **KEY POINTS**
>
> - Topical medications used to treat glaucoma have systemic side effects.
> - The peripheral visual field defects of glaucoma are asymptomatic and are not identified by the routine visual acuity checks in the primary care setting.

## Cataract

### Clinical Presentation and Evaluation

Cataract, or any opacification of the otherwise optically clear lens behind the pupil and iris, is the most common cause of blindness and low vision worldwide. In the United States, the prevalence of cataract is approximately 17% in persons 40 years or older. Risk factors include older age, smoking, ultraviolet B radiation exposure, diabetes (two-fold risk), a family history of cataracts, and corticosteroid use (systemic, topical, ophthalmic); inhaled corticosteroids may increase cataract risk, but the evidence is unclear.

Patients with cataracts may report glare, reduced visual acuity, loss of contrast, or monocular diplopia. On direct ophthalmoscopic examination, lens opacities may be observed, especially when using the magnifying lenses (green numbers).

For cataract prevention, smoking cessation and ultraviolet B eye protection (sunglasses) may be beneficial. N-acetylcarnosine (NAC) has shown promise in early, but small, clinical trials. NAC is a powerful antioxidant applied topically that inhibits lipid peroxidation (a process thought to contribute to cataract formation) and is available without a prescription.

### Treatment

Treatment of cataracts is surgical removal, most commonly using phacoemulsification, in which an ultrasonic probe inserted through a small incision emulsifies the lens, which is then removed via suction, leaving the posterior capsule intact for placement of an intraocular lens. Indications for surgery include loss of visual acuity that impairs daily activities or a need to effectively evaluate and treat other eye diseases, such as diabetic retinopathy. Delaying indicated cataract surgery for more than 6 months has been associated with an increased risk of falls, reduced visual acuity, and worsening quality of life compared with those who have indicated surgery within 6 weeks. Routine perioperative medical consultation is usually unnecessary for patients undergoing cataract surgery with local anesthesia and perioperative sedation.

Complications from cataract surgery are rare (<2%) but include ongoing pain and inflammation, which may last for weeks, and impaired visual acuity owing to corneal edema or cystic macular edema. Endophthalmitis is a serious complication that requires prompt ophthalmologic evaluation (see Eye Emergencies, below). The most common late complication is opacification of the posterior capsule (up to 25% of eyes), which can be treated with laser capsulotomy.

> **KEY POINT**
>
> - Routine perioperative medical consultation is unnecessary for patients undergoing cataract surgery with local anesthesia and perioperative sedation.

## Dry Eyes

Dry eyes affect 8% to 14% of adults and may be a manifestation of local or systemic disease. Dry eyes result from either decreased tear secretion or increased evaporation, which can lead to pathologic changes (keratoconjunctivitis sicca). Decreased tear secretion may originate in the lacrimal gland (Sjögren syndrome, rheumatoid arthritis, systemic lupus erythematosus) or result from decreased corneal sensation. Decreased corneal sensation may result from diabetes mellitus, herpes zoster infection, or following a laser-assisted intrastromal keratomileusis (LASIK) procedure; decreased corneal sensation can lead to dry eye by reducing a reflex arc that stimulates tear production. Increased evaporation results from an increased palpebral distance (Graves disease) or meibomian gland dysfunction. Dry eye symptoms begin gradually over weeks to months, progressing to a persistent sandy, gritty, or burning sensation. Symptoms typically worsen as the day progresses, are aggravated by irritants such as smoke and low humidity, and relieved with eye closing and humidity. In most patients, the condition is annoying but rarely leads to serious problems. Occasional patients with connective tissue disease, Graves ophthalmopathy, or Bell palsy may develop corneal damage secondary to drying and are at risk for corneal infection.

Systemic symptoms (dry mouth, fatigue, arthralgia) may suggest Sjögren syndrome or rheumatoid arthritis and prompt further serologic testing. The lid should be examined for inflammation or acne rosacea (meibomian gland dysfunction) and increased palpebral width (>10 mm) or incomplete closure of the eye (Graves disease, Bell palsy). The Schirmer test screens for adequate tear production: a filter paper strip is placed in the lower conjunctival sac and the eyes are closed; less than 5 mm of wetting after 5 minutes is abnormal.

Treatment of dry eye involves suppressing inflammation and addressing lid pathology. Artificial tears 4 times daily and a nighttime lubricant are beneficial for patients with incomplete lid closure. Warm compresses for 5 minutes in the early morning and mid-afternoon may provide significant relief. Lid inflammation may respond to an oral tetracycline, which has anti-inflammatory properties. Gentle scrubs with dilute, nontearing shampoo may relieve meibomian gland dysfunction or meibomitis. Topical corticosteroids can improve symptoms within days, but long-term side effects (cataracts, increased IOP) limit long-term use. Topical cyclosporine 0.05% is a potent anti-inflammatory medication that targets the underlying inflammatory process and appears to be safe for long-term use in patients with keratoconjunctivitis sicca.

## Excessive Tearing

Excessive tearing results from overproduction (lacrimation) or impaired drainage (epiphora). Overproduction is usually intermittent, bilateral, and without discharge. Epiphora is usually unilateral, frequent or constant, and may be associated with pain, edema, erythema, or frank infection (dacryocystitis) in the medial canthus or lacrimal sac.

Examination should include the cornea and conjunctiva for evidence of foreign bodies; the lids (and facial muscles) for ectropion (eversion) of the lower lid or inability to close the lids; the medial canthus for tenderness, inflammation, or even extrusion of pus from the punctum (suggesting infection); and the nasal cavity to determine whether the region of the middle and inferior turbinates is patent for tear drainage. Referral to an ophthalmologist for further evaluation is often necessary. Treatment involves correcting the underlying condition (such as systemic antibiotics for dacryocystitis) or surgical intervention for outflow obstructions and strictures.

## Eye Emergencies

The outpatient management of various ocular emergencies is summarized in **Table 47**.

Central retinal artery occlusion (CRAO) classically presents in a 50- to 70-year-old patient as a painless, abrupt loss of vision that occurs in the early morning hours—usually between midnight and 6 AM and second most commonly between 6 AM and noon. It results from an embolic or thrombotic event in the ophthalmic artery. It may occur as a complication of coronary angiography or ocular trauma or from an underlying condition, such as giant cell arteritis, systemic lupus erythematosus, homocystinemia, a patent foramen ovale, or posterior scleritis.

On examination of patients with CRAO, the patient's visual acuity is markedly diminished in the affected eye to either finger counting or light perception. There is an afferent papillary defect. On funduscopic examination, the retina appears pale, although the fovea may appear as a cherry red spot because the darkly pigmented choroid is more visible in this region (**Figure 25**). Because irreversible loss of vision may occur within 100 minutes of symptom onset, immediate therapy is necessary in addition to emergent ophthalmologic consultation. Ocular massage for 15 minutes (repeated direct pressure and release on the eyeball) should be attempted, as this may allow the causative plaque or clot to migrate more distally.

Giant cell arteritis may result in abrupt loss of vision due to thrombosis, most commonly of the posterior ciliary artery or the ophthalmic artery. In a patient with sudden vision loss and signs and symptoms of giant cell arteritis (headache in a patient >50 years, tenderness over the temporal artery, jaw claudication, symptoms of polymyalgia rheumatica, elevated erythrocyte sedimentation rate), treatment with systemic corticosteroids must begin promptly and not be delayed while

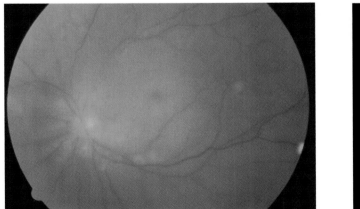 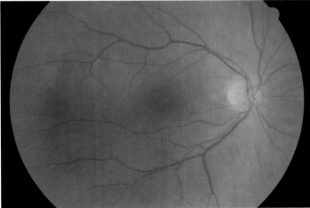

**FIGURE 25.**
**Central retinal artery occlusion.**
Central retinal artery occlusion (CRAO) (*left*); normal fundus (*right*). In comparison to the normal fundus, note the pale fundus in the eye with CRAO.

Image courtesy of Linda Lippa, MD, University of California, Irvine.

**TABLE 47** Diagnosis and Initial Outpatient Treatment of Ocular Emergencies

| Disorder | Signs and Symptoms | Initial Treatment |
|---|---|---|
| Mechanical injury to the globe | Normal or damaged cornea; irregular or deviated pupil toward the direction of injury; hyphema; red eye/subconjunctival hemorrhage in the area 360 degrees around the cornea; moderate to severe pain; normal or decreased vision | Leave embedded foreign object in place; avoid direct pressure on orbit; protect with eye shield; tonometry contraindicated<br><br>Analgesia and antiemetics; update tetanus immunization<br><br>*Immediate referral to ophthalmologist* |
| Chemical injury | Cornea may have minor epithelial damage or be opaque; moderate to severe pain; blurred vision; reflex blepharospasm; photophobia; sensation of foreign body; red eye/conjunctiva | Eye irrigation with normal saline or lactated Ringer solution (usually a minimum 1-2 L of fluid); continue eye wash on way to emergency department or ophthalmologist<br><br>*Immediate referral to ophthalmologist* |
| Central retinal artery occlusion | Sudden, painless transient or permanent visual loss: onset often in early morning hours; patient age 50-70 years; clear cornea; attenuation of the retinal arteries; red eye/conjunctiva; pale fundus; pupil may be dilated and react poorly to light; afferent pupillary defect. Permanent visual loss possible within 100 min of symptom onset | Reduce intraocular pressure with ocular digital massage, intravenous mannitol, oral acetazolamide, oral nitrates, or by laying the patient on his or her back<br><br>*Immediate referral to ophthalmologist* |
| Acute angle-closure glaucoma | Acute onset to severe pain; blurred vision; frontal headache; halos around lights; increased intraocular pressure; red eye/conjunctiva; mid-dilate and sluggish pupil; normal or hazy cornea | *Immediate referral to ophthalmologist* |
| Retinal detachment | Normal to peripheral or central vision loss; absence of pain; increasing floaters; unilateral photopsia; metamorphopsia; normal conjunctiva and cornea; normal pupil; pale, detached retina | Antitussives or antiemetics (if needed)<br><br>*Referral to ophthalmologist within 24 hours* |
| Herpes zoster ophthalmicus | Tingling, pain in brow, lids, tip of nose, distribution of trigeminal nerve; vesicular skin eruption; red eye; cornea may be involved; involvement of tip of the nose (Hutchinson sign) confers a high risk of corneal involvement | Begin antiviral agent (acyclovir, valacyclovir, or famciclovir)<br><br>*Urgent referral to ophthalmologist within 24 hours* |
| Endophthalmitis (infectious) | If postoperative, usually occurs within 6 weeks of surgery (>6 weeks considered delayed)<br><br>Decreased visual acuity; red eye/conjunctival injection; pain, photophobia; corneal edema/opacification; hypopyon (pus in anterior chamber); symptoms of infection in adjacent structures or distant site | *Immediate referral to ophthalmologist* (for intravitreal antibiotic treatment) |
| Orbital or preseptal cellulitis | Preseptal: erythema, edema of lids, periocular structures<br><br>Orbital: eye pain, decreased visual acuity, pain with eye movement, unilateral proptosis, afferent pupillary defect | Intravenous antibiotics targeting likely organisms<br><br>*Immediate referral/consultation with ophthalmologist* |

Adapted with permission from Pokhrel PK, Loftus SA. Ocular Emergencies. Am Fam Physician. 2007;76(6):829-836. [PMID: 17910297] Copyright 2007, American Academy of Family Physicians.

awaiting biopsy or referral to an ophthalmologist, as visual loss may be permanent (see MKSAP 15 Rheumatology).

Chemical burns pose an immediate threat to vision. Alkali burns, which can be caused by lye, drain cleaners, fertilizers, and firecrackers, are the most serious and can rapidly cause corneal-scleral melting. Emergency treatment in the office includes immediate and copious irrigation, which must be continued while the patient is transported to the emergency department or an ophthalmologist. Acid burns can also cause serious corneal damage, and initial management also consists of irrigation. Base should never be used to neutralize acid, and vice versa.

Globe trauma can range from blunt to penetrating trauma from a variety of projectiles, such as metal, rock, or glass. Failure to recognize globe penetration can lead to endophthalmitis, a serious infection of the globe. A blowout fracture results from direct trauma to the eyeball in which the force of the blow is transmitted through the floor of the orbit, resulting in the eyeball being trapped in the maxillary sinus; physical examination findings include the orbit being posterior and inferior but in the eye socket and an inability to perform an upward gaze (**Figure 26**).

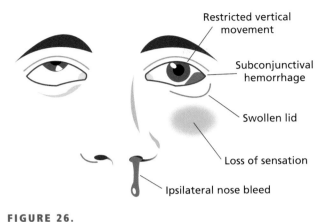

**FIGURE 26.**
**Blowout fracture.**
Signs of a left orbital blowout fracture (patient looking upward).

Restricted vertical movement
Subconjunctival hemorrhage
Swollen lid
Loss of sensation
Ipsilateral nose bleed

Reprinted with permission from Khaw PT, Shah P, Elkington AR. Injury to the eye. BMJ. 2004;328(7430):38. [PMID: 14703545] Copyright 2000, BMJ Publishing Group Ltd.

When trauma is suspected, the globe must be protected from further injury with a shield; the bottom half of a paper cup taped in place will suffice if a shield is not available. CT scanning of the orbits may be needed to fully define the extent of trauma or presence of foreign bodies. Systemic antibiotics should be targeted to likely organisms (streptococcal and staphylococcal species; gram-negative organisms and fungi in trauma caused by organic material; *Pasteurella* species in trauma from cats).

Angle-closure glaucoma is characterized by narrowing or closure of the anterior chamber angle, which impedes the trabecular drainage system in the anterior chamber, resulting in elevated intraocular pressure and damage to the optic nerve. In susceptible individuals, rapid increases in intraocular pressure can be triggered by abrupt dilation of the eyes from topical medications, systemic medications such as sulfa derivatives or topiramate, or by moving from brightly to dimly lit environments. Typical signs and symptoms include significant pain, diminished visual acuity, seeing halos around lights, a red eye, headache, and a dilated pupil. The globe may feel firm owing to increased intraocular pressure (often to 30 mm Hg or higher).

Retinal detachment is a separation of the neurosensory layer of the retina from the choroid beneath (**Figure 27**). It may result from trauma or occur spontaneously, particularly in persons with myopia. Symptoms include diminished vision, photopsia (flashes of light), abrupt onset of multiple floaters in the vision, or metamorphopsia (wavy vision). Direct ophthalmoscopic examination may help identify a detachment, but referral to an ophthalmologist is necessary.

Infections involving the eye include endophthalmitis, an intraocular infection that can occur as a complication of eye surgery (developing several days after the procedure), as a result of globe penetration, or from hematogenous or local extension of an infection (for example, from the ethmoid or maxillary sinus). Preseptal and periorbital cellulitis may result

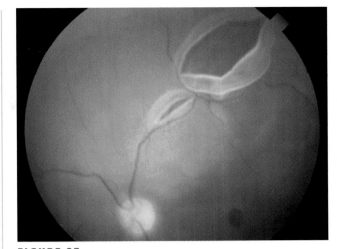

**FIGURE 27.**
**Retinal detachment.**
Folding and tearing of the retina characteristic of retinal detachment.

Image courtesy of Edward A. Jaeger, MD, Jefferson Medical College, Wills Eye Institute, Philadelphia, PA.

from direct trauma, contiguous skin infection, or sinusitis; CT or MRI may be necessary to assess for deep infections. Orbital cellulitis may result from a dental, soft tissue, or ethmoid sinus infection; direct trauma; or hematogenous spread. Untreated, orbital cellulitis can result in meningitis or cavernous sinus thrombosis.

**KEY POINTS**

- Central retinal artery occlusion causes an abrupt, painless loss of vision and requires restoration of blood flow within 100 minutes.
- Chemical burns to the eye should be irrigated copiously with fluid for at least 30 minutes, even while transporting the patient for definitive care.
- Traumatic eye injuries must be protected with a shield while awaiting ophthalmologic intervention.

## Bibliography

Bourla DH, Young TA. Age-related macular degeneration: a practical approach to a challenging disease. J Am Geriatr Soc. 2006;54(7): 1130-1135. [PMID: 16866687]

Chong EW, Wong TY, Kreis AJ, Simpson JA, Guymer RH. Dietary antioxidants and primary prevention of age related macular degeneration: systematic review and meta-analysis. BMJ. 2007;335(7623): 755. [PMID: 17923720]

Hodge W, Horsley T, Albiani D, et al. The consequences of waiting for cataract surgery: a systematic review. CMAJ. 2007;176(9):1285-1290. [PMID: 17452662]

Naradzay J, Barish RA. Approach to ophthalmologic emergencies. Med Clin North Am. 2006;90 (2):305-328. [PMID: 16448877]

Vass C, Hirn C, Sycha T, Findl O, Bauer P, Schmetterer L. Medical interventions for primary open angle glaucoma and ocular hypertension. Cochrane Database Syst Rev. 2007;(4):CD003167. [PMID: 17943780]

Zaldívar RA, Buerger DE, Buerger DG, Woog JJ. Office evaluation of lacrimal and orbital disease. Otolaryngol Clin North Am. 2006;39(5): 911-922. [PMID: 16982254]

# Ear, Nose, Mouth, and Throat Disorders

## Evaluation of Hearing Loss

The two basic types of hearing loss are *conductive*, which involves any cause that limits external sound from reaching the inner ear, and *sensorineural*, which involves the inner ear, cochlea, or auditory nerve. Patients with conductive hearing loss are likely to report simple hearing loss, to have ear pain, and to have drainage. Patients with sensorineural hearing loss have more trouble understanding speech, especially faint or high-pitched voices. In addition, hearing loss is more likely to be sensorineural if accompanied by tinnitus, dizziness, or true vertigo.

Other important historical items include onset and progression; trauma, including noise and barotrauma; surgery; and family history. **Table 48** lists common causes of hearing loss.

A hearing evaluation can be performed by assessing the patient's ability to hear a whispered voice (2 feet from the ear, with the examiner behind the patient and the examiner's finger occluding and simultaneously rubbing the opposite external ear canal, the examiner whispers three numbers/letters after exhalation). Alternatively, an audioscope (a handheld combination screening audiometer and otoscope) can be used. The Weber and Rinne tests can help to distinguish conductive from sensorineural hearing loss. In the Weber test, a vibrating tuning fork is placed on the forehead, the crown, or the nose. If the sound is louder on the unaffected side,

| **TABLE 48** Differential Diagnosis of Hearing Loss | |
|---|---|
| **Disease** | **Notes** |
| **Conductive Hearing Loss** | |
| Otosclerosis | Fixation of the stapes footplate eventually causes a conductive hearing loss. Affects both ears in most patients. Stapedectomy or stapedotomy are the standard treatments. A hearing aid may also be helpful. |
| Cholesteatoma | A middle ear mass composed of keratinized epithelial debris. Causes ossicular disruption or may impede the tympanic membrane's capacity to vibrate. Usually presents as a pearly white mass. Any suspicion of cholesteatoma (whitish, middle ear mass; continually draining ear, over weeks to months) should prompt an otolaryngology consultation. |
| Tympanic membrane perforation | A large tympanic membrane perforation prevents the tympanic membrane from vibrating normally. Most tympanic membrane perforations can be treated surgically. Rule out cholesteatoma. |
| Foreign body | Foreign bodies may enter the external auditory canal and become impacted. Foreign bodies should be removed by an otolaryngologist. |
| Cerumen impaction | Cerumen may completely obstruct the ear canal. |
| Infection | Bacterial infection may involve the external ear (otitis externa) or middle ear (otitis media), thereby producing a conductive hearing loss. Chronic ear infections may produce tympanosclerosis or ossicular disruption, producing a conductive hearing loss. |
| **Sensorineural Hearing Loss** | |
| Noise-induced | Chronic noise exposure or sudden, short exposure to noise blast can produce hearing loss. Noise exposure produces temporary threshold shifts, which eventually become permanent. |
| Drug-induced | History of ototoxic medication use (aminoglycosides, loop diuretics, chemotherapeutic agents) |
| Presbycusis | Age-related hearing loss; typically high-frequency hearing loss that is symmetric with good speech discrimination scores. Hearing aids are the mainstay of therapy for presbycusis. |
| Sudden sensorineural hearing loss | Unclear etiology. Considered an otologic emergency because early treatment may improve prognosis. |
| Meniere disease | Classically presents as a triad of sensorineural hearing loss, tinnitus, and vertigo, although all three are not necessarily present. Electronystagmography and electrocochleography are important tests in the diagnosis, although history usually suggests the disorder. |
| Vestibular schwannoma (acoustic neuroma) | Benign neoplasms that arise in the cerebellopontine angle, usually causing sensorineural hearing loss, tinnitus, and sometimes vertigo. In advanced cases, facial nerve function is affected. |
| Perilymph fistula | Usually sudden onset of hearing loss accompanied by dizziness, with history of straining or trauma. Pneumatic otoscopy with bulb insufflation may cause dizziness (Hennebert sign), sometimes referred to as a "positive fistula test." |
| Inherited hearing loss | Numerous genetic conditions (Waardenburg syndrome, Cogan syndrome) have sensorineural hearing loss as a component. |
| Autoimmune hearing loss | An idiopathic form of hearing loss that is typically bilateral and progressive. Thus far, corticosteroid treatment has been the only therapy with proven benefit. |

Information from Limb CJ, Williams MF. Hearing Loss. http://pier.acponline.org/physicians/diseases/d333/tables/d333-tables.html. In PIER (online database). Philadelphia: American College of Physicians, 2009. Accessed July 7, 2009.

sensorineural hearing loss is suggested; if the sound is louder on the side with hearing loss, conductive hearing loss is suggested. The Rinne test is performed by touching the vibrating fork to the mastoid tip of each ear (to assess bone conduction) and then holding it over the external auditory canal (to assess air conduction). An abnormal Rinne test (hearing is better with bone conduction) is consistent with conductive loss and is more accurate than the Weber test in diagnosing conductive hearing loss. With normal hearing or sensorineural hearing loss, hearing is better with air conduction. Compared with audiometry, the sensitivity of the Rinne test is approximately 80%.

Examination of the ear should include visualization of the tympanic membrane and pneumoscopy to evaluate its mobility. A nonmobile tympanic membrane may indicate fluid or a mass in the middle ear or retraction from negative middle ear pressure.

If no obvious cause of hearing loss is found (such as cerumen impaction or otitis media), the patient should have formal audiologic testing. Patients with hearing loss of unclear etiology should be referred for otolaryngologic evaluation. Asymmetric sensorineural hearing loss not clearly due to Meniere disease should be evaluated with an MRI or CT scan of the posterior fossa and internal auditory canal to exclude acoustic neuroma and meningioma.

Sudden sensorineural hearing loss (SSNHL) is an alarming problem that is defined as hearing loss occurring in 3 days or less. Patients often report immediate or rapid hearing loss or loss of hearing upon awakening. Ninety percent have unilateral hearing loss, and some have tinnitus, ear fullness, and vertigo. SSNHL constitutes a considerable diagnostic challenge because it may be caused by many conditions, including infection, neoplasm, trauma, autoimmune disease, vascular events, and ototoxic drugs. Immediate otolaryngologic referral is required. Improvement occurs in about two thirds of patients. Oral corticosteroids are usually given, although randomized trials differ in their conclusions regarding efficacy.

**KEY POINTS**

- Hearing loss accompanied by ear pain and drainage is more likely to be conductive.

- Hearing loss associated with dizziness and vertigo is more likely to be sensorineural.

## Tinnitus

Tinnitus is an auditory perception of sound that is not present in the external environment. It affects up to 7% of the U.S. population, with incidence increasing with age. Tinnitus is usually minor and is noted only in quiet environments, but for about 25% of patients it interferes with daily life, sometimes to a significant degree.

Pulsatile tinnitus is often vascular in origin and may be due to an arteriovenous fistula, arteriovenous malformation, arterial aneurysm, tumor, or atherosclerotic disease. A head and neck examination should include auscultation for bruits over the neck, eyes, and around the ear. The effect of positioning of the head and neck and of arterial and venous compression on the tinnitus should be noted. Patients with frequent or constant pulsatile tinnitus should have otolaryngologic evaluation and may require CT, magnetic resonance, or interventional angiography.

Tinnitus that is clicking may be caused by myoclonus of the palatal muscles or muscles of the middle ear and may be an indication of neurologic disease, including multiple sclerosis. Clicking from palatal myoclonus may be stopped with wide jaw opening.

Continuous tinnitus most often originates within the auditory system and is usually a consequence of sensorineural hearing loss. A high-pitched continuous tone is most common. Low-pitched tinnitus may be seen in patients with Meniere disease. Other causes are noise exposure, ototoxic medications (**Table 49**), presbycusis, otosclerosis, acoustic neuroma, and barotrauma. Correcting a reversible cause of conductive hearing loss (such as cerumen impaction or otitis media) may eliminate tinnitus that results from attenuation of background sounds. Patients with continuous tinnitus should have audiologic testing and further evaluation if hearing asymmetry is present.

Treatment of tinnitus should first be directed at the underlying disorder. For those with severe sensorineural hearing loss, cochlear implants may improve tinnitus. Other therapies include sound-masking devices and inducing habituation to tinnitus. Behavioral therapies include biofeedback, stress reduction, and cognitive-behavioral therapy directed at improving the patient's ability to cope with tinnitus.

**KEY POINTS**

- Pulsatile tinnitus most often is vascular in origin and should prompt specialty referral and may require angiography.

- Continuous tinnitus most often originates within the auditory system and is usually a consequence of sensorineural hearing loss.

| **TABLE 49** Drugs that May Cause or Exacerbate Tinnitus |
|---|
| Aminoglycoside antibiotics |
| Antimalarial drugs (chloroquine, hydroxychloroquine) |
| Benzodiazepines |
| Carbamazepine |
| Loop diuretics |
| Quinidine |
| Salicylates |
| NSAIDs |
| Tricyclic antidepressants |

# Otitis Media and Otitis Externa

## Otitis Media

Otitis media is the most frequent bacterial infection in children, but it is much less common in adults. It is usually preceded by viral upper respiratory tract infection. The microbiology of otitis media in adults appears to be similar to that of children: *Streptococcus pneumoniae*: 21% to 63%; *Haemophilus influenzae*: 11% to 26%; *Staphylococcus aureus*: 3% to 12%; *Moraxella catarrhalis*: 3%. Thirty percent of bacterial cultures of middle ear effusions are sterile. Complications of otitis media include conductive hearing loss from persistent middle ear effusion, tympanic membrane perforation, mastoiditis, and, rarely, meningitis or intracranial abscess.

To diagnose acute otitis media, there should be a history of an acute onset, signs of middle ear effusion (using a pneumatic otoscope to document lack of tympanic membrane movement), and signs of middle ear inflammation (erythema of the tympanic membrane). Because the frequency of bacterial and viral pathogens cultured in bullous myringitis is similar for otitis media without bullae, bullous myringitis is probably not a separate clinical entity but rather otitis media with blisters on the tympanic membrane.

Treatment of otitis media in adults has not been well studied. There are no guidelines for antibiotic use in adults separate from those for children. In children older than 2 years without severe illness, outcomes appear to be similar for observation without antibiotics compared with antibiotic treatment. This strategy to reduce use of antimicrobials has not been evaluated in adults, and it is not known if antibiotics are associated with improved short- or long-term outcomes. If antibiotics are used, amoxicillin is the recommended antibiotic because of its proven efficacy and safety, relatively low cost, and narrow spectrum. Cephalosporins (cefdinir, cefuroxime, cefpodoxime) or macrolides (azithromycin, clarithromycin) can be used in patients who are allergic to penicillin. In the case of treatment failure after 48 to 72 hours of initial management with an antibiotic, amoxicillin-clavulanate or ceftriaxone is recommended. Decongestants and antihistamines are not recommended.

### KEY POINTS

- Acute otitis media is characterized by middle ear effusion and signs of middle ear inflammation (erythema of the tympanic membrane).

- It is not known whether antibiotic use for acute otitis media in adults is associated with improved short or long-term outcomes.

## Otitis Externa

Acute otitis externa is diffuse inflammation of the external ear canal. Factors that predispose to otitis externa are regular cleaning of the ear canal with removal of cerumen, which is an important barrier to moisture and infection; debris from dermatologic conditions; local trauma from attempts at self-cleaning, irrigation, and hearing aids; and increased exposure to water. In the United States, nearly all external otitis is bacterial, primarily *Pseudomonas aeruginosa* and *Staphylococcus aureus*. Polymicrobial infection occurs in about one third of cases.

Acute otitis externa usually has a rapid onset, typically within 48 hours but sometimes up to 3 weeks. Symptoms include otalgia, itching or fullness with or without hearing loss, and pain intensified by jaw motion. Signs include internal tenderness when the tragus or pinna is pushed or pulled and diffuse ear canal edema and erythema, with or without otorrhea. Otitis externa can cause erythema of the tympanic membrane and mimic otitis media. In otitis externa, however, pneumatic otoscopy shows good tympanic membrane mobility. Conditions that may mimic otitis externa are an external canal furuncle; inflammatory dermatologic conditions such as eczema and seborrhea; contact dermatitis of the ear and ear canal from ear drops, earrings, or hearing aids; and herpes zoster, which may cause the Ramsay Hunt syndrome (**Figure 28**), characterized by herpetic lesions in the external canal and ipsilateral facial palsy.

The most serious complication of acute otitis externa is necrotizing otitis externa, which occurs when the infection spreads beyond the ear canal to the surrounding tissue, cartilage, and bone. The most common cause is *P. aeruginosa*, and it is most likely to occur in elderly patients with diabetes mellitus and immunocompromised patients. Patients suspected of having necrotizing otitis externa should be referred to an otolaryngologist; the diagnosis may require confirmation with CT or MRI.

Topical antimicrobials for 7 days is the recommended treatment for acute otitis externa. A systematic review found

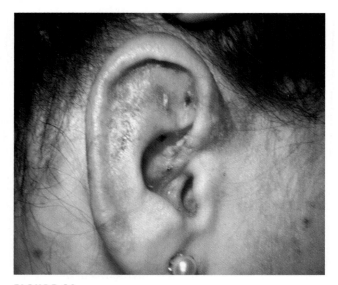

**FIGURE 28.**
**Ramsay Hunt syndrome.**
The triad of ipsilateral facial paralysis, ear pain, and *Herpes zoster* vesicles in the auditory canal and auricle define the Ramsay Hunt syndrome.

no significant differences in clinical outcomes after use of antiseptic or antimicrobial preparations, fluoroquinolone antibiotic or nonfluoroquinolone antibiotic preparations, and corticosteroid-antimicrobial or antimicrobial-alone preparations. The combination corticosteroid-antimicrobial drops may relieve pain faster and may be considered in patients with more severe pain.

Oral antibiotics should not be used for otitis externa unless the infection has spread beyond the ear canal or the patient has immunodeficiency, diabetes mellitus, a history of radiation to the ear, or occlusion of the ear canal precluding delivery of topical medication. The antibiotic choice should cover *P. aeruginosa* and *S. aureus*. Often an oral fluoroquinolone is appropriate. If the ear canal is obstructed, referral to an otolaryngologist for cleaning the canal or placing a wick may be warranted.

**KEY POINTS**

- Topical antimicrobials are the recommended treatment for uncomplicated acute otitis externa.

- Necrotizing otitis externa is a serious complication of acute otitis externa that occurs when the infection spreads beyond the ear canal to the surrounding tissue, cartilage, and bone.

## Cerumen Impaction

Cerumen is composed of the secretions of sebaceous and ceruminous glands located in the outer third of the external ear canal, mixed with desquamated epithelial cells, shed hairs, and foreign bodies. Normally, the ear canal is self-cleaning owing to the outward migration of the squamous epithelium from the tympanic membrane. Although the cause of cerumen impaction in most patients in unknown, it can be due to narrowing of the ear canal, occlusion by hearing aids, certain skin conditions, and inappropriate efforts to clean the ear canal (for example, with a cotton swab). Complete occlusion causes moderate conductive hearing loss.

It is unnecessary to remove ear wax unless there is hearing loss or symptoms requiring visualization of the ear canal or tympanic membrane. Removal of cerumen from the outer third of the canal may be performed using an ear curet or spoon. This should be done under direct visualization and with care taken to avoid trauma to the skin. A cooperative patient is necessary. Gentle irrigation with water at body temperature is often effective, and direct visualization of the ear canal is not necessary for irrigation. The canal should be straightened during irrigation with gentle traction upward and backward on the external ear. If initially unsuccessful, it may be repeated after leaving water or a ceruminolytic in place for 15 to 30 minutes. If the initial attempt to clear the canal is unsuccessful, the patient can use a ceruminolytic for several days, followed by another trial of irrigation. Otolaryngology referral may be appropriate in selected

patients. A recent systematic review concluded that no ceruminolytic has been shown to be superior to any other ceruminolytic or to water or saline solution. For patients with frequent cerumen impaction, weekly or monthly use of several drops of mineral oil, olive oil, or other emollient in the external canal will keep cerumen softer and facilitate the normal cerumen elimination mechanism.

**KEY POINTS**

- It is unnecessary to remove cerumen unless there is hearing loss or symptoms requiring visualization of the ear canal or tympanic membrane.

- No ceruminolytic has been shown to be superior to any other ceruminolytic or to water or saline solution.

# Upper Respiratory Tract Disorders

## Sinusitis

Sinusitis, also called rhinosinusitis, represents one of the most common reasons for office visits in the United States. Sinusitis is responsible for 25 million office visits annually, and a primary care physician may see 50 or more cases per year. Although most patients do not have a confirmed diagnosis or proven bacterial cause, 92% of patients receive an antibiotic. The consequences of unnecessary antibiotic use are $2.4 billion per year in costs and increasing antibiotic resistance. The term *acute sinusitis* describes cases with a duration of symptoms of less than 4 weeks. Recurrent sinusitis is defined as more than three episodes per year, and chronic sinusitis is defined as the presence of symptoms for more than 12 weeks.

The symptoms of acute sinusitis include nasal congestion, rhinorrhea, and facial pain; more severe infections may include fever and malaise. Most infections are viral in origin, with only 0.5% to 2% having a bacterial cause. Typical organisms include *Streptococcus pneumoniae, Haemophilus influenzae,* and, occasionally, *Moraxella catarrhalis.* The gold standard for diagnosis of bacterial sinusitis is sinus aspiration with culture-positive purulent material. In some studies, radiologic diagnosis correlates well with direct aspiration. However, neither radiography nor aspiration is typically indicated in primary care practice. Imaging, including CT, should be considered in patients with AIDS or in other immunocompromised patients to evaluate for fungal infection or other atypical infections.

Various clinical criteria have been proposed to predict the likelihood of true sinusitis among suspected cases. One such clinical prediction rule assigns one point each for maxillary toothache, history of colored nasal discharge, no improvement with decongestants, abnormal transillumination, and purulent secretion on examination of the nares. The overall probability of radiographically confirmed sinusitis is 37%, and patients with 3, 4, and 5 points have approximately 60%, 80%, and 90% probability of sinusitis, respectively.

Antibiotics have been found to have little, if any, role in the treatment of acute sinusitis in the primary care setting. Nonetheless, some current guidelines conclude that antibiotics (amoxicillin) are reasonable if at least two of the following features are present: symptoms for longer than 7 days, facial pain, and purulent nasal discharge. A recent review concluded that after 10 days of rhinosinusitis symptoms, antibiotic therapy and watchful waiting are equally acceptable. In penicillin-allergic patients, doxycycline or trimethoprim-sulfamethoxazole may be used. No well-designed, randomized studies have addressed the efficacy of sinus irrigation, nasal sprays, or other nondrug therapies, but they are often prescribed. Their effectiveness is unknown. Endoscopic sinus surgery with lavage and drainage may be indicated in refractory infections.

Complications of acute sinusitis are unusual but important to recognize and treat promptly. Patients with cavernous sinus thrombosis are acutely ill and may have fever, nausea, vomiting, headache, orbital edema, or cranial nerve involvement. Osteomyelitis presents with fever, leukocytosis, frontal headache, and edema over the affected frontal sinus (Pott puffy tumor). Brain abscess should be suspected in patients with headache, vomiting, and neurologic signs. In patients with fever, stiff neck, headache, photophobia, vomiting, or seizures, bacterial meningitis should be suspected. Consultation is indicated when any of the above complications is suspected.

---

**KEY POINTS**

- Antibiotics should usually not be prescribed for patients with suspected sinusitis unless at least two of the following features are present: symptoms lasting for more than 7 days, facial pain, and purulent nasal discharge.
- Patients with suspected sinusitis who appear acutely ill, have fever, periorbital edema, or neurologic signs may have serious complications of sinusitis and should be evaluated further.

## Allergic Rhinitis

Allergic rhinitis is characterized by nasal congestion, rhinorrhea, sneezing, and itchiness due to inflammation of the nasal mucosa. Allergic rhinitis is a common problem, accounting for more than $2 billion in health care expenditures in the United States annually. Allergic rhinitis is seen in patients with atopy (one or more findings of allergic rhinitis, asthma, or atopic eczema) or a family history of allergic rhinitis. Typical outdoor allergic triggers include pollen and molds. Indoor allergens include house mites, molds, and pet dander. Occupational exposures can be irritants or allergic triggers. Nonallergic rhinitis (vasomotor or irritant rhinitis) is similar in frequency to allergic rhinitis and is caused by increased sensitivity to irritants in the air. The pathophysiology is less clear than that of allergic rhinitis, but the chemical mediators that result in symptoms are similar. Other causes of rhinitis include viral infection, pregnancy, hypothyroidism, decongestant overuse, and vasculitis (**Table 50**).

---

**TABLE 50** Differential Diagnosis of Allergic Rhinitis

| Disease | Notes |
|---|---|
| Rhinitis in pregnancy | Hormonal changes in pregnancy can cause nasal congestion. |
| Hypothyroidism | Resolves with treatment of hypothyroidism. |
| Hypertrophic turbinates or adenoids, foreign body, nasal tumors | Causes of fixed obstruction. Physical examination and endoscopy helpful. Lateral neck radiograph, sinus CT may be helpful. Tumors can be benign or malignant. Hypertrophic adenoids and foreign bodies seen more in children than in adults. |
| Wegener granulomatosis | Usually accompanied by systemic illness. Can cause nasal ulceration or chronic sinusitis. |
| Sarcoidosis | Usually accompanied by systemic illness. Causes granulomatous inflammation. |
| Sjögren syndrome | May cause nasal dryness and eye irritation. Sicca syndrome can cause rhinitis and conjunctivitis. |
| Cerebrospinal fluid rhinorrhea | History of trauma or surgery may be present. Head CT or MRI for diagnosis. May require surgical correction. Screening by fluid glucose level of nasal secretions. |
| Cystic fibrosis | Younger age group, nasal polyposis, or chronic sinusitis present. Sweat chloride test of choice. |
| Vasomotor rhinitis | Allergy skin tests negative or positive without correlating history. Nonseasonal. |
| Nasal polyposis | Causes obstruction and rhinorrhea. Seen on physical examination or rhinoscopy. |
| Sinusitis | Infectious or inflammatory. May be difficult to distinguish from allergic rhinitis, or may coexist with allergic rhinitis. |
| Deviated nasal septum | Causes fixed obstruction. May cause unilateral symptoms. |
| Rhinitis medicamentosa | Refractory nasal congestion. Overuse of topical nasal decongestants. |

Adapted from Li JT. Allergic rhinitis. http://pier.acponline.org/physicians/diseases/d095/tables/d095-tables.html. In PIER (online database). Philadelphia: American College of Physicians, 2009. Accessed July 7, 2009.

When evaluating the patient with allergic rhinitis, the history should include questions about seasonal occurrence, color of mucus, nasal obstruction (unilateral or bilateral), eye symptoms, coughing, and wheezing. Lower respiratory tract symptoms may suggest concomitant asthma. Additional historical items that are important in distinguishing allergic from nonallergic rhinitis include information about occupational exposures and medications, including aspirin, NSAIDs, and systemic and local decongestants that can be associated with symptoms of rhinitis. Important physical examination findings relevant to allergic rhinitis include a horizontal nasal crease (in children, from pushing upward on the nose), a widened nasal bridge (seen in nasal polyposis), and darkness under the eyes (due to venous engorgement). Nasal polyps, due to prolapsed inflamed nasal or sinus mucosa, can be seen as yellowish gray nodules that are separate from the side wall of the nose. A depressed nasal bridge is seen in patients with cocaine abuse and Wegener granulomatosis (types of nonallergic rhinitis).

Skin prick tests remain the most cost-effective and specific diagnostic method to confirm allergic rhinitis. Serum immunoassays for allergen-specific IgE (cap-radioallergosorbent [CAP-RAST] tests) are available, but they are more expensive and less sensitive than skin tests. Nasal secretion Wright smear may help differentiate allergic rhinitis (predominance of eosinophils) from infection (predominance of neutrophils), but the specificity of this test is poor. If rhinitis is persistent, spirometry should be performed to evaluate for asthma. If the spirometry results are consistent with asthma (partially reversible airflow obstruction), further evaluation and treatment of asthma should be initiated according to the National Asthma Education and Prevention Program of the National Heart, Lung, and Blood Institute.

Topical nasal corticosteroids are first-line therapy for allergic rhinitis. Fluticasone and mometasone have minimal systemic side effects. Topical corticosteroids are considered safe in pregnancy after the first trimester. Second-generation (nonsedating) antihistamines can be used as additional therapy or alone for mild symptoms. Topical azelastine improves nasal congestion, but it is less effective at improving other symptoms. Ipratropium bromide is effective for severe rhinorrhea. Nasal saline irrigation has been shown to relieve symptoms and may be most helpful for patients with concomitant sinusitis.

Montelukast has been approved for the treatment of allergic rhinitis, but its effectiveness is limited. Topical cromolyn has some effectiveness but needs to be used every 4 hours. Rarely, systemic corticosteroids may be needed for patients with severe rhinitis. Subcutaneous allergen immunotherapy, using extracts of pollen, house dust mites, and animal dander, is effective for patients with confirmed allergic rhinitis who do not respond to the above therapies.

Patient education should include information about avoiding allergens, proper use of nasal sprays, the long-term nature of the condition, and the limitations of therapy. Avoiding pets may be helpful, but it takes months for cat allergens to be cleared from the home. Mite-proof bed covers have not been proved to be effective as a single measure.

The most consistently effective treatments for chronic nonallergic rhinitis are topical intranasal corticosteroids, topical intranasal antihistamines, and topical ipratropium bromide; however, nonallergic rhinitis is less responsive to therapy than allergic rhinitis.

**KEY POINTS**

- Physicians should always consider the possibility of coexisting asthma in patients with allergic rhinitis.
- Intranasal corticosteroids are first-line therapy for allergic rhinitis and are superior to antihistamines.

## Pharyngitis

Acute pharyngitis accounts for 1% to 2% of all visits to physician offices. Pharyngitis may present as a primary symptom or as a component of a constellation of upper respiratory tract symptoms. The differential diagnosis of sore throat includes viral and bacterial pharyngitis, irritation from posterior pharyngeal drainage of mucus, and gastroesophageal reflux disease. Most patients with pharyngitis presenting to a primary care physician have a viral illness due to rhinovirus, adenovirus, coronavirus, or Epstein-Barr virus. The physician's task is to differentiate these patients from those who have bacterial infections and require antibiotic treatment, mainly group A β-hemolytic streptococcal (GABHS) infection. Pharyngitis caused by *Neisseria gonorrhoeae* requires antibiotic treatment and there is some evidence that non-GABHS streptococcal organisms (for example, group C or G) can cause symptomatic disease and should also be treated with antibiotics.

Physicians should consider infectious mononucleosis in patients with fever, headache, palatine petechiae, marked lymphadenopathy (especially posterior cervical or diffuse), splenomegaly, and malaise. HIV infection should be considered in patients at risk for this disease. Pharyngitis due to *N. gonorrhoeae* should be suspected in individuals who have engaged in oral-genital sex, but the appearance of the pharynx has no characteristic features. Pharyngitis due to *Corynebacterium diphtheriae* should be suspected if the characteristic gray membrane is seen during inspection of the pharynx. The appearance of non-GABHS streptococcal pharyngitis is indistinguishable from GABHS.

Use of the four-point Centor criteria is a reasonable way to triage patients to empiric treatment with antibiotics, symptomatic treatment only, or testing with treatment if the test is positive (**Table 51**). One point is given for each of the following: fever (subjective or measured >38.1 °C

**TABLE 51 Testing and Treatment Guidelines for Adult Pharyngitis**

| Centor Score[a] | Recommended Testing | Treatment |
|---|---|---|
| 0 | No test | No treatment |
| 1 | No test | No treatment |
| 2 | RADT | Penicillin V if test is positive |
| 3 | No test[b] | Empiric penicillin V[b] |
|   | RADT | Penicillin V if test is positive |
| 4 | No test | Empiric penicillin V |

RADT = rapid antigen detection test.

[a]One point is given for each of fever, absence of cough, tender anterior cervical lymphadenopathy, and tonsillar exudates.

[b]Strategy endorsed by Centor RM, Allison JJ, Cohen SJ. Pharyngitis management: defining the controversy. J Gen Intern Med. 2007;22(1):127-130. [PMID: 17351852]

[100.5 °F]), absence of cough, tender anterior cervical lymphadenopathy, and tonsillar exudates. Patients with all four criteria have a 40% or greater chance of having GABHS pharyngitis; patients with zero or one criterion have a low (<3%) probability of GABHS pharyngitis. Patients with two or three criteria have an intermediate probability of GABHS pharyngitis; for these patients, some guidelines recommend throat culture and others recommend the rapid antigen detection test (RADT) with confirmation of negative results. The advantage of RADT is the immediate availability of the results. RADT has comparable sensitivity and specificity to throat culture. The throat swab for either culture or RADT should be obtained from both tonsils or tonsillar fossae and the posterior pharyngeal wall. A recent analysis of all current recommendations concluded that empirically treating all patients with Centor scores of three or four would optimally balance potential over- and undertreatment of patients in these categories. Use of the Centor criteria would decrease antibiotic usage from 73% to 35%.

The treatment of choice for GABHS pharyngitis is penicillin V (500 mg twice daily for 10 days) or, in penicillin-allergic patients, erythromycin. Antibiotic therapy instituted within 2 to 3 days of symptom onset decreases symptom duration by 1 to 2 days if GABHS is confirmed, but this effect is not seen in GABHS-negative patients. Tonsillectomy in patients with recurrent GABHS pharyngitis (three or more episodes of pharyngitis in 6 months or four episodes in 12 months) is associated with decreased recurrence of GABHS pharyngitis and fewer days of sore throat pain.

Complications of untreated GABHS pharyngitis include peritonsillar abscess ("quinsy"), poststreptococcal glomerulonephritis, and rheumatic fever. About half of patients with peritonsillar abscess present first with this complication; among those who present first with sore throat and then develop peritonsillar abscess, only one quarter have GABHS pharyngitis. Poststreptococcal acute glomerulonephritis is very rare, and there are no studies showing that antibiotics prevent this complication. Rheumatic fever is rare in adults. The number needed to treat to prevent one case of acute rheumatic fever was approximately 63 in initial studies but is probably closer to 3000 today. Treatment to prevent rheumatic fever can be delayed for up to 9 days after the onset of symptoms.

**KEY POINT**

- Antibiotics are not recommended for group A β-hemolytic streptococcal pharyngitis in patients with only zero or one of the following features: fever, tender cervical lymphadenopathy, tonsillar exudate, and absence of cough.

## Epistaxis

The incidence of epistaxis has a bimodal distribution, peaking at ages younger than 10 years and older than 50 years. Most episodes occur in the anterior part of the nose in the Kiesselbach plexus, the vascular watershed area of the nasal septum. Posterior bleeds most often arise from branches of the sphenopalatine arteries, behind the posterior portion of the middle turbinate or at the posterior superior roof of the nasal cavity. Common local causes are nose picking, trauma, irritants (including medications), low humidity, foreign bodies, rhinitis from viral infections or allergies, tumors, septal perforation, vascular malformation, and telangiectasias. Common systemic causes include anticoagulation therapy, antiplatelet therapy, thrombocytopenia, and other bleeding disorders. Most causes of epistaxis can be identified by a directed history and physical examination. Laboratory studies, including prothrombin time, complete blood count, platelet count, and blood type and cross-match, should be obtained when appropriate.

Initial management of stable patients should included application of direct pressure to the septal area for up to 20 minutes. Control of bleeding with this maneuver suggests an anterior bleed. If needed, further treatment of anterior bleeding can include topical application of phenylephrine or oxymetazoline to the septal area and repeated periods of direct pressure. Chemical cautery of a bleeding point with silver nitrate may be used for simple anterior epistaxis. To avoid septal necrosis, only one side of the septum should be cauterized. If these maneuvers do not control anterior bleeding, either urgent otolaryngology referral or anterior nasal packing is recommended. Patients with posterior bleeds, anterior bleeds not responding to treatment, or severe blood loss require appropriate stabilizing interventions and urgent otolaryngology consultation.

- Initial management of stable patients with epistaxis should included application of direct pressure to the septal area for up to 20 minutes.

# Oral Health

## Oral Infections and Ulcers

### Oral Candidiasis

Oropharyngeal candidiasis, usually caused by *Candida albicans*, has variable symptoms, ranging from none to a sore, painful mouth with burning tongue and altered taste. Pseudomembranous candidiasis (thrush) is characterized by white, curd-like, discrete plaques on an erythematous base that can be exposed by scraping a plaque (**Figure 29**). It is found on the buccal mucosa, throat, tongue, and gingivae. Erythematous candidiasis is characterized by smooth red patches on the hard or soft palate, tongue, or buccal mucosa and is associated with chronic salivary hypofunction (as in Sjögren syndrome or from anticholinergic drug effects). Hyperplastic candidiasis has white, firmly adherent patches or plaques that cannot be scraped off. Denture-induced candidiasis presents as smooth or granular erythema in the denture-bearing areas, often associated with angular cheilitis (red, fissured lesions at the corners of the mouth). Causes of oral candidiasis include immunosuppression, broad-spectrum antibiotic use, inhaled or systemic corticosteroids, xerostomia, diabetes, and dentures.

In patients without HIV disease, topical treatment with nystatin or clotrimazole should be tried first. If the response is inadequate, oral fluconazole should be used. In HIV-positive patients, the occurrence of oral candidiasis usually indicates significant immunosuppression. In patients with mild oral candidiasis, topical therapy may be tried. For those with moderate or severe disease and for those with odynophagia and suspected esophageal candidiasis, oral fluconazole should be used. When possible, the underlying cause of the candidiasis should be addressed.

### Herpes Labialis

Herpes simplex virus persisting in a latent state in the trigeminal ganglion may reactivate, typically causing a localized cluster of vesicles along the vermilion border of the lip (**Figure 30**). The vesicles rupture and crust within 24 to 48 hours and heal over the ensuing 7 to 10 days without scarring. An outbreak may be triggered by sunlight, stress, or fatigue. In immunocompetent patients, herpes labialis is a mild, self-limited illness. Oral herpes zoster occurs less often and can be distinguished from herpes simplex by being unilateral and corresponding to specific sensory nerve distributions.

Treatment of recurrent herpes labialis with oral or topical antiviral agents is largely unsuccessful owing to the difficulty of recognizing the onset of recurrence early enough to start the medication in time to affect the disease course. In those patients who have a recognizable prodrome, however, oral antiviral agents (acyclovir, valacyclovir, famciclovir) or penciclovir cream can result in modest reductions in duration of pain and time to healing. For those with frequent recurrences, oral antiviral agents given prophylactically may reduce the frequency and severity of attacks.

### Aphthous Ulcers

Aphthous ulcers are painful, well-defined, circular ulcerations that occur most commonly on the buccal and labial mucosa (**Figure 31**). They may occur on all areas of the oral mucosa except the hard palate, gingiva, and vermilion border. They may be single or multiple. Most adults experience them at some time during their life, and the incidence lessens with advancing age. Minor aphthous ulcers are flat, are less than 1 cm in diameter, and last 5 to 10 days. Major aphthous ulcers

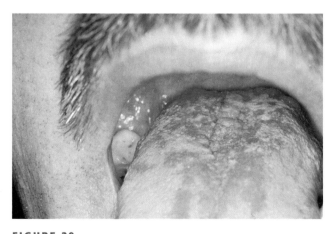

**FIGURE 29.**
**Oral candidiasis.**
Oropharyngeal candidiasis (thrush) is characterized by white, curd-like discrete plaques on an erythematous base typically located on the buccal mucosa, throat, tongue, and gingivae.

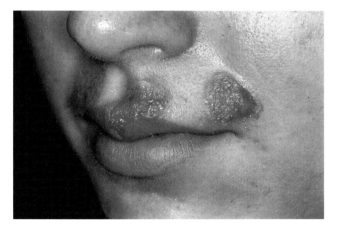

**FIGURE 30.**
**Herpes labialis.**
Herpes labialis is recognized as a localized cluster of vesicles and erosions along the vermilion border of the lip.

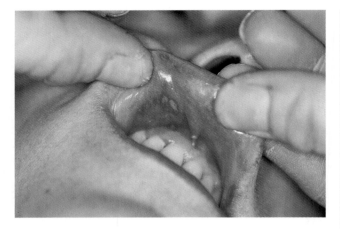

**FIGURE 31.**
**Aphthous ulcer.**
Aphthous ulcer is characterized by a painful, discrete shallow, round, to oval ulcer with a grayish base typically less than 1 cm in diameter.

are greater than 1 cm, have raised borders, may last for weeks or months, and may require biopsy to exclude malignancy. Herpetiform aphthous ulcers resemble recurrent herpetic lesions but are not preceded by vesicles, and viral cultures are negative. Severe ulcers may be associated with inflammatory bowel disease, celiac disease, HIV infection, and Behçet syndrome, which is characterized by aphthous ulcers plus urogenital ulcerations and iridocyclitis. Chlorhexidine mouth rinses and topical corticosteroids in dental paste may reduce ulcer severity and pain. In smokers, the risk of recurrence may decrease if smoking is given up.

### Oral Lichen Planus

Lichen planus occurs in about 1% of the population, predominantly in adults older than 40 years, and is of unknown etiology (see MKSAP 15 Dermatology). Oral lichen planus may occur with skin disease or may be the only manifestation of the disease. Oral lesions may appear as white, lace-like striae on the buccal mucosa or as hyperkeratosis or painful erosive changes of the oral cavity (**Figure 32**). Oral lichen planus tends to be chronic and may be associated with an increased risk of oral cancer. In patients with a symptomatic mouth lesion, topical corticosteroids may be used. Topical calcineurin inhibitors have been used for patients with highly symptomatic disease responding poorly to topical corticosteroids (off-label use) and should only be prescribed by specialists in the management of oral lichen planus.

## Oral Tumors

Tori are benign, bony protuberances considered to be developmental anomalies that usually do not appear until adulthood. They occur in 20% to 35% of the U.S. population. Tori may occur along the midline of the hard palate (torus palatinus) and along the lingual aspect of the mandible (torus mandibularis). Removal is usually only required if the torus interferes with dentures.

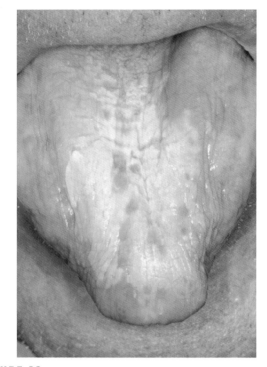

**FIGURE 32.**
**Oral lichen planus.**
Oral lichen planus appears as white, lace-like striae on the buccal mucosa or as hyperkeratosis or painful erosive changes of the oral cavity.

Mucoceles are cystic structures resulting from trauma to a salivary gland duct. They usually are found on the lower lip (**Figure 33**). There is often a history of trauma and episodes of recurrent swelling and rupture. Treatment is surgical excision.

Oral pyogenic granulomas may occur on the gingiva, lip, tongue, or buccal mucosa. They are rapidly growing nodules that range in size from a few millimeters to several centimeters and are erythematous, painless, smooth, and friable. They may develop in response to local irritation, trauma, or increased hormone levels in pregnancy. Surgical excision is

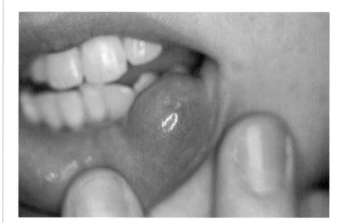

**FIGURE 33.**
**Mucocele.**
A large, shiny, nontender nodule on the lip suggests mucocele.

usually indicated in patients in whom in which a clinical diagnosis is uncertain or to rule out malignancy.

Oral leukoplakia and erythroplakia are oral lesions that present as white or red patches or plaques with changes in the mucosal surface texture (**Figure 34**). They are particularly common in smokeless tobacco users. Leukoplakia is premalignant, with 1% to 20% of lesions progressing to cancer over 10 years. Erythroplakia includes severe dysplasia or malignancy in 50% of cases. Unclassified red or white lesions that persist for longer than several weeks should be referred for evaluation and biopsy. Tobacco users should be counseled to stop.

Oropharyngeal cancers are the ninth most common cancer in the United States. The vast majority of these are squamous cell carcinomas. Tobacco and alcohol use are strong risk factors. Squamous cell carcinoma is locally invasive and metastasizes by lymphatic spread. Any lesion of the mucosal surface that cannot be identified readily should be biopsied. Other malignancies that occur in the oral cavity and oropharynx include cancers of the salivary glands, lymphomas, Kaposi sarcoma (in patients with HIV infection), and, rarely, mucosal melanoma.

### KEY POINT

- Unclassified red or white lesions that persist for longer than several weeks should be referred for evaluation and biopsy.

## Dental Infection

Although dental care is not usually in the domain of general medicine practitioners, patients sometimes have oral complaints that are dental in nature, and some dental diseases can progress to require medical treatment. Dental pain from exposed and infected dental pulp is one of the most frequent reasons that patients seek emergency dental care. Treatment is removal of the tooth or removal of the nerve with cleaning the root canal. A recent Cochrane review found one small

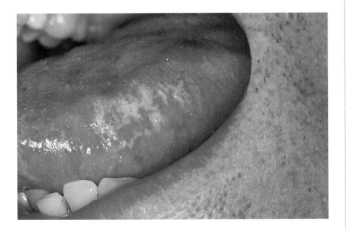

**FIGURE 34.**
**Leukoplakia.**
Leukoplakia is a precancerous lesion that presents as white patches or plaques of the oral mucosa with changes in the mucosal surface texture.

randomized trial comparing the use of a systemic antibiotic (penicillin) to placebo for treatment of acute pulpitis without operative endodontic treatment. Although the study had limited statistical power, no pain relief benefit from the antibiotic was found.

Periodontal disease is caused by a shift in microorganisms within the subgingival dental plaque from sparse gram-positive organisms to a complex flora with a preponderance of anaerobic gram-negative bacteria and motile organisms. There is resulting inflammation (gingivitis), destruction of the periodontium, gingival recession, increase in the depth of periodontal pockets, and bone loss. Age and tobacco use are risk factors for gingivitis. Prevention and treatment of periodontal disease include thorough brushing with fluoridated toothpaste and dental flossing after each meal, decreased intake of carbohydrate-rich foods, smoking cessation, and regular dental care.

Suppurative odontogenic infection occurs when an endodontic infection perforates the alveolar bone and extends along planes of least resistance to potential fascial spaces in the orofacial and peripharyngeal areas. The location of the infection can help in identifying the infected tooth. In addition, periodontal abscesses may occur adjacent to areas of periodontitis. Management involves surgical drainage and appropriate antibiotics.

## Halitosis

Halitosis is a frequent complaint in people of all ages. The most common source is the mouth, where bacteria degrade amino acids into volatile sulfur compounds. This is made possible by accumulation of food debris and dental plaque on the teeth and tongue from poor oral hygiene, gingivitis, and periodontitis. Xerostomia (dry mouth), a side effect of many medications, results in lack of normal oral cleansing from saliva and may cause or enhance halitosis. This is often the source of "morning breath"—the mild and transient oral malodor that occurs after sleep. The second most common source of halitosis is the nasal passages. Causes include sinusitis, malignancy, obstructing nasal polyps, or a foreign body. Garlic, onions, alcohol, tobacco, and some drugs have been implicated.

Clinical evaluation of halitosis should include a subjective assessment of the patient's breath from 5 to 10 cm away, both when the patient is mouth breathing and again when the patient is breathing out of the nose. If the odor is the same from both sites, there may be a systemic cause, such as hepatic failure, renal failure, pulmonary disease, or an esophageal diverticulum.

For mouth sources of halitosis, treatment should including improved oral hygiene, regular dental care, increased water intake, cleaning dentures and bridges nightly, and avoiding foods and habits that worsen the problem. A recent Cochrane review concluded that any beneficial effects of tongue scrapers or cleaners on halitosis are modest and short-lived.

Some patients have greatly exaggerated concerns about bad breath without objective evidence of having it (halitophobia). In such patients, the presence or absence of an odor should be confirmed by a family member or close friend and by scheduling a follow-up appointment for re-evaluation. If an odor cannot be confirmed, efforts can be made to reassure the patient as well as to explore psychosocial factors that may play a role.

> **KEY POINT**
>
> - Treatment of halitosis should be focused on brushing and flossing of teeth, regular dental care, increased water intake, cleaning dentures and bridges nightly, and avoiding foods and habits that worsen the problem.

## Tongue Syndromes

Geographic tongue, also known as migratory glossitis, is present on the dorsal tongue in about 2% of the population. There are well defined areas of atrophied filiform papillae (erythematous areas) surrounded by slightly elevated, curving borders of normal or hyperplastic filiform papillae (white rim) in an irregular or "geographic" shape. The location of these areas changes gradually over time. Geographic tongue appears in young and middle-aged adults and waxes and wanes over a lifetime. It is often noticed by the patient and brought to the attention of the physician because of unrelated mouth problems. Patients should be reassured that the condition is benign and requires no special treatment.

Fissured tongue, also known as "scrotal" tongue, is present in about 5% of the population and often coexists with geographic tongue. There are numerous linear deep "valleys" on the dorsal tongue covered by normal epithelium. This condition persists and may become more exaggerated throughout life. Patients should be reassured that the condition is benign. In some, removal of trapped debris in the fissures may be necessary by brushing the tongue.

Hairy tongue is a common disorder in which the filiform papillae on the dorsal surface of the tongue become elongated and hypertrophied as a result of slowing of the normal removal of the scales from the tips of the papillae. Hairy tongue is usually pigmented black, brown, or yellow owing to overgrowth of pigment-forming bacteria. It is precipitated by reduced normal salivary flow, such as occurs with dehydration, fever, and medications that cause a dry mouth. It is associated with smoking and poor oral hygiene. The condition usually disappears when the causative factors resolve or are eliminated. To speed the process, local measures may be used, including antibacterial mouthwashes and brushing the tongue.

> **KEY POINT**
>
> - Geographic, fissured, and hairy tongue are benign conditions that typically require simple reassurance without specific treatment.

## Temporomandibular Disorder

Temporomandibular disorder (TMD) is not a single entity but rather a cluster of pain-related conditions in the masticatory muscles, temporomandibular joint (TMJ), and associated structures. TMD pain occurs in about 3% to 10% of the general population, with a peak onset between the ages of 20 and 45 years and a 1.5- to 2-times greater prevalence in women. There is about a 30% to 60% comorbidity between TMD and tension headache, and TMD also occurs at higher rates among persons with irritable bowel syndrome, fibromyalgia, chronic fatigue syndrome, and other functional somatic conditions. Pain is present in at least 75% to 80% of patients with TMD, either as TMJ arthralgia or myalgia in the muscles of mastication; most patients have both types of pain. Other common symptoms include TMJ clicking or popping (60%), jaw clenching during the day (30%-40%) or while asleep (bruxism, 30%), TMJ locking or catching (15%-20%), and limitations in chewing (15%-20%). The diagnosis is largely clinical; neither imaging nor other laboratory testing is routinely recommended.

Self-care strategies include jaw relaxation, efforts to reduce abnormal clenching while awake, hot packs, passive opening stretches, suggestions about stress reduction, and NSAIDs. Another conservative therapy is hard or soft splint therapy, which is usually provided in the dentist's office. Splints are worn overnight and a few hours each day. A recent clinical trial randomized 200 subjects to one of three groups: hard splint plus self-care, soft splint plus self-care, and self-care only. There were no differences in clinical outcomes among the groups at 3, 6, or 12 months. Thus, self-care recommendations should be the initial approach; patients with persistent symptoms should be referred to a dentist to determine if splint therapy is warranted. Patients with TMD frequently have comorbid depressive, anxiety, or somatoform disorders that may warrant treatment. Surgical treatment for those with objective TMJ derangements is a last resort, and controlled clinical trials regarding its effectiveness are lacking.

> **KEY POINT**
>
> - Self-care strategies and hard or soft splints are equally effective in the initial treatment of temporomandibular disorder.

## Bibliography

Ah-See KW, Evans AS. Sinusitis and its management. BMJ. 2007;334(7589):358-361. [PMID: 17303885]

Alho OP, Koivunen P, Penna T, Teppo H, Koskela M, Luotonen J. Tonsillectomy versus watchful waiting in recurrent streptococcal pharyngitis in adults: randomized controlled trial. BMJ. 2007;334(7600):939. [PMID: 17347187]

American Academy of Pediatrics Subcommittee on Management of Acute Otitis Media. Diagnosis and management of acute otitis media. Pediatrics. 2004;113(5):1451-1465. [PMID: 15121972]

Bagai A, Thavendiranathan P, Detsky AS. Does this patient have hearing impairment? JAMA. 2006;295(4):416-428. [PMID: 16434632]

Centor RM, Allison JJ, Cohen SJ. Pharyngitis management: defining the controversy. J Gen Intern Med. 2007;22(1):127-130. [PMID: 17351852]

Hwang PH. A 51-year-old woman with acute onset of facial pressure, rhinorrhea, and tooth pain: review of acute rhinosinusitis. JAMA. 2009;301(17):1798-1807. [PMID: 19336696]

Keenan JV, Farman AG, Fedorowicz Z, Newton JT. Antibiotic use for irreversible pulpitis. Cochrane Database of Syst Rev. 2005,(2):CD004969. [PMID: 15846738]

Kucik CJ, Clenney T. Management of epistaxis. Am Fam Physician. 2005;71(2):305-311. [PMID: 15686301]

McCarter DF, Courtney AU, Pollart SM. Cerumen Impaction. Am Fam Physician. 2007;75(1):1523-1528. [PMID: 17555144]

Porter SR, Scully C. Oral malodour (halitosis). BMJ. 2006;333(7569): 632-635. [PMID: 16990322]

Rosenfeld RM, Brown L, Cannon CR, et al. Clinical practice guideline: acute otitis externa. Otolaryngol Head Neck Surg. 2006;134(4 Suppl):S4-S23. [PMID: 16638473]

Scadding GK, Durham SR, Mirakian R, et al; British Society for Allergy and Clinical Immunology. BSACI guidelines for the management of allergic and non-allergic rhinitis. Clin Exp Allergy. 2008;38(1):19-42. [PMID: 18081563]

Truelove E, Huggins KH, Mancl L, Dworkin SF. The efficacy of traditional, low-cost and nonsplint therapies for temporomandibular disorder: a randomized controlled trial. J Am Dent Assoc. 2006; 137(8):1099-1107. [PMID: 16873325]

Williamson IG, Rumsby K, Benge S, et al. Antibiotics and topical nasal steroid for treatment of acute maxillary sinusitis: a randomized controlled trial. JAMA. 2007;298(21):2487-2496. [PMID: 18056902]

# Mental and Behavioral Health

## Depression

Depression is the second most commonly encountered condition in primary care, following hypertension. Approximately one in six Americans will suffer an episode of major depression; for many, it is a chronic disease, as the likelihood of recurrence is 50% after a single episode, rises to 70% after a second, and 90% after a third. Depression is more common in those with significant medical problems, including heart disease, stroke, diabetes mellitus, and cancer; it also has a negative impact on the outcome of such conditions. Overall, depression is associated with reduced productivity, missed work, greater health care expenditures, and higher mortality rates. The nine depressive symptoms can be recalled by the mnemonic SPACEDIGS:

- Sleep disturbance
- Psychomotor agitation or retardation
- Appetite disturbance
- Concentration impairment
- Energy level low
- Depressed mood
- Interest in activities lost (anhedonia)
- Guilt or worthlessness
- Suicidal ideation

Ultra-brief screening measures consisting of two to three questions have been validated. Simply asking about whether one of the two core depressive symptoms (depressed mood and anhedonia) have been present most days in the past 2 weeks has been shown to be 90% sensitive for depressive disorders. The PHQ-4, a screen for anxiety and depression, assesses these two core symptoms (**Table 52**).

### Types of Depression

Major depression is characterized by the presence of at least five of the nine criteria for major depression, including at least one of the two hallmark features (depressed mood and anhedonia). Minor depression (subsyndromal depression) is characterized by the presence, for at least 2 weeks, of two to four depressive symptoms, associated with impaired social functioning, mental health, and health perceptions. *Dysthymia* is similar to minor depression with regard to the number of symptoms, but requires at least 2 years' duration to make the diagnosis. Whereas some symptoms of depression are typically part of the bereavement process after the death of a loved one, serious consideration should be give to treatment of the bereaved who still meet criteria for major depression 2 months after their loss.

Seasonal affective disorder is a cyclical subtype of depression that most often recurs in fall and winter months, with improvement in spring and summer. Bright light therapy is particularly effective for seasonal affective disorder; antidepressants and cognitive-behavioral therapy are also effective.

| **TABLE 52** The PHQ-4 Screen for Depression and Anxiety | | | | |
|---|---|---|---|---|
| **Over the last 2 weeks, how often have you been bothered by the following problems?** | **Not at all** | **Several days** | **More than half the days** | **Nearly every day** |
| 1. Feeling nervous, anxious, or on edge | 0 | 1 | 2 | 3 |
| 2. Not being able to stop or control worrying | 0 | 1 | 2 | 3 |
| 3. Little interest or pleasure in doing things | 0 | 1 | 2 | 3 |
| 4. Feeling down, depressed, or hopeless | 0 | 1 | 2 | 3 |

Scoring: Questions 1 and 2 constitute an anxiety subscale and questions 3 and 4 constitute a depression subscale. Scores on each subscale can range from 0 to 6, and a subscale score of 3 or greater suggests that further evaluation for clinically significant anxiety or depression is warranted.

Information from Kroenke K, Spitzer RL, Williams JBW, Löwe B. An ultra-brief screening scale for anxiety and depression: the PHQ-4. Psychosomatics. In press.

Several mood disorders are unique to women. Premenstrual dysphoric disorder (PMDD) occurs in 3% to 5% of menstruating women and is characterized by the cyclical recurrence of five or more symptoms of depression, anxiety, and emotional lability that have their onset within 1 week prior to menstruation and resolution within 1 week after menstruation. Whereas most women experience some heightened emotional lability in the days immediately following giving birth, major depression has been identified in 10% to 15% of women 1 to 6 months after delivery. Risks for postpartum depression include prior depression, life stressors, stillbirth, and miscarriage.

Depressed patients must be asked about suicidal thoughts, intent, and plans. Such questioning does not increase the likelihood of committing suicide and may be helpful in detecting those at risk for carrying out a planned suicide. Patients with suicidal ideation but without a plan or intent should have treatment initiated, and their suicidal ideation should be closely monitored. Patients with a suicide plan warrant urgent referral to a psychiatrist or emergency referral for hospitalization and psychiatric assessment, depending upon the clinical situation.

## Treatment

Referral to a psychiatrist is advisable for patients with any one of several features: (1) significant suicidal or homicidal ideation; (2) psychotic symptoms; (3) bipolar disorder; or (4) lack of response to two or more antidepressants. Some of these patients may require hospitalization, whereas others may require more complex management than is practical for the primary care physician to provide.

The care of most depressed patients has been facilitated for the primary care physician by the advent of a wide range of relatively safe, easy to administer antidepressants. As different classes of antidepressants appear to be equally effective, the selection of a particular agent should be driven by its side-effect profile, other comorbid disorders, and cost, matching the medication to the individual patient (**Table 53**). Antidepressants have been associated with a rare risk of

| **TABLE 53** Selected Frequently Prescribed Antidepressants | | |
|---|---|---|
| **Agent** | **Advantages** | **Disadvantages** |
| **SSRIs** | | |
| Citalopram | Few drug interactions; safe in cardiovascular disease | |
| Escitalopram | Few drug interactions | |
| Fluoxetine | Effective for OCD, GAD, bulimia, PMDD. Long half-life (good for missed doses, poor adherence) | Long half-life (can lead to accumulation); affects cytochrome P-450 system and drug interactions are common |
| Paroxetine | Effective for panic disorder, GAD, PTSD, OCD, social phobia | Highest risk (class D) in pregnancy; affects cytochrome P-450 system and drug interactions are common; weight gain |
| Sertraline | Few drug interactions; effective for panic disorder, PTSD, OCD, social phobia, PMDD; safe in cardiovascular disease | |
| **SNRIs** | | |
| Venlafaxine | Effective for anxiety spectrum disorders; few drug interactions | Nausea; can exacerbate hypertension |
| Duloxetine | Effective in pain conditions and GAD | Nausea |
| **Serotonin Antagonist (and Noradrenergic Enhancement)** | | |
| Mirtazapine (tetracyclic) | Facilitates improved sleep; few drug interactions | Weight gain; sedation |
| **Tricyclic Antidepressant** | | |
| Nortriptyline | Drug levels can be monitored; analgesic effect | Anticholinergic side effects (dry mouth, sedation, weight gain); cardiac toxicity with overdose |
| **Norepinephrine and Dopamine Reuptake Inhibitor** | | |
| Bupropion | Effective in smoking cessation; less sexual side effects than SSRIs; less weight gain; lowest risk (class B) in pregnancy | Seizure risk |

GAD = generalized anxiety disorder; OCD = obsessive compulsive disorder; PMDD = premenstrual dysphoric disorder; PTSD = posttraumatic stress disorder; SNRI = selective serotonin-norepinephrine reuptake inhibitor; SSRI = selective serotonin reuptake inhibitor.

precipitating suicidal ideation in children, and a potential risk has been identified in persons up to the age of 24 years. The U.S. Food and Drug Administration (FDA) is currently analyzing data to determine whether a similar risk exists in adults. Although a "black box" warning to this effect exists for all antidepressants, the risk of suicide from untreated depression is far more significant. In patients with bipolar disorder, initiation of an antidepressant can trigger a manic episode. Therefore, it is important to rule out bipolar disorder prior to initiating antidepressant therapy.

Selective serotonin reuptake inhibitors (SSRIs) are the most commonly prescribed class of antidepressants and are effective for anxiety as well as depression. In general, SSRIs are well tolerated with low toxicity; however, sexual side effects are common. Fluoxetine has a significantly longer half-life, which may be helpful in cases of missed doses or cessation of therapy, but also can lead to greater accumulation, which must be considered when switching to other antidepressants.

Bupropion is a good alternative for those with intolerable sexual dysfunction on SSRIs. It can lower the seizure threshold in patients at risk of seizures, although this is a rare event. Mirtazapine is often a good choice for thin depressed patients or those with insomnia because it is more likely to cause weight gain and somnolence. Serotonin-norepinephrine reuptake inhibitors (SNRIs) appear to be more effective than SSRIs in patients with comorbid pain. Duloxetine is FDA-approved for neuropathic pain and fibromyalgia, and venlafaxine has also shown some efficacy for pain relief, although it lacks a specific FDA indication for pain.

Successful treatment of depression often requires more than one medication. The Sequenced Treatment Alternatives to Relieve Depression (STAR*D) trial treated more than 4000 depressed patients at multiple sites. Initial treatment with the SSRI citalopram alone achieved a 30% remission rate. Random assignment of treatments to nonresponders at multiple steps eventually resulted in remission in approximately two thirds of patients. There was no difference whether inadequate responders were randomized to receive a different SSRI, a non-SSRI antidepressant, a combination of two antidepressants, augmentation with lithium or thyroxine, or cognitive therapy. These results suggest that depression is similar to chronic medical disorders in which multiple treatments may be equally effective, and monitoring outcomes and adjusting therapy are essential to optimizing outcomes.

Nonpharmacologic therapy appears to have similar efficacy to pharmacotherapy in mild to moderate depression, and referral for psychotherapy should be considered in patients who are reluctant to take medication or seem to have a good degree of insight. For more severe depression, there is good evidence that a combination of psychotherapy and pharmacotherapy is superior to either alone. Another alternative is electroconvulsive therapy, especially in severely depressed patients, such as those with profound suicidal ideation or psychotic features in whom a rapid response to therapy is particularly desirable.

The goal of treatment is to achieve complete remission within 6 to 12 weeks and continue treatment for 4 to 9 months thereafter. Up to 50% of patients will experience recurrent symptoms and will require long-term maintenance pharmacotherapy. Patients should be assessed 2 and 4 weeks after starting therapy for adherence, adverse drug reactions, and suicide risk and again at 6 to 8 weeks for response to therapy. At this point, patients should complete a formal tool for severity assessment (such as the PHQ-9) and are considered to have responded if a 50% or greater decrease in symptom score has occurred. After severity assessment, patients can be classified as complete, partial, or nonresponders. Complete responders should continue the same therapy modality for an additional 4 to 9 months. Treatment options for partial responders include using a higher dose of the same agent, adding a second agent, or adding psychotherapy. Patients with no response should be switched to a different category of drug or to psychotherapy. Any change in therapy requires periodic follow-up as outlined above.

**KEY POINTS**

- The presence of either depressed mood or anhedonia for most days in the past 2 weeks has a 90% sensitivity for a diagnosis of major depression.
- Referral to a psychiatrist is advisable for depressed patients with psychotic features, suicidal or homicidal ideation, bipolar depression, or lack of response to two or more antidepressants.
- It is important to ask about current bipolar disorder symptoms or history prior to initiating antidepressant therapy.
- The choice of an antidepressant should be based on matching the side effect profile to the individual patient.
- For partial responders to an antidepressant, maximize the dose and then add a second agent; for nonresponders, change to a different agent.

## Anxiety

The anxiety disorder spectrum includes generalized anxiety disorder (GAD), panic disorder with and without agoraphobia, posttraumatic stress disorder (PTSD), obsessive compulsive disorder (OCD), social anxiety disorder, and specific phobias. Overall, anxiety disorders are perhaps even more common than depression, and total direct and indirect costs are similar to those associated with depression.

### Generalized Anxiety Disorder and Panic Disorder

GAD has a prevalence of 4% to 6%. The disorder is characterized by excessive anxiety and worry about a variety of events or activities over at least a 6-month period; difficulty exercising control over worrying; several symptoms associated with the anxiety, such as fatigue, irritability, restlessness, sleep disturbance, and difficulty concentrating; and functional impairment. GAD can be easily screened for, either by asking, "Are you bothered by nerves?" which had a 100% sensitivity and 59% specificity in a study of primary care patients, or with the two-item GAD-2. The GAD-2 (scored 0 to 6) had a sensitivity of 86% and specificity of 83% when using a cut-off score of 3. Using a cut-off score of 2, the GAD-2 also has a sensitivity above 85% in screening for three other common anxiety disorders: panic disorder, PTSD, and social anxiety disorder. The GAD-2 was recently combined with the two highly sensitive screening questions for depression into the PHQ-4, providing an ultra-brief screen for depression and anxiety (see Table 52).

Panic disorder is characterized by recurrent, unexpected panic attacks with the abrupt onset of numerous somatic symptoms, including palpitations, sweating, tremulousness, dyspnea, chest pain, nausea, dizziness, and numbness. Symptoms typically peak within 10 minutes of onset, and attacks usually have a duration from 15 to 60 minutes. Although as many as 30% of Americans may experience a panic attack during their lifetime, the prevalence of panic disorder is only 1% to 2% because its diagnosis also requires that one or more of the attacks be followed by at least 1 month of persistent worry about having another attack, about the implications of the attack, or about its consequences; or a significant change in behavior related to the attacks. Up to half of those with panic disorder also have agoraphobia, characterized by a fear of being in places from which escape might be difficult (such as in crowds, on a train or plane, on a bridge, or in a tunnel). Persons with agoraphobia either avoid such situations or endure them with marked distress, even experiencing symptoms of panic.

Effective therapies are available for both GAD and panic disorder. Cognitive-behavioral therapy (CBT) is the best-evidenced nonpharmacologic therapy for these conditions, supported by many randomized controlled trials and several meta-analyses. Several recent studies provide evidence that relatively brief courses of CBT, or even self-help CBT, may be effective for panic disorder, whereas GAD may require longer courses, such as 12 to 20 sessions. CBT seems to have a more durable effect, with lower relapse rates than pharmacologic therapy, and use of CBT in patients who failed to benefit from pharmacologic therapy also showed significant efficacy. Panic disorder stands alone among the anxiety spectrum disorders as the condition for which there is clear evidence that the combination of CBT and pharmacotherapy is superior to either alone.

There is good evidence that SSRIs, as well as venlafaxine, are far superior to placebo in the treatment of both GAD and panic disorder. Duloxetine has also been approved for GAD. Second-line therapies have been shown to have some utility but all have drawbacks, including tricyclic antidepressants such as imipramine (risk of fatal cardiac arrhythmias in overdose, anticholinergic side effects), benzodiazepines (dependence and tolerance issues), and buspirone (relatively delayed onset of action).

## Posttraumatic Stress Disorder

PTSD is unique among the anxiety disorders because it has a clear precipitant—exposure to a traumatic event, such as war, disaster, or an assault, that involves an actual or threatened death or serious injury to one's self or others. To meet criteria for PTSD, the trauma must be followed by at least 1 month of disabling symptoms in three different categories: re-experiencing the event, avoiding reminders of the trauma, and heightened arousal.

Although many individuals have experienced trauma sufficient to induce PTSD, most of those exposed are resilient, so that the overall likelihood of developing PTSD after a traumatic event is estimated at 9% to 25%. Community surveys identify an 8% to 12% lifetime prevalence for PTSD. PTSD was documented in 39% of patients referred by their primary care providers for mental health services based on suspicion of depression or anxiety. The four-item PC-PTSD is a useful screen for PTSD, using a cut-off of two or more positive replies: Have you ever had any experience that was so frightening, horrible, or upsetting that in the past month you . . .

(1) . . . have had nightmares about it or thought about it when you did not want to?

(2) . . . tried hard not to think about it or went out of your way to avoid situations that remind you of it?

(3) . . . were constantly on guard, watchful, or easily startled?

(4) . . . felt numb or detached from others, activities, or your surroundings?

The preferred treatment for PTSD is CBT with exposure therapy. Exposure therapy helps patients to confront stimuli (thoughts, images, objects, situations, or activities) associated with the traumatic experience through progressively more intense exposure. Imaginal exposure has been the most widely employed approach, wherein the therapist asks the patient to recall the traumatic experience in progressively greater detail. This process is often supplemented by in vivo exposure, in which the patient confronts real-life circumstances that have triggered symptoms. Because avoidance is a cardinal feature of PTSD, patients often are unwilling or unable to effectively engage in exposure therapy. Virtual reality therapy may help overcome avoidance by immersing patients in an environment reminiscent of their trauma to facilitate recall. Although CBT is effective for most anxiety disorders, its effect is most robust for GAD and PTSD.

SSRIs are the most effective pharmacotherapy for PTSD, but the best reported response rates are only 40% to 60%, and relapse after discontinuation of medication is common. The α-blocker prazosin appears to reduce the frequency and intensity of intrusive nightmares. A meta-analysis comparing trials of pharmacotherapy with psychotherapy found that although both approaches were effective, the effect size for psychotherapy was significantly greater (1.17 versus 0.69), and the drop-out rate was lower (14% versus 32%).

## Social Anxiety Disorder

Formerly known as social phobia, social anxiety disorder is one of the most common psychiatric disorders, with a lifetime prevalence of more than 13%. The primary feature is a severe and persistent fear of social or performance situations, such as public speaking or taking an examination. In such situations, blushing and other anxiety symptoms are commonly experienced, although full-blown panic attacks usually are not. Persons with more generalized social anxiety disorder avoid many occupational and social situations because of fears of interacting with other people. Persons with social anxiety disorder recognize that their fear is excessive (except children sometimes do not), are characteristically markedly distressed about the condition, and either avoid precipitating situations or endure them with dread. CBT, especially regimens that incorporate elements of either imaginal or virtual exposure therapy, has been proved effective for social anxiety disorder, and SSRIs are the most evidence-based pharmacotherapy. Although β-blockers or benzodiazepines are sometimes used clinically for nongeneralized social anxiety, usually related to test-taking or public speaking, reports of efficacy are mostly anecdotal.

## Obsessive-Compulsive Disorder

The hallmark of obsessive-compulsive disorder (OCD) is the presence of recurrent obsessions or compulsions that are of sufficient severity to occupy at least 1 hour per day or to result in marked distress or functional impairment. The individual should recognize the obsessions or compulsions as excessive or unreasonable. *Obsessions* are defined as persistent ideas, thoughts, impulses, or images that are experienced as intrusive, inappropriate, and associated with significant anxiety or distress. Common obsessions include worries about having left a door unlocked, fears of contamination related to contact with others, or a need to have things in a specific order. *Compulsions* are repetitive behaviors, such as handwashing, checking, and ordering, or mental acts, such as counting or repeating words silently, that are performed to try to decrease the anxiety or stress associated with the obsessions. OCD has a prevalence of 2.3% in U.S. adults.

CBT with an exposure therapy element is the treatment of choice for OCD. SSRIs are the most effective pharmacotherapy and should be used in patients who are resistant or only partially responsive to CBT and in those with more severe OCD or in whom a rapid response is critical. Higher SSRI doses are often needed to treat OCD as compared with depression, and the dose may be escalated at 2- to 4-week intervals. Adjunctive use of antipsychotics has some evidence of benefit.

> **KEY POINT**
>
> - Cognitive-behavioral therapy achieves the highest response rates and has the most durable effect of all treatments for the anxiety spectrum disorders.

# Bipolar Disorder

Bipolar disorder is subdivided into type I (featuring manic or mixed manic-depressive episodes, typically with periods of major depression as well) and type II (characterized by periods of major depression with a history of at least one hypomanic period). The prevalence of bipolar disorder in the U.S. population has been estimated at 1% to 4%; the Epidemiologic Catchment Area Study identified type I in 0.8% of the population studied, type II in 0.5%, and another 5.1% with subthreshold bipolar symptoms. Some studies suggest that as many as one in five of all depressed patients in primary care have bipolar disorder, although it is frequently misdiagnosed, with 50% having seen at least three professionals before being correctly diagnosed as having bipolar disorder. The Mood Disorders Questionnaire (MDQ) (**Figure 35**) is a relatively brief, validated questionnaire to screen for bipolar disorder. A cut-off of seven or more positive responses on Question 1 yields a sensitivity of 73% and specificity of 90%. Because of the strong genetic component of bipolar disorder, family history is also important. Primary care physicians should briefly assess for a personal or family history of diagnosed bipolar disorder and ask about some of the characteristic features in Question 1 of the MDQ prior to initiating antidepressant therapy. If not administered initially, the full MDQ should be administered to those who do not respond to an initial course of therapy for unipolar depression.

Pharmacotherapy for bipolar disorder is more complicated than for unipolar depression, and a psychiatrist should be involved in the care of most patients with the disorder. Lithium has long been a mainstay of bipolar disorder therapy; however, it has a narrow therapeutic window and is teratogenic, nephrotoxic, and can cause hypothyroidism. Alternative first-line therapies include the anticonvulsant agents valproic acid, carbamazepine, and lamotrigine; as well as second-generation antipsychotic agents, such as quetiapine, olanzapine, and risperidone. There is evidence that adjunctive psychotherapy, particularly psychoeducation, is associated with improved outcomes. Pharmacotherapy should be continued for at least 1 year after achieving a response, and many will require lifelong treatment.

> **KEY POINTS**
>
> - Nearly 20% of nonrespondents to treatment for unipolar depression may meet criteria for bipolar disorder.
> - First-line treatments for bipolar disorder include lithium, anticonvulsant agents, and second-generation antipsychotic agents.

**1. Has there ever been a period of time when you were not your usual self and...**

| | Yes | No |
|---|---|---|
| ...you felt so good or so hyper that other people thought you were not your normal self or you were so hyper that you got into trouble? | ☐ | ☐ |
| ...you were so irritable that you shouted at people or started fights or arguments? | ☐ | ☐ |
| ...you felt much more self-confident than usual? | ☐ | ☐ |
| ...you got much less sleep than usual and found you didn't really miss it? | ☐ | ☐ |
| ...you were much more talkative or spoke much faster than usual? | ☐ | ☐ |
| ...thoughts raced through your head or you couldn't slow your mind down? | ☐ | ☐ |
| ...you were so easily distracted by things around you that you had trouble concentrating or staying on track? | ☐ | ☐ |
| ...you had so much more energy than usual? | ☐ | ☐ |
| ...you were much more active or did many more things than usual? | ☐ | ☐ |
| ...you were much more social or outgoing than usual; for example, you telephoned friends in the middle of the night? | ☐ | ☐ |
| ...you were much more interested in sex than usual? | ☐ | ☐ |
| ...you did things that were unusual for you or that other people might have thought were excessive, foolish, or risky? | ☐ | ☐ |
| ...spending money got you or your family into trouble? | ☐ | ☐ |

**2. If you answered YES to more than one of the above, have several of these happened during the same period of time?**

☐ Yes     ☐ No

**3. How much of a problem did any of these cause you—like being unable to work; having family, money, or legal troubles; getting into arguments or fights? (Please check one response only.)**

☐ No problem     ☐ Minor problem     ☐ Moderate problem     ☐ Serious problem

**FIGURE 35.**
**Mood disorders questionnaire.**
Scoring: a positive screen is indicated by 7 or more positive answers on question 1, *yes* to question 2, and either *moderate* or *serious* for question 3.

Adapted with permission from Hirschfeld RM, Williams JB, Spitzer RL, et al. Development and validation of a screening instrument for bipolar spectrum disorder: The Mood Disorder Questionnaire. Am J Psychiatry. 2000;157(11);1873-1875. [PMID: 11058490]

# Somatoform Disorders

Somatoform disorders are defined by the presence of physical symptoms in patients who have no demonstrable organic disease to explain the symptoms. Somatic symptoms are common, accounting for 400 million office visits each year in the United States. The care of patients with somatoform disorders is challenging for physicians and costly for society. These patients generate medical costs nine times that of the average patient. It is important for clinicians to learn to care for patients with somatoform disorders, because when doctors directly or indirectly refuse to care for them, they tend to seek care from other physicians, resulting in repeated unnecessary, costly, and sometimes harmful investigations.

## Types of Somatoform Disorders

Somatoform disorders, as classified by the Diagnostic and Statistical Manual of Mental Disorders, Fourth Edition (DSM-IV), include conversion disorder, hypochondriasis, pain disorder, body dysmorphic disorder, somatization disorder, factitious disorders, and malingering. Except for factitious disorders and malingering, none of these involve conscious intent by the patient. Factitious disorders and malingering are not discussed here.

Conversion disorder is manifested by a psychologically caused voluntary motor or sensory deficit that mimics a neurologic condition. Hypochondriasis, perhaps better called "health anxiety disorder," is the preoccupation with the belief that a serious disease is the cause of a bodily complaint. The worry about an underlying disease tends to be more prominent than in somatization disorder. Pain disorder is characterized by chronic pain for which psychological factors play a major role. Body dysmorphic disorder refers to preoccupation with an imagined or exaggerated defect in physical appearance.

Somatization disorder (including its less severe abridged or subthreshold variants) is probably the most frequently encountered somatoform disorder by primary care physicians and is characterized by multiple unexplained physical symptoms for at least 6 months, along with symptom-related social or occupational impairment. Current DSM-IV criteria require at least four pain symptoms, two gastrointestinal symptoms, one pseudoneurologic symptom, and one sexual symptom. Patients attribute their symptoms to an undiagnosed disorder despite multiple negative evaluations and are often not reassured despite repeated work-ups.

## Management

The principles of therapy for patients with somatization disorder include regular office appointments with one physician so that the patient does not feel he or she needs to develop new symptoms to see the doctor. The frequency of visits, which initially may need to occur monthly, can be decreased over time. Patient-centered communication during office visits is recommended. The physician should acknowledge the patient's suffering and convey a sense of partnership in dealing with the complaints. The patient should be reassured that life-threatening conditions have been ruled out and should be given a plausible explanation for the symptoms (such as muscle strain, neurotransmitter imbalance, fibromyalgia). The physician should gradually steer the conversation away from discussions about symptoms and toward what is going on in the patient's life. It is unrealistic for the patient or the physician to expect complete resolution of the symptoms. A more realistic goal is a decrease in the number of urgent phone calls to the physician, visits to the emergency department, referrals to specialists, and invasive tests and procedures. A major treatment goal should be increased functioning rather than eradication of symptoms. For pain management, narcotics should be avoided if possible. Among all treatments, CBT has the broadest evidence of benefit across a number of somatoform disorders.

It is often difficult for physicians to decide whether a new complaint represents significant disease or another somatic symptom. Extreme approaches by the physician to this dilemma include ignoring the new complaint completely or performing extensive evaluations. The first extreme risks missing important disease—somatizing patients can, of course, develop life-threatening diseases. The latter approach often results in false-positive test results requiring further testing and potential harm from invasive testing and procedures (including unnecessary surgical procedures). A reasonable approach is to investigate new symptoms as in any patient but to avoid repeated work-ups of previously evaluated chronic symptoms.

Depression and anxiety are commonly present in patients with somatization, and various physical complaints can be presenting symptoms for mood disorders. Thus, detecting and treating depression and anxiety are essential.

**KEY POINTS**

- Patients with somatoform disorders are distressed by medically unexplained physical symptoms in several areas of the body, seek help from multiple physicians, and are typically not reassured by negative test results.
- Cognitive-behavioral therapy is the most evidence-based treatment for somatoform disorders.

# Eating Disorders

Eating disorders are especially common among young females, with a variety of societal trends inducing girls as young as ages 5 to 9 years to desire to lose weight, not infrequently through dieting or even purging. Eating disorders are categorized in DSM-IV as follows: anorexia nervosa, bulimia nervosa, binge-eating disorder, and eating disorder not otherwise specified (EDNOS). Unfortunately, physicians make a diagnosis in fewer than 10% of patients, and therefore most do not receive treatment. Moreover, these categories are poorly validated, and in clinical practice, the great majority of patients are given a diagnosis of EDNOS; those in the EDNOS category have similar attitudes, behaviors, and comorbidities as those with anorexia nervosa or bulimia nervosa. The SCOFF questionnaire (**Table 54**) is a validated screening tool for eating disorders. Compared with a detailed clinical interview, the SCOFF had a sensitivity of 84.6% and specificity of 89.6% for all eating disorders in the primary care setting and was able to identify all patients with anorexia nervosa and bulimia nervosa.

## Types of Eating Disorders

Anorexia nervosa has a lifetime prevalence of 0.5% to 3.7%, and the highest mortality rate of any mental disorder, with the best estimate being approximately 6%. More than 90% of cases occur in females. Anorexia nervosa is defined by four diagnostic criteria: (1) refusal to maintain body weight at or above a minimally normal level (arbitrarily set at 85% of expected body weight); (2) intense fear of gaining weight or becoming fat, even though underweight; (3) a disturbance in the perception of one's body weight or shape or denial of the

**TABLE 54** SCOFF Questionnaire for Screening for Eating Disorders

Do you make yourself **S**ick because you feel uncomfortably full?

Do you worry that you have lost **C**ontrol over how much you eat?

Have you recently lost more than **O**ne stone (14 pounds) in a 3-month period?

Do you believe yourself to be **F**at when others say you are too thin?

Would you say **F**ood dominates your life?

Score one point for each *yes*. A score of two or more points indicates a likely diagnosis of anorexia nervosa or bulimia.

Adapted with permission from Morgan JF, Reid F, Lacey JH. The SCOFF questionnaire: assessment of a new screening tool for eating disorders. BMJ. 1999;319(7223):1467-1468. [PMID: 10582927] Copyright 1999, BMJ Publishing Group Ltd.

seriousness of low body weight; and (4) amenorrhea for at least 3 months in postmenarchal (reproductive-age) females. The 85% body weight cut-off lacks empiric validity, and the amenorrhea criterion excludes men and prepubescent girls from the diagnosis. One large study found that nearly half the EDNOS admissions to an eating disorders unit were anorexia nervosa without amenorrhea. The DSM-IV includes two types of anorexia nervosa: a restricting type characterized by drastic limitation of caloric intake and a binge-eating/purging type that is characterized by repetitive binge-eating or purging. However, these subtypes seem to represent two ends of a spectrum rather than two distinct clinically useful categories.

Bulimia is present in approximately 1% to 3% of women, with the highest rates in college-aged women. Although bulimia nervosa occurs in men, it is up to 10 times more common in women. Bulimia nervosa is characterized by recurrently eating an unusually large amount of food within a discrete time frame, along with feeling unable to stop or to control how much food is eaten. In addition, the patient recurrently engages in inappropriate compensatory behavior to prevent weight gain, such as inducing vomiting, using laxatives or diuretics, fasting, or excessive exercise. For a diagnosis of bulimia nervosa, both of these behaviors need to occur at least twice weekly for 3 months. Furthermore, the patient's self-evaluation is excessively dependent upon body shape and weight. What constitutes a sufficiently large amount of food or loss of control is purely subjective; the significance of the frequency and duration of binges and purges is not well-defined.

Binge-eating disorder is characterized by binge eating at least twice a week for 6 weeks, featuring rapid eating, eating until uncomfortable, and feeling guilty after bingeing, but no purging. Those with binge-eating disorder tend to have a later age of onset and are more often males or minorities, in comparison with persons with anorexia nervosa or bulimia nervosa, although perceptions of body weight and shape, as well as comorbidity and functional impairment, are similar.

There is evidence that binge-eating disorder is more persistent than either anorexia nervosa or bulimia nervosa. Genetics may play a role in binge-eating disorder that is independent of obesity, which is a frequent complication.

## Medical Complications of Eating Disorders

Primary care physicians often see patients with eating disorders because of medical complications. Physical complications associated with anorexia nervosa include hypokalemia and hypomagnesemia, which may cause significant cardiac arrhythmias and osteopenia or osteoporosis, which can lead to fractures. Malnutrition and vitamin deficiencies can lead to anemia (iron and vitamin $B_{12}$ deficiencies), easy bruising or bleeding (vitamin K deficiency), or the "three D's" of niacin deficiency: diarrhea, dementia, and dermatitis. Hypophosphatemia may occur and can be particularly profound when malnourished patients begin to increase caloric intake (whether orally or intravenously), resulting in the refeeding syndrome. It is important to closely monitor, and replete, electrolytes when replenishing the nutritional status of patients with anorexia.

## Treatment of Eating Disorders

Systematic reviews and expert panels have identified CBT as the most effective therapy for eating disorders, achieving higher responses than antidepressants, which are in turn better than placebo. There is mixed evidence as to whether CBT plus antidepressants is better than CBT alone, although the combination is clearly better than antidepressants alone. The available evidence is strongest for bulimia nervosa, in which CBT eliminates bingeing and purging in 30% to 50% of patients, with many others also showing some improvement. CBT improves body image, self-esteem, and dietary discretion in bulimia nervosa. There is less evidence for the benefits of CBT in anorexia nervosa and binge-eating disorder.

**KEY POINTS**

- Anorexia nervosa has the highest mortality rate of any mental disorder.
- Cognitive-behavioral therapy is the best-evidenced treatment for eating disorders.

# Schizophrenia

Psychosis encompasses delusions, hallucinations, disorganized speech, and disorganized or catatonic behavior. Psychotic features may occur in depression as well as other psychiatric or organic disorders, but schizophrenia is a disorder in which psychosis is a defining feature. The diagnosis requires at least 6 months of symptoms, including 1 month or more of at least two active-phase symptoms, such as hallucinations, delusions, disorganized speech, grossly disorganized or catatonic behavior; and negative symptoms, such as flattened affect. There must also be significant impairment in social or occupational function. Behavioral manifestations may include grossly disheveled appearance or inappropriate dress (wearing an overcoat, hat, scarf, and gloves in the heat of summer) or unprovoked agitation, such as yelling or profanity in public. Impaired cognition, including decrements in short-term memory and attention, is also characteristic of schizophrenia. Schizophrenia has a lifetime prevalence of 1% to 2%, most often presenting in late adolescence or early adulthood.

Second-generation antipsychotics have a favorable side effect profile compared with the older neuroleptics and thus appear better tolerated in schizophrenia, but selecting a drug involves a complicated individual assessment of risks and benefits. Second-generation antipsychotics are associated with significantly increased rates of diabetes mellitus, especially in patients younger than 60 years. In a large study comparing perphenazine, olanzapine, risperidone, quetiapine, and ziprasidone in patients with chronic schizophrenia, efficacy was generally similar among treatments; however, time to antipsychotic discontinuation for any reason was shortest for olanzapine. Olanzapine was associated with discontinuations due to weight gain, whereas perphenazine was associated with the discontinuations for extrapyramidal symptoms. Significant elevations in triglycerides, cholesterol, and hemoglobin $A_{1c}$ levels were most apparent with olanzapine.

## Attention-Deficit/Hyperactivity Disorder

Attention-deficit/hyperactivity disorder (ADHD) is characterized by difficulty paying attention, impulsivity, and motor restlessness or hyperactivity, with onset before the age of 7 years. There must also be some impairment in social, occupational, or academic functioning, and the symptoms must be manifest in at least two different environments, such as school and home. There are three subtypes: predominantly inattentive, predominantly hyperactive, and a combined type.

Comorbidity with mood and anxiety disorders, substance abuse, and personality disorders is common. Between 3% to 9% of children in the United States may have ADHD, with diagnosis several times more common in boys than girls; this equalizes, however, in late adolescence, and among young adults, the disorder is actually more common in women. Genetics play a role (patients with ADHD are five times more likely to have a close relative with ADHD), and it is not uncommon for adults to recognize that they might have ADHD when one of their children is diagnosed. Presentation in adulthood tends to be characterized less by problems with hyperactivity and more by inattention, with frequent difficulty focusing on academic or workplace tasks and higher rates of motor vehicle accidents.

Two classes of drugs have proved particularly efficacious in ADHD: stimulants and antidepressants. Stimulants such as dex-amphetamine and methylphenidate that influence both the noradrenergic and dopaminergic pathways are available in both short-acting and slow-release forms. Atomoxetine is a serotonin-norepinephrine reuptake inhibitor (SNRI) recently approved for treatment of ADHD in both children and adults. Another SNRI, venlafaxine, and bupropion, which acts on dopaminergic pathways, have less robust evidence to support their use, but can be considered as secondary alternatives. Behavioral therapy added to pharmacotherapy is also beneficial in some patients and may allow lower doses of medication.

**KEY POINTS**
- A diagnosis of attention-deficit/hyperactivity disorder requires that the onset of symptoms occurred before the age of 7 years.
- Stimulants and some antidepressants are effective for the treatment of attention-deficit/hyperactivity disorder.

## Autism Spectrum Disorders

Autism is characterized by a triad of impaired communication; impaired social interactions; and restrictive, repetitive, and stereotyped behaviors and interests (**Table 55**). In addition,

**TABLE 55 Triad of Impairments Characteristic of Autism**

| Impairment | Examples |
|---|---|
| Social interaction | Impaired use of nonverbal behaviors, such as facial expressions, body posture, and gestures |
| | Difficulty making friends ("loners") |
| | Lack of empathy or understanding of others' emotions |
| | Lack of appreciation of social cues |
| Communication | Delayed language development (for example, no single words before age 2 years, no phrases before age 3 years) |
| | Abnormalities in speech volume and prosody; echolalia |
| | Perseveration on a topic regardless of listener's level of interest |
| Behavior | Abnormal focus on one or more stereotyped and restricted patterns of interest |
| | Inflexible adherence to nonfunctional routines or rituals |
| | Preference for "sameness" in environment; functioning is better if there is clear structure in the environment; prompts are needed to carry out infrequent tasks |
| | Repetitive or stereotyped motor mannerisms |

classic autism is often associated with some degree of learning disability or mental retardation and is typically diagnosed in early childhood. Less severe variants include high-functioning autism (HFA) and Asperger syndrome, which may not be diagnosed until adolescence or even adulthood. HFA is a category of autistic disorder with less severe clinical features and without cognitive impairment. Asperger syndrome differs from HFA in that early language development is not delayed. Many experts believe that autism, HFA, and Asperger syndrome are variants along a single spectrum.

There is a paucity of evidence-based treatments for autism. In children, parents and the school system typically are key partners in reducing behaviors that interfere with social integration; in teaching the child to recognize others' emotions and nonverbal cues; in facilitating adaptation to new situations outside the child's "comfort zone" of routine, ritualized activities; and in implementing other behavioral and psychoeducational interventions. Applied behavioral therapy is currently the most effective therapy. There is a relative dearth of evidence regarding effective pharmacologic treatments. A recent review found only five randomized controlled trials involving a total of 149 patients; all studies had small sample sizes (median = 30) and brief treatment durations (≤12 weeks). Most of these trials focused on older patients, either adolescents or adults. Two trials of risperidone (mean dose of 2-3 mg/d), one trial of fluvoxamine (mean dose of 277 mg/d), and one trial of haloperidol, suggested that the active drug was superior to placebo in reducing repetitive behaviors, aggression, hyperactivity, and selected mood states (depression, irritability and nervousness). Improvements were less evident for social functioning or language outcomes. One trial of naltrexone showed no benefits.

---

**KEY POINTS**

- Autism is characterized by a triad of impaired communication; impaired social interactions; and restrictive, repetitive and stereotyped behaviors and interests.

- Asperger syndrome is a less severe variant of autism in which language development is not delayed; diagnosis may not occur until late childhood or adolescence.

---

## Bibliography

Broadstock M, Doughty C, Eggleston M. Systematic review of the effectiveness of pharmacological treatments for adolescents and adults with autism spectrum disorder. Autism. 2007;11(4):335-348. [PMID: 17656398]

Hill LS, Reid F, Morgan JF, Lacey JH. SCOFF, the development of an eating disorder screening questionnaire. Int J Eat Disord. 2009. [Epub ahead of print] [PMID: 19343793]

Hirschfeld RM. Screening for bipolar disorder. Am J Manag Care. 2007;13(7 Suppl):S164-S169. [PMID: 18041877]

Kroenke K. Efficacy of treatment for somatoform disorders: a review of randomized clinical trials. Psychosom Med. 2007;69(9):881-888. [PMID: 18040099]

Kroenke K. Somatoform disorders and recent diagnostic controversies. Psychiatr Clin North Am. 2007;30(4):593-619. [PMID: 17938036]

Kroenke K, Spitzer RL, Williams JBW, Lowe B. An ultra-brief screening scale for anxiety and depression: the PHQ-4. Psychosomatics. In press.

Lieberman JA, Stroup TS, McEvoy JP, et al; Clinical Antipsychotic Trials of Intervention Effectiveness (CATIE) Investigators. Effectiveness of antipsychotic drugs in patients with chronic schizophrenia. N Engl J Med. 2005;353(12):1209-1223. [PMID: 16172203]

Mitchell AJ, Coyne JC. Do ultra-short screening instruments accurately detect depression in primary care? A pooled analysis and meta-analysis of 22 studies. Br J Gen Pract. 2007;57(535):144-151. [PMID: 17263931]

Norton PJ, Price EC. A meta-analytic review of adult cognitive-behavioral treatment outcome across the anxiety disorders. J Nerv Ment Dis. 2007;195(6):521-531. [PMID: 17568301]

Papadopoulos FC, Ekbom A, Brandt L, Ekselius L. Excess mortality, causes of death and prognostic factors in anorexia nervosa. Br J Psychiatry. 2009;194(1):10-17. [PMID: 19118319]

Rush JA, Trivedi MH, Wisniewski SR, et al; STAR*D Study Team. Bupropion-SR, sertraline, or venlafaxine-XR after failure of SSRIs for depression. N Engl J Med. 2006;354(12):1231-1242. [PMID: 16554525]

Trivedi MH, Fava M, Wisniewski SR, et al; STAR*D Study Team. Medication augmentation after the failure of SSRIs for depression. N Engl J Med. 2006;354(12):1243-1252. [PMID: 16554526]

# Geriatric Medicine

## Functional Assessment

The evaluation of a geriatric patient differs from the usual medical evaluation by having an emphasis on functional ability, independence, and quality of life. The comprehensive geriatric assessment addresses functional ability, physical health, sensory capacity, cognitive and mental health, and socio-environmental limitations that can affect the lives of elderly patients and their caregivers. Possible benefits of the geriatric assessment include greater diagnostic accuracy, improved functional and mental status, reduced mortality, decreased use of nursing homes and acute care hospitals, and greater satisfaction with care.

## Hearing

Hearing loss affects one third of adults older than 60 years and one half of those older than 85 years. For the older adult, hearing loss interferes with performance of activities of daily living and is isolating, more so because it tends to cause frustration in others, whereas other disabilities, such as blindness, typically engender compassion. The most common cause of hearing loss in the elderly is presbycusis, the diagnosis given to age-related hearing loss caused by various factors, including aging, accumulated noise toxicity, genetic factors, and ototoxic medications. Presbycusis is a sensorineural hearing loss that initially impairs high frequency hearing, then progresses to loss of ability to hear frequencies important to speech. This results in the common complaint of inability to understand speech rather than an inability to hear.

In a systematic review evaluating screening tools for hearing impairment, it was concluded that the best strategy for determining a need for formal audiometric testing is a combination of self-reported hearing loss (a positive answer to the question, "Do you have trouble hearing?") and the whispered voice test (see Ear, Nose, Mouth, and Throat Disorders), performed in sequence. Although a family member's claim that a patient has difficulty hearing was not formally addressed by the review, that information may also be an important factor in deciding on formal testing. A handheld audioscope has diagnostic accuracy characteristics similar to the whispered voice test and should be used if the examiner is unsure of his or her ability to perform the whispered voice test reliably. The Rinne test, Weber test, and Hearing Handicap Inventory (a 10-item self-administered questionnaire) do not have a role in screening for hearing impairment.

**KEY POINT**

- Older adults should be screened for hearing loss with the whispered voice test or an audioscope and undergo audiometry if they fail either of those tests or report hearing loss.

## Vision

Visual impairment is a common problem among the elderly. Thirteen percent of those older than 65 years have visual acuity of less than 20/40 as measured with a Snellen vision chart. Legal blindness (visual acuity <20/200) occurs in 3% of persons aged 60 years and 11% of those aged 80 years. Underreporting of vision problems by patients is common. As many as one third of geriatric patients have unrecognized severe vision loss, and up to 25% are wearing improper corrective lenses. The most common causes of visual impairment in the elderly are presbyopia (the universal age-related diminishing ability of the lens to accommodate), cataracts, primary open-angle glaucoma, age-related macular degeneration, and diabetic retinopathy, all of which are potentially treatable (see Eye Disorders).

Because visual impairment and disability are common in the elderly, the U.S. Preventive Services Task Force recommends periodic Snellen visual acuity testing. Multiple professional organizations, including the American College of Physicians, recommend that patients with diabetes undergo annual screening, by an eye professional, with a dilated ophthalmoscopic examination or stereoscopic fundus photography. There is also consensus that accurate detection of the intraocular changes of age-related macular degeneration and glaucoma is difficult in a primary care setting. Therefore, periodic examination by an eye professional of patients older than 65 years is prudent, especially for those patients with risk factors for these disorders.

Presbyopia and other refractive errors are easily addressed with corrective lenses. In the Baltimore Eye Survey, half of those screened had improved vision after receiving appropriate corrective lenses.

**KEY POINTS**

- The most common causes of vision loss among the elderly—presbyopia, cataracts, age-related macular degeneration, glaucoma, and diabetic retinopathy—are all potentially treatable.
- Elderly patients should undergo periodic Snellen visual acuity testing.
- Because age-related macular degeneration and glaucoma may be difficult to detect in a primary care setting, periodic examination by an eye professional of those older than 65 years is prudent, especially for patients with risk factors for these disorders.

## Depression

Depression is common in later life. Major and minor depression have been reported in 3% to 26% of older adults living in the community, 10% of older medical outpatients, 23% of older acute care inpatients, and 16% to 30% of nursing home residents. Risk factors for depression include older age, stressful life events, personal or family history of depression, and chronic medical conditions. In older adults, somatic symptoms such as pain or poor memory may mask underlying depressive symptoms and lead to underdiagnosis.

A quick and effective two-item screen for major depression has a sensitivity of 96% and specificity of 57% for major depression. A positive response to either question constitutes a positive screen:

- "Over the past 2 weeks have you felt down, depressed, or hopeless?"
- "Over the past 2 weeks have you felt little interest or pleasure in doing things?"

Further information about diagnosing and treating depression is presented in the Mental and Behavioral Health section.

## Activities of Daily Living

Activities of daily living (ADLs) are the basic physical, mental, and emotional skills necessary to accomplish everyday routines, such as eating, dressing, bathing, and grooming, and include those skills necessary to provide for one's own personal care and to move through one's environment. Patients unable to perform these activities and obtain adequate nutrition usually require caregiver support. Instrumental activities of daily living (IADLs) are those skills necessary for independent living, such as using the telephone, handling finances, shopping, preparing food, and taking medications. Patients with deficits in ADLs and IADLs should be further evaluated regarding their home environment and caregiver availability.

It is generally not necessary to do structured ADL and IADL assessments in all older patients, as the physician may know the patient well from prior contacts or can quickly determine his or her abilities during an office visit. For example, showing up for an office visit and completing the requisite interactions during the visit can be seen as tests of function. However, the physician must be alert for IADL "triggers" that should prompt more in-depth inquiry. For example, weight loss should not be assumed to be due to an undiagnosed malignancy or other new medical problem but should prompt an inquiry into dietary intake, meal preparation, grocery shopping, and social support. Other examples of IADL triggers are mail and bills being left to pile up, a cluttered house, spoiled food in the refrigerator, repeatedly wearing the same clothes, missed appointments, multiple or inappropriate phone calls, family concerns about driving, taking medications incorrectly, and inappropriate behavior. Patient self-reports regarding function should be interpreted cautiously and validated by direct observation or reliable sources. Family members, caregivers, or friends are often good sources of information regarding how a person is doing at home. Office personnel, both nursing and front office staff, should be asked to share concerns regarding patient function based on their interactions with the patient.

When a potential problem is identified, a more thorough discussion can be initiated, using a structured assessment tool such as those shown in **Table 56**. Potential causes of functional decline warranting evaluation may be cognitive (delirium, dementia), psychosocial (depression, anxiety, loss of caregiver, inadequate financial resources), environmental (dangerous neighborhood, stairs, broken car or appliance), or physical (a new medical problem affecting gait or balance).

**KEY POINT**

- Although routine periodic screening for activities of daily living and instrumental activities of daily living function is not warranted, any indication of decline in ability to perform instrumental activities of daily living should trigger an investigation into potential causes.

## Falls

Falls are common in older patients and cause mortality, morbidity, reduced functioning, and premature nursing home admissions. Thirty percent to 40% of community dwellers older than 65 years fall each year, increasing to 50% of those aged 80 years and older. Because falls have multiple causes (**Table 57**) and multiple predisposing risk factors, the evaluation of patients who fall and the initiation of preventive measures present a complex clinical challenge. The risk for falling increases dramatically as the number of risk factors increases. Because some risk factors are amenable to amelioration or treatment, risk factor identification is a useful first step in preventing falls. The stronger risk factors are lower-extremity weakness, history of falls, gait and balance deficits, vision problems, and arthritis. **Figure 36** presents the American Geriatrics Society's recommended algorithm for

**TABLE 56** Indices to Assess Basic and Instrumental Activities of Daily Living

| Index | Functional Activities Assessed |
|---|---|
| Katz Index of Independence in Activities of Daily Living[a] | Bathing |
| | Dressing |
| | Toileting |
| | Transferring |
| | Continence |
| | Feeding |
| Barthel Index[b] | Feeding |
| | Bathing |
| | Grooming |
| | Dressing |
| | Bowels |
| | Bladder |
| | Toilet use |
| | Transfers |
| | Mobility |
| | Stairs |
| Lawton and Brody Instrumental Activities of Daily Living Scale[c] | Ability to use a telephone |
| | Shopping |
| | Food preparation |
| | Housekeeping |
| | Laundry |
| | Mode of transportation |
| | Responsibility for own medications |
| | Ability to handle finances |

[a]The Katz index is scored by assigning a score of 1 to each activity if it can be completed independently, which is defined as having no supervision, direction, or personal assistance; scores are then added for a range of 0 to 6.

[b]The Barthel index results in a score of 0 to 100, with higher scores reflecting independence.

[c]The Lawton and Brody scale results in a score of 0 to 8, with a score of 8 representing independence and 0 representing total dependence for activities of daily living.

the assessment and management of falls. In addition, low vitamin D levels are common in the elderly and have been shown to be associated with muscle weakness, functional impairment, and increased risk of falls and fractures.

As part of the routine care of older persons, the American Geriatrics Society recommends that clinicians periodically ask about fall history. Patients who report a single fall should undergo balance and gait screening with the "get up and go" test. This test is appropriate for screening because it is a quantitative evaluation of general functional mobility. Persons are timed in their ability to rise from a chair, walk 10 feet, turn,

**TABLE 57** Causes of Falls in Older Persons

| Cause | Mean (%) |
| --- | --- |
| Accident and environment related | 31 |
| Gait and balance disorders or weakness | 17 |
| Dizziness and vertigo | 13 |
| Drop attack | 9 |
| Confusion | 5 |
| Postural hypotension | 3 |
| Visual disorder | 2 |
| Syncope | 0.3 |
| Other specified cause | 15 |
| Unknown | 5 |

Adapted with permission from Rubenstein LZ, Josephson KR. Falls and their prevention in elderly people: What does the evidence show? Med Clin North Am. 2006;90(5):810. [PMID: 16962843] Copyright 2006, with permission from Elsevier.

and then return to the chair. Most adults can complete this task in 10 seconds, and most frail elderly persons, in 11 to 20 seconds. Those requiring more than 20 seconds should be considered for a comprehensive evaluation. A strong association exists between performance on this test and a person's functional independence in activities of daily living.

Patients with recurrent falls or who are at increased risk for falls should undergo a fall evaluation. Typically, this consists of a focused history covering fall circumstances, prescribed and over-the-counter medications, acute and chronic medical problems, and mobility level. Physical examination should include vision; gait and balance; lower extremity strength and joint function; neurologic examination, including mental status, sensory function, proprioception, and cerebellar function; and a cardiac evaluation, including postural pulse and blood pressure. Further evaluation, including measurement of 25-hydroxyvitamin D levels, should be directed according to findings in the individual patient.

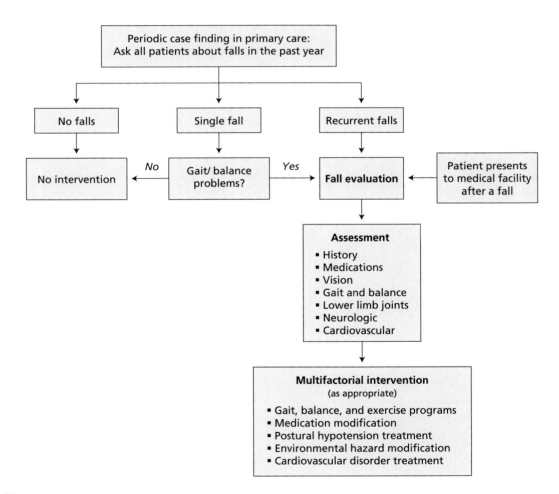

**FIGURE 36.**
**Assessment and management of falls.**

Reprinted from Guideline for the prevention of falls in older persons. American Geriatrics Society, British Geriatrics Society, and American Academy of Orthopaedic Surgeons Panel on Falls Prevention. J Am Geriatr Soc. 2001;49(5):664-672. [PMID: 11380764] Copyright 2001, the American Geriatrics Society with permission from Blackwell Publishing Ltd.

A Cochrane review concluded that a multidisciplinary, multifactorial intervention program tailored to the patient's needs is most like to be beneficial in preventing falls in elderly persons living in the community, reducing the relative risk of falls by about 20%. This type of program should include multiple interventions targeted to modify the identified risk factors, including gait training by physical therapists; prescription of and teaching the use of assistive devices by occupational therapists; exercise programs, including balance training; review and modification of medications (especially psychotropic agents); modification of home hazards; and treatment of cardiac problems, including postural hypotension. Single interventions likely to be beneficial include muscle strengthening and balance training at home by a trained professional; home hazard assessment and modification directed by a trained professional; withdrawal of psychotropic medication; cardiac pacing for patients with carotid sinus hypersensitivity; and tai chi group exercises. A Cochrane review concluded that hip protectors in older people who fall are ineffective in preventing hip fractures, partly owing to limited patient acceptance and adherence because of discomfort. A meta-analysis of five randomized controlled trials plus more recent trials suggest that vitamin D supplementation in elderly patients reduces the relative risk of falls by about 20% (number needed to treat = 15). The vitamin D dose should be 1000 IU daily with the goal of achieving a serum 25-hydroxyvitamin D level of 30 ng/mL (74.9 nmol/L) or greater.

---

**KEY POINTS**

- For elderly persons with a single fall, the "get up and go" test is a good screening test for gait and balance problems that warrant further evaluation.
- Fall prevention should take a multifactorial approach that addresses all potentially treatable risk factors, including vitamin D deficiency.

## Home Safety

In the United States, unintentional injuries are the ninth leading cause of death in persons aged 65 years and older. Falls rank first as the cause of accidental death, followed by fires and poisoning. For every fatal home injury, there are 650 nonfatal injuries. However, older adults value their independence and often prefer to "age in place," even though their safety may be compromised by declining function. This desire often leads them to conceal problems with their home environment due to the fear that they will be taken from their home, instead of asking for help. Reluctance by older adults to make home modifications may be due to beliefs such as "my disability is temporary," "modifications are unattractive and too expensive," or "my landlord will not allow it." It is often up to a family member, friend, home health nurse, or other caregiver to identify home safety problems and initiate remedies. When questions arise about the safety of a patient

at home, a home health referral for a home safety assessment is often warranted, particularly in preparation for discharge home after a hospitalization or a rehabilitation facility stay.

A Cochrane review found no studies demonstrating a reduction in injuries from modification of the home environment to reduce hazards; however, two studies were identified that demonstrated a reduction in falls. The review concluded that better designed studies were needed. **Table 58** lists some

| **TABLE 58** Home Safety Interventions |
|---|
| **Fire Prevention** |
| Have smoke alarms that work |
| Make a home escape plan |
| Keep escape routes clear |
| Keep a phone where it can be used to call for help |
| Smoke safely: use large deep ashtrays on sturdy surfaces; do not smoke in bed or when sleepy |
| Stay in the kitchen when food is cooking on the stove; consider using a microwave oven |
| Make sure space heaters have adequate space away from things that can burn; turn them off if you leave the room, or do not use them |
| Make sure electrical cords and appliances are in good shape; do not overload electrical outlets |
| Have fire extinguishers that you know how to use and are not out of date |
| **Falls Prevention** |
| Have handrails on both sides of stairs and steps, extending the full length |
| Have adequate lighting at both the top and bottom of stairs |
| Tape small rugs to the floor or do not use them at all |
| Have night lights in bedroom, hall, and bathroom |
| Have grab bars in tub and shower |
| Keep sidewalks and paths clear |
| Repair broken steps and walkways |
| Remove clutter from floor |
| Keep wires and cords away from walking areas |
| Move things you use from higher shelves to lower ones |
| If you need a step stool, make sure it has a wide base and a bar to hold on to |
| Use non-skid mat in tub and shower |
| Wear shoes at all times |
| Have a phone near the floor in case of a fall |
| Consider wearing an alarm device |
| **Poison Control** |
| Use a pill box or other system to follow medicine dosages carefully |
| Install a carbon monoxide detector |

Recommendations from the Home Safety Council, www.homesafetycouncil.org/SafetyGuide. Accessed July 7, 2009.

commonly recommended safety interventions. Educational resources on home safety are available from the Home Safety Council, the National Resource Center for Safe Aging, the National Center for Injury Prevention and Control, the National Fire Protection Association, and the Consumer Product Safety Commission.

**KEY POINT**

- A home health referral for a home safety assessment may be indicated if safety is a concern in an elderly person, particularly in preparation for discharge home after a hospitalization or a rehabilitation facility stay.

## Assessment of the Elderly Driver

Although older drivers do not have high overall rates of motor vehicle crashes, they are involved in more fatalities and crashes per mile driven than any other age group except those aged 16 to 24 years. Any report of an accident or moving violation involving an elderly patient should trigger an assessment of the person's driving capacity. In addition, patients with known cognitive losses, limitations in movement of the neck or extremities, cardiac arrhythmias, or a history of falls should be considered as high risk and require closer evaluation. All patients who drive should be routinely asked about recent accidents or moving violations. Driving restrictions in patients with dementia are discussed in MKSAP 15 Neurology.

## Mild Cognitive Impairment and Dementia

The normal aging process has many effects on memory. The ability to memorize, acquire and retain new information, and recall names diminishes with advancing age, particularly in those older than 70 years. This process is also referred to as *benign senescent forgetfulness*. Memory problems in clinical practice represent a spectrum of diagnoses, from mild forgetfulness, with no objective decline in cognition or effects on functioning, to dementia, with significant deficits in various aspects of cognition and functioning. Mild cognitive impairment (MCI) is defined as a decline in memory or other domain of cognition without impact on patient functioning (that is, the process is not dementia). MCI and dementia are discussed more fully in MKSAP 15 Neurology.

Screening asymptomatic patients for MCI might be a reasonable strategy if MCI consistently progressed to dementia and there were treatments to prevent or delay the progression of MCI to dementia. However, the heterogeneity of MCI is revealed in the fact that 20% to 25% of patients with MCI return to normal, thus making discussions of prognosis difficult. Furthermore, no pharmacotherapy has been proved to prevent MCI or slow its transition to dementia, including cholinesterase inhibitors (donepezil, rivastigmine, galantamine, which all have adverse effects), statins, folate with or without vitamin $B_{12}$, vitamin E, melatonin, ginkgo biloba, or omega-3 fatty acids. Lifestyle modifications (such as moderate

exercise, dancing, or doing crossword puzzles) have not been shown to be effective in preventing or treating MCI, but observational evidence supports their use, and the associated risks may be small. Control of cardiovascular risk factors (hypertension, diabetes mellitus, hyperlipidemia) should follow established national guidelines.

For reports or suspicion of memory or cognitive impairment (from patients or family members), the most frequently used and most extensively studied dementia evaluation test is the Mini–Mental State Examination (MMSE). Scores below 24 points (out of a possible 30) are highly correlated with cognitive loss, but the MMSE is insufficiently sensitive to test memory. The most sensitive tool for assessing impairment of short-term memory is the three-word recall test. The clock-drawing test is useful to evaluate cognitive deterioration over time. The National Institute of Aging Consortium to Establish a Registry for Alzheimer's Disease (CERAD) 10-word list tests multiple cognitive domains and may be more useful in detecting the earliest changes of Alzheimer disease. There is no consensus about the role of full neuropsychiatric testing, or the need for neuroimaging, in patients believed to have MCI.

Patients with MCI and their caregivers should be made aware of the uncertain nature of MCI and the unpredictability of progression. They should be educated about signs and symptoms of progression to dementia and followed at regular intervals (for example, every 6 months).

**KEY POINT**

- Presently, there is no effective pharmacotherapy to prevent mild cognitive impairment or slow its transition to dementia.

# Incontinence
## Epidemiology and Detection

The three types of urinary incontinence (UI) are stress, urge, and mixed (with features of both stress and urge UI), each accounting for roughly one third of cases (although in some studies, stress UI accounts for up to half of cases). In women, stress UI is most common, beginning to be a problem following childbirth and in middle age. Prevalence of UI in community-dwelling women increases with age, from 19% in women younger than 45 years to 29% in women 80 years and older. In community-dwelling men, the prevalence ranges from 5% in men younger than 45 years of age to 21% in men 65 years and older. Prevalence in nursing homes is much higher, with rates of 60% to 78% in women and 45% to 72% in men. Caregiver burden related to UI is a common factor leading to institutionalization. Besides sex and age, other risk factors for UI include trauma (childbirth, prostatectomy, radiation), obesity, limited physical inactivity, neuropsychiatric conditions (multiple sclerosis, dementia, stroke, diabetic neuropathy), and constipation or other bowel disorders.

Moderate to severe UI leads to embarrassment, stigma, and impaired social and occupational functioning. This leads to patients hiding UI from their families as well as their physicians: fewer than half spontaneously report their symptoms during health care visits. A simple screening question for identifying patients with UI (or fecal incontinence) is: "How often do you leak urine or stool?" A suggested follow-up question for those who respond positively is: "Do you use pads or protective garments?"

## Evaluation

A practical approach to the office assessment of UI is outlined in **Table 59**. After detecting UI either by a patient's spontaneous report or by the use of screening questions, it is important to first consider transient (reversible) causes that are extrinsic to the bladder, sphincter, and neurogenic regulation. Once transient causes are excluded or are identified and treated, a voiding diary that records frequency, volume, timing (daytime vs. nocturnal), and antecedent factors may be useful. Downloadable voiding diaries can be found at

| **TABLE 59** Office Evaluation of the Patient with Urinary Incontinence | |
| --- | --- |
| Screening questions | How often do you leak urine or stool? *If the patient reports incontinence, ask:* <br>• Do you use pads or protective garments? <br>• Has this problem made you cut down on activities or stay home more? |
| Rule out transient (reversible) causes ("DIAPERS") | Drugs (diuretics, medications with autonomic effects) <br>Infections (urinary tract) <br>Atrophic vaginitis <br>Psychiatric/central nervous system (depression, delirium, dementia) <br>Endocrine/metabolic (such as hyperglycemia, hypercalcemia) <br>Restricted mobility (neurologic or musculoskeletal problems) <br>Stool impaction |
| History | Stress incontinence features? (small volume after cough, exercise, straining) <br>Urge incontinence features? (larger volume after sense of urgency to void) <br>Voiding diary (3 days) to determine frequency, volume, and triggers <br>Prior surgery (abdominal, urologic, gynecologic, orthopedic) <br>Prior genitourinary trauma or instrumentation |
| Physical examination | Abdominal (palpable bladder suggesting possible overflow incontinence) <br>Genitourinary: <br>• Pelvic examination in women (uterine prolapse; atrophic vaginitis; cysto- or rectoceles) <br>• Prostate examination in men (enlargement) <br>Lower extremity neurologic (screening for neurogenic bladder) |
| Postvoid residual volume assessment | In selected situations, determine postvoid residual volume by in-and-out catheter or by ultrasonography after patient voids. (Normal is less than 50-100 mL; abnormal may be above 200-300 mL.) |
| Laboratory studies | Urinalysis or urine dipstick (culture if there is pyuria or hematuria) |
| Indications for referral | Hematuria <br>Voiding difficulty <br>Pelvic mass or prostate enlargement or abnormality <br>Palpable bladder on bimanual or abdominal examination after voiding <br>Possible overflow incontinence (e.g., neurogenic bladder or obstruction; postvoid residual urine >300 mL) <br>Symptomatic prolapse at or below the vaginal introitus <br>Persistent bladder or urethral pain <br>Associated fecal incontinence <br>Suspected neurologic disease <br>Suspected urogenital fistula <br>Previous continence surgery, prostate surgery, or pelvic surgery or radiation therapy |

www.augs.org. A 3-day period is typically sufficient to characterize a patient's voiding profile.

The history, augmented with a voiding diary when necessary, is often adequate to classify the patient's UI as stress, urge, or mixed, along with a focused physical examination and urinalysis. Postvoid residual urine volume determination is most useful if overflow incontinence due to outlet obstruction or a flaccid neurogenic bladder is suspected. Detailed urologic evaluations, such as cytoscopy and urodynamic testing, are unnecessary in uncomplicated UI.

## Treatment

Interventions for UI comprise three major categories: behavioral, pharmacologic, and surgical. As UI disproportionately affects women, and much of the research into the management of UI relates to women, treatment of UI in women is first reviewed, followed by a brief discussion of issues unique to men.

**Table 60** highlights the interventions for UI in women supported by the strongest evidence from randomized, controlled trials. In pelvic floor muscle training (PFMT), women learn repetitive exercises (Kegel exercises) to strengthen the voluntary urethral sphincter and levator ani muscles. For PFMT to be effective, it is important that the patient learn to correctly contract her muscles without straining, which increases abdominal pressure. Each contraction is held for approximately 10 seconds, followed by an equal relaxation period. The number of repetitions should be increased weekly until the patient is performing 8 to 12 repetitions three times daily, every day or at least 3 to 4 days per week.

Because only 30% of women can perform an ideal pelvic floor muscle contraction after written or verbal instruction, many trials have augmented PFMT with biofeedback, which

**TABLE 60** Evidence-Based Interventions for Stress and Urge Incontinence in Women

| Intervention | Indication[a] | | Description | Comments |
|---|---|---|---|---|
| | Stress | Urge | | |
| **Behavioral** | | | | |
| Pelvic floor muscle training (PFMT) | +++ | + | At least 24 contractions daily (eight contractions 3 times daily) at least 3-4 times per week for ≥6 weeks | 30 RCTs tested PFMT alone or combined with bladder training. Most of the RCTs (22/30) used biofeedback to enhance PFMT. More long-term follow-up studies are needed to determine if continued exercises are necessary to sustain benefits. |
| Bladder training (timed voiding) | ± | + | Increase voiding interval by 15-30 min/week to attain a 2-3 h voiding interval | Five RCTs (but four combined with PFMT). Most commonly used for urge incontinence, although sometimes a component of PFMT trials for stress incontinence. The single trial (N = 131) that studied bladder training alone showed that it did improve incontinence. |
| **Pharmacologic** | | | | |
| Anticholinergic | | +++ | Oxybutynin 5-10 mg three times daily (or extended release 10-15 mg/d)  Tolterodine extended release 4 mg/d | Cochrane review included 61 RCTs of overactive bladder in adults. Another six RCTs focused on women only. Dry mouth is most common side effect. |
| Duloxetine | +++ | | 20-80 mg/d, with no clear dose-response relationship | 10 RCTs (n = 3633) showed improvements in incontinence. Approved in Europe for SUI. In the United States, approved as antidepressant, but does not have an FDA indication for SUI. |
| **Surgical** | | | | |
| Retropubic suspension | ++ | | Permanent sutures placed through suprapubic incision | Sutures at bladder neck supported to either Cooper ligament (Burch colposuspension) or the periosteum of the pubic symphysis (Marshall-Marchetti-Krantz procedure). |
| Pubovaginal sling | ++ | | A strip of tissue or mesh is used to support bladder neck | Efficacy similar to retropubic suspension, although long-term outcomes less well-established. A modification is the midurethral tension-free vaginal tape procedure. |

PFMT = pelvic floor muscle training; RCT = randomized controlled trial; SUI = stress urinary incontinence.

[a]Strength of evidence from randomized clinical trials by type of incontinence.

Data from Shamliyan TA, Kane RL, Wyman J, Wilt TJ. Systematic review: randomized, controlled trials of nonsurgical treatments for urinary incontinence in women. Ann Intern Med. 2008;148(6):459-473. [PMID: 18268288] Copyright 2008, American College of Physicians.

can be done by the examiner, the patient, or with specialized equipment. The patient is advised to contract the circumvaginal muscles as if she is interrupting her urinary stream or preventing flatus. If the examiner's fingers are drawn inward during a vaginal examination, this indicates appropriate levator ani contraction; if the fingers are pushed outward, inappropriate abdominal muscle contraction has occurred. The patient can perform this maneuver at home with self-palpation of the vagina during PFMT, usually during or immediately following bathing. Another option for providing feedback is to contract the pelvic floor muscles while seated in a chair. This strategy should produce proprioceptive awareness of tightening the entire horseshoe-shaped levator ani, combined with tightening and slight elevation of the anal sphincter. Patients who have difficulty isolating the pelvic floor muscles can place a hand over the rectus abdominis during contraction, providing tactile feedback as they perceive contraction of the abdominal muscles with a simultaneous rise in abdominal pressure. Patients who cannot learn to identify, contract, and relax the pelvic floor muscles after 4 weeks of self-directed PFMT should be referred for computer-enhanced electromyographic or manometric biofeedback.

Bladder training is a formalized toileting technique to increase functional bladder capacity and reduce UI frequency by gradually increasing the time between voiding. It can be used in motivated patients with stress, urge, or mixed UI. During waking hours, the patient is taught to void routinely by the clock, regardless of the desire to urinate. No attempt is made to regulate nighttime voiding patterns. The time interval between voiding is gradually increased, usually by 15 to 30 minutes on a weekly basis, to attain a 2- to 3-hour voiding interval. Episodes of urgency between scheduled toileting times are managed by urge suppression, consisting of slow deep breathing and three to five rapid pelvic floor muscle contractions. The patient is also encouraged to distract herself by counting backward from 100 by sevens or by silently repeating a self-affirming statement, such as "I will conquer my urgency." Once the urge has subsided, the patient should walk to the bathroom to urinate without rushing, but without excessive delays.

Pharmacologic treatments for which there is strong evidence from randomized, controlled trials include duloxetine for stress UI (off-label indication in the United States) and anticholinergic drugs for urge UI. Oral estrogens were once commonly prescribed for UI in postmenopausal women with atrophic vaginitis, but recent studies have shown that these agents actually worsen UI. Transdermal and vaginal administration of estrogen have proved beneficial in some trials, although the results have been inconsistent. The tricyclic antidepressant imipramine has been used to treat incontinence, but evidence regarding its effectiveness is inconclusive. Adrenergic drugs have not proved effective.

Surgery is used mainly in the treatment of stress UI. Options include retropubic suspension (urethropexy) and pubovaginal slings. Long-term studies of retropubic suspension have shown 5-year cure rates of 82% and 10-year cure rates of 55% to 69%. Sling procedures have a cure rate and an improvement rate equal to retropubic suspensions but with less information about long-term outcomes.

Catheterization may be necessary in patients with persistent urinary retention that causes overflow incontinence, symptomatic infections, or renal dysfunction. This most commonly occurs in individuals with a flaccid neurogenic bladder due to diabetic neuropathy or neurologic disorders or injuries causing lower motor denervation. Intermittent catheterization is preferred if the patient or caregiver can perform the technique. Long-term indwelling catheterization may be indicated for: (1) chronic retention in patients unable to manage intermittent catheterization; (2) urine contamination of skin wounds or pressure sores; or (3) distress and disruption caused by bed and clothing changes. Indwelling suprapubic catheters are an alternative that may cause lower rates of urinary tract infections and urethral complications.

Medical devices, such as vaginal cones, incontinence pessaries, or disposable intravaginal devices, have not shown benefit in randomized, controlled trials. Treatments for which the evidence is inconclusive include injectable bulking agents and electrostimulation. Although obesity is a risk factor for incontinence, evidence to determine whether weight loss improves incontinence is lacking. Patients with UI are often advised to avoid excessive fluid intake (>3 to 4 L daily) in general, and caffeinated beverages and alcohol in particular, although to what degree this dietary manipulation is effective for UI is uncertain. Absorbent products, handheld urinals, and toileting aids may be used as coping strategies while awaiting definitive treatment or as an adjunct to ongoing therapy, but should be used in long-term management of UI only after other treatment options have been explored.

## Male Incontinence

Incontinence in men typically begins in later years and most commonly is caused by detrusor instability (urge UI); prostatic disease and its complications or treatment; and central nervous system disorders, such as stroke, dementia, and Parkinson disease. Benign prostatic hyperplasia is a common cause of voiding problems but seldom causes incontinence unless obstruction is severe enough to cause urinary retention.

Evidence-based treatments that have proved effective for urge UI in women, particularly bladder training and anticholinergic medications, may also be beneficial in men. As stress and mixed incontinence can occur in men, PFMT may also play a role, particularly in the setting of prostate disease or its treatment. Guidelines regarding intermittent and indwelling catheterization for UI in women also apply to men. Condom catheters are often considered an option in men but can predispose to urinary tract and skin infections.

- Stress incontinence is characterized by leakage of a small volume of urine after coughing, exercise, or straining.
- Urge incontinence is characterized by leakage of a large volume of urine after a sense of urgency to void.
- Pelvic floor muscle training exercises are beneficial in stress urinary incontinence; anticholinergic medications are beneficial in urge incontinence.
- Effective surgical treatments for stress urinary incontinence are retropubic suspension and pubovaginal slings.

## Pressure Ulcers

### Risk Factors and Prevention

Pressure ulcers may result from continuous pressure, friction (such as from repositioning a patient in bed without lifting), and shear forces to the skin (as from raising the head of a bed more than 30 degrees). Pressure ulcers occur in up to 38% of hospitalized patients, up to 24% of nursing home patients, and up to 17% of home care populations. Bony prominences below the waist are most prone to developing pressure ulcers. Risk factors include increased age, reduced mobility, sensory impairment, reduced level of consciousness, acute and chronic illness, malnutrition, vascular disease, incontinence, and poor skin condition.

A targeted preventive approach is less costly than one focused on treatment of established ulcers. Patients at risk of developing pressure ulcers should be identified soon after each hospital or nursing home admission, with reassessment if there is a change in the patient's condition. Expert opinion recommends the consistent use of a validated risk assessment tool, such as the Braden Scale for Predicting Pressure Sore Risk (www.bradenscale.com), supplemented by clinical judgment. Skin inspection of those at risk should occur regularly, and patients who are willing and able to should inspect their own skin.

A variety of therapeutic support surfaces have been developed with the goal of preventing pressure ulcers in patients at risk. A recent systematic review of such interventions concluded that specialized foam mattresses or overlays and specialized sheepskin overlays reduce the incidence of pressure ulcers compared with standard hospital mattresses and that mattress overlays on operating tables decrease the incidence of postoperative pressure ulcers. Any additional advantage from "higher-tech" constant low-pressure and alternating-pressure mattresses is unclear. Cost and patient preference may be the important factors in choosing among these preventive strategies. Air-filled vinyl boots, water-filled gloves, regular sheepskin, and doughnut-type devices are likely to be harmful and should not be used. Although there is limited scientific evidence for regular repositioning ("turning"), nutritional supplements, various seat cushions, and lotions, these interventions have a role in many situations. It is important to avoid friction, shear, and excessive skin moisture, which may result from perspiration, urinary or fecal incontinence, or excessive wound drainage.

### Treatment

Classification of pressure ulcers is shown in **Table 61** and is useful for documenting the examination findings and planning treatment. Treatment of pressure ulcers is best managed with an interdisciplinary team approach, with a care plan directed toward addressing the factors that predisposed to the development of the ulcer. Dressings should be chosen to maintain a moist wound environment and manage exudates. When present, infection should be controlled with topical therapies and the addition of systemic antibiotics when cellulitis is present. The possibility of underlying osteomyelitis

| **TABLE 61** Classification of Pressure Ulcers | |
|---|---|
| **Stage** | **Description** |
| Suspected deep tissue injury | Purple or maroon localized area of discolored, intact skin or blood-filled blister due to damage of underlying soft tissue from pressure and/or shear. May be difficult to detect in persons with dark skin tones. |
| Stage I | Intact skin with nonblanchable redness of a localized area, usually over a bony prominence. Darkly pigmented skin may not have visible blanching; its color may differ from the surrounding area. |
| Stage II | Partial-thickness loss of dermis presenting as a shallow open ulcer with a red-pink wound bed, without slough. May also present as an intact or open/ruptured serum-filled blister. |
| Stage III | Full-thickness tissue loss. Subcutaneous fat may be visible but bone, tendon, or muscle are not exposed. Slough may be present but does not obscure the depth of tissue loss. May include undermining and tunneling. Depth varies by anatomic location and may be extremely deep in areas of significant adiposity. |
| Stage IV | Full-thickness tissue loss with exposed bone, tendon, or muscle. Slough or eschar may be present on some parts of the wound bed. Often includes undermining and tunneling. |
| Unstageable | Full-thickness tissue loss in which the base of the ulcer is covered by slough (yellow, tan, gray, green, or brown) and/or eschar (tan, brown, or black) in the wound bed. |

Adapted with permission from National Pressure Ulcer Advisory Panel. Pressure ulcer stages revised by NPUAP. http://npuap.org/pr2.htm. Published February 2007. Accessed July 14, 2009.

should be considered. Surgical or nonsurgical débridement of eschars and nonviable tissue may be needed. Protective creams or solid barrier dressings should be used to protect the skin surrounding the wound. Air-fluidized beds are likely to improve healing compared with other pressure relief devices, although they make it harder for people to get in and out of bed independently. Cochrane reviews do not support a role for electromagnetic therapy, ultrasound therapy, or hyperbaric oxygen in pressure ulcer treatment.

### KEY POINT

- Specialized foam mattresses/overlays and specialized sheepskin overlays reduce the incidence of pressure ulcers compared with standard hospital mattresses.

### Bibliography

Bagai A, Thavendiranathan P, Detsky AS. Does this patient have hearing impairment? JAMA. 2006;295(4):416-428. [PMID: 16434632]

Fung CH, Spencer B, Eslami M, Crandall C. Quality indicators for the screening and care of urinary incontinence in vulnerable elders. J Am Geriatr Soc. 2007;55 Suppl 2:S443-S449. [PMID: 17910569]

Landefeld CS, Bowers BJ, Feld AD, et al. National Institutes of Health state-of-the-science statement: prevention of fecal and urinary incontinence in adults. Ann Intern Med 2008;148(6):449-458. [PMID: 18268289]

Lyons RA, John A, Brophy S, et al. Modification of the home environment for the reduction of injuries. Cochrane Database System Rev. 2006;(4):CD003600. [PMID: 17054179]

Mariani E, Monastero R, Mecocci P. Mild cognitive impairment: a systematic review. J Alzheimers Dis. 2007;12(1):23-35. [PMID: 17851192]

Norton P, Brubaker L. Urinary incontinence in women. Lancet. 2006;367(9504):57-67. [PMID: 16399154]

Prince RL, Austin H, Devine A, Dick IM, Bruce D, Zhu K. Effects of ergocalciferol added to calcium on the risk of falls in elderly high-risk women. Arch Intern Med. 2008;168(1):103-108. [PMID: 18195202]

Reddy M, Gill SS, Kalkar SR, Wu W, Anderson PJ, Rochon PA. Treatment of pressure ulcers: a systematic review. JAMA. 2008;300(22):2647-2662. [PMID: 19066385]

Reddy M, Gill SS, Rochon PA. Preventing pressure ulcers: a systematic review. JAMA. 2006;296(8):974-984. [PMID: 16926357]

Rubenstein LZ, Josephson KR. Falls and their prevention in elderly people: what does the evidence show? Med Clin N Am. 2006;90(5):807-824. [PMID: 16962843]

Trenkle DL, Shankle WR, Azen SP. Detecting cognitive impairment in primary care: performance assessment of three screening instruments. J Alzheimers Dis. 2007;11(3):323-335. [PMID: 17851183]

# Perioperative Medicine

## General Approach

The role of the medical consultant for preoperative evaluation is to assess and minimize risk by evaluating the patient's medical problems, including severity and degree of control and need for further testing; optimizing medical treatment; and recommending risk reduction strategies. Personal communication with the surgeon and anesthesiologist is key, both

to clarify the specific question being asked and to discuss the management plan. To improve adherence to recommendations, recommendations should be limited, specific, and focused on the central issues, and follow-up should be provided.

### Preoperative Laboratory Testing

Preoperative testing should be selective, based on the likelihood of finding an abnormality and, more importantly, that the result will change management. The results of most screening tests will be normal, and any abnormalities found usually do not affect management. Additionally, patients with previously normal laboratory studies in the 4 months prior to surgery and no change in their clinical condition rarely warrant repeat testing. However, most hospital policies continue to require preoperative screening tests despite the evidence to the contrary.

### KEY POINT

- Preoperative testing should be selective and based on the likelihood of finding an abnormality that will change management.

### Perioperative Medication Management

Preoperative medicine reconciliation is an important safety measure, and the medical consultant should obtain a complete list of the patient's medications, including prescription medications, over-the-counter drugs, and herbal products. In assessing whether a medication should be continued, modified, or discontinued prior to surgery, considerations include the indication and need for the medication, the effect on the disease if the drug is stopped, the pharmacokinetics of the drug, and the risk of adverse effects or interactions with anesthetics if the drug is continued. Certain medications are essential, and most can be continued safely. Medications that should be discontinued or modified before surgery include antiplatelet agents, anticoagulants, hypoglycemic drugs, and corticosteroids (discussed in subsequent sections). In addition, the potential benefits of prophylactically starting a drug (for example, a β-blocker) should be assessed. Recommendations for perioperative management of various medications are summarized in **Table 62**.

### KEY POINT

- Medications that should be discontinued or modified before surgery include antiplatelet agents, anticoagulants, hypoglycemic drugs, and corticosteroids.

## Cardiovascular Perioperative Medicine

### Cardiac Medication Management

Most cardiac medications and antihypertensive agents should be continued perioperatively, including on the morning of

**TABLE 62** Perioperative Medication Management

| Medication Class | Recommendation |
|---|---|
| Anticoagulant | Continue for minor surgery. Discontinue before major surgery: 6 h for intravenous heparin; 12-24 h for LMWH; 3-5 d for warfarin; Patients on chronic warfarin therapy may require a heparin "bridge" if at high risk for thrombosis. |
| Antiplatelet | Clopidogrel: discontinue 3-7 d before surgery. Aspirin: continue if minor surgery or recent myocardial infarction (up to 6 months), percutaneous coronary intervention, or stroke; otherwise, discontinue 5-10 d before major surgery. NSAIDs and COX-2 inhibitors are usually discontinued 1-3 d before surgery. |
| Cardiovascular | Continue β-blockers, calcium channel blockers, nitrates, ACEIs, and ARBs. Diuretics optional (usually withheld). |
| Lipid lowering | Continue statins; hold cholestyramine. |
| Pulmonary | Continue controller and rescue inhalers. Probably continue leukotriene antagonists (montelukast, zafirlukast) and lipoxygenase inhibitors. |
| Gastrointestinal | Continue $H_2$ receptor blockers, proton pump inhibitors, and immunomodulators (azathioprine, 6-mercaptopurine, infliximab) |
| Hypoglycemic agents | Oral hypoglycemics: discontinue 12-72 h before surgery depending upon half-life of the drug and risk of hypoglycemia. Intermediate-acting insulin: give 1/2 to 2/3 of usual AM dose. Basal insulin: continue or reduce dose. |
| Thyroid | Continue thyroid replacement, propylthiouracil, methimazole, and potassium iodide. |
| Corticosteroids | Continue; increase to stress doses if indicated. |
| Estrogen | Discontinue hormone replacement therapy several weeks before surgery (or continue oral contraceptives and increase level of DVT prophylaxis). |
| Psychiatric | Discontinue MAOIs 10-14 d before surgery; consider withholding SSRIs 2-3 weeks before neurosurgery. Continue antipsychotic medications. Tricyclic antidepressants and lithium may be continued, although some experts taper and discontinue several days before surgery. |
| Neurologic | Continue anticonvulsants. May continue antiparkinsonian agents, although some experts may discontinue the night before surgery. Discontinue Alzheimer drugs. |
| Herbal | Discontinue up to 1 week before surgery. |

ACEI = angiotensin-converting enzyme inhibitor; ARB = angiotensin receptor blocker; DVT = deep venous thrombosis; LMWH = low-molecular-weight heparin; MAOI = monoamine oxidase inhibitor; SSRI = selective serotonin reuptake inhibitor.

surgery. Diuretics should be withheld if there is a suggestion of hypovolemia. Angiotensin-converting enzyme inhibitors and angiotensin receptor blockers may increase the risk of hypotension with induction of anesthesia, and discontinuation of these agents may be considered, although they have not been associated with increased risk of myocardial infarction or death.

Somewhat controversial is the perioperative management of antiplatelet therapy, especially in patients with coronary stents. The risk of discontinuing antiplatelet therapy needs to be compared with the risk of bleeding if it is continued. Aspirin and clopidogrel cause irreversible platelet inhibition and are typically discontinued several before surgery in patients without stents. In a patient with a coronary stent, elective noncardiac surgery should be postponed until the recommended course of dual antiplatelet therapy has been completed (see MKSAP 15 Cardiovascular Medicine). If surgery is urgent or emergent, the American College of Cardiology/American Heart Association (ACC/AHA) recommends that aspirin be continued if possible and clopidogrel be restarted as soon as possible after the surgery.

## Risk Assessment

The ACC/AHA recommends a five-step approach to assessing cardiovascular risk prior to noncardiac surgery (**Figure 37**).

The ACC/AHA approach includes the urgency of surgery, the presence of active cardiac conditions, the risk of the surgery, the patient's functional capacity, and the presence of other clinical risk predictors as defined by the Revised Cardiac Risk Index (RCRI). The RCRI is based on six factors that predict major cardiac complications: high-risk surgery; history of ischemic heart disease, heart failure, or cerebrovascular disease; diabetes mellitus treated with insulin; and renal insufficiency (serum creatinine >2 mg/dL [176.8 µmol/L]). Cardiac complications occurred in approximately 1% of patients with zero or one risk factor, 5% of those with two risk factors, and 10% of those with three or more risk factors.

Patients with active cardiac conditions (see Figure 37) are at high risk for complications and require further testing and/or treatment prior to elective surgery. If the surgical procedure is low risk, additional testing or interventions are unlikely to lower risk. Functional capacity tends to correlate with complications, and if a patient has adequate exercise capacity (≥4 metabolic equivalents: ability to climb a flight of stairs, walk up a hill, or walk on level ground at 4 miles/hour), no further cardiac testing is usually necessary. For those patients not meeting any of the above criteria, the RCRI factors are used to decide whether further testing is indicated. In general, the overriding theme of the ACC/AHA

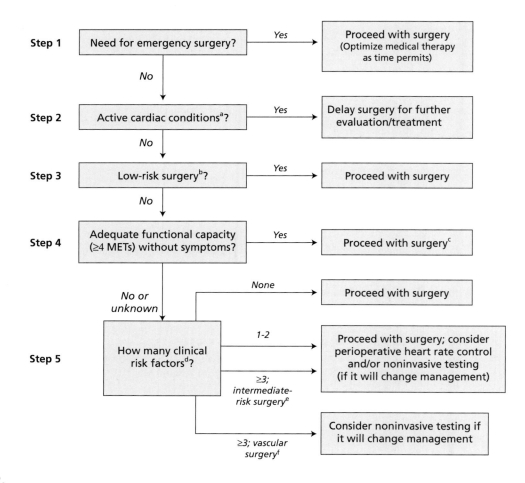

**FIGURE 37.**
**Perioperative cardiac evaluation and care for noncardiac surgery.**

MET = metabolic equivalent.

[a]Active cardiac conditions: unstable coronary syndromes (myocardial infarction <30 days ago, unstable or severe angina), decompensated heart failure, significant arrhythmia, severe valvular disease.

[b]Low-risk surgical procedure examples: endoscopic, superficial, breast, cataract, ambulatory.

[c]Consider noninvasive testing in patients undergoing vascular surgery with ≥1-2 risk factors if it will change management.

[d]Clinical risk factors: (1) history of heart disease, (2) history of compensated or prior heart failure, (3) history of cerebrovascular disease, (4) diabetes mellitus, (5) renal insufficiency.

[e]Intermediate-risk surgery: intraperitoneal, intrathoracic, endovascular aortic aneurysm repair, carotid endarterectomy, head/neck, orthopedic, prostate.

[f]Vascular surgery: aortic or other major vascular surgery; peripheral vascular surgery.

Recommendations from Fleisher LA, Beckman JA, Brown KA, et al. ACC/AHA 2007 Guidelines on Perioperative Cardiovascular Evaluation and Care for Noncardiac Surgery: Executive Summary: A Report of the American College of Cardiology/American Heart Association Task Force on Practice Guidelines (Writing Committee to Revise the 2002 Guidelines on Perioperative Cardiovascular Evaluation for Noncardiac Surgery). Developed in Collaboration With the American Society of Echocardiography, American Society of Nuclear Cardiology, Heart Rhythm Society, Society of Cardiovascular Anesthesiologists, Society for Cardiovascular Angiography and Interventions, Society for Vascular Medicine and Biology, and Society for Vascular Surgery [erratum in Circulation. 2008;118(9):e141-142. Circulation. 2007 Oct 23;116(17):1981. [PMID: 17901356] Copyright 2007 American Heart Association, Inc.

algorithm is that testing should only be done if the results will affect management, and prophylactic revascularization is rarely necessary just to get a patient through surgery.

## Risk Reduction Strategies

Perioperative myocardial infarctions may result from ischemia due to a supply and demand mismatch or plaque rupture. To prevent these complications, interventions addressing these mechanisms include revascularization, β-blockers, and statins. Observational data from patients in the Coronary Artery Surgery Study (CASS) suggested that patients who had

undergone coronary artery bypass grafting (CABG) had fewer postoperative myocardial infarctions and lower mortality rates after subsequent noncardiac surgery. This beneficial effect of CABG appeared to last approximately 4 to 6 years, but there was no benefit for patients undergoing low-risk surgical procedures, and the morbidity and mortality of CABG itself were not taken into account. More recently, the only randomized, controlled trial for coronary artery revascularization prophylaxis (CARP) failed to demonstrate a benefit in patients with stable cardiac symptoms undergoing elective vascular surgery, either for short-term outcome (30-day risk of myocardial infarction or death) or long-term mortality after an average of 2.7 years. However, patients with unstable symptoms, left main coronary artery disease, a left ventricular ejection fraction below 20%, or significant aortic stenosis were excluded. Percutaneous coronary intervention (PCI) is a lower-risk alternative to CABG for patients with amenable lesions. In patients who undergo angioplasty without stenting, the ACC/AHA recommends delaying surgery for at least 2 weeks following completion of the procedure. For patients who received angioplasty and stenting, elective surgery should be postponed for at least 4 to 6 weeks after bare metal stent placement and 12 months after a drug-eluting stent in order to complete the recommended course of dual antiplatelet therapy.

The 2007 ACC/AHA guideline update recommends continuing β-blockers for patients on chronic β-blocker therapy. Otherwise, the guidelines recommend restricting β-blockers to patients with inducible ischemia who are undergoing elective vascular surgery. In addition, β-blockers may be considered for high-risk patients (RCRI score ≥3) undergoing vascular or nonvascular surgery. However, recent findings have emphasized the need for caution when considering the initiation of perioperative β-blockers. The 2008 POISE trial randomized more than 8000 patients to fixed-dose extended-release metoprolol versus placebo. (A high dose of metoprolol was used, and it was not titrated to the patient's blood pressure or heart rate.) Patients receiving metoprolol had fewer perioperative myocardial infarctions and cardiac deaths; however, this was offset by higher overall mortality and more strokes. There was significantly more hypotension and bradycardia in the β-blocker group. A 2008 meta-analysis of 33 trials that included more than 12,000 patients found that β-blockers were not associated with any significant reduction in all-cause mortality, cardiovascular mortality, or heart failure, but were associated with a decrease in nonfatal myocardial infarction and myocardial ischemia and an increase in strokes. Until the risks and benefits of perioperative β-blockade are further clarified, patients already taking β-blockers should continue taking them during the perioperative period. For patients in whom the preoperative evaluation identifies an indication for β-blockade, the β-blocker should be initiated at least several days prior to surgery to allow for safe titration of the β-blocker dose. All patients who receive a β-blocker in the perioperative period must be observed carefully for perioperative hypotension and bradycardia. In the absence of a clear indication, β-blockers should not be routinely started preoperatively.

Observational studies suggest perioperative statins may be beneficial in patients undergoing major surgery; however, large randomized trials of prophylactic statin use are still lacking. A benefit is most likely due to the anti-inflammatory and plaque-stabilizing effects of statins, which are independent of their cholesterol-lowering effect. The ACC/AHA guidelines recommend continuing statins perioperatively in patients already taking them. The initiation of perioperative statin therapy in patients who are undergoing major vascular surgery with or without clinical risk factors is considered reasonable.

Heart failure is a major risk factor that should be treated before elective surgery. Preoperative B-type natriuretic peptide level is being evaluated as a predictor of cardiac complications, but its current role should be considered investigational.

Patients with symptomatic or severe valvular heart disease (primarily aortic stenosis) are at increased risk for cardiac complications and ideally are candidates for valve replacement prior to elective surgery. However, if patients are deemed too high risk for cardiac surgery or refuse surgery, it is often possible to safely get them through noncardiac surgery with medical therapy and close perioperative monitoring. Hypertension is usually considered a minor surgical risk factor, and blood pressure 180/110 mm Hg or below is not associated with an increased risk for postoperative cardiac complications.

**KEY POINTS**

- Most cardiac medications should be continued perioperatively, with the exception of diuretics in patients who may be hypovolemic and antiplatelet agents.

- In patients with active cardiac conditions, noncardiac elective surgery should be delayed or canceled pending further evaluation and treatment.

- Patients with adequate functional capacity and without active cardiac conditions can usually proceed to surgery without preoperative cardiovascular testing.

- β-Blockers and statins should be continued perioperatively in patients already taking these agents, and their use should be considered in high-risk patients scheduled for high-risk surgery.

## Pulmonary Perioperative Medicine

### Risk Assessment

Although postoperative pulmonary complications are as common as cardiac complications, there are fewer good-quality studies of risk assessment. According to American College of Physicians guidelines for reducing perioperative pulmonary complications, the type, location, and duration (>3 hours) of surgery are the strongest predictors of pulmonary complications, with intrathoracic and upper abdominal procedures having the greatest risk followed by lower abdominal procedures. These operations reduce $FEV_1$ and FVC by approximately 50% and 25%, respectively. Surgery not invading the chest or abdomen has little effect on pulmonary function. Other surgery-specific risk factors include emergency surgery, general anesthesia, longer-acting neuromuscular blockers (especially pancuronium), and routine use of nasogastric tubes.

Patient-specific risk factors include chronic obstructive pulmonary disease (but not stable asthma), older age (>60 years), higher American Society of Anesthesiologists (ASA) class (≥II), heart failure, and functional dependence. Cigarette smoking increases risk in current smokers and possibly very recent quitters. A low serum albumin level (<3.5g/dL [35 g/L]) was also associated with postoperative pulmonary complications, but improving nutritional status by enteral or parenteral hyperalimentation failed to improve outcome. Surprisingly, obesity was not associated with increased risk of pulmonary complications, although obstructive sleep apnea was related to development of minor pulmonary complications.

## Risk Reduction Strategies

The American College of Physicians guidelines found good evidence to support the use of routine lung expansion maneuvers—either deep breathing exercises or incentive spirometry—to prevent postoperative pulmonary complications. Evidence was fair for other modalities, including selective nasogastric tube decompression (only used for symptoms or abdominal distention) and use of short-acting neuromuscular blockers. There is conflicting evidence regarding the use of neuraxial anesthesia and analgesia compared with general anesthesia and other methods of pain management. Similarly, smoking cessation more than 8 weeks before surgery improves pulmonary function and may decrease the incidence of complications; however, smoking cessation shortly before surgery does not prevent pulmonary complications, and controversy exists as to whether it may actually increase the risk of complications. Evidence regarding laparoscopic surgery is insufficient. Intraoperatively, laparoscopic surgery may compromise pulmonary function, but postoperatively, patients have less pain and better pulmonary function, and therefore may be at lower risk compared with patients who undergo open surgical procedures.

Consensus opinion supports the use of preoperative spirometry for lung resection candidates to estimate postoperative pulmonary function. Spirometry also may be useful in patients with undiagnosed but suspected chronic obstructive pulmonary disease. Preoperative spirometry should not be used routinely for predicting risk for postoperative pulmonary complications. Spirometry does not usually add information beyond what was known or suspected clinically and rarely changes management. Patients diagnosed with symptomatic obstructive airway disease should have their treatment optimized with corticosteroids and inhaled β-agonists and anticholinergic agents.

Evidence suggests that physicians are capable of predicting findings on most abnormal preoperative chest radiographs by history and physical examination alone and that radiographic results rarely influence preoperative management. There is some evidence that chest radiography is helpful for patients with known cardiopulmonary disease and those older than 50 years who are undergoing upper abdominal, thoracic, or abdominal aortic aneurysm surgery.

Medications for pulmonary disease should be continued perioperatively.

### KEY POINTS

- Smoking cessation more than 8 weeks before surgery improves pulmonary function and may decrease the incidence of complications.

- Good evidence supports the use of routine lung expansion maneuvers to prevent postoperative pulmonary complications.

- Preoperative spirometry and chest radiography should not be used routinely for predicting risk for postoperative pulmonary complications.

# Hematologic Perioperative Medicine

## Venous Thromboembolism Prophylaxis

Preventing venous thromboembolism (VTE) was the highest ranked intervention for patient safety in a recent Agency for Healthcare Research and Quality (AHRQ) report. Appropriate prophylaxis can reduce these rates by approximately two-thirds; however, various studies have shown suboptimal use of prophylaxis in both medical and surgical patients.

Methods of VTE prophylaxis can be mechanical, pharmacologic, or both. Mechanical prophylaxis measures include early ambulation, gradient elastic compression stockings, sequential compression devices, and inferior vena cava filters. In general, sequential compression devices are recommended for adjunct therapy or as sole therapy only if there are contraindications to pharmacologic methods. Inferior vena cava filters are not currently recommended for primary prophylaxis, although they are frequently used in trauma, neurosurgical, and oncology patients.

In general, VTE prophylaxis is indicated for most surgical patients. Prevention techniques include the following: low-molecular-weight heparin (LMWH) once daily; low-dose unfractionated heparin two or three times daily; vitamin K antagonists to maintain the INR between 2 and 3; fondaparinux; and combination gradient compression stockings or intermittent pneumatic compression and LMWH or low-dose unfractionated heparin.

In patients with renal impairment, dosing of LMWH must be adjusted (glomerular filtration rate <30 mL/min/ $1.73$ m$^2$) and fondaparinux is contraindicated. American College of Chest Physicians (ACCP) guidelines state that aspirin should not be used as sole prophylaxis in any group, although guidelines from the American Academy of Orthopaedic Surgeons (AAOS) recommend aspirin for preventing fatal pulmonary emboli in total hip or knee arthroplasty.

ACCP recommendations for prophylaxis are based on the surgery-specific risk for VTE (major versus minor surgery; bleeding risk; and presence of additional risk factors, including prior VTE, malignancy, or hypercoagulable state) (**Table 63**). In general, higher or more frequent dosing and combined modalities are recommended as the risk category increases. Prophylaxis should be initiated preoperatively and continued throughout the patient's hospitalization. In certain procedures (hip replacement, hip fracture repair, knee replacement, and abdominal surgery for cancer), extended prophylaxis beyond hospitalization is recommended because of the ongoing risk of VTE weeks after surgery. Routine noninvasive screening for deep venous thrombosis in asymptomatic patients before discharge is not recommended.

Recommendations for perioperative management of patients on chronic anticoagulation are reviewed in MKSAP 15 Hematology and Oncology.

## Bleeding Disorders

In the absence of a personal or family history of abnormal bleeding, liver disease, significant alcohol use, malabsorption, or anticoagulation therapy, the likelihood of a bleeding disorder is low, and no further preoperative testing is required. Patients with any of these risk factors should be screened with a prothrombin time (PT/INR), activated partial thromboplastin time (aPTT), and platelet count. In addition, plasma fibrinogen measurement and von Willebrand factor testing are considerations in patients with a history of bleeding problems. PT should be within 3 seconds of control, INR 1.5 or below, aPTT within 10 seconds of control, and platelet count greater than 80,000 to 100,000/μL (80 to 100 × 10$^9$/L). Platelet transfusion and hematologic consultation may be warranted for platelet counts below 50,000/μL (50 × 10$^9$/L). The decision to transfuse platelets in patients with platelet counts between 50,000/μL and 80,000/μL (50 and 80 × 10$^9$/L) should be individualized based on the underlying cause and the type of surgery. Bleeding times are rarely performed, as they are nonspecific and do not correlate with bleeding problems.

In patients with bleeding disorders, the use of antithrombotic drugs with neuraxial anesthesia may increase the risk of paraspinal hematomas and should be avoided. In patients without a bleeding disorder, aspirin and NSAIDs do not increase risk. Data on clopidogrel are limited, but expert opinion recommends that it should be stopped 5 days prior to neuraxial anesthesia. In patients undergoing neuraxial anesthesia, insertion of a spinal needle or epidural catheter should be delayed for at least 12 hours after a prophylactic dose of LMWH or 24 hours after a full anticoagulation dose, and removal of an epidural catheter should be done when the anticoagulant effect is at a minimum. The resumption of prophylactic anticoagulation should be delayed at least 2 hours after the epidural catheter is removed.

## Anemia

Anemia is commonly encountered in surgical patients. A study in elderly patients found that even mild degrees of anemia or polycythemia were associated with an increased risk of short-term mortality and cardiac events; however, normalizing the hematocrit does not necessarily improve outcomes. Despite the common practice of giving blood transfusions to patients with hemoglobin levels below 10 g/dL (100 g/L) or a hematocrit below 30%, there is no evidence or physiologic basis to support this practice. The decision to provide blood transfusion depends on whether the anemia is acute or chronic, the expected blood loss of the surgical procedure, and whether or not the patient has cardiac or pulmonary disease that would impair the normal compensatory mechanisms. Although there is no clear cut-off for blood transfusion, it is thought to be somewhere between 7 and 8

| **TABLE 63** Venous Thromboembolism Prevention in Surgical Patients | | | | | |
|---|---|---|---|---|---|
| **Risk Category**[a] | **LMWH** | **LDUFH** | **VKA** | **Fondaparinux** | **Other** |
| Low risk (<10%): minor surgery, mobile patient | No | No | No | No | Early and "aggressive" ambulation |
| Moderate risk (10%-40%): most general, open gynecologic, or urologic surgery | Yes (at recommended doses) | 5000 U twice or three times daily | No | Yes (not FDA approved for non-orthopedic surgery) | Mechanical prophylaxis alone if high bleeding risk |
| High risk (40%-80%): Hip or knee arthroplasty, hip fracture surgery, major trauma, spinal cord injury | Yes (at recommended doses) | No | Yes (INR range 2-3) | Yes | Mechanical prophylaxis as adjunct or use alone if high bleeding risk |

FDA = U.S. Food and Drug Administration; LDUFH = low-dose unfractionated heparin; LMWH = low-molecular-weight heparin; VKA = vitamin K antagonist.

[a]Deep venous thrombosis risk without prophylaxis.

Recommendations based on Geerts WH, Bergqvist D, Pineo GF, et al; American College of Chest Physicians. Prevention of venous thromboembolism: American College of Chest Physicians Evidence-Based Clinical Practice Guidelines (8th Edition). Chest. 2008;133(6 Suppl):381S-453S. [PMID: 18574271] Copyright 2008, American College of Chest Physicians.

g/dL (70 and 80 g/L) of hemoglobin in otherwise stable asymptomatic patients and somewhat higher in patients with cardiopulmonary disease. Simple transfusion rather than exchange transfusion can be given in patients with sickle cell anemia undergoing major surgery.

---

**KEY POINTS**

- Sequential compression devices should only be used as sole prophylaxis for venous thromboembolism in patients at high risk for bleeding or with contraindications to pharmacologic prophylaxis.

- The risk for venous thromboembolism (VTE) is highest in patients with multiple risk factors for VTE and in those undergoing hip or knee arthroplasty, hip fracture surgery, and surgery for major trauma or spinal cord injury.

- Effective preventive strategies for patients at highest risk for venous thromboembolism include low-molecular-weight heparin, vitamin K antagonist, and fondaparinux.

- Screening tests for coagulopathy are indicated only in patients with a personal or family history of a bleeding disorder or in patients with alcohol or drug abuse, liver disease, or on anticoagulants.

- Although there is no clear cut-off for perioperative blood transfusion in patients with anemia, a threshold hemoglobin level of 7 to 8 g/dL (70-80 g/L) in otherwise stable asymptomatic patients is generally recommended.

---

## Endocrine Perioperative Medicine

### Perioperative Glycemic Control

Stress-induced hyperglycemia is common in surgical patients without diabetes. The physiologic stress of anesthesia and surgery stimulates the production of counter-regulatory hormones, including epinephrine, norepinephrine, cortisol, and growth hormone, that decrease insulin production. Additionally, lipolysis, ketogenesis, and decreased caloric intake can further impair glycemic control. The value of glucose control in nondiabetic patients with stress-induced hyperglycemia is currently unknown. Although an earlier study of surgical intensive care unit patients found a benefit with tight glucose control (target <110 versus 180-220 mg/dL [6.11 versus 9.99-12.21 mmol/L]), more recent studies have either found no benefit or reported harm. Current recommendations are to keep the glucose level between 110 and 180 mg/dL (6.11 and 9.99 mmol/L).

Patients with type 2 diabetes taking oral hypoglycemic agents should have the drug stopped either on the morning of surgery or 24 to 72 hours before, depending on the half-life of the drug. Although it is usually recommended that metformin be stopped 48 hours before surgery to minimize the likelihood of developing lactic acidosis, there is no evidence that metformin is more likely than any other hypoglycemic agent to cause this problem in the absence of renal insufficiency, hepatic impairment, or heart failure. Choices for perioperative management of patients with type 2 diabetes who take insulin range from continuous intravenous infusion of short-acting insulin, to a reduction in dose (to one-half to two-thirds of the usual dose) of intermediate-acting insulin, to no glucose and no insulin on the morning of surgery. All patients with type 1 diabetes should receive perioperative insulin. Basal insulin can usually be continued at the same dose; however, if the procedure will be delayed until later in the day and the patient will receive nothing by mouth for a prolonged period, a reduction in dose may be indicated. Regardless of the perioperative hypoglycemic regimen, all patients with diabetes should be monitored frequently and receive additional short-acting insulin if needed.

### Thyroid Disease

Mild to moderate hypothyroidism does not confer any significant perioperative risk, and there is no reason to delay surgery in these patients. Thyroid replacement medication should be continued, but intravenous substitution is rarely necessary owing to the long half-life of levothyroxine. Elective surgery should be delayed in patients with severe hypothyroidism or myxedema, in order to provide replacement therapy.

Conversely, surgery should be postponed in patients with hyperthyroidism, as surgery itself can trigger thyroid storm. If surgery is urgent, treatment should include propylthiouracil and potassium iodide to block production of thyroid hormone and inhibit its release and conversion, and β-blockers to block its peripheral effects. In addition, corticosteroids should be administered to block thyroxine to triiodothyronine conversion and prevent possible hypoadrenalism.

### Chronic Corticosteroid Use

Suppression of the hypothalamic-pituitary-adrenal (HPA) axis should be suspected in a patient who has cushingoid features or who has received the equivalent of 20 mg/d or more of prednisone for 3 or more weeks during the preceding 6 months (possibly longer). Suppression is uncertain in patients with daily doses between 5 and 20 mg, and suppression is unlikely in those with daily doses below 5 mg or who are on alternate-day therapy. If suppression is uncertain, management options include performing a cosyntropin stimulation test or empirically prescribing supplemental corticosteroids.

For minor procedures, no additional corticosteroids are necessary. Recommendations for moderate-risk surgery are intravenous hydrocortisone, 50 mg preoperatively followed by 25 mg every 8 hours for 1 to 2 days; and for major or high-risk surgery, hydrocortisone, 100 mg preoperatively followed by

50 mg every 8 hours for 2 to 3 days. Once the stressful period is over, patients can resume their usual preoperative dose.

KEY POINTS

- Most experts do not recommend intensive insulin control for critically ill patients, including surgical patients in the intensive care unit.
- Mild to moderate hypothyroidism does not increase surgical risk, but hyperthyroidism does and should be treated preoperatively.
- Patients with a history of corticosteroid use should be considered for stress-dose coverage if they took more than the equivalent of 20 mg/d prednisone for at least 3 weeks within the past 6 to 12 months.

## Renal Perioperative Medicine

Chronic kidney disease is a predictor of increased postoperative cardiopulmonary complications and worsening postoperative renal function. A recent observational study in patients with normal renal function undergoing general surgery identified seven independent preoperative factors that predicted development of postoperative acute renal failure: age 59 years or older, emergency surgery, high-risk surgery, liver disease, peripheral arterial disease, BMI of 32 or greater, and chronic obstructive pulmonary disease requiring bronchodilator therapy. Intraoperative risk factors include diuretic use and the need for and total dose of vasopressors. The presence of three or more risk factors was associated with acute renal failure in 4.3% of the patients, a 16-fold increase in risk. Acute renal failure was also associated with increased short- and long-term mortality.

Patients on hemodialysis are at increased risk of perioperative complications due to comorbid conditions (coronary artery disease, diabetes, hypertension), platelet dysfunction, and fluid-electrolyte abnormalities. Ideally, patients should be dialyzed the day before surgery to minimize acute shifts in fluid-electrolyte and acid-base balance and should be followed by a nephrologist perioperatively.

KEY POINT

- Predictors of postoperative renal failure include older age, emergency or high-risk surgery, liver disease, peripheral arterial disease, BMI of 32 or greater, chronic obstructive pulmonary disease requiring bronchodilator therapy, intraoperative vasopressors, and diuretic use.

## Hepatic Perioperative Medicine

Surgery and general anesthesia may result in decreased hepatic blood flow, transient elevation in aminotransferases, and other metabolic changes. Elective surgery should be delayed in patients with acute viral or alcoholic hepatitis pending normalization of liver function. Chronic hepatitis that is medically stable does not usually significantly increase surgical risk.

Perioperative risk for patients with cirrhosis is best evaluated using the Child-Turcotte-Pugh (CTP) score or the Model for End-stage Liver Disease (MELD) score, although these indices were not intended for this purpose. Mortality rates for patients with CTP class A, B, or C liver disease are approximately 10%, 30%, and 80%, respectively. Preoperative treatment to improve encephalopathy, ascites, and coagulopathy appears to reduce risk in these patients.

KEY POINT

- Chronic hepatitis that is medically stable does not usually significantly increase surgical risk.

## Neurologic Perioperative Medicine

The incidence of perioperative stroke is related to the type of surgery, urgency, previous stroke history, and coexisting conditions. The risk of stroke after noncardiac, nonvascular surgery is less than 1% but may be as high as 3% to 6% after coronary artery bypass surgery or carotid endarterectomy. Asymptomatic bruits are not correlated with risk of postoperative stroke and rarely warrant further investigation preoperatively. Most postoperative strokes are embolic and have a bimodal distribution with a smaller peak occurring within 24 hours of surgery (mainly after coronary artery bypass or carotid endarterectomy) and the majority occurring later in the postoperative period. It is generally recommended that elective surgery be postponed for at least 2 weeks after a stroke. There is some evidence that perioperative statins may decrease stroke risk. Patients with symptomatic carotid artery disease should be considered for carotid endarterectomy prior to elective surgery.

Postoperative cognitive dysfunction is common after hospital discharge, and elderly patients are at increased risk for long-term impairment and risk of death. Of the various risk factors for postoperative delirium, preexisting cognitive impairment and psychotropic drug use were found to be the best predictors in a recent systematic review. Other risk factors from previous studies include poor functional status, polypharmacy, advanced age, glucose and electrolyte abnormalities, alcohol abuse, prolonged surgery (thoracic and vascular, especially aortic surgery), pain, tobacco abuse, hypoxia, and anemia. Management of postoperative delirium includes treating the precipitating causes, maintaining a quiet environment, avoiding physical restraints, and use of low-dose haloperidol, which may reduce the severity and duration of delirium. Risperidone and olanzapine can also be used but have not been found to be superior to haloperidol.

## Bibliography

Bangalore S, Wetterslev J, Pranesh S, Sawhney S, Gluud C, Messerli FH. Perioperative beta blockers in patients having non-cardiac surgery: a meta-analysis. Lancet. 2008;372(9654):1962-1976. [PMID: 19012955]

Kapoor AS, Kanji H, Buckingham J, Devereaux PJ, McAlister FA. Strength of evidence for perioperative use of statins to reduce cardiovascular risk: systematic review of controlled studies. BMJ. 2006; 333(7579):1149. [PMID: 17088313]

Kheterpal S, Tremper KK, Englesbe MJ, et al. Predictors of postoperative acute renal failure after noncardiac surgery in patients with previously normal renal function [erratum in Anesthesiology. 2008;108(5):969]. Anesthesiology. 2007;107(6):892-902. [PMID: 18043057]

McFalls EO, Ward HB, Moritz TE, et al. Coronary-artery revascularization before elective major vascular surgery. N Engl J Med. 2004;351(27):2795-2804. [PMID: 15625331]

Newman S, Stygall J, Hirani S, Shaefi S, Maze M. Postoperative cognitive dysfunction after noncardiac surgery: a systematic review. Anesthesiology. 2007;106(3):572-590. [PMID: 17325517]

NICE-SUGAR Study Investigators, Finfer S, Chittock DR, et al. Intensive versus conventional glucose control in critically ill patients. N Engl J Med. 2009;360(13):1283-1297. [PMID: 19318384]

POISE Study Group, Devereaux PJ, Yang H, et al. Effects of extended-release metoprolol succinate in patients undergoing non-cardiac surgery (POISE trial): a randomised controlled trial. Lancet. 2008;371 (9627):1839-1847. [PMID: 18479744]

Qaseem A, Snow V, Fitterman N, et al. Clinical Efficacy Assessment Subcommittee of the American College of Physicians. Risk assessment for and strategies to reduce perioperative pulmonary complications for patients undergoing noncardiothoracic surgery: a guideline from the American College of Physicians. Ann Intern Med. 2006;144(8):575-580. [PMID: 16618955]

Salerno SM, Hurst FP, Halvorson S, Mercado DL. Principles of effective consultation: an update for the 21st-century consultant. Arch Intern Med. 2007;167(3):271-275. [PMID: 17296883]

Selim M. Perioperative stroke. N Engl J Med. 2007;356(7):706-713. [PMID: 17301301]

Teh SH, Nagorney DM, Stevens SR, et al. Risk factors for mortality after surgery in patients with cirrhosis. Gastroenterology. 2007;132(4): 1261-1269. [PMID: 17408652]

Wu WC, Schifftner TL, Henderson WG, et al. Preoperative hematocrit levels and postoperative outcomes in older patients undergoing noncardiac surgery. JAMA. 2007;297(22):2481-2488. [PMID: 17565082]

# Self-Assessment Test

This self-assessment test contains one-best-answer multiple-choice questions. Please read these directions carefully before answering the questions. Answers, critiques, and bibliographies immediately follow these multiple-choice questions. The American College of Physicians is accredited by the Accreditation Council for Continuing Medical Education (ACCME) to provide continuing medical education for physicians.

The American College of Physicians designates MKSAP 15 General Internal Medicine for a maximum of 22 *AMA PRA Category 1 Credits*™. Physicians should only claim credit commensurate with the extent of their participation in the activity. Separate answer sheets are provided for each book of the MKSAP program. Please use one of these answer sheets to complete the General Internal Medicine self-assessment test. Indicate in Section H on the answer sheet the actual number of credits you earned, up to the maximum of 22, in ¼-credit increments. (One credit equals one hour of time spent on this educational activity.)

Use the self-addressed envelope provided with your program to mail your completed answer sheet(s) to the MKSAP Processing Center for scoring. Remember to provide your MKSAP 15 order and ACP ID numbers in the appropriate spaces on the answer sheet. The order and ACP ID numbers are printed on your mailing label. If you have *not* received these numbers with your MKSAP 15 purchase, you will need to acquire them to earn CME credits. E-mail ACP's customer service center at custserv@acponline.org. In the subject line, write "MKSAP 15 order/ACP ID numbers." In the body of the e-mail, make sure you include your e-mail address as well as your full name, address, city, state, ZIP code, country, and telephone number. Also identify where you have made your MKSAP 15 purchase. You will receive your MKSAP 15 order and ACP ID numbers by e-mail within 72 business hours.

CME credit is available from the publication date of July 31, 2009, until July 31, 2012. You may submit your answer sheets at any time during this period.

# Self-Scoring Instructions:

# General Internal Medicine

**Compute your percent correct score as follows:**

**Step 1**: Give yourself 1 point for each correct response to a question.

**Step 2**: Divide your total points by the total number of questions: 133.

The result, expressed as a percentage, is your percent correct score.

|  | Example | Your Calculations |
|---|---|---|
| Step 1 | 133 | |
| Step 2 | 113 ÷ 133 | ÷ 133 |
| % Correct | 85% | % |

*Each of the numbered items is followed by lettered answers. Select the **ONE** lettered answer that is **BEST** in each case.*

## Item 1

An 83-year-old man is hospitalized for cholecystitis. He is prescribed subcutaneous unfractionated heparin, 5000 units every 8 hours, for prevention of venous thromboembolism. By accident, the nurse uses a vial with a more concentrated heparin and administers 50,000 units to the patient. She immediately tells her supervisor. An incident report is filed and an immediate partial thromboplastin time is requested.

**When or under which circumstances should the error be reported to the patient?**

(A) As soon as possible

(B) If additional therapy is required

(C) If the partial thromboplastin time is greater than 100 sec

(D) If there is clinical bleeding

## Item 2

A 45-year-old man is evaluated because of the acute onset of right ear pain. The patient was well until 10 days ago, when he developed symptoms of an upper respiratory tract infection, including nasal congestion and a nonproductive cough. Although these symptoms are resolving, pain and some loss of hearing in the right ear first occurred last night. He does not have fever, sore throat, or drainage from the ear. Medical history is unremarkable. The patient has no allergies and takes no medications.

On physical examination, vital signs, including temperature, are normal. The right tympanic membrane is erythematous, opacified, and immobile, but the external auditory canal is normal. The left ear and posterior pharynx are normal. Examination of the chest is unremarkable.

**Which of the following is the best initial antibiotic choice in this patient?**

(A) Amoxicillin

(B) Amoxicillin-clavulanate

(C) Azithromycin

(D) Ceftriaxone

## Item 3

A 29-year-old woman has an 8-month history of insomnia, difficulties concentrating, fatigue, and irritability. She has trouble falling asleep, awakens after 2 or 3 hours, and has difficulty returning to sleep. The patient is concerned that her impaired concentration is interfering with her work as an attorney and has tried to compensate by spending long hours in the office. Her social activities have decreased because of the extended work hours. She broke up with her boyfriend several months ago and is concerned that she will soon be 30 years old and that "her biological clock is ticking." She frequently lies awake in bed wondering if she will make partner at her law firm as well as whether she will ever get married and have children. She has occasional episodes of crampy abdominal pain, but her appetite is unchanged and her weight has been stable.

Findings on physical examination are unremarkable. BMI is 24. Results of routine laboratory studies, including thyroid function tests, are normal. The patient refuses to see a psychotherapist because she finds "talk therapy" difficult.

**Which of the following is the most appropriate pharmacologic agent at this time?**

(A) Alprazolam

(B) Imipramine

(C) Quetiapine

(D) Sertraline

## Item 4

A 48-year-old woman is evaluated for a cough that has lasted for 3 months. She describes the cough as occurring daily, nonproductive, and without hemoptysis. She has experienced no associated dyspnea, wheezing, fever, weight loss, night sweats, or recent illness. She has not traveled recently or been exposed to anyone else who has been ill. She has never smoked. She was diagnosed with essential hypertension 6 months ago and has taken lisinopril daily since her diagnosis.

Physical examination is unremarkable. She has no oral or pharyngeal exudates or drainage. A chest radiograph is normal.

**Which of the following is the most appropriate management option for this patient at this time?**

(A) Discontinue the lisinopril

(B) Order a chest CT

(C) Order spirometry

(D) Start an antihistamine/decongestant combination

(E) Start a proton-pump inhibitor

## Item 5

A 66-year-old woman, who resides in a nursing home following a stroke, is hospitalized because of loose stools and confusion. On the second hospital day, the patient has two episodes of urinary incontinence. Neither the nursing-home staff nor family members report previous problems with incontinence. Medical history is significant for a cerebrovascular accident with severe aphasia and left hemiparesis, hypertension, and type 2 diabetes mellitus. Current medications are aspirin, dipyridamole, lisinopril, and glipizide.

On physical examination, temperature is 36.8 °C (98.2 °F), blood pressure is 164/96 mm Hg, pulse rate is 92/min, and respiration rate is 18/min. Arterial oxygen saturation is 98% on ambient air. Results of cardiopulmonary, abdominal, and rectal examinations are normal. On neurologic examination, the patient is not oriented to place or date and she keeps trying to climb out of bed.

There is expressive aphasia and moderate weakness of the left arm and leg.

**Laboratory studies:**

| | |
|---|---|
| Complete blood count | Normal |
| Calcium | 8.6 mg/dL (2.15 mmol/L) |
| Creatinine | 1.2 mg/dL (106.1 μmol/L) |
| Glucose | 100 mg/dL (5.55 mmol/L) |
| Electrolytes | Normal |
| Urinalysis | 2+ glucose, moderate protein, 10-20 leukocytes and 3-5 erythrocytes/hpf |

Results of urine and blood cultures are pending. An electrocardiogram and chest radiograph are normal.

**Which of the following is the best management for this patient's incontinence?**

(A) Begin ciprofloxacin
(B) Discontinue glipizide
(C) Insert an indwelling urinary catheter
(D) Schedule a CT scan of the head

## Item 6

A 35-year-old man has a 16-year history of recurrent nasal congestion, sneezing, and rhinorrhea that begin in the early spring. He feels uncomfortable and is having difficulty concentrating at work. The patient had eczema as a child. Medical history is otherwise unremarkable. He has no allergies and takes no medications. A sister has asthma.

Vital signs, including temperature, are normal. Examination of the nose reveals a widened bridge, a horizontal nasal crease, pale nasal mucosa, and a clear mucoid discharge. The lungs are clear to auscultation.

**Which of the following is the most efficacious initial treatment?**

(A) Intranasal azelastine
(B) Intranasal fluticasone
(C) Oral fexofenadine
(D) Oral pseudoephedrine

## Item 7

A 51-year-old woman is evaluated during a routine physical examination. She has no history of hypertension and has never used tobacco. There is no family history of heart disease. Her only medication is daily oral conjugated estrogens combined with medroxyprogesterone acetate for intolerable hot flushes.

Physical examination is normal. BMI is 31. A fasting lipid panel is obtained with the following results: total cholesterol, 218 mg/dL (5.65 mmol/L); HDL cholesterol, 42 mg/dL (1.09 mmol/L); LDL cholesterol, 128 mg/dL (3.32 mmol/L); triglycerides, 240 mg/dL (2.71 mmol/L).

**Which of the following is the most appropriate next step in the management of this patient?**

(A) Calculate Framingham risk score
(B) Calculate non-HDL cholesterol level

(C) Prescribe atorvastatin
(D) Prescribe gemfibrozil

## Item 8

A 52-year-old man is evaluated during a routine examination that includes a discussion of health maintenance issues. After discussing screening for colorectal cancer, he refuses colonoscopy because of lack of insurance coverage. He is willing to consider other options for screening and states that if an abnormality is found, he would be willing to undergo colonoscopy. There is no family history of colorectal cancer, and no previous colonoscopy. On physical examination, vital signs and the heart, lungs, and abdomen are normal.

**Which of the following is the most appropriate colorectal cancer screening strategy for this patient?**

(A) Annual home fecal occult blood testing
(B) Annual office rectal examination and fecal occult blood testing
(C) Double-contrast barium enema every 10 years
(D) Flexible sigmoidoscopy every 10 years

## Item 9

A 52-year-old man is evaluated for a daily cough for the past 6 months. It occurs throughout the day and occasionally at night, but he does not notice any specific triggers. There is occasional production of small amounts of white sputum but no hemoptysis. He does not have any known allergies, has no new pets or exposures, and does not smoke. He does have nasal discharge. He has not noticed any wheezing and has no history of asthma. He has no symptoms of heartburn. He has had no fever, weight loss, or foreign travel, and takes no medications.

Vital signs are normal. There is no cobblestone appearance of the oropharyngeal mucosa or mucus dripping down the oropharynx. Lungs are clear to auscultation. A chest radiograph is normal.

**Which of the following is the most appropriate management for this patient?**

(A) Antihistamine/decongestant combination
(B) CT scan of chest
(C) Inhaled fluticasone
(D) Proton-pump inhibitor
(E) Pulmonary function testing

## Item 10

A 29-year-old woman is evaluated for bilateral breast pain, which she has experienced off and on for 6 months. The pain is diffuse, aching, radiates to her upper arms and axillae, and typically occurs or worsens towards the end of her menstrual cycle. She denies any localized pain, mass, or nipple discharge. Medical and family history are unremarkable.

She takes no medications and has no allergies. The patient has never had a mammogram.

On physical examination, vital signs are normal. BMI is 30. Her breasts have mild tenderness bilaterally. There is no mass or nodularity, no skin changes or nipple discharge, and no lymphadenopathy.

**After reassuring the patient that her pain is unlikely to be due to breast cancer, which of the following is the next management option?**

(A) Bilateral mammography
(B) Breast ultrasound
(C) Danazol
(D) Tamoxifen
(E) Well-fitting support bra

## Item 11

An 85-year-old terminally ill woman is evaluated in a home hospice setting. She has metastatic breast cancer to the spine, lungs, and liver. She has had progressive anorexia and weight loss and is dependent on family for all activities of daily living. She has an advance directive stating she does not want cardiopulmonary resuscitation or artificial nutrition. Her pain has been well controlled on a fentanyl transdermal patch and immediate-release morphine as needed for pain. These medications have been stable over the past month. Last night, the patient became confused and agitated, trying to get out of bed and repeatedly stating she needed to look for her deceased husband. There is no dyspnea, fever, dysuria, chest discomfort, or abdominal discomfort. She rates her back pain as 1 on a scale of 1 to 10. She continues to require immediate-release morphine.

Vital signs are normal. The patient is alert and oriented to name and place but cannot remember the year or date. The patient is still agitated and confused, picking at her clothes during the examination.

**Which of the following is the most appropriate management for this patient?**

(A) Discontinue fentanyl patch
(B) Initiate haloperidol
(C) Initiate lorazepam
(D) Measure serum electrolytes, calcium, and renal and hepatic function
(E) Schedule MRI brain scan

## Item 12

A 52-year-old woman is evaluated at a routine appointment and seeks advice on smoking cessation. She smokes one and one half packs of cigarettes daily and wants help to stop. She has tried to stop smoking on three previous occasions, each time using nicotine replacement therapy, and she would like to try something different. She has a seizure disorder that is well controlled on valproate.

**In addition to brief smoking cessation counseling, which of the following is the most appropriate pharmacologic therapy to offer?**

(A) Bupropion
(B) Nortriptyline
(C) Sertraline
(D) Varenicline

## Item 13

An 87-year-old woman comes to the office for a routine evaluation. She reports that she has fallen once or twice a month for the past 4 months. The falls happen at various times of the day and occur immediately after standing up or after standing for some time. She does not experience dizziness, lightheadedness, vertigo, palpitations, chest pain or tightness, focal weakness, loss of consciousness, or injury at the time of the falls. The patient lives alone. Medical history includes hypertension and degenerative joint disease of both knees. Medications are acetaminophen and hydrochlorothiazide.

On physical examination, temperature is normal, blood pressure is 135/85 mm Hg without postural change, pulse rate is 72/min, and respiration rate is 16/min. Visual acuity with glasses is 20/40 on the right and 20/60 on the left. Cardiopulmonary examination is normal. There is bony enlargement of both knees without warmth or effusion. On balance and gait screening with the "get up and go" test, the patient must use her arms to rise from the chair. Neurologic examination, including cerebellar testing and a Romberg test, is normal. The patient's score on the Mini–Mental State Examination is 26/30 (normal ≥24/30).

Results of a complete blood count and blood chemistry studies are normal.

**Which of the following should be included as part of her management at this time?**

(A) Begin risedronate
(B) Measure serum 25-hydroxyvitamin D level
(C) Prescribe hip protectors
(D) Schedule 24-hour electrocardiographic monitoring

## Item 14

A 52-year-old man is evaluated for a 3-month history of perineal and suprapubic pain. He has experienced urinary frequency and dysuria for 4 to 6 weeks. The patient reports fatigue, insomnia, and low mood for the past 6 months. He has hypertension. Current medications are hydrochlorothiazide and acetaminophen as needed for pain.

On physical examination, temperature is normal, blood pressure is 138/80 mm Hg, and pulse rate is 78/min. BMI is 29. Abdominal examination is normal with mild suprapubic tenderness. The prostate is not enlarged; it is mildly tender without nodularity. Testicular examination is normal.

On laboratory study, urinalysis is normal, and urine culture is negative. Prostate-specific antigen level is 0.8 ng/mL (0.8 µg/L).

**Which of the following is the most appropriate treatment for this patient?**

(A) Levofloxacin
(B) Naproxen
(C) Oxybutynin
(D) Saw palmetto
(E) Terazosin

## Item 15

A 24-year-old woman tearfully calls her physician's office while on vacation at a resort in another state, concerned that the condom broke last night while she was having intercourse with her husband. She and her husband are interested in having children some day, but she is in graduate school, and they would like to have a more settled life before having children. Her last menstrual period was 2 weeks ago, and she has never been pregnant.

**Which of the following is the most appropriate management option for this patient?**

(A) Copper intrauterine device
(B) Oral ethinyl estradiol and levonorgestrel
(C) Oral levonorgestrel (Plan B)
(D) Oral mifepristone

## Item 16

A 38-year-old man is evaluated for severe nontraumatic neck pain that has been present for the last 48 hours, which began after driving for 6 hours. The patient has had intermittent episodes of neck pain over the past few years. The pain usually resolved after 24 to 72 hours, and the patient has not sought prior treatment. He has no history of paresthesia, weight loss, muscle weakness or decreased grip strength, or fever. He has no other medical problems, and his only current medication is ibuprofen.

On physical examination, there is tenderness over the paravertebral musculature at the C4-C5 level on the left side. There is decreased range of motion secondary to pain. Passive range of motion is normal, but with pain and stiffness noted. Strength and reflexes in the upper and lower extremities are normal. Disk spaces are nontender.

**Which of the following is the most appropriate management of this patient's neck pain?**

(A) Epidural corticosteroid injection
(B) MRI of the cervical spine
(C) NSAIDs
(D) Plain films of the cervical spine
(E) Transcutaneous electrical nerve stimulation

## Item 17

A 25-year-old woman presents for evaluation of recurrent, bilateral eye pain and redness. Symptoms began several months ago without a specific inciting event. With each episode, she has deep or boring pain that is constant and has awakened her from sleep. She has had photophobia, tearing, and decreased vision during the episodes.

Vital signs are normal. Visual acuity is 20/40 bilaterally. There is photophobia. The pupils are equal, round, and reactive to light. Extraocular movements are intact but painful. The corneas appear clear. On the lateral aspect of both eyes, there is a localized area of raised erythema, with superficial blood vessels coursing over top of erythema but no white sclera visible between the blood vessels. There is no discharge or crusting of the lids.

**Which of the following is the most likely diagnosis regarding her eyes?**

(A) Episcleritis
(B) Scleritis
(C) Subconjunctival hematoma
(D) Uveitis
(E) Viral conjunctivitis

## Item 18

A 68-year-old woman is evaluated during a routine examination. She states that last year she had a painful rash on the right side of her back that was self-limited. She does not recall a history of childhood chickenpox. She takes no medications and has no allergies.

Vital signs are normal and the physical examination is unremarkable. Complete blood count, liver enzymes, and serum chemistry studies are all normal. She is scheduled to receive her annual influenza vaccination today.

**Which of the following is the most appropriate vaccine administration strategy to prevent herpes zoster in this patient?**

(A) Zoster vaccination if negative for varicella antibodies
(B) Zoster vaccination if positive for varicella antibodies
(C) Zoster vaccination now
(D) Zoster vaccination now and in 6 months
(E) Zoster vaccination not indicated

## Item 19

A 70-year-old woman is evaluated before undergoing cystoscopy for microscopic hematuria. She is currently asymptomatic. Medical history is significant for hypertension, type 2 diabetes mellitus, cholecystectomy, and appendectomy. Both surgical procedures were uncomplicated, and the patient has no history of easy bruising or bleeding disorders. Current medications are hydrochlorothiazide, glyburide, and aspirin. She does not drink alcohol and has never smoked cigarettes. An electrocardiogram 6 months ago was normal. The most recent hemoglobin $A_{1c}$ measurement was 6.5%.

Vital signs are normal, and the remainder of the physical examination is unremarkable.

**Which of the following preoperative studies should be done next?**

(A) Chest radiograph

(B) Complete blood count

(C) Electrocardiogram

(D) Prothrombin time, activated partial thromboplastin time, and INR

(E) No additional diagnostic studies are needed

## Item 20

A 22-year-old woman is evaluated because of decreased energy, increased sleep, weight gain, and feeling depressed. The patient always did very well academically, but since her graduation from college several months ago, she has been unable to find a job so she had to move back in with her parents. She states that her life is not working out well but denies thinking about suicide. She previously had periods of unlimited energy when she could stay up all night to do schoolwork or socialize without ever feeling tired. During some of these periods, she had several sexual partners, sometimes with men she met for the first time in a bar, and occasionally did not use condoms.

Medical history is unremarkable. She has never been treated for depression and takes no medications, including oral contraceptive agents. Findings on physical examination are unremarkable.

**Which of the following is the most likely diagnosis?**

(A) Attention-deficit/hyperactivity disorder

(B) Bipolar disorder

(C) Borderline personality disorder

(D) Generalized anxiety disorder

## Item 21

A 48-year-old overweight woman is evaluated for buttock pain. She began jogging 1 week ago to lose weight. Over the last 2 days, pain has developed deep in the left gluteal area. The pain is an ache that she first noticed while lying in bed on her left side. It was somewhat relieved by lying on her right side. The pain has become severe enough that she avoids putting weight her left leg while climbing stairs. The pain does not radiate. Ibuprofen has helped the pain somewhat. She is on no other medications.

On physical examination, there is tenderness elicited over the left sciatic notch when pressure is applied with the thumb. When lying on the right side, abduction of the leg is painful. The hip joint has no pain with full range of motion. There is no tenderness in the groin or over the lateral thigh, and FABER (Flexion, ABduction, and External Rotation of the hip) test results are normal. Reflexes and the straight-leg-raising test are normal.

**Which of the following is the most likely diagnosis?**

(A) Left hip osteoarthritis

(B) Left trochanteric bursitis

(C) L4-L5 disk herniation

(D) Piriformis syndrome

## Item 22

A 39-year-old woman is evaluated for a 6-month history of gradually increasing bilateral tinnitus that is low-pitched, louder in the left ear, and often pulsatile. The patient does not have ear pain or discharge, vertigo, previous ear problems, or exposure to excessive loud noise. Medical history is unremarkable, and she takes no medications. There is no family history of hearing loss.

On physical examination, vital signs are normal. She is able to hear equally whispered numbers 2 feet from each ear with the opposite ear covered. The left and right external auditory canals and tympanic membranes are normal. There are no carotid bruits, and the cardiovascular examination is normal without evidence of murmurs, extra sounds, or jugular venous distention.

**Which of the following is the most likely cause or source of the tinnitus?**

(A) Meniere disease

(B) Palatal myoclonus

(C) Presbycusis

(D) Vascular malformation

## Item 23

A 72-year-old woman has a 6-month history of almost daily urinary incontinence that frequently occurs without warning. She was diagnosed with urge incontinence 6 weeks ago, and oxybutynin was started. Although the frequency of episodes has decreased, incontinence still occurs two to three times each week, especially when she is away from home and not near a bathroom. There is no dysuria or nocturia.

Results of the physical examination are unremarkable. Relevant laboratory results, including urinalysis and urine culture, are normal.

**Which of the following is the best treatment for this patient's persisting urge incontinence?**

(A) Bladder training

(B) Pubovaginal sling surgery

(C) Transanal electrostimulation

(D) Vaginal estrogen cream

(E) Vaginal pessary

## Item 24

A 65-year-old woman undergoes preoperative evaluation prior to elective cholecystectomy. Medical history is significant for chronic obstructive pulmonary disease, hypertension, and type 2 diabetes mellitus. Current medications are albuterol, ipratropium, and corticosteroid inhalers; chlorthalidone; metformin; and aspirin. The patient is a current smoker with a 40-pack-year smoking history. She does not have chest pain, dyspnea, or cough.

On physical examination, temperature is 37.0 °C (98.6 °F), blood pressure is 130/85 mm Hg, pulse rate is 80/min, and respiration rate is 14/min. BMI is 34. The lungs are clear; no wheezing is heard. A chest radiograph shows no active pulmonary disease.

**Which of the following preoperative interventions is most likely to reduce the risk of postoperative pulmonary complications in this patient?**

(A) Intravenous aminophylline
(B) Intravenous corticosteroids
(C) Preoperative spirometry (pulmonary function testing)
(D) Prophylactic antibiotics
(E) Smoking cessation

## Item 25

A 64-year-old man with intermittent acute gout is evaluated in the office for a swollen right elbow of 2 days' duration. He recalls no inciting trauma. His last attack of gout occurred 4 months ago and involved his right knee. He takes no medications.

On physical examination, temperature is 38.1 °C (100.5 °F). The right elbow is warm with minimal erythema. Musculoskeletal examination reveals slight fullness and tenderness over the right olecranon process. Passive and active extension of the right elbow is painless, but passive flexion greater than 90 degrees elicits pain. Rotation of the forearm is painless. He is able to extend the arm fully without discomfort.

**Which of the following is the most appropriate next step in this patient's management?**

(A) Empiric trial of colchicine
(B) Measurement of erythrocyte sedimentation rate
(C) Radiograph of the right elbow and forearm
(D) Right elbow joint aspiration
(E) Right olecranon bursa aspiration

## Item 26

A 70-year-old woman is evaluated because of depressed mood, anhedonia, decreased appetite, impaired sleep, and decreased energy. Although the patient feels somewhat hopeless about the future, she adamantly states that she would never take her own life. Her judgment appears intact. Medical history is unremarkable, and she has not had previous episodes of depression. She is taking no medications. Findings on physical examination are unremarkable.

Sertraline, 50 mg/d, is begun. The patient returns for a follow-up visit 5 weeks later and reports that she is tolerating the medication well but has no significant change in symptoms, which is validated with a standardized symptom assessment tool. The sertraline is therefore increased to 100 mg/d. Six weeks later, she again reports no side effects and no improvement.

**Which of the following is most appropriate at this time?**

(A) Add methylphenidate
(B) Discontinue sertraline and begin citalopram
(C) Reassess in 4 weeks
(D) Refer for electroconvulsive therapy

## Item 27

A 35-year-old woman is evaluated in the office for a 5-day history of acute right knee pain that began when she hopped down from the bed of a truck, twisting her knee. She experienced a popping sensation and a gradual onset of knee joint swelling over the next several hours. Since then, she has continued to have moderate pain, particularly when walking up or down stairs. She reports no locking or giving way of the knee or any previous knee injury.

On physical examination, the right knee has a minimal effusion with full range of motion. The medial aspect of the joint line is tender to palpation. Maximally flexing the hip and knee and applying abduction (valgus) force to the knee while externally rotating the foot and passively extending the knee (McMurray test) result in a palpable snap but no crepitus.

**Which of the following is the most likely diagnosis?**

(A) Anserine bursitis
(B) Anterior cruciate ligament tear
(C) Meniscal tear
(D) Patellofemoral pain syndrome

## Item 28

A 68-year-old man is evaluated during a routine examination. He has a 5 pack-year cigarette smoking history but stopped 12 years ago. He has no history of hypertension, diabetes mellitus, stroke, or transient ischemic attack. He has no claudication. He is being treated for hyperlipidemia. There is no family history of premature coronary artery disease. He has noted no change in his bowel movements, and his most recent screening colonoscopy, performed at age 60 years, was normal. His only current medication is lovastatin.

Blood pressure is 130/82 mm Hg. BMI is 24. Physical examination reveals no abnormalities. Total cholesterol level on his most recent lipid profile was 213 mg/dL (5.52 mmol/L), and his HDL cholesterol level was 48 mg/dL (1.24 mmol/L).

**Which of the following is the most appropriate screening test for this patient?**

(A) Abdominal ultrasonography
(B) Colonoscopy
(C) Low-dose CT of the chest
(D) Office spirometry

## Item 29

A 24-year-old male truck driver comes for a routine examination in order to renew his commercial driver's license. The patient is asymptomatic. Medical history is unremarkable. He does not engage in risky sexual behavior or take any medications. A recent HIV test was negative. He has used smokeless tobacco for 14 years.

On physical examination, vital signs are normal. Dentition is poor. An oral mucosal lesion is shown on the next page. There are no oral masses or ulcers and no cervical lymphadenopathy. The remainder of the examination is normal.

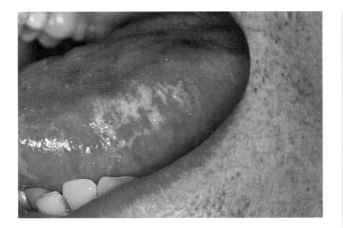

**Which of the following is the most likely diagnosis?**

(A) Candidiasis
(B) Leukoplakia
(C) Lichen planus
(D) Oral hairy leukoplakia

## Item 30

A 21-year-old woman is evaluated after missing her last two menstrual periods. She reports that a home pregnancy test was positive, and she wants to discuss termination of her pregnancy. Although she wants a child, she says that her husband is upset about the pregnancy and blames her for "not being more careful." She also says that he has always been jealous, but since she became pregnant, his behavior has been worse, accusing her of being unfaithful, controlling how she spends her time, and becoming angry when she goes out without asking his permission. She reports that he has "an alcohol problem," and when he is drinking, he has slapped and choked her. She reports that she is becoming afraid for herself and the pregnancy.

**Which of the following is the most appropriate next management option for this patient?**

(A) Obtain previous medical records
(B) Refer for marital counseling
(C) Safety planning
(D) Schedule a joint appointment with her husband

## Item 31

A 62-year-old woman is evaluated during a follow-up visit for diabetes mellitus. Her diabetes has been previously very well controlled, with her most recent hemoglobin $A_{1c}$ level 6.5%. Her husband died unexpectedly 2 months ago, and during a visit 1 month ago, she noted that she had not been sleeping well. She was prescribed zolpidem for sleep.

Today, she reports that her sleep has improved. She is concerned, however, that her morning glucose level over the past 3 weeks has averaged 240 mg/dL (13.32 mmol/L), over her usual baseline of 104 mg/dL (5.77 mmol/L). She reports finding food on the kitchen counter each morning that she cannot account for as well as used dishes and

serving ware. She reports she is not awakening at night, not having dreams, and is not sweaty. She states that she has been taking all of her medications. She has gained 3.6 kg (8 lb) in the past 2 weeks. Current medications are metformin, insulin glargine, low-dose aspirin, and zolpidem.

Vital signs are normal. BMI is 28. Her weight has increased 4.1 kg (9 lb) since the last appointment. The remainder of the physical examination is normal.

**Which of the following is the most likely reason for this patient's elevated morning glucose level?**

(A) Complex sleep-related behavior
(B) Gastroparesis
(C) Medication nonadherence
(D) Somogyi effect

## Item 32

A 67-year-old woman is admitted into the care of a hospitalist physician for treatment of an exacerbation of chronic obstructive pulmonary disease. The following morning, the hospitalist transfers the care of the patient to the attending physician. During the transfer, the hospitalist conveys that the patient's condition is improving, but she has leukocytosis from the recently initiated corticosteroid therapy.

On examination by the attending physician, the patient is comfortable but appears diaphoretic and distractible. Temperature is 37.7 °C (99.8 °F), blood pressure is 110/60 mm Hg, heart rate is 108/min, and oxygen saturation on 3 L of oxygen by nasal cannula is 93%. An internal jugular venous catheter and urinary catheter are in place. Breath sounds are decreased bilaterally; the remainder of the physical examination is normal. No changes in the patient's evaluation or care are ordered by the attending physician. Five hours later, the patient develops fever, increased tachycardia, and hypotension.

**Which of the following categories of diagnostic errors is most likely responsible for the attending physician missing the correct diagnosis?**

(A) Anchoring heuristic
(B) Availability heuristic
(C) No-fault error
(D) System-related error

## Item 33

A 46-year-old woman is evaluated for a 2-year history of fatigue and not feeling rested despite sleeping 9 to 10 hours per night. Before this period, she ran 2 to 3 miles daily. Now, she tries to walk 1 to 2 miles two or three times per week but feels much too tired to run. After walking, she feels extremely fatigued, and her joints and muscles ache. Her appetite is about the same, and she has gained a few pounds, with a current BMI of 27. She denies difficulty getting to sleep or staying asleep, and her husband has not noticed any snoring or apnea. She denies depressed mood or anhedonia.

Her physical examination is unremarkable. Complete blood count, erythrocyte sedimentation rate, serum chemistry studies, and thyroid-stimulating hormone level are normal.

**Which of the following is the most effective treatment for this patient at this time?**

(A) Acclydine
(B) Acyclovir
(C) Cognitive-behavioral therapy
(D) Fluoxetine

## Item 34

An 89-year-old woman is evaluated for dizziness that she has had for the past year, mainly while standing and ambulating. The dizziness is described as a sense of unsteadiness. The symptoms can last for minutes to hours, and she has at least 4 to 5 episodes per day. There are no reproducible activities that cause the dizziness. She does not describe hearing loss, headache, diplopia, or other motor or sensory symptoms. Medical history is remarkable for a 15-year history of type 2 diabetes mellitus, hypertension, hyperlipidemia, osteoporosis, and mild dementia. Current medications are hydrochlorothiazide, ramipril, simvastatin, metformin, insulin glargine, low-dose aspirin, and donepezil. She has not started any new medications recently, and she has no known drug allergies.

Vital signs are normal; there is no evidence of orthostasis. BMI is 27. A cardiopulmonary examination is normal. The patient has a positive Romberg sign and is unsteady on tandem gait. Rapid alternating movements are slowed. The patient has a corrected visual acuity of 20/50 in the right eye and 20/70 in the left eye. Vibratory sense and light touch are diminished in a stocking pattern in the lower extremities, and ankle jerk reflexes are 1+. The patient's Mini-Mental State Examination score is 26/30 (normal ≥24/30), unchanged from 1 year ago. She has no motor abnormalities and no cranial nerve abnormalities. A Dix-Hallpike maneuver does not elicit vertigo or nystagmus.

A complete blood count, metabolic profile, and thyroid function studies are normal.

**Which of the following management options is the best choice for this patient?**

(A) Brain MRI
(B) Meclizine
(C) Physical therapy
(D) Replace aspirin with aspirin/extended-release dipyridamole

## Item 35

A 19-year-old woman is requesting birth control. She took oral contraceptives previously, but had difficulty remembering to take them regularly.

**In addition to recommending condoms to prevent sexually transmitted diseases, which of the following is the most appropriate birth control option for this patient?**

(A) Depot injection of medroxyprogesterone acetate
(B) Diaphragm
(C) Progestin-only pill
(D) Tubal ligation

## Item 36

A 72-year-old woman is evaluated for a 8-month history of aching in her left wrist that keeps her awake at night. She is in a knitting group and has found it increasingly difficult to perform fine hand movements. Using the Katz hand diagram, the patient indicates the presence of sensory changes in the first through third digits. She also reports wrist pain with sparing of the palm and some pain into the forearm. Her only medication is acetaminophen.

On physical examination, there is weakness of thumb abduction, hypalgesia in a median nerve distribution, and thenar atrophy. Vascular assessment in the hand is normal. A nerve conduction study and electromyogram demonstrate medial neuropathy.

**Which of the following is the most appropriate management option for this patient?**

(A) Corticosteroid injection
(B) NSAIDs
(C) Surgery
(D) Ultrasound treatment
(E) Wrist splint

## Item 37

A 32-year-old woman is evaluated as a new patient for a 5-year history of diffuse abdominal pain, headache, tongue burning, intermittent vomiting and diarrhea, pelvic pain, and right arm numbness. She has consulted two other physicians this past year, neither of whom was able to help her. She denies depressed mood and anhedonia but says she has no interest in sexual activity. She takes zolpidem 10 mg each night for difficulty in falling asleep and staying asleep plus five over-the-counter supplements for her symptoms.

Vital signs are normal and there is no orthostatic hypotension. BMI is 32. Mild diffuse abdominal tenderness is present that decreases when the patient is distracted. Neurologic examination is normal; there is no sensory deficit or weakness of the right arm. The remainder of the examination, including pelvic examination, is unremarkable.

Results of laboratory studies obtained 2 months ago were normal. These included a complete blood count, erythrocyte sedimentation rate, thyroid function studies, vitamin $B_{12}$ and folate levels, metabolic profile, antinuclear antibody titer, measurement of serum complement levels and serum quantitative immunoglobulin levels, and serum protein electrophoresis. A chest radiograph and CT scan of the abdomen and pelvis were also normal.

**In addition to regular and frequent office visits, which of the following is the best initial management for this patient?**

(A) Abdominal MRI
(B) Cognitive-behavioral therapy
(C) Electromyography of the right arm
(D) Sertraline

## Item 38

A 35-year-old man is evaluated for a 5-month history of difficulty sleeping, which began during a time of high stress at work. The situation at work has since resolved. Since then, however, he has continued to have trouble falling asleep and staying asleep. It can take up to an hour before he falls asleep, and he awakens one or two times per night. At night, he finds himself watching the clock. He watches television in bed to help him fall asleep or when he awakens during the night. He has tried over-the-counter sleep remedies or drinking alcohol, neither of which has helped. He says his wife has not complained about him snoring, and he has no lower extremity symptoms in the evenings. He denies illicit drug use.

Vital signs are normal. BMI is 24. Physical examination is normal. PHQ-9 depression screening is normal.

**Which of the following is the most appropriate management option for this patient?**

(A) Order thyroid-stimulating hormone level
(B) Polysomnography
(C) Prescribe ramelteon
(D) Sleep hygiene and stimulus control

## Item 39

A 48-year-old woman is evaluated for red, irritated eyes. The symptoms began to develop over the past several months, but she cannot identify an exact precipitant or start to her symptoms. She describes a gritty feeling to her eyes but no itching. Generally, symptoms feel better in the morning upon awakening but get worse as the day progresses. Symptoms are worse when she is outdoors or in the wind. She has no history of eye problems and has not had any eye surgery. She does not have a history of seasonal allergies, coughing, or asthma.

Vital signs are normal. Conjunctiva is mildly injected. No foreign bodies are evident. There is no lid crusting or exudate. Lids are nontender, with no masses on the lids or medial canthus. There is no erythema on the lids. Visual acuity is normal bilaterally. There are no lesions or discharge of the nares. The mouth is moist. There are no skin lesions.

**Which of the following is the most likely diagnosis?**

(A) Allergic conjunctivitis
(B) Blepharitis
(C) Dry eyes
(D) Meibomitis

## Item 40

A 45-year-old woman is evaluated for a 2-month history of right heel pain. She has been trying to lose weight and had begun walking, but the pain has limited her ability to continue. The pain is worse in the morning particularly the first steps in the morning or after resting. She has had decreased pain when taking NSAIDs, but overall, the condition has worsened. Her only medication is ibuprofen.

On physical examination, there is tenderness along the anterior edge of the right calcaneus. Pressing into the sole at the level of the heel elicits pain. When the ankle is maximally dorsiflexed, and the toes are then dorsiflexed by the examiner, the pain is reproduced.

**Which of the following is the most appropriate next step in this patient's management?**

(A) Corticosteroid injection
(B) Heel magnet inserts
(C) MRI
(D) Plain film radiography
(E) Plantar fascial stretching exercises

## Item 41

A 47-year-old man is evaluated in the office for right lateral shoulder pain. He has been pitching during batting practice for his son's baseball team for the past 2 months. He has shoulder pain when lifting his right arm overhead and also when lying on the shoulder while sleeping. Acetaminophen does not relieve the pain.

On physical examination, he has no shoulder deformities or swelling. Range of motion is normal. He has subacromial tenderness to palpation, with shoulder pain elicited at 60 degrees of passive abduction. He also has pain with resisted mid-arc abduction but no pain with resisted elbow flexion or forearm supination. He is able to lower his right arm smoothly from a fully abducted position, and his arm strength for abduction and external rotation against resistance is normal.

**Which of the following is the most likely diagnosis?**

(A) Adhesive capsulitis
(B) Bicipital tendinitis
(C) Glenohumeral arthritis
(D) Rotator cuff tear (complete)
(E) Rotator cuff tendinitis

## Item 42

A 79-year-old woman is evaluated at home by a visiting hospice nurse for dyspnea that began 4 days ago and has worsened in the past 24 hours. The patient has breast cancer metastatic to the lung, liver, and spine. She has executed a do-not-resuscitate order and has discontinued treatment for the cancer. She desires no other interventions. Over the past 6 weeks her oral intake has worsened, and she cannot walk without assistance because of diffuse weakness. She takes extended-release morphine (15 mg twice daily) for musculoskeletal pain and immediate-release morphine (20 mg) as needed for breakthrough pain.

The hospice nurse reports that the patient is alert and oriented to person, place, time, and date. Her temperature is normal, pulse is 94/min, respiration rate is 24/min, and blood pressure is 145/88 mm Hg. Oxygen saturation is 97% on ambient air. She has crackles and early inspiratory wheezing over both lung fields and a reduced cough effort. She has mild dullness to percussion and reduced breath sounds over the right base. There is no $S_3$, jugular venous distention, or peripheral edema. Her last dose of extended-release morphine was 6 hours ago, and her last dose of immediate-release morphine was yesterday.

**How should this patient's dyspnea be managed?**

(A) A supplemental dose of immediate-release morphine
(B) Emergency department evaluation
(C) Initiate furosemide
(D) Initiate home oxygen therapy

## Item 43

A 65-year-old man with chronic stable angina is evaluated for a 1-year history of erectile dysfunction. His libido is intact and he would like to resume sexual activity. He experiences occasional exertional chest pain after quickly walking six to eight blocks or three flights of stairs, but has no chest pain at rest or with usual activities and no dyspnea. This symptom has been stable for the past few years, and he has not used any nitroglycerin for it. He has hypertension. He has no history of myocardial infarction or diabetes mellitus. He does not smoke or drink alcohol. Current medications are aspirin, metoprolol, atorvastatin, and enalapril.

Results of physical examination and laboratory studies are unremarkable. An electrocardiogram reveals normal sinus rhythm and left ventricular hypertrophy with no ischemic changes.

**Which of the following is the most appropriate management option for this patient?**

(A) Cardiac stress test
(B) Serum testosterone level
(C) Start a phosphodiesterase-5 inhibitor
(D) Start yohimbine
(E) Advise against treatment of erectile dysfunction

## Item 44

A 75-year-old man is admitted to a nursing home after having a stroke 2 weeks ago. The patient has residual right-sided paralysis, aphasia and urinary incontinence. He can respond to verbal commands but cannot speak well enough to make his needs known. His ability to walk is greatly impaired, and he spends most of the day in bed or in a chair. He is unable to change position independently and needs assistance with all activities of daily living. The patient has a poor appetite, cannot use his right arm to feed himself, and is eating only half his meals. He also has intermittent urinary incontinence.

**Which of the following is the most appropriate intervention for preventing pressure ulcers in this patient?**

(A) An air-fluidized bed
(B) A doughnut cushion when seated
(C) A foam mattress overlay
(D) Bladder catheterization
(E) Massage of skin over pressure points

## Item 45

A 32-year-old woman has a 6-month history of aching pain in her jaws that is exacerbated by eating. She clenches her jaws during the day, and her husband states that she grinds her teeth in her sleep. The patient also reports fatigue, difficulty sleeping, and depression. Medical history is significant for irritable bowel syndrome since adolescence and fibromyalgia for the past 6 years. Current medications are loperamide as needed for loose stools and nortriptyline at bedtime for fibromyalgia.

Physical examination of the head and neck discloses intermittent locking and catching at the temporomandibular joints (TMJ) when the patient opens and closes her mouth. The remainder of the examination is normal.

**Which of the following is the best initial management?**

(A) Arthroscopic surgery of the TMJ
(B) Corticosteroid injection into the TMJ
(C) CT scan of the TMJ
(D) Jaw exercises and NSAIDs

## Item 46

A 79-year-old man is evaluated in the emergency department for vertigo that began suddenly about 1 hour ago, associated with severe nausea and vomiting. He noticed that he could not seem to sit up straight and could not walk without assistance. The patient denies confusion, motor weakness, hearing loss, dysarthria, diplopia, fever, or paresthesias. Medical history is remarkable for hypertension, hyperlipidemia, and type 2 diabetes mellitus. Current medications are lisinopril, atorvastatin, low-dose aspirin, insulin glargine, metformin, and atenolol. There are no allergies.

Vital signs are normal. The patient demonstrates unsteadiness on finger-to-nose testing in the right upper extremity and is unable to walk more than a few steps or stand without assistance. Motor strength and reflexes are normal. Visual acuity and visual fields are normal. An otoscopic examination and cursory evaluation of hearing are normal. Cardiopulmonary examination is normal.

A complete blood count, liver chemistry studies, and renal function studies are normal. Plasma glucose level is 168 mg/dL (9.32 mmol/L). An electrocardiogram is normal except for evidence of an old inferior myocardial infarction, unchanged from an electrocardiogram 1 year ago.

**Which of the following is the most appropriate management option for this patient?**

(A) Admit for telemetry
(B) Brain MRI
(C) Intravenous methylprednisolone
(D) Oral meclizine

## Item 47

A 60-year-old woman is evaluated before undergoing a lumpectomy for breast cancer tomorrow. Medical history is significant for hypertension, type 2 diabetes mellitus, chronic kidney disease, a myocardial infarction 2 years ago, and a stroke 1 year ago with residual right-sided hemiparesis. The patient does not have chest pain or shortness of breath and is otherwise asymptomatic. She uses a walker to ambulate. Current medications are metoprolol, simvastatin, furosemide, losartan, nifedipine, insulin glargine, insulin aspart, and aspirin.

On physical examination, temperature is 36.8 °C (98.3 °F), blood pressure is 160/90 mm Hg, pulse rate is 66/min, and respiration rate is 14/min. Examination is normal except for right-sided hemiparesis and mild bilateral pedal edema. Pertinent laboratory results: blood urea nitrogen, 35 mg/dL (12.5 mmol/L); creatinine, 2.2 mg/dL (194.5 μmol/L); random glucose, 180 mg/dL (9.99 mmol/L); hemoglobin $A_{1c}$, 8.1%.

An electrocardiogram shows normal sinus rhythm, left ventricular hypertrophy, first-degree atrioventricular block, and nonspecific ST-T wave changes.

**Which of the following is the most appropriate preoperative management?**

(A) Postpone surgery until blood pressure is below 140/90 mm Hg
(B) Postpone surgery until dobutamine stress echocardiography is obtained
(C) Postpone surgery until fasting glucose is below 110 mg/dL (6.11 mmol/L)
(D) Proceed with surgery

## Item 48

A 56-year-old woman is evaluated for hot flushes that have been interfering with her sleep and causing discomfort while at work. She wants some relief from her symptoms, which have been persistent since she experienced menopause 3 years ago. She is a nonsmoker and has no history of thromboembolic disease and no personal or family history of cancer.

**Which of the following is the most appropriate treatment?**

(A) Black cohosh
(B) Bupropion
(C) Estrogen replacement therapy
(D) Raloxifene

## Item 49

A 44-year-old obese man is evaluated at a follow-up of chronic medical problems. He has been trying to follow a restricted-calorie Mediterranean-style diet for the past year after being unable to comply with a low-carbohydrate, high-protein diet the year before. He has been on sibutramine to lose weight for the past 2 years and has attended a medically supervised weight loss clinic. The patient initially lost 4.5 kg (10 lb) but gained 2.3 kg (5 lb) back. Efforts to increase aerobic activity have been difficult owing to right knee osteoarthritis. He also has type 2 diabetes mellitus, hyperlipidemia, and hypertension. Current medications are hydrochlorothiazide, lisinopril, atorvastatin, aspirin, metformin, insulin glargine, sibutramine, and acetaminophen.

On physical examination, temperature is normal, blood pressure is 144/78 mm Hg, pulse rate is 70/min, and respiration rate is 14/min. BMI is 43. Hemoglobin $A_{1c}$ is 8.2%, and random plasma glucose is 186 mg/dL (10.32 mmol/L). Laboratory results, including complete blood count, hepatic enzymes, and serum chemistry studies, are otherwise normal.

**Which of the following is the most appropriate management option for this patient?**

(A) Bariatric surgery
(B) Begin a very-low-calorie diet (800 kcal/d)
(C) Continue sibutramine
(D) Discontinue sibutramine and prescribe orlistat

## Item 50

A 60-year-old man is evaluated for persistent pain following an episode of herpes zoster infection 3 weeks ago involving the right-sided T4 dermatome. He reports that the pain is interfering with his sleep. His medical history is otherwise unremarkable. On physical examination, his vital signs are normal. The lesions have crusted over and appear to be healed.

**Which of the following is the most appropriate treatment for this patient's pain?**

(A) Acyclovir
(B) Codeine
(C) Gabapentin
(D) Ibuprofen
(E) Topical capsaicin

## Item 51

A 68-year-old woman is evaluated in the emergency department for difficulty seeing out of her left eye. The symptoms were first present upon awakening 45 minutes earlier. She describes her vision as "looking through a dark veil." Her right eye is unaffected. There is no associated pain, headache, muscle aching, or difficulty chewing, and no trauma or history of a similar episode. She has hypertension, hypercholesterolemia, and chronic open-angle glaucoma. Current medications are ramipril, hydrochlorothiazide, atorvastatin, aspirin, and timolol ophthalmic solution.

Vital signs are normal. Visual acuity in the right eye is 20/30, corrected for glasses; in the left eye, visual acuity is restricted to finger counting. Both globes are nontender to palpation. There is no conjunctival injection. Ophthalmoscopic examination of the right eye is normal. Findings in the left eye are shown on the next page. Venous pulsations are noted. Pupils are equal. The right pupil reacts to direct and consensual light stimulus. The left pupil has sluggish response to direct light, but normal consensual response. Cardiac and neurologic examinations and electrocardiogram are normal.

**Which of the following is the most likely diagnosis?**

(A) Acute angle-closure glaucoma
(B) Acute occipital stroke

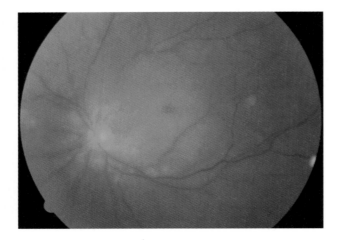

(C) Central retinal artery occlusion

(D) Central retinal vein occlusion

(E) Retinal detachment

## Item 52

A 34-year-old woman has a 2-week history of increasingly severe left groin pain. Her pain awakens her at night and causes significant difficulty in walking. There is no history of trauma, and she has not had hip pain prior to this time. She has a 10-year history of systemic lupus erythematosus. Eighteen months ago she developed glomerulonephritis, which was treated with corticosteroids and cyclophosphamide for 14 months. Her current medications are NSAIDs for arthralgia and hydroxychloroquine for lupus-related skin disease.

On physical examination, she has an obvious left leg limp. The vital signs are normal. There is restricted flexion and internal rotation of the left hip due to pain located in the groin. There is no tenderness to palpation over the lateral hip, sacroiliac joints, or sciatic notch. There is no evidence of other joint involvement.

Plain radiographs of the pelvic region and hips are normal.

**Which of the following is the best test to evaluate her hip pain?**

(A) Arthrocentesis of the left hip

(B) Bone densitometry

(C) MRI of the left hip

(D) Radionuclide bone scan

## Item 53

A 63-year-old man is evaluated during a follow-up appointment. One month ago, he had a transient ischemic attack. Carotid ultrasound revealed a 60% left internal carotid artery stenosis, and transthoracic echocardiogram revealed left ventricular hypertrophy. He is currently asymptomatic. He has hypertension and quit smoking 10 years ago. He has no history of coronary artery disease and no family history of premature coronary artery disease. Current medications are hydrochlorothiazide and aspirin. An LDL cholesterol

level 6 months ago was 138 mg/dL (3.57 mmol/L), and he has been compliant with recommended lifestyle modifications, including diet and exercise.

On physical examination, blood pressure is 132/84 mm Hg. There are no focal neurologic abnormalities. Fasting lipid levels are as follows: total cholesterol, 206 mg/dL (5.34 mmol/L); HDL cholesterol, 50 mg/dL (1.3 mmol/L); LDL cholesterol, 128 mg/dL (3.32 mmol/L); triglycerides, 144 mg/dL (1.63 mmol/L).

**In addition to continuing therapeutic lifestyle changes, which of the following is the most appropriate management option for this patient?**

(A) Add atorvastatin

(B) Add nicotinic acid

(C) Change hydrochlorothiazide to amlodipine

(D) Change hydrochlorothiazide to carvedilol

## Item 54

A 46-year-old man has a 1-year history of almost daily non-seasonal nasal congestion associated with a clear nasal discharge but without sneezing or itchy eyes. Symptoms are worse on humid days or days when the air quality is poor. There is no relationship to spicy foods. The patient has not had headache, facial pain or pressure, fatigue, malaise, fever, sore throat, cough, or change in sense of smell. Oral antihistamines do not relieve his symptoms, and he has not used any nasal sprays. Medical history is significant for hypertension managed with hydrochlorothiazide. There is no family history of asthma or hay fever.

Vital signs, including temperature, are normal. Examination of the nose shows only a clear mucoid discharge. The sclerae are not erythematous. The lungs are clear to auscultation.

**Which of the following is the most likely diagnosis?**

(A) Allergic rhinitis

(B) Chronic sinusitis

(C) Chronic vasomotor rhinitis

(D) Rhinitis medicamentosa

## Item 55

A 78-year-old man comes for a routine annual physical examination. The patient feels well. He is accompanied by his wife, who is concerned about his hearing. The review of systems is normal, and the patient states that he does not have any difficulty hearing.

**Which of the following is the best way to screen this patient for hearing impairment?**

(A) Administer the Screening Hearing Handicap Inventory

(B) Perform the Weber and Rinne tests

(C) Perform the whispered-voice test

(D) Refer for audiometric testing

(E) No further evaluation is needed

## Item 56

A 36-year-old man is evaluated for follow-up after a recently obtained fasting lipid profile that revealed a low HDL cholesterol level. He denies chest pain. He currently smokes, and has a 10 pack-year smoking history. He is overweight and does not exercise regularly. There is no family history of coronary artery disease.

On physical examination, blood pressure is 133/82 mm/Hg and BMI is 29. Heart examination reveals regular rhythm without murmur or gallop. Fasting lipid levels are as follows: total cholesterol, 198 mg/dL (5.13 mmol/L); HDL cholesterol, 33 mg/dL (0.85 mmol/L); LDL cholesterol, 129 mg/dL (3.34 mmol/L); and triglycerides, 183 mg/dL (2.07 mmol/L).

**Which of the following is the most appropriate management option for this patient?**

(A) Exercise stress test
(B) Gemfibrozil
(C) Nicotinic acid
(D) Pravastatin
(E) Therapeutic lifestyle modification

## Item 57

A 21-year-old man is evaluated in the emergency department 1 hour after twisting his ankle while playing basketball. The pain was immediate and has hurt constantly since. His coach immediately wrapped his ankle in ice.

On physical examination, there is swelling in the ankle and significant lateral bruising. It is tender on palpation, but not on the medial or lateral malleolus. When the foot is inverted by the examiner, there is no laxity of the calcaneofibular ligament. The patient is able to ambulate 10 steps with pain.

**Which of the following is the next most appropriate management option?**

(A) Ankle joint corticosteroid injection
(B) Ankle radiograph
(C) Ankle splint
(D) MRI of ankle

## Item 58

A 65-year-old man with a 2-year history of severe osteoarthritis of the right knee is evaluated before undergoing total knee replacement surgery. Until 1 month ago, the patient was able to walk four or more blocks and four flights of stairs but now can only walk one block because of severe knee pain. He has a 3-year history of occasional chest pain that occurs less than once each month and develops only after walking too quickly. There has been no change in the severity or frequency of the chest pain and no dyspnea. Medical history is significant for a myocardial infarction 4 years ago, type 2 diabetes mellitus, and hypertension. Current medications are metoprolol, fosinopril, atorvastatin, insulin glargine, metformin, and aspirin.

Blood pressure is 140/80 mm Hg, pulse rate is 60/min. BMI is 30. There is no jugular venous distention. The lungs are clear. There are no murmurs or gallops. Serum creatinine is 1.5 mg/dL (132.6 μmol/L). An electrocardiogram shows normal sinus rhythm with Q waves in leads II, III, and aVF; nonspecific ST-T wave changes; and left ventricular hypertrophy. A chest radiograph is normal.

**Which of the following is the most appropriate preoperative cardiac testing?**

(A) Coronary angiography
(B) Dobutamine stress echocardiography
(C) Exercise (treadmill) thallium imaging
(D) Resting two-dimensional echocardiography
(E) No additional testing is indicated

## Item 59

A 45-year-old woman is evaluated because of the gradual onset of right-sided hearing loss and a 3-year history of tinnitus. She does not have ear pain or drainage, dizziness, or headache. There is no history of trauma to the ear or excessive exposure to loud noises.

On examination, the patient is unable to hear numbers whispered 2 feet from the right ear with the left auditory canal blocked. Examination of the external auditory canals and tympanic membranes is normal. Neurologic examination is normal. When a tuning fork is placed on the top of her head, she reports that the sound is heard toward the left ear (Weber test). Results of audiometry show normal hearing on the left and 45-decibel high-frequency hearing loss on the right.

**Which of the following is the most likely diagnosis?**

(A) Acoustic neuroma
(B) Cholesteatoma
(C) Meniere disease
(D) Otosclerosis
(E) Presbycusis

## Item 60

An 82-year-old woman is evaluated after having fallen in her home 2 days ago and landing on her right wrist and hip. She could not get up on her own but was able to reach a phone and call an ambulance. Evaluation in the emergency department included radiographs of the right wrist and hip, an electrocardiogram, a complete blood count, and other routine laboratory studies, all of which were normal. She was subsequently released and advised to seek follow-up care.

The patient does not recall why she fell and states that she "must have tripped." She did not have prodromal symptoms, including loss of consciousness, dizziness, lightheadedness, or imbalance. There is no history of falls. Medical history is significant for hypertension and mitral valve prolapse. Current medications are hydrochlorothiazide, lisinopril, and amlodipine.

On physical examination, the patient is alert and oriented. Temperature is 36.9 °C (98.5 °F), blood pressure is

140/85 mm Hg without postural changes, pulse rate is 74/min, and respiration rate is 17/min. BMI is 36. Visual acuity is 20/40 in both eyes with glasses. The lungs are clear. A grade 2/6 holosystolic murmur is heard at the cardiac apex. An ecchymosis is present over the right hip. Neurologic examination is normal.

**Which of the following diagnostic studies should be done next?**

(A) CT scan of the head
(B) "Get up and go" test
(C) 24-Hour electrocardiographic monitoring
(D) Transthoracic echocardiography

## Item 61

A 58-year-old man is evaluated as a new patient. He reports that he is healthy, he drinks one martini before dinner, and has wine with dinner. There is no family history of alcohol problems. He has recently retired.

**Which of the following is the best choice to screen this patient for alcohol problems?**

(A) Alanine and aspartate aminotransferase concentrations
(B) CAGE questionnaire
(C) Complete blood count and mean corpuscular volume
(D) Ethanol level

## Item 62

A 57-year-old woman is seen following a stenting procedure of the left main coronary artery. The patient has type 2 diabetes mellitus. Her father had a myocardial infarction at age 62 years. Current medications are rosuvastatin, 40 mg/d; aspirin, 81 mg/d; and glipizide, 10 mg/d.

On physical examination, blood pressure is 152/92 mm Hg. Lungs are clear. Cardiac examination reveals no murmurs, and the point of maximal impulse is not displaced. Fasting lipid levels are as follows: total cholesterol, 200 mg/dL (5.18 mmol/L); HDL cholesterol, 42 mg/dL (1.09 mmol/L); LDL cholesterol, 121 mg/dL (3.13 mmol/L); triglycerides, 183 mg/dL (2.07 mmol/L). Hemoglobin $A_{1c}$ is 6.9%.

**Which of the following is the most appropriate treatment for this patient?**

(A) Add a second lipid-lowering drug
(B) Increase the dose of rosuvastatin
(C) Substitute fenofibrate for rosuvastatin
(D) Substitute metformin for glipizide

## Item 63

A 75-year-old man treated with a fentanyl patch for chronic pain due to spinal stenosis seeks advice regarding the use of alternative therapies to help with pain relief. He does not want surgery but does not feel he has been getting sufficient pain relief with the fentanyl, and did not like the sedation that was associated with oral narcotics in the past. His medical history is significant for atrial fibrillation, hypertension, hyperlipidemia, and type 2 diabetes mellitus. Current medications are warfarin, hydrochlorothiazide, and metformin. He denies anhedonia or feeling down, depressed, or hopeless. On examination, there is no tenderness over the spine or paraspinous muscles, and no tightness or spasm of the paraspinous muscles is detected.

**Which of the following is the best management option for this patient?**

(A) Ginkgo
(B) Graduated exercise program
(C) Local application of ice
(D) St. John's wort (Hypericum)
(E) Traction

## Item 64

A 69-year-old man is evaluated for low back discomfort. He has a history of metastatic prostate cancer to the spine without evidence of spinal cord compression. He is ambulatory and functional in all activities of daily living. He recently received palliative radiation therapy to treat metastatic disease in L1 and L3. The treatment improved but did not eliminate his discomfort. He rates his discomfort as 5 on a scale of 1 to 10. He denies any radiation of the pain, fever, motor weakness, or difficulties with bowel or bladder control. The patient takes at least two naproxen 250-mg tablets daily. The pain medication reduces but does not eliminate his back discomfort.

On physical examination, temperature is normal, blood pressure is 150/88 mm Hg, pulse rate is 88/min, and respiration rate is 16/min. BMI is 28. Neurologic and mental status examinations are normal. There is no point tenderness over the lumbar vertebrae.

**Which of the following is the most appropriate strategy for pain management in this patient?**

(A) Add an extended-release opioid
(B) Add fentanyl patch
(C) Add a short-acting opioid
(D) Discontinue naproxen and substitute ibuprofen

## Item 65

A 57-year-old man is evaluated during a routine examination. He has hypertension, which is well controlled on hydrochlorothiazide. He asks if he should get a prostate-specific antigen (PSA) test. Medical history is otherwise unremarkable. There is no family history of cancer. Blood pressure is 132/86 mm Hg, and results of the physical examination are unremarkable.

**Which of the following is the best prostate cancer screening option for this patient?**

(A) Discuss the risks and benefits of screening for prostate cancer
(B) Order PSA testing

(C) Order PSA testing and perform digital rectal examination (DRE)

(D) Perform DRE

## Item 66

A 78-year-old asymptomatic man comes for an initial routine office visit. Medical history is significant for hypertension and hyperlipidemia, and current medications are hydrochlorothiazide, atenolol, and simvastatin. The patient has never smoked. His wife recently had a stroke, and the couple just moved from their home of many years to live in an assisted living facility. The results of a routine screening examination and laboratory tests are normal.

**Which of the following screening tests should be done next?**

(A) Abdominal ultrasonography

(B) Ankle-brachial index

(C) Depression screening

(D) Mini–Mental State Examination

## Item 67

A physician is observed being confrontational with a nurse. He eventually shouts at her and storms off the floor. During the past few weeks, he has been observed engaging in similar behavior, which was previously out of character for this physician. At a recent hospital social outing, he was drinking heavily and was boisterous at times. In addition, he has recently appeared disheveled.

**Which of the following is the best course of action for a colleague to take in this situation?**

(A) Apologize to the nurse for the physician's actions

(B) Determine if other physicians have witnessed similar behavior

(C) Notify the physician's chief of service

(D) Question the physician's staff about his behavior

## Item 68

A 68-year-old man has a 6-month history of urinary incontinence that occurs two to three times each week and results in loss of about one cup of urine each time. Before most episodes, he feels the need to urinate but often is unable to get to the bathroom in time. He started wearing adult diapers 1 month ago. The patient has not had dysuria, urinary frequency or hesitancy, nocturia, or postvoid dribbling. He has recently noted some memory loss. Although his wife has taken over managing their finances, the patient continues to drive and perform all activities of daily living but has stopped playing golf because of embarrassment about his incontinence. Medical history is significant for osteoarthritis of the right knee and hyperlipidemia. Current medications are naproxen and pravastatin.

Vital signs are normal. BMI is 28. Abdominal examination shows no suprapubic mass or tenderness. On rectal examination, the prostate gland is normal. His score on the Mini–Mental State Examination is 23/30 (normal is ≥24/30). The remainder of the neurologic examination is normal. Pertinent laboratory results, including serum creatinine, electrolytes, and prostate-specific antigen levels, are normal. A urinalysis is normal, and a urine culture is negative.

**Which of the following medications should be prescribed?**

(A) Doxazosin

(B) Imipramine

(C) Phenylpropanolamine

(D) Tolterodine

## Item 69

A 32-year-old man has a 5-day history of persistent nasal congestion and pain in the right forehead area associated with a clear nasal discharge and mild cough. The patient reports that he has had similar episodes in the past that were helped by antibiotics. Medical history is otherwise unremarkable, and he currently takes no medications.

On physical examination, vital signs, including temperature, are normal. Mild right suborbital ridge tenderness is present. The nares are patent with a clear mucoid discharge. There is no pharyngeal erythema or exudate. The lungs are clear to auscultation.

**Which of the following is the best initial management?**

(A) Amoxicillin

(B) CT scan of the sinuses

(C) Plain films of sinuses

(D) Symptomatic treatment

(E) Trimethoprim-sulfamethoxazole

## Item 70

A 43-year-old woman with fibromyalgia is evaluated for continued diffuse myalgia, fatigue, and difficulty sleeping. She has cut back on her activity level because of the pain. She denies depression or significant worries. Her only medications are acetaminophen or ibuprofen for occasional headaches. She has tried various tricyclic antidepressants and selective serotonin reuptake inhibitors in the past for her fibromyalgia pain, and while helpful, she could not tolerate the side effects of these medications.

Physical examination is unremarkable, with the exception of ill-defined tenderness over the shoulders, back, and hips. Complete blood count, serum chemistry studies, and thyroid-stimulating hormone level are normal. Erythrocyte sedimentation rate is 29 mm/h.

**In addition to instituting a graded exercise program, which of the following is the most appropriate treatment for this patient's fibromyalgia?**

(A) Naproxen

(B) Oral oxycodone

(C) Prednisone

(D) Pregabalin

## Item 71

An 18-year-old female college student has a 2-week history of painful oral ulcers. The patient has had several similar episodes in the past year. Medical history is unremarkable. She is a nonsmoker and takes no medications. She reports considerable stress because of preparation for final examinations and difficulties with her boyfriend.

Physical examination discloses four very tender white ulcers with a surrounding halo of erythema and swelling involving the buccal and labial mucosa and underside of the tongue. The largest lesion measures 0.5 cm in diameter. A representative ulcer is shown. Dentition is good. Several nontender 1-cm anterior jugular lymph nodes are palpated.

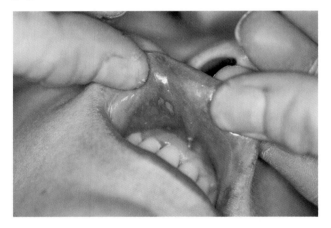

**Which of the following is the best initial management?**

(A) Antinuclear antibody assay

(B) Biopsy of an ulcer

(C) Nystatin swish and swallow

(D) Oral acyclovir

(E) Topical corticosteroids

## Item 72

A 44-year-old woman is evaluated during a routine appointment. She has been trying to lose weight over the past 3 years. The patient has tried several diets and has also attempted to increase her physical activity. Medical history is remarkable for type 2 diabetes mellitus, hypertension, and hyperlipidemia. Current medications are lisinopril, simvastatin, aspirin, metformin, and glipizide.

On physical examination, temperature is normal, blood pressure is 138/90 mm Hg, pulse rate is 72/min, and respiration rate is 14/min. BMI is 34. Her hemoglobin $A_{1c}$ is 6.9%.

**In addition to encouraging continued efforts at dieting and exercise, which of the following is the most appropriate management option for this patient?**

(A) Add orlistat

(B) Add sibutramine

(C) Discontinue glipizide, initiate insulin glargine

(D) Refer for bariatric surgery

## Item 73

A 25-year-old woman develops nasal congestion, rhinorrhea, sneezing, and itching when she visits her grandmother, about once a month. Her grandmother has a cat, and the patient has developed similar symptoms when exposed to cats at other times. Medical history is unremarkable. She does not have other allergies, asthma, sinusitis, or obstructive sleep apnea and takes no medications. She has tried oral antihistamines but they made her drowsy.

**Other than avoiding contact with cats, which of the following is the best initial management?**

(A) Intranasal corticosteroids

(B) Intranasal cromolyn sodium

(C) Nasal smear for detection of eosinophils

(D) Serum immunoassay for specific IgE antibodies

## Item 74

A 19-year-old asymptomatic woman is evaluated at a routine annual physical examination. The patient states she is not sexually active and has not engaged in prior sexual activity. She has a boyfriend whom she has dated for the past year. The patient completed her menstrual cycle 3 days ago. She has no pertinent family history or known drug allergies and takes no medications. She has not received a human papillomavirus vaccine.

Results of the physical examination, including a breast and pelvic examination, are normal.

**Which of the following is the most appropriate management option for prevention of human papillomavirus infection for this patient?**

(A) Human papillomavirus (HPV) vaccine at age 21 years

(B) HPV vaccine at onset of sexual activity

(C) HPV vaccine at time of HPV seroconversion

(D) HPV vaccine now

## Item 75

A 61-year-old man is evaluated for dizziness that started about 2 days ago while he was looking over his shoulder. He describes the symptoms as "room spinning" dizziness and mild nausea. The symptoms resolved within several minutes when he lay back on the couch and was perfectly still. They recurred several hours later while turning in bed and the next day while backing out of his driveway. He denies diplopia, slurred speech, confusion, motor weakness, paresthesias, tinnitus, antecedent infection, or hearing loss. He has no other medical problems and takes no medications.

Vital signs are normal. The cardiopulmonary examination is normal. Peripheral nystagmus and reproduction of symptoms on the Dix-Hallpike maneuver when the head is turned right are demonstrated. There are no focal neurologic defects. Visual acuity and hearing are normal.

**Which of the following management options is the best choice for this patient?**

(A) Audiometry
(B) Brain MRI with magnetic resonance angiography
(C) Cardiac event monitor recording
(D) Epley canalith repositioning maneuver
(E) Methylprednisolone

## Item 76

A 67-year-old woman is admitted to the hospital with endocarditis. Two weeks ago, she was discharged from the same hospital, where she was treated for heart failure. During the previous admission, an echocardiogram revealed "mild calcific mitral stenosis with a mobile vegetation on the anterior leaflet."

In the patient's chart from the index hospitalization, the attending physician made no mention of the mobile component on the leaflet in his notes. Two days prior to the patient's discharge, he signed off the case and transferred care to another attending physician, who completed the hospitalization and discharge without noting the abnormal echocardiogram. During that admission, two subspecialty consultants and three trainees all had access to the echocardiogram report, but none had noted the abnormal report.

The original attending physician explained that the echocardiogram report had been communicated to him by a physician assistant, and he had not read the actual report.

**Which of the following quality improvement tools will be most helpful in analyzing the reason the echocardiogram report was missed?**

(A) Chart audit
(B) Root-cause analysis
(C) Standardized protocols
(D) Team "time out"

## Item 77

A 46-year-old man is evaluated for an 8-year history of episodic chest pain associated with dyspnea, tachycardia, diaphoresis, and dizziness that occurs several times each week. The symptoms develop suddenly, are often so severe that he feels that he is going to die, and improve significantly within 20 to 30 minutes. The patient does not know what precipitates these episodes or whether anything makes the symptoms better or worse.

Previous medical evaluations have been unremarkable. Studies have included electrocardiographic exercise stress testing, 24-hour electrocardiographic monitoring, echocardiography, cardiac catheterization, and upper endoscopy. The patient takes no medications. Findings on physical examination are unremarkable.

**Which of the following is the most effective treatment for this patient?**

(A) Buspirone
(B) Cognitive-behavioral therapy
(C) Cognitive-behavioral therapy plus paroxetine

(D) Paroxetine
(E) Venlafaxine

## Item 78

A 52-year-old woman is brought to the emergency department because of a 1-day history of abdominal pain and urinary incontinence accompanied by decreased episodes of spontaneous voiding. She is surprised by the loss of urine because she does not feel that her bladder is full. The patient does not have dysuria, hematuria, nocturia, or urinary urgency. Medical history is significant for type 1 diabetes mellitus that was diagnosed 24 years ago and fibromyalgia. Current medications are insulin glargine and insulin lispro. Nortriptyline was also started 1 week ago for treatment of fibromyalgia. Review of systems reveals paresthesias involving the lower extremities in a "stocking" pattern and episodes of lightheadedness when she stands up quickly.

On physical examination, temperature is 37.2 °C (99.0 °F), blood pressure is 150/92 mm Hg (sitting) and 110/72 mm Hg (standing), pulse rate is 102/min. BMI is 26. Abdominal examination reveals some tenderness and increased dullness to percussion in the suprapubic region. Rectal and bimanual pelvic examinations are normal. Neurologic examination reveals loss of vibratory sensation at the ankles bilaterally.

Results of serum calcium, creatinine, and electrolyte measurements and urinalysis are normal. A plain radiograph of the abdomen is normal.

**Which of the following diagnostic studies should be done next to evaluate the most likely cause of this patient's urinary incontinence?**

(A) CT scans of the abdomen and pelvis
(B) Cystoscopy
(C) Plasma glucose measurement
(D) Postvoid residual urine volume measurement
(E) Urine culture

## Item 79

A 48-year-old woman presents with a history of heavy painless menstrual bleeding for the past 4 days. Her last period was 20 days ago, but before that, her periods had become more irregular over the previous 2 years, with lighter than usual bleeding. She has been sexually active with her husband, but had a tubal ligation after the birth of her fourth child 6 years ago.

On physical examination, the vital signs are normal. There is no evidence of hypovolemia or conjunctival pallor. The skin examination is negative for ecchymoses and petechiae. The bimanual pelvic examination reveals a nontender, normal-sized, and regular uterus. Speculum examination reveals a normal-appearing cervix with dark blood in the cervical os but no other abnormalities. A Pap smear is performed. A urine pregnancy test is negative.

**Which of the following is the most appropriate next step in the management of this patient?**

(A) Endometrial biopsy

(B) Measure serum luteinizing hormone and follicle-stimulating hormone

(C) Oral contraceptive

(D) Pelvic ultrasonography

## Item 80

A 60-year-old man is hospitalized because of lower gastrointestinal bleeding secondary to diverticular disease diagnosed by colonoscopy. The bleeding stops after blood transfusions are given. This is his third episode of bleeding, and the patient is being considered for possible hemicolectomy. He has cirrhosis secondary to a 25-year history of alcohol abuse, and his last drink was 1 week ago. The patient has no known allergies and takes no medications.

On physical examination, temperature is 36.7 °C (98.0 °F), blood pressure is 110/60 mm Hg, pulse rate is 96/min, and respiration rate is 14/min. The patient is alert and oriented. There is no scleral icterus. Gynecomastia is present. Abdominal examination shows mild ascites. There is no tremor, and neurologic examination is normal.

His Child-Turcotte-Pugh score is calculated as class C and his Model for End-stage Liver Disease (MELD) score is 23.

**Which of the following is the best recommendation regarding elective surgery?**

(A) Delay surgery for 7 to 10 days

(B) Delay surgery indefinitely until risk improves

(C) Proceed with surgery at any time

(D) Recommend against elective surgery at any time

## Item 81

A 78-year-old man is evaluated in the emergency department following a syncopal episode. He was at home when he suddenly developed severe back pain and he then collapsed. On the way to the hospital, he regained consciousness. He has no history of syncope prior to this episode.

On physical examination, temperature is normal, blood pressure is 148/80 mm Hg in the right arm and 125/70 mm Hg in the left arm, pulse is 65/min and regular, and respiration rate is 12/min. The patient is awake and in significant pain. Cardiac examination shows a normal $S_1$ and $S_2$ with no murmur. The lungs are clear. Neurologic examination shows left facial droop and right hemiparesis. Right upper extremity pulse is 2+; left upper extremity pulse is 1+.

Complete blood count, electrolytes, and cardiac enzymes are normal. Electrocardiogram shows sinus rhythm with no acute ST-T wave changes. A chest radiograph shows no infiltrates, effusions, or mediastinal widening.

**Which of the following is the most appropriate diagnostic test?**

(A) Carotid duplex ultrasound

(B) CT angiography of the chest and aorta

(C) MRI of the brain

(D) Transthoracic echocardiogram

## Item 82

A 38-year-old man is evaluated at a routine appointment with a new primary care physician. There is no history of major illnesses. He has a 15 pack-year smoking history. There is no family history of coronary artery disease or diabetes mellitus. His only current medication is a multivitamin.

On physical examination, blood pressure is 126/78 mm Hg and pulse rate is 72/min. BMI is 24. The remainder of the examination is normal.

**Which of the following is the most appropriate screening test in the management of this patient?**

(A) Chest radiograph

(B) Complete blood count

(C) Comprehensive metabolic profile

(D) Fasting blood sugar

(E) Fasting lipid profile

## Item 83

A 42-year-old woman is evaluated for discomfort during intercourse. Over the past 2 to 3 years, she has noted increasing discomfort and pain that initially had a burning quality during intercourse. Over time, intercourse has become more uncomfortable and feels like her husband is "hitting a wall" during insertion. She has also noted similar discomfort with inserting a tampon. She is able to achieve orgasm without difficulty. She continues to have sexual desire, and she experiences vaginal lubrication during intimacy. She believes her marriage is healthy and feels supported by her husband. Nevertheless, she is bothered by this pain and is worried how this might affect her marriage. Her menses remain regular without any recent change. She is not taking any medications.

On physical examination, vital signs are normal. BMI is 25. External genitalia are normal. During speculum examination, there is difficulty inserting the speculum, with the smallest possible speculum causing discomfort. The cervix is normal. Bimanual examination causes significant discomfort on insertion of one finger, with some resistance. The uterus and adnexa are normal. A Pap smear is obtained.

**Which of the following is the most likely diagnosis?**

(A) Androgen deficiency

(B) Dyspareunia

(C) Vaginismus

(D) Vulvodynia

## Item 84

A 46-year-old man is evaluated for worsening of previously mild asthma. He was last seen 4 months ago, and at that time, his asthma was well controlled on low-dose inhaled corticosteroids. In the past 3 weeks, he has awakened twice coughing and needed to use his rescue inhaler. He was diagnosed with glaucoma 3 months ago following a routine eye examination, and treatment was initiated. Current medications are fluticasone, timolol ophthalmic drops, and a daily multivitamin.

Vital signs are normal. BMI is 24. There is occasional expiratory wheezing on lung examination, but good air movement. The patient's peak expiratory flow in the office is 75% of his best at symptom-free baseline.

**Which of the following is the most appropriate management option for this patient?**

(A) Add a long-acting β-agonist
(B) Discontinue timolol
(C) Increase fluticasone
(D) Order chest radiography

## Item 85

An 84-year-old man is evaluated for a 6-month history of slow urinary stream, urinary hesitancy, postvoid dribbling, and a need to get up an average of three times each night to urinate. He has chronic obstructive pulmonary disease and is on inhaled albuterol as needed and 2 L/min of home oxygen.

On physical examination, temperature is normal, blood pressure is 140/76 mm Hg, and pulse rate is 76/min. Abdominal examination is normal without tenderness or masses or evidence of a distended bladder. Digital rectal examination reveals a symmetrically enlarged prostate without any discrete nodules or tenderness.

**Which of the following is the most useful test for evaluating this patient's urinary symptoms?**

(A) Postvoid residual urine volume measurement
(B) Prostate-specific antigen
(C) Prostate ultrasound
(D) Serum creatinine
(E) Urinalysis

## Item 86

A 28-year-old woman has a 3-day history of a sore throat, malaise, and fatigue without cough or fever. Medical history is unremarkable. She has no known drug allergies and takes no medications.

On physical examination, vital signs, including temperature, are normal. Bilateral tonsillar exudates are present. There is no cervical lymphadenopathy.

**Which of the following is the best management step at this time?**

(A) Erythromycin
(B) Heterophile antibody (Monospot) test
(C) Penicillin
(D) Rapid streptococcal antigen test
(E) Throat culture

## Item 87

A 72-year-old man is evaluated at the hospital for colorectal cancer that has metastasized to the liver. A decision needs to be made regarding whether to initiate chemotherapy, which is not expected to be curative but could prolong the patient's life by 12 to 18 months. The patient has experienced memory loss over the past 2 years, and his wife has taken over management of family finances and driving. A Mini–Mental State Examination reveals a score of 22 (normal ≥24/30). The remainder of the neurologic examination is normal. In consultation with the oncologist, the benefits and risks of chemotherapy as well as alternative treatments are explained to the patient and his wife.

**Which of the following is the best way to arrive at a decision regarding chemotherapy for this patient?**

(A) Ask the patient if he wants chemotherapy
(B) Ask the patient if he wants chemotherapy now and ask him again later today
(C) Ask the patient to repeat the key benefits and risks of chemotherapy
(D) Ask the patient why he does or does not want chemotherapy
(E) Defer decision to the patient's wife

## Item 88

A 65-year-old woman is evaluated for a 2-month history of left lateral hip pain. It began after an outing to a nature preserve, where she walked 2 to 3 miles. The pain is burning and constant. She has tried NSAIDs without success. The pain increases with walking but continues even while at rest. Medical history is remarkable for osteoarthritis of the left hip that has been treated with acetaminophen. The patient reports that this new pain is different in nature and location from her arthritic hip pain. The pain has not responded to rest, application of heat, or a trial of a maximum dosage of ibuprofen. She has had no other medical problems.

On physical examination, there is point tenderness elicited directly over the left greater trochanter. Pain worsens with active range of motion, particularly leg abduction. There is no tenderness in the groin, over the sacroiliac joint, or over the sciatic notch. Reflexes and sensation in the lower extremities are normal.

**Which of the following treatments is most likely to improve this patient's left lateral hip pain?**

(A) Indomethacin
(B) Local corticosteroid injection
(C) Pregabalin
(D) Topical capsaicin

## Item 89

A 60-year-old man is evaluated before undergoing a colectomy for colon cancer under general anesthesia. Medical history is significant for chronic obstructive pulmonary disease (for which he was last hospitalized 1 year ago), hypertension, and obesity. The patient has a 45-pack-year smoking history and stopped smoking 5 years ago. He has dyspnea on exertion after walking three blocks or climbing one flight of stairs. There is no history of coronary artery disease or heart failure, and he does not have chest pain. Current medications are hydrochlorothiazide, albuterol, ipratropium, and a corticosteroid inhaler.

On physical examination, temperature is 36.7 °C (98.0 °F), blood pressure is 140/85 mm Hg, pulse rate is 84/min, and respiration rate is 16/min. BMI is 32. Examination of the chest discloses coarse breath sounds without wheezing. There are no cardiac murmurs or gallops and no lower-extremity edema.

A chest radiograph shows hyperinflation but no pulmonary infiltrates.

**Which of the following is most likely to reduce this patient's risk of developing postoperative pulmonary complications?**

(A) Incentive spirometry
(B) Postoperative nasogastric decompression
(C) Prophylactic systemic corticosteroids
(D) Right heart catheterization
(E) Routine intravenous nutritional support

## Item 90

A 40-year-old male college professor is planning a week-long bicycle trip involving cycling 20 miles daily. He has a sedentary lifestyle, with his most vigorous activity being walking on campus to classes. He wants to know if it is safe for him to go on the bike trip. His medical history is unremarkable, he takes no medications, there is no family history of early coronary artery disease, and he does not smoke cigarettes. His blood pressure is 124/82 mm Hg and his BMI is 32. Heart and lung examinations are normal. Recent cholesterol test results included total cholesterol, 182 mg/dL (4.71 mmol/L); HDL cholesterol, 45 mg/dL (1.17 mmol/L); and LDL cholesterol, 127 mg/dL (3.29 mmol/L).

**Which of the following is the most appropriate evaluation strategy for this patient?**

(A) Carotid intimal medial thickness measurement
(B) Coronary artery calcium scoring
(C) Electrocardiographic treadmill stress test
(D) Nuclear stress test
(E) No testing

## Item 91

A 37-year-old woman is evaluated in the office for major depression that was diagnosed 3 months ago and treated with sertraline. Five weeks after initiation of treatment, she had no suicidal ideation, and her depressive symptoms had improved, with a 5-point decrease in her Patient Health Questionnaire–9 (PHQ-9) score. During today's visit, she reports that her depressive symptoms have continued to improve, although she has experienced sexual dysfunction manifested by bothersome anorgasmia. She is also overweight and is worried about gaining more weight.

Blood pressure is 140/80 mm Hg. Her BMI is 29. The remainder of the physical examination is normal.

**Which of the following is the most appropriate alternative treatment option for this patient's depression?**

(A) Bupropion
(B) Citalopram
(C) Fluoxetine
(D) Mirtazapine

## Item 92

A 49-year-old woman is evaluated after noticing a small lump in her right breast 3 weeks ago. It is painless and has not changed in size. She has no other pertinent medical history and did not use oral contraceptives. She had menarche at age 12 years and is still menstruating. Her last menstrual period was 2 weeks ago. She has two children, the first at age 25 years and the second at age 30 years. Her mother had breast cancer at age 55 years; there is no other family history of cancer.

On physical examination, vital signs are normal. There is a 1.0 cm × 1.5 cm firm, discrete, mobile mass in the upper outer quadrant of the right breast. There is no lymphadenopathy or other abnormalities on examination.

A mammogram done 18 months ago was normal. A bilateral mammogram does not reveal any suspicious lesion in either breast.

**Which of the following is the most appropriate management option for this patient?**

(A) Aspiration or biopsy
(B) Clinical reevaluation in 1 month
(C) MRI of both breasts
(D) Repeat mammogram in 6 months

## Item 93

A 66-year-old man is evaluated because of a 1-year history of difficulty with memory. The patient continues to work as an executive but has had trouble remembering meetings or whether he has completed an assigned task. The patient's wife has also noted these changes. He is still able to shop, drive without difficulty, and care for himself. He continues to maintain interest in his usual activities. He has had no sleep disturbance, change in appetite, feelings of guilt or hopelessness, or difficulty concentrating. He has no medical problems and no family history of Alzheimer disease.

On physical examination, he is afebrile, blood pressure is 142/92 mm Hg, and pulse rate is 78/min. BMI is 28. Results of general examination, including neurologic examination, are unremarkable. The patient's score on the Mini–Mental State Examination is 28/30 (normal ≥24/30); two points were deducted because he could not recall two of three items after 5 minutes.

Fasting laboratory results reveal a glucose of 102 mg/dL (5.66 mmol/L), total cholesterol of 230 mg/dL (5.96 mmol/L), LDL cholesterol is 160 mg/dL (4.14 mmol/L), HDL cholesterol is 40 mg/dL (1.04 mmol/L), and triglycerides are 150 mg/dL (1.70 mmol/L).

**Which of the following is the best management of his memory loss at this time?**

(A) Begin a cholinesterase inhibitor
(B) Begin ginkgo supplements
(C) Begin vitamin E supplements
(D) Control cardiovascular risk factors
(E) Reassure the patient

## Item 94

An 80-year-old widow with multiple medical problems is diagnosed with lung cancer. She does not want to undergo surgery, chemotherapy, or radiation therapy, saying she is too old and has lived a good life. She has a son, who is a physician, and an older daughter with whom she lives. She requests that no information be released regarding her condition. You determine that she is not depressed and is mentally competent to make that decision. She signs a do-not-resuscitate order and advance directives stating that she does not want to be kept alive by artificial means.

Both the son and daughter call requesting information about their mother's medical condition.

**With which of the following family members may the patient's condition be discussed?**

(A) The daughter
(B) The son
(C) Both daughter and son
(D) Neither daughter nor son

## Item 95

A 65-year-old woman comes for a preoperative evaluation before elective right knee arthroplasty. The patient has severe pain and disability due to osteoarthritis of the right knee. She had a myocardial infarction 4 months ago and required a percutaneous coronary intervention with placement of a paclitaxel drug-eluting stent in the left anterior descending coronary artery. The patient also has hypertension and type 2 diabetes mellitus. She currently has no chest pain or dyspnea but can only walk two blocks and climb one flight of stairs because of the osteoarthritis. Current medications are clopidogrel, metoprolol, atorvastatin, losartan, metformin, aspirin, acetaminophen, and tramadol.

Vital signs are normal. Other than evidence of bony hypertrophy of the knees and a small effusion in the right knee, the remainder of the examination is unremarkable.

An electrocardiogram shows normal sinus rhythm; Q waves in leads II, III, and aVF; and left ventricular hypertrophy.

**Which of the following is the best preoperative management?**

(A) Postpone surgery for 6 months after stent was placed
(B) Postpone surgery for 12 months after stent was placed
(C) Proceed with surgery; continue aspirin but temporarily stop the clopidogrel
(D) Proceed with surgery; continue both aspirin and clopidogrel
(E) Proceed with surgery; temporarily discontinue aspirin and clopidogrel

## Item 96

An 83-year-old woman who is recuperating from hip replacement surgery was evaluated on the orthopedic floor of a hospital when she became confused and was found on the floor of her room at about 3 am. Her assessment found no sign of injury, and vital signs were normal. The patient was released from the hospital without further incident 2 days later. The patient's medical history is significant for osteoporosis and hypothyroidism. A geriatric assessment within the past year revealed a Mini–Mental State Examination score of 29/30 (normal ≥24/30) and full activity of daily living capability. Current medications are hydrocodone, levothyroxine, diphenhydramine, aspirin, and fondaparinux.

The patient's records show that hydrocodone was ordered on a routine schedule, and an additional hydrocodone order was to be given for breakthrough pain. The patient had received the two doses of hydrocodone during the 6 hours prior to the incident. Diphenhydramine was ordered as a routine sleep aid.

**Which of the following system-level interventions will be most helpful in preventing future falls in other patients in similar circumstances?**

(A) Begin collecting adverse drug event prevalence data
(B) Implement a fall-risk prediction tool for newly admitted patients
(C) Re-engineer the hospital room architecture to decrease fall risk
(D) Standardize protocols for management of opiate medications

## Item 97

A 62-year-old woman is evaluated during a follow-up visit for hypertension. She has no complaints and is monogamous with her husband of 35 years. Her only current medication is hydrochlorothiazide. On physical examination, blood pressure is 136/72 mm Hg and weight is 62 kg (136 lb). Physical examination is normal. Total cholesterol is 188 mg/dL (4.87 mmol/L) and HDL cholesterol is 54 mg/dL (1.40 mmol/L). She received an influenza vaccination 3 months ago and a herpes zoster vaccination 1 year ago. Her last Pap smear was 14 months ago and it was normal, as were the previous three annual Pap smears.

**Which of the following is the most appropriate health maintenance option for this patient?**

(A) Abdominal ultrasonography
(B) Dual-energy x-ray absorptiometry
(C) Pap smear
(D) Pneumococcal vaccine

## Item 98

A 22-year-old woman is evaluated in the office for feelings of sadness and guilt 6 weeks after an uncomplicated delivery of twins. Her symptoms have been present for 3 weeks but have worsened over the past week, and she cannot sleep, is preoccupied about the babies' health, and has discontinued all social activities. She says that her husband is supportive and that they have no marital problems. She is willing to start treatment for her disorder, but she is concerned about the potential impact of medication because she is breastfeeding, and is interested in alternative treatments.

**Which of the following is the best treatment option for this patient?**

(A) Fluoxetine
(B) Psychotherapy
(C) Reassurance with follow-up in 2 weeks
(D) St. John's wort

## Item 99

A 36-year-old woman presents with a 12- to 14-month history of persistent pelvic pain. She reports no relation to dietary factors or bowel movements and denies diarrhea, constipation, melena, hematochezia, dysuria, or hematuria. She has had negative evaluations by multiple providers, with normal colonoscopy, ultrasonography and CT of the abdomen and pelvis, and cystoscopy. She underwent a hysterectomy and salpingo-oophorectomy for possible endometriosis 9 months ago, without relief of her symptoms. Her medical history is significant for chronic migraine headaches and chronic lower back pain. She is taking estrogen replacement therapy. She has two children, and has not been sexually active since her divorce from her husband more than 2 years ago.

Her BMI is 30. Mild nonfocal tenderness is present on abdominal and pelvic examinations, with normal bowel sounds, no rebound, no masses, and no vaginal bleeding or discharge.

**Which of the following is the most appropriate management for this patient?**

(A) Cognitive-behavioral therapy
(B) Naproxen
(C) Reassurance with follow-up at 3 to 4 weeks
(D) Sertraline

## Item 100

An 86-year-old man with metastatic lung cancer is evaluated at a follow-up appointment; he is accompanied by his daughter. The patient's daughter reports that he has been in steady decline over the past month. He has anorexia and a 4.5 kg (10 lb) weight loss, and has become reliant on her for many routine tasks, including dressing, bathing, and eating. He is unable to ambulate due to dyspnea and fatigue and requires assistance to get out of bed to a chair and to a bedside commode. He discontinued chemotherapy 2 months ago owing to progression of his disease despite treatment. The patient has chronic kidney disease and has been on hemodialysis for the past 8 years. The patient wants to discontinue dialysis because the treatments are increasingly unpleasant owing to fatigue, but he denies dialysis-related pain or dyspnea. He says that he is aware that stopping dialysis will result in near-term death. He has an advanced directive that states that he does not want cardiopulmonary resuscitation, artificial nutrition, or hydration. A depression screen is negative, and a mental status examination is normal. The patient's wife is deceased, and his daughter is the surrogate decision maker in his health care power of attorney.

**Which of the following is the most appropriate option regarding continuation of this patient's dialysis?**

(A) Consult with psychiatry
(B) Consult with the patient's daughter
(C) Coordinate discontinuation of dialysis
(D) Obtain approval of the patient's nephrologist

## Item 101

A 15-year-old male is evaluated in the emergency department for an eye injury. The patient was hammering pieces of copper for an art project when a foreign object hit his eye. Medical history is unremarkable. All childhood immunizations were on schedule, but he cannot recall his last tetanus booster.

The patient is holding his hand over his left eye, and when his hand is removed from the eye, he wants to keep it shut. There are no lacerations to the lids, brow, or surrounding tissue. There is photophobia. There is a subconjunctival collection of blood surrounding the iris. Direct visualization shows no visible metal in the eye. The pupil is elongated, pointing toward the inferolateral part of the eye. The right pupil reacts normally to direct and consensual light reflex. The left pupil reacts to direct and consensual light reflex but is sluggish. Visual acuity is 20/50 in the left eye and 20/20 in the right eye. The orbital rim is nontender to palpation. Extraocular movements are intact.

**In addition to an emergency ophthalmology evaluation, which of the following interventions should be done first?**

(A) Administer broad-spectrum antibiotics
(B) Administer tetanus booster
(C) Obtain CT of the orbits
(D) Place a shield over the affected eye

## Item 102

A 60-year-old man who requires hemodialysis because of chronic kidney disease is evaluated before undergoing revision of his nonfunctioning arteriovenous fistula. Medical history is significant for hypertension and type 2 diabetes mellitus. The patient does not have chest pain or dyspnea. Current medications are nifedipine, sevelamer, clonidine, aspirin, and regular and NPH insulin.

On physical examination, temperature is 36.8 °C (98.3 °F), blood pressure is 160/95 mm Hg, pulse rate is 80/min, and respiration rate is 14/min. There is no evidence of jugular venous distention, extracardiac sounds, pulmonary crackles, or peripheral edema. The remainder of the examination is normal. Post-dialysis laboratory studies are shown.

**Laboratory studies:**

| | |
|---|---|
| Hemoglobin | 11.0 g/dL (110 g/L) |
| Blood urea nitrogen | 40 mg/dL (14.3 mmol/L) (usual pre-dialysis result: 60 mg/dL [21.4 mmol/L]) |

| | |
|---|---|
| Creatinine | 4.8 mg/dL (424.3 µmol/L) (usual pre-dialysis result: 7.0 mg/dL [618.8 µmol/L]) |
| Potassium | 3.3 meq/L (3.3 mmol/L) (usual pre-dialysis result: 4.8 meq/L [4.8 mmol/L]) |
| Glucose | 120 mg/dL (6.66 mmol/L) |

An electrocardiogram shows normal sinus rhythm and left ventricular hypertrophy.

**Which of the following is most appropriate to optimize this patient's medical management and minimize surgical risk before graft revision?**

(A) Administer erythropoietin
(B) Administer potassium supplements
(C) Postpone surgery until blood pressure is less than 130/80 mm Hg
(D) Schedule hemodialysis the day before surgery

## Item 103

A 25-year-old woman is evaluated for a 2-month history of feeling "down" and hopeless after her fiancé ended their engagement. She believes that the broken engagement was somehow her fault. The patient also reports spending less time with friends, restricting previously enjoyable social activities, and having difficulty concentrating. During the past week, she has been thinking increasingly about ending her life and has been fingering a knife when at home alone while contemplating cutting her wrists. She lives at home with her mother and two sisters, who are concerned and have expressed feelings of support and willingness to help. The patient is willing to make a "no-harm contract" of calling or going to the emergency department if suicide feelings intensify. She has no history of previous suicide attempts. Medical history is unremarkable, and she takes no medications. Her father committed suicide several years ago. Findings on physical examination are unremarkable.

**Which of the following is the most appropriate initial care for this patient?**

(A) Corroborate her account by contacting her former fiancé
(B) Reassurance and careful follow-up and observation
(C) Start an antidepressant and follow up in 2 weeks
(D) Urgent mental health referral

## Item 104

A 64-year-old man is evaluated for a new right-sided headache that began 1 day ago. He awoke yesterday with a dull ache over his right forehead that has gradually increased in intensity. He also notes some right eye discomfort, sensitivity to light, and that his eye is red.

Vital signs are normal. The patient is uncomfortable and prefers to have the lights dimmed. Physical examination findings are shown. The right eye has diffusely injected conjunctiva and the cornea appears clear. The left eye is normal.

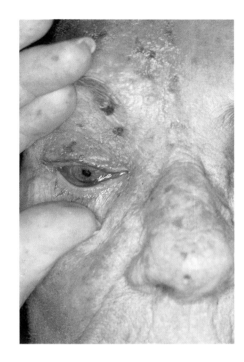

The pupils are equal and reactive. Visual acuity is normal. Cranial nerves are intact.

**Which of the following is the most likely diagnosis?**

(A) Herpes simplex virus keratitis
(B) Herpes zoster ophthalmicus
(C) Scleritis
(D) Trigeminal neuralgia

## Item 105

A 36-year-old woman is evaluated in the emergency department after collapsing suddenly while waiting in line at a county fair on a hot summer day. The patient states she felt nauseated and became diaphoretic and lightheaded. She sat on the ground and then lost consciousness. According to her son, she was unconscious for less than a minute, exhibited some twitching movements when she first lost consciousness, but had no incontinence or symptoms of confusion upon awakening. She had no further symptoms upon regaining consciousness. She has a history of hypertension and hyperlipidemia. Current medications are lisinopril and lovastatin.

On physical examination, temperature is normal, blood pressure is 142/80 mm Hg (supine) and 138/78 mm Hg (standing), pulse rate is 84/min (supine) and 92/min (standing), and respiration rate is 14/min. BMI is 35. Cardiac and neurologic examinations are normal. An electrocardiogram is normal.

**Which of the following is the most appropriate management option for this patient?**

(A) Echocardiogram
(B) Electroencephalogram
(C) Exercise stress test

(D) Tilt-table testing

(E) No further testing

## Item 106

A 64-year-old woman is evaluated for a urinary tract infection. She has had three urinary tract infections in the past 2 years. She is not sexually active. She has no other medical problems and takes no medications. A pelvic examination reveals pale, dry vaginal epithelium that is smooth and shiny with loss of most rugation. Urinalysis reveals 2+ leukocyte esterase, leukocytes too numerous to count, and 10 to 20 erythrocytes/hpf. Urine culture grows *Escherichia coli*.

**In addition to treating the current urinary tract infection, which of the following is the most reasonable management option for this patient?**

(A) Continuous antibiotic prophylaxis

(B) CT imaging of the abdomen and pelvis

(C) Topical estrogen therapy

(D) Vaginal lubricants

## Item 107

A 75-year-old man has a 1-month history of intermittent nosebleeds that occur from either naris. Last night, he experienced a more severe episode. There is no history of trauma to the nose, bleeding disorders, recent upper respiratory tract infections, or recent use of nasal decongestants. The patient uses tissues to remove scabs and mucus from his nares. He has been using his home heater more often because of unusually cold weather. Medical history is significant for hypertension. Current medications are hydrochlorothiazide, atenolol, and low-dose aspirin.

Vital signs are normal. No bleeding site is identified in either naris, and examination of the ears, nose, and throat is normal.

**Which of the following is the best treatment?**

(A) Cauterization of the anterior septum bilaterally

(B) Intranasal fluticasone

(C) Oxymetazoline spray

(D) Packing of one or both anterior nares

(E) Topical petrolatum and home humidification

## Item 108

A 34-year-old man is evaluated at the urging of his wife because of a 3-month history of nightmares, increased irritability, outbursts of anger, and social isolation. He recently returned from reserve duty in Iraq. The nightmares are especially frequent and troubling around the time of his monthly weekend reserve duty, and he has started to drink heavily at these times to try to block out the dreams. The patient has lost interest in his usual activities, does not play with his children, spends much time alone, won't watch the news on television, and is very uncomfortable in crowded places, such as restaurants. He has avoided repeated efforts by his wife to talk about his experiences in Iraq. Findings on physical examination are unremarkable.

**Which of the following is the most effective treatment for this patient?**

(A) Prescribe fluoxetine

(B) Prescribe zolpidem and alcohol counseling

(C) Provide brief counseling for the patient and his wife

(D) Refer for cognitive-behavioral therapy

(E) Refer for psychodynamic therapy

## Item 109

A 42-year-old man has a 15-day history of a cough that was initially associated with rhinorrhea, nasal congestion, and a sore throat. All symptoms have resolved except the cough, which is productive of purulent sputum. The patient has not had fever, malaise, dyspnea, pleuritic chest pain, myalgia, paroxysms of coughing, or posttussive vomiting. Medical history is unremarkable, and he takes no medications.

On physical examination, vital signs, including temperature, are normal. There is no pharyngeal erythema or exudate and no lymphadenopathy. The lungs are clear to auscultation.

**Which of the following is the best initial management?**

(A) Albuterol inhaler

(B) Azithromycin

(C) Chest radiograph

(D) Nasopharyngeal swab for influenza virus culture

(E) Symptomatic treatment

## Item 110

A 72-year-old woman is evaluated for a 4-month history of insomnia, with difficulty falling asleep. The patient was the major caretaker for her husband, who had advanced heart failure and died suddenly 4 months ago. She has lost 3.6 kg (8 lb) and does not have much of an appetite. The patient used to volunteer at the hospital, but she does not enjoy going there any longer. She also does not have much energy. The patient is tearful and says that nearly everything reminds her of her husband. Medical history is otherwise unremarkable. The physical examination is unremarkable.

**Which of the following is the most appropriate management option for this patient?**

(A) Begin dextroamphetamine

(B) Begin mirtazapine at bedtime

(C) Begin zolpidem at bedtime

(D) Reassure the patient and schedule a follow-up appointment in 3 months

## Item 111

A 70-year-old man with severe disability due to claudication in his right leg and a 2-month history of increasingly frequent chest pain undergoes preoperative cardiovascular evaluation prior to elective right femoropopliteal bypass graft surgery. The patient can only walk one block because of claudication and chest pain despite adequate medical treatment. Medical history is significant for coronary artery disease, a myocardial infarction 4 years ago, hypertension, and type 2 diabetes mellitus. The patient underwent left femoropopliteal bypass graft surgery 2 years ago under general anesthesia without complications. He has a 55 pack-year smoking history but stopped smoking 2 years ago. Current medications are metoprolol, atorvastatin, amlodipine, fosinopril, isosorbide mononitrate, insulin glargine, insulin aspart, and aspirin.

Vital signs are normal. There is no jugular venous distention. Cardiopulmonary examination is normal. Pulses in the right calf are decreased. There is no calf tenderness and no peripheral edema. An electrocardiogram shows Q waves in the inferior leads.

**Which of the following is the best preoperative management?**

(A) Coronary angiography
(B) Dipyridamole nuclear imaging stress testing
(C) Dobutamine stress echocardiography
(D) Two-dimensional echocardiography
(E) No testing needed

## Item 112

An 18-year-old male college freshman is brought for evaluation by his parents because of difficulty focusing and completing tasks during his first college semester. The patient did fairly well in high school but now reports being unable to concentrate, especially in his dormitory, where he is easily distracted by music, television, and other students' conversations. He also has difficulty completing assignments on time. Both parents had to supervise the patient in high school to make sure that he remained focused. His elementary school teachers reported that he was very bright but had difficulty paying attention and following directions. The patient drinks socially on weekends and does not use illicit drugs. He enjoys playing his guitar and attending fraternity parties. He does not feel depressed or anxious, other than worrying about his grades. Medical history is unremarkable, and he takes no medications. He is alert and oriented to person, place, and time, and physical examination is normal.

**Which of the following is the most likely diagnosis?**

(A) Attention-deficit/hyperactivity disorder
(B) Generalized anxiety disorder
(C) Major depression
(D) Paranoid schizophrenia

## Item 113

A 64-year-old man is evaluated at a follow-up appointment. He had a left inguinal hernia diagnosed 6 months ago and has since had mild intermittent pain that is tolerable and does not interfere with his daily activities. He has not had previous hernia surgery, and he has had no episodes of bowel obstruction. The patient is reluctant to have surgery. He had a myocardial infarction 9 months ago, but has had no chest pain or other cardiopulmonary symptoms since then. Current medications are tamsulosin, aspirin, metoprolol, pravastatin, and lisinopril.

On physical examination, the prostate is enlarged, and there is a left inguinal hernia that arises above the inguinal ligament and moves toward the scrotum with the Valsalva maneuver.

**Which of the following is the most appropriate management option for this patient?**

(A) Defer surgery and monitor
(B) Laparoscopic hernia repair
(C) Open surgical hernia repair
(D) Prescribe a hernia truss

## Item 114

A 30-year-old woman is evaluated during a routine appointment. She has no symptoms other than fatigue, which she attributes to long work hours. She denies daytime somnolence and a history of snoring.

She is a lawyer and, owing to stress at work, she finds it difficult to eat healthy foods and get exercise. She gained 9.1 kg (20 lb) with the birth of her first child last year and has been unable to lose the weight. The patient had gestational diabetes. She states that her menstrual periods are normal. She is taking no medications.

Vital signs are normal. She is 177.8 cm (70 in) tall. BMI is 32. Her thyroid examination is normal. She has normal hair distribution and normal skin color with no evidence of striae.

**In addition to a fasting plasma glucose, lipid panel, and thyroid-stimulating hormone assay, which of the following should be done next?**

(A) 24-Hour urine cortisol
(B) Pelvic ultrasonography
(C) Serum insulin-like growth factor 1 (IGF-1) concentration
(D) Waist circumference measurement

## Item 115

A 64-year-old woman is evaluated during a health maintenance examination. She has hypertension and hypercholesterolemia. She has no symptoms to report. She is a current smoker, with a 20 pack-year history. Current medications are atenolol and hydrochlorothiazide.

Vital signs are normal. BMI is 28. Funduscopic examination reveals bright, yellow, refractile deposits scattered in the retina of the right eye, with approximately five deposits seen on direct ophthalmoscopy. The left fundus appears normal. On visual acuity testing, near vision is 20/20 with reading glasses, and distance vision is 20/25 for both eyes. The remainder of the physical examination is normal.

A lipid panel obtained prior to today's visit reveals a total cholesterol of 190 mg/dL (4.92 mmol/L); LDL cholesterol of 120 mg/dL (3.11 mmol/L); HDL cholesterol of 40 mg/dL (1.04 mmol/L); and triglycerides of 150 mg/dL (1.70 mmol/L).

**Which of the following is the most effective management option for this patient's ocular findings?**

(A) Antioxidant supplements

(B) Atorvastatin

(C) Lower blood pressure to below 130/85 mm Hg

(D) Smoking cessation

## Item 116

A 62-year-old man is evaluated for a syncopal event two nights ago. On his way to the bathroom during the night, he felt very dizzy and the next thing he remembered was waking up on the floor in the hallway to the bathroom. He went back to bed, and the symptoms did not recur the following morning. He notes that he often feels a little dizzy when he stands up. Medical history is remarkable for hypertension, benign prostatic hyperplasia, and hyperlipidemia. Two weeks ago, he started doxazosin, 2 mg before bedtime, for benign prostatic hyperplasia. Other current medications are lisinopril, atenolol, and atorvastatin.

On physical examination, temperature is normal, blood pressure is 142/78 mm Hg (supine) and 106/64 mm Hg (standing), pulse rate is 74/min (supine) and 80/min (standing), and respiration rate is 16/min. He experiences lightheadedness when he stands up. BMI is 31. Cardiac and neurologic examinations are normal. An electrocardiogram is normal.

**Which of the following is the most appropriate management option for this patient?**

(A) Admit to hospital for cardiovascular evaluation

(B) Brain MRI

(C) Discontinue doxazosin

(D) 24-Hour ambulatory electrocardiographic monitoring

## Item 117

A 54-year-old woman is evaluated for pain in the right posterior hip and pelvic area that she noticed upon awakening 3 days ago. She had been moving and lifting boxes the day before the onset of pain. She has experienced similar pain several times over the last 2 years, but it has never lasted so long.

On physical examination, BMI is 30. The FABER test (Flexion, ABduction, and External Rotation of the hip) elicits pain in the right posterior pelvis. There is tenderness on palpation over the right posterior pelvic girdle. Flexing the hip is painful. There is no tenderness in the right groin, the right trochanter, or the right gluteal notch. Passive range of motion of the right hip reveals no pain. Straight-leg-raising test is negative, and deep tendon reflexes are normal.

**Which of the following is the most likely diagnosis?**

(A) Osteoarthritis of the right hip

(B) Piriformis syndrome

(C) Right L5 radiculitis

(D) Right sacroiliitis

(E) Right trochanteric bursitis

## Item 118

A 21-year-old female college student is referred by the student health center for evaluation of a possible eating disorder. The patient acknowledges that she sometimes eats very large amounts of food and is unable to stop herself until she has consumed an entire container of ice cream or a bag of potato chips. She says that this eating behavior occurs almost daily while preparing for final examinations but may only occur once or twice weekly during less stressful times. She has never induced vomiting but does take laxatives and exercises for hours after one of these eating episodes. She also feels that her hips are too wide. Her older sister has required hospitalization several times for anorexia nervosa.

Findings on physical examination are unremarkable. BMI is 22.

**Which of the following is the most likely diagnosis?**

(A) Anorexia nervosa, binge-eating/purging type

(B) Anorexia nervosa, restricting type

(C) Binge-eating disorder

(D) Bulimia nervosa

## Item 119

A 76-year-old woman with significant bilateral vision loss is evaluated for visual hallucinations. She is accompanied by her daughter. Over the past 4 months, she has had episodes seeing images of her deceased husband's face and of objects, such as books or buildings. The images usually last for a few minutes but some have lasted up to several hours. She is aware that the images are not real, but she is worried that she might have Alzheimer disease. She denies any auditory hallucinations. She has hypertension, overactive bladder, and advanced macular degeneration. She has no history of mental health problems. Her daughter notes no changes in her mother's demeanor, mental status, or functional capabilities at home. Current medications are ramipril, hydrochlorothiazide, tolterodine, aspirin, and a daily antioxidant supplement, with no medication changes in the past year.

Vital signs are normal. The patient is alert and oriented to person, place, and time. Her judgment, reasoning, and concentration are normal. Visual acuity is 20/200 in both eyes, with no change from 2 months ago. The neurologic and cardiac examinations are normal.

**Which of the following is the most likely diagnosis?**

(A) Alzheimer dementia

(B) Intracranial mass

(C) Medication side effect

(D) Stroke

(E) Visual loss–associated hallucinations

## Item 120

An 81-year-old woman with metastatic breast cancer is admitted to the hospital for a pleurodesis by tube thoracostomy. Her disease was in remission until 2 months ago, when she presented with several bony metastases, dyspnea, and a recurrent malignant pleural effusion, treated with thoracentesis. The patient is considering several palliative therapy options.

The patient lives with her daughter. Prior to the recurrence of her disease, she enjoyed playing with her grandchildren. She used to enjoy going to book club meetings, but stopped going about 2 months ago. The patient appears withdrawn and complains of loss of energy. She has become tearful at times, stating she is a burden on her daughter and that she does not want to go home as she will "just end up in the hospital again." Current medication is oxycodone, which adequately controls her low back pain.

Neurologic and mental status examinations are normal. There is dullness to percussion in the left lower thorax.

**In addition to the tube thoracostomy and pleurodesis, which of the following is the most appropriate management option for this patient?**

(A) Initiate citalopram
(B) Initiate lorazepam
(C) Order brain MRI with gadolinium
(D) Reassess patient after treatment for bony metastases

## Item 121

A 64-year-old man is evaluated for a 1-year history of slow urinary stream, urinary hesitancy, and postvoid dribbling. Previously, he got up once a night to urinate, but in the past 2 months, his nocturia has increased to three times per night. His American Urological Association prostate symptom score is 9 (score >7 indicates moderately severe symptoms).

On physical examination, temperature is normal, blood pressure is 146/80 mm Hg, and pulse rate is 74/min. Abdominal examination is normal without tenderness or masses or evidence of a distended bladder. Digital rectal examination reveals a slightly enlarged prostate without discrete nodules or tenderness. Routine laboratory studies and urinalysis are normal. Prostate-specific antigen level is 1.0 ng/mL (1.0 μg/L). A urine culture shows no growth.

**In addition to decreasing total fluid intake and voiding just before bedtime, which of the following is the most appropriate treatment for this patient?**

(A) Doxazosin
(B) Finasteride
(C) Saw palmetto
(D) Transurethral microwave therapy

## Item 122

A 38-year-old man is evaluated during a follow-up visit. A fasting lipid panel was performed 3 weeks ago and repeated 2 weeks later to confirm the presence of hyperlipidemia. The patient does not use tobacco and has no history of heart disease, stroke, transient ischemic attack, diabetes mellitus, or renal, liver, or thyroid disease. His father has hypertension. He takes no medications and has no allergies.

Blood pressure is 132/72 mm Hg, pulse rate is 68/min, and respiration rate is 12/min. BMI is 32. Physical examination is unremarkable. Fasting lipid levels are as follows: total cholesterol, 234 mg/dL (6.06 mmol/L);

HDL cholesterol, 48 mg/dL (1.24 mmol/L); LDL cholesterol, 158 mg/dL (4.09 mmol/L); triglycerides: 142 mg/dL (1.60 mmol/L). All other laboratory findings are within normal limits.

**Which of the following is the most appropriate management option for this patient?**

(A) Begin therapy with a fibrate
(B) Begin therapy with a statin
(C) Obtain lipoprotein(a) level
(D) Repeat lipid screening in 1 to 2 years

## Item 123

An 18-year-old woman is evaluated because of perceived halitosis that she first became aware of at age 12 years, when a friend told her that she had bad breath. The patient subsequently became very self-conscious about her breath. She covers her mouth when talking to anyone, brushes her teeth repeatedly, and constantly chews gum and mints. Because of her concern about her breath, the patient has never had a boyfriend. Her mother does not agree that she has bad breath. Medical history is unremarkable. She does not snore, have difficulty breathing, smoke, or drink alcohol. She sees a dentist regularly.

Examination of the nose, mouth, and posterior pharynx is normal. There is no noticeable odor when the patient breathes out through the mouth or nose at a distance of 5 to 10 cm from the examiner. Scrapings from the back of the tongue do not have an odor.

**Which of the following is the most likely diagnosis?**

(A) Gastroesophageal reflux disease
(B) Halitophobia
(C) Nasal polyps
(D) Obstructive sleep apnea
(E) Periodontal disease

## Item 124

A 78-year-old woman is evaluated because of concerns about her ability to drive. She has trouble seeing on bright, sunny days and also at night because of the glare from headlights of oncoming cars. The patient has type 2 diabetes mellitus and a 55-pack-year smoking history. Her current medications include metformin and glipizide.

**This patient's history is most suggestive of which of the following ophthalmologic disorders?**

(A) Age-related macular degeneration
(B) Cataracts
(C) Presbyopia
(D) Primary open-angle glaucoma
(E) Proliferative diabetic retinopathy

## Item 125

A 50-year-old man is evaluated because of complete hearing loss in his left ear that was present for the first time when he awoke this morning. Hearing was normal when he went to bed. He has tinnitus in the left ear but does not have pain, drainage, dizziness, or a history of trauma or recent upper respiratory tract infections. Medical history is unremarkable, and he takes no medications.

On examination, the patient is unable to hear numbers whispered 2 feet from the left ear with the right auditory canal blocked. Both external auditory canals are normal. The tympanic membranes are also normal and are mobile following air insufflation. When a tuning fork is placed on the top of his head, he reports that the sound is heard toward the right ear (Weber test).

**Which of the following is the most likely diagnosis?**

(A) Cholesteatoma
(B) Eustachian tube dysfunction
(C) Otosclerosis
(D) Sudden sensorineural hearing loss

## Item 126

A 42-year-old man is seen in the office for low back pain that began after lifting a box 5 days ago. The pain is moderately severe, and almost any movement makes it worse. He tried lying down and experienced some, but not complete, relief. He reports that he has had no trouble urinating. He has no other symptoms and is otherwise healthy.

Physical examination reveals tenderness over the L4 paravertebral musculature bilaterally. His gait is slow owing to the pain. Results of a straight-leg-raising test are normal. There are no signs of motor weakness or sensory loss, including perineal sensation. Deep tendon reflexes are normal bilaterally.

**Which of the following is the best initial management option?**

(A) Acetaminophen
(B) Epidural corticosteroid injection
(C) MRI of the lumbar spine
(D) Plain radiographs of the lumbar spine
(E) Strict bed rest

## Item 127

A 19-year-old man is evaluated for increasing pain in the left testicular region for 2 days. It is tender when he palpates the scrotum or moves. He has had some mild dysuria but has not noted any urethral discharge. He is taking no medications, has not had any procedures or trauma to the region, and has no history of similar symptoms. He feels generally ill today with some mild nausea and a poor appetite but no vomiting.

On physical examination, temperature is 38.4 °C (101.2 °F) and other vital signs are normal. There is mild erythema overlying the left side of the scrotum. There is no edema of the scrotum. An area superior and posterior to the left testicle is moderately tender to palpation, with mild fullness and bogginess. The left testicle is nontender, similar in size to the right testicle, and sits lower in the scrotum than the right testicle. The cremasteric reflex is intact bilaterally. The penis and right testicle are normal.

**Which of the following is the most likely diagnosis?**

(A) Epididymitis
(B) Hernia
(C) Orchitis
(D) Testicular torsion

## Item 128

A 74-year-old man with metastatic lung cancer to the liver and pelvis is evaluated for low back pain. The pain is localized to the right ischial region and has progressively worsened over the past month, despite the use of immediate-release morphine (15 mg) every 6 hours. He states the pain returns about 4 hours after taking his medication. The patient has no fever, no bowel or bladder dysfunction, no radiation of pain, and no motor weakness. The patient previously underwent palliative chemotherapy and radiation therapy, but elected to discontinue therapy owing to a steady increase in tumor size. He has declined radiation therapy for his bony lesions.

On physical examination, temperature is 36.6 °C (97.8 °F), blood pressure is 100/58 mm Hg, pulse rate is 90/min, and respiration rate is 18/min. BMI is 18. Neurologic and mental status examinations are normal.

**Which of the following is the most appropriate strategy for managing this patient's pain?**

(A) Add gabapentin three times daily
(B) Increase frequency of immediate-release morphine to every 4 hours
(C) Switch to immediate-release oxycodone every 4 hours
(D) Switch to sustained-release morphine twice daily

## Item 129

A 51-year-old woman has a 2-year history of involuntary leakage of small amounts of urine. Episodes are more frequent after coughing or exercising. There is no urinary frequency, dysuria, or nocturia. The patient is gravida 3, para 3. All three pregnancies were uncomplicated and resulted in normal vaginal deliveries. She has not had a menstrual period for the past 3 years.

On physical examination, vital signs are normal. BMI is 32. Abdominal examination is unremarkable except for moderate obesity, and pelvic examination is normal except for some vaginal atrophy and mild uterine prolapse.

Results of complete blood count, blood chemistry studies, and urinalysis are normal.

**Which of the following is the best treatment at this time?**

(A) Bladder training
(B) Oral estrogen therapy
(C) Oxybutynin
(D) Pelvic floor muscle exercises
(E) Retrograde suspension surgery

## Item 130

A 17-year-old boy is brought for an evaluation by his mother, who is concerned about her son's lack of friends, poor school performance, and unemployment. The patient dropped out of high school last year and has never held a job. His mother states that since childhood, he has always been interested in only a few activities and becomes frustrated when his normal routine is changed.

During the interview, the patient talks in a monotone voice, tends to perseverate instead of easily moving from one topic to another, and seems to avoid eye contact. Use of hand or body gestures while talking is limited. He denies having a depressed mood, loss of interest in his usual activities, anxiety, hallucinations, or delusions. His speech is organized and logical. Mental status examination is normal.

**Which of the following is the most likely diagnosis?**

(A) Asperger syndrome
(B) Attention-deficit/hyperactivity disorder
(C) Major depressive disorder
(D) Schizophrenia
(E) Social anxiety disorder

## Item 131

A 41-year-old woman is evaluated for persistent nausea and vomiting after laparoscopic gastric bypass surgery 6 weeks ago for morbid obesity. The patient sometimes notices dull epigastric discomfort after the vomiting. She also has early satiety. The patient has tried to eat six small meals per day and has no history of an eating disorder or purging after meals. The patient has lost 4.5 kg (10 lb) since her surgery. She takes naproxen for osteoarthritis.

On physical examination, temperature is normal, blood pressure is 118/62 mm Hg, pulse rate is 86/min, and respiration rate is 16/min. BMI is 43. There is no abdominal discomfort to deep palpation.

Complete blood count, hepatic enzymes, and serum chemistry studies are normal.

**Which of the following management options is the best choice for this patient?**

(A) Omeprazole
(B) Right upper quadrant ultrasound
(C) Surgical laparotomy
(D) Upper endoscopy

## Item 132

A 37-year-old woman is evaluated for a 2-week history of bilateral anterior knee pain. The pain is described as aching in nature; it worsens when she descends steps or kneels, and requires her get up from her chair at work every few hours to relieve stiffness and discomfort. The patient runs several times a week but has not had any traumatic injury to the knees. She has no other medical problems.

On physical examination, there is no swelling, warmth, redness, or instability of the knees. Pressing the patella against the femur and moving it inferiorly and superiorly reproduces the pain.

**Which of the following is the most likely cause of this patient's knee pain?**

(A) Osteoarthritis
(B) Patellofemoral pain syndrome
(C) Pes anserine bursitis
(D) Prepatellar bursitis

## Item 133

A 24-year-old woman is evaluated for a 2-week history of vaginal itch and a discharge. She has tried douching and an over-the-counter vaginal cream without success. She and her partner have been together for 2 years, and they have been considering getting pregnant. Current medications are a vaginal benzocaine cream and an oral contraceptive.

On speculum examination, she has a cloudy, thin discharge coating the vaginal walls with a fishy odor to the discharge when potassium hydroxide is applied. The cervix appears normal. A bimanual examination is normal. The vaginal discharge has a pH level of 5.0. Clue cells are seen on wet mount.

**Which of the following is the most appropriate management option for this patient?**

(A) Clotrimazole for patient and partner
(B) Clotrimazole for patient only
(C) Lactobacillus intravaginal suppositories
(D) Metronidazole orally for patient and partner
(E) Metronidazole orally for patient only

# Answers and Critiques

## Item 1     Answer: A

**Educational Objective:** Understanding disclosure relating to medical errors.

The most appropriate management option is to disclose the error to the patient regardless of the partial thromboplastin time or bleeding or need for additional therapy. In general, physicians should disclose to patients information about procedural or judgment errors made in the course of patient care if it is material to the patient's well-being. Although this may represent a potential conflict of interest to the physician, most hospitals and risk management departments recommend disclosure of medical errors and near misses to the patient. This is best done as soon as possible after the incident rather than after an adverse event occurs, in which case it may appear to the patient that the staff tried to cover up the mistake. Failure to disclose a medical error may be considered unethical.

### KEY POINT

- Physicians should disclose to patients information about procedural or judgment errors made in the course of patient care if it is material to the patient's well-being.

**Bibliography**

Calvert JF Jr, Hollander-Rodriguez J, Atlas M, Johnson KE. Clinical inquiries. What are the repercussions of disclosing a medical error? J Fam Pract. 2008;57(2):124-125. [PMID: 18248735]

## Item 2     Answer: A

**Educational Objective:** Treat otitis media in an adult patient.

The best initial antibiotic for this patient is amoxicillin. Although otitis media is the most frequent bacterial infection in children, it is much less common in adults. In most cases of acute otitis media, a viral upper respiratory tract infection precedes the ear infection. Eustachian tube obstruction occurs secondary to inflammation. Bacteria subsequently enter the middle ear by means of a compliant eustachian tube, aided by other factors, including nose blowing, sniffing, and negative middle ear pressure. The microbiology of otitis media in adults is similar to that of children: *Streptococcus pneumoniae,* 21% to 63%; *Haemophilus influenzae,* 11% to 26%; *Staphylococcus aureus,* 3% to 12%; and *Moraxella catarrhalis,* 3%. Thirty percent of bacterial cultures of the middle ear show no growth.

Antibiotic therapy should be reserved for patients in whom evidence of purulent otitis exists. There are no antibiotic treatment trials in adults. Guidelines for antibiotic use are the same in children and adults. Amoxicillin is the recommended initial antibiotic because of its proven efficacy, safety, relatively low cost, and narrow spectrum of activity. If symptoms do not improve after 48 to 72 hours of amoxicillin therapy, initiation of amoxicillin-clavulanate, cefuroxime, or ceftriaxone is recommended. Alternative agents for patients with penicillin allergy are oral macrolides (azithromycin, clarithromycin). Patients should not use nasal decongestants or antihistamines. Follow-up of these patients is not necessary unless symptoms persist or progress.

### KEY POINT

- Amoxicillin is the recommended antibiotic for treating acute otitis media in adults because of its proven efficacy, safety, relatively low cost, and narrow spectrum of activity.

**Bibliography**

Ramakrishnan K, Sparks RA, Berryhill WE. Diagnosis and treatment of otitis media [erratum in Am Fam Physician. 2008;78(1):30]. Am Fam Physician. 2007;76(11):1650-1658. [PMID: 18092706]

## Item 3     Answer: D

**Educational Objective:** Treat generalized anxiety disorder.

This patient's presentation is characteristic of generalized anxiety disorder (GAD). Psychotherapy and pharmacotherapy are effective in treating patients with GAD, and cognitive-behavioral therapy is the psychotherapy of choice in these patients. In this patient who is resistant to "talk therapy," a selective serotonin reuptake inhibitor (SSRI) such as sertraline is appropriate. SSRIs have proven efficacy in treating GAD and are approved by the U.S. Food and Drug Administration (FDA) for this indication. In addition, SSRIs are relatively safe and well-tolerated.

GAD is defined by excessive anxiety and worry about a variety of events or activities over at least a 6-month period; difficulty exercising control over worrying; the presence of several symptoms associated with the anxiety, such as fatigue, irritability, restlessness, sleep disturbance, and difficulty concentrating; and functional impairment.

Alprazolam (a benzodiazepine) and buspirone (an azapirone) are also approved by the FDA for treating GAD. However, alprazolam may cause dependence and tolerance, and there is less robust evidence to support the efficacy of buspirone for this indication. In addition, buspirone takes longer to induce a response than the other pharmacologic agents listed.

Some evidence suggests that imipramine (a tricyclic antidepressant) may be effective in treating GAD. However, imipramine is not approved by the FDA for this indication. In addition, this antidepressant causes anticholinergic side effects and has the potential to cause fatal cardiac arrhythmias. Quetiapine (an atypical antipsychotic agent) may also be useful for treating unipolar and bipolar depression, but there is no evidence of its efficacy for treating GAD.

**KEY POINT**

- **Selective serotonin reuptake inhibitors are the most effective pharmacologic agents for treating generalized anxiety disorder.**

**Bibliography**

Bandelow B, Seidler-Brandler U, Becker A, Wedekind D, Ruther E. Meta-analysis of randomized controlled comparisons of psychopharmacological and psychological treatments for anxiety disorders. World J Biol Psychiatry. 2007;8(3):175-187. [PMID: 17654408]

## Item 4          Answer:   A

**Educational Objective:** Manage chronic cough.

The most appropriate management option for this patient is to discontinue the angiotensin-converting enzyme (ACE) inhibitor, lisinopril. This patient presents with a cough of longer than 8 weeks' duration and thus meets the definition for chronic cough. According to American College of Chest Physicians guidelines, the initial evaluation of all patients with a chronic cough involves a history and physical examination to determine likely etiologies, followed by a chest radiograph to identify obvious abnormalities. If the chest radiograph is normal, one should recommend discontinuing ACE inhibitors and smoking, if these factors are identified in the history, or pursue empiric management of chronic cough if the patient is a nonsmoker and is not taking an ACE inhibitor. There may be no obvious temporal relationship between the initiation of ACE inhibitor therapy and the onset of cough. The median time to resolution is 26 days from withdrawal of the ACE inhibitor.

In patients with chronic cough and a normal chest radiograph, a chest CT is only indicated for those at high risk for lung cancer. A chest CT is not indicated in this young, otherwise healthy, nonsmoking patient.

Asthma and nonallergic eosinophilic bronchitis may present without any symptoms other than cough. Spirometry would be indicated in the evaluation of chronic cough that has not resolved after the initial management measures (history, physical examination, chest radiograph, cessation of ACE inhibitor, treatment for upper airway cough syndrome).

Upper airway cough syndrome (UACS) is a common cause of chronic cough. A trial of a first-generation antihistamine/decongestant combination for several weeks is appropriate treatment for UACS. In a nonsmoking patient who is taking an ACE inhibitor, however, the ACE inhibitor should be discontinued for several weeks before treating for UACS. Similarly, although empiric therapy for gastroesophageal reflux disease (GERD) is appropriate if prominent symptoms of GERD accompany the cough or if

initial management measures fail, discontinuing the ACE inhibitor always should precede empiric therapy for either UACS or GERD.

**KEY POINT**

- **In patients taking an angiotensin-converting enzyme inhibitor who present with a chronic cough and a normal chest radiograph, discontinuing the angiotensin-converting enzyme inhibitor may be both diagnostic and therapeutic.**

**Bibliography**

Irwin RS, Baumann MH, Bolser DC, et al; American College of Chest Physicians (ACCP). Diagnosis and management of cough executive summary: ACCP evidence-based clinical practice guidelines. Chest. 2006;129(1 Suppl):1S-23S. [PMID: 16428686]

## Item 5          Answer:   A

**Educational Objective:** Manage reversible causes of urinary incontinence.

This patient with new-onset urinary incontinence should first be evaluated for transient, reversible causes, for which the mnemonic DIAPERS may be useful: Drugs, Infection, Atrophic vaginitis, Psychological (depression, delirium, dementia), Endocrine (hyperglycemia, hypercalcemia), Restricted mobility, and Stool impaction. Urinary tract infection is a very common cause of transient incontinence in the elderly, particularly if other contributing factors such as cognitive impairment or impaired mobility are present. The presence of significant pyuria in this setting generally justifies administration of empiric antibiotic therapy pending urine culture results. Therefore, beginning ciprofloxacin is appropriate for this patient.

Although some medications may induce transient incontinence, causative agents are most often diuretics or drugs that affect autonomic nervous system or bladder function. Oral hypoglycemic agents do not typically cause incontinence, and discontinuing these agents in a patient with diabetes mellitus could precipitate hyperglycemia and increased incontinence.

Indwelling catheterization is a treatment of last resort for patients who have chronic incontinence that is unresponsive to other therapy and in whom intermittent catheterization is not feasible.

This patient's confusion is more consistent with delirium in an elderly patient as a generalized response to an acute illness rather than a focal neurologic event. CT scan of the head is typically not helpful in such patients and is unlikely to provide an explanation for this patient's incontinence.

**KEY POINT**

- **Empiric antibiotic treatment pending the results of a urine culture may be warranted in elderly patients with new-onset urinary incontinence and pyuria.**

Bibliography

Holroyd-Leduc JM, Straus SE. Management of urinary incontinence in women: clinical applications. JAMA. 2004;291(8):996-999. [PMID: 14982916]

## Item 6     Answer:   B

**Educational Objective:**   Treat allergic rhinitis.

This patient has allergic rhinitis, for which intranasal corticosteroids are the most efficacious therapy. Intranasal corticosteroids, oral antihistamines, intranasal antihistamines, oral antihistamine/oral decongestant combination products, and intranasal cromolyn sodium are all superior to placebo. Studies have shown that intranasal corticosteroids are superior to both intranasal and oral antihistamines for relief of sneezing and nasal obstruction. Some corticosteroid preparations (for example, fluticasone) may also relieve ocular symptoms such as itching and tearing. Although intranasal corticosteroids are associated with minimal systemic bioavailability, this finding should not limit their use. Growth retardation has been reported with long-term administration of intranasal beclomethasone in children but has not been reported with use of other intranasal corticosteroid preparations. Epistaxis is the most common side effect of intranasal corticosteroids and occurs in approximately 10% of patients. However, this is not usually severe enough to warrant discontinuation of the drug. The rare side effect of nasal perforation can be avoided by using proper spray technique.

Oral second-generation (nonsedating) antihistamines (for example, fexofenadine) can either be used alone or as additional therapy for control of mild symptoms. However, the patient described here has more severe symptoms that are affecting his comfort and ability to work and therefore make intranasal corticosteroids the preferred therapy.

Azelastine is an intranasal H$_1$-antihistamine that improves nasal congestion but is less effective than corticosteroids in relieving other symptoms.

Oral decongestants, including pseudoephedrine, also relieve nasal congestion but not rhinorrhea, itching, or sneezing.

Other effective therapeutic agents for allergic rhinitis include oral leukotriene modifiers (to be used as add-on therapy only), topical cromolyn sodium, and nasal saline irrigation. Immunotherapy may be considered when symptoms are not well controlled by other agents. Oral corticosteroids may also be used for brief periods to relieve severe symptoms. Intranasal ipratropium bromide is generally indicated for patients with nonallergic rhinitis but can also be used for patients with allergic rhinitis associated with profuse rhinorrhea.

**KEY POINT**

- **Intranasal corticosteroids are superior to antihistamines for treating patients with allergic rhinitis.**

Bibliography

Drugs for allergic disorders [erratum in Treat Guidel Med Lett. 2007;5(61):88]. Treat Guidelines Med Lett. 2007;5(60):71-80.

## Item 7     Answer:   B

**Educational Objective:**   Manage hypertriglyceridemia.

The most appropriate management option for this patient is to calculate her non-HDL cholesterol level. This patient has a high triglyceride level (>200 mg/dL [2.26 mmol/L]). According to the Adult Treatment Panel III guidelines, the next step in the management of a patient with a triglyceride level between 200 mg/dL and 500 mg/dL (2.26 and 5.65 mmol/L) is to calculate non-HDL cholesterol (total cholesterol minus HDL cholesterol) to determine whether triglyceride-lowering medication is indicated. In addition, reversible causes of hypertriglyceridemia should be sought. These include excessive alcohol intake, obesity, high carbohydrate intake, physical inactivity, type 2 diabetes mellitus, renal disease, and certain medications (corticosteroids, β-blockers, estrogens, and protease inhibitors).

LDL cholesterol goal is based on the presence or absence of five major risk factors (smoking, hypertension, older age, low HDL cholesterol, family history of premature coronary artery disease). This patient does not have any of these risk factors; therefore, her LDL cholesterol goal is 160 mg/dL (4.14 mmol/L), and she does not need a statin.

The second therapeutic target is the non-HDL cholesterol. The non-HDL cholesterol goal is set at the LDL goal plus 30 mg/dL (0.78 mmol/L); therefore, her non-HDL cholesterol goal is 190 mg/dL (4.92 mmol/L). This patient's non-HDL cholesterol level is 176 mg/dL (4.56 mmol/L); therefore, triglyceride-lowering medication (gemfibrozil or other fibrate medication) is not indicated. Triglyceride-lowering medication should be considered in patients with a personal or family history of premature coronary artery disease regardless of non-HDL cholesterol level. The patient presented has no family history of premature coronary artery disease.

The Framingham risk score, used to further stratify some patients with elevated LDL cholesterol, does not have to be calculated in this patient because her LDL cholesterol of 128 mg/dL (3.32 mmol/L) is below the goal of 160 mg/dL (4.14 mmol/L). Calculating the Framingham risk score is most helpful in making management decisions when patients have an LDL cholesterol level above their target goal.

**KEY POINT**

- **In patients with a triglyceride level between 200 mg/dL and 500 mg/dL (2.26 and 5.65 mmol/L), the need for medication to lower the triglyceride level is determined by calculating the non-HDL cholesterol level.**

Bibliography

Brunzell JD. Hypertriglyceridemia. N Engl J Med. 2007;357(10): 1009-1017. [PMID: 17804845]

## Item 8     Answer:   A

**Educational Objective:**   Screen for colorectal cancer.

The most appropriate management option for this patient is annual home fecal occult blood testing. Patients should be offered several methods of screening, because personal preference and insurance coverage variations may render some methods more appropriate than others for individual patients. Even though sensitivity and specificity vary among the different screening methods, it is more important to choose and follow a screening program than it is to be concerned about which method is used. Screening methods include structural tests (such as colonoscopy and sigmoidoscopy) that can accomplish both detection and prevention (by identification and removal of precursor lesions) and stool-based tests (such as fecal occult blood testing [FOBT]), which detect existing cancers and, to a lesser degree, polyps. Annual home high-sensitivity FOBT, sampling two to three consecutive specimens, is a method recommended by the U.S. Preventive Services Task Force (USPSTF) for screening if the patient is willing to undergo colonoscopy if results are positive. Other screening programs recommended by the USPSTF are colonoscopy every 10 years or flexible sigmoidoscopy every 5 years combined with high-sensitivity FOBT every 3 years.

Annual rectal examination with office FOBT is not considered adequate screening for colorectal cancer because of poor sensitivity (4.9% for advanced neoplasia and only 9% for cancer).

The American Cancer Society, U.S. Multi-Society Task Force on Colorectal Cancer, and American College of Radiology joint task force considers double-contrast barium enema an acceptable screening method; however, it should be performed every 5 years.

Flexible sigmoidoscopy is an acceptable screening method with detection limited to the sigmoid colon. The USPSTF-recommended frequency for flexible sigmoidoscopy is every 5 years together with high-sensitivity FOBT every 3 years.

### KEY POINT

- Acceptable colorectal cancer screening methods for average-risk patients include annual home stool testing, colonoscopy every 10 years, and flexible sigmoidoscopy every 5 years together with high-sensitivity fecal occult blood testing every 3 years.

Bibliography

Levin B, Lieberman DA, McFarland B, et al. Screening and Surveillance for the Early Detection of Colorectal Cancer and Adenomatous Polyps, 2008: A Joint Guideline from the American Cancer Society, the US Multi-Society Task Force on Colorectal Cancer, and the American College of Radiology. CA Cancer J Clin. 2008;58(3): 130-160. [PMID: 18322143]

## Item 9     Answer:   A

**Educational Objective:**   Initiate empiric management for chronic cough.

The most appropriate treatment for this patient is a trial of an antihistamine/decongestant combination. The initial approach in patients with chronic cough (>8 weeks in duration) is to conduct a history and physical examination looking for identifiable causes, determine whether the patient is taking an angiotensin-converting enzyme (ACE) inhibitor, and obtain a chest radiograph. In the population of patients who do not smoke, do not take an ACE inhibitor, and have a normal chest radiograph, upper airway cough syndrome (UACS) (previously termed *postnasal drip*), asthma, and gastroesophageal reflux disease (GERD) are responsible for approximately 99% of cases of chronic cough. When the etiology of a chronic cough is unclear, the American College of Chest Physicians recommends initial treatment with a first-generation antihistamine/decongestant combination to treat UACS. This is true even in the absence of evidence of a postnasal drip. The diagnosis of chronic cough is often based upon the patient's response to empiric therapy, and it may take weeks or even months for the cough to resolve with appropriate therapy.

In a nonsmoking patient with a normal chest radiograph and no systemic symptoms, CT scan of the chest is not indicated.

Asthma is a common cause for a chronic cough and may present only with a cough (cough-variant asthma). However, pursuing pulmonary function testing or initiating empiric β-agonist therapy for asthma is premature unless the patient fails to respond to empiric treatment of UACS.

In the absence of GERD symptoms, proton-pump inhibitors should be reserved for patients with chronic cough who have a normal chest radiograph, are not taking an ACE inhibitor, do not smoke, and who have failed to improve with treatment for UACS, asthma, and nonallergic eosinophilic bronchitis.

### KEY POINT

- Empiric treatment of chronic cough in a non-smoking patient not taking an angiotensin-converting enzyme inhibitor who has a normal chest radiograph begins with treatment for upper airway cough syndrome.

Bibliography

Pavord ID, Chung KF. Management of chronic cough. Lancet. 2008;371(9621):1375-1384. [PMID: 18424326]

## Item 10     Answer:   E

**Educational Objective:**   Manage breast pain in a young woman.

This patient most likely has cyclic mastalgia. The pain of cyclic mastalgia is typically dull, heavy, or aching; diffuse; and bilateral; involving the upper outer breast region with radiation to the upper arm and axilla. Noncyclic mastalgia is constant or intermittent. It is usually unilateral and localized within a quadrant. It tends to occur at a later age and is not associated with the menstrual cycle. The cause of cyclic mastalgia is not known. Cyclical breast pain resolves spontaneously within 3 months in 20% to 30% of women. Among women who undergo treatment for breast pain, up to 60% experience recurrent symptoms within 2 years. Reassurance alone is often highly effective in alleviating symptoms and associated anxiety. The simplest first-line recommendations are to wear a well-fitting support bra (underwire for routine use and sports bra for activities) and use local measures (heat, topical NSAIDs) or oral analgesics (NSAIDs or acetaminophen). Changes in diet and lifestyle (avoidance of dietary fat, caffeine, nicotine) and the use of dietary supplements (vitamin E, evening primrose oil) have been advocated by some, but in general, there is inadequate evidence to support these measures.

In the absence of any focal findings, it is unlikely that this woman has cancer, and specific imaging tests are not required. While some experts recommend mammography in patients with generalized breast pain who are older than 30 years, there are scant outcome research results to support this approach. Age-appropriate breast cancer screening protocols can be followed.

If the patient's pain is significant and does not respond to first-line treatments, the antiestrogen tamoxifen or androgenic corticosteroid danazol can be considered as second-line treatment.

### KEY POINT

- **Reassurance and the use of a well-fitting support bra should be the first-line treatment for cyclic mastalgia.**

**Bibliography**

Rosolowich V, Saettler E, Szuck B, et al; Society of Obstetricians and Gynecologists of Canada (SOGC). Mastalgia. J Obstet Gynaecol Can. 2006;28(1):49-71. [PMID: 16533457]

## Item 11    Answer:  B

**Educational Objective:** Treat delirium in a terminally ill patient.

The most appropriate treatment for this terminally ill patient is to initiate haloperidol. During the terminal phases of hospice care, most patients experience at least some form of altered mental status. This patient demonstrates confusion, agitation, and a deficit in attention, pointing to a likely diagnosis of delirium. There are no U.S. Food and Drug Administration–approved therapies for delirium. However, there is evidence demonstrating that low-dose antipsychotic agents are effective in the treatment of delirium.

Even though this patient is confused, she is able to articulate whether she is in pain. Confusion after a recent increase in narcotic dose is common in terminally ill patients. This patient has been on a stable fentanyl dose for 1 month, however, making this cause less likely. Discontinuation of

her pain medication may subject her to inappropriate discomfort, as she still has some baseline pain.

As benzodiazepines, including lorazepam, can cause or worsen delirium, they should only be used if there is a strong component of patient anxiety or if the antipsychotic medication is ineffective after upward titration.

As this patient is in hospice care, the only reason for diagnostic testing, such as laboratory evaluation or brain MRI, would be to guide active interventions, which would result in only temporary stabilization of her condition. Such diagnostic testing is, therefore, inappropriate.

### KEY POINT

- **Antipsychotic medications in small doses are effective treatment for delirium in a terminally ill patient.**

**Bibliography**

Lonergan E, Britton AM, Luxenberg J, Wyller T. Antipsychotics for delirium. Cochrane Database Syst Rev. 2007;(2):CD005594. [PMID: 17443602]

## Item 12    Answer:  D

**Educational Objective:** Manage a patient interested in smoking cessation.

The U.S. Public Health Service has recommended brief smoking cessation counseling interventions for smokers interested in quitting. Potential quitters should be warned of withdrawal symptoms (which will improve in several weeks), plan a coping strategy for cravings (such as chewing gum), avoid high-risk smoking situations, and anticipate some weight gain.

For this patient who would like to try an alternative to nicotine replacement therapy, varenicline would be the best option. Cochrane systematic reviews have addressed a number of pharmacologic approaches to smoking cessation treatment. Varenicline for 12 weeks increased the odds of long-term smoking cessation approximately threefold compared with placebo. When compared directly with bupropion, varenicline was the more effective drug. The main side effect was nausea, which usually subsided over time. Two trials tested varenicline for an additional 12 weeks without adverse effects. No randomized trial has compared varenicline with nicotine replacement therapy alone. Nicotine replacement therapy should not be combined with varenicline, since the combination may increase the risk of nausea, vomiting, headache, dizziness, and other adverse effects. Varenicline for smoking cessation may be associated with depressed mood, agitation, and suicidal thoughts, and safety review by the U.S. Food and Drug Administration is ongoing.

When used as sole pharmacotherapy, bupropion and nortriptyline doubled the odds of cessation compared with placebo. However, although bupropion and nortriptyline appear to be equally effective and of similar efficacy to nicotine replacement therapy, they appear to be less effective than varenicline. There is a risk of 1 in 1000 of seizures associated with bupropion use, making bupropion a poor choice for this patient. Adverse effects of bupropion include insomnia, dry mouth, and nausea; those of nortriptyline include dry mouth, constipation, nausea, and sedation.

Trials of selective serotonin reuptake inhibitors, including sertraline, have shown no evidence of significant benefit for smoking cessation.

### KEY POINT

- **For smoking cessation, bupropion and nortriptyline appear to be equally effective and of similar efficacy to nicotine replacement therapy but less effective than varenicline.**

**Bibliography**

Cahill K, Stead LF, Lancaster T. Nicotine receptor partial agonists for smoking cessation. Cochrane Database Syst Rev. 2007;(1): CD006103. [PMID: 17253581]

## Item 13     Answer: B

**Educational Objective:** Manage recurrent falls in an elderly patient.

Low serum vitamin D levels are common in elderly persons and have been shown to be associated with muscle weakness, functional impairment, and increased risk of falls and fractures. A meta-analysis of five randomized controlled trials, in addition to more recent studies, suggests that vitamin D supplementation in elderly persons reduces falls by about 20%. Therefore, the initial study in the patient described here should be measurement of a serum 25-hydroxyvitamin D level. If the vitamin D level is low, this patient should take ergocalciferol or cholecalciferol, 50,000 units weekly for 6 to 8 weeks, followed by 800 to 1000 units of vitamin D daily along with calcium supplementation (at least 1200 mg of elemental calcium [diet plus supplementation]). Although vitamin D deficiency is common in the elderly, routine vitamin D level screening is not recommended. Rather, vitamin D plus calcium supplementation as described above is recommended for all elderly persons.

In the absence of clinical manifestations of osteoporosis (such as vertebral, hip, or wrist fracture) or a low bone mineral density measurement, use of medications such as risedronate to treat osteoporosis is not warranted.

A Cochrane systematic review concluded that hip protectors are ineffective in preventing hip fractures in elderly persons who fall, partly as a result of limited patient acceptance and adherence because of discomfort. There is no proven value of performing routine 24-hour electrocardiographic monitoring in elderly persons who fall.

### KEY POINT

- **Vitamin D supplementation reduces falls in elderly persons by about 20%.**

**Bibliography**

Bischoff-Ferrari HA, Dawson-Hughes BD, Willett WC, et al. Effect of vitamin D on falls: A meta-analysis. JAMA. 2004;291(16):1999-2006. [PMID: 15113819]

## Item 14     Answer: E

**Educational Objective:** Treat chronic pelvic pain syndrome.

The most appropriate treatment for this patient is terazosin. This patient has chronic prostatitis/chronic pelvic pain syndrome (CP/CPPS). CP/CPPS is manifested by genitourinary/pelvic pain and voiding symptoms. There are no diagnostic physical or laboratory findings. Urine cultures are typically negative, and the presence or absence of leukocytes in the urine has limited clinical utility in diagnosis or in predicting treatment response.

α-Blockers have the most evidence of efficacy among pharmacologic therapies for the treatment of CP/CPPS. Several specific α-blockers have been evaluated in randomized clinical trials, including terazosin, in doses ranging from 1 to 5 mg/d. Other α-blockers tested in trials include tamsulosin and alfuzosin. Clinical response is often modest, however, and long-term efficacy is uncertain.

Current evidence does not support a bacterial cause of CP/CPPS. Although a 4- to 6-week trial of antibiotics is still commonly prescribed, there is a lack of clinical trial evidence supporting their use. In contrast to bacterial prostatitis, in which urinalysis and urine culture typically show signs of an infection, results of these tests are normal in CP/CPPS. Acute bacterial prostatitis is unlikely in this patient with an indolent course of symptoms and a prostate that on examination is only mildly rather than exquisitely tender.

NSAIDs are another class of drugs commonly recommended as empiric treatment, and there is preliminary evidence that inflammatory markers such as interleukin and tumor necrosis factor are elevated in patients with CP/CPPS. However, only one randomized controlled trial has been conducted, which showed modest benefits for rofecoxib, a COX-2 inhibitor. The efficacy of other NSAIDs has not been established.

Anticholinergic drugs such as oxybutynin are effective therapy for urge incontinence but are not indicated for other genitourinary syndromes.

Quercetin, a bioflavonoid found in red wine, onions, and other foods, has proven beneficial in one small trial, but other popular "prostate health" supplements, including saw palmetto, do not appear effective for CP/CPPS.

### KEY POINT

- **α-Blockers may be effective in the treatment of chronic prostatitis/chronic pelvic pain syndrome.**

**Bibliography**

Schaeffer AJ, Datta NS, Fowler JE Jr, et al; Chronic Prostatitis Collaborative Research Network. Overview summary statement: diagnosis and management of chronic prostatitis/chronic pelvic pain syndrome (CP/CPPS). Urology. 2002;60(6 Suppl):1-4. [PMID: 12521576]

**Item 15      Answer:  C**

**Educational Objective:**  Prescribe emergency contraception.

Two types of pills are available for emergency contraception. Both must be taken as soon as possible, or within 5 days of a risked pregnancy, and a second dose is taken 12 hours later. Levonorgestrel (Plan B) is the preferred formulation of emergency contraception because it is more efficacious and has fewer side effects (nausea 20% and vomiting 6%) than the other option, which is a combination of ethinyl estradiol and levonorgestrel. Forty percent of women experience severe nausea and vomiting when using ethinyl estradiol and levonorgestrel; an antiemetic agent can be given 1 hour before the first dose of this formulation. This patient should, therefore, be prescribed oral levonorgestrel. The usual contraindications to oral hormonal contraceptives are not applicable to women using the two-dose method for emergency contraception. Specifically, emergency contraception with oral levonorgestrel is believed to have acceptable risks in patients with cardiovascular disease, thrombophilic disorders, migraine, liver disease, and for patients who are breastfeeding. A routine follow-up office visit is not required after taking emergency contraception with either of these two methods.

A copper intrauterine device is even more effective than either oral levonorgestrel or mifepristone, but requires insertion, which carries a 1 in 3000 risk of fundal perforation and is impractical for this patient who is not in town.

Mifepristone (RU-486) is an antiprogestin that has been approved by the U.S. Food and Drug Administration for termination of intrauterine pregnancies of 7 weeks or less. In randomized trials, mifepristone as an emergency contraceptive has been shown to have similar efficacy and tolerability to levonorgestrel, but is not available in pharmacies. Access is limited to direct sale to registered health care providers only. In addition, the optimum dose has not yet been established.

**KEY POINT**

- **Levonorgestrel is the preferred method of emergency contraception based on its availability, efficacy, and side effect profile.**

**Bibliography**

Cheng L, Gülmezoglu AM, Piaggio G, Ezcurra E, Van Look PF. Interventions for emergency contraception. Cochrane Database Syst Rev. 2008;(2):CD001324. [PMID: 18425871]

**Item 16      Answer:  C**

**Educational Objective:**  Manage musculoskeletal neck pain.

This patient has neck pain caused by musculoskeletal strain. Sometimes called cervicalgia or cervical strain, this is a nonspecific diagnosis describing an injury to paraspinal soft tissues that causes spasm of the neck and upper back muscles. The diagnosis is established in patients presenting with acute neck and trapezius muscle pain without neurologic findings. Neck pain typically results from ordinary activities that cause stress to the cervical muscles and ligaments, such as poor posture, an awkward sleeping position, or even abruptly turning the head and neck. Patients complain of pain, stiffness, and tightness in the upper back or shoulder, which may last 1 to 2 days or even up to 6 weeks. The mainstays of therapy are NSAIDs and physical therapy. A Cochrane systematic review found strong evidence favoring a multimodal approach consisting of exercise, mobilization, or manipulation for subacute and chronic mechanical neck disorders.

Epidural corticosteroid injection might be considered in patients with neck pain and stable neurologic symptoms and signs who have not responded to conservative treatment. As this patient has not attempted conservative therapy, corticosteroid injection in not indicated.

Radiographic diagnostic procedures for neck pain have little validity and utility for patients with neck pain without a history of severe trauma or radicular symptoms. As this patient has no such history, neck imaging with plain radiography or MRI is not indicated.

The effectiveness of transcutaneous electrical nerve stimulation (TENS) for treating acute neck pain has not been established.

**KEY POINT**

- **Radiographic diagnostic procedures for neck pain have little validity and utility for patients with neck pain without a history of severe trauma or radicular symptoms.**

**Bibliography**

Binder AI. Cervical spondylosis and neck pain. BMJ. 2007 Mar;334 (7592):527-531. [PMID: 17347239]

**Item 17      Answer:  B**

**Educational Objective:**  Diagnose scleritis.

Painful red eye should prompt consideration of conjunctivitis, episcleritis, scleritis, keratitis or corneal ulcer, iritis, endophthalmitis, uveitis, and glaucoma. This patient has severe bilateral eye pain that is described as deep and boring, has awakened her from sleep, and has associated photophobia, tearing, and eye findings of erythema localized to the sclera. The most likely diagnosis is scleritis.

Scleritis is a serious eye condition that can lead to permanent visual loss or globe rupture and should be treated urgently in consultation with an ophthalmologist. Nearly half of patients with scleritis have an underlying systemic problem, often a connective tissue disease.

Episcleritis is an inflammation of the superficial blood vessels overlying the sclera. Patients may present with no symptoms or mild ocular pain and redness, which may occur abruptly. The blood vessels appear prominent and engorged, but normal white sclera may be visible between the blood vessels, helping to distinguish this from scleritis. This patient's severe pain and raised erythematous lesions make scleritis the more likely diagnosis.

Subconjunctival hematoma causes an often well-localized area of bright erythema that overlies but does not involve the sclera. It causes a painless red eye and resolves spontaneously and does not affect visual acuity. This patient's red eyes are associated with diminished visual acuity, severe pain, and involve the sclera, ruling out subconjunctival hematoma.

Patients with anterior uveitis present with the abrupt onset of eye pain and redness. The redness is typically adjacent and circumferential to the iris. Patients may have photophobia, tearing, decreased vision, and headache. As the inflammation involves the iris and ciliary body, patients may have an irregular pupil. Uveitis requires emergency ophthalmology consultation. The patient's focal inflammation and equal pupils make anterior uveitis an unlikely diagnosis.

Viral conjunctivitis can present with the abrupt onset of diffuse conjunctival erythema and injection associated with a foreign body sensation and discharge. This patient's deep, severe pain and localized, raised erythema and diminished visual acuity are more consistent with scleritis.

**KEY POINT**

- **Patients with a severely painful, red eye should be considered to have a sight-threatening condition until proven otherwise.**

**Bibliography**

Mahmood AR, Narang AT. Diagnosis and management of the acute red eye. Emerg Med Clin North Am. 2008;26(1):35-55. [PMID: 18249256]

## Item 18      Answer:   C

**Educational Objective:**  Provide the appropriate herpes zoster vaccination strategy.

The zoster vaccine is indicated in all patients older than 60 years for prevention of herpes zoster (shingles). A randomized, double-blind, placebo-controlled trial showed that live attenuated zoster vaccine in adults 60 years or older reduced the incidence of herpes zoster by 51% and postherpetic neuralgia by 67%. The vaccine was more efficacious in preventing herpes zoster among adults 60 to 69 years of age than among those 70 years or older. On the

other hand, the vaccine prevented postherpetic neuralgia to a greater extent among adults aged 70 years or more.

The zoster vaccine is a live vaccine and is contraindicated in people with active, untreated tuberculosis; in pregnant women; in immunocompromised patients; and in patients receiving chemotherapy, radiotherapy, or large doses of corticosteroids. Immunization should be avoided if an immunocompromised person is living in the household.

Zoster vaccine can be given concomitantly with all other live and inactivated vaccines, including influenza and pneumococcal vaccine. Zoster vaccine is given as a single subcutaneous dose. A booster dose is not recommended.

More than 99% of patients 40 years or older have serologic evidence of prior varicella infection. Therefore, routine serologic testing for varicella antibodies to determine who should be vaccinated is not cost-effective or necessary.

A reported history of possible herpes zoster is not a contraindication to vaccination. While recurrence of herpes zoster is rare, there are no recognized safety concerns in giving the vaccine to a patient with a history of shingles. It is felt that excluding patients with a possible history would be a barrier to vaccination and impose a burden on physicians to assess the reliability of the prior diagnosis.

**KEY POINT**

- **Zoster vaccine is indicated in all patients age 60 years and older without contraindications, regardless of history of prior chickenpox infection.**

**Bibliography**

Yawn BP, Saddier S, Wollan P, St Sauver JS, Kurland M, Sy L. A population-based study of the incidence and complications of herpes zoster before zoster vaccine introduction [erratum in Mayo Clin Proc. 2008;83(2):255]. Mayo Clin Proc. 2007;82(11):1341-1349. [PMID: 17976353]

## Item 19      Answer:   E

**Educational Objective:**  Evaluate need for preoperative testing in a patient undergoing a low-risk procedure.

Various criteria and algorithms have been proposed for preoperative screening tests. Although most screening test results are normal, even the few abnormal results rarely cause a change in management and even fewer will lead to an improved outcome. Therefore, preoperative testing should be individualized and directed towards evaluating pre-existing diseases or finding abnormalities based on specific factors (for example, medical history, medications). In general, a test should not be done if the results are unlikely to alter management. Additionally, if tests were done recently (within 3 months) and were normal, evidence suggests that repeat tests will also be normal, unless the patient's clinical condition or medications have changed.

This patient is scheduled to have a low-risk procedure in which testing is unlikely to alter management. A finding of mild anemia, renal insufficiency, or hyperglycemia (plasma glucose <200 to 300 mg/dL [11.1 to 16.65 mmol/L]) would not change management. Therefore, despite the patient's age and history of hypertension and diabetes mellitus, additional testing is not indicated. Similarly, an abnormal activated partial thromboplastin time would be unlikely to indicate a significant bleeding disorder in the absence of a clinical history of bleeding. A chest radiograph is not indicated despite the patient's age, as it is unlikely to show any significant abnormality and would not alter management. Age alone should not be the criterion for testing. In the absence of a cardiac history or change in symptoms, an electrocardiogram is unlikely to show anything that would change management for a low-risk procedure, especially if a relatively recent electrocardiogram was normal.

**KEY POINT**

- **Although most preoperative screening test results are normal, even the few abnormal results rarely cause a change in management and even fewer will lead to an improved outcome.**

**Bibliography**

Smetana GW, Macpherson DS. The case against routine preoperative laboratory testing. Med Clin North Am. 2003;87(1):7-40. [PMID: 12575882]

## Item 20    Answer:  B

**Educational Objective:** Diagnose bipolar disorder.

This patient most likely has bipolar disorder. Although she presents with symptoms of depression, her history includes episodes of mania or hypomania. Diagnostic criteria for mania include a distinct period of abnormally and persistently elevated, expansive, or irritable mood lasting at least 1 week. Typical symptoms include inflated self-esteem or grandiosity, decreased need for sleep, distractibility, increased goal-directed behavior, and excessive involvement in pleasurable activities that have a high potential for consequences (unrestrained buying sprees, sexual indiscretions). It is important to ask depressed patients about a personal and family history of manic symptoms in order to select an appropriate therapy.

The diagnosis of attention-deficit/hyperactivity disorder (ADHD) requires documentation of multiple symptoms of inattention or hyperactivity and impulsivity dating back to at least age 7 years. There is no history provided to indicate either these symptoms or related impairment in two or more settings, such as school and home, so ADHD appears an unlikely diagnosis.

There is also no history provided of self-harm, dysfunctional relationships, or intense anger to suggest borderline personality disorder. Although the impulsive sexual behavior could be a manifestation of borderline personality disorder, it can also be characteristic of mania or hypomania, and the overall presentation is more consistent with bipolar disorder. While there is overlap between depression and generalized anxiety disorder (GAD), with impaired concentration, sleep disturbance, and fatigue being common to both, this patient reports depression as a prominent symptom and has a history of depression as well as a history of prior manic or hypomanic periods. Thus, a diagnosis of bipolar disorder is much more apt than GAD.

**KEY POINT**

- **It is important to ask depressed patients about a personal and family history of manic symptoms in order to select an appropriate therapy.**

**Bibliography**

Beyer JL. An evidence-based medicine strategy for achieving remission in bipolar disorder. J Clin Psychiatry. 2008;69 Suppl 3:31-37. [PMID: 18533760]

## Item 21    Answer:  D

**Educational Objective:** Diagnose piriformis syndrome.

This patient most likely has piriformis syndrome, a common source of sciatic nerve pain resulting from irritation and hypertrophy of the piriformis muscle. Prolonged sitting or carrying a large wallet in the back pocket can predispose to piriformis syndrome, which is characterized by chronic posterior pain. Other causes of sciatic nerve injury should be ruled out, such as a herniated nucleus pulposus. However, when examination findings localize to the sciatic notch and there is no other sign of neurologic compromise, it is reasonable to diagnose piriformis syndrome. The management is conservative, with NSAIDs and stretching exercises.

True hip pain usually presents as groin pain and typically worsens with weight bearing. Active and passive range of motion may intensify pain from the hip joint, and motion may be restricted with advanced disease. As this patient's hip pain is posterior rather than anterior and is not reproduced with hip motion, osteoarthritis is an unlikely diagnosis.

Trochanteric bursitis can be confirmed in patients in whom hip adduction intensifies the pain or in those in whom the examination reveals pain and tenderness over the bursa, which is located over the lateral projection of the greater trochanter.

Sciatica, a sharp, burning pain that radiates down the leg and is often associated with leg numbness or paresthesias, is a highly sensitive (95%) and specific (88%) finding for herniated disk. This patient does not have sciatic pain, and she has normal deep tendon reflexes and a normal straight-leg-raising test. The absence of these findings argues strongly against an L4-L5 disk herniation as the cause of her buttock pain.

**KEY POINT**

- **Piriformis syndrome is a likely diagnosis in patients with sciatic pain when examination findings localize to the sciatic notch and there are no other signs of neurologic compromise.**

**Bibliography**
Papadopoulos EC, Khan SN. Piriformis syndrome and low back pain: a new classification and review of the literature. Orthop Clin North Am. 2004;35(1):65-71. [PMID: 15062719]

## Item 22    Answer:  D
**Educational Objective:** Evaluate pulsatile tinnitus.

This patient has pulsatile tinnitus, which is often vascular in origin and may be due to an arteriovenous fistula, arteriovenous malformation, arterial aneurysm, tumor, or atherosclerotic disease. A head and neck examination is required, including auscultation for bruits over the neck, eyes, and around the ears. The effect on the tinnitus of positioning the head and neck and compressing the arteries and veins of the neck should be determined. Patients with frequent or constant pulsatile tinnitus should have an otorhinolaryngologic evaluation and may require imaging with CT angiography or MR angiography

Meniere disease is characterized by three cardinal symptoms: tinnitus, sensorineural hearing loss, and episodic vertigo. Meniere disease is an unlikely cause of this patient's symptoms because of the frequently pulsatile nature of her tinnitus, apparently normal hearing, and lack of vertigo.

Palatal spasm or contractions of the tensor tympani or stapedius muscles may create clicking sounds. This source of tinnitus is often objective (may be heard by the examining physician), is benign, and requires no particular intervention other than patient reassurance.

The most common cause of chronic sensorineural hearing loss (>90%) is the aging ear (presbycusis). This condition is usually gradual, bilateral, worse in the presence of high-frequency sound, and may be accompanied by tinnitus. Clinically bothersome tinnitus may improve with the use of hearing aids, cochlear implants, or otologic surgery for conductive hearing loss. Presbycusis does not cause pulsatile tinnitus and would be unusual in a 39-year-old woman.

**KEY POINT**
- Patients with frequent or constant pulsatile tinnitus should be referred for otorhinolaryngologic evaluation and may require CT angiography or MR angiography.

**Bibliography**
Liyanage SH, Singh A, Savundra P, Kalan A. Pulsatile tinnitus. J Laryngol Otol. 2006;120(2):93-97. [PMID: 16359136]

## Item 23    Answer:  A
**Educational Objective:**  Treat urge urinary incontinence that has only partially responded to anticholinergic medication.

This patient's signs and symptoms are most consistent with urge urinary incontinence, the most common type of incontinence in elderly women. It is typically due to detrusor sphincter instability that increases with aging. Episodes are usually preceded by a normal sensation of needing to void. Factors that impair mobility (for example, Parkinson disease and osteoarthritis) may increase the risk of incontinent episodes by impeding the patient's ability to get to the bathroom promptly.

Anticholinergic agents such as oxybutynin are effective in many patients with urge incontinence but may need to be combined with behavioral therapy or other treatment if a complete response is not achieved. Because oxybutynin has been only partially effective in this patient, she may benefit from bladder training, which is a formalized toileting technique to increase functional bladder capacity by gradually increasing the time between voiding.

Surgical procedures, such as pubovaginal sling procedures and retropubic suspension, are indicated for patients with moderate to severe stress urinary incontinence that is unresponsive to pelvic floor muscle training. However, surgery is not indicated for urge incontinence.

Transanal electrostimulation of the bladder is accomplished by applying a small device in either the vagina or anus. Some experts believe that this treatment has some efficacy for urge incontinence, but objective findings are inconclusive, and this therapy cannot be recommended at this time.

Results of randomized clinical trials have shown possible but inconsistent improvement in urinary incontinence with estrogen delivered by transdermal patch or vaginal cream or gel. However, these studies have typically been in women with stress, rather than urge, incontinence.

Medical devices such as vaginal pessaries or cones are not indicated for urge incontinence. Although these devices are commonly prescribed for stress incontinence, they have not been shown to be effective for this indication.

**KEY POINT**
- Surgery is not indicated for patients with urge urinary incontinence.

**Bibliography**
Ostaszkiewicz J, Roe B, Johnston L. Effects of timed voiding for the management of urinary incontinence in adults: systematic review. J Adv Nurs. 2005;52(4):420-431. [PMID: 16268846]

## Item 24    Answer:  E
**Educational Objective:** Identify strategies to reduce postoperative pulmonary complications.

There is fair evidence that smoking cessation, if begun at least 8 weeks before surgery, may improve pulmonary function and reduce the risk of postoperative pulmonary complications.

The addition of intravenous corticosteroids or aminophylline is appropriate in patients with refractory bronchospasm if needed but is not indicated in patients in the absence of wheezing.

Reasonable, but untested, indications for preoperative spirometry include dyspnea of unclear etiology and chronic obstructive pulmonary disease or asthma in patients in whom it is uncertain that airflow limitation has been maximally reduced. There is no evidence that routine preoperative spirometry affects important management decisions and prevents pulmonary complications.

Prophylactic antibiotics do not prevent postoperative pulmonary complications and may predispose to respiratory colonization with resistant organisms.

**KEY POINT**

- Smoking cessation, if begun at least 8 weeks before surgery, may improve pulmonary function and reduce the risk of postoperative pulmonary complications.

**Bibliography**

Lawrence VA, Cornell JE, Smetana GW; American College of Physicians. Strategies to reduce postoperative pulmonary complications after noncardiothoracic surgery: systematic review for the American College of Physicians. Ann Intern Med. 2006;144(8):596-608. [PMID: 16618957]

## Item 25    Answer:  E

**Educational Objective:** Manage olecranon bursitis.

Immediate aspiration of the right olecranon bursa is indicated for this patient. There is a strong clinical suspicion for olecranon bursitis, which may be infectious, crystalline, or traumatic. Synovial fluid analysis will help guide therapy in this setting. Acute crystalline or infectious synovitis usually is associated with extreme pain on passive joint motion. This patient has pain only on full flexion of the joint, most likely because this movement causes tautness of the bursa and surrounding soft tissue.

If gout were evident on the synovial fluid analysis, a trial of colchicine would be reasonable.

Measurement of the erythrocyte sedimentation rate will not help to distinguish between crystal-induced arthritis and infection.

Radiography is useful in evaluating traumatic causes of acute pain near a joint but would not help to differentiate between crystalline and infectious arthritis or to diagnose bursitis. Nuclear scanning and MRI are similarly not particularly useful in establishing a diagnosis among these conditions.

Joint aspiration is not indicated in the absence of convincing evidence that the joint itself is the source of the problem, such as painful elbow joint rotation or extension.

**KEY POINT**

- Olecranon bursitis is typically associated with painful full elbow flexion; acute crystalline or infectious synovitis is usually associated with pain on any passive joint motion.

**Bibliography**

Cardone DA, Tallia AF. Diagnostic and therapeutic injection of the elbow region. Am Fam Physician. 2002;66(11):2097-2100. [PMID: 12484691]

## Item 26    Answer:  B

**Educational Objective:** Treat depression that does not respond to initial therapy.

The goal of depression therapy should not be simply improvement of symptoms but rather remission of depressive symptoms whenever possible. Patients with no response to full-dose therapy within 6 weeks should receive another medication or referral for psychotherapy. The STAR*D trial found that 25% of patients with major depression who did not respond to an initial antidepressant achieved remission when another agent was substituted for the initial drug. Because this patient has not responded to an appropriate dose of sertraline after a reasonable period of time, changing to another antidepressant such as citalopram is indicated. Although both citalopram and sertraline are selective serotonin reuptake inhibitors (SSRIs), the STAR*D trial reported essentially identical responses when one SSRI was substituted for another or when an SSRI was changed to an antidepressant from a different class.

This patient has had a complete lack of response to sertraline after 3 months. Therefore, continuing this agent at the same dose for another 4 weeks is unlikely to be helpful. Similarly, augmentation with a second agent might be considered if a partial response had been achieved with sertraline, but that is not the case here. Although several case reports suggested methylphenidate might be an effective augmenter, a randomized, double-blind, placebo-controlled trial found no benefit for methylphenidate augmentation in treatment-resistant depression.

Electroconvulsive therapy is reserved for situations warranting immediate change and should be considered if profound suicidal ideation or psychotic features are present or if the patient fails to respond to multiple antidepressants. However, a trial of at least one other agent is warranted before considering electroconvulsive therapy in the absence of compelling urgency to achieve a prompt response.

**KEY POINT**

- A patient with major depression who has not responded to one antidepressant at an appropriate dose for an adequate period should be given a different antidepressant.

**Bibliography**

Patkar AA, Masand PS, Pae CU, et al. A randomized, double-blind, placebo-controlled trial of augmentation with an extended release formulation of methylphenidate in outpatients with treatment-resistant depression. J Clin Psychopharmacol. 2006;26(6):653-656. [PMID: 17110825]

## Item 27    Answer:  C

**Educational Objective:**  Diagnose meniscal tear.

The patient's history is suspicious for a meniscal tear. Patients typically describe a twisting injury with the foot in a weight-bearing position, in which a popping or tearing sensation is often felt, followed by severe pain. Swelling occurs over several hours, in contrast to ligamentous injuries, in which swelling is immediate. Patients with meniscal tears may report a clicking or locking of the knee secondary to loose cartilage in the knee but often have pain only on walking, particularly going up or down stairs. Pain along the joint line is 76% sensitive for a meniscal tear, and an audible pop or snap on the McMurray test is 97% specific for a meniscal tear.

Anserine bursitis is characterized by pain and tenderness over the anteromedial aspect of the lower leg below the joint line of the knee. The location of the patient's pain and her abnormal physical examination findings do not support the diagnosis of anserine bursitis.

Ligamentous damage usually occurs as a result of forceful stress or direct blows to the knee while the extremity is bearing weight. Excessive medial rotation with a planted foot stresses the anterior cruciate ligament. A popping or tearing sensation is frequently reported in patients with ligamentous damage. This patient's physical examination findings, particularly the result of the McMurray test, support a diagnosis of meniscal, rather than ligamentous, injury.

Patellofemoral pain syndrome is the most common cause of chronic knee pain in active adults, particularly women, younger than 45 years. The exacerbation of the pain by going down steps and the development of knee stiffness and pain at rest when the knee is flexed for an extended period of time are clues to the diagnosis. Reproducing the pain by firmly moving the patella along the femur confirms the diagnosis. This patient's history and physical examination findings are consistent with acute injury to the meniscus rather than the patellofemoral pain syndrome.

### KEY POINT

- **Pain along the joint line is 76% sensitive for a meniscal tear, and a pop or snap on the McMurray test is 97% specific.**

**Bibliography**

Jackson JL, O'Malley PG, Kroenke K. Evaluation of acute knee pain in primary care. Ann Intern Med. 2003;139(7):575-588. [PMID: 14530229]

## Item 28    Answer:  A

**Educational Objective:**  Screen for abdominal aortic aneurysm.

An abdominal ultrasonography is the most appropriate test for this patient. In a large randomized trial, abdominal duplex ultrasound screening in men aged 65 to 75 years who had ever smoked reduced mortality from abdominal aortic aneurysm (AAA) rupture. AAA repair prevents rupture, and the benefits of repair appear to outweigh its risks for large AAAs (>5.5 cm) in good-operative-risk patients. The U.S. Preventive Services Task Force (USPSTF) recommends a one-time screening by ultrasonography for AAA in men aged 65 to 75 years who have ever smoked, makes no recommendation for men who have never smoked, and recommends against screening in women.

The USPSTF recommends using one of the following protocols to screen for colorectal cancer in average-risk persons: annual high-sensitivity fecal occult blood testing, sigmoidoscopy every 5 years combined with high-sensitivity fecal occult blood testing every 3 years, and screening colonoscopy at intervals of 10 years. This patient's last colonoscopy was 8 years ago; therefore, a colonoscopy at this time is not indicated.

Although low-dose CT is more sensitive than chest radiograph for the detection of lung cancer, there is insufficient evidence to recommend for or against this test to screen for lung cancer. In this former smoker, the fact that his risk of lung cancer is significantly less than that of a current smoker would further diminish screening test performance.

The USPSTF recommends against using spirometry to screen for chronic obstructive pulmonary disease. This recommendation is based on the findings that harms (time and effort required by patients and the health care system, false-positive results, and adverse effects of subsequent unnecessary therapy) exceed benefits (improvement in respiratory-related health status).

### KEY POINT

- **Abdominal duplex ultrasound screening in men aged 65 to 75 years who have ever smoked reduces mortality related to abdominal aortic aneurysm rupture.**

**Bibliography**

Kim LG, P Scott RA, Ashton HA, Thompson SG; Multicentre Aneurysm Screening Study Group. A sustained mortality benefit from screening for abdominal aortic aneurysm [erratum in Ann Intern Med. 2007;147(3):216]. Ann Intern Med. 2007;146(10):699-706. [PMID: 17502630]

## Item 29    Answer:  B

**Educational Objective:**  Diagnose leukoplakia.

This patient's oral lesion is most likely leukoplakia, a precancerous condition that represents hyperplasia of the squamous epithelium and is particularly common in smokeless tobacco users. Leukoplakia presents as a white patch or plaque with changes in the mucosal surface texture. About 1% to 20% of lesions will progress to cancer over 10 years. However, most lesions resolve within 2 to 6 weeks of cessation of smokeless tobacco use. A related lesion, erythroplakia, is characterized by a red mucosal patch or plaque. Biopsy of the lesion shows severe dysplasia or malignancy in

50% of patients. Patients with either red or white oral lesions that persist for longer than several weeks should be referred for evaluation and biopsy. The patient should be counseled to stop chewing tobacco.

Candidiasis causes white plaques on the buccal mucosa, palate, tongue, or oropharynx. Risk factors include diabetes mellitus, immunosuppression, use of inhaled corticosteroids, or wearing dentures. This patient has none of these risk factors, which makes candidiasis very unlikely. The plaque can easily be scraped off, and if the diagnosis is uncertain, a potassium hydroxide smear can be done on the scrapings, which will show budding yeasts with or without pseudohyphae.

Lichen planus is a disease of unknown cause that occurs on the skin, nails, and mucous membranes in middle-aged adults. Oral lesions may be the only manifestations. It is typically characterized by a network of white, lacy-appearing hypertrophic mucosa on the buccal mucosa, gingiva, and tongue. Additional clinical presentations include papular, atrophic, and painful erosive lesions.

Oral hairy leukoplakia is characterized by white, corrugated, painless plaques that typically develop on the lateral tongue but also occur on the floor of the mouth, palate, and buccal mucosa. Unlike the plaque due to candidiasis, the plaque caused by oral hairy leukoplakia cannot be scraped off. Although it may resemble leukoplakia on physical examination, it is not premalignant. It occurs almost exclusively in patients with HIV infection and for that reason is unlikely in this patient. It is caused by the Epstein-Barr virus and may respond to antiviral therapy.

**KEY POINT**

- Leukoplakia is a precancerous lesion that represents hyperplasia of the squamous epithelium and is particularly common in smokeless tobacco users.

**Bibliography**

Kademani D. Oral cancer [erratum in Mayo Clin Proc. 2007;82(8): 1017]. Mayo Clin Proc. 2007;82(7):878-887. [PMID: 17605971]

## Item 30      Answer:  C

**Educational Objective:** Manage a patient experiencing intimate partner violence.

This patient reports a clear pattern of domestic abuse that is escalating. When such a situation is identified, the patient may not be ready to leave the abuser because of fear of retaliation, financial dependence on the abuser, having no place to go, a belief that the abuse will stop, or a belief that the abuse is the patient's fault. According to expert opinion, the most important initial intervention is to conduct an assessment for safety, looking for escalating verbal or physical abuse as well as the presence of weapons. Safety planning should then be discussed in detail, including whether the patient wants to leave home or return home and whether an attempt should be made to remove the abuser from the household (for example, by contacting the police). Interventions designed to enhance safety provided by clinicians appear to be efficacious but lack rigorous scientific proof. Additional important interventions include validation of the patient's perception of being abused, assuring the patient of your support, performing and documenting an appropriate examination, asking if the patient wants to file a police report or obtain a restraining order, and providing information about community resources. Such resources include local and national domestic violence hot lines (800-799-SAFE; www.ndvh.org), shelters, legal advocacy groups, and social services. Calling from the physician's office and going directly to a shelter may be appropriate in some circumstances.

Marital counseling or scheduling a joint appointment with her husband may be useful, but should not be the next step. Obtaining previous medical records that could provide evidence of a pattern of abuse may also be useful, but safety planning should come first. Reporting to the local department of social services is mandatory for domestic violence involving a child. However, a minority of states require reporting injuries from domestic violence against competent women.

**KEY POINT**

- When an abusive situation is identified, it is important to address immediate safety needs.

**Bibliography**

Wathen CN, MacMillan HL. Interventions for violence against women: scientific review. JAMA. 2003;289(5):589-600. [PMID: 12578492]

## Item 31      Answer:  A

**Educational Objective:** Diagnose complex sleep-related behavior.

This patient with diabetes mellitus presents with a recent loss of control of her morning glucose levels following institution of a sedative hypnotic, zolpidem. The most likely explanation is complex sleep-related behavior, specifically sleep eating, that is contributing to her elevated glucose levels. All sedative hypnotics may be associated with complex sleep-related behaviors, which include preparing and eating food, driving, making phone calls, and engaging in sexual activity, all of which the patient may be unaware of or unable to recall. Patients who are prescribed sleep aids must be warned of the potential for these side effects, and the lowest effective dosage for the shortest period of time should be used.

Gastroparesis can lead to symptoms of early satiety, variation in glucose control, heartburn, upper abdominal pain, and vomiting. This patient has loss of glucose control and weight gain and no other symptoms associated with gastroparesis.

Whereas nonadherence should be considered in a patient whose glucose is not well controlled, this is not a likely explanation in this patient who has evidence of complex sleep-related behavior.

The Somogyi effect represents a rare rebound hyperglycemia in response to nocturnal hypoglycemia. The finding of weight gain and remnants of meals in the morning makes the Somogyi effect an unlikely cause of her blood glucose elevations.

**KEY POINT**

- **Sedative hypnotics may be associated with complex sleep-related behaviors that may exacerbate chronic medical conditions.**

**Bibliography**

Wilson JF. In the clinic. Insomnia. Ann Intern Med. 2008;148(1): ITC13-1-ITC13-16. [PMID: 18166757]

## Item 32      Answer:   A

**Educational Objective:**  Recognize anchoring heuristic as a cause of diagnostic error.

Heuristics are the problem-solving shortcuts built into clinicians' thinking that help make associations between a problem and the solution. In the instance described in the patient scenario, the physician made a heuristic error known as an *anchoring heuristic*, which occurred when her colleague told her the leukocytosis was from corticosteroids. She became "anchored" to the diagnosis, unable or subconsciously unwilling to consider another diagnosis. Tools that can reduce anchoring heuristic errors include intentionally expanding a differential diagnosis, using prospective hindsight (for example, asking, "*What is the one thing that might cause this patient to die today?*"), and employing metacognitive aids, such as information search engines.

An *availability heuristic* is a shortcut based on a recent occurrence of a phenomenon. For instance, a person sees a red bird and is told it is a cardinal. The next time the person sees a red bird, the shortcut in her mind says, "a cardinal." This may be correct. But what if the bird was another species of red bird? If the clinician had recently seen a patient with leukocytosis from myelodysplasia and incorrectly assumed that this patient's leukocytosis likewise stemmed from myelodysplasia, the error would be based upon an availability heuristic.

A no-fault error is one in which the presentation is misleading and the clinician really has no opportunity to pick up clues based on any data that there is an underlying problem. A system-related error is one in which processes intended to facilitate routine health care fail, such as a lab error giving an erroneous test result. Neither of these types of error are involved in the case described.

**KEY POINT**

- **Anchoring heuristic errors occur when a clinician holds to an initial impression, such as might occur when accepting a previous diagnosis at face value.**

**Bibliography**

Graber ML, Franklin N, Gordon R. Diagnostic Error in Internal Medicine. Arch Intern Med. 2005;165(13):1493-1499. [PMID: 16009864]

## Item 33      Answer:   C

**Educational Objective:**  Treat chronic fatigue syndrome.

This patient meets criteria for chronic fatigue syndrome (CFS), based on the history of at least 6 months of fatigue along with sleep that is not refreshing, exertional malaise, and joint and muscle pain. A systematic review of interventions for CFS reported that only two interventions, cognitive-behavioral therapy (CBT) and graded exercise, were found to be consistently beneficial in improving, but not curing, symptoms. Therefore, this patient should be referred for CBT. CBT has been shown to reduce fatigue and cognitive impairment and to improve functional status. Graded exercise programs also can provide some benefit, and while this patient seems to be making an effort to engage in physical activity, she might also benefit from specific guidance to make sure she is not engaging in a cycle of pushing too far and then exacerbating her fatigue.

Acclydine, a food supplement purported to increase insulin-like growth factor, has not been shown to be effective in treating CFS. In a randomized, placebo-controlled, double-blind trial of adult patients with CFS, acclydine did not result in treatment benefits compared with placebo.

Efforts to establish a relationship between Epstein-Barr virus and CFS have failed to establish a connection, nor has acyclovir shown any benefit for CFS.

As many as 75% of all patients with CFS also meet the criteria for depression and/or anxiety syndromes. In addition, antidepressants have a specific role in reducing pain and improving sleep; however, evidence suggesting an overall improvement in symptoms with the use of these agents is mixed. Many experts suggest that a trial of antidepressant medication as an adjunct to CBT and a graded exercise program may be worthwhile, but antidepressant therapy is likely to be ineffective if used as sole therapy.

**KEY POINT**

- **Cognitive-behavioral therapy and a graded exercise program can improve functional status in patients with chronic fatigue syndrome.**

**Bibliography**

Jackson JL, O'Malley PG, Kroenke K. Antidepressants and cognitive-behavioral therapy for symptom syndromes. CNS Spectr. 2006; 11(3):212-222. [PMID: 16575378]

## Item 34      Answer:   C

**Educational Objective:**  Manage multifactorial dizziness in a geriatric patient.

Disequilibrium in the elderly is often described as a vague sense of unsteadiness, most often occurring while standing or walking. It is different than orthostatic hypotension in that symptoms are not always temporally related to moving from a seated to a standing position and are not associated with a drop in blood pressure. Disequilibrium in the elderly is often multifactorial, with contributors including peripheral neuropathy, visual loss, a decline in bilateral vestibular function, deconditioning, autonomic neuropathy, and medication side effects. Treatment of disequilibrium involves reducing polypharmacy, installing safety features in patients' homes, providing assistive devices such as walkers and canes, correcting eyesight and hearing if possible, and instituting physical therapy to improve muscle strength. Referral to physical therapy would be an appropriate first step for this patient.

Neuroimaging should usually be reserved for patients with signs suggesting potentially serious underlying conditions, such as cerebellar or focal neurologic symptoms or vertical nystagmus. There is no evidence that this patient has a new neurologic lesion. Therefore, obtaining an MRI is not indicated.

Meclizine can be of use in patients with prolonged or sustained vertigo such as in acute viral labyrinthitis. However, for intermittent episodes of unsteadiness, it is not likely to be of benefit and will add to her polypharmacy.

The combination of aspirin and dipyridamole is an effective strategy for the secondary prevention of ischemic stroke. However, there is no evidence that such treatment improves disequilibrium in the elderly.

**KEY POINT**

- **Dizziness in geriatric patients is often multifactorial and caused by deficits in multiple sensory systems and medication side effects.**

**Bibliography**

Eaton DA, Roland PS. Dizziness in the older adult, Part 2. Treatments for causes of the four most common symptoms. Geriatrics. 2003;58(4):46, 49-52. [PMID: 12708155]

## Item 35          Answer:  A

**Educational Objective:** Advise a woman in choosing a contraceptive method.

The most appropriate birth control option for this patient is a depot injection of medroxyprogesterone acetate. Long-acting progesterone compounds with intramuscular depot medroxyprogesterone acetate are an especially good choice for teenagers or other women who may have difficulty remembering to take a pill each day. Medroxyprogesterone acetate injection is 99.7% effective and is administered every 3 months. It is also useful for women who cannot take estrogen because of current breast-feeding or problems with estrogen's side effects.

Other hormonal contraceptives that do not require daily administration by the patient are the topical patch and vaginal ring, which may also be acceptable options for this patient, although each does require some action by the patient, making them less desirable options. The patch, which contains ethinyl estradiol and norelgestromin, is applied weekly for 3 concurrent weeks and then removed during the fourth week, when withdrawal bleeding should occur. Efficacy and adverse effects are similar to those of the pill. The vaginal ring is inserted into the vagina and remains in place for 3 weeks. It releases continuous estradiol and etonogestrel until it is removed at week 4 to allow withdrawal bleeding to occur. Its efficacy and adverse effects are similar to those of the pill, except for an increased incidence of vaginal infection, irritation, and discharge associated with the vaginal ring.

Condoms and diaphragms are less reliable and effective (particularly in the absence of concomitant spermicide use) because they must be on hand at the time of need and an action must be taken at that time. However, condoms do provide important protection against HIV infection and other sexually transmitted diseases, so their adjunctive use should be advised for patients whose sexual behavior places them at risk for sexually transmitted diseases.

The progestin-only pill is taken daily, and dose timing must be very regular. The failure rate of this contraceptive is slightly higher than that of the combined estrogen-progestin pills. The effectiveness of this contraceptive is dependent upon regular timing of the dose; therefore, it would not be a good choice for a woman having trouble remembering to take her oral contraceptive on a daily basis.

While tubal ligation is a highly effective method of birth control, it is not a good choice for a young woman who will likely desire to have children at some point.

**KEY POINT**

- **Long-acting depot or implantable progesterone compounds provide effective contraception in teens or others more likely to forget daily oral contraceptive pills.**

**Bibliography**

Zurawin RK, Ayensu-Coker L. Innovations in contraception: a review. Clin Obstet Gynecol. 2007;50(2):425-439. [PMID: 17513928]

## Item 36          Answer:  C

**Educational Objective:** Manage carpal tunnel syndrome.

This patient has multiple signs and symptoms of carpal tunnel syndrome (CTS), including aching wrist pain with sparing of the palm, sensory changes in the median nerve distribution of the fingers, and weakness of the thenar muscles. Symptoms of clinically severe CTS include intolerable pain and progressive numbness and weakness, particularly if present for 6 or more months. Patients with clinically or electrodiagnostically severe CTS, such as this patient, should undergo surgical decompression as first-line treatment.

Corticosteroid injection into the carpal tunnel should be considered in patients with mild to moderate CTS (intermittent or mild persistent symptoms) if it has not been tried before and if noninvasive treatments are ineffective. Corticosteroid injection is more effective for short-term treatment than placebo or oral corticosteroids for the treatment of CTS. Over the long term, however, corticosteroid injection has not been shown to improve outcomes compared with NSAIDs or splinting. Corticosteroid injection is not indicated for patients with moderate to severe symptoms, as experienced by this patient, because injection therapy will not provide long-term improvement for the patient's neuromuscular symptoms.

Although NSAIDs are recommended and widely used as an initial drug therapy for CTS, there is no strong evidence that they are useful.

Splints and ultrasound therapy have been shown to be effective for mild to moderate CTS. Although most guidelines emphasize noninvasive therapies before invasive treatment for mild to moderate CTS, the evidence is not sufficient to show whether drug or nondrug modalities are more effective, which should be tried first, or whether a combination of therapeutic approaches would be more useful. Particularly for advanced symptoms and signs, surgical correction is safe and effective compared with conservative treatments.

**KEY POINT**

- **Patients with advanced symptoms and signs of carpal tunnel syndrome should be referred for carpal tunnel release.**

**Bibliography**

Gerritsen AA, de Vet HC, Scholten RJ, Bertelsmann FW, de Krom MC, Bouter LM. Splinting vs surgery in the treatment of carpal tunnel syndrome: a randomized controlled trial. JAMA. 2002; 288(10):1245-1251. [PMID: 12215131]

## Item 37    Answer:  B

**Educational Objective:**  **Manage a patient with somatization disorder.**

This patient meets the American Psychiatric Association Diagnostic and Statistical Manual IV (DSM IV) criteria for somatization disorder (a history of somatic symptoms prior to the age of 30 years; pain in at least four different sites; two gastrointestinal problems, such as vomiting or diarrhea [not including gastrointestinal pain]; one sexual symptom, such as lack of interest or erectile dysfunction; one pseudoneurologic symptom similar to those seen in conversion disorder, such as fainting, numbness, or blindness). Cognitive-behavioral therapy (CBT) is the most effective specific therapy for somatization disorder.

This patient's seeking help from multiple physicians and lack of reassurance after numerous negative test results are also typical of somatization. It is important for the physician to try to break the cycle of "doctor shopping" by establishing a relationship with the patient and by planning frequent and regular office visits so that the patient does not feel the need to develop new symptoms or escalate existing

symptoms in order to be seen. Office visits should include a reasonable evaluation of symptoms (not more or less intensive than for patients without somatization), acknowledgment of the patient's suffering, and an attempt to shift the focus of the visit toward what is going on in the patient's life. Eventually, the frequency of visits can be decreased.

An abdominal MRI is not likely to be helpful in a patient with a nonspecific history, normal physical examination findings, and a recent normal CT scan. Electromyography is not indicated in the initial evaluation of this patient who has no motor or sensory deficit involving the arm. The patient discussed here does not meet criteria for depression on initial screening and does not require treatment with sertraline, but should undergo further evaluation for depression and anxiety.

**KEY POINT**

- **Cognitive-behavioral therapy (CBT) is the most effective specific therapy for somatization disorder.**

**Bibliography**

Kroenke K. Efficacy of treatment for somatoform disorders: a review of randomized controlled trials. Psychosom Med. 2007;69(9):881-888. [PMID: 18040099]

## Item 38    Answer:  D

**Educational Objective:**  **Manage chronic primary insomnia.**

This patient has difficulty falling asleep and maintaining sleep. Whereas most cases of chronic insomnia are secondary to an underlying medical condition, this patient likely has primary insomnia that was triggered initially by stress at work but has now persisted and become a focus of worry, despite the resolution of the previous stressor.

Given the nature of his symptoms and his maladaptive responses, the most appropriate next step is to instruct this patient on proper sleep hygiene and stimulus control. Stimulus control seeks to remove sources of stimulation around bedtime and help the patient reassociate the bedroom with rest. Measures include using the bedroom only for sleep and sexual activity (not reading or watching television); and going to bed only when sleepy. In addition, he should be instructed that if he is unable to initiate sleep within 15 to 20 minutes, he should leave the bedroom and engage in quiet, relaxing activities (such as reading) elsewhere, returning to bed only when sleepy.

This patient does not have a history to suggest thyroid dysfunction as an underlying reason for the insomnia; therefore, thyroid function testing is not indicated.

A polysomnogram is indicated in patients in whom an underlying sleep disorder, such as obstructive sleep apnea or periodic limb movements, is suspected. This patient's presentation does not point to an underlying sleep disorder.

Ramelteon is a melatonin receptor agonist and promotes the initiation of sleep, although it does not help with sleep maintenance and should not replace behavioral modification as the first-line therapy for primary insomnia.

- **Stimulus control is an effective behavioral strategy for treating primary insomnia.**

**Bibliography**

Wilson JF. In the clinic. Insomnia. Ann Intern Med. 2008;148(1): ITC13-1-ITC13-16. [PMID: 18166757]

## Item 39     Answer: C

**Educational Objective:** Diagnose dry eyes.

This patient is presenting with signs and symptoms of dry eyes. Common symptoms include a feeling of grittiness in the eyes. The eyes often feel better in the morning owing to the lids being closed and retaining tears. Also, humidity can improve symptoms. Symptoms often worsen upon exposure to irritants such as dust, smoke, wind, or pollen, and in low humidity. Dry eyes result from decreased tear production, increased tear evaporation, or some combination of both. Dry eyes may be a symptom of systemic disease, particularly Sjögren syndrome.

Treatment of dry eyes is guided by the severity and frequency of symptoms and is aimed at reducing the local inflammatory response common to dry eyes. Warm compresses (humidity), and artificial tears (no more than four times daily) may be all that is necessary for episodic dry eyes. For patients with persistent dry eyes and/or evidence of ongoing inflammation despite artificial tears, topical cyclosporine 0.5% solution appears to be safe for long-term use (and targets the inflammatory response).

Allergic conjunctivitis can also cause a sandy, gritty sensation in the eyes. Patients also typically complain of itching, which is absent in this patient. Furthermore, the symptoms may have a seasonal variation or vary in accordance to exposure to known allergens.

Blepharitis is an acute or chronic eyelid inflammation often associated with conjunctival inflammation. This patient has no evidence of eyelid inflammation, crusting, or exudate, making blepharitis an unlikely diagnosis.

Meibomitis, an inflammation of the meibomian glands in the eyelids, can cause symptoms similar to those seen in dry eyes. However, the symptoms of meibomitis are typically worse upon awakening, as the inflamed meibomian glands have been in direct contact with the surface of the eye overnight.

- **The symptoms from dry eyes worsen as the day progresses and improve with humidity.**

**Bibliography**

Gilbard JP. The diagnosis and management of dry eyes. Otolaryngol Clin North Am. 2005;38(5):871-885. [PMID: 16214564]

## Item 40     Answer: E

**Educational Objective:** Manage plantar fasciitis.

This patient most likely has plantar fasciitis, and plantar fascial stretching exercises are the most appropriate initial therapy. Plantar fasciitis, the most common cause of inferior heel pain, is characterized by pain that worsens with walking, especially with the first steps in the morning or after resting, in addition to localized tenderness along the plantar fascia or the calcaneal insertion site. Obesity, prolonged standing, and repetitive microtrauma from running or dancing are risk factors for this condition.

Symptoms of plantar fasciitis resolve in more than 80% of patients within 1 year. Conservative treatment is appropriate, although systematic reviews have found little evidence to guide clinical practice. A controlled trial showed that plantar fascial stretching exercises more effectively relieved pain than Achilles tendon stretches, although dropout rates in this study were substantial. The benefits of orthotic devices, NSAIDs, avoidance of flat shoes and walking barefoot, and night splints are uncertain, although these are safe, inexpensive interventions. Heel inserts may provide increased relief compared with stretching exercises alone. Plantar fasciotomy is reserved for the few patients with severe, persistent symptoms.

Corticosteroid injections show short-term benefit compared with placebo in patients with plantar fasciitis but are associated with a substantial risk of fascial rupture (number needed to harm = 14). Magnets have been studied in plantar fasciitis and have not shown a benefit.

Plantar fasciitis is usually diagnosed clinically; radiographic bone spurs are neither specific nor sensitive findings in these patients. Imaging, including plain film radiography, bone scans, ultrasonography, and MRI, is usually reserved for selected patients in whom the diagnosis of plantar fasciitis is uncertain or for evaluation of other causes of heel pain if conservative therapy is unsuccessful.

- **Plantar fasciitis is characterized by pain that worsens with walking, especially with the first steps in the morning or after resting, in addition to localized tenderness along the plantar fascia or the calcaneal insertion site.**

**Bibliography**

Buchbinder R. Clinical practice. Plantar fasciitis. N Engl J Med. 2004;350(21):2159-2166. [PMID: 15152061]

## Item 41     Answer: E

**Educational Objective:** Diagnose rotator cuff tendinitis.

Rotator cuff tendinitis, an inflammation of the supraspinatus and/or infraspinatus tendon that can also involve the subacromial bursa, is a common overuse injury. This injury is characterized by subacromial tenderness and impingement—painful compression of the rotator cuff tendons and subacromial bursa between the humeral head and the acromion with arm elevation. Pain in patients with rotator cuff tendinitis often occurs with reaching overhead and when lying on the shoulder. The passive painful-arc maneuver assesses the degree of impingement. The examiner places one hand on the acromion and the other on the forearm and abducts the arm while preventing the patient from shrugging. Subacromial pain at 60 to 70 degrees of abduction suggests moderate impingement, while pain at 45 degrees or less suggests severe impingement. Pain with resisted mid-arc abduction is a specific finding for rotator cuff tendinitis. Appropriate treatments for acute tendinitis include NSAIDs, ice, and exercises; overhead reaching and lifting should be limited.

Adhesive capsulitis (frozen shoulder) is characterized by a decreased range of shoulder motion predominantly resulting from stiffness rather than from pain or weakness.

Bicipital tendinitis is also an overuse injury in which the bicipital groove may be tender, and anterior shoulder pain is elicited with resisted forearm supination or elbow flexion.

Glenohumeral arthritis is often related to trauma and the gradual onset of pain and stiffness over months to years.

A torn rotator cuff usually results in arm weakness, particularly with abduction and/or external rotation. A positive drop-arm test (inability to smoothly lower the affected arm from full abduction) is a very specific but relatively insensitive method for diagnosing rotator cuff tear.

### KEY POINT

- **Rotator cuff tendinitis is characterized by subacromial tenderness and impingement; pain often occurs with reaching overhead and when lying on the shoulder.**

**Bibliography**

Koester MC, George MS, Kuhn JE. Shoulder impingement syndrome. Am J Med. 2005;118(5):452-455. [PMID: 15866244]

## Item 42     Answer: A

**Educational Objective:** Treat dyspnea in a palliative care setting.

The home hospice nurse of this patient should be advised to administer the immediate-release morphine to treat the dyspnea. In terminally ill patients with malignancy or cardiopulmonary disease, narcotics can be an effective treatment for dyspnea. In a randomized trial that evaluated narcotics for dyspnea in patients already on these medications for pain, the intensity of dyspnea and the respiration rate improved with administration of a supplemental dose of opioid. In a study of cancer patients who were not oxygen dependent, cautious titration of parenteral opioids was not associated with respiratory depression. Similar studies have not been performed with oral agents.

An emergency department visit is unlikely to provide long-term improvements in comfort or prognosis and is generally inappropriate for a hospice patient.

The results of the patient's physical examination are consistent with a right pleural effusion. A right pleural effusion could be a sign of heart failure; however, the patient does not have any other signs suggestive of heart failure. Therefore, a diuretic such as furosemide is not indicated.

Although supplemental oxygen is often used in the palliative care setting to relieve dyspnea in nonhypoxemic patients with malignancy, this approach is not effective. A meta-analysis demonstrated no improvement in patients' perception of dyspnea at activity or at rest after receiving 4 to 10 L/min of oxygen.

### KEY POINT

- **Morphine is effective in treating cancer-related dyspnea as well as dyspnea related to end-stage cardiopulmonary disorders.**

**Bibliography**

Estfan B, Mahmoud F, Shaheen P, et al. Respiratory function during parenteral opioid titration for cancer pain. Palliat Med. 2007;21(2): 81-86. [PMID: 17344255]

## Item 43     Answer: C

**Educational Objective:** Manage erectile dysfunction in a patient with coronary artery disease.

The most appropriate management option for this patient is to begin a phosphodiesterase-5 (PDE-5) inhibitor, such as sildenafil, tadalafil, or vardenafil. The usual energy expenditure for sexual intercourse is less than or equal to 4 metabolic equivalents (METs), which correlates with the ability to walk at least two blocks at a good pace or climb at least one flight of stairs without stopping or developing symptoms (chest pain or shortness of breath). The Princeton Consensus Conference guidelines for the management of erectile dysfunction in the cardiovascular patient can be used to determine the need for further cardiac evaluation and whether it is safe to prescribe treatment to allow the patient to resume sexual activity. This patient's self-reported activity is greater than 4 METs, and his angina is mild and stable. According to the Princeton guidelines, he is low risk and he does not require further cardiac evaluation, and as long as he is not being treated with nitrates, it is safe to prescribe a PDE-5 inhibitor for his erectile dysfunction.

Most patients with heart disease are low risk. The Princeton guidelines define *low risk* as patients with:

- No symptoms and fewer than three major cardiovascular risk factors (excluding gender) (this category applies to patients without known heart disease)
- Controlled hypertension
- Mild stable angina

- Post–successful coronary revascularization
- Uncomplicated myocardial infarction 6-8 weeks previously in patients who do not have exercise-induced ischemia or who have undergone coronary revascularization
- Mild valvular disease
- Asymptomatic left ventricular dysfunction

If this patient does not respond to an adequate trial of the PDE-5 inhibitor, it would be reasonable to obtain a testosterone level; however, a testosterone level does not need to be obtained at the time of the initial evaluation unless there is decreased libido or physical signs suggestive of hypogonadism, which are not present in this patient.

The $\alpha_2$-adrenergic receptor blocker yohimbine has been suggested as an effective treatment for men with psychogenic erectile dysfunction, but clinical studies have demonstrated limited efficacy. Furthermore, because of its cardiovascular side effects, including tachycardia and hypertension, yohimbine is best avoided in patients with cardiovascular disease.

**KEY POINT**

- **Patients classified by the Princeton Consensus Conference guidelines as low risk for sexual activity can safely initiate or resume sexual activity and can be treated for sexual dysfunction without additional cardiovascular evaluation.**

**Bibliography**
McVary KT. Clinical practice. Erectile dysfunction. N Engl J Med. 2007;357(24):2472-2481. [PMID: 18077811]

## Item 44     Answer: C

**Educational Objective:** **Manage a patient at high risk for developing pressure ulcers.**

This patient has many risk factors for pressure ulcers, including advanced age, reduced mobility, inadequate nutrition, and urinary incontinence. The most appropriate preventive measure for this patient is a foam mattress overlay. A systematic review concluded that specialized foam mattresses/overlays and specialized sheepskin overlays reduce the incidence of pressure ulcers compared with standard hospital mattresses.

Since a targeted preventive approach to pressure ulcers is less costly than one focused on treating established ulcers, evaluation of patients by health care providers should include identifying patients at risk as quickly as possible. Expert opinion recommends the consistent use of a validated risk assessment tool, such as the Braden and Norton scales, supplemented by clinical judgment. Health care workers should regularly inspect the skin of patients at risk, and patients who are willing and able should be instructed to inspect their own skin.

Whether there is any additional advantage for ulcer prevention by using a "higher-tech" air-fluidized bed is unclear. These beds are much more expensive, are difficult to move, make nursing care more difficult, and are usually reserved for treating patients with established ulcers, mostly in a hospital setting.

The preferred seat cushion is one that distributes pressure uniformly over the weight-bearing body surface. Doughnut cushions do not do this and should not be used.

Avoiding friction, shear, and excessive skin moisture (for example, from perspiration, urinary or fecal incontinence, or excessive wound drainage) is important and should be part of routine care. Underpads on the bed or adult diapers, combined with consistent skin cleansing, are adequate for managing most patients with urinary incontinence. An indwelling or condom catheter is sometimes needed when treating an ulcer, but its use is probably unnecessary and potentially harmful in this patient with occasional incontinence. Massaging of pressure points adds to skin friction and increases the risk of early skin breakdown and should be avoided.

**KEY POINT**

- **Specialized foam mattresses/overlays reduce the incidence of pressure ulcers compared with standard hospital mattresses.**

**Bibliography**
Reddy M, Gill SS, Rochon, PA. Preventing pressure ulcers: a systematic review. JAMA. 2006;296(8):974-984. [PMID: 16926357]

## Item 45     Answer: D

**Educational Objective:** **Manage temporomandibular joint disorder.**

Chronic jaw aching aggravated by chewing or other activities that require opening and closing the mouth is consistent with a diagnosis of temporomandibular joint (TMJ) disorder. Clenching of the jaws during the day, grinding the teeth (bruxism) at night, and locking or catching of the TMJ may also be present. Common comorbid conditions include depression and functional somatic disorders such as irritable bowel syndrome, fibromyalgia, and chronic fatigue syndrome. Self-care measures are initially recommended for management of TMJ disorders. Jaw exercises, including relaxation and passive stretching, and NSAIDs may be beneficial. Other self-care strategies considered to be effective include efforts to reduce abnormal clenching while awake, application of hot packs, and counseling regarding stress reduction.

Arthroscopic surgery for patients with objective TMJ derangements is a treatment of last resort, although controlled clinical trials regarding the efficacy of surgery are lacking. There is also no evidence to support the use of intra-articular corticosteroid injections for treating this disorder.

Because TMJ disorder is primarily a clinical diagnosis, neither imaging studies, such as CT scans, nor laboratory tests are routinely recommended or helpful.

A recent clinical trial that randomized patients to receiving hard intraoral splints plus self-care, soft intraoral splints plus self-care, and self-care alone found no differences in clinical outcomes among the groups at 3, 6, and 12 months. Therefore, intraoral splints are not indicated as initial therapy. However, patients with persistent symptoms should be referred to a dentist to determine if splinting is warranted.

> **KEY POINT**
> - Self-care measures, including jaw exercises and NSAIDs, are the initial therapy for patients with temporomandibular joint disorder.

**Bibliography**
Truelove E, Huggins KH, Mancl L, Dworkin SF. The efficacy of traditional, low-cost and nonsplint therapies for temporomandibular disorder: a randomized controlled trial. J Am Dent Assoc. 2006; 137(8):1099-1107. [PMID: 16873325]

## Item 46    Answer:  B
**Educational Objective:** Evaluate vertigo in a patient with risk factors for stroke.

This patient with severe vertigo has symptoms concerning for a cerebellar infarction. In addition, he has several risk factors for stroke, including diabetes mellitus, hypertension, hyperlipidemia, and age. The finding of ataxia involving the right upper extremity further suggests a focal cerebellar lesion. He should undergo immediate MRI of the brain.

The patient had a normal cardiac examination and an unchanged electrocardiogram. Although the patient has a history of cardiac disease, further cardiac testing and monitoring for arrhythmias is not a priority in the absence of symptoms or electrocardiographic changes and is unlikely to uncover an etiology for acute vertigo.

Constant, severe vertigo that is not self limited and may be associated with nausea and vomiting is characteristic of both posterior circulation cerebrovascular disease and vestibular neuronitis. Vestibular neuronitis is often difficult to differentiate from posterior circulation cerebral ischemia. The disorders are differentiated by characteristic examination findings on the Dix-Hallpike maneuver, the presence of associated neurologic findings in stroke, general preservation of auditory function in stroke, and neuroimaging studies. If this patient were able to tolerate a Dix-Hallpike maneuver, nonfatiguing vertical nystagmus with no latent period would have supported a central cause of vertigo, such as stroke, rather than a peripheral cause, such as vestibular neuronitis. However, truncal ataxia and limb ataxia are more characteristic of a cerebellar infarction than vestibular neuronitis. Therefore, treatment for vestibular neuronitis with methylprednisolone is not indicated.

Treatment with meclizine may help the patient's vertigo symptoms; however, he needs a brain MRI to rule out stroke.

> **KEY POINT**
> - Patients with risk factors for stroke who present with acute vertigo should undergo brain MRI.

**Bibliography**
Savitz SI, Caplan LR. Vertebrobasilar disease. N Engl J Med. 2005;352(25):2618-2626. [PMID: 15972868]

## Item 47    Answer:  D
**Educational Objective:** Determine the appropriate preoperative cardiac evaluation for a patient at low risk for cardiac disease.

This patient with multiple medical problems is scheduled for a low-risk surgical procedure (<1% cardiac complications), and it is unlikely that any intervention will decrease this risk even more. The American College of Cardiology/American Heart Association (ACC/AHA) guidelines recommend no additional testing before low-risk surgery, assuming that a patient has no "active cardiac conditions" (unstable coronary syndromes, decompensated heart failure, hemodynamically significant arrhythmias, severe valvular heart disease).

Although this patient's blood pressure and glucose values are not optimally controlled based on long-term target goals, there is no evidence that these findings will increase the risk of postoperative complications for low-risk procedures. Hypertension is not an independent predictor of postoperative cardiac complications. Blood pressure less than or equal to 180/110 mm Hg does not appear to increase the risk for perioperative cardiac complications. There is no clear evidence regarding desirable targets for glucose control in patients with diabetes mellitus, as reflected in the varying glucose targets recommended by different guidelines. Therefore, surgery should not be postponed in order to improve glucose control.

> **KEY POINT**
> - There is no benefit for cardiac testing prior to low-risk surgery in the absence of unstable coronary syndromes, decompensated heart failure, hemodynamically significant arrhythmias, or severe valvular heart disease.

**Bibliography**
Fleisher LA, Beckman JA, Brown KA, et al. ACC/AHA 2007 Guidelines on Perioperative Cardiovascular Evaluation and Care for Noncardiac Surgery: Executive Summary: A Report of the American College of Cardiology/American Heart Association Task Force on Practice Guidelines (Writing Committee to Revise the 2002 Guidelines on Perioperative Cardiovascular Evaluation for Noncardiac Surgery) Developed in Collaboration With the American Society of Echocardiography, American Society of Nuclear Cardiology, Heart Rhythm Society, Society of Cardiovascular Anesthesiologists, Society for Cardiovascular Angiography and Interventions, Society for Vascular Medicine and Biology, and Society for Vascular Surgery [erratum in J Am Coll Cardiol. 2008;52(9):794-797]. J Am Coll Cardiol. 2007;50(17):1707-1732. [PMID: 17950159]

## Item 48    Answer:  C
**Educational Objective:** Treat perimenopausal symptoms.

Estrogen replacement therapy (ERT) provides significant relief for hot flushes associated with menopause in 50% to

90% of patients. There is no clear benefit of one estrogen-containing product over another. Relief of hot flushes is the primary (arguably the only) indication for ERT, although it also reduces the rate of postmenopausal bone density loss. However, the benefits of ERT must be weighed against the risks, which include potential increased rates of breast cancer, thromboembolic events, and cardiac events.

Contraindications to estrogen use include undiagnosed vaginal bleeding, breast cancer, other estrogen-sensitive cancers, current or previous history of venous or arterial thrombosis, and liver dysfunction or disease. The U.S. Food and Drug Administration recommends use of the smallest effective dose of hormone replacement therapy for the shortest duration possible to treat menopausal symptoms.

Although some studies have reported positive results with black cohosh, reports have been inconsistent, and the methodologically strongest studies have found no evidence of benefit. Conclusive evidence is similarly lacking for other alternative medicines such as soy proteins and red clover.

Prescription treatments for which there is some evidence of benefit in patients with hot flushes include the selective serotonin and norepinephrine reuptake inhibitors venlafaxine and desvenlafaxine and selective serotonin reuptake inhibitors such as citalopram, paroxetine, fluvoxamine, and fluoxetine. These can be considered as second-line agents, especially in women who also have some symptoms of mood or anxiety disorders. It is hypothesized that hot flushes are pathophysiologically associated with increased noradrenergic activity and decreased serotonergic activity, so it is likely that the blockage of serotonin reuptake is responsible for the benefits with these agents. Other agents that may relieve hot flushes include mirtazapine and gabapentin. Conversely, an agent such a bupropion, which acts primarily on the noradrenergic system without serotonergic effects, would be less likely to be effective. The lack of efficacy of bupropion in the relief of hot flushes was, in fact, demonstrated in one small study.

Raloxifene is a selective estrogen receptor modulator that is approved for the prevention of postmenopausal bone mass loss, but it does not help with hot flushes or other postmenopausal symptoms, and may even worsen them.

**KEY POINT**

- Estrogen replacement therapy provides effective relief of hot flushes, but its use must be weighed against the potential adverse effects.

**Bibliography**

Alexander JL, Burger H, Dennerstein L, et al. Treatment of vasomotor symptoms in the menopausal transition and postmenopausally: psychiatric comorbidity. Expert Rev Neurother. 2007;7(11 Suppl):S115-S137. [PMID: 18039061]

## Item 49          Answer:  A
**Educational Objective:**  Manage morbid obesity.

This patient has been unable to lose sufficient weight on two different types of diet, exercise, pharmacologic therapy,

and counseling. A 2005 American College of Physicians clinical guideline recommends that surgery should be considered as a treatment option for patients with a BMI of 40 or greater in whom an adequate exercise and diet program (with or without adjunctive drug therapy) has failed and who present with obesity-related comorbid conditions. One recent study demonstrated weight losses from baseline were 25% for gastric bypass and 14% for gastric banding. When adjusted for age, sex, and comorbidities, the surgical group (bypass and banding groups combined) had a significant 29% reduction in mortality compared with the control (nonsurgical treatment) group.

Very-low-calorie diets of less than 800 kcal/d are difficult to administer and are associated with an increased risk of adverse effects and are not generally recommended. Furthermore, switching to a very-low-calorie diet is unlikely to be successful, as the patient could not comply with a low-carbohydrate diet in the past.

Continuing sibutramine is not an appropriate option because the patient has been on sibutramine for 2 years, the maximum recommended by the manufacturer. Patients on orlistat lost an average of 2.9 kg (6.4 lb) in a recent meta-analysis. Even assuming that he does not gain weight after stopping sibutramine, given the amount of weight loss likely with orlistat, his BMI would still be above 40. Sustained weight loss with bariatric surgery will reduce his cardiovascular risk and potentially improve his comorbid conditions, as well.

**KEY POINT**

- Bariatric surgery should be considered in patients with a BMI above 40 who have acceptable surgical risk, have failed to benefit from nonsurgical weight loss, and have serious comorbidities.

**Bibliography**

Sjöström L, Narbro K; Sjöström CD, et al; Swedish Obese Subjects Study. Effects of bariatric surgery on mortality in Swedish obese subjects. N Engl J Med. 2007;357(8):741-752. [PMID: 17715408]

## Item 50          Answer:  C
**Educational Objective:** Treat postherpetic neuralgia.

Herpes zoster (shingles), which is caused by reactivation of the varicella-zoster virus, is usually a self-limited disease in immunocompetent patients. However, treatment is warranted because of the frequent complications of acute pain and postherpetic neuralgia, a debilitating disorder that occurs most often in persons 60 years of age and older. Gabapentin is approved by the U.S. Food and Drug Administration for the treatment of postherpetic neuralgia; it is an effective and well-tolerated treatment for neuropathic pain. In addition, immunization of immunocompetent adults older than 60 years reduces the incidence and severity of herpes zoster and postherpetic neuralgia.

The major risk factors for postherpetic neuralgia are increasing age and severity of the acute infection (pain and extent of rash) but not immunosuppression. Spontaneous resolution of postherpetic neuralgia is common, particularly in the first 6 months after presentation; however, medical treatment may be indicated for pain that interferes with functioning or sleep. Several studies have demonstrated decreased pain and improved sleep in patients with postherpetic neuralgia who took gabapentin.

Clinical trials with antiviral drugs for herpes zoster have focused on patients presenting within 72 hours of lesion onset; the value of antiviral therapy in the treatment of acute infection for patients presenting beyond 72 hours has not been adequately studied, and the late use of acyclovir has not shown efficacy in reducing postherpetic neuralgia.

NSAIDs such as ibuprofen are effective for somatic pain, but have not been shown to provide significant benefit for neuropathic pain and, in particular, randomized controlled studies have failed to demonstrate effectiveness in the treatment of postherpetic neuralgia.

Topical application of capsaicin (a hot pepper extract that depletes substance P from nerve endings) can provide relief of postherpetic neuralgia. However, the local stinging and burning associated with application of capsaicin cream may be intolerable for some patients and up to one third of patients discontinue capsaicin owing to intolerable discomfort. Capsaicin is not considered a first-line therapy for postherpetic neuralgia.

### KEY POINT

- **Gabapentin is an effective and well tolerated treatment for neuropathic pain and is approved for the treatment of postherpetic neuralgia.**

**Bibliography**

Hempenstall K, Nurmikko TJ, Johnson RW, A'Hern RP, Rice AS. Analgesic therapy in postherpetic neuralgia: a quantitative systemic review. PLoS Med 2005;2(7):e164. [PMID: 16013891]

## Item 51    Answer:  C

**Educational Objective:** Diagnose acute central retinal artery occlusion.

This patient presents with the acute onset of painless visual loss, which should immediately raise concern for an ischemic vascular event, in this case a central retinal artery occlusion (CRAO). CRAO classically presents in a 50- to 70-year-old patient, often in the early morning hours, with an abrupt but painless loss of vision. Risk factors include atherosclerosis, diabetes mellitus, hypertension, hypercholesterolemia, hypercoagulable states, and migraine. This patient has notable physical examination findings typical of CRAO: markedly diminished visual acuity; an afferent pupillary defect; and a pale fundus, with a "cherry red spot" near the fovea. Central visual acuity may be preserved if the retina is perfused by the cilioretinal artery.

CRAO represents a "stroke to the eye." Interventions to restore perfusion are essential, as permanent visual loss may result within 90 to 100 minutes from symptom onset,

although the most effective intervention is not known. Immediate consultation with an ophthalmologist is essential. Ocular massage for 15 minutes, agents to lower the intraocular pressure, and lying the patient flat may help the plaque or clot to migrate and can be initiated immediately.

Acute angle-closure glaucoma can result in acute visual loss that is typically painful, in contrast to this patient's presentation. Additionally, patients present with headache, seeing halos around lights, conjunctival injection, a pupil that is mid-dilated and sluggish or fixed in reaction to light, and sometimes a clouded cornea.

An acute stroke may cause loss of vision. Neurologic findings in this patient are absent, other than for monocular visual loss, which would be unusual as the sole presenting feature of an occipital stroke. Furthermore, the funduscopic findings are typical of CRAO and would not be seen in an ischemic event to the occipital lobes.

Central retinal vein occlusion (CRVO) may also present with the abrupt onset of painless, monocular visual loss. In contrast to CRAO, however, the retina is notable for hemorrhages, "cotton wool" spots, or the classic "blood and thunder" appearance of extensive edema and hemorrhages.

Symptoms of retinal detachment include the relatively sudden and painless onset of floaters. The peripheral vision is usually affected first, and then symptoms may progress over days or weeks to involve the central vision. The abrupt onset of near complete monocular visual loss and the appearance of the retina in this patient make retinal detachment unlikely.

### KEY POINT

- **The acute onset of painless visual loss suggests the possibility of a central retinal artery occlusion, which is a medical emergency.**

**Bibliography**

Vortmann M, Schneider JI. Acute monocular visual loss. Emerg Med Clin North Am. 2008;26(1):73-96. [PMID: 18249258]

## Item 52    Answer:  C

**Educational Objective:** Diagnose osteonecrosis of the hip.

This patient most likely has osteonecrosis of the hip. Osteonecrosis, or avascular necrosis of the femoral head in adults, is often associated with trauma, sickle cell disease, alcohol abuse, gout, corticosteroid use, and hypercoagulable states; it can also be idiopathic. Pain is the most common symptom and is usually located in the groin; thigh and buttock pain is also common. Plain film radiography is often the initial diagnostic test, and early findings may include increased density, reflecting marrow infarction and calcification. However, changes on plain film radiography may take weeks to months to appear and, therefore, this modality is insensitive in the diagnosis of early osteonecrosis. MRI has a reported sensitivity for osteonecrosis that exceeds 90% and is positive when other studies are negative. It is the preferred imaging modality, particularly if initial plain radiographs are normal.

Septic arthritis should always be considered in a patient with acute monoarticular arthritis. However, in the absence of previous hip disease or prosthesis, septic arthritis of the hip is relatively rare. The history of systemic lupus erythematosus and long-term corticosteroid use makes osteonecrosis a much more likely diagnosis and dictates MRI as the initial diagnostic study, rather than arthrocentesis.

Localized osteoporosis may occur in patients with injuries and is a prominent feature of complex regional pain syndrome (reflex sympathetic dystrophy), characterized by pain in the extremities associated with swelling, limited range of motion, vasomotor instability, and skin changes. Bone densitometry is not indicated in this patient because she has no history of injury and none of the symptoms characteristic of complex regional pain syndrome.

Radionuclide bone scan is also a sensitive indicator of osteonecrosis that is likely to be abnormal when plain radiography is nondiagnostic. Radionuclide bone scan is typically reserved for patients who have a contraindication for MRI (for example, metal implants).

**KEY POINT**

- **MRI is more than 90% sensitive in the diagnosis of osteonecrosis and is positive when other studies are negative.**

**Bibliography**

Petrigliano FA, Lieberman JR. Osteonecrosis of the hip: novel approaches to evaluation and treatment. Clin Orthop Relat Res. 2007;465:53-62. [PMID: 17906590]

## Item 53    Answer:  A

**Educational Objective:**  Manage hyperlipidemia in a patient with a history of transient ischemic attack.

This patient with carotid artery disease and transient ischemic attack (TIA) is considered by the Adult Treatment Panel III to have coronary artery–equivalent disease. In such patients, the LDL cholesterol goal is lower than 100 mg/dL (2.59 mmol/L) to reduce the risk for future coronary events. Additionally, the American Heart Association/American Stroke Association and the National Stroke Association recommend aggressive risk factor reduction for the secondary prevention of stroke following an ischemic stroke or TIA. There is also accumulating evidence that reduction of blood pressure and treatment with a statin may prevent recurrent stroke even in patients with no evidence of hypertension or hyperlipidemia based upon current thresholds for treatment.

The SPARCL study first demonstrated that in patients with stroke or TIA, secondary prevention with a statin reduced the incidence of a second ischemic stroke. Although a posthoc analysis also demonstrated an increased incidence of hemorrhagic stroke, the number needed to treat to prevent one stroke was 51 and the number needed to harm to cause one hemorrhagic stroke was 110; therefore, the benefits of statin therapy outweigh the risks in patients with a previous ischemic stroke or TIA.

Changing antihypertensive medication to a β-blocker or calcium channel blocker in this patient is not indicated. The 2006 American Heart Association/American Stroke Association guidelines recommend antihypertensive therapy for all patients with a stroke and TIA, and support the use of diuretics and the combination of diuretics and an angiotensin-converting enzyme inhibitor.

Nicotinic acid is a lipid-lowering agent that, in addition to reducing LDL cholesterol level, reduces triglyceride level and increases HDL cholesterol level. However, statins are first-line therapy for LDL cholesterol lowering in the absence of contraindications, and this patient has normal levels of triglycerides and HDL cholesterol.

**KEY POINT**

- **In patients who have had a stroke or transient ischemic attack, the LDL cholesterol goal is less than 100 mg/dL (2.59 mmol/L) to lower coronary event risk; statin therapy should also be considered to prevent recurrence of ischemic stroke.**

**Bibliography**

O'Regan C, Wu P, Arora D, Perri D, Mills EJ. Statin therapy in stroke prevention: a meta-analysis involving 121,000 patients. Am J Med. 2008;121(1):24-33. [PMID: 18187070]

## Item 54    Answer:  C

**Educational Objective:**  Diagnose vasomotor (nonallergic) rhinitis.

This patient has chronic vasomotor (nonallergic) rhinitis, which is caused by increased sensitivity to irritants in the air. The pathophysiology of vasomotor rhinitis is less clear than that of allergic rhinitis, but the chemical mediators causing symptoms are similar in both conditions. Symptoms of vasomotor rhinitis include nasal congestion and rhinorrhea and may develop after exposure to odors, humidity, temperature change, and alcohol. Sneezing and itching occur less often than in allergic rhinitis. Some experts consider the diagnosis one of exclusion. Results of skin tests and radioallergosorbent tests are normal in patients with vasomotor rhinitis and can be used to differentiate this condition from allergic rhinitis. Some patients have both allergic and nonallergic rhinitis. Chronic nonallergic rhinitis is less responsive to therapy than is allergic rhinitis. Topical intranasal corticosteroids, topical intranasal antihistamine, and topical ipratropium are the most consistently effective treatments.

Allergic rhinitis is unlikely in this patient because his symptoms are increased by humidity and pollutants, and there is no seasonal variation in symptoms, no family history of allergies, and no constitutional symptoms associated with allergic rhinitis. In addition, most patients develop allergic rhinitis before 20 years of age.

Chronic sinusitis is unlikely in this patient because of the absence of mucopurulent nasal drainage, facial pain or pressure, or decreased sense of smell.

Rhinitis medicamentosa refers to the syndrome of rebound nasal congestion after discontinuing topical α-adrenergic decongestant sprays. Symptoms may occur after using these sprays for 5 or more days and resolve with prolonged discontinuation of these agents. However, this patient has not used nasal sprays. Rhinitis may be induced by other drugs, as well. Medications generally associated with drug-induced rhinitis include aspirin, NSAIDs, oral contraceptive agents, angiotensin-converting enzyme inhibitors, prazosin, methyldopa, β-blockers, and chlorpromazine.

### KEY POINT

- **Chronic vasomotor (nonallergic) rhinitis should be considered in patients who develop perennial nasal congestion and rhinorrhea after 20 years of age, whose symptoms are exacerbated by irritant rather than allergic triggers, and who do not have a family history of allergies.**

**Bibliography**

Quillen DM, Feller DB. Diagnosing rhinitis: allergic vs. nonallergic. Am Fam Physician. 2006;73(9):1583-1590. [PMID: 16719251]

## Item 55     Answer:  C

**Educational Objective:**  Screen for hearing impairment in an elderly patient.

Screening for hearing loss is important in elderly persons because hearing impairment is prevalent but frequently underdiagnosed in this population. In addition, significant hearing loss is still possible despite a patient's denial of having trouble hearing. A recent systematic review evaluated the accuracy and precision of office clinical maneuvers for diagnosing hearing impairment. The whispered-voice test is a quick and easy assessment tool that has the best test characteristics among the office maneuvers. This test assesses the ability to hear a whispered voice with the examiner standing behind the patient 2 feet from the patient's ear while occluding and simultaneously rubbing the opposite external auditory canal and whispering three numbers or letters. Using a battery-powered handheld audioscope is an acceptable alternative screening modality.

The systematic review also found that the Screening Hearing Handicap Inventory and the Weber and Rinne tests did not perform as well as the whispered-voice test in detecting hearing impairment.

Referring patients for formal audiometry, although the gold standard for evaluating hearing loss, is expensive and time consuming. It is also unnecessary to do routinely, since a normal result on the whispered-voice test effectively rules out significant hearing loss.

### KEY POINT

- **Elderly persons should be screened for hearing impairment with the whispered-voice test or the handheld audioscopy, even if they deny having a hearing problem.**

**Bibliography**

Bagai A, Thavendiranathan P, Detsky AS. Does this patient have hearing impairment? JAMA. 2006;295(4):416-428. [PMID: 16434632]

## Item 56     Answer:  E

**Educational Objective:**  Manage a patient with a low HDL cholesterol level.

The most appropriate management option for this patient is therapeutic lifestyle modification. This patient's HDL cholesterol is low, total cholesterol is below 200 mg/dL (5.18 mmol/L), and triglyceride level is borderline high. HDL cholesterol levels are inversely related to risk for the development of coronary artery disease (CAD). Patients such as this one, who have low HDL cholesterol as the primary lipid abnormality and who have no CAD, are managed with therapeutic lifestyle modification. Because exercise, weight loss, and tobacco cessation raise HDL cholesterol, physicians should counsel patients about these lifestyle changes.

Although this patient's risk for the development of CAD is increased because of his low HDL cholesterol level, his weight, his sedentary lifestyle, and his smoking status, a cardiac stress test is not indicated because he has no complaints of chest pain or CAD equivalents.

Medications such as gemfibrozil or nicotinic acid to treat isolated low HDL cholesterol are only indicated in the setting of CAD. Although in practice, nicotinic acid is often used for patients such as this one, therapeutic lifestyle changes should be attempted first.

LDL cholesterol goal is based on the presence or absence of five cardiovascular risk factors: smoking, hypertension (≥140/90 mm Hg or taking antihypertensive medication), older age (men ≥45 years, women ≥55 years), low HDL cholesterol (<40 mg/dL [1.04 mmol/L]), and family history of premature CAD (male first-degree relative <55 years or female first-degree relative <65 years). This patient has two major risk factors: cigarette smoking and low HDL cholesterol; therefore, his LDL cholesterol goal is 130 mg/dL (3.37 mmol/L). A statin is not indicated because his LDL cholesterol level is already below this goal.

### KEY POINT

- **Patients with low HDL cholesterol level as the primary lipid abnormality but no coronary artery disease should be treated with therapeutic lifestyle modification.**

**Bibliography**

Rubins HB, Robins SJ, Collins D, et al. Gemfibrozil for the secondary prevention of coronary heart disease in men with low levels of high-density lipoprotein cholesterol. Veterans Affairs High-Density

Lipoprotein Cholesterol Intervention Trial Study Group. N Engl J Med. 1999;341(6):410-418. [PMID: 10438259]

## Item 57 Answer: C

**Educational Objective:** Manage ankle sprain.

This patient's ability to bear weight and the absence of instability on examination are consistent with a grade I or II ankle sprain. Most patients with grade I sprains, which involve stretching of a ligament with mild pain and swelling but no joint instability or difficulty ambulating, do not seek medical care. Grade II sprains involve partial tears and are accompanied by moderate pain and disability and some difficulty bearing weight. Grade III sprains involve complete rupture of ligaments with significant swelling, tenderness, and an inability to bear weight. Fifteen percent of patients with sprains have complications involving fractures of the ankle or midfoot; however, decisions about routine radiography should be guided by the Ottawa ankle rules. These rules do not recommend a radiograph for an ankle injury unless there is bone tenderness at the posterior edge of either malleolus, pain and bone tenderness in the midfoot, or an inability to bear weight. A systematic review has determined this instrument to be nearly 100% sensitive and able to reduce the number of unnecessary radiographs by 30% to 40%. Because this patient is able to bear weight and does not have tenderness on the medial or lateral malleolus, neither plain film radiographs nor an MRI of the ankle would be appropriate.

The initial management of a sprained ankle is to Protect, Rest, Ice, Compress, and Elevate the injured ankle (PRICE treatment). The patient should have the PRICE treatment for 3 days, and then the injury should be reassessed. If the patient does not improve with conservative therapy, plain radiography may then be employed to look for fractures that were not apparent on the initial examination.

While an ankle joint corticosteroid injection might be appropriate for certain inflammatory arthropathies, it is not appropriate in an ankle sprain.

> ### KEY POINT
> - **The Ottawa ankle rules do not recommend a radiograph for an ankle injury unless there is bone tenderness at the posterior edge of either malleolus, pain and bone tenderness in the midfoot, or an inability to bear weight.**

### Bibliography
van Rijn RM, van Os AG, Bernsen RM, Luijsterburg PA, Koes BW, Bierma-Zeinstra SM. What is the clinical course of acute ankle sprains? A systematic literature review. Am J Med. 2008;121(4):324-331. [PMID: 18374692]

## Item 58 Answer: E

**Educational Objective:** Assess preoperative risk and need for cardiac testing in a patient undergoing total knee replacement.

According to the American College of Cardiology/American Heart Association guidelines, no further preoperative cardiac testing is indicated in a patient without "active cardiac conditions" (unstable coronary syndrome, decompensated heart failure, significant arrhythmia, or severe valvular heart disease) who has adequate exercise capacity. This patient was able to walk four or more blocks until 1 month ago, when his arthritis symptoms worsened, but he is still considered to have adequate exercise capacity. Despite multiple cardiac risk factors, he has stable cardiac symptoms and is on optimal medical therapy with good control of heart rate. A study of intermediate-cardiac-risk patients randomized to testing or no testing found no benefit to noninvasive cardiac testing if the heart rate was adequately controlled with β-blockers.

Coronary angiography is only indicated for patients with severe or unstable coronary artery disease or significant ischemia detected by noninvasive testing.

The goal of noninvasive testing is to identify a high-risk subgroup of patients who may benefit from coronary artery revascularization (patients with three or more cardiac risk factors and five or more abnormal segments on dobutamine stress echocardiography). Because this patient has adequate exercise capacity and only two clinical cardiac risk factors (history of ischemic heart disease, diabetes mellitus), noninvasive testing with dobutamine stress echocardiography would probably not alter management.

Even if the patient described here required cardiac testing, an exercise test (without a pharmacologic stressor) with nuclear imaging would be inadequate in someone who can only walk one block because he will not achieve 85% of his maximum heart rate. A resting echocardiogram has not been found to predict ischemic complications, but may be helpful in a patient with suspected valvular disease or heart failure, which this patient does not have.

> ### KEY POINT
> - **Preoperative cardiac testing is not indicated in a patient without active cardiac conditions (unstable coronary syndrome, decompensated heart failure, significant arrhythmia, or severe valvular heart disease) who has adequate exercise capacity.**

### Bibliography
Fleisher LA, Beckman JA, Brown KA, et al. ACC/AHA 2007 Guidelines on Perioperative Cardiovascular Evaluation and Care for Noncardiac Surgery: Executive Summary: A Report of the American College of Cardiology/American Heart Association Task Force on Practice Guidelines (Writing Committee to Revise the 2002 Guidelines on Perioperative Cardiovascular Evaluation for Noncardiac Surgery) Developed in Collaboration With the American Society of Echocardiography, American Society of Nuclear Cardiology, Heart Rhythm Society, Society of Cardiovascular Anesthesiologists, Society for Cardiovascular Angiography and Interventions, Society for Vascular Medicine and Biology, and Society for Vascular Surgery [erratum in J Am Coll Cardiol. 2008;52(9):794-797]. J Am Coll Cardiol. 2007;50(17):1707-1732. [PMID: 17950159]

## Item 59    Answer:    A

**Educational Objective:** Diagnose gradual hearing loss from acoustic neuroma.

This patient most likely has an acoustic neuroma, which is an important cause of asymmetric sensorineural hearing loss that usually originates from the vestibular portion of the acoustic nerve. The two major symptoms are hearing loss and tinnitus. Unilateral hearing loss occurs in approximately 90% of patients with this disorder, but many patients may be unaware of the deficit. Two thirds of patients have tinnitus. Both hearing loss and tinnitus are present, on average, slightly more than 3 years prior to diagnosis, although acoustic neuroma can cause sudden acute hearing loss. Other symptoms include dizziness and headaches. MRI is the imaging modality of choice because it is more sensitive than CT for detecting small tumors.

Cholesteatoma is a growth of desquamated, stratified, squamous epithelium within the middle ear. Patients may present with otorrhea, pain, hearing loss, or neurologic symptoms. Otosclerosis is a bony overgrowth that involves the footplate of the stapes, eventually resulting in total fixation and inability to transmit vibration from the tympanic membrane along the ossicular chain. Cholesteatomas and otosclerosis cause a conductive hearing loss rather than a sensorineural loss.

Although Meniere disease also causes unilateral sensorineural hearing loss, this is most often a low-frequency loss. Patients with Meniere disease usually have episodic vertigo that lasts for several hours and is associated with tinnitus and a sensation of aural fullness. Occasionally, patients experience episodic low-frequency hearing loss that develops on a daily, weekly, or monthly basis and remits within 12 to 24 hours.

Presbycusis is the term used to describe sensorineural hearing loss associated with aging. It is typically symmetric, starts in the high-frequency range, becomes more noticeable in the sixth decade, and steadily progresses. Patients experience problems understanding speech in a crowded or noisy environment and often have tinnitus. Unilateral or asymmetric hearing loss is not typical for presbycusis and requires further evaluation when present.

### KEY POINT
- **Hearing loss is unilateral in approximately 90% of patients with acoustic neuroma.**

**Bibliography**
Spoelhof GD. When to suspect an acoustic neuroma. Am Fam Physician. 1995;52(6):1768-1774. [PMID: 7484687]

## Item 60    Answer:    B

**Educational Objective:** Evaluate a fall in an elderly patient.

Risk factors for falling include lower extremity weakness, gait deficit, arthritis, impaired activities of daily living, female sex, and age over 80 years. Other risk factors for falls include balance deficits, impaired vision, depression, cognitive impairment, psychotropic drug use, and use of an assistive device. Because falls often have multiple causes and more than one predisposing risk factor, there is no standard diagnostic evaluation for patients who fall or are at risk for falling. However, evaluations should begin with balance and gait screening, such as the "get up and go" test. The "get up and go" test is appropriate for screening because it is a quantitative evaluation of general functional mobility. A strong association exists between performance on this test and a person's functional independence in activities of daily living. Persons are timed in their ability to rise from a chair, walk 10 feet, turn, and then return to the chair. Most adults can complete this task in 10 seconds, and most frail elderly persons, in 11 to 20 seconds. Those requiring more than 20 seconds should undergo a fall evaluation. Typically, this consists of a focused history and physical examination, much of which has already been performed in this patient. Further evaluation, including measurement of 25-hydroxyvitamin D levels, should be directed according to findings of the evaluation. Interventions to prevent falls should be tailored to the patient's needs.

A CT scan of the head, 24-hour electrocardiographic monitoring, and echocardiography are not routine studies for fall evaluation and should not be done before balance and gait screening.

### KEY POINT
- **For elderly persons following a single fall, the "get up and go" test is a good screening test for gait and balance problems that may warrant further evaluation.**

**Bibliography**
Kannus P, Sievänen H, Palvanen M, Järvinen T, Parkkari J. Prevention of falls and consequent injuries in elderly people. Lancet. 2005;366(9500):1885-1893. [PMID: 16310556]

## Item 61    Answer:    B

**Educational Objective:** Screen a patient for alcohol problems.

Alcohol abuse may be difficult to diagnose. Patients often present with complaints that may be attributable to other medical conditions but actually are caused by alcohol consumption. These problems might include depression, insomnia, injuries, gastroesophageal reflux disease, uncontrolled hypertension, and important social problems. Other potential clues to alcohol misuse are recurrent legal or marital problems, absenteeism or loss of employment, and committing or being the victim of violence. The U.S. Preventive Services Task Force (USPSTF) recommends routine screening of adults with either directed questioning or use of a standardized tool to identify persons whose alcohol use puts them at risk. More likely to be at risk are those with prior alcohol problems, young adults, and smokers. The USPSTF found good evidence that brief behavioral counseling interventions with follow-up produce small to moderate reductions in alcohol consumption that are sustained over 6- to 12-month periods or longer.

Although the optimal interval for screening is not known, screening at the time of an initial visit is clearly important. There are multiple screening instruments; the CAGE questionnaire is one of the most widely used. Two positive responses indicate that further assessment for alcohol misuse is warranted.

**C** Have you ever felt you should *cut down* on your drinking?

**A** Have people *annoyed* you by criticizing your drinking?

**G** Have you ever felt bad or *guilty* about your drinking?

**E** *Eye opener*. Have you ever had a drink first thing in the morning to steady your nerves or to get rid of a hangover?

The CAGE questionnaire has a reported sensitivity ranging from 43% to 94% and specificity ranging from 70% to 97%.

Laboratory tests such as an elevated mean corpuscular volume (sensitivity 63%; specificity 48%) and an elevated aspartate aminotransferase/alanine aminotransferase ratio (sensitivity 12%; specificity 91%) can be suggestive but are not diagnostic of alcohol abuse and dependence. Their relatively low sensitivities make them unsuited for screening.

Because of the short half-life of ethanol, a random ethanol level should not be used to screen for alcoholism.

**KEY POINT**

- **Screening instruments such as the CAGE questionnaire are effective for alcohol misuse screening in the primary care setting.**

**Bibliography**

Saitz R. Clinical practice. Unhealthy alcohol use. N Engl J Med. 2005;352(6):596-607. [PMID: 15703424]

## Item 62     Answer:  A

**Educational Objective:** Manage hyperlipidemia in a patient with coronary artery disease.

LDL cholesterol should be less than 100 mg/dL (2.59 mmol/L) in patients with coronary artery disease (CAD) or CAD-equivalent disease. In patients at very high risk, decreasing LDL cholesterol to less than 70 mg/dL (1.81 mmol/L) is considered a therapeutic option. This patient is at very high risk of future major cardiac events because she has diabetes mellitus and CAD. Most authorities would recommend using more aggressive drug therapy by adding a second lipid-lowering drug to further lower LDL cholesterol in patients such as this one.

Although increasing the statin dose for patients still above their LDL goal is a therapeutic option often employed in practice, the incremental reduction in LDL cholesterol by increasing the dose of a statin that is already near the maximal recommended dose is less than that which could be achieved by using combination therapy. In this patient, rosuvastatin is already at the maximum recommended dose. Adding a resin, nicotinic acid, or ezetimibe are reasonable options. Although the ENHANCE trial did not show a benefit of adding ezetimibe to simvastatin when carotid intimal thickness was used as the outcome, the American College of Cardiology Statement on the ENHANCE trial (www.acc.org/enhance.htm) concluded that major decisions could not be made on the basis of that trial and that ezetimibe remains a reasonable option for patients who cannot tolerate statins or do not reach goal with statins alone. Adding gemfibrozil in this patient would require lowering the dose of rosuvastatin to reduce the risk of myopathy. Because fenofibrate does not interfere with statin catabolism, there is less risk of myopathy if this is the fibrate chosen.

Substituting fenofibrate for rosuvastatin would further lower the triglyceride level, but, despite the fact that this patient's non-HDL cholesterol (158 mg/dL [4.09 mmol/L]) is above her goal of 130 mg/dL (3.37 mmol/L), LDL cholesterol lowering is the higher priority in this very-high-risk patient.

Substituting metformin for glipizide may have a beneficial effect on this patient's diabetes control, but her hemoglobin $A_{1c}$ is already less than 7%, and LDL cholesterol lowering is the higher priority.

**KEY POINT**

- **Combination lipid-lowering therapy is often necessary to reach lipid goals for very-high-risk patients.**

**Bibliography**

Drugs for Lipids. Treat Guidel Med Lett. 2008;6(66):9-16. [PMID: 18216759]

## Item 63     Answer:  B

**Educational Objective:** Treat chronic pain nonpharmacologically.

A systematic review jointly conducted by the American Pain Society and the American College of Physicians found that exercise is slightly to moderately superior to no treatment for chronic low back pain for pain relief at earliest follow-up. Several other reviews drew similar conclusions, and one review identified reduced sick leave in the first year, as well as a higher percentage of patients returning to work at 1 year. Other nonpharmacologic methods with some evidence to support them include cognitive-behavioral therapy, spinal manipulation, and interdisciplinary rehabilitation.

Ginkgo should be discouraged for this patient. While there are some studies of debatable quality suggesting potential benefits with ginkgo in depression, anxiety, and memory difficulties, there is very little evidence of efficacy in chronic pain. More concerning for this particular patient is that ginkgo can increase bleeding time or cause spontaneous hemorrhage.

There is some evidence of modest benefit with the local application of heat for chronic low back pain, but none for ice. Although St. John's wort is unlikely to be harmful, it is also unlikely to be of significant benefit, as the only condition for which it has some evidence of efficacy is mild to moderate depression. The Cochrane review of therapies for low back pain found that traction was no better than placebo, sham, or no treatment for any reported outcome.

### KEY POINT

- Nonpharmacologic therapies that may be helpful for chronic pain include graduated exercise, cognitive-behavioral therapy, spinal manipulation, and interdisciplinary rehabilitation.

### Bibliography

Chou R, Huffman LH; American Pain Society; American College of Physicians. Nonpharmacologic therapies for acute and chronic low back pain: a review of the evidence for an American Pain Society/American College of Physicians clinical practice guideline [erratum in Ann Intern Med. 2008;148(3):247-248]. Ann Intern Med. 2007;147(7):492-504. [PMID: 17909210]

## Item 64    Answer:   C

**Educational Objective:** Manage narcotic medications in a terminally ill patient with mild to moderate pain.

Patients with advanced malignancy often exceed the ability of non-narcotic analgesics to control their pain. In cancer patients with mild to moderate pain such as this one, an effective strategy is moving to step 2 on the World Health Organization three-step pain relief ladder by prescribing an intermittent low-dose narcotic in addition to adjuvant, non-narcotic pain medicine. The most appropriate management for this patient is adding a short-acting opioid medication such as immediate-release formulations of oxycodone, morphine, or oxymorphone.

Initiating a long-acting narcotic such as a fentanyl transdermal patch or extended-release oxycodone is not indicated until the patient's pain is adequately controlled with short-acting narcotics, which can be rapidly titrated to achieve adequate pain control. Once pain control is established, the cumulative dose of the short-acting opioid can be used to calculate an effective dose of a long-acting opioid, remembering to reduce the dose by 30% to 50% and maintaining access to a short-acting opioid for breakthrough pain. If the short-acting opioid is needed more than three times daily, the amount of long-acting opioid is increased. Long-acting opioids should not be used as initial therapy for moderate to severe pain because their long-half lives makes it impossible to quickly titrate the dose and control the patient's pain.

Changing the NSAID is much less likely to control this patient's pain than is adding a short-acting opioid analgesic.

### KEY POINT

- Low-dose narcotic pain medications combined with non-narcotic analgesics are often an effective treatment strategy for mild to moderate cancer-associated pain.

### Bibliography

Bruera E, Kim HN. Cancer Pain. JAMA. 2003;290(18):2476-2479. [PMID: 14612485]

## Item 65    Answer:   A

**Educational Objective:** Manage prostate cancer screening.

This 57-year-old asymptomatic man should participate in a discussion with his doctor about risks and benefits of screening for prostate cancer. In 2002, the U.S. Preventive Services Task Force (USPSTF) concluded that the evidence was insufficient to recommend for or against screening for prostate cancer using prostate-specific antigen (PSA) testing or digital rectal examination (DRE) and recommended that physicians discuss potential but uncertain benefits and possible harms (complications of future diagnostic testing and therapies, including incontinence, erectile dysfunction, and bowel dysfunction) before ordering PSA testing. In a 2008 update of the 2002 recommendations, the USPSTF recommended against screening for prostate cancer in men age 75 years or older. They noted that if screening is performed, men ages 50 to 70 years would benefit most. The USPSTF stated that men should be informed of the gaps and conflicting results in the evidence and should be assisted in considering their personal preferences before deciding whether to be tested. The American Cancer Society recommends that PSA testing be offered to men at age 50 years (age 45 years for men at high risk owing to a positive family history of prostate cancer or who are black) and that information about limitations and benefits be provided.

Two large randomized screening trials studied the effect of screening on rate of death from prostate cancer. There was no difference in the rate of death from prostate cancer between screened and control groups in the PLCO study. In the ERSPC trial, the prostate cancer death rate per 1000 person-years was 0.35 in the screened group versus 0.41 in the control group ($P = 0.04$). The number needed to screen was 1410 and the number needed to treat to prevent one prostate-cancer death over a 10-year period was 48. About 50% to 75% of those 48 men would be expected to have some complication of treatment. In evaluating the limited benefit seen in the ERSPC trial, one must consider the increased number of false diagnoses (false-positive rate of 75.9% of those undergoing biopsy) and unnecessary treatments.

### KEY POINT

- Physicians should discuss potential but uncertain benefits and possible harms before ordering prostate-specific antigen testing.

**Bibliography**

Barry MJ. Screening for prostate cancer—the controversy that refuses to die. NEJM. 2009;360(13):1351-1354. [PMID: 19297564]

## Item 66    Answer:    C

**Educational Objective:** Screen an older patient for depression.

This asymptomatic elderly man should be screened for depression. Depression is common in later life. Risk factors include older age, neurologic conditions including stroke and Parkinson disease, stressful life events, a personal or family history of depression, and other medical illnesses. The U.S. Preventive Services Task Force (USPSTF) has documented that screening adults in primary care settings leads to accurate identification of depression, a disorder for which treatment is often effective. The USPSTF recommends that screening be restricted to primary care settings in which an accurate diagnosis of depression can be made, effective treatment can be provided, and follow-up care is available. Screening should be considered in patients with the risk factors listed above (such as the stressful life events in the patient discussed here) and in those with unexplained or unrelated somatic symptoms; other psychological conditions, such as anxiety or substance abuse; chronic pain; or lack of response to usually effective treatment of other medical conditions.

A two-item screening instrument has a sensitivity of 96% and specificity of 57% for diagnosing depression. A "yes" response to either of the following questions constitutes a positive screen: *"Over the past 2 weeks have you felt down, depressed, or hopeless?"* and *"Over the past 2 weeks have you felt little interest or pleasure in doing things?"* A positive result on either of these screening measures should be followed by a full diagnostic interview to determine the presence of a depressive disorder.

Although the USPSTF recommends one-time ultrasonographic screening for abdominal aortic aneurysm in men 65 to 75 years of age who are current or former smokers, it does not extend this recommendation to never-smokers because of the lower risk of large aneurysms in this population.

The USPSTF does not recommend for or against screening for the diagnosis of peripheral arterial disease (such as determination of the ankle-brachial index) because there is little evidence that treatment, other than therapy based on standard cardiovascular risk factor assessment, is beneficial during the asymptomatic phase of this disease.

The USPSTF does not recommend for or against screening for dementia with instruments such as the Mini–Mental State Examination because of the potential harm of inaccurate diagnosis and the modest benefits of drug therapy for this disorder.

**KEY POINT**

- **Screening adults for depressive disorders in the primary care setting is recommended by the U.S. Preventive Services Task Force.**

**Bibliography**

Williams JW Jr, Noël PH, Cordes JA, Ramirez G, Pignone M. Is this patient clinically depressed? JAMA. 2002;287(9):1160-1170. [PMID: 11879114]

## Item 67    Answer:    C

**Educational Objective:** Recognize and manage an impaired physician.

It is often difficult to recognize impairment in a physician colleague because physicians are skilled at hiding the impairment. The physician presented has several behaviors that should raise concern for impairment. Signs of impairment at work may include frequent absences, missed appointments, secretive or inappropriate behavior, mood swings, conflict with colleagues, and heavy drinking at hospital functions. Impaired physicians may exhibit poor personal hygiene, bloodshot eyes, stumbling, or changes in speech patterns. Changes in clinical performance may appear late and indicate advanced impairment. Although physicians may be reluctant to report suspected physician impairment because of the desire to protect colleagues, fear of mislabeling a colleague as impaired, or fear of reprisals, every physician is responsible for protecting patients from an impaired physician. Physicians should report their concerns about colleagues to the hospital impaired physician program, or, lacking such a program, to the chief of the appropriate clinical service or to the hospital chief of staff.

Although showing support for the nurse involved may help temporarily defuse the situation, it does nothing to protect patients or get the impaired physician into treatment.

If a physician witnesses possible signs of impairment in a colleague, he or she has an obligation to report the suspected impairment regardless of whether others have similar suspicions. Determining if other physicians have witnessed similar behavior may delay reporting obligations based on one's own observations. If left unrecognized and untreated, remission and cure are unlikely. With appropriate treatment, 75% to 85% of physicians can be expected to return to work.

It is not appropriate to question the physician's staff about their employer's behavior nor does it contribute in any meaningful way to the resolution of the perceived problem. The best course of action is to use the established hierarchy in the health system to report concerns.

**KEY POINT**

- **Every physician is responsible for protecting patients from an impaired physician and should report any concerns to the hospital impaired physician program, or, lacking such a program, to the chief of the appropriate clinical service or to the hospital chief of staff.**

**Bibliography**

Baldisseri MR. Impaired healthcare professional. Crit Care Med. 2007;35(2 Suppl):S106-S116. [PMID: 17242598]

## Item 68      Answer:  D

**Educational Objective:**  Treat urge urinary incontinence.

This patient's symptoms are most consistent with urge urinary incontinence (overactive bladder), which is manifested by involuntary leakage of large amounts of urine. The incontinence is frequently preceded by a sense of urgency but an inability to get to the bathroom in time. This patient's memory loss and findings on the Mini–Mental State Examination could indicate early dementia, which is a risk factor for urge incontinence.

An anticholinergic agent such as tolterodine is effective in reducing episodes of urge incontinence. Oxybutynin is an alternative agent in the same drug class with similar efficacy. Although this patient has no signs or symptoms of benign prostatic hyperplasia, he should be monitored for difficulty urinating or urinary retention following initiation of any anticholinergic agent.

Doxazosin, like other α-adrenergic blockers, is effective for the urinary symptoms associated with benign prostatic hyperplasia, such as slow urinary stream, urinary hesitancy, and nocturia. However, doxazosin is not indicated for the treatment of urge incontinence.

Although tricyclic antidepressants such as imipramine have been used to treat urge incontinence, there is no strong evidence from clinical trials supporting their effectiveness in this setting.

Adrenergic drugs (phenylpropanolamine, norepinephrine, clenbuterol) have been principally studied for treatment of stress urinary incontinence in women, but have not proved superior to placebo or pelvic floor muscle training.

> **KEY POINT**
>
> - **Tolterodine and oxybutynin are anticholinergic agents that are effective for treating urge urinary incontinence.**

**Bibliography**

Gibbs CF, Johnson TM 2nd, Ouslander JG. Office management of geriatric urinary incontinence. Am J Med. 2007;120(3):211-220. [PMID: 17349439]

## Item 69      Answer:  D

**Educational Objective:**  Manage acute sinusitis.

This patient most likely has acute sinusitis. Most cases of acute sinusitis are due to a virus; only 0.5% to 2% are caused by bacteria. Signs and symptoms are not reliable for diagnostic purposes. A meta-analysis found that no symptoms or signs, including unilateral facial pain, pain in the teeth, pain on bending, or purulent nasal discharge, were precise enough to establish the diagnosis. In most patients, symptoms last up to 2 weeks and resolve without additional studies or administration of antibiotics.

Antibiotics are not indicated for this patient. Even though most patients with suspected acute sinusitis do receive antibiotics, there is little evidence to support the effectiveness of this practice. A randomized trial found that the duration of symptoms did not differ between patients who did and did not receive antibiotics. A meta-analysis found that although patients with more severe symptoms had a longer period of illness, antibiotics did not decrease symptom severity or duration of infection. However, some guidelines still recommend administration of antibiotics. If these agents are used, they should be limited to patients with at least two of the following findings: symptoms lasting longer than 7 days, facial pain, and purulent nasal discharge. The data as a whole suggest that if antibiotics are to be used, amoxicillin or doxycycline are adequate first-line agents. Trimethoprim-sulfamethoxazole is acceptable for β-lactam–allergic adults. The patient described here has only facial pain and does not meet the criteria for antibiotic administration by most guidelines.

Several randomized studies have addressed the use of various ancillary drug therapies, including a proteolytic enzyme (bromelain), α-adrenergic agonists (xylometazoline and oxymetazoline), a mucolytic agent (bromhexine), intranasal corticosteroids (budesonide and flunisolide), and an antihistamine (loratadine). In most patients, these agents were used in conjunction with antibiotics, and studies did not exclude patients with chronic sinusitis. Efficacy varied, but generally favorable trends were reported. When prescribing symptomatic treatment, selection of modalities should factor in cost, potential side effects, and strength of evidence supporting use.

Imaging studies, including CT or plain films of the sinuses and sinus aspiration, should be considered only in patients with predisposing factors for atypical microbial causes, such as pseudomonal or fungal infection, and in patients with AIDS or who are otherwise immunocompromised.

Patients who appear acutely ill or have a high fever, periorbital swelling, or neurologic signs may have serious complications of sinusitis and require further evaluation. When complications such as periorbital cellulitis or venous sinus thrombosis are suspected, urgent consultation with an ophthalmologist, neurosurgeon, infectious disease specialist, or neurologist is advised.

> **KEY POINT**
>
> - **Antibiotics are unlikely to be effective for most patients with suspected acute sinusitis.**

**Bibliography**

Young J, De Sutter A, Merenstein D, et al. Antibiotics for adults with clinically diagnosed acute rhinosinusitis: A meta-analysis of individual patient data. Lancet. 2008;371(9616):908-914. [PMID: 18342685]

## Item 70      Answer:  D

**Educational Objective:**  Treat fibromyalgia pain.

Fibromyalgia syndrome (FMS) is difficult to treat. Cognitive-behavioral therapy has been shown to be effective, as have rehabilitative outpatient programs based on appropriately managed increases in activity. The mainstay of adjunctive drug therapy in patients with FMS continues to be antidepressant drugs, which may be helpful for mood, pain, and sleep symptoms, but have a limited effect on overall health outcomes. Patients who have pain and require nighttime sedation may be treated with tricyclic antidepressants, which have been shown to be effective in combination with selective serotonin reuptake inhibitors (SSRIs) (for example, fluoxetine [off-label use]). Higher doses of SSRIs than those typically used for treating depression may be required to achieve a therapeutic response in some patients. Duloxetine, a selective serotonin and norepinephrine reuptake inhibitor, has been shown to be efficacious in alleviating most symptoms of fibromyalgia in patients with or without depression. As an alternative to antidepressant therapy or for patients who cannot tolerate antidepressant therapy, pregabalin is the most appropriate treatment to relieve this patient's symptoms. In a randomized, placebo-controlled trial, pregabalin significantly improved pain, sleep, fatigue, and health-related quality of life in patients with FMS. The most prominent side effects are somnolence and dizziness. Pregabalin and duloxetine are both approved by the U.S. Food and Drug Administration for treatment of fibromyalgia.

NSAIDs are no more effective in reducing FMS symptoms than placebo. There is limited evidence that combining NSAIDs with centrally acting drugs (off-label use) such as antidepressants or anticonvulsants may have a synergistic effect in treating FMS. However, adding naproxen alone will not provide significant relief of central sensitization pain for this patient. Similarly, prednisone is not beneficial in treating the symptoms of FMS, and there is a serious risk of short- and long-term side effects.

Narcotics such as oxycodone are best avoided in fibromyalgia and other central sensitization pain syndromes because of the potential for abuse and addiction, little evidence of efficacy, and undesirable side effects, such as sedation and constipation.

**KEY POINT**

- **Pregabalin reduces pain and improves functional status in patients with fibromyalgia.**

**Bibliography**

Abeles M, Solitar BM, Pillinger NH, Abeles AM. Update on fibromyalgia therapy. Am J Med. 2008;121(7):555-561. [PMID: 18589048]

## Item 71　　Answer:　E
**Educational Objective:**　Manage aphthous ulcers.

This patient has the characteristic findings of aphthous ulcers, including painful, well-defined, circular ulcerations that occur most often on the buccal and labial mucosa. Aphthous ulcers can develop on all areas of the oral mucosa except the hard palate, gingiva, and vermilion border (that is, the colored portion of the lips). Although these lesions are associated with inflammatory bowel disease, celiac disease, HIV infection, and Behçet syndrome, they are also idiopathic. Treatment is focused on providing symptomatic relief with topical corticosteroids in dental paste, topical over-the-counter analgesic agents, or chlorhexidine mouth rinses.

Oral ulcers are also associated with systemic lupus erythematosus (SLE). However, ulcers are rarely the first sign of disease activity in patients who have SLE with mucosal involvement, and ulcers that do develop most often involve the hard palate and vermilion border as well as the buccal mucosa. Therefore, an antinuclear antibody assay to diagnose SLE is not needed.

Biopsy to exclude malignancy is only indicated for patients with "major" aphthous ulcers, that is, lesions measuring greater than 1 cm with raised borders that have been present for 1 month or longer.

Nystatin is used to treat oral candidiasis, which is not usually associated with painful ulcers. In addition, this patient does not have the characteristic discrete white plaques on an erythematous base typical of this disorder.

Acyclovir is indicated for patients with herpes simplex virus infection. Although this virus also causes painful ulcers ("cold sores"), herpetic ulcers typically are clustered, measure 1 to 2 mm in diameter, become less painful in 1 or 2 days, and proceed from vesicles to crusting lesions in about 8 days. Recurrent oral herpes simplex lesions occur at the vermilion border, whereas aphthous ulcers never occur on keratinized skin surfaces.

**KEY POINT**

- **Treatment of aphthous ulcers is symptomatic and includes agents such as topical corticosteroids in dental paste, topical over-the-counter analgesic agents, or chlorhexidine rinses.**

**Bibliography**

Scully C. Clinical practice. Aphthous ulceration. N Engl J Med. 2006; 355(2):165-172. [PMID: 16837680]

## Item 72　　Answer:　A
**Educational Objective:**　Treat obesity.

The best management option for this patient is to add a weight loss medication such as orlistat with meals, with continued encouragement of diet and exercise. A meta-analysis of orlistat trials demonstrated an average weight loss of 2.9 kg (6.4 lb) compared with placebo. Repeated attempts at dietary modification and exercise have failed to treat this patient's obesity, which is likely a contributing factor to her hyperlipidemia, hypertension, and type 2 diabetes mellitus. According to the American College of Physicians clinical guideline, drug therapy can be offered to obese patients who have failed to achieve their weight loss goals through diet and exercise alone. Before initiating drug therapy, it is important to have a frank discussion with the patient regarding the drugs' side effects, safety data, and the temporary nature of the weight loss achieved with medications.

Sibutramine is a sympathomimetic agent that suppresses appetite and food intake. Like orlistat, it is an effective drug for weight loss. However, sibutramine increases systolic blood pressure and pulse and should not be used in patients with uncontrolled or poorly controlled hypertension or a history of cardiac disease. This patient's blood pressure is above target for a person with diabetes (130/80 mm Hg), and sibutramine would not be the best choice for her.

Medications are a common contributing factor to obesity, and sulfonylureas such as glipizide have been associated with weight gain. However, insulin is also associated with weight gain, and switching the patient's medication from glipizide to insulin is unlikely to be of benefit.

Referring the patient for bariatric surgery is not indicated, as the patient does not meet commonly established referral guidelines (BMI ≥40 or ≥35 with medical comorbidities such as sleep apnea, obesity-related cardiomyopathy, severe arthritis, hyperlipidemia, diabetes, or glucose intolerance).

> **KEY POINT**
> - **Pharmacologic treatment may be considered when obese patients fail to lose weight after an adequate trial of diet and exercise and treatment of any contributing comorbidities.**

**Bibliography**

Rucker D, Padwal R, Li SK, Curioni C, Lau DC. Long term pharmacotherapy for obesity and overweight: updated meta-analysis [erratum in BMJ. 2007 Nov 24;335(7629)]. BMJ. 2007;335(7631):1194-1199. [PMID: 18006966]

## Item 73    Answer:  B

**Educational Objective:** Manage episodic allergic rhinitis.

This patient has episodic allergic rhinitis characterized by typical symptoms of nasal congestion, rhinorrhea, sneezing, and itching with exposure to an allergen (in this instance a pet cat). Symptoms occur when a patient is exposed to inhalant aeroallergens that are not usually present in his or her indoor or outdoor environment. Other types of allergic rhinitis are seasonal, perennial, or perennial with seasonal exacerbations. This patient can best be managed by preventing symptoms from developing when she visits her grandmother. Intranasal cromolyn sodium is effective for symptom prevention, and the protective effect can last for 4 to 8 hours.

Intranasal corticosteroids are the most effective therapy once symptoms have occurred but do not prevent attacks of episodic allergic rhinitis. Other agents that can be administered once symptoms develop are topical decongestants for short-term use, intranasal antihistamines, intranasal anticholinergic agents, and oral antihistamines.

This patient has typical symptoms of episodic allergic rhinitis and does not require additional tests. Nasal smears for detection of eosinophils are usually indicated only for patients with atypical symptoms, as the presence of eosinophils can help differentiate allergic from nonallergic rhinitis. The presence of neutrophils would suggest, but not be diagnostic of, an infectious cause. Finding large numbers of eosinophils (>5% to 20%) would suggest nonallergic rhinitis with eosinophilia syndrome (NARES). Patients with NARES have profuse watery rhinorrhea and other typical symptoms of rhinitis.

Serum immunoassay for specific IgE antibodies has limited value and should not be performed routinely, especially when a patient has typical symptoms related to exposure to a specific allergen.

> **KEY POINT**
> - **Symptoms of episodic allergic rhinitis can be prevented by use of intranasal cromolyn sodium before exposure to the allergen.**

**Bibliography**

Wallace DV, Dykewicz MS, Bernstein DI, et al; Joint Task Force on Practice; American Academy of Allergy; Asthma & Immunology; American College of Allergy; Asthma and Immunology; Joint Council of Allergy, Asthma and Immunology. The diagnosis and management of rhinitis: an updated practice parameter. J Allergy Clin Immunol. 2008;122(2 Suppl):S1-S84. [PMID: 18662584]

## Item 74    Answer:  D

**Educational Objective:** Appropriately administer the human papillomavirus vaccine.

The Advisory Committee on Immunization Practices of the Centers for Disease Control and Prevention recommends the quadrivalent human papillomavirus (HPV) vaccine for cervical cancer prevention. The vaccine is recommended for all females between ages 9 and 26 years regardless of sexual activity. The vaccine has a high success rate in preventing infections with HPV strains 6, 11, 16, and 18, which cause most cases of genital warts and cervical cancer.

HPV infection is predominantly spread by sexual contact. This patient states she is not sexually active. However, the vaccine should be recommended now as it is of low risk, and vaccine efficacy lasts for at least several years. The vaccine does not protect against all types of HPV, and roughly 30% of cervical cancers will not be prevented by the vaccine, so women should continue to get regular Pap smears even after completing the vaccination series.

The HPV quadrivalent vaccine is not effective in preventing HPV-related diseases in women who have an established infection at the time of vaccination; therefore, waiting for HPV seroconversion prior to vaccination is inappropriate.

Although the HPV vaccine is well tolerated in men, and high rates of seroconversion against pathologic HPV have been demonstrated, efficacy of male vaccination in preventing clinical disease in men and women remains uncertain, and cost-effectiveness is unproven. Studies are underway to resolve some of these controversies, and the vaccine is not currently indicated for men.

---

**KEY POINT**

- A human papillomavirus quadrivalent vaccination series should be offered to all girls and women ages 9 through 26 years, and women should continue to get regular Pap smears even after completing the vaccination series.

---

**Bibliography**

Garland SM, Hernandez-Avila M, Wheeler CM, et al; Females United to Unilaterally Reduce Endo/Ectocervical Disease (FUTURE) I Investigators. Quadrivalent Vaccine against Human Papillomavirus to Prevent Anogenital Diseases. N Engl J Med. 2007;356(19): 1928-1943. [PMID: 17494926]

## Item 75     Answer: D

**Educational Objective:** Manage benign paroxysmal positional vertigo.

The patient has benign paroxysmal positional vertigo. Key diagnostic features are precipitation with head movement; recurrent episodes over days to weeks that last for several minutes each; reproduction of symptoms and peripheral nystagmus with a Dix-Hallpike maneuver; and a lack of associated hearing loss, tinnitus, or neurologic findings. The disease typically is self-limited and may recur months to years later. The Epley maneuver to reposition otolith debris within the patient's semicircular canal is effective in eliminating symptoms and has minimal adverse effects.

Audiometry is most useful in patients with signs and symptoms suggestive of Meniere disease or acoustic neuroma and is not routinely indicated in most patients with vertigo. Meniere disease is usually associated with unilateral tinnitus, ear fullness, and hearing loss. An acoustic neuroma most often presents with unilateral hearing loss or tinnitus and nonspecific feelings of imbalance. Severe acute vertigo as a presenting symptom is unusual for an acoustic neuroma.

Neuroimaging should usually be reserved for patients with cerebellar or focal neurologic symptoms or vertical nystagmus; brain MRI with magnetic resonance angiography is not indicated in this patient.

Methylprednisolone is an effective therapy for acute vestibular neuronitis. However, this patient does not have persistent symptoms, severe symptoms, or a history of antecedent infection that would be more characteristic of vestibular neuronitis. Therefore, treatment with methylprednisolone is not indicated.

A cardiac dysrhythmia could cause episodic symptoms lasting for minutes spread out over days to weeks and may be detected by an event monitor. However, this patient has positive findings on a Dix-Hallpike maneuver, and the last three episodes all occurred in the context of head-turning.

---

**KEY POINT**

- The Epley maneuver is effective at relieving short-term symptoms of benign paroxysmal positional vertigo and has minimal adverse effects.

---

**Bibliography**

Hilton M, Pinder D. The Epley (canalith repositioning) maneuver for benign paroxysmal positional vertigo. Cochrane Database of Syst Rev. 2004;(2):CD003162. [PMID: 15106194]

## Item 76     Answer: B

**Educational Objective:** Use root-cause analysis to assess the etiology of a medical error.

Most errors in health systems stem from multiple breakdowns culminating into one adverse event. This kind of sentinel event should trigger a performance improvement (PI) team evaluation. The PI team convenes a meeting of the key clinicians who interacted with the patient during the situation when the error occurred. Through an interactive group discussion with these clinicians, the PI team develops a root-cause analysis (which can be illustrated by a fishbone diagram) to uncover all the factors related to the error. The PI team uses the analysis to develop an intervention (or interventions) to prevent further errors. Two quality improvement principles are paramount. First, focus on processes, not people. Most processes devolve to chaos unless structured and maintained. Second, redundancy must be built into processes to ensure backup plans at key points. A commonly used methodology for developing a potential intervention is called a PDSA cycle—Plan a change, Do the change, Study the impact of the change, and Act upon the results.

A chart audit is an important initial task of the PI team but does not help in understanding the full scope of the team dynamics, the limitations of the technology, and exact course of events that may not have been recorded in the chart.

Standardized protocols are highly effective interventions used by PI teams to create force-functions that eliminate or decrease system-type errors. Likewise, a team "time out" is a highly effective intervention implemented to decrease errors in procedures, such as surgeries. However, neither of these would be useful in analyzing the source of an error.

---

**KEY POINT**

- A root-cause analysis is used by a performance improvement team to determine the multiple factors associated with patient care errors.

---

**Bibliography**

VA's Approach to Patient Safety. Culture Change: Prevention, not Punishment. United States Department of Veteran's Affairs Web site. www.va.gov/ncps/vision.html. Accessed August 5, 2009.

## Item 77    Answer:  C

**Educational Objective:**  Treat panic disorder.

This patient's presentation is characteristic of panic disorder. Panic disorder is characterized by recurrent, unexpected panic attacks that feature the abrupt onset of numerous somatic symptoms such as palpitations, sweating, tremulousness, dyspnea, chest pain, nausea, dizziness, and numbness. Symptoms typically peak within 10 minutes of onset and attacks usually have a duration from 15 to 60 minutes. The most appropriate treatment for panic disorder is cognitive-behavioral therapy (CBT) and a selective serotonin reuptake inhibitor, such as paroxetine. Panic disorder is the only anxiety spectrum disorder for which there is clear evidence that the combination of CBT and pharmacotherapy achieves better results than those achieved with either therapeutic intervention alone. Despite evidence that combined pharmacologic and nonpharmacologic therapy is superior to either approach alone, many physicians use a stepped care approach, starting with one form of treatment and supplementing it with the other if needed. The initial selection is often based upon availability; insufficient access to therapists trained in CBT is often the determinant favoring an initial pharmacologic approach.

Because the symptoms of panic disorder are primarily physical, most patients with this disorder present to their primary care physicians or to emergency departments for evaluation. Patients with panic disorder are evaluated, on average, by 10 clinicians before the diagnosis is established. The alarming nature of their symptoms prompts patients with panic disorder to seek medical attention; consequently, they have very high health care utilization rates.

The other options, used individually, have some efficacy in treating panic attacks. CBT has been shown to be the most effective nonpharmacologic therapy if pharmacologic agents are contraindicated or are refused by the patient. Venlafaxine and paroxetine (as well as other selective serotonin reuptake inhibitors) are superior to placebo but are less effective when used without CBT. Buspirone is a second-line therapeutic agent because of the less compelling evidence of efficacy and the longer period required to achieve a response.

**KEY POINT**

- **For treatment of panic disorder, the combination of cognitive-behavioral therapy and pharmacotherapy achieves better results than those achieved with either therapeutic intervention alone.**

### Bibliography

Bandelow B, Seidler-Brandler U, Becker A, Wedekind D, Rüther E. Meta-analysis of randomized controlled comparisons of psychopharmacological and psychological treatments for anxiety disorders. World J Biol Psychiatry. 2007;8(3):175-177. [PMID: 17654408]

## Item 78    Answer:  D

**Educational Objective:**  Evaluate overflow urinary incontinence.

This patient with long-standing diabetes mellitus most likely has overflow urinary incontinence due to a neurogenic bladder. This diagnosis is supported by symptoms and findings that suggest the presence of a peripheral and autonomic neuropathy, including paresthesias, loss of vibration sensation in the feet and ankles, and orthostatic hypotension. The abdominal examination suggests possible bladder distention. The incontinence was probably triggered by the anticholinergic effects of the recently prescribed nortriptyline.

The most appropriate diagnostic study at this time is measurement of postvoid residual urine volume, which can be determined with in-and-out catheterization after the patient spontaneously voids or postvoid bladder ultrasound. This study is most useful if overflow incontinence due to outlet obstruction or a flaccid neurogenic bladder is suspected. A postvoid residual urine volume of less than 50 to 100 mL is normal, and greater than 200 to 300 mL is abnormal.

Detailed urologic evaluation, such as cystoscopy, urodynamic testing, and imaging studies, is not needed in patients with uncomplicated urinary incontinence. If this patient is found to have increased postvoid residual urine volume and her incontinence resolves with discontinuation of nortriptyline, more invasive testing would not be indicated.

Measuring the plasma glucose level would be useful in determining adequate control of this patient's diabetes mellitus. However, incontinence associated with hyperglycemia would usually be urge incontinence with a sense of urgency but inability to get to the bathroom in time, rather than decreased episodes of spontaneous voiding.

Urinary tract infection may be a cause of transient incontinence, but typically would be associated with urge incontinence rather than overflow incontinence. The likelihood of a urinary tract infection is considerably decreased because of the normal urinalysis, and a urine culture would not help evaluate the most likely cause of this patient's incontinence.

**KEY POINT**

- **Urinary incontinence with a postvoid residual urine volume greater than 200 to 300 mL suggests a diagnosis of overflow incontinence.**

### Bibliography

American College of Obstetricians and Gynecologists. Urinary incontinence in women. Obstet Gynecol 2005;105(6):1533-1545. [PMID: 15932869]

## Item 79    Answer:  A

**Educational Objective:**  Manage menstrual irregularities in a perimenopausal woman.

The most appropriate next step in the management of this patient with abnormal uterine bleeding is to obtain an endometrial biopsy. In all patients with abnormal bleeding, physical examination should include a pelvic examination and Pap smear. In pre- or perimenopausal patients, a urine pregnancy test is also appropriate. Further laboratory testing depends on the findings of the history and physical examination and may include cultures for gonorrhea and *Chlamydia trachomatis*, complete blood count, thyroid function tests, plasma glucose measurement, prolactin levels, and coagulation studies. After performing appropriate laboratory studies, an assessment of the endometrial lining with an endometrial biopsy is appropriate to rule out endometrial cancer or hyperplasia in patients older than 35 years of age with abnormal uterine bleeding.

Pelvic ultrasonography is a useful test in the evaluation of abnormal uterine bleeding. It is typically indicated in the evaluation of women who have uncertain findings on pelvic examination and in the assessment of the endometrium and uterine wall in ovulatory women. Performance of ultrasonography is not indicated in every woman with abnormal uterine bleeding, however, and it is frequently omitted in the initial evaluation of patients in whom a reasonable diagnosis for the bleeding has been established (for example, an endocervical polyp or anovulation). If ultrasonography is indicated, most experts recommend both transabdominal and transvaginal imaging.

Luteinizing hormone and follicle-stimulating hormone levels may be able to confirm the menopausal state, but these tests cannot exclude the possibility of endometrial carcinoma.

In patients with anovulatory bleeding, initiation of oral contraceptives or cyclic progestins can help to maintain regular cycles. However, this intervention would be inappropriate without first eliminating the possibility of endometrial cancer as the cause of the abnormal uterine bleeding in this patient.

**KEY POINT**

- An assessment of the endometrial lining with an endometrial biopsy is appropriate to rule out endometrial cancer or hyperplasia in patients older than 35 years with abnormal uterine bleeding.

**Bibliography**

Fazio SB, Ship AN. Abnormal uterine bleeding. South Med J. 2007;100(4):376-382. [PMID: 17458397]

## Item 80      Answer:  D

**Educational Objective:**  Evaluate the risk for postoperative mortality in a patient with cirrhosis.

This patient has a high surgical risk and should be advised to avoid elective surgery. Although various risk indices for patients with cirrhosis were developed to predict outcome after shunt procedures or liver transplantation, they have also been used to predict outcome after other surgical procedures. The Child-Turcotte-Pugh (CTP) score is based on the presence of ascites and encephalopathy, as well as serum bilirubin, albumin, and INR values. Patients with CTP class A (0-6 points), class B (7-9 points), and class C (≥10 points) scores have postoperative mortality rates of approximately 10%, 30%, and 80%, respectively. The Model for End-stage Liver Disease (MELD) score is based on serum bilirubin, INR, and creatinine values, and scores of <10, 10-15, and >15 tend to correlate with CTP class A, B, and C scores.

Other risk factors for postoperative mortality in patients with cirrhosis include age greater than 70 years, obstructive jaundice, portal hypertension, and advanced American Society of Anesthesiologists class. Patients with a CTP class A score or MELD score of less than 10 can usually undergo elective surgery at acceptable risk without further workup. Those with a CTP class C score or MELD score of greater than 15 are at high risk and are usually advised to avoid elective surgery. Intermediate-risk patients require optimal therapy to treat coagulopathy, ascites, encephalopathy, and other disorders before being considered for surgery.

**KEY POINT**

- Patients with a Child-Turcotte-Pugh class C score or Model for End-stage Liver Disease (MELD) score of greater than 15 are at high surgical risk and are usually advised to avoid elective surgery.

**Bibliography**

Teh SH, Nagorney DM, Stevens SR, et al. Risk factors for mortality after surgery in patients with cirrhosis. Gastroenterology. 2007;132(4):1261-1269. [PMID: 17408652]

## Item 81      Answer:  B

**Educational Objective:**  Diagnose acute aortic dissection.

This patient presents with syncope, back pain, neurologic deficits, and blood pressure and pulse differentials between the upper extremities. The most likely diagnosis is acute aortic dissection; therefore, diagnostic evaluation of the aorta is indicated. Patients who present with syncope associated with severe chest or back pain should be presumed to have an aortic dissection or pulmonary embolism until proven otherwise.

Patients with dissection of the thoracic aorta typically present with abrupt onset of severe, sharp, or tearing pain of the back or chest. Decreased cardiac output associated with aortic dissection may cause syncope, and an associated carotid or coronary artery occlusion or dissection may cause stroke or myocardial infarction, respectively. A pulse differential is one of the most useful findings (positive likelihood ratio = 5.7). Focal neurologic deficits can be present in a minority of patients but are highly suggestive of aortic dissection. Although a widened mediastinum on chest radiograph is a common initial finding, it is absent in at least 40% of patients and thus lacks sufficient sensitivity to rule out aortic dissection.

When aortic dissection is suspected, imaging is indicated. The most common imaging studies to diagnose aortic dissection include MRI or CT angiography of the chest and transesophageal echocardiography, all of which have excellent test characteristics (sensitivity and specificity 98%-100%).

A patient presenting with neurologic deficits in the distribution of the left internal carotid artery may well have had a thrombotic or embolic cerebrovascular accident. However, a stroke would not explain the severe back pain or the blood pressure and pulse differentials noted in this patient. Therefore, an MRI of the brain and carotid duplex ultrasound are not the best initial diagnostic studies.

Transthoracic echocardiography may be helpful in diagnosing ascending dissections, but its overall test characteristics (sensitivity of 59%-85% and specificity of 93%-96%) make it a poor diagnostic test for aortic dissection compared with MRI, CT, or transesophageal echocardiography.

**KEY POINT**

- Patients who present with syncope associated with chest pain should be presumed to have an aortic dissection or pulmonary embolism as the cause of their chest pain until proven otherwise.

**Bibliography**
Kelly BS. Evaluation of the elderly patient with acute chest pain. Clin Geriatr Med. 2007;23(2):327-349. [PMID: 17462520]

## Item 82    Answer:  E

**Educational Objective:** Choose the appropriate screening test for an asymptomatic patient.

Screening for dyslipidemia is recommended by the U.S. Preventive Services Task Force (USPSTF) for all men older than 35 years regardless of risk factors. In addition, men and women older than 20 years who have other risk factors for cardiovascular disease should undergo cholesterol screening. These include diabetes mellitus, history of coronary or noncoronary atherosclerosis, family history of premature cardiovascular disease (<50 years in male relatives and <60 years in female relatives), tobacco use, hypertension, and obesity (BMI >30). In addition, this patient should be provided smoking cessation counseling.

Chest radiography has not been shown to be effective in screening for lung cancer in any group, including smokers, due to poor specificity and lack of evidence for decreasing mortality from lung cancer or overall mortality.

Many of the diseases that can be detected by a screening complete blood count have a low prevalence (for example, leukemia). In addition, a complete blood count often has limited sensitivity and specificity to detect target conditions (such as iron-deficiency anemia) and there is no proven benefit from their early detection.

Many diseases detected by a comprehensive metabolic profile (CMP) have very low prevalence, and changes in patient management occur in fewer than 1% of patients screened. Therefore, CMP screening is not indicated in this or other asymptomatic persons.

Fasting blood sugar (FBS) for screening purposes is recommended for patients with hypertension according to the USPSTF, because lower blood pressure goals reduce cardiovascular risk in patients with diabetes. Similarly, screening for type 2 diabetes in adults with dyslipidemia should be considered because diabetes is one of the conditions that lowers LDL cholesterol target levels. The American Diabetes Association (ADA) recommends a screening FBS in adults older than 45 years and in those 45 years or younger if they are overweight (BMI ≥25) and have one or more additional risk factors for diabetes. The ADA recommends that adults older than 45 years who have normal weight and no risk factors should be screened every 3 years; adults of any age who are overweight and have additional risk factors should be screened annually. FBS assessment is not indicated in this patient.

**KEY POINT**

- Men should be screened for dyslipidemia starting at age 35 years.

**Bibliography**
Guide to Clinical Preventive Services, 2008. Recommendations of the U.S. Preventive Services Task Force. Agency for Healthcare Research and Quality. www.ahrq.gov/clinic/pocketgd.htm. Accessed August 5, 2009.

## Item 83    Answer:  C

**Educational Objective:** Diagnose vaginismus.

This patient presents with pain during sexual intercourse typical of vaginismus. Vaginismus is caused by the involuntary spasm of the muscles of the outer third of the vagina, making intercourse (or the insertion of a finger, speculum, or tampon) uncomfortable or even impossible. Symptoms can include a sensation of burning during or after intercourse or a sensation of the penis or object hitting a barrier. The involuntary spasm can occur with the anticipation of vaginal penetration. Vaginismus may be a symptom related to a prior sexual trauma. Treatment is centered on cognitive-behavioral interventions.

Symptoms and signs of androgen deficiency include low desire, poor sexual well-being, persistent vasomotor symptoms of menopause even with estrogen replacement, fatigue and low motivation, and loss of axillary and/or pubic hair. Testosterone levels correlate poorly with desire and have no role in assessing female sexual dysfunction. The pain described by the patient cannot be explained by androgen deficiency.

Dyspareunia is pain that occurs with intercourse that is not caused by lack of lubrication or vaginismus. It may be caused by processes that affect insertion, such as Bartholin cysts or vulvodynia, or may be related to deeper penetration, which could reflect pelvic pathology. In this patient, the history and examination are consistent with vaginismus.

Generalized vulvodynia is pain or discomfort localized to the vulva (labia majora, labia minora, vestibule) or perineum, mons pubis, or thighs. In this patient, the duration of her symptoms, their association with intercourse, and the description of a barrier to insertion rather than primarily pain are consistent with vaginismus rather than vulvodynia.

**KEY POINT**

- **Vaginismus is an involuntary spasm of the outer third of the vagina that may lead to painful intercourse or prevent intercourse.**

**Bibliography**

Kammerer-Doak D, Rogers RG. Female sexual function and dysfunction. Obstet Gynecol Clin North Am. 2008;35(2):169-183. [PMID: 18486835]

## Item 84    Answer:  B

**Educational Objective:**  Manage the systemic side effects of glaucoma treatment.

The most appropriate management option for this patient is to discontinue timolol ophthalmic drops. Topical medications used to treat glaucoma can have systemic side effects, and for topical β-blockers, these effects include bradycardia, lethargy, decreased libido, erectile dysfunction, and bronchospasm. In this patient, this seems the most likely etiology of the asthma exacerbation. Discontinuing the timolol and asking the ophthalmologist to substitute a topical prostaglandin will most likely return his asthma control to his previous baseline.

Escalating therapy for asthma that is not well controlled is important and may be accomplished by either increasing the dose of the inhaled corticosteroid or by adding a long-acting β-agonist. However, this patient is well controlled at baseline and is presenting with a mild exacerbation of his symptoms. As there appears to be a likely precipitant to his worsening asthma, therapy can first be aimed at removing the offending agent.

A chest radiograph is not indicated as there are no history or physical examination findings to suggest pneumonia or another pulmonary process to explain the patient's symptoms.

**KEY POINT**

- **Medications used to treat glaucoma, including topical medications, may have systemic side effects and interact with other drugs.**

**Bibliography**

Kirwan JF, Nightingale JA, Bunce C, Wormald R. Do selective topical beta antagonists for glaucoma have respiratory side effects? Br J Ophthalmol. 2004;88(2):196-198. [PMID: 14736772]

## Item 85    Answer:  E

**Educational Objective:**  Evaluate benign prostatic hyperplasia.

This elderly man has voiding symptoms that are most consistent with benign prostatic hyperplasia (BPH), a diagnosis that is further supported by the findings of a symmetrically enlarged prostate on physical examination. A urinalysis is the laboratory test experts most strongly recommend in order to screen for urinary abnormalities and evidence of a urinary tract infection. A urine culture may also be desirable, particularly if there is pyuria or bacteriuria noted on urinalysis.

Postvoid residual urine volume can be determined with in-and-out catheterization after the patient spontaneously voids, and is most useful if one suspects overflow incontinence due to outlet obstruction (such as from prostatic hyperplasia) or a flaccid neurogenic bladder (due to conditions affecting the lower motor neurons, such as diabetes mellitus). Incontinence, however, is not part of this patient's symptom complex.

Prostate cancer seldom causes lower urinary tract symptoms. The American Urological Association guidelines recommend a serum prostate-specific antigen (PSA) level be obtained as a prostate cancer screening test for men with BPH who have more than a 10-year life expectancy and for those for whom PSA levels may influence BPH treatment. In an 84-year-old man with oxygen-dependent chronic obstructive pulmonary disease, a routine PSA would not be warranted. Moreover, an evidence-based review of quality indicators for BPH in the elderly recommended a urinalysis as a routine initial test but did not report the same degree of evidence for routine PSA testing.

A prostate ultrasound is most useful in evaluating suspected prostate cancer and therefore would not be initially ordered to evaluate voiding complaints.

Measurement of serum creatinine is no longer routinely recommended for patients with suspected BPH because multiple long-term, placebo-controlled trials have shown that the incidence of renal insufficiency in men with BPH is the same as in the general population.

**KEY POINT**

- **A urinalysis is the laboratory test experts most strongly recommend for initial evaluation of voiding symptoms in a man with suspected benign prostatic hyperplasia.**

**Bibliography**

Saigal CS. Quality indicators for benign prostatic hyperplasia in vulnerable elders. J Am Geriatr Soc. 2007;55 Suppl 2:S253-S257. [PMID: 17910545]

## Item 86    Answer:  D

**Educational Objective:**  Manage acute pharyngitis.

Managing patients with pharyngitis includes estimating the probability of the presence of group A β-hemolytic streptococcal (GABHS) infection. The four-point Centor criteria (fever, tonsillar exudates, tender anterior cervical lymphadenopathy, and absence of cough) are often used as a prediction rule in patients with suspected GABHS infection. Patients with two Centor criteria, such as the patient described here, have an intermediate probability for GABHS infection, and rapid streptococcal antigen testing (sensitivity of 88% and specificity of 94%) is a reasonable strategy for these patients. Patients with 0 or 1 criterion have a low (<3%) probability of GABHS, and neither testing nor antibiotic treatment is recommended. Empiric antibiotic therapy is recommended for patients who meet all four Centor criteria because the probability of GABHS is 40% or greater. Opinion differs regarding the management of patients with three criteria, and either empiric antibiotic treatment or testing and then treating only if test results are positive is acceptable. Patients with Centor scores of 3 or 4 who have negative rapid antigen testing should then undergo throat cultures to guide treatment decisions. A throat culture prior to a negative rapid antigen test would be unnecessarily expensive.

The diagnosis of infectious mononucleosis should be considered in patients presenting with pharyngitis associated with fever and lymphadenopathy (most often enlargement of the posterior cervical lymph nodes). Because this patient does not have these findings, a heterophile antibody (Monospot) test to diagnose infectious mononucleosis is not indicated.

Antibiotics are not indicated for this patient before rapid streptococcal antigen testing is done to determine whether they are needed. If treatment is indicated, the antibiotic of choice is penicillin. Macrolide antibiotics and first- and second-generation cephalosporins are alternative choices for penicillin-allergic patients.

### KEY POINT

- **Rapid streptococcal antigen testing is a reasonable strategy for patients with pharyngitis who have two of the four Centor criteria (fever, tonsillar exudates, tender anterior cervical lymphadenopathy, and absence of cough).**

**Bibliography**

Centor RM, Allison JJ, Cohen SJ. Pharyngitis management: defining the controversy. J Gen Intern Med. 2007;22(1):127-130. [PMID: 17351852]

## Item 87      Answer:  D

**Educational Objective:** Evaluate medical decision-making capacity.

Soliciting a patient's decision after explaining the benefits and risks of a particular treatment as well as alternative treatments is appropriate, but a mere yes or no answer does not guarantee that the patient has fully understood the consequences. A more stringent criterion, appropriate for a complex or potentially burdensome treatment, is to not only ask

what a patient wants, but the reasons why he or she makes a particular treatment choice. In this patient in whom mental status testing has revealed mild dementia, it is appropriate to inquire about the reasons behind his decision regarding chemotherapy.

Asking the patient to reiterate his treatment preferences at a later point in time is a useful way to assess the consistency of his responses and to avoid acting upon an initial reply that may have been random or confused. Evidencing a choice—whether once or multiple times—may be adequate for life-saving or simple treatments, but is not sufficient for more complex treatment decisions in which benefits and harms may be closely balanced.

Asking a patient to repeat the benefits and risks of a particular therapy that have just been explained to him or her is a higher test of decision-making capacity than simply accepting or refusing treatment. It reflects recall of specific information and not just general cognitive capacity as determined by mental status examination. However, for potentially burdensome treatments with marginal benefits, asking for the patient's rationale for a treatment choice is an even better criterion of medical decision-making capacity.

Surrogate decision-making is appropriate when the patient is incompetent to exercise his or her own choice, such as a comatose patient or one with very advanced dementia. However, this patient's dementia appears to be mild, and assessing the patient's rationale for a decision is reasonable prior to turning to a surrogate decision maker.

### KEY POINT

- **For potentially burdensome treatments with marginal benefits, it is best to not only ascertain the patient's acceptance or refusal of a specific treatment but also the reasons why he or she makes a particular choice.**

**Bibliography**

Kitamura T, Takahashi N. Ethical and conceptual aspects of capacity assessments in psychiatry. Curr Opin Psychiatry. 2007;20(6):578-581. [PMID: 17921758]

## Item 88      Answer:  B

**Educational Objective:** Treat trochanteric bursitis.

This patient has a burning, constant pain with point tenderness directly over the greater trochanter, consistent with trochanteric bursitis. Typically, patients with trochanteric bursitis have a history of a recent change in activity. Treatment of trochanteric bursitis includes relative rest, NSAIDs, and topical modalities such as ice or heat. Range-of-motion activities may speed healing. Additional treatment modalities include aspiration of the bursa with or without injection of an anesthetic (lidocaine) and corticosteroid mixture. Local injection into the bursa with corticosteroids is a highly effective treatment and should be offered to this patient as rest, heat, and NSAIDs have failed to improve her symptoms.

Indomethacin is unlikely to be helpful in a patient who has failed to respond to a maximum dosage of ibuprofen. Pregabalin is indicated in the treatment of fibromyalgia and painful peripheral neuropathy. This patient's localized pain, reproduced with direct pressure over the greater trochanter and associated with pain upon movement of the hip, is most characteristic of bursitis, not a peripheral neuropathy. Topical capsaicin administered two to four times daily has been shown to reduce pain in osteoarthritis. Topical capsaicin is not an anti-inflammatory agent and is unlikely to be helpful in treating this patient's underlying soft tissue inflammatory disorder.

**KEY POINT**

- **Trochanteric bursitis responds favorably to local corticosteroid injection.**

**Bibliography**

Segal NA, Felson DT, Torner JC, et al; Multicenter Osteoarthritis Study Group. Greater trochanteric pain syndrome: epidemiology and associated factors. Arch Phys Med Rehabil. 2007;88(8):988-992. [PMID: 17678660]

## Item 89     Answer:   A

**Educational Objective:**  Reduce a patient's risk for postoperative pulmonary complications.

The overriding factor in determining a patient's risk of postoperative pulmonary complications is the type of surgery and proximity to the diaphragm. Procedures associated with the greatest risk of complications are aortic aneurysm repair, intrathoracic surgery, and upper abdominal surgery. Pulmonary function ($FEV_1$ and FVC) declines by approximately 50% after these procedures. In this patient undergoing a colectomy, therefore, maneuvers to help prevent postoperative pulmonary complications should be undertaken. There is good evidence supporting routine lung expansion with incentive spirometry and deep-breathing exercises to prevent postoperative pulmonary complications. No one pulmonary expansion modality has been found to be clearly superior to the other.

There is good evidence supporting selective nasogastric decompression after abdominal surgery in patients with nausea, vomiting, or abdominal distention only. The evidence does not support routine nasogastric decompression after abdominal surgery until bowel function returns. Evidence to support prophylactic corticosteroids in the prevention of postoperative pulmonary complications is insufficient, and corticosteroids cannot be recommended in patients without evidence of wheezing that is not controlled by inhaled medications. Right heart catheterization and routine nutritional support for malnutrition have not been found to prevent postoperative pulmonary complications.

**KEY POINT**

- **Routine lung expansion with incentive spirometry and deep-breathing exercises helps prevent postoperative pulmonary complications.**

**Bibliography**

Lawrence VA, Cornell JE, Smetana GW; American College of Physicians. Strategies to reduce postoperative pulmonary complications after noncardiothoracic surgery: systematic review for the American College of Physicians. Ann Intern Med. 2006;144(8):596-608. [PMID: 16618957]

## Item 90     Answer:   E

**Educational Objective:**  Evaluate a patient prior to beginning an exercise program.

Asymptomatic adults at low risk for coronary artery disease (CAD) who plan to be physically active at moderate levels do not need to consult with a physician prior to beginning exercise unless they have a specific medical question. According to the U.S. Preventive Services Task Force, routine stress testing prior to beginning an exercise program in these patients is not warranted owing to the poor predictive value of stress testing in this setting for acute cardiac events. The American Heart Association concurs that exercise stress testing is not necessary in all individuals prior to beginning a moderate intensity exercise program. Alternatively, the American College of Sports Medicine has recommended exercise testing before vigorous exercise for men 45 years or older and women 55 years or older, and in persons with two or more major cardiac risk factors; signs or symptoms of CAD; or those with cardiac, pulmonary, or metabolic disease, despite the lack of data to substantiate this approach. This patient meets none of these criteria for preparticipatory stress testing.

In adults, there is a moderate relationship between carotid intimal thickness and the presence of coronary atherosclerosis and risk of future cardiovascular events, but this association assumes less predictive importance when traditional risk factors are taken into account. Measurement of the carotid intimal medial thickness is not, therefore, indicated.

Coronary artery calcium scoring may be considered for asymptomatic patients with a 10-year risk of a cardiovascular event between 10% and 20% if the result might lead to a change in management based upon reclassification to a lower or higher risk group. This patient's 10-year Framingham risk is estimated to be 1%; therefore, coronary artery calcium scoring is not indicated.

Electrocardiographic (ECG) treadmill stress testing with or without nuclear imaging is typically the initial test for a patient with suspected CAD after a baseline ECG. Neither of these tests is appropriate in an asymptomatic patient.

**KEY POINT**

- **Asymptomatic adults at low risk for coronary artery disease who plan to be physically active at moderate levels do not need to consult with a physician prior to beginning exercise unless they have a specific medical question.**

**Bibliography**

Haskell WL, Lee IM, Pate RR, et al. Physical activity and public health: updated recommendations for adults from the American College of Sports Medicine and the American Heart Association. Circulation. 2007;116(9):1081-1093. [PMID: 17671237]

## Item 91     Answer: A

**Educational Objective:** Treat depression in a patient with sexual dysfunction who is taking a selective serotonin reuptake inhibitor.

Bupropion is the best treatment option for this patient because it has the least proclivity toward sexual dysfunction and does not cause weight gain. Anorgasmia is a common side effect of selective serotonin reuptake inhibitors (SSRIs), including citalopram and fluoxetine, and there is no good evidence suggesting one SSRI has fewer sexual side effects than another SSRI. Although mirtazapine is associated with fewer sexual side effects than are SSRIs, it stimulates the appetite, resulting in weight gain; therefore, although mirtazapine might be a good treatment choice in a thin patient who may have had weight loss as part of a depressive episode, it is not appropriate in this overweight patient who is concerned about further weight gain.

Other options that could be considered are a reduction in the dose of the sertraline by taking a "drug holiday" on Fridays and Saturdays. One small study found that drug holidays were associated with improved sexual function, without significant rates of relapse in depressive symptoms. However, since 2 of 30 patients did have an increase in depression scores, if this approach is taken, patients should be monitored closely. This approach does not seem to help with sexual dysfunction in patients taking fluoxetine, which has a much longer half-life.

### KEY POINT

- **Bupropion has the least proclivity toward sexual dysfunction and does not cause weight gain.**

**Bibliography**

Kroenke K, West SL, Swindle R, et al. Similar effectiveness of paroxetine, fluoxetine, and sertraline in primary care: a randomized trial. JAMA. 2001;286(23):2947-2955. [PMID: 11743835]

## Item 92     Answer: A

**Educational Objective:** Manage a breast mass.

The most appropriate management option is fine-needle aspiration or biopsy of the breast mass. A patient with a breast mass requires triple assessment: palpation, mammography with or without ultrasound, and surgical evaluation for biopsy. Mammograms may be normal in 10% to 15% of patients with breast lumps, some of which may be cancerous. After performance of bilateral diagnostic mammography, the initial focus of the workup of a dominant breast mass is to distinguish a simple cyst from a solid mass by fine-needle aspiration (FNA) or ultrasonography. If the fluid from FNA is bloody, the fluid should undergo cytologic evaluation. Women with simple cysts should undergo a breast examination 4 to 6 weeks after cyst aspiration to evaluate for cyst recurrence or a residual lump. A solid mass requires a tissue diagnosis by fine-needle aspiration biopsy (FNAB), core-needle biopsy, or excisional biopsy. Patients with benign FNAB or core-needle biopsy results and negative mammography require close clinical follow-up of the breast abnormality.

It is inappropriate to observe the patient without further workup or to just repeat the mammogram later, as she has a discrete mass that may represent a breast cancer despite the normal mammographic findings. Even if an ultrasound is negative, the patient requires tissue sampling.

The role of breast MRI for screening high-risk patients is currently being evaluated. In patients with an established diagnosis of breast cancer, it may be of value in determining the extent of disease. In this patient, a breast MRI would not obviate the need for fine-needle aspiration or biopsy and is much more expensive than ultrasound.

### KEY POINT

- **A patient with a breast mass requires triple assessment: palpation, mammography with or without ultrasound, and biopsy.**

**Bibliography**

Kerlikowske K, Smith-Bindman R, Ljung BM, Grady D. Evaluation of abnormal mammography results and palpable breast abnormalities. Ann Intern Med 2003;139(4):274-284. [PMID: 12965983]

## Item 93     Answer: D

**Educational Objective:** Manage mild cognitive impairment.

This patient has mild cognitive impairment (MCI), which is believed to represent an intermediate stage between normal age-related changes in memory and dementia. There is no effective treatment for MCI, but control of cardiovascular risk factors and close clinical follow-up are recommended. There have been no randomized controlled clinical trials to support this recommendation, but control of hypertension has been shown to reduce the incidence of dementia in the general population. There is less compelling evidence for treatment of hyperlipidemia or management of diabetes in the treatment of MCI or prevention of dementia.

MCI is a heterogeneous disorder and current diagnostic criteria include:

1. A memory complaint by the patient that is corroborated by an informant

2. An objective impairment in memory or another cognitive domain (for example, problem solving, word finding)

3. Essentially normal general cognitive functioning

4. Essentially normal instrumental activities of daily living

5. No evidence of dementia (that is, the memory disturbance does not impair function in more than one domain).

Studies have shown no benefit, and possible harm, from the use of cholinesterase inhibitors to prevent progression of

MCI to dementia. Vitamin E, folate with or without vitamin $B_{12}$, melatonin, ginkgo, and omega-3 fatty acids have not shown benefit in preventing or treating MCI.

Approximately 50% of patients with MCI will develop dementia over 5 years. However, up to 25% of patients regress to normal, making discussions about prognosis very challenging. Patients with MCI should not be falsely reassured that they have normal age-related findings.

**KEY POINT**

- **Mild cognitive impairment is a heterogeneous clinical disorder but may represent a prodromal state to progression to dementia.**

**Bibliography**

Chertkow H, Massoud F, Nasreddine Z, et al. Diagnosis and treatment of dementia: 3. Mild cognitive impairment and cognitive impairment without dementia. CMAJ. 2008;178(10):1273-1285. [PMID: 18458258]

## Item 94    Answer:  D

**Educational Objective:**  Manage a request for information regarding a patient.

Confidentiality involves respecting the privacy and wishes of a patient, and a physician should not release a patient's personal medical information without his or her consent. Exceptions to this policy may occur to protect individuals or the public or to disclose or report information as required by law.

In this case, the patient made a deliberate decision to keep her diagnosis private and specifically requested that no one be told about her condition. This is considered "privileged communication," and unless she changes her mind or signs a release of information, her physician (and all personnel involved in her care) should respect that decision. The fact that her son is a physician is not relevant as he is not personally involved in her medical care. The next of kin or other family members are also not entitled to this information without the patient's consent.

**KEY POINT**

- **A physician should respect the privacy and wishes of a patient and not release a patient's personal medical information (privileged communication) without his or her consent.**

**Bibliography**

Snyder L, Leffler C; Ethics and Human Rights Committee, American College of Physicians. Ethics manual: fifth edition. Ann Intern Med. 2005;142(7):560-582. [PMID: 15809467]

## Item 95    Answer:  B

**Educational Objective:**  Manage a patient with a recently placed drug-eluting stent who requires non-cardiac surgery.

The American College of Cardiology/American Heart Association currently recommends that patients with recently placed paclitaxel or sirolimus drug-eluting stents continue uninterrupted dual antiplatelet therapy with aspirin and clopidogrel for at least 12 months, if possible, to minimize the possibility of in-stent thrombosis. Previous recommendations were dual antiplatelet therapy for at least 3 months for patients with sirolimus stents and 6 months for those with paclitaxel stents. The patient described here, whose stent was placed 4 months ago, should postpone surgery for an additional 8 months to reduce the risk of stent thrombosis. In patients who must undergo nonelective surgery, the risk of prematurely discontinuing one or both antiplatelet agents must be balanced against the risk of perioperative bleeding if these agents are continued.

**KEY POINT**

- **For patients with recently placed paclitaxel or sirolimus drug-eluting stents, dual antiplatelet therapy with aspirin and clopidogrel should be continued uninterrupted for at least 12 months, if possible, to minimize the possibility of in-stent thrombosis.**

**Bibliography**

Grines CL, Bonow RO, Casey DE Jr, et al; American Heart Association; American College of Cardiology; Society for Cardiovascular Angiography and Interventions; American College of Surgeons; American Dental Association; American College of Physicians. Prevention of premature discontinuation of dual antiplatelet therapy in patients with coronary artery stents: a science advisory from the American Heart Association, American College of Cardiology, Society for Cardiovascular Angiography and Interventions, American College of Surgeons, and American Dental Association, with representation from the American College of Physicians. J Am Coll Cardiol. 2007;49(6):734-739. [PMID: 17291948]

## Item 96    Answer:  D

**Educational Objective:**  Implement systems-based initiatives to improve patient safety.

Standardized protocols to decrease opiate-related adverse drug events (ADEs) include using order sets that have standardized dosing with monitoring parameters, both of which were lacking in this case. Minimizing the strength and dosing on the order sets is a key intervention. Also, having a protocol for the use of reversal agents without a physician being contacted is another best-practice recommendation. Protocols for use in elderly patients should always be devised with attention to the Beers list of medications that should be avoided in the geriatric population. Diphenhydramine is a particularly concerning sedative medication in the elderly and likely added to the patient's confusion and fall risk. Efforts to curtail the use of sedating drugs with real-time, computer-based pharmacy reminders to clinicians are effective. Hospital formularies should stock only low-dose, moderate sedation agents as a limiting factor.

A "sentinel event" such as this provides an opportunity for the hospital to assess and improve its safety controls. Beginning to collect ADE prevalence data will help to demonstrate the impact of an intervention but will not, by itself, prevent ADEs from occurring.

Fall-risk prediction tools alone have not been shown to decrease falls and have disappointing sensitivity and specificity, failing to identify up to 25% of patients who will fall. All patient care areas should be screened for optimal patient-safety architecture. However, most patient falls are more related to patient-specific factors (medications, weakness, poor gait) than to environmental issues.

> **KEY POINT**
> - Standardized protocols that minimize the strength and dosing of psychotropic and opiate medications may help prevent adverse drug events in the elderly.

**Bibliography**
Federico F. Preventing Harm from High-Alert Medications. Jt Comm J Qual Patient Saf. 2007;33(9):537-542. [PMID: 17915527]

## Item 97    Answer:   B
**Educational Objective:**  Screen for osteoporosis.

Dual-energy x-ray absorptiometry is an appropriate screening test for this patient. Guidelines recommend that screening for osteoporosis begin at age 65 years for women. Women aged 60 to 64 years should be screened if they are at higher than average risk for osteoporosis. The most predictive risk factor for osteoporosis is weight below 70 kg (154 lb), as in the patient presented. A screening interval of 2 years is appropriate for women 65 years or older but can reasonably be extended to 5 years for women younger than 65 years.

Osteoporosis in men is underdiagnosed. A clinical practice guideline from the American College of Physicians recommends that clinicians periodically perform individualized assessment of risk factors for osteoporosis in older men; screening for osteoporosis is recommended for men who are at increased risk for osteoporosis and are candidates for drug therapy. The most important risk factors in men are age older than 70 years, low body weight (BMI 20-25 or below), weight loss in recent years, physical inactivity, use of oral corticosteroids, and previous fragility fracture.

The U.S. Preventive Services Task Force (USPSTF) recommends against screening for abdominal aortic aneurysm in women because of the low prevalence of abdominal aortic aneurysm in this group. Abdominal ultrasonography, therefore, is not indicated.

After three consecutive negative annual cytology smears, the risk of cervical cancer is reduced to approximately 1/100,000 person-years. In this monogamous patient with three consecutive normal Pap smears whose last Pap smear was 14 months ago, it would be reasonable to increase the screening interval to every 2 to 3 years, with consideration of stopping screening at age 65 years if her Pap smears continue to be normal.

Pneumococcal vaccine is indicated for persons aged 65 years and older or for those younger than 65 years who live in long-term care facilities or who have chronic illnesses, or who are Alaskan natives or American Indians. This patient has no indication for pneumococcal vaccination at this time.

> **KEY POINT**
> - Screening for osteoporosis is recommended for women aged 65 years and older and in women 60 to 64 years old who are at increased risk for osteoporosis.

**Bibliography**
Guide to Clinical Preventive Services, 2008. Recommendations of the U.S. Preventive Services Task Force. Agency for Healthcare Research and Quality. www.ahrq.gov/clinic/pocketgd.htm. Accessed August 5, 2009.

## Item 98    Answer:   B
**Educational Objective:**  Treat postpartum depression in a patient reluctant to take medication.

This patient has postpartum depression, and psychotherapy alone is an effective nonpharmacologic treatment. Prevalence studies estimate that up to 20% of women have a nonpsychotic major depression within the first 6 months after parturition. In addition to meeting criteria for major depressive disorder according to the American Psychiatric Association Diagnostic and Statistical Manual-IV (DSM-IV) guidelines, women with postpartum depression may have predominant symptoms of anxiety and upsetting and unwanted thoughts of harming their infant. Because of the risks associated with untreated postpartum depression, reassurance with follow-up is not an adequate treatment approach. For breastfeeding women who do not wish to take antidepressant medication because of concerns about exposure of the infant, nondrug treatments, such as psychotherapy, are a first-line choice.

Fluoxetine is a selective serotonin reuptake inhibitor (SSRI) that is secreted in significant concentrations in breast milk and has a very long half-life, so it is not a desirable choice for this patient. Sertraline and paroxetine are SSRIs that do not reach as high levels in breast milk and have shorter half-lives, making them the preferred pharmacologic agents for moderate to severe postpartum depression in breastfeeding mothers who require drug therapy.

St. John's wort (*Hypericum perforatum*) is an herbal remedy for which numerous controlled trials have shown some efficacy in mild to moderate depression. However, more recent trials of larger size and stronger methodology, as well as meta-analyses, have found either no effect or a significantly diminished effect. In addition, there is no good evidence regarding whether it is secreted in breast milk or what effect it might have on children, so it is not recommended for women who are nursing.

somatocognitive therapy: results of a 1-year follow-up study. Am J Obstet Gynecol. 2008;199(6):615. [PMID: 18845283]

**KEY POINT**

- Psychotherapy alone is an effective nonpharmacologic therapy for postpartum depression.

**Bibliography**

Shaw E, Levitt C, Wong S, Kaczorowski J; The McMaster University Postpartum Research Group. Systematic review of the literature on postpartum care: effectiveness of postpartum support to improve maternal parenting, mental health, quality of life, and physical health. Birth. 2006;33(3):210-220. [PMID: 16948721]

## Item 99    Answer:   A

**Educational Objective:**  Manage chronic pelvic pain.

Pelvic pain is considered chronic when it persists for longer than 3 to 6 months. Chronic pelvic pain is not a disease but a syndrome, thought to be a complex multifactorial entity related to neurologic, musculoskeletal, endocrine, and psychologic factors. It is a frustrating entity for both patients and clinicians, with ill-defined symptoms and, frequently, without a definitive diagnosis, but it nevertheless is treatable. Cognitive-behavioral therapy (CBT) has been shown to be effective across this spectrum of symptom syndromes. One CBT-based approach reduced pain scores in patients with chronic pelvic pain by 50% compared with usual gynecologic care, and continued improvement was seen in psychological distress, pain, and motor function 9 months after completion of therapy.

The four most common disorders associated with chronic pelvic pain are endometriosis, adhesions, interstitial cystitis, and irritable bowel syndrome. In this patient, the imaging studies and lack of response to surgery render endometriosis and adhesions improbable explanations, and the normal cystoscopy rules out interstitial cystitis. In the absence of a specific underlying etiology, pharmacotherapy has generally been unsuccessful in treating chronic pelvic pain. NSAIDs such as naproxen have utility in dysmenorrhea, but a Cochrane review found insufficient evidence to recommend them in endometriosis, and although an empiric trial has sometimes been recommended in chronic pelvic pain of undetermined etiology, there is no evidence to support this practice. Controlled trials of antidepressants such as sertraline have improved depressive symptoms in those patients for whom such symptoms are prominent, but have not been associated with significant reduction in pain.

Reassurance and follow-up would be inappropriate for this woman who has had no relief from her symptoms for more than a year.

**KEY POINT**

- Cognitive-behavioral therapy has been shown to be effective in the treatment of chronic pelvic pain syndrome.

**Bibliography**

Haugstad GK, Haugstad TS, Kirste UM, et al. Continued improvement of chronic pelvic pain in women after short-term Mensendieck

## Item 100    Answer:   C

**Educational Objective:**  Manage withdrawal of life-sustaining therapy in a terminally ill patient.

When a patient requests discontinuation of a life-sustaining treatment such as dialysis, it is important to ensure the patient's mental status is not impaired and the patient understands the consequences of his or her actions and has a realistic understanding of the prognosis. In this case, because the patient is essentially chair- or bed-bound, has reduced oral intake, and is dependent on his daughter for his activities of daily living, he has a palliative performance score of about 30, predicting that he will likely die within 2 months. He appears to have a clear understanding of the consequences of stopping dialysis. It is appropriate to honor this patient's wishes and coordinate the discontinuation of dialysis with his nephrologist. If hospice care has not already been initiated, this would be appropriate as well.

If the patient remains firm in his desire to stop dialysis, the consent of the patient's nephrologist would not be needed. If his mental status is normal, his daughter's permission would also not be needed. A psychiatric evaluation prior to withdrawal of care is not indicated unless the physician feels his mental status is impaired owing to organic or psychiatric disease.

**KEY POINT**

- A patient with a normal mental status and no evidence of psychiatric illness can choose to discontinue therapy without the consent of family or a psychiatrist.

**Bibliography**

Fissell RB, Bragg-Gresham JL, Lopes AA, et al. Factors associated with "do not resuscitate" orders and rates of withdrawal from hemodialysis in the international DOPPS. Kidney Int. 2005;68(3):1282-1288. [PMID: 16105062]

## Item 101    Answer:   D

**Educational Objective:**  Manage initial presentation of ocular trauma.

This patient has a history and examination findings consistent with a penetrating globe injury with a possible intraorbital foreign body, and emergency ophthalmology consultation is indicated. The most important next step is to protect the eye from further damage. Inadvertent pressure or manipulation of the eye could lead to extravasation of aqueous or vitreous humor and could be vision-threatening. A metal shield, or a shield fabricated out of the bottom half of a paper cup and gently taped in place over the affected eye, will help prevent further damage.

Hammering, especially metal on metal, is the most common mechanism of injury for penetrating eye injuries. Findings in this patient consistent with a penetrating globe injury include mechanism of injury, immediate eye pain, distorted pupil, circumferential subconjunctival hemorrhage, and reduced visual acuity. A point of entry may not be seen on examination, but this does not exclude penetrating eye injury.

Endophthalmitis occurs in up to 13% of patients with penetrating eye injuries and may develop after weeks or months. Early administration of systemic antibiotics can reduce the risk of endophthalmitis and would be indicated in this patient. However, protection of the eye should not be delayed to administer antibiotics. Likewise, although a tetanus booster would be needed in this patient, immunization can be delayed while addressing the immediate visual threat.

Intraorbital foreign bodies can be difficult to visualize on plain radiographs, and a CT of the orbits would be the procedure of choice if looking for fractures or intraorbital foreign bodies (especially metal). However, the eye needs protection while making such arrangements.

**KEY POINT**

- Protecting an eye that has been traumatized is critical to preventing further damage.

**Bibliography**
Bord SP, Linden J. Trauma to the globe and orbit. Emerg Med Clin North Am. 2008;26(1):97-123. [PMID: 18249259]

## Item 102    Answer:  D
**Educational Objective:** Provide preoperative management for a patient on hemodialysis.

Patients with chronic kidney disease are potentially at increased risk for postoperative complications because of electrolyte abnormalities, platelet dysfunction, and the presence of any comorbid conditions (for example, hypertension, diabetes mellitus, coronary artery disease). Ideally, patients with end-stage kidney disease should undergo hemodialysis the day before surgery to minimize acute acid-base shifts and electrolyte and volume changes and therefore avoid last-minute cancellation of the surgical procedure.

Patients requiring hemodialysis are typically anemic for various reasons, one of which is a lack of erythropoietin. For most patients with chronic kidney disease, the threshold for erythropoietin therapy is a hemoglobin level below 10 g/dL (100 g/L) with a target hemoglobin of 11 to 12 g/dL (110 to 120 g/L). Mild chronic anemia does not increase surgical risk, particularly if the expected blood loss is low and the patient does not have significant cardiopulmonary disease. This patient is at the target hemoglobin level, and studies have demonstrated treatment to a hemoglobin level above 12 g/dL (120 g/L) may be associated with more deaths, hypertension, and heart failure in patients with chronic kidney disease. Therefore, erythropoietin or blood transfusions are not indicated.

A serum potassium level between 3.0 and 3.5 meq/L (3.0 and 3.5 mmol/L) is not associated with an increased risk for perioperative cardiac arrhythmias. Furthermore, potassium replacement therapy is not warranted in a patient whose potassium level will increase in the time period up to the next hemodialysis appointment.

Although this patient has hypertension and requires better long-term blood pressure control, reducing his blood pressure to the normal range will not decrease his perioperative risk, and surgery should not be postponed in order to do this.

**KEY POINT**

- Patients with end-stage kidney disease who require surgery should undergo hemodialysis the day before surgery, if possible, to minimize acute acid-base shifts and electrolyte and volume changes.

**Bibliography**
Joseph AJ, Cohn SL. Perioperative care of the patient with renal failure. Med Clin North Am. 2003;87(1):193-210. [PMID: 12575890]

## Item 103    Answer:  D
**Educational Objective:** Manage a patient with depression with suicidal features.

This patient with major depression with suicidal ideation should be urgently referred to a mental health professional. Major depression is characterized by the presence of at least five of the nine criteria for this disorder, including at least one of the two hallmark features of depressed mood and anhedonia. The nine depressive symptoms are as follows: sleep disturbance, psychomotor agitation or retardation, appetite disturbance, concentration impairment, low energy level, depressed mood, lost interest in activities, guilt or worthlessness, and suicidal ideation. This patient describes five of these symptoms (poor concentration, depressed mood, lack of interest, guilt, suicidal ideation). Urgent referral to a psychiatrist is appropriate for patients with suicidal ideation and a plan. In evaluating a patient with major depression, previous suicide attempts should be considered the best predictor of completed suicide.

Patients with suicidal ideation can be further risk stratified by assessing the level of social support and the willingness to make a *no-harm contract*, in which the suicidal patient is asked to agree not to harm or kill herself or himself for a particular period of time. Patients with good social support who are willing to enter into a no-harm contract can likely be safely referred to a psychiatrist for management. Patients with poor social support, who are unable to make a contract for safety, or who are currently intoxicated would best be managed with emergency referral for hospitalization and psychiatric assessment.

Reassurance and careful follow-up is an insufficient course of action for a patient with features of major depression, suicidal ideation, and a plan, particularly if there is no planned therapeutic intervention. Speaking with her fiancé is similarly inadequate, given her presentation; the patient clearly meets criteria for major depression, and a treatment plan should be implemented immediately rather than delaying to gather further information.

Initiation of an antidepressant with follow-up in 2 weeks would be an acceptable approach for moderate depression, but not for a patient with significant suicidal or homicidal ideation or psychotic features.

**KEY POINT**

- Patients with suicidal ideation and a plan should be either urgently referred to a psychiatrist or hospitalized for psychiatric assessment.

**Bibliography**

Mann JJ. The medical management of depression. N Engl J Med. 2005;353(17):1819-1834. [PMID: 16251538]

## Item 104    Answer:    B

**Educational Objective:** Diagnose herpes zoster ophthalmicus.

This patient has a localized headache associated with unilateral eye pain. There is conjunctival injection localized to same side of the headache and a skin eruption in the distribution of the first branch of the trigeminal nerve. This presentation is most consistent with a diagnosis of herpes zoster ophthalmicus. A zoster eruption in the first branch of the trigeminal nerve may involve the eye and cause blepharitis, conjunctivitis, keratitis, uveitis, ophthalmoplegia, or optic neuritis.

Herpes zoster ophthalmicus (which includes any involvement of the structures of the eye) is an ophthalmologic emergency, as it is potentially sight threatening. A particularly high-risk lesion is when zoster involves the tip of the nose, as this is the nasociliary branch of the trigeminal nerve and thus also innervates the cornea. All patients with a zoster eruption in the territory of the first branch of the trigeminal nerve should be emergently referred to an ophthalmologist to rule out eye involvement, even if only the skin appears to be involved, as deeper structures of the eye can be affected.

Herpes zoster ophthalmicus should be distinguished from herpes simplex virus (HSV) infection of the eye, which can cause inflammation and infection of the cornea (keratitis). HSV keratitis presents acutely with pain, blurred vision, and eye weeping; chemosis and conjunctivitis are present on physical examination. HSV keratitis differs from the conjunctivitis of herpes zoster in that it is not associated with a cutaneous eruption in a dermatomal pattern.

Scleritis is a painful, localized or diffuse, raised hyperemic lesion. Scleritis can cause deep, boring ocular pain but is not associated with a cutaneous eruption, making it an unlikely diagnosis for this patient.

Trigeminal neuralgia is typically characterized by excruciating, paroxysmal pain in the distribution of the trigeminal nerve. Although this patient's pain was localized to the trigeminal region, the presence of a skin eruption makes this an unlikely diagnosis.

**KEY POINT**

- Herpes zoster ophthalmicus is an ophthalmologic emergency and requires immediate referral to an ophthalmologist and institution of antiviral therapy.

**Bibliography**

Mahmood AR, Narang AT. Diagnosis and management of the acute red eye. Emerg Med Clin North Am. 2008;26(1):35-55. [PMID: 18249256]

## Item 105    Answer:    E

**Educational Objective:** Manage vasovagal syncope.

The patient's history is consistent with vasovagal (neurocardiogenic) syncope based on the history of prolonged standing and prodromal symptoms of nausea, lightheadedness, and diaphoresis. These presyncopal warning symptoms are highly sensitive for the diagnosis of vasovagal syncope if lasting for more than 10 seconds. Brief myoclonic jerking after losing consciousness is not unusual with syncope, especially vasovagal syncope. In addition, the normal physical examination, electrocardiogram, and lack of orthostasis on vital sign assessment all point toward vasovagal syncope.

Advanced cardiovascular diagnostic testing, such as an echocardiogram or exercise stress test, is not needed after a first episode of syncope when symptoms are characteristic for vasovagal syncope.

In suspected vasovagal syncope, a tilt-table test can be useful, providing a diagnosis in up to 60% of patients when done with pharmacologic stimulation. This test is indicated in patients with recurrent syncope as well as those with one episode who are at high risk based upon their occupation. However, this test has poor sensitivity, specificity, and reproducibility, and it is not indicated in most patients with suspected vasovagal syncope.

An electroencephalogram might be indicated to evaluate a first, unprovoked seizure, but despite this patient's few myoclonic jerks, there is no evidence of seizure activity, such as tongue biting, incontinence, or postictal confusion.

**KEY POINT**

- Vasovagal syncope is typically associated with a prodrome of nausea, lightheadedness, and diaphoresis.

**Bibliography**

Huff JS, Decker WW, Quinn JV, et al; American College of Emergency Physicians. Clinical policy: critical issues in the evaluation and management of adult patients presenting to the emergency department with syncope. Ann Emerg Med. 2007;49(4):431-437. [PMID: 17371707]

## Item 106    Answer:    C

**Educational Objective:** Prevent recurrent urinary tract infection in a postmenopausal woman.

This patient has evidence of atrophic vaginitis, and this condition puts her at risk for recurrent urinary tract infections

(UTIs). Recurrent UTIs are common in women and are believed to represent new infection rather than relapse of a previous episode. Postmenopausal women are at risk because reduced estrogen levels favor colonization by uropathogenic gram-negative bacteria because of less acidic vaginal secretions, a decrease in vaginal secretions, and thinning of the vulva and vaginal walls. Use of topical estrogen can restore altered genital mucosa and thus reduce the risk of UTIs. A recent Cochrane review found evidence to support the efficacy of vaginal estrogen cream in preventing recurrent UTIs in postmenopausal women.

Continuous antibiotic prophylaxis is not a recommended strategy to prevent recurrent UTIs because of the greater incidence of antibiotic-related side effects and the risk of promoting the emergence of resistant bacteria.

Evaluation for subtle predisposing factors (such as CT imaging to evaluate for anatomic urinary tract abnormalities) is seldom useful and cannot be recommended in this otherwise healthy woman. Inquiring about behavioral practices can be helpful, however. Sexual intercourse is a risk factor for acute or recurrent UTIs, as is the use of spermicides or spermicides plus a diaphragm.

For women with mild urogenital atrophy symptoms, vaginal moisturizing agents and lubricants may be helpful, particularly in the treatment and prevention of dyspareunia in sexually active women. However, vaginal lubricants do not restore the natural protective effect of estrogen on the vaginal mucosa and are not associated with a decreased incidence of recurrent UTIs.

### KEY POINT

- **In patients with atrophic vaginitis, use of topical estrogen can restore altered genital mucosa and thus reduce the risk of urinary tract infection.**

**Bibliography**

Perrotta C, Aznar M, Mejia R, Albert X, Ng CW. Oestrogens for preventing recurrent urinary tract infection in postmenopausal women. Cochrane Database Syst Rev. 2008;(2):CD005131. [PMID: 18425910]

## Item 107    Answer:  E
**Educational Objective:**  Treat recurrent epistaxis.

Most episodes of epistaxis are anterior and occur in Kiesselbach plexus, which is the vascular watershed area of the nasal septum. Common local causes are nose picking; trauma; irritants such as medications, low humidity, foreign bodies, or rhinitis from viral infections or allergies; tumors; septal perforations; vascular malformations; and telangiectasias. Common systemic causes are thrombocytopenia, bleeding disorders, and use of anticoagulants (including antiplatelet therapy). In this patient, low humidity, nose picking, and aspirin may be factors leading to the recurrences. However, his most recent episode has resolved, and no bleeding site has been identified. Therefore, no specific treatment is indicated. The patient should be advised to avoid picking his nose, use petrolatum to prevent drying of the nares, and use a home humidifier. A decision regarding discontinuation of low-dose aspirin should be individualized on the basis of the patient's cardiovascular risk.

Chemical cautery of a bleeding point with silver nitrate sticks may be useful for some patients with active bleeding. However, only one side of the septum should be treated at any one time to limit the risk of septal perforation. The patient described here does not require this procedure.

There is no role for fluticasone in epistaxis. Rather, intranasal corticosteroids may cause epistaxis. Therapies such as administration of phenylephrine or oxymetazoline spray for vasoconstriction are occasionally beneficial for acute epistaxis but have no role as prophylactic therapy in patients who are not currently bleeding.

Anterior packing of one or both nares should be performed if cautery does not stop the bleeding or if bleeding continues despite a search for the bleeding site, but has no role in the absence of active bleeding.

### KEY POINT

- **Most episodes of epistaxis occur from an anterior nasal site.**

**Bibliography**

Kucik CJ, Clenny C. Management of epistaxis. Am Fam Physician. 2005;71(2):305-311. [PMID: 15686301]

## Item 108    Answer:  D
**Educational Objective:**  Treat posttraumatic stress disorder.

This patient's presentation is consistent with a diagnosis of posttraumatic stress disorder (PTSD). The combination of cognitive-behavioral therapy (CBT) with exposure therapy is the evidence-based treatment of choice for PTSD and is associated with higher response rates and lower drop-out rates than those achieved with pharmacotherapy. An expert panel convened by the Institute of Medicine concluded that CBT with exposure therapy is the only treatment for which there is sufficient evidence to recommend it for PTSD.

Unlike other anxiety disorders, PTSD is preceded by a clear precipitating trauma, such as war, an accident, or experiencing or witnessing a violent assault. To meet criteria for PTSD, the trauma must be followed by at least 1 month of disabling symptoms in three different categories: re-experiencing the event, avoiding reminders of the trauma, and heightened arousal.

Although selective serotonin reuptake inhibitors such as fluoxetine are better than other pharmacologic agents for treating PTSD, they have a lower response rate and less durable effect than CBT with exposure therapy. Administration of zolpidem and a decrease in alcohol intake may possibly help with this patient's sleep difficulties. However, the sleep disturbance is primarily secondary to nightmares, which is only one of the manifestations of PTSD displayed by this patient, and this approach does not address the underlying problem. There is no compelling evidence to support brief counseling or psychodynamic therapy as being effective for treating PTSD.

- **Cognitive-behavioral therapy with exposure therapy is the evidence-based treatment of choice for posttraumatic stress disorder.**

**Bibliography**

Committee on Treatment of Posttraumatic Stress Disorder, Institute of Medicine. Treatment of Posttraumatic Stress Disorder: An assessment of the evidence. Washington, D.C.: National Academies Press; 2008.

## Item 109    Answer:  E

**Educational Objective:** Manage acute bronchitis.

Whether a cough is due to acute bronchitis or an upper respiratory tract infection is difficult to determine during the first few days. However, a cough caused by bronchial infection typically persists for 10 to 20 days. Since this patient has been coughing for 15 days, he most likely has acute bronchitis. Approximately 50% of patients with acute bronchitis have purulent sputum, but this is not a reliable predictor of bacterial infection.

Treatment of acute bronchitis is usually symptomatic. There is no evidence to support the use of most over-the-counter and prescription antitussive medications. However, some studies have shown that NSAIDs, with or without an antihistamine, decrease cough severity. A trial of ibuprofen may be reasonable for this patient, provided there are no contraindications.

Albuterol in a metered-dose inhaler may help to decrease cough severity and duration in adults with acute bronchitis when there is evidence of wheezing. However, β-agonist inhalers have not been shown to be helpful in the absence of wheezing and, therefore, probably would not benefit this patient.

Most studies fail to show that antibiotic administration significantly improves outcomes in patients with acute bronchitis, including symptom resolution and early return to work. In patients with an acute exacerbation of chronic obstructive pulmonary disease, antibiotic therapy is most likely to be helpful in those with at least two of the following: increased sputum purulence (change in sputum color), increased sputum volume, or increased dyspnea. Antibiotics are appropriate for patients with pertussis in order to decrease disease transmission, although these agents have a limited effect on symptoms. Pertussis should be suspected when a community outbreak has been reported. Symptoms may include coughing paroxysms and posttussive vomiting, but are not reliable indicators of infection.

A chest radiograph is not indicated in a patient with acute bronchitis who does not have signs or symptoms of pneumonia, such as fever, dyspnea, and pleuritic chest pain.

Cough that persists for more than 3 weeks is atypical for acute bronchitis, and a chest radiograph is generally indicated as the initial diagnostic test. Influenza virus culture is not needed in a patient without fever, myalgia, or malaise because the probability of influenza virus infection would be very low.

- **Antibiotics are not beneficial for patients with acute bronchitis.**

**Bibliography**

Wenzel RP, Fowler AA 3rd. Clinical Practice. Acute bronchitis. N Engl J Med. 2006;355(2):2125-2130. [PMID: 17108344]

## Item 110    Answer:  B

**Educational Objective:** Manage bereavement-associated depression.

The most appropriate management option for this patient is to initiate an antidepressant. Between 20% and 30% of spouses experience depression or complicated grief after the loss of a loved one. Most negative symptoms of bereavement peak before 6 months, and most family members are able to resume social activities and other activities of daily living by 6 months after their loved one's loss. Patients who meet symptoms of major depression for at least 2 consecutive weeks, 8 or more weeks after their loved one's death, are candidates for pharmacologic therapy.

Major depression in the setting of bereavement cannot be diagnosed unless the symptoms persist for more than 2 months or include substantive functional impairment, morbid preoccupation with worthlessness, suicidal ideation, psychotic symptoms, or psychomotor retardation. In this patient, the symptoms have persisted for more than 2 months and therapy is indicated. Mirtazapine would be an appropriate initial choice in this patient because it is an effective antidepressant and it has a side effect of sedation. Also, weight gain sometimes occurs with mirtazapine, which may be advantageous in a depressed patient with weight loss.

Complicated grief may present as persistent symptoms (>6 months after the loved one's death) of difficulty accepting the death, feelings of a meaningless future or empty life, difficulty moving on, detachment from other life activities, agitation, bitterness, and difficulty in forming relationships and trusting others. This patient is at risk for complicated grief and should be reassessed in several weeks.

Psychostimulants such as dextroamphetamine have been studied as an initial treatment of depression but with inconsistent efficacy results. Treating the insomnia with zolpidem would not treat the underlying cause of the insomnia. Reassuring the patient and offering follow-up in 3 months do not adequately address the underlying problem, for which there is effective treatment.

Practice Guidelines (Writing Committee to Revise the 2002 Guidelines on Perioperative Cardiovascular Evaluation for Noncardiac Surgery) Developed in Collaboration With the American Society of Echocardiography, American Society of Nuclear Cardiology, Heart Rhythm Society, Society of Cardiovascular Anesthesiologists, Society for Cardiovascular Angiography and Interventions, Society for Vascular Medicine and Biology, and Society for Vascular Surgery [erratum in J Am Coll Cardiol. 2008;52(9):794-797]. J Am Coll Cardiol. 2007;50(17):1707-1732. [PMID: 17950159]

**KEY POINT**

- Caregivers under stress or with prior mental health disorders should receive careful follow up and treatment for depression and complicated grief after their loved one dies.

**Bibliography**

Stroebe M, Schut H, Stroebe W. Health outcomes of bereavement. Lancet. 2007;370(9603):1960-1973. [PMID: 18068517]

## Item 111    Answer:  A

**Educational Objective:**  Manage the preoperative evaluation of a high-risk patient.

This patient, who is to undergo elective vascular surgery, has severe angina (class III-IV) that appears to be getting worse despite multiple medications. He has not benefited from medical therapy and meets the criteria for coronary angiography independent of his need for a femoropopliteal bypass graft. As long as surgery is elective, there is time for further cardiac evaluation and possible coronary artery revascularization.

Intensive medical therapy with β-blockers and statins may be as effective as a revascularization procedure in stable patients. However, this patient has increasing symptoms despite maximal medical therapy and therefore warrants further evaluation despite the potential risks associated with the contrast medium used in coronary angiography, even in the presence of diabetes mellitus or chronic kidney disease.

Although the Coronary Artery Revascularization Prophylaxis trial failed to show either a short-term or long-term benefit of prophylactic revascularization in patients with stable cardiac symptoms before elective vascular surgery, this patient has angina that is progressing despite medical therapy, and the results of this trial cannot be generalized to this patient.

Pharmacologic stress testing is not indicated for this patient with known coronary artery disease and a high pretest probability of an abnormal test result.

Resting two-dimensional echocardiography is useful for evaluating suspected significant valvular heart disease or left ventricular function in a patient with heart failure in order to clarify the cause and extent of cardiac dysfunction. It is not a good predictor of perioperative ischemic events.

**KEY POINT**

- Preoperative prophylactic revascularization in patients with coronary artery disease who require an elective noncardiac surgical procedure should be restricted to patients with criteria for coronary artery revascularization independent of their need for surgery.

**Bibliography**

Fleisher LA, Beckman JA, Brown KA, et al. ACC/AHA 2007 Guidelines on Perioperative Cardiovascular Evaluation and Care for Noncardiac Surgery: Executive Summary: A Report of the American College of Cardiology/American Heart Association Task Force on

## Item 112    Answer:  A

**Educational Objective:**  Diagnose attention-deficit/hyperactivity disorder.

This patient's presentation is suggestive of attention-deficit/hyperactivity disorder (ADHD). ADHD is characterized by difficulty paying attention, impulsivity, and motor restlessness or hyperactivity, with onset before the age of 7 years. There must also be some impairment in social, occupational, or academic functioning, and the symptoms must be manifest in at least two different environments, such as school and home. When diagnosing an adult with ADHD, the diagnosis should be established by a mental health professional because of the multiple symptoms that must be confirmed, the possible presence of comorbid mental disorders, and the need to verify that the symptoms began before the patient was 7 years old. Although evidence of symptoms dating back to age 7 years is required to make the diagnosis, patients are often identified in their first year of college or graduate school, presumably because they have been intelligent enough to compensate for the disorder until the level of work becomes too great.

Generalized anxiety disorder (GAD) is characterized by difficulty exercising control over worrying, as well as other symptoms such as fatigue, irritability, restlessness, sleep disturbance, and difficulty concentrating. This patient does not report worrying that is excessive or difficult to control, and his inability to concentrate, given the accompanying symptoms, is much better explained by ADHD than GAD.

Although impaired concentration is a feature of major depression, this patient does not present with depressed mood or anhedonia, and there is no report of appetite or sleep disturbance, fatigue, guilt, or suicidal ideation.

Although schizophrenia often presents at this age, there is no history provided of delusions, hallucinations, disorganized speech or behavior, or affective flattening to support the diagnosis.

**KEY POINT**

- Although attention-deficit/hyperactivity disorder (ADHD) often comes to medical attention in late adolescence or early adulthood, symptoms must have had their onset prior to age 7 years to diagnose ADHD.

**Bibliography**

Newcorn JH, Weiss M, Stein MA. The complexity of ADHD: diagnosis and treatment of the adult patient with comorbidities. CNS Spectr. 2007;12(8 Suppl 12):1-14. [PMID: 17667893]

## Item 113    Answer:  A

**Educational Objective:**  Manage a patient with an inguinal hernia.

Watchful waiting with deferred surgery is an appropriate management option for this patient who is reluctant to have surgery and has minimal symptoms of an inguinal hernia. In selected patients with asymptomatic inguinal hernia, a wait-and-watch policy can be employed to avoid the risks of surgery (infection, chronic pain, recurrence) and anesthesia-related problems. The risk of developing obstruction is small in asymptomatic inguinal hernias, but it increases slowly over a period of time and requires symptom monitoring.

If symptoms worsen, the patient can then opt for surgery. A previous myocardial infarction or mild stable angina is not a contraindication to surgery, and inguinal hernia repair is a relatively low-risk surgical procedure. Two surgical techniques are commonly available: open mesh repair and laparoscopic repair. An open mesh repair is a quicker procedure and has lower rates of major complications compared with laparoscopic repair. Local anesthesia is the least expensive and most cost-effective option and is associated with fewer postoperative medical and urologic complications than general anesthesia or regional anesthesia. Laparoscopic surgery is usually preferable for bilateral hernias because it is less painful, less invasive, recovery is faster, and there is a lower incidence of numbness and pain. The increased cost of laparoscopic repair in patients with bilateral hernias is offset by earlier return to work.

No studies have shown that hernia trusses offer good control of symptoms. In fact, they may lead to spermatic cord atrophy or fusion to the hernial sac and atrophy of the fascial elements of the groin, which are important for the integrity of the groin after repair. Therefore, a hernia truss is not recommended for this patient.

**KEY POINT**

- **Watchful waiting is a reasonable option for patients with an inguinal hernia with minimal symptoms, and incarceration is a relatively uncommon complication.**

**Bibliography**
Fitzgibbons RJ Jr, Giobbie-Hurder A, Gibbs JO, et al. Watchful waiting vs repair of inguinal hernia in minimally symptomatic men: a randomized clinical trial [erratum in JAMA. 2006;295(23):2726]. JAMA. 2006;295(3):285-292. [PMID: 16418463]

## Item 114    Answer:  D

**Educational Objective:**  Evaluate a patient with obesity.

The evaluation of the patient with an initial diagnosis of overweight or obesity should include measurement of waist circumference and a review of eating and exercise habits. Higher levels of abdominal obesity are associated with increased risk of coronary artery disease, type 2 diabetes mellitus, dyslipidemia, and hypertension. In adults with a BMI of 25 to 34.9, a waist circumference greater than 102 cm (40 in) for men and 88 cm (35 in) for women is associated with greater risk than that determined by BMI alone. In patients with a BMI of 35 or greater, the measurement is less helpful, as nearly all these patients have abdominal obesity. In Asian populations, a male waist circumference greater than 90 cm (35 in) and a female waist circumference greater than 80 cm (32 in) are considered abnormal.

Patients should also be screened for diseases that are caused or worsened by obesity, including hyperlipidemia, diabetes mellitus, hypertension, and obstructive sleep apnea, particularly in patients who complain of unrefreshing sleep, daytime somnolence, or have a history of snoring.

Screening for Cushing syndrome may be indicated in patients with truncal obesity, plethora, wide purple striae, hypertension, or hirsutism, but these findings are absent in this patient. Measurement of 24-hour cortisol is, therefore, not necessary. The regularity of her menstrual periods, her ability to conceive, and absence of androgen excess make polycystic ovary syndrome unlikely, and pelvic ultrasonography is unnecessary. A patient with growth hormone deficiency and obesity would be expected to have short stature, but this patient is relatively tall, and an insulin-like growth factor 1 (IGF-1) concentration in not indicated.

**KEY POINT**

- **Waist circumference should be measured in all overweight and obese patients with a BMI of less than 35.**

**Bibliography**
Janssen I, Katzmarzyk PT, Ross R. Body mass index, waist circumference, and health risk: evidence in support of current National Institutes of Health guidelines. Arch Intern Med. 2002;162(18):2074-2079. [PMID: 12374515]

## Item 115    Answer:  D

**Educational Objective:**  Manage early age-related macular degeneration.

This patient has early age-related macular degeneration (AMD), which can affect one or both eyes. Early AMD is characterized by the finding of drusen (yellow deposits in the retina, as noted on examination in this patient) or retinal pigment changes. (A few small, scattered drusen are a normal part of aging.) The clearest risk factors for the development of AMD are increasing age and smoking (>10 pack-year history). Thus, all smokers with AMD, regardless of stage, should be advised to quit smoking. Patients who have quit smoking for more than 20 years are at no higher risk of AMD than nonsmokers.

There is no indication for initiating antioxidant supplementation in patients with early AMD, as it has not been shown to prevent progression. Patients with intermediate AMD in one or both eyes, or advanced AMD in one eye, should be treated with antioxidant therapy; for these patients, the Age-Related Eye Disease Study demonstrated significant reduction in the risk of progression of visual loss, and in some patients, improvement in vision, in those taking a combination of antioxidants (vitamin C, vitamin E, β-carotene) plus zinc and copper daily. However, patients who are smokers should not take β-carotene supplements, as this may increase the risk of lung cancer, and vitamin E supplementation can increase the risk of heart failure in patients with diabetes mellitus or coronary artery disease. In these subgroups, supplementation with zinc and copper alone may be just as effective.

Hypertension and hypercholesterolemia should be treated according to national guidelines regardless of the presence of AMD. Further reduction of this patient's LDL cholesterol level or blood pressure will have no additional beneficial effect on this patient's AMD.

### KEY POINT

- All patients with age-related macular degeneration, regardless of stage, should be counseled to quit smoking.

**Bibliography**

Jager RD, Mieler WF, Miller JW. Age-related macular degeneration. NEJM. 2008;358(24):2606-2617. [PMID: 18550876]

## Item 116      Answer:   C

**Educational Objective:** Diagnose orthostatic hypotension as a cause of syncope.

The patient's history and examination findings are consistent with orthostatic hypotension. A drop in systolic blood pressure of 20 mm Hg or more or diastolic blood pressure of 10 mm Hg or more after standing for 3 minutes is diagnostic of orthostatic hypotension. Medications are a common cause of orthostatic hypotension, and α-adrenergic blockers, such as doxazosin, are a class of medications that may precipitate this condition. As the episode of syncope was temporally related to initiation of the doxazosin, a prudent strategy would be to discontinue the medication.

Structural heart disease is common in this patient's age group, but nothing in his clinical history or physical examination suggests a cardiac abnormality. In the presence of a likely explanation for his syncope, there is no indication for admitting him for inpatient cardiovascular evaluation.

Cerebrovascular causes of syncope are invariably associated with neurologic signs and symptoms, such as ataxia, vertigo, and diplopia. Since the patient has no neurologic signs, a cerebrovascular cause is unlikely and a brain MRI would be of limited use.

24-Hour ambulatory electrocardiographic monitoring has poor yield in the evaluation of syncope unless the patient has frequent episodes of syncope or lightheadedness that could be captured during testing. For patients with infrequent symptoms, continuous-loop recorders are recommended. However, in a patient with historical and clinical findings strongly suggesting orthostatic hypotension, additional diagnostic evaluation for arrhythmia is not indicated.

### KEY POINT

- Orthostatic hypotension is usually diagnosed by a suggestive history or a systolic blood pressure decrease of at least 20 mm Hg or a diastolic blood pressure decrease of at least 10 mm Hg within 3 minutes of standing.

**Bibliography**

Gupta V, Lipsitz LA. Orthostatic hypotension in the elderly: diagnosis and treatment. Am J Med. 2007;120(10):841-847. [PMID: 17904451]

## Item 117      Answer:   D

**Educational Objective:** Diagnose sacroiliac joint pain.

This patient is probably suffering from right sacroiliitis from strain. The sacroiliac joint is susceptible to strain injuries, particularly in overweight patients who do not routinely exercise. Pain in the posterior pelvic region when performing the FABER test (Flexion, ABduction, and External Rotation of the hip) with the absence of pain on passive hip rotation is fairly specific for sacroiliac joint pathology.

Hip pain from osteoarthritis usually presents as groin pain and occasionally radiates to the knee and localizes to the buttock. Weight bearing is often painful, and patients usually have evidence of osteoarthritis elsewhere. Osteoarthritis of the hip is also associated with pain during both passive and active range of motion, which is not present in this patient. Furthermore, the diagnosis of osteoarthritis, a chronic medical condition, is unlikely in a patient who presents with the acute onset of symptoms of 3 days' duration.

Piriformis syndrome is a common source of sciatic nerve pain resulting from irritation and hypertrophy of the piriformis muscle. Pain is reproduced by applying pressure to the sciatic notch, a finding that was absent in this patient.

Most patients with a herniated disk and associated radiculitis will have a positive straight-leg-raising test, which is absent in this patient.

Trochanteric bursitis can be confirmed in patients in whom hip adduction intensifies the pain or in those in whom the examination reveals pain and tenderness over the bursa. The absence of lateral hip pain in this patient makes trochanteric bursitis unlikely.

### KEY POINT

- Pain in the posterior pelvic region when performing the FABER test (Flexion, ABduction, and External Rotation of the hip) with the absence of pain on passive hip rotation is fairly specific for sacroiliac joint pathology.

**Bibliography**

Foley BS, Buschbacher RM. Sacroiliac joint pain: anatomy, biomechanics, diagnosis, and treatment. Am J Phys Med Rehabil. 2006;85(12):997-1006. [PMID: 17117004]

## Item 118    Answer:  D

**Educational Objective:**  Diagnose bulimia nervosa.

This patient's presentation is consistent with a diagnosis of bulimia nervosa. Bulimia incidence peaks in college-aged students. Diagnostic criteria for this disorder are episodes of bingeing with loss of control occurring a minimum of two times per week for 3 months, followed by purging or other compensatory behavior, such as fasting, strict dieting, or excessive exercise. Purging includes vomiting or abuse of laxatives or diuretics. Patients with bulimia usually have normal weight, but many have depression or anxiety. The medical complications of bulimia nervosa result from the method and frequency of purging and can involve acid-induced dental disease, esophageal tears, and electrolyte derangements. Clues for the presence of bulimia include low serum potassium or high serum bicarbonate levels in otherwise healthy patients. Patients with this disorder respond well to psychotherapy and pharmacotherapy, the combination of which may be better than either therapy alone, although some data suggest patients prefer psychotherapy.

There are two types of anorexia nervosa: *restricting type*, in which patients restrict intake, and *binge-eating/ purging type*, in which they binge and then purge to control weight. Diagnostic criteria for anorexia nervosa consist of refusal to maintain weight within 15% of normal, fear of weight gain, distorted body image, and amenorrhea or lack of onset of menstruation. This patient's weight is normal; therefore, she does not meet the diagnostic criteria for either type of anorexia nervosa.

Binge-eating disorder is present in patients who binge at least 2 days per week for 6 months, bingeing with rapid eating, eating until uncomfortable, and feeling disgusted or guilty after the binge. Binge-eating disorder does not involve purging.

**KEY POINT**

- **Diagnostic criteria for bulimia nervosa are episodes of bingeing with loss of control occurring a minimum of two times per week for 3 months, followed by purging or other compensatory behavior.**

**Bibliography**

Wilfley DE, Bishop ME, Wilson GT, Agras WS. Classification of eating disorders: Toward DSM-V. Int J Eat Disord 2007;40 Suppl:S123-S129. [PMID: 17685383]

## Item 119    Answer:  E

**Educational Objective:**  Diagnose hallucinations in a patient with low vision.

Visual hallucinations are a normal finding in patients with severely diminished vision. These hallucinations, known as Charles Bonnet syndrome, are present in approximately 10% to 15% of patients with low vision. The visual hallucinations that people describe can vary from simple geometric figures to vivid images of faces and scenes that they may recognize or that may be distinctly unusual or nonsensical. The hallucinations may be integrated with normal vision and perception but are not accompanied by auditory hallucinations or other sensory findings. The images themselves are rarely disturbing; patients know that they are not real and may be able to make them disappear by closing their eyes. The visual hallucinations are a benign process, and patients should be reassured about their benign nature. There is currently no consensus on effective treatment, and the hallucinations may persist for years.

This patient, although limited by her diminished vision, has no findings to suggest dementia as a cause of her hallucinations. The normal neurologic examination makes either stroke or intracranial mass unlikely.

Medication side effects, from prescription and over-the-counter medications, should always be considered in an elderly patient with complaints of hallucinations or mental status changes. Tolterodine can cause hallucinations; however, she has had no changes in her medications in the past year, making this an unlikely cause of her symptoms.

**KEY POINT**

- **Patients with markedly diminished visual acuity may develop vivid visual hallucinations that they recognize as not real and are benign.**

**Bibliography**

Khan JC, Shahid H, Thurlby DA, Yates JR, Moore AT. Charles Bonnet syndrome in age-related macular degeneration: the nature and frequency of images in subjects with end-stage disease. Ophthalmic Epidemiol. 2008;15(3):202-208. [PMID: 18569816]

## Item 120    Answer:  A

**Educational Objective:**  Manage depression in a terminally ill patient.

The most appropriate management option is to initiate an antidepressant, such as citalopram. Weight loss and anorexia, sleeping difficulty, fatigue, and reduced concentration—features used as diagnostic criteria for major depression—are often found in patients with malignancy in the absence of depression. For this reason, substitute criteria of tearfulness, social withdrawal, self-pity/pessimism, and lack of reactivity have been suggested as alternative markers of clinical depression. This patient meets diagnostic criteria for major depression, including depressed mood or anhedonia, and treatment should be initiated. Low-dose citalopram or another selective serotonin reuptake inhibitor that does not have multiple drug-drug interactions would be an appropriate first-choice therapy. Tricyclic antidepressants are also effective. There are no evidence-based studies comparing efficacy of antidepressants in palliative care.

Lorazepam would be effective in treating patients in a palliative care setting who had symptoms of anxiety. However, lorazepam would not be beneficial in treating this patient, who does not have symptoms of anxiety and has symptoms of depression.

A metastasis to the brain can cause mood changes and could be detected by an MRI. However, this is an unlikely diagnosis without other focal neurologic symptoms.

While an improvement in her physical symptoms and functional status following treatment for bony metastases may result in a more positive outlook, this is uncertain, and it would be inappropriate to withhold offering effective antidepressant therapy in the meantime.

### KEY POINT

- **Depression is both common and treatable in patients receiving palliative care.**

**Bibliography**
Qaseem A, Snow V, Shekelle P, et al. Evidence-based interventions to improve the palliative care of pain, dyspnea, and depression at the end of life: a clinical practice guideline from the American College of Physicians. Ann Intern Med. 2008;148(2):141-146. [PMID: 18195338]

## Item 121      Answer:  A

**Educational Objective:**  Treat benign prostatic hyperplasia.

The most appropriate treatment for this patient is doxazosin. His symptoms and American Urological Association (AUA) prostate symptom score are consistent with moderately severe benign prostatic hyperplasia (BPH). α-Blockers act rapidly (usually within 48 hours) and are considered first-line treatment, producing a clinical response in 70% of men. α-Blockers approved in the United States for symptomatic BPH are doxazosin, terazosin, tamsulosin, and alfuzosin. All four appear equally effective, causing on average a 4- to 6-point improvement in the AUA prostate symptom score, which most patients perceive as a meaningful change.

Conservative treatment (such as decreasing fluid intake, dietary and medication changes, timed voiding) would be warranted in a patient with mild symptoms (AUA symptom score of ≤7) or those wishing to avoid medication or procedural interventions. Because 5α-reductase inhibitors (finasteride, dutasteride) shrink prostate tissue, symptoms often do not improve until after 6 months of therapy. They are indicated in patients who have failed to benefit from or do not tolerate α-blockers, those with severe symptoms, and those with an obviously enlarged prostate or a prostate-specific antigen level greater than 1.4 ng/mL (1.4 μg/L). They can also be combined with α-blockers in patients with an inadequate response to monotherapy.

Some studies suggest that *Serenoa repens* (saw palmetto berry) and *Pygeum africanum* (red stinkwood or African plum) may be beneficial for BPH symptoms. However, the trials have often been poorly designed, and the extracts available have not undergone the same scrutiny as conventional drugs for efficacy, purity, and safety. Consensus guidelines therefore do not recommend herbal treatments at the present time.

Minimally invasive therapies such as transurethral microwave thermotherapy are a treatment option in patients with an inadequate response to pharmacotherapy as well as those who do not tolerate or desire to take chronic medications.

### KEY POINT

- **α-Blockers act rapidly and are considered first-line treatment for benign prostatic hyperplasia symptoms.**

**Bibliography**
Kaplan S. Update on the American Urological Association guidelines for the treatment of benign prostatic hyperplasia. Rev Urol. 2006;8 Suppl 4:S10–S17. [PMID: 17215996]

## Item 122      Answer:  D

**Educational Objective:**  Manage hyperlipidemia.

The best management for this patient is to repeat a fasting lipid level in the future. This patient has hyperlipidemia, defined by a total cholesterol level above 200 mg/dL (5.18 mmol/L). The LDL cholesterol goal varies depending on the presence or absence of five major cardiovascular risk factors: cigarette smoking, hypertension, older age, low HDL cholesterol (<40 mg/dL [1.04 mmol/L]), and a family history of coronary artery disease (CAD).

In patients with zero or one risk factor, the LDL cholesterol goal is below 160 mg/dL (4.14 mmol/L). This patient has no major risk factors. Because his current LDL cholesterol level is below goal, no therapy is indicated. The U.S. Preventive Services Task Force concluded that the optimal interval for repeat screening is uncertain. It would be reasonable to repeat screening every 5 years, as recommended by the National Cholesterol Education Program or select a shorter interval if the lipid levels are close to the threshold for treatment, as in this patient.

Fibrate therapy would be indicated for hypertriglyceridemia (>200 mg/dL [2.26 mmol/L]) in the setting of elevated non-HDL cholesterol. This patient's triglyceride level is in the normal range and his non-HDL cholesterol level is 186 mg/dL (4.82 mmol/L), which is below his non-HDL cholesterol goal of 190 mg/dL (4.92 mmol/L).

Statin therapy would be appropriate for this patient with no risk factors if his LDL cholesterol level were above 190 mg/dL (4.92 mmol/L) and would be optional if the level were between 160 mg/dL and 190 mg/dL (4.14 and 4.92 mmol/L).

Lipoprotein(a) [Lp(a)] level determination is not recommended for routine practice. Lp(a) is associated with increased risk for CAD, but does not appear to be an independent predictor of risk of CAD. Moreover, treatment of elevated Lp(a) with statins is not effective in lowering Lp(a) levels appreciably, and there are no clinical trials that show benefit from treatment.

- In patients with zero or one cardiovascular risk factor, the LDL cholesterol goal is below 160 mg/dL (4.14 mmol/L).

**Bibliography**

Grundy SM, Cleeman JI, Merz CN, et al; National Heart, Lung, and Blood Institute; American College of Cardiology Foundation; American Heart Association. Implications of recent clinical trials for the National Cholesterol Education Program Adult Treatment Panel III guidelines. Circulation [erratum in Circulation. 2004;110(6):763]. 2004;110(2):227-239. [PMID: 15249516]

## Item 123   Answer:   B
**Educational Objective:** Evaluate possible halitosis.

This patient's concern about her breath has become an obsession, resulting in major restrictions in her social interactions. The clinical evaluation of possible halitosis begins with an assessment of odor. In this patient, there is no confirmation of odor during an examination that includes a subjective assessment of her breath during mouth breathing and nose breathing. Also, scrapings of the back of her tongue do not have an odor. Additionally, her mother does not confirm the presence of halitosis.

The patient should be re-examined for halitosis on another day after not eating, drinking, or brushing her teeth. A family member or close friend should also provide objective evidence of odor at this time. If no significant odor is detected by the examiner and family member or friend, she likely has halitophobia (exaggerated concerns about bad breath without objective evidence). Halitophobia is diagnosed in about 25% of persons being evaluated for complaints of bad breath. Efforts should be made to reassure the patient as well as to explore any psychosocial factors that may be playing a role. If the distorted breath odor image does not resolve, referral to a mental health professional with experience in treating this disorder is indicated because if its significant impact on this patient's life.

The esophagus, stomach, and intestines are rarely causes of halitosis. Therefore, even if the patient has gastroesophageal reflux disease, which is unlikely based upon her symptoms, she would not have halitosis as a result of this disorder.

The most common source of halitosis is the mouth (poor oral hygiene, gingivitis, periodontitis). This patient has normal teeth and gums and has had regular dental examinations, ruling out periodontal disease. The nasal passages are the second most common source of halitosis. Because this patient has no odor detected during nose breathing, nasal polyps as a cause of bad breath are unlikely.

Obstructive sleep apnea is unlikely in a patient who does not snore. Sleep apnea may contribute to "morning breath," the mild transient oral odor that occurs after sleep and is exacerbated by xerostomia, but this odor would not persist throughout the day.

- Clinical evaluation of perceived halitosis should include a subjective assessment of the patient's breath, both when mouth breathing and nose breathing.

**Bibliography**

Porter SR, Scully C. Oral malodour (halitosis). BMJ. 2006;333 (7569):632-635. [PMID: 16990322]

## Item 124   Answer:   B
**Educational Objective:** Diagnose vision loss in an elderly patient.

This patient's symptoms are typical for cataracts, which commonly cause reduced illumination, reduced contrast sensitivity, increased glare, and impaired blue-yellow color vision. She also has diabetes mellitus and smokes, which are both risk factors for cataract formation. Other risk factors are excessive sunlight exposure and heavy alcohol consumption.

Age-related macular degeneration, presbyopia, primary open-angle glaucoma, and proliferative diabetic retinopathy are the other common ophthalmologic problems in elderly persons. Macular degeneration affects the macula and typically causes decreased visual acuity and, in particular, loss of central vision. There is also loss of contrast sensitivity and the perception of straight lines as wavy (metamorphopsia).

Presbyopia is part of the natural aging process and is manifested by decreased visual acuity and focusing ability. Primary open-angle glaucoma is usually asymptomatic until late in its course because loss of peripheral vision occurs first and loss of central vision occurs much later. Risk factors include age, family history, myopia, black race, and diabetes mellitus.

Proliferative diabetic retinopathy may result in reduced visual acuity, scotomata, a sensation of a "curtain falling" as a result of vitreous bleeding, and floaters due to a resolving episode of vitreous bleeding. Risk factors include hypertension, poor control of diabetes, the duration of diabetes, excessive alcohol consumption, and smoking.

Since visual impairment and disability are common in the elderly, the U.S. Preventive Services Task Force recommends periodic Snellen visual acuity testing. Many professional organizations, including the American College of Physicians, recommend annual screening of patients with diabetes by means of a dilated ophthalmoscopic examination or stereoscopic fundus photography. Consensus also exists that most internists have uncertain ability to detect the intraocular changes of age-related macular degeneration and glaucoma. Therefore, periodic examination by an eye professional is recommended for persons over 65 years of age, especially persons with risk factors for age-related ophthalmologic disorders.

- Periodic examination by an eye professional is recommended for all persons over 65 years of age, especially persons with risk factors for age-related ophthalmologic disorders.

**Bibliography**

Rosenthal BP. Ophthalmology. Screening and treatment of age-related and pathologic vision changes. Geriatrics. 2001;56(12):27-31; quiz 32. [PMID: 11766560]

## Item 125    Answer:  D

**Educational Objective:**  Diagnose sudden sensorineural hearing loss.

This patient has sudden sensorineural hearing loss in his left ear (Weber test lateralizes to the good ear), which is defined as hearing loss that occurs in 3 days or less. Patients often report immediate or rapid loss of hearing or find that they cannot hear upon awakening. Approximately 90% of patients have unilateral hearing loss, and some have tinnitus, ear fullness, or vertigo. Diagnosing sudden sensorineural hearing loss is a challenge because it may be caused by many diverse conditions, including viral infections and autoimmune disorders. Immediate referral to an otorhinolaryngologist is required. Oral corticosteroids are usually given, although results of randomized trials differ regarding the efficacy of this therapy.

Cholesteatoma is a growth of desquamated, stratified, squamous epithelium within the middle ear. It is typically visible on otoscopy as an opaque or ivory colored mass behind the tympanic membrane. With growth, the cholesteatoma may erode the ossicles, resulting in a conductive hearing loss. If left untreated, erosion into the inner ear may cause sensorineural hearing loss. Patients may present with otorrhea, pain, hearing loss, or neurologic symptoms. This patient's presentation is not compatible with a cholesteatoma.

Eustachian tube dysfunction can cause muffled hearing and intermittent popping sounds in the ear. The Weber test is typically normal. This patient's sudden hearing loss and tinnitus are not compatible with eustachian tube dysfunction.

Otosclerosis is a bony overgrowth that involves the footplate of the stapes, eventually resulting in total fixation and inability to transmit vibration from the tympanic membrane along the ossicular chain. This results in a gradually progressive conductive hearing loss. The patient's sudden sensorineural hearing loss is not compatible with the diagnosis of otosclerosis.

- Patients with sudden sensorineural hearing loss require immediate referral to an otorhinolaryngologist.

**Bibliography**

Rauch SD. Clinical practice. Idiopathic sudden sensorineural hearing loss. N Engl J Med. 2008;359(8):833-840. [PMID: 18716300]

## Item 126    Answer:  A

**Educational Objective:**  Manage acute nonspecific low back pain.

This patient has acute low back pain resulting from a recent injury. He has no signs of neurologic compromise or potentially serious underlying conditions. Guidelines published by the American College of Physicians and the American Pain Society recommend acetaminophen or NSAIDs for first-line treatment of acute nonspecific low back pain. Opioid analgesics or tramadol is an option when used judiciously in patients with severe, disabling acute low back pain that is not controlled (or is unlikely to be controlled) with acetaminophen or NSAIDs. Patients should be informed that the prognosis for acute lower back pain is generally good and that most patients improve within 1 month.

An epidural corticosteroid injection may be appropriate treatment for a patient with persistent symptoms or if radiculopathy is suspected; however, this patient's pain is of recent onset, and he does not have signs of nerve root involvement.

The patient has no signs of neurologic compromise or features suggesting a potentially serious condition; therefore, MRI would not be necessary. Even if there were signs of disk herniation (a positive straight-leg-raising test), an MRI would not be necessary unless the patient had evidence of motor impairment, had not responded to therapy, or symptoms were increasing.

Lumbar plain radiographs are generally not recommended in the evaluation of low back pain because there is no evidence that routine plain radiography in patients with nonspecific low back pain is associated with a greater improvement in patient outcomes than selective imaging. Plain radiographs would be appropriate if a vertebral compression fracture is suspected.

Studies have not demonstrated that bed rest is helpful in acute lumbago, and it may impair recovery time.

- Acetaminophen or NSAIDs are first-line therapy for acute nonspecific low back pain.

**Bibliography**

Chou R, Qaseem A, Snow V, Casey D, Cross JT Jr, Shekelle P, Owens DK; Clinical Efficacy Assessment Subcommittee of the American College of Physicians; American College of Physicians; American Pain Society Low Back Pain Guidelines Panel. Diagnosis and treatment of low back pain: a joint clinical practice guideline from the American College of Physicians and the American Pain Society [erratum in Ann Intern Med. 2008;148(3):247-248]. Ann Intern Med. 2007;147(7):478-91. [PMID: 17909209]

## Item 127    Answer:  A

**Educational Objective:** Diagnose epididymitis.

This patient has gradual onset of pain and discomfort localized to the left testicular region, with associated dysuria, fever, mild systemic symptoms, scrotal erythema, and tenderness localized to the epididymis. The most likely diagnosis is acute epididymitis, an infection of the epididymis. Acute epididymitis (presenting with symptoms over hours or days) or subacute epididymitis (symptoms present for up to 6 weeks) is often caused by bacterial infection. Epididymitis before age 35 years is usually caused by a sexually transmitted disease, but may result from a urinary tract infection with retrograde flow from the bladder through the vas deferens to the epididymis.

Hernias may present with scrotal pain or masses but should not present with infectious symptoms, as in this patient.

Orchitis, an inflammation of the testicle, presents with a diffusely tender testicle with the gradual onset of pain over hours to days. This patient presents with scrotal pain over hours to days, but the pain is well localized to the epididymis and does not involve the testicle, making acute orchitis unlikely.

Testicular torsion is characterized by the abrupt onset of severe pain. The testicle may sit higher in the scrotum than normal, may lie transversely, or a knot may be palpated in the spermatic cord. This patient presented with a gradual onset of pain more typical of epididymitis, and there were no physical examination findings suggestive of torsion. An absent cremasteric reflex on the affected side is nearly 99% sensitive for torsion; this patient had a normal testicular lie and an intact cremasteric reflex, making torsion unlikely.

### KEY POINT

- **Bacterial epididymitis presents with gradual onset of pain and discomfort localized to the involved testicle, with associated dysuria, fever, systemic symptoms (nausea, poor appetite), and tenderness localized to the epididymis.**

**Bibliography**
Tracy CR, Steers WD, Costabile R. Diagnosis and management of epididymitis. Urol Clin North Am. 2008;35(1):101-108. [PMID: 18061028]

## Item 128    Answer:  D

**Educational Objective:** Manage narcotic medications in a terminally ill patient with moderate to severe pain.

Pain control is a common management issue in the terminally ill patient. As-needed doses of opioid analgesics combined with non-opioid adjunctive therapy is an effective management strategy for mild to moderate cancer pain. When this strategy no longer suffices, however, additional pain relief must be given. This patient has discomfort from pain that returns before his next scheduled dose of analgesic therapy, and he is taking the medication on a continual basis. This patient would benefit the most from the addition of a longer-acting narcotic to treat his pain. An appropriate solution would be to give sustained-release morphine twice daily. A breakthrough pain strategy should be continued so the patient has options if the longer-acting pain medication does not provide complete relief. When adding a long-acting opioid, a strategy to avoid overmedication is to start with 30% to 50% of the patient's average 24-hour dosage of narcotic.

Gabapentin can be useful to treat neuropathic pain, but would likely not be useful to reduce pain from a bony metastasis. Increasing the frequency of the immediate-release medication is not the best answer because of the need of the patient to re-dose frequently owing to multiple recurrent bouts of pain. The goal of palliative therapy for pain is to have the patient free of significant pain for most of the day with infrequent need for additional doses of immediate-release pain medication. Switching the medication from one immediate-release formulation to another is also unlikely to make the patient more comfortable.

### KEY POINT

- **Long-acting narcotics are useful in pain control for patients with inadequate pain relief on short-acting, as-needed narcotic therapy.**

**Bibliography**
Bruera E, Kim HN. Cancer Pain. JAMA. 2003;290(18):2476-2479. [PMID: 14612485]

## Item 129    Answer:  D

**Educational Objective:** Treat stress urinary incontinence.

This patient has mild stress urinary incontinence, which is manifested by involuntary leakage of small amounts of urine and is frequently precipitated by activities that increase intra-abdominal pressure, such as coughing, exercise, or straining. Stress urinary incontinence is particularly common in middle-aged to older women in whom the pelvic musculature that supports the bladder has weakened as a result of childbearing, aging, or other factors.

Numerous clinical trials has shown that pelvic floor muscle exercises (such as Kegel exercises), either alone or with bladder training, have proven efficacy in managing stress urinary incontinence. For patients who have difficulty learning or performing these exercises, training can occur in conjunction with biofeedback.

Oral estrogen therapy was once considered a potentially effective treatment for stress urinary incontinence in postmenopausal women, presumably because vaginal atrophy may aggravate urethral sphincter incompetence. However, numerous clinical trials have shown that oral estrogens (with or without progestin) may actually increase stress or urge incontinence.

Bladder training, which includes scheduled voiding, may have modest benefits for urge incontinence (overactive bladder), but the evidence of the efficacy of this method for stress incontinence in inconclusive. Oxybutynin and several other anticholinergic agents are effective for urge incontinence but are not indicated for the treatment of stress incontinence.

Surgical procedures to correct stress urinary incontinence include retropubic suspension and pubovaginal slings. However, a trial of a nonoperative therapy, particularly pelvic floor muscle training, is usually indicated first in a patient with early or mild stress urinary incontinence.

**KEY POINT**

- **Pelvic floor muscle exercises are effective for treating early or mild stress urinary incontinence.**

**Bibliography**

Choi H, Palmer MH, Park J. Meta-analysis of pelvic floor muscle training: randomized controlled trials in incontinent women. Nursing Research. 2007;56(4):226-234. [PMID: 17625461]

## Item 130    Answer:  A

**Educational Objective:**  Diagnose Asperger syndrome.

This patient most likely has Asperger syndrome, which is a form of autism. Autism is characterized by a triad of impaired communication, impaired social interactions, and restrictive, repetitive, and stereotyped behaviors and interests. Asperger syndrome is a high-functioning type of autism in which early language development is not delayed. The syndrome is often diagnosed in adolescence or early adulthood. This patient's lack of friends and social isolation, lack of normal prosody and gesturing in speech, restricted interests, desire for routine, and poor school and employment history are all consistent with this syndrome.

Attention-deficit/hyperactivity disorder (ADHD) is characterized by difficulty concentrating, impulsivity, and motor restlessness or hyperactivity. ADHD usually develops before 7 years of age. Although impairment in social, occupational, and/or academic functioning occurs, the speech abnormalities and restricted interests typical of patients with Asperger syndrome are not characteristic of those with ADHD.

The diagnosis of major depressive disorder requires the presence of depressed mood or loss of interest in usual activities (anhedonia). This patient states that he is not depressed. Although his activities are limited, there is no evidence that he has lost interest in the few activities that he does maintain.

The diagnosis of schizophrenia requires a history of at least two psychotic symptoms for 1 or more months. Symptoms may include hallucinations, delusions, disorganized speech, grossly disorganized or catatonic behavior, and flattening of the affect. This patient's speech is flattened but not disorganized, and he does not have other psychotic findings.

The primary feature of social anxiety disorder is a severe and persistent fear of social or performance situations, such as public speaking or taking an examination. This patient does not attribute his social problems to such fears or anxiety, and his communication style and restricted interests are characteristic of an autistic rather than an anxiety disorder.

**KEY POINT**

- **Asperger syndrome is a high-functioning type of autism in which early language development is not delayed.**

**Bibliography**

Macintosh KE, Dissanayake C. Annotation: The similarities and differences between autistic disorder and Asperger's disorder: a review of the empirical evidence. J Child Psychol Psychiatry. 2004;45(3): 421-434. [PMID: 15055363]

## Item 131    Answer:  D

**Educational Objective:**  Diagnose short-term complications after gastric bypass surgery.

The patient should receive an upper endoscopy to rule out a complication from her recent laparoscopic gastric bypass surgery, especially stomal stenosis (a stricture at the anastomosis of the gastric pouch and jejunum) or marginal ulcerations or erosions. If a stricture is diagnosed at the time of endoscopy, dilation of the stricture endoscopically often results in relief of symptoms without the need for repeat surgery.

Stomal stenosis typically presents with symptoms of nausea, vomiting, and inability to eat. Either barium swallow or upper endoscopy can establish the diagnosis. Endoscopy may be more appropriate than barium swallow in this patient because of the possibility of stomal erosion, which is more difficult to diagnose with barium radiography. Because the patient has not had other signs of upper gastrointestinal bleeding or anemia with her persistent symptoms, stricture is more likely; however, the patient takes naproxen, and therefore, ulceration at the anastomotic site should also be excluded. Another cause of post–gastric bypass vomiting is poor compliance with diet or an eating disorder such as bulimia. However, the patient denies eating patterns characteristic for an eating disorder.

Marginal erosions or ulcerations can be treated with proton pump inhibitors and cessation of the NSAID in most patients; however, this therapy is not indicated until a diagnosis is established.

A right upper quadrant ultrasound would be useful for the diagnosis of biliary colic. Gallstones are very common after gastric bypass surgery with rapid weight loss. However, the close proximity to the surgery, normal hepatic enzymes, and prominent recurrent vomiting associated with this patient's symptoms argue against this diagnosis.

Surgical laparotomy should not be performed unless endoscopy fails to diagnose a treatable cause of her symptoms that can be managed less invasively.

**KEY POINT**

- Stomal stenosis, inappropriate eating habits and eating disorders, and marginal ulceration should be ruled out when persistent nausea and vomiting occur within the first few months after gastric bypass surgery.

**Bibliography**

Schneider BE, Villegas L, Blackburn GL, Mun EC, Critchlow JF, Jones DB. Laparoscopic gastric bypass surgery: outcomes. J Laparoendosc Adv Surg Tech A. 2003;13(4):247-255. [PMID: 14561253]

## Item 132    Answer:  B

**Educational Objective:**  Diagnose patellofemoral pain syndrome.

This patient's history and physical examination are typical of the patellofemoral pain syndrome (chondromalacia patellae), the most common cause of knee pain in active adults younger than 45 years. The exacerbation of the pain by going down steps and the development of knee stiffness and pain at rest when the knee is flexed for an extended period are clues to the diagnosis. Reproducing the pain by firmly moving the patella along the femur confirms the diagnosis. Patellofemoral pain syndrome is self-limited and responds to rest and NSAIDs.

The patient has no history of worsening pain over the course of the day that is typical for osteoarthritis. Patients with knee osteoarthritis may have crepitus with joint movement and bone tenderness and enlargement. The absence of these signs and symptoms excludes the diagnosis of osteoarthritis in this patient.

Pes anserine bursitis is another common overuse injury characterized by tenderness directly over the pes anserine bursa on the medial aspect of the leg just below the knee. This patient's presentation is consistent with patellofemoral pain syndrome rather than anserine bursitis.

Prepatellar bursitis is nearly always unilateral and often asymptomatic. Typically, there is a history of knee trauma or repetitive or extended kneeling preceding the knee pain. On palpation, there is tenderness over the entire bursal sac and a collection of fluid directly over the patella; these findings are absent in this patient, excluding this diagnosis.

**KEY POINT**

- The typical patient with patellofemoral pain syndrome is an active young woman with anterior knee pain worsened by going down steps.

**Bibliography**

Dixit S, Difiori J, Burton M, Mines B. Management of patellofemoral pain syndrome. Am Fam Phys. 2007;75(2):194-203. [PMID: 17263214]

## Item 133    Answer:  E

**Educational Objective:**  Manage bacterial vaginosis.

The patient has bacterial vaginosis, the most common cause of vaginal discharge in young healthy women. Symptoms of bacterial vaginosis include increased malodorous discharge without irritation or pain. The diagnosis of bacterial vaginosis is based on the presence of three of the four Amsel criteria: a positive "whiff" test, a thin white discharge, clue cells (squamous epithelial cells with edges that are obscured with bacteria) on wet mount, and discharge with a pH greater than 4.5. The recommended treatment is metronidazole, 500 mg orally twice daily for 7 days. Bacterial vaginosis is related to sexual activity, but studies have been unable to demonstrate spread between partners. Therefore, the Centers for Disease Control and Prevention do not recommend treating the partner when treating the patient. There is no evidence to support withholding treatment of women during pregnancy.

Although bacterial vaginosis is associated with changes in the normal flora of the vagina, studies of lactobacillus probiotics to restore the proper bacterial balance have been disappointing, and lactobacillus intravaginal suppositories have not been found effective.

Studies have found that the least effective treatment for bacterial vaginosis is a one-time high dose of metronidazole, and this regimen is no longer used.

Symptoms of vaginal candidiasis include pruritus, external and internal erythema, and nonodorous, white, curd-like discharge. Lack of pruritus makes this diagnosis less likely. Because this patient does not have vaginal candidiasis, treatment of her or her partner with clotrimazole is inappropriate.

**KEY POINT**

- The recommended treatment for bacterial vaginosis is metronidazole, 500 mg orally twice daily for 7 days; sexual partners of women with bacterial vaginosis are not treated.

**Bibliography**

Barrons R, Tassone D. Use of Lactobacillus probiotics for bacterial genitourinary infections in women: a review. Clin Ther. 2008;30 (3):453-468. [PMID: 18405785]

# Index